D1284691

Yearbook 118

2016 New In Chess - The Netherlands

Colophon

Editor-in-chief: Jan Timman
Managing Editor: Peter Boel
Supervisor: René Olthof
Editorial assistant: Frank Erwich
Translation: Ken Neat
Proofreading: Piet Verhagen, Maaike Keetman
Production: Joop de Groot, Anton Schermer

Cover photo: New In Chess

CIP-code Koninklijke Bibliotheek, Den Haag

New In Chess Yearbook
periodical analysis of current opening practice
ed. by Jan Timman
ISSN 0168-7697
4 times a year
Yearbook 118 (2016)
ISBN: 978-90-5691-640-4 geb./hardcover
ISBN: 978-90-5691-639-8 ing./softcover
SISO 621.25 UDC 794.1.05(058)
Trefw.: schaken; openingen

© INTERCHESS BV
No part of this book may be reproduced, stored in a retrieval
system or transmitted in any form or by any means, electronic,
mechanical, photocopying, recording or otherwise, without the
prior written permission from the publisher.

All photos: New In Chess Archives, unless indicated otherwise.

Interchess BV, Rochdalestraat 4A, 1814 TH Alkmaar.
P.O. Box 1093, 1810 KB Alkmaar, The Netherlands
Phone: 00-31-(0)72 - 5.127.137
E-mail: editors@newinchess.com
Subscriptions: www.newinchess.com

Code System

White stands slightly better	±	excellent move	!!	see	–
Black stands slightly better	∓	bad move	?	editorial comment	RR
White stands better	±	blunder	??	Yearbook	YB
Black stands better	∓	interesting move	!?	championship	ch
White has a decisive advantage	+−	dubious move	?!	zonal tournament	zt
Black has a decisive advantage	−+	only move	□	interzonal tournament	izt
balanced position	=	with the idea	△	candidates tournament	ct
unclear position	∞	attack	→	team tournament	tt
compensation for the material	⯑	initiative	↑	olympiad	ol
strong (sufficient)	>	counterplay	⇄	match	m
weak (insufficient)	<	mate	#	correspondence	cr
better is	≥	novelty	N	junior	jr
weaker is	≤	zugzwang	Z		
good move	!	time	T		

NEW IN CHESS
Yearbook
118

Contributing Authors

Adorjan • I.Almasi • Antic • Aronian • Benjamin • Bosch • Debashis • De Dovitiis • Erwich
Flear • Fogarasi • Gonda • Hazai • Ikonnikov • Ilczuk • Ivanisevic • Karolyi • S.Kasparov
A.Kuzmin • Lalic • Lukacs • Marin • Mchedlishvili • Ninov • Panczyk • Perunovic
Prasanna • Rodi • Schroeder • So • Stoica • Svidler • K.Szabo • Timman • Tomashevsky
Tuncer • Vachier-Lagrave • Van der Tak • Van der Werf • Vigorito • Vilela • Wolochowicz

CHESS OPENING NEWS

Edited by Jan Timman

Opening Highlights

Maxime Vachier-Lagrave

A lot of sympathy went out to the Frenchman (justifiably dubbed 'our strongest countryman since Philidor' by Europe Échecs) when he missed the Candidates' tournament in a highly unfortunate way last year. He'll get over it. A friendly and flexible guy in daily life, Maxime is and will remain **a monster at the board – especially when his bishop is on g7 in the Najdorf** Sicilian, as Nikolay Ninov demonstrates in his Survey on page 49.

Peter Svidler

Svidler did make it to the Candidates', but that didn't mean his year was any less dramatic. At the World Cup in Baku he let Sergey Karjakin get away in a mind-boggling final. In two Surveys we see the Russian as an opening pioneer – first in **an intricate Marshall endgame** (Lukacs and Hazai, page 117), and then in Tibor Fogarasi's Grünfeld Survey on page 187, in which Svidler's successful reversed Stonewall idea will be subjected to close scrutiny.

Ivan Ivanisevic

Like his tennis-playing namesake, the Serbian grandmaster has a wicked serve, which makes him a suitable Yearbook contributor! When the fourfold champion of his country was preparing **the 4.g3 Slav** line for black for a game against Alexander Grischuk, he discovered that it **held quite promising possibilities for White**, and decided to play it on that side of the board! Ivanisevic nevertheless presents a good practical solution for Black in his Survey on page 166.

Milos Perunovic

Like his fellow countryman Ivanisevic, Perunovic is a respected opening theoretician. His first Yearbook Survey contains **a very interesting update for the modern Benko Gambit** Sergey Kasparov introduced to us in Yearbook 114. As Kasparov wrote then, the Benko remains alive, but this new approach is evolving very fast. Perunovic, partly drawing from his own experience, analyses two interesting new weapons for White on page 200.

Jan Timman

The editorship of the Yearbook has changed hands. After 32 years of invaluable work for this series, Genna Sosonko has handed over the baton to none other than Jan Timman! Of course, the Dutch chess legend, still very active as a player and with a broad repertoire, will write Surveys like his predecessor did. His first one (page 221) is about **a sharp approach to the Symmetrical English**, adopted by Levon Aronian to beat Veselin Topalov at London 2015.

David Vigorito

Acclaimed opening book writer David Vigorito joined us for this issue. For his Survey on page 181, he delved into the Grünfeld Indian, about which the American master wrote a well-received monograph in 2013. **In the Fianchetto Variation, members of the notorious Armenian team cooked up the 'exotic' move 10.♘h4!?**. The real extent of Black's problems is not yet clear, but the move certainly is a game-changer.

Das Debashis

Das Debashis is a young representative of the rapidly expanding Indian chess contingent. The grandmaster from Bhubaneswar is coached by another Yearbook contributor, Mikheil Mchedlishvili, who has taught him a great deal. Together, master and pupil wrote a Survey about **an unexpectedly early knight swap on c6 in the Richter-Rauzer Sicilian** (page 75). It has surprise value, but may become mainstream, so remember where you saw it first.

Mark van der Werf

Now that Magnus Carlsen has started playing **the London System**, we can say that **it has definitely become salonfähig**. Mark van der Werf is the President of the Royal Dutch Chess Federation, a strong international master and an expert on this underrated system. Have a look on page 205, where the Dutchman analyses the game which just about earned the World Champion first prize against Yu Yangyi at the Qatar Open – and much more.

Your Variations

Trends & Opinions

Forum

Surveys

1.e4 openings

HOT! = a trendy line or an important discovery

SOS = an early deviation

GAMBIT = a pawn sacrifice in the opening

TRENDS & OPINIONS

Forum

Tributes and Eye-Openers

The FORUM is a platform for discussion of developments in chess opening theory in general and particularly in variations discussed in previous Yearbook issues.

Contributions to these pages should be sent to:
Editors Yearbook
P.O. Box 1093
NL 1810 KB Alkmaar
The Netherlands.
Or by e-mail to:
editors@newinchess.com

A Big Thanks and a Big Welcome
by Allard Hoogland

From its very birth onwards, editor Genna Sosonko has put an indelible stamp on the Yearbook with a highly varied output. He started out together with colleague grandmaster Paul van der Sterren in 1984. Sosonko wrote a whopping 61 high-quality Surveys, and from Yearbook 48 through 97 entertained each and every one of our readers with his famous 'Sosonko's Corner' – another 50 articles on many different aspects of opening theory in 12½ years! Genna was closely involved with the making of each issue, always ready to give advice in his own colourful way – and in those rare cases that he couldn't give an answer, he would ask one of his many friends in the chess world.

Jan Timman

However, all good things come to an end, and after 32 years Genna Sosonko has decided to step down as editor. This is clearly a big loss for our Yearbook series, but we are of course very grateful for everything Genna has done for us. I am very happy to present a worthy successor to you: none other than our legendary grand-master Jan Timman! Jan has been, of course, co-editor-in-chief of New In Chess Magazine for many years. After taking a step back there (though he will continue writing his popular column in the magazine) he has now taken the Yearbooks under his wing. On page 221 of this issue you will find Timman's first opening Survey. I hope this marks the beginning of a long and fruitful cooperation with our Yearbook staff.

Sincerely,
Allard Hoogland
Publisher, New In Chess

Genna Sosonko

And the Winner is...

by the Editorial Staff

SI 24.1 (B40)

Actually there was hardly any doubt about who would win the Novelty of the Year Award for 2015. Wei Yi's 21.♘d5! against Lazaro Bruzon Batista, which introduced one of the most brilliant chess games ever, got almost twice as many votes as the number two, Anish Giri, for his ingenious 19.♘d1! in the King's Indian against Ding Liren. Anish in his turn was hotly pursued by Viswanathan Anand (10.♘g5 in the Closed Ruy Lopez against Wesley So).

Wei Yi
Lazaro Bruzon Batista
Danzhou 2015 (2)

1.e4 c5 2.♘f3 e6 3.♘c3 a6 4.♗e2 ♘c6 5.d4 cxd4 6.♘xd4 ♕c7 7.0-0 ♘f6 8.♗e3 ♗e7 9.f4 d6 10.♔h1 0-0 11.♕e1 ♘xd4 12.♗xd4 b5 13.♕g3 ♗b7 14.a3 ♖ad8 15.♖ae1 ♖d7 16.♗d3 ♕d8 17.♕h3 g6 18.f5 e5 19.♗e3 ♖e8 20.fxg6 hxg6

21.♘d5!

'An opening novelty – and the start of a fantastic combination!', Alexey Kuzmin wrote in his Harvest column in Yearbook 116. On move 36 Bruzon had to throw in the towel, faced with an inevitable mate, as every chess fan on the planet knows by now.

Our shortlist was quite long this time – there were no less than 9 highly interesting novelties. The list included a second novelty by Wei Yi (11.h3! against Maxim Rodshtein in the Four Knights Game), and in fact when our colleague Dirk Jan ten Geuzendam handed him the prize in Wijk aan Zee the young Chinese asked him: 'For which novelty?'

The total of 379 voters (not counting invalid or double votes) was exactly the same as last year! But this time they were divided over 9 instead of 6 candidates. So the 99 votes for the winner may not sound as impressive as Fabiano Caruana's 121 from last year, but in fact Vladimir Kramnik earned 96 votes last year as the number 2, whereas Giri's 19.♘d1! (see Kuzmin's Harvest, Yearbook 114) earned him 54 votes. Competition was stronger! As said, Anand's 10.♘g5 (Kuzmin's Harvest, Yearbook 115) came third with 53 votes.

Alexander Grischuk was still quite close to these two with 48 votes for his 8.♘g1! against Jon Ludwig Hammer in the Reversed Sicilian (Survey Jeroen Bosch in Yearbook 116, page 208). And Wesley So did not do badly either with 41 votes for his 9...♘b8 against last year's winner Caruana in the Closed Ruy Lopez – to which Anand's novelty was a reaction (Kuzmin's Harvest, Yearbook 114).

The tail-enders still got quite a few votes. 29 went to Andrea Stella for his 17.♘d5! sacrifice against Aroshidze's Hedgehog (Survey by Carlos Matamoros and Andrea Stella on page 219 of Yearbook 117). Wei Yi's second novelty (11.h3 in the Four Knights, featured also in Kuzmin's Harvest in Yearbook 116) got 26. 17 votes went to Husein Aziz Nezad for 12.b5! in the Classical King's Indian against Emre Can (Kuzmin's Harvest, Yearbook 117), and 12 to Evgeny Tomashevsky for his 9.♘h3! in the 4.♗g5 Grünfeld against Maxime Vachier-Lagrave (also Kuzmin's Harvest, Yearbook 117).

Wei Yi received 350 euro for his by now famous novelty. Dutchman Eric de Haan, one of the voters for the 'Chinese Carlsen', won the raffle, and will receive a one-year Yearbook subscription.

Happy New Year Magnus!

by Luis Rodi

GI 1.1 (D70)

YB 48, 86, 91, 107, 113, 116, 117

World Champion Magnus Carlsen closed off the year 2015 with a deserved victory in the Qatar Open in Doha. In that tournament,

he played a masterpiece against Li Chao, in a line of Alekhine's Anti-Grünfeld I revised in a three-part Yearbook Survey published recently.

I want to show this game to the reader for two reasons: first, because is a good complement to the Survey (in a variation that had been left out due to space limitations); secondly and most importantly, because it's a really wonderful game, featuring some of the better characteristics in Carlsen's play.

Magnus Carlsen
Li Chao
Doha 2015 (5)

1.d4 ♘f6 2.c4 g6 3.f3 d5 4.cxd5 ♘xd5 5.e4 ♘b6 6.♘c3 ♗g7 7.♗e3 0-0 8.♕d2 ♘c6 9.0-0-0 f5!?

The Chinese grandmaster avoids the main line 9...♕d6 in favour of this move, which leads to positions with a more or less closed centre, putting up a light-square blockade.

10.e5
According to Svetushkin, premature is 10.h4 fxe4 11.h5 because of 11...gxh5 12.♖xh5 ♗f5 with counterplay. The move by the World Champion is considered better.

10...♘b4
Black starts to make the blockade work.
The main ideas are ...♗e6, ...♘4(6)d5 and ...c7-c6.

11.♘h3!

In this way, the knight participates actively in the fight for the central squares. Later it can be directed to f4 (or g5), and White can consider a kingside initiative with h4-h5.

11...♕e8!?
A new idea. The queen joins the battle for the light squares, and can play on both sides of the board. The main line is 11...♗e6 12.♔b1 and now 12...♘4d5 is the latest preference (after 12...♕d7 13.♘f4 ♗f7 14.a3 a5 Svetushkin recommends 15.♗b5 c6 16.d5, saying that 'the possibility of this move defines White's advantage': 16...♗xe5 17.♗xb6 cxb5 18.♖he1± and 'White rules in the centre and he has a strong initiative' (Svetushkin), Bitan-Vokarev, Bhubaneswar 2010) 13.♘g5 ♘xc3+ 14.♕xc3 ♗d5 15.h4 c6 (15...♕d7 16.♗d3 ♖ac8 17.♗c2± Ivanisevic-Gabrielian, Plovdiv 2012) 16.♗d3± Simantsev-Nurkiewicz, Gora 2014; earlier in the year, the alternative 11...a5 was played, with the continuation 12.a3 (12.♔b1!?) 12...♘4d5 (12...♗e6!?) 13.♘f4 ♘xf4 14.♗xf4 ♘d5 15.h4±, Le Quang-Li Chao, Ho Chi Minh City 2015.

12.♔b1 a5 13.♗e2 c6 14.♖c1!
A typical move for Carlsen, who has no equal in the art of improving his pieces in an almost imperceptible way. On this square, the rook provides additional protection of the possible target squares c2 and c4, and has more space than on the closed d-file.

14...♔h8?!
A serious loss of time. Instead, the following moves could be considered:

A) 14...♘6d5 15.♘xd5 ♘xd5 16.♗c4 ♗e6. Here Black achieves an effective blockade, but the resulting position is passive. An illustrative line is 17.♘g5 (17.♗xd5 ♗xd5 18.♘f4 ♖d8 19.♕c3± is another possibility) 17...♗h6 18.♘xe6 ♗xe3 19.♕e2 ♗xc1 20.♗xd5 cxd5 21.♖xc1 ♖c8 22.♖xc8 ♕xc8 23.♘xf8 ♔xf8 24.♕b5±;

B) 14...♗e6 15.♘f4 ♕f7 (15...♗c4 16.h4±) 16.♘xe6 ♕xe6 17.a3 ♖fd8 (17...♘4d5 18.♘xd5 ♘xd5 and now 19.h4 or 19.♗c4 b5 20.♗b3 a4 21.♗a2 with a better position for White, due to the bishop pair and the initiative on the c- and h-files) 18.f4 ♘4d5 (18...♘c4 seems natural, but after 19.♗xc4 ♕xc4 comes a forced variation, long and complex, that seems to be better for the first player: 20.axb4 axb4 21.♘a4 ♕d5 22.♘b6 ♕a2+ 23.♔c2 ♖a3 24.♔d1 ♖b3 25.♖c2 ♕a1+ 26.♕c1 ♕a6 27.d5 ♕d3+ 28.♖d2 ♕xe3 29.♕c4 ♔h8 30.♖e1 ♕xb6 31.♕xb3±) 19.♗f2 with a white initiative on the kingside, or by way of the c-file. Black is ready to reply to White's h2-h4 with another light-square blockade move, ...h7-h5. Then White can consider h2-h3 and g2-g4.

15.♔a1 ♗e6 16.♘f4 ♕f7

17.h4!!
A great assessment, and a clever pawn sacrifice by the World Champion!
17.♘xe6 ♕xe6 18.h4 is the computer's recommendation.

17...♗xa2?

The game continuation shows that this decision – though very tempting – is not correct. Objectively better was, for example, the useful 17...♖fd8! when White has a choice between 18.h5!? – here this is not so clear because of the reply 18...g5, but still worthy of investigation – and 18.♘xe6 ♕xe6 19.f4 (19.h5!?) 19...h5!? 20.♗f3 with White's initiative.

18.h5 ♔g8

A tacit recognition of his inaccuracy on the 14th move, but the alternatives are not better: 18...♕b3 19.hxg6+–; 18...g5 19.♘g6+ ♔g8 20.♘xf8 ♗xf8 (20...f4 21.♘xh7! fxe3 22.♕xe3 ♗xh7 23.h6 ♗f8 24.d5!±) 21.♗xg5 a4 22.♘b5! ♘d5 23.♘c7 (23.♘a3!?±) 23...♘c2+ 24.♕xc2 ♘xc7 25.g4+–.

19.hxg6 hxg6

Superficially it seems that both sides have made progress with their attack, and have weakened the security of the respective enemy kings. But that is an illusion; a deeper analysis shows that the quality of the two initiatives is very different. White's attack fits neatly into the theory of attacking in positions with opposite castling: first advancing the pawns, with the objective of opening lines for the pieces, and his conduct of the attack is perfectly natural.

20.g4!

Initiative! The strong advance of the g-pawn has two objectives: a) further exposing the enemy king's position; b) enabling the passage of the queen to h2. Instead, 20.♘xg6?!, even though it destroys part of Black's defences, allows counterplay after 20...♕xg6 21.♘xa2 f4!.

20...♗b3

This move attends to one of Black's problems: the lack of coordination between Black's attacking pieces, planning to follow up with ...a5-a4 without

Magnus Carlsen

allowing the reply b2-b3. Some alternatives are:

A) The immediate 20...a4 is possible, when 21.gxf5! a3 22.b3! reveals one of White's main defensive resources: 22...♕xb3 23.♘xg6 ♘d5 24.♘xd5 ♕b2+ 25.♕xb2 axb2+ 26.♔xb2 ♘xd5 27.♗h6 ♖xf5 28.♖cg1+–;

B) 20...fxg4 21.fxg4 a4 22.♘e4 a3 23.♕xb4 ♘d5 24.♘xd5 axb2+ 25.♔xb2 ♗xd5 26.♘c3 ♗xh1 27.♖xh1+–;

C) 20...g5 21.♘h3 f4 is an attempt to close the position, but after 22.♗f2 it is evident that Black cannot take care of a2 and g5 at the same time: 22...♗b3 23.♘xg5 ♕g6 24.♘ce4+–.

21.♗d1 a4

21...♗xd1 22.♕h2 (also 22.e6+–) 22...♘c2+ (22...♕b3 allows mate: 23.♕h7+ ♔f7 24.♕xg6+ ♔g8 25.♘e6 ♖f7 26.♕h7#) 23.♖xc2 ♗h6 24.♘xd1+–.

22.♕h2 ♖fd8 23.♕h7+ ♔f8

Here, the most obvious choice is to take on g6 with check, but this is not the strongest move. Time for some concrete calculation!

24.d5!

This strong break, with the basic double threat of 25.♘e6+ and 25.♗xb6, causes a short circuit in Black's position, cutting off the communication between his offensive and defensive zones – now the queen cannot attack, and the ♗b3 cannot defend.

24...♘c4!?

In the circumstances, an excellent practical decision.

25.♘xg6+!

Always be careful! The other check with this piece, 25.♘e6+?, loses after 25...♕xe6!, for instance 26.dxe6 a3 27.bxa3 ♖xa3+ 28.♔b1 ♗xd1! (28...♖d2 29.♗xd2 ♘xd2+ 30.♔b2 ♘c4+ is a curious draw) 29.♖hxd1 ♖b3+ 30.♔a1 ♖a8+ with mate in two moves.

25...♔e8

Here the queen sacrifice doesn't help: 25...♕xg6 26.♕xg6 a3 (or 26...♘xe5 27.♖h8+) 27.♖h8+ ♗xh8 28.♗h6+ ♗g7 29.♗xg7+ and White gives mate.

26.e6 a3

A further escalation. Black gives his queen, but in the future White's timing will have to be perfect.

27.exf7+ ♔d7 28.♘e5+! ♗xe5 29.♕xf5+ ♔c7 30.♕xe5+ ♘xe5

This capture was a sad necessity; 30...♔c8 would be consistent, but it loses after 31.♕e6+ ♔b8 32.♗f4+ ♔a7 33.bxa3+–; 30...♖d6 31.♕xe7+ ♖d7 32.♘b5+ cxb5 33.♖xc4+ ♗xc4 34.♕c5+ and White is winning.

31.♗xb3 axb2+ 32.♔xb2 ♘bd3+ 33.♔b1 ♘xc1 34.♖xc1

The game now enters a simple technical phase with a material and positional advantage for the first player, with a starring role for his dangerous passed pawns.

34...♔c8 35.dxc6 bxc6 36.f4

In this utterly hopeless position, Black resigned. A great achievement, creatively and technically, by Carlsen.

Shyam Pays Tribute to Yearbook Authors

by Peter Boel

CA 3.2 (E04)

In Yearbook 116 (page 158), Bogdan Lalic discussed a line in the Central Variation of the Queen's Gambit Accepted where Black sacrifices an exchange on a8. This exchange sac appears in many shapes and sizes. In the decisive game in the Groningen Open the eventual co-winner showed a way to do it in the Catalan.

Avital Boruchovsky
Sundar Shyam
Groningen 2015 (9)

1.d4 ♘f6 2.c4 e6 3.♘f3 d5 4.g3 dxc4 5.♗g2 ♘bd7 6.♘bd2

6...b5!?
This comes down to an exchange sac, which by the way has been known since the 1970s, a time when several of our first YB authors were active players. It turns out to be a good choice against the young Israeli, who had beaten the eventual number 1 of the tournament, the even younger Dutch hope Jorden van Foreest, in the previous round.

7.♘e5 ♘xe5 8.♗xa8 ♕xd4 9.0-0 ♗c5
Shyam opts for quick development. Some of the other tries have been:

A) 9...♘d5 10.a4 c6 11.axb5 cxb5 12.♘b1 ♗c5 13.♕xd4 ♗xd4 14.♖d1 ♗b6 15.♗xd5

exd5 16.♘c3 ♘g4 17.e3 (it looks as if White has consolidated and can now mop Black up, but things still aren't very clear-cut) 17...0-0 18.♘xd5 ♖e8 19.♘xb6 axb6 20.♖a8 ♘e5 21.♖d6 ♘f3+ 22.♔h1 ♘e5 23.e4 ♘d3 24.♖c6 ♗d7 25.♖xe8+ ♗xe8 26.♖c8 ♔f8 27.♗e3 ♘xb2 28.♗xb6 ♘d3 29.♔g2 ♔e7 30.♗d4 f6 31.♔f3 ♗d7 32.♖g8 ♔f7 33.♖b8 b4?! 34.♔e3 ♔e7 35.f4 h6? (35...♔d6 keeps the disadvantage within limits) 36.e5 fxe5 37.♗xe5 and the king intervened decisively in a game by our previous editor, Genna Sosonko, against Comp Mephisto, Amsterdam 1985;

B) 9...♕b6 10.♘f3 ♕b8 11.♗f4 ♕xa8 (11...♘g6 12.♗c6+) 12.♗xe5 ♗c5 13.a4 b4 14.♗d4 ♗e7! 15.♖c1 ♗a6 16.♕c2 0-0 17.♖fd1 (now everything works for Black: 17.♘d2 b3 18.♕c3 c5 19.♗e5 ♘d5 20.♕f3 f6 21.♗c3 ♕c6 etc.) 17...♘d5 18.e4 b3 19.♕e2 ♘b4 20.♗c3 ♘d3 21.♖a1 ♗c5 22.♖f1 ♕c6 23.♘d2 f5! (opening the f-file and/or the long diagonal, and winning) 24.exf5 ♗b7 0-1 Vukic-Hübner, Sombor 1970.

10.♘f3
10.♘e4! ♕xd1 11.♘xf6+ gxf6 12.♖xd1 may be a little better, weakening Black's structure a little. But Black also has 10...♘xe4 11.♕xd4 ♗xd4 12.♗xe4 0-0, which is about equal.

10...♘xf3+ 11.♗xf3

11...♕xd1
Black is not afraid of the ending. In fact he has all the fun there.

11...♔e7 12.♕c2 ♘d5 13.♗d2 ♕e5 14.♖ad1 ♗b7 15.a3 ♖d8 16.♕xh7 ♘f6 17.♕g7 ♗xf3 18.exf3 ♕xb2 ½-½ was Langeweg (yet another prominent Yearbook author over the years!)-Osmanovic, Sarajevo 1981. White has some initiative after 19.♗e3 ♖xd1 20.♗xc5+ ♖d6 21.♕g5 but probably the Dutch master didn't trust that c-pawn.

12.♖xd1 ♔e7 13.♗f4 ♗d6 14.♗c6 ♗d7 15.♗xd7 ♘xd7 16.a4 ♖b8
Now the position gets hoovered, which appears to be to the advantage of the side with the two rooks, i.e. White. However things are not that simple.

Nevertheless, 16...b4 looked stronger: 17.♖ac1 c3 18.bxc3 ♗xf4 19.gxf4 b3 and rook, knight and passed pawn will make a dangerous combination.

17.axb5 ♖xb5 18.♖xa7 ♖xb2
The black pawns look a lot less dangerous now, but there are still two of them!

19.♔f1 e5 20.♗d2 ♔e6

21.♗e3?
Better 21.♗a5, e.g. 21...♖a2 22.♗b6. Now the c-pawn becomes dangerous after all.

21...c3 22.♖c1 ♖b3
22...c2! 23.♖a4 ♔d5 with control!

23.♖a4 ♗a3 24.♖e1 ♘b6 25.♖a7 ♘d5 26.♖a6+ ♔e7
26...♗d6 was more circumspect, followed by bringing on the king.

27.♗c1 ♗b2 28.♖a5 ♔e6 29.♖d1?!
After 29.♖a6+ Black would have had to find something clever.

29...♘b4! 30.♗xb2 cxb2
31.♖b1 ♔d6 32.♖a8 ♔d7
33.♖a5 ♔d6 34.♖a8 ♔d5
35.♔e1 ♘c2+
In the end the knight would get to
a3 anyway.
36.♔d2 ♘a3 37.♖xa3 ♖xa3
38.♖xb2 ♖a7 39.h4 c5 40.f3
f5 41.♖b8 ♖a2+ 42.♔e3 f4+
43.gxf4 exf4+ 44.♔f2 c4
45.♖b7

45...c3! 46.♖xg7 ♖a6?!
46...♔c4 was simpler; after
47.♖xh7 c2 48.♖c7+ ♔b3 49.h5
♔b2 the rook can hold the white
pawns remarkably easily.
**47.e4+! ♔c4 48.♖c7+ ♔b3
49.♖b7+ ♔a3 50.♔e2**
This is the difference; the king
can hold the c-pawn, and the win
becomes problematic.
**50...♖d6 51.♖xh7 c2 52.♖c7
♔b2 53.♖b7+ ♔c1 54.h5 ♖d2+
55.♔e1 ♖d1+ 56.♔e2 ♖h1
57.♖b5 ♖h3**

58.♖c5?
Here White appears to miss a
draw with 58.♖g5: 58...♖h2+
(58...♖g3!? 59.♖g6 (59.♖a5
♖g2+60.♔d3 ♖f2!−+) 59...♖xg6
60.hxg6 ♔b2 61.g7 c1♕ 62.g8♕

Sundar Shyam

♕e3+ 63.♔f1 ♕xf3+ may not be
a win, but it's still torture) 59.♔d3
♖f2 60.♖g1+ ♔b2 61.e5 ♖xf3+
62.♔e4 and in this line the white
rook's placement is much better
– it's a draw after e.g. 62...♖g3
63.♖f1 f3 64.e6 ♖g8 65.e7 ♖e8
66.♔xf3 ♖xe7 67.♔g4 and the
black rook cannot beat the white
pawn (variation by Herman
Grooten on Schaaksite).
Another interesting line is 58.e5!?
♖xh5 59.♖c5 with a kind of status
quo that Black cannot break, e.g.
59...♖h7 (or 59...♔b2 60.♖b5+
♔c3 61.♖c5+ ♔b3 62.♔d3 ♖xe5
63.♖c3+ ♔b4 64.♖c4+! ♔b5
65.♖xc2 ♖e3+ 66.♔d4 ♖xf3
67.♔e4) 60.e6 ♖h2+ 61.♔e1
(61.♔d3?? ♔d1) 61...♖h6
62.♖c6! and if the black king
moves, White has checks.
58...♖h2+ 59.♔f1
59.♔d3 ♖d2+ 60.♔c4 ♔d1 and
the white pawns are remarkably
slow here, e.g. 61.♔b5 (61.♔b3
c1♕ 62.♖xc1+ ♔xc1 63.h6
♖d3+ 64.♔c4 ♖xf3 65.h7 ♖h3
etc.) 61...♖h2! 62.♔c6 c1♕
63.♖xc1+ ♔xc1 64.♔d6 ♖xh5
65.e5 ♔d2.
59...♖d2 60.♔g1 ♖xh5   0-1
This win brought Shyam on 7.5
out of 9, and shared first place
with young Dutchman Jorden van
Foreest, who was declared the
tournament winner.

One-Sided Character Attack
by Erik Kislik

RL 26.8 (C92)   YB 115, 117

I recently saw the article in New in
Chess Yearbook 117 by Kuzmin,
which described me as a plagiarist
and a 'petty trickster'. I wish
that Kuzmin had contacted me
before publishing that, because
it's a very one-sided character
attack. It is unprofessional from
both sides (the author and the
publication). Interestingly, one of
my grandmaster students named
the variation, not me.
The question here is: what
justification is needed to name
an opening after someone? In
the chess world, the three main
reasons we accept someone's
name on an opening are if:
a) they developed the main ideas
in the proper handling of the
variation (Chebanenko);
b) they helped popularize the
variation;
c) they were the first titled player
to play the variation.
In any of those cases, one can
make a very valid claim that
naming an opening after that
person has good logic behind it.
In this interesting case, I did
actually develop the main ideas
in the proper handling of the
variation, as can be seen by how
I proposed dealing with all of
White's main tries in my actual
article. Additionally, I was the
sole reason that the variation
became popularized (Svidler told
me he only found out it was a
good line after my student played
it against him).
Interestingly, when I check the
position after 12...exd4, I see
Kislik as the first titled player
playing the line, followed by
6(!) games in a row by my students (Kjartansson, Kjartansson,
Kjartansson, Stefansson, Narayanan, Narayanan). Three months
later, another grandmaster played
it, and then one month later,

COURTESY GRONINGEN CHESS FESTIVAL

Svidler tried it for himself and the line gradually became more popular. As we can see, all three of the usual criteria for naming an opening after someone are met. I could understand the claim that attaching my name to the variation is questionable if only one of the criteria was met, but here there is no confusion or contention.

I addressed Kuzmin's main point about the move order in the initial article. Kuzmin states that 10...♘d7 is the correct move order. I wrote in my article that 11.♗c2 was the reason I rejected this, and came to the correct move order that all of my students adopted. This is not some small subtlety, but a vital innovation to make this variation playable.

Kuzmin's article is potentially damaging to my reputation as an author and coach. I am currently ranked the number one online chess vendor in sales among native English speaking coaches. In other words, being the most popular online chess coach from America, my reputation is important. Overall, this is just a really needless and senseless character attack in poor taste. Strong judgments are made about my character with insufficient information and no evidence of my motives, which is very poor argumentation. To write a professional, meaningful article, he should honestly evaluate my reasons for naming the variation this way, and simply explain where my mistake was. To declare I'm a petty trickster and a plagiarist is a pretty large insult, not justified in any sense or with any logic or evidence. The criticism of my name on the variation also has no logical coherence to it (it's merely a question of if this is a valid reason to name it after me. Meeting all three criteria makes it as crystal clear as it could be).

Best regards,
Erik Kislik

Erik Kislik

Reply by Alexey Kuzmin:
The initial position of the variation – the position after Black's 14th move – was clearly pointed out even in Kislik's Survey (Yearbook 115). In fact, the 'Saratov team' can be considered the first serious developer of this variation: the coach, Pavel Lobach, introduced it, and his students Pogonina and Kovanova regularly used the variation in the years 2008-2010. Later the variation was played by Svetushkin.

In my Harvest column (Yearbook 117), exactly the above-mentioned was used as the main argument to close the discussion about Kislik's pretention to the authorship of this variation. I can hardly believe that Kislik does not understand this. Yet, in his letter he writes: 'I addressed Kuzmin's main point about the move order...', ignoring one more time the real main argument – the fact that numerous players had used this variation previously.

According to Kislik's letter he deals with the initial position after 10...♖e8 11.♘bd2 exd4. But in his Survey, Kislik analyses games by Elianov and Svetushkin, who used the order 10...♘d7 11.♘bd2 exd4. Actually the move order that was analysed and recommended by Kislik gave a strong impulse to the development of the

variation. But this is merely a question of move order. The fact that someone has improved the move order leading to the initial position of a variation does not mean that he is the author of the variation. Furthermore, this move order – 11...exd4 12.cxd4 ♘d7 13.♘f1 ♘a5 14.♗c2 ♗f6 – was previously seen in email games. So, if we put it quite strictly, Kislik was not even the author of this more exact move order leading to the initial position of the variation, which had earlier been developed to some level by the 'Saratov team' and others.

Two more points concerning Kislik's Survey in Yearbook 115:
1) Kislik's analyses show the benefits of the move order he recommends. However, his sentence: 'Kuzmin states that 10...♘d7 is the correct move order' is not correct, for the simple reason that I didn't write it! In general, I agree with Kislik's assessments.
2) Kislik has made and showed a deep analysis of a position that was previously met in several dozens of games, including games by grandmasters.
But even if we take all this together, this does not mean that he can pretend to the authorship of this variation.

An Eye-Opener in the Keres Variation
by Frank Erwich
NI 12.8 (E43)

At the end of 2015, Magnus Carlsen won the Qatar Masters by defeating Yu Yangyi convincingly in a blitz playoff. In the first round Carlsen outplayed the Chinese in the London System (check the Survey by Mark van der Werf elsewhere in this issue!), which meant that a draw in the second game was sufficient to win the match and thus the tournament. Thanks to a novelty, the World Champion reached an equal position, but he could never have expected to win the game only five moves later!

Let's have a look:

Yu Yangyi
Magnus Carlsen
Doha 2015 playoff blitz (2)

1.d4 ♘f6 2.c4 e6 3.♘c3 ♗b4 4.♘f3 b6 5.e3 ♗b7 6.♗d3 0-0 7.0-0 c5 8.♘a4 cxd4 9.exd4 ♖e8 10.a3 ♗f8 11.♗f4

Not a frequently played move (six times according to my database). However, Magnus played this move himself in 2011 against Karjakin!

11...♗xf3!
Carlsen-Karjakin, Medias 2011, continued with 11...d6 12.♖e1 ♘bd7 13.♖c1 e5! 14.dxe5 ♗xf3 15.♕xf3 ♘xe5 16.♗xe5 dxe5 and Black was doing fine. However, 13.♘c3 seems to be an improvement on White's play.
12.♕xf3 ♘c6 13.d5?!
After 13.♗e3, which is of course a waste of time, the idea of the exchange becomes clear: 13...e5! 14.d5 (14.dxe5 ♘xe5 15.♕d1 d5∓) 14...e4! 15.♗xe4 ♘e5! 16.♕f4 ♖c8 and Black is already better.
Chances are more or less balanced after 13.♕e3 (not a great square for the queen though, in a vis-à-vis with the rook and taking away squares of its own bishop).
13...exd5 14.cxd5 ♘e5 15.♕d1??

15.♗xe5 ♖xe5 16.♘c3 should be equal, although Black's position seems easier to play.

15...♘xd3 16.♕xd3 ♖e4
And Black resigned. After 17.♗d2 ♖xa4 18.b4 a5 the rook on a4 cannot be trapped.

The idea of giving the bishop for the knight is not new:

position after 10...♗f8

If White plays a healthy move like 11.♖e1, which after 11.b4 is the most frequently played move, a majority of players continue with 11...d6 (see Kramnik-Polgar, Hoogeveen 2011), but 11...♗xf3! is again an important equalizer! 12.♕xf3 ♘c6 13.♗e3 (compared to the Carlsen game White has saved a tempo here in the line with 13.♗e3, but still Black is doing absolutely fine!) 13...e5! 14.dxe5 (14.d5 e4 15.♗xe4 ♘e5 16.♕f4 ♘xe4 17.♕xe4 ♖c8 should be familiar by now) 14...♘xe5 15.♕d1 d5!= 16.c5? d4! 17.♗xd4? ♘xd3 18.♖xe8 ♘xe8 19.♕xd3 bxc5 −+.
In addition, 11.♗g5!? will not prevent Black's idea either: 11...

h6 12.♗h4 ♗xf3 13.♕xf3 ♘c6 14.♕e3 with an equal position in Chatalbashev-Iordachescu, Baden-Baden 2013.

Is taking the knight with the bishop always a good idea? Well, in the line with 11.b4 White seems to be doing slightly better, because White's dark-squared bishop can be put on the a1-h8 diagonal: 11...♗xf3!? 12.♕xf3 ♘c6 13.♗b2 e5 14.dxe5 ♘xe5 15.♕h3±.

The bishop is better placed on b2 than on f4 or g5.
Of course Black is not obliged to go 11...♗xf3!? in this line. Magnus reached a comfortable game against Bruzon Batista (Mexico City rapid 2012) after 11...a5 12.b5 d6 13.♗b2 ♘bd7 14.♖e1 ♖c8 15.♖c1 g6 16.h3 d5 17.♘d2 dxc4 18.♘xc4 ♘d5.

Yu Yangyi

11.♘c3 seems to be a good alternative. White keeps open the option to play b2-b4 and also anticipates the exchange. 11...♗xf3 is not a good idea here, because after 12.♕xf3 ♘c6 13.♗e3 e5 14.d5 e4 15.♘xe4 ♘e5 White is a healthy pawn up after taking the knight on f6 with check(!): 16.♘xf6+.

In short, Magnus' idea is not applicable in all circumstances. See for another example the next diagram:

position after 9.exd4

9...♗xf3?! (as we have already seen, 9...♖e8 is the main move here) is too early. Black will miss the rook on e8: 10.♕xf3 ♘c6 11.♗e3 e5 12.d5 e4 13.♗xe4 ♘e5 14.♕f5! ♘xc4? (14...♖e8 15.♗g5!±) 15.♗g5! and White is winning.

The final example:

position after 9.a3

An important idea behind 9...♖e8 is to make space for the bishop on b4. This is a good reason for

White to be smart and play the zwischenzug 9.a3. Now a very interesting possibility for Black is 9...♗d6!. Let me first show you a game between Speelman and Ivanchuk (Roquebrune rapid 1992):
9...♗e7 10.exd4 ♗xf3 11.♕xf3 ♘c6 12.♗e3 e5 13.d5 e4 14.♗xe4 ♘e5 15.♕f4

15...♗d6
How nice would it be if the bishop was already standing on this square? The game continued with **16.c5 ♘g6 17.♕f3 ♘h4 18.♕h3 ♘xe4 19.cxd6**
And around fifty moves later the game ended in a draw.
Let's see what the difference is if the bishop goes to d6 immediately (you won't be surprised): 9...♗d6 10.exd4

10...♗xf3 (Kortchnoi introduced this idea in his game against Lukacs, Austria Bundesliga 1996) 11.♕xf3 ♘c6 12.♗e3 (12.♖d1 ♘xd4 13.♗xh7+ ♘xh7 14.♖xd4 ♗e5! is no problem at all for Black. See Kortchnoi-Lukacs, Leitao-Nisipeanu, Las Vegas 1999, and Zilberman-Wells, Herzliya 2000) 12...e5.

A) If White decides to play 13.d5? we can already dream up Black's next moves: 13...e4! 14.♗xe4 ♘e5! 15.♕f4 and now we have almost the same position as in Speelman-Ivanchuk, but Black is a tempo up! After 15...♕c7! Black is much better (15...♘xc4? 16.♗xh7+!±);
B) 13.dxe5 ♘xe5 14.♕d1 ♕c7 led to equality in Romanov-Fedoseev, St Petersburg 2013;
C) An interesting try is 13.c5!, but Black should not be worried after 13...exd4 14.cxd6 dxe3 15.♕xe3 ♖e8 (Ushenina-Pogonina, Istanbul 2012, and Arnaudov-Adams, Eilat 2012).

After his victory in Doha, in Wijk aan Zee Carlsen won his third tournament in a row! And what about Yu Yangyi? He participated in Gibraltar and played the London System for the first time in an official game! He drew against Maze. but maybe next time he will be more successful playing the Keres Variation!

Avoiding a Bind
by IM José L. Vilela

PU 16.8 (B08)   YB 53

It is not a common event to see a high-level game where the defensive side comes up with a radically new idea that completely changes the evaluation of a line. But this seems to have been the case in a game from the recent European Club Chess

Championship in Skopje. The encounter is Leinier Dominguez-Christian Bauer, played in round 5, on the 2nd board of the match Mednyi Vsadnik-Schachgesellschaft Zürich. Let us take a close look at it:

Leinier Dominguez Perez
Christian Bauer
Skopje tt 2015

1.♘f3 g6 2.d4 d6 3.e4 ♘f6 4.♘c3 ♗g7 5.♗e2 0-0 6.0-0

What started as a probable 1.d4 opening has turned into an 1.e4 opening, a Pirc Defence in one of its more quiet lines, the system where White plays ♘f3, ♗e2 and 0-0.

6...♘c6

If you check in the databases, you will see that this is the 3rd most popular option in this position. The two most played lines are 6...c6 and 6...♗g4. Several other alternatives are also played.

7.d5

The most principled reply; White attacks the knight while gaining space in the centre.

7...♘b8 8.h3

A typical restrictive move, which also gives air to the king.

8...e5 9.dxe6 ♗xe6 10.♗g5

The main move in frequency and overall result percentage.

10...h6 11.♗e3 ♘c6 12.♕d2

One of the ideas of developing the bishop to g5 is to induce the move ...h7-h6, so as now to play 12.♕d2 with tempo due to the attack on h6. Apparently Black has to defend the pawn, but...

12...d5!N

Previously Black had always played 12...♔h7; after the centralization 13.♖ad1 there are 3 games in MegaBase, with two wins for White (Piket-Gulko, Amsterdam 1989; Hatanbaatar-Rudin, Manila ol 1992) and one draw (Gruenfeld-Smirin, Israel tt 1997).

After 12...♔h7 13.♖ad1 White's position is undoubtedly more pleasant, not only because he has prevented the central break ...d6-d5 and remains with an advantage in space, but also because it is not easy for Black to generate counterplay, even if his position is still solid. But after the surprising text move Black is no longer caring about defending h6; he counterattacks in the centre at the latest possible moment.

13.exd5

The first point of Black's move is 13.♗xh6 dxe4, when already Black does not have the slightest problem. The second point is that advancing 13.e5 does not provide White any benefit after the counter 13...♘e4!. Dominguez' reply is the best one, given the circumstances.

13...♘xd5 14.♘xd5

This was the first moment where White could have captured the pawn on h6: after 14.♗xh6 ♘xc3 15.bxc3 ♕xd2 16.♗xd2 White's deteriorated queenside pawn structure and the excellent placement of Black's minor pieces quite clearly compensate for the minus pawn.

14...♕xd5 15.♕xd5

After this simplification, equality is complete. A last try to create some sort of unbalance would have been 15.♗xh6 ♕xd2 16.♗xd2 ♗xb2 17.♖ab1. Now Black can avoid losing the pawn on b7 by 17...♗d4 18.♘xd4 (18.♖xb7 ♗b6, trapping the rook) 18...♘xd4. In this position White has the bishop pair and there is some weakness of Black's dark squares on the kingside, but Black's better pawn structure compensates for that and

Christian Bauer

objectively the position should be considered balanced after, for example, 19.♗d3 b6.

15...♗xd5 16.♖fd1 ♖ad8 17.c3 ♖fe8 18.♔f1 g5 19.♖d2 a6 20.a3 ♗b3 21.♖xd8 ♖xd8 22.♘d2 ♗d5 23.♖d1 ♗f6 24.♘f3 ♔g7 25.♘d4 ♘xd4 26.♗xd4 ♗xd4 27.♖xd4 ♖d6 28.f4 gxf4 29.♖xf4 ♖f6 30.♖xf6 ♔xf6 31.♔f2 a5 32.g3 b6 33.h4 ♔e5 34.♔e3 c5 35.♗d3 f6 36.♗c2 ♗c6 37.♗d3 ♗d5 38.♗c2 ♗c6 39.♗d3 ♗d5 40.♗c2 ½-½

Although there are still a couple of moments where White could have tried to unbalance the game, it seems to this annotator that the novelty 12...d5! is a very serious blow to any white hope of getting something tangible in this line.

Not So Clear
by A.C. van der Tak

KG 5.9 (C30)　　　　　　　　YB 69

In Yearbook 69 I wrote about the position after 1.e4 e5 2.f4 ♗c5 3.♘f3 d6 4.♘c3 ♘f6 5.♗c4 ♘c6 6.d3 a6 and now 7.♖f1, which may or may not have been Charousek's move. An important game in that Survey was Bouverot-Colucci, cr 1995: 7...♗g4 8.h3 ♗xf3 9.♕xf3 ♘d4 10.♕g3 0-0!? and Black didn't have too many problems.

John Shaw, too, in his much-praised book *The King's Gambit* (Quality Chess 2013), gives this game as a way to achieve approximate equality for Black. Shaw recommends the option 7.♘d5! for White, and analyses this move further to a white advantage: 'Black has several playable responses, but I was unable to find a clear path to equality.' Roman Ovetchkin and Sergei Soloviov also recommend 7.♘d5 in their book *The Modern Vienna Game* (Chess Stars 2015): '... a very useful move. White trades the enemy knight on f6, since it protects Black's kingside'. All the same, the situation isn't clear at all, as after 7...♘xd5 8.♗xd5 it appears that Black has a good possibility in 8...0-0!? 9.f5 ♘e7!? (not 9...♘d4?!, as given in the above-mentioned books), or also 8...♗g4 9.c3 0-0, and now, after 10.f5, again 10...♘e7!?. See the games given below.

Frank Meissen
Frank Penzler
cr 2015

1.e4 e5 2.♘c3 ♗c5 3.f4 d6 4.♘f3 ♘f6 5.♗c4 ♘c6 6.d3 a6 7.♘d5 ♘xd5 8.♗xd5 ♗g4 9.c3 0-0 10.f5

10.h3!? Shaw.

10...♘e7 11.♗b3

11.♗g5 h6 (11...♕e8!= Ovetchkin/Soloviov) 12.♗h4 c6 13.♗b3 d5 14.h3 ♗xf3 15.♕xf3 f6 16.0-0-0± Zulfugaryi-Dovliatov, Baku ch-AZE 2000.

11...d5 12.h3 ♗xf3 13.♕xf3 ♕d6

14.g4

14.♖f1 (↑ Ovetchkin/Soloviov) 14...f6 15.exd5 ♔h8 16.g4 a5 17.a4 ♖ad8=.

14...a5

14...dxe4 15.dxe4 a5 16.g5 ♖fd8=.

15.a4 ♖ad8 16.♔d2

16.exd5 ♘xd5 (16...♖fe8!?) 17.♗xd5 ♕xd5 18.♕xd5 ♖xd5 19.♔e2=; 16.♖f1 dxe4 17.dxe4 ♕b6 18.♗c4 ♘c8 19.f6 g6=.

16...dxe4 17.♕xe4 ♘d5= 18.g5 ♕c6 19.♖e1 ♖d6 20.♔c2

20.♕xe5?! ♘b4∓.

20...♘f2 21.♗xd5 ♕xd5 22.♕xd5 ♖xd5 23.♖e2 ♗g3 24.♗e3 ♖fd8 25.♖d1 g6 26.♖f1 ♖xd3 27.♗d4 ♖8xd4 28.cxd4 ♖xd4 29.f6 ♖c4+= 30.♔b1 ♖d4 31.♖f3 ♗f4 32.♖c2 ♗xg5 33.♖xc7 ♖d1+ 34.♔a2 h5 35.♖e7 ♖d5 36.♖e8+ ♔h7 37.♖b3 ♗xf6 38.♖xb7 ♔g7 39.♖b5 ♖d3 40.b4 axb4 41.♖xb4 ♖d4 42.♖b2 ♖d7 43.♖e2 ♗h4 44.♔b3 f5 45.♖8xe5 ½-½

Willem-Jan Pannekoek
Jaap Niewold
cr 2015

1.e4 e5 2.♘c3 ♗c5 3.♗c4 ♘f6 4.f4 d6 5.♘f3 ♘c6 6.d3 a6 7.♘d5 0-0 8.f5 ♘xd5 9.♗xd5 ♘d4?!

10.♘g5!?

10.c3 ♘xf3+ 11.♕xf3 c6 12.♗b3 b5 13.h4 ♔h8∞ A.Sokolov-Karpatchev, Nizhnij Novgorod 1998; 10.♘xd4! ♗xd4 11.♕h5! c6 12.♗b3 d5 13.c3 ♗a7 (Hresc-Wieckiewicz, Kirchheim rapid 1990) 14.♖f1!±→ Shaw.

10...h6 11.h4!?

11.♕h5 ♕f6! (11...hxg5? 12.h4 g4 13.♗g5 ♕e8 14.f6 ♘e6 15.♔d2!+−→ Ovetchkin/Soloviov) 12.♔d1 c6 13.♗xf7+ ♖xf7 14.♘xf7 ♕xf7 15.♕xf7+ ♔xf7∓.

11...c6?!

A) 11...hxg5? 12.hxg5 ♘xc2+ 13.♔f1+−;

B) 11...♕f6? 12.♘h7!+−;

C) 11...♕e7 12.c3 ♘e6 13.♕g4 c6 14.♗b3±→.

12.♗xf7+ ♖xf7 13.♘xf7 ♔xf7 14.c3 ♘b5 15.♕h5+ ♔g8

15...♕e7 16.a4 ♘c7 17.b4 ♗b6 18.♗xh6 gxh6 19.f6+ ♔e6 20.♕g4+ ♔f7 21.♕g7++−.

16.♖h3≌→ ♕f8 17.♖g3 ♔h7 18.♖g6 ♗d7 19.a4 ♘c7 20.d4!

20.f6? ♗e8∓.

20...♗xd4

20...exd4 21.f6+−.

21.cxd4 ♗e8 22.dxe5 dxe5 23.♗xh6+− gxh6 24.0-0-0 ♘d5 25.exd5 cxd5 26.♖xd5 ♖c8+ 27.♔d1 ♗xa4+ 28.♔e2 ♖c2+ 29.♔f1 1-0

Andrea Sorcinelli
Wladyslaw Krol
cr 2009

1.e4 e5 2.♗c4 ♘f6 3.d3 ♗c5 4.♘c3 ♘c6 5.f4 d6 6.♘f3 ♘d5 7.♘d5 ♘xd5 8.♗xd5 0-0!? 9.f5 ♘e7!?

10.♗b3

10.♗g5 h6 11.♗h4 ♕d7 12.♗b3 a5 13.a4 ♔h8 14.♕d2 (14.f6 ♘g6 15.♕d2 ♘xh4 16.♘xh4 ♕g4 17.♘f3 ♗e6=) 14...f6 15.g4 d5= 16.♗f2 dxe4 17.dxe4 ♕xd2+ 18.♘xd2 ♗xf2+ 19.♔xf2 ♗d7 20.♔e3 ♖ad8 21.♖ad1 ½-½ Eberl-Poljak, cr 2009.

10...d5 11.♕e2

11.♘xe5 ♘xf5 12.exf5 ♕h4+ 13.g3 ♕d4 14.♕e2 ♖e8 15.♔d1 (15.♗f4?! ♕xb2 16.♖d1 c6 17.♔f1 ♗xf5 18.♔g2 f6 19.♕f3 ♕d4∓→) 15...♕xe5 16.♕xe5 ♖xe5 17.g4 c6=; 11.f6?! gxf6 12.♗h6 ♖e8 (12...dxe4!?) 13.♘d2 c6 14.♖f1 (14.♕f3 f5∓) 14...♔h8 15.♕f3 ♘g8∓.

11...a5 12.a3

12.a4 ♕d6 13.♗e3 ♗xe3 14.♕xe3 ♔h8!? (14...♗d7 15.g4 ♖ab8 16.0-0↑ 'White's hands are free for a kingside offensive', Ovetchkin/Soloviov) 15.0-0 f6=. Black's position looks safe. Is it?

12...♕d6= 13.♗e3 b6 14.♕f2 f6 15.♘d2 ♗xe3 16.♕xe3 b5 17.0-0 ♗b7 18.♕f2 a4 19.♗a2 ♖fd8 20.exd5 ½-½

At this moment, the game material is indeed a bit sparse, but I have no doubt that we will experience new developments in this sub-variation in the future.

Komodo's Dynamic Line

by Bogdan Lalic

RE 7.4 (A11)   YB 9, 100

I had maybe less than an hour time to prepare for the 1st round of the Kilkenny open tournament. I saw that my opponent always plays the Réti Opening with white, starting as the English (1.c4) but transposing after 2.g3. The system with 2...c6 is known to be the best antidote against White's early fianchetto. I also saw that my opponent had some experience when Black defends the pawn on c4 after ...b7-b5, so I decided to surprise him in the opening with the early move 5...e5, which was a pet line of Paul Keres.
Usually players who start to play the Réti Opening tend to know better the lines in which Black takes on c4 and later plays ...b7-b5, thus keeping an extra pawn, but most of these positions are very unclear because White gets

long-lasting positional compensation for the pawn. I think White's move 6.♕c2 is already dubious – after it White is slightly worse in all the lines. Critical for this Keres line is allowing Black to play ...e5-e4, after which an interesting recommendation for White is to sacrifice the exchange while Black's king is uncastled – White doesn't even have a pawn for the exchange but Komodo confidently claims that White is better! What a difference from the old days. Now computers play and assess positions very dynamically, often much more dynamically than humans!

Frans Smit
Bogdan Lalic
Kilkenny 2015 (1)

1.c4 ♘f6 2.g3 c6 3.♗g2 d5 4.♘f3

4.cxd5 cxd5 5.d4 ♘c6 6.♘f3 ♗f5 7.♘c3 e6 8.0-0.

4...dxc4 5.♘a3

A) 5.♕c2 b5;
B) 5.0-0 ♘bd7 6.♘a3 (6.a4?! e5 7.♕c2 e4 8.♘g5 ♘c5 9.♕xc4 ♕d5 10.♕xd5 cxd5 11.d3 h6 12.♘h3 ♘b3 13.♖a2 ♗g4! 14.dxe4 ♗xe2 15.♖e1 ♘xc1 16.♖xc1 dxe4 17.♘c3 ♗g4 18.♘f4 ♗f5 19.♘cd5 ♘xd5 20.♘xd5 ♖d8 21.♘c7+ ♔d7 22.♘b5 ♔e6 23.♘xa7 ♖d2↑) 6...♗b6 7.♕c2 ♕d5!? and now:
B1) 8.b3♙;
B2) 8.♘e1∞;
B3) 8.♘h4∞.

5...e5

5...b5 6.♘e5 ♕c7 7.d4 ♗b7 8.0-0 e6 9.b3 c3 10.♕d3♙ Keres.

Paul Keres

6.♕c2?!

Better is 6.♘xc4 e4 and now:
A) 7.♘fe5 b5 8.♘e3□ ♕d4 (8...♗d6 9.f4 exf3 10.♘xf3 0-0 11.0-0∞) 9.f4∞;
B) 7.♘g5 ♗c5 8.♕c2!? (8.0-0 h6 9.♘xe4 ♘xe4 10.♗xe4 ♗h3 11.d4!? (11.♖e1? ♕d4 12.d3 ♕xf2+ 13.♔h1 ♘d7∓ Komodo 9.1) 11...♗xf1 12.♗e3 ♗xe2 13.♕xe2 ♗e7 14.♕g4♙ Komodo 9.1) 8...♗f5 (8...♗xf2+?? 9.♔xf2 ♘g4+ 10.♔e1 ♕xg5 11.♘d6+! ♔e7 12.♘xc8+ ♖xc8 13.♕xe4+ ♔f8 14.♕b4++− Komodo 9.1) and now:
B1) 9.0-0 ♕e7 10.d3 exd3 11.exd3 0-0 12.♗f4 ♘a6 13.♖fe1 ♕d8=;
B2) 9.♘xf7 ♔xf7 10.♘e5+ ♔e6! 11.♕xc5 ♘a6 12.♕c3 ♘d5 13.♘xc6 bxc6 14.♕xc6+ ♕d6∞ Komodo 9.1;
B3) 9.♘xe4?! ♗xe4 10.♗xe4 ♕d4 11.♗f3 ♕xf2+ 12.♔d1 0-0∓;
B4) 9.♘xe4! ♗xe4 10.♘xe4 0-0 11.d3± Komodo 9.1.

6...♗xa3 7.bxa3 ♕d5 8.♗b2 ♘bd7 9.0-0

9.♘h4 ♕e6 10.♘f5 0-0∓.

9...e4 10.♘d4 0-0 11.f3!?⇄ exf3 12.♘xf3

12.♖xf3 ♕c5 (12...♕e4 13.♖f4!? (13.♕c1 ♕e7 14.♘f5→ ♕xe2 15.♘xg7! ♔xg7 16.♗xf6+ ♘xf6 17.♕c3 ♔g8 18.♕xf6 ♕xd2 19.♖f4 ♕d8∞) 13...♘xc2

14.♘xc2 ♘b6! 15.♗xf6 gxf6
16.♘e3 ♗e6 17.♖xf6 ♖fd8∓)
13.♔h1 ♘e5 14.♖f4 ♘d5∓.
12...♕e4 13.♕d1
13.d3!? ♕e3+ 14.♔h1 cxd3
15.exd3 ♕c5 16.♕d2 ♘d5∓
17.♖ae1 ♘7f6 18.♗d4!? ♕xa3
19.♘g5⩲ h6?! (19...♕b4!?)
20.♗xd5□ ♘xd5□ 21.♘xf7!→
♗h3? (21...♕b4! 22.♘xh6+
♔h7! 23.♕xb4 ♖xf1+□ 24.♖xf1
♘xb4 25.♘f7 b6! 26.h4 c5∓)
22.♘xh6+ ♔h7 23.♕g5!+−.
13...♕e7 14.♖c1 ♘b6 15.♔h1?!
15.a4!? ♗e6 16.♘d4 ♕b4!
17.♘xe6 fxe6 18.♖b1 ♖ad8!
19.♗c3 (19.♗xf6 ♕c5+∓)
19...♕e7 20.♕c2 ♘fd5∓
21.♗e4? ♘xc3 22.♗xh7+? ♔h8
23.dxc3 ♖xf1+ 24.♖xf1 ♘d5
25.♕e4 ♕c5+ 26.♔h1 ♖f8!!
27.♖xf8+ ♕xf8 28.♔g2 ♘f6−+
Komodo 9.1.

15...♘e4!∓ 16.♘e5??
16.♕c2 ♗f5 17.d3 cxd3
(17...♘d6!? 18.e4 ♗e6 (18...
cxd3?? 19.♕c3+−) 19.d4 f5!↑
20.e5 ♘e4∓) 18.exd3 ♘d6
19.♘d4 ♗g6 20.♖ce1 ♕d7
21.♘b3 f6 22.♘c5 ♕f7∓.
16...c3!−+   0-1
As a surprise weapon I think
Keres' line is quite a practical
option for Black.

Black is More than OK in the Alapin with 5.♗c4

by Anssi Manninen

SI 47.3 (B22)   YB 76, 117

I recently read *Ivan's Chess Journey: Games and Stories* by
Ivan Sokolov (Thinkers Publishing, 2016). Both Sokolov and Ulf Andersson were the seconds of Jan Timman, so Sokolov certainly had a clue about Andersson's abilities. In analyses, he 'simply saw everything', as Sokolov put it. In order to find a compromise between his love for chess and his 'damaged' nervous system (i.e. his inability to withstand the pressure during an over-the-board game), Andersson started to play correspondence chess. And indeed he saw pretty much everything! In 2002, Andersson had the highest correspondence Elo rating in the world.
But let's get down to business. The following correspondence game demonstrates that Black has nothing to fear in the Alapin Variation of the Sicilian Defence with 5.♗c4. If anything, it seems to me it is White who has to play precisely to maintain the balance.

Petr Dolezal
Anssi Manninen
cr World Cup 21 prelim 2015
1.e4 c5 2.c3
No Dragon today? So far I have played three correspondence games in the Dragon with the black pieces and I have scored 2.5 points. Admittedly, only one of my opponents played a serious line; nevertheless, in my street Black is OK in the Dragon!
The Basman-Sale variation of the Sicilian received a lot of publicity in Yearbook 117. Without going into details, I would like to suggest a new chess rule: if your opponent wants to play the Basman-Sale, don't prevent it! That is what the great Petrosian used to say about the Dutch Defence.
As far as the Alapin Variation is concerned, the world-renowned opening expert Andras Adorjan is clearly not a big fan of it (see Yearbook 117).
2...♘f6
This is considered best by Sveshnikov, but Adorjan seems
to prefer 2...d5. Also, the 'King of the Sicilian' himself chose 2... d5 against Deep Blue, so it is certainly a viable alternative.
3.e5 ♘d5 4.♘f3 ♘c6 5.♗c4 ♘b6 6.♗b3 c4 7.♗c2

7...d6
My opponent played quite slowly, so I had several 'free' days to compare different options; the positional 7...g6 was recommended by Kotronias in *Chess Informant*, while Sveshnikov prefers the aggressive 7...♕c7 8.♕e2 g5. However, I came to the conclusion that the 'boring' line played in the game fully equalizes without any risk.
After all, Black is not advised to take any risks in the opening, right? Perhaps that is why Karpov almost always played the 'Dull Kann'. Of course, real men play the Sicilian! ('I promised you, dad, not to do the things you've done. I walk away from trouble when I can. Now please don't think I'm weak, I didn't turn the other cheek. Papa, I should hope you understand, sometimes you gotta fight when you're a man' – *Coward of the County*).
7...d6 was recommended by Aagaard in *Experts on the Anti-Sicilian* (Quality Chess, 2011). His general conclusion was that we will reach an equal position, which is easier to play with the black pieces. I believe this game supports his conclusion; it is White who has to play precisely to maintain the balance.
8.exd6 ♕xd6
8...e5!?.

Ivan Sokolov

9.0-0 ♗g4 10.♖e1 0-0-0

'I have honestly never understood players who carry on playing a system which in my opinion permits Black to achieve a promising position without too much difficulty.' So harsh was the statement by Adorjan regarding the Alapin Variation in Yearbook 117. But let's take a look after 10 moves: Black is developing quickly and harmoniously, and he even has a small advantage in space. It is very rare that Black has a space advantage after a mere 10 moves. This may seem insignificant and temporary, but let's see what happens:

11.h3 ♗h5 12.b3 ♕f6 13.♗e4 ♘e5 14.g4 ♘xf3+ 15.♕xf3 ♕xf3 16.♗xf3 ♗g6 17.♘a3 e6 18.♘xc4 ♘xc4 19.bxc4 ♗d3 20.♗e2?!

The first inaccuracy. This move is suggested by Houdini 4, but it does not make any sense. Houdini

is very strong in certain types of positions, but this is not one of them. Black could not care less about White's miserable c4-pawn, so why waste time to defend it? Of course, 19...♗d3 was played to block White's d-pawn, not to win the c4-pawn.

Perhaps 20.a4 could keep the balance. 20.♖e5 has been played in some games but Black keeps a slight pull.

20...♗e7 21.♔g2 ♗g5 22.a4 ♗f4!

I am not sure if this move is objectively stronger than, let's say, 22...♗xe2 23.♖xe2 ♖d3, as suggested by the latest version of Stockfish. However, as White has no counterplay, it makes sense to not force matters and just keep White bottled up. Just look at that 'tall pawn' on c1; apparently, it is just waiting for the next game to start, as this one should not last very long.

After 22...♗f4, the e5-square is controlled so the potentially forthcoming ...h7-h5 break will gain strength. Also, around here I came to the conclusion that my opponent was playing under the authority of Houdini, and it suggested a weak response to 22...♗f4. ('Son, I've made a life out of readin' people's faces knowin' what the cards were by the way they held their eyes' – *The Gambler*).

Finally, it is always nice to attach an exclamation mark to your own move, even if you're a patzer like yours truly.

23.♗f3?

This was the above-mentioned weak move suggested by Houdini. It makes no sense whatsoever. Now the bishop may look active on the h1-a8 diagonal but what exactly is it doing there? Absolutely nothing. Furthermore, now the ...e6-e5-e4 advance will come with tempo. In a higher sense, White is already lost.

23...h5! 24.gxh5 e5 25.a5 f5 26.♖g1

Another dubious move suggested by Houdini, but it seems that nothing could have saved White any more. Houdini believes Black has only a microscopic edge. After a longer period of calculation, Stockfish and Komodo start to realize that White is in trouble. From the human perspective, we can conclude that White is completely busted. Black's whole army is getting more and more active, while White's pieces cannot do anything but sit and wait.

I have many chess friends who think that correspondence games are decided by engine analysis, but nothing could be further from the truth. All serious correspondence players utilize computer-assisted analysis; nevertheless, some players win and others lose. Perhaps in 2025 we can kiss correspondence chess goodbye, as the strongest engines will be so powerful that almost all computer-assisted games will end in draws. Just imagine Stockfish 22 or Komodo 24 with an Elo rating of 4200!

26...e4 27.♗d1 g6!

Now the kingside will be opened up, with fatal consequences.

28.Kh1

A quite bizarre position, with all White's pieces standing on the back rank. Who said Black's space advantage was insignificant and temporary?!

28...gxh5 29.a6 b6

And more thinking in this position can only prolong the inevitable.

In his classic *Think Like a Grandmaster*, Alexander Kotov wrote about players who were over-confident, complacent in their recognition of the fact that they had a massive advantage, and so their vigilance was blunted. 'Dizziness due to success', as Kotov put it.

So, 'You never count your money [or Elo points] when you're sittin' at the table. There'll be time enough for countin' when the dealin's done' – *The Gambler*.

Another Boring Berliner

by Peter Boel

RL 7.4 (C65)   YB 113

The daily reports in London are sardined with complaints about all those Berlin games that seem to be played only at the Classic. Perhaps it is for this reason that not much attention was given to a rather clever novelty in this infamous line by Anish Giri.

The Berlin boring? Come on, people. It's a chess opening variation. It can't be boring!

Maxime Vachier-Lagrave
Anish Giri
London 2015 (5)

1.e4 e5 2.♘f3 ♘c6 3.♗b5 ♘f6 4.0-0 ♘xe4 5.d4 ♘d6 6.♗xc6 dxc6 7.dxe5 ♘f5 8.♕xd8+ ♔xd8 9.h3 ♔e8

This is the 'hot' line at this moment.

10.♘c3 h5 11.♗f4 ♗e7 12.♖ad1 ♗e6 13.♘g5 ♖h6 14.g3

Still the first choice.

14...♗c4

But here the simplifying 14...♗xg5 15.♗xg5 ♖g6 16.h4 f6, with a little something for White, is mostly preferred – which may change after this game.

15.♖fe1 ♖g6 16.♘ce4 ♖d8 17.♖xd8+ ♗xd8 18.b3 ♗d5 19.c4

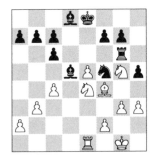

Now 19...♗xg5 20.♘xg5 ♗e6 21.♔g2 was in fact OK for Black in Adams-Kramnik, in the London Classic one year earlier (...), but Black's kingside still looks a bit jam-packed. Giri had found a radical solution in this position:

19...♘d4! 20.cxd5

Untangling, since on 20.♖d1 follows 20...♘f3+ 21.♘xf3 ♗xe4 with liberation.

20...cxd5 21.♘d6+

White cannot avoid giving back the piece; if 21.♖d1 ♘e2+.

Anish Giri

21...cxd6 22.exd6+ ♘e6 23.♘f3 ♗f6 24.♗e3 ♔d7 25.♗xa7

25...♖h6!

What an arrogant little move! Black does not have to take back the pawn yet; he has time to go all the way back with his rook to improve it.

26.♖d1 ♔xd6 27.♗b8+ ♔c6 28.♖c1+ ♔d7 29.♖d1 ♔c6 30.♖c1+ ♔d7 31.♖d1

And yes – the draw was agreed.

Two Errata in Yearbook 117

by the Editorial Staff

YB 117

As various of our readers have pointed out, we placed a picture of the wrong Marc Lacrosse in the FORUM section on page 12 of Yearbook 117. The player depicted is not the Marc Lacrosse described by Srdjan Sale in his article (i.e. the Marc Lacrosse who passed away in 2009), but another Belgian player called Marc Lacrosse, who was born in 1958 and is still alive.

We sincerely apologize to all concerned for this painful mistake.

In the same FORUM section there is another mistake on page 23. The black player who faced Mikhail Ulibin in the featured game is not Viacheslav Zakhartsov, but his son Vladimir Zakhartsov, as was indicated in the text above the game.

Isolated Incidents

by Joel Benjamin

In this series of columns, grandmaster Joel Benjamin helps club players to build up a good, practical opening repertoire. He will make his point by using examples of the chess stars, but also gives advice that is more suitable for club players. Learn from an experienced grandmaster/trainer and find out what openings suit your style best!

It can be hard work remembering sequences of opening moves, and, as Yearbook readers well know, theory can change so quickly. Developing understanding of the strategy of typical positions provides knowledge for the long-term. In this column we will explore one of the most important structures in all of chess – the isolated d-pawn (IQP).

As a chess coach, I am privileged to work with many talented juniors. I always feel a little disappointed when I see discomfort in playing IQP positions (and I often do). Today's kids have such good tools for learning opening specifics that they may shy away from positions of a more general strategic nature. In my youth, information on the openings was hard to come by; we were happy to have Informants every six months, and ECOs (sadly, New In Chess had not come along yet). My boyhood

Maxim Dlugy

teacher George Kane had the wisdom to educate me on IQP strategy early in my career, and I have enjoyed playing those positions for a lifetime.

IQP positions matter so much because they can arise out of almost any opening. So far I have focused on lines for 1.e4 players, and I will here as well. But IQP positions occur quite frequently from 1.d4 openings (arguably more so) and Englishes, too. Positions from the Panov Attack in the Caro-Kann may be indistinguishable from ones in the Nimzo-Indian.

Nothing illustrates the point like the following position:

I reached this position via two different move orders in the Panov Attack in games twenty years apart! The first game came out of a conventional move order.

Joel Benjamin
Maxim Dlugy
Estes Park ch-USA 1985
1.e4 c6 2.d4 d5 3.exd5 cxd5
4.c4 ♘f6 5.♘c3 e6 6.♘f3 ♗e7
7.cxd5

It is not necessarily to Black's advantage to occupy the blockading square. Sometimes there will be issues with his development; sometimes Black will prefer to have direct pressure on the d-pawn.

7...♘xd5 8.♗c4

8.♗d3 is the alternative development, and I will investigate that a bit later. In my experience, both deployments are of roughly equal value.

8...♘f6

This is what my opponents tend to do, though it may seem strange to the uninitiated. White has some ideas to capture on d5, though it won't really be a threat due to counterattacks on the d4-pawn. But Black will need to develop his queen's bishop, and ♗c4xd5 can be effective against an attempted

Jonathan Grant

26

fianchetto. Still, White has to feel good in saving a tempo over 7.♗d3 dxc4 8.♗xc4.

9.0-0 ♘c6 10.a3 0-0 11.♖e1 a6 12.♗a2 b5 13.d5!

A very young Patrick Wolff fed me this idea, which takes advantage of White's quicker development. Black is already in trouble, as evidenced by White's 85% score from here. But also 49 players, including a GM here and there, have fallen into this trap.

13...exd5 14.♘xd5 ♘xd5 15.♕xd5 ♗b7 16.♕h5!

The kingside is under fire, and I don't think Black can do much better than Dlugy did here.

16...♕d6 17.♗g5 ♖ad8 18.♗xe7 ♘xe7 19.♘g5 ♕g6 20.♕xh7+ ♕xh7 21.♘xh7 ♔xh7 22.♖xe7

Dlugy outplayed me and held a draw in the endgame, though it obviously isn't an easy task for Black.

Now watch lightning strike again:

**Joel Benjamin
Jonathan Grant**
Cork ch-EU 2005

[Yes, I really did play in the EU Championship. I'm Irish on my wife's side]

1.e4 c6 2.c4

Reversing the order of White's first two moves demonstrates a useful anti-Slav approach. It does allow Black to go for an Old Indian with 2...e5, but that opening is less well regarded than the Caro-Kann, and your opponent likely doesn't normally play it.

2...d5 3.exd5

If White intends to take twice, 3.cxd5 makes sense because the text permits 3...♘f6. It only matters if you intend to try to hold the d5-pawn with 5.♗b5+ or 5.♕a4+, neither of which appeals to me.

3...cxd5 4.cxd5 ♘f6 5.♘c3 ♘xd5 6.♘f3 e6

6...♘c6 7.♗b5 e6 8.0-0 ♗e7 9.d4 0-0 10.♖e1 leads to a position where White's bishop is placed oddly but effectively.

Black should be content with 10...♗d7, whereupon the bishop will generally retreat to d3, often with a trade on d5. The resulting positions look innocent but can build into something more substantial, e.g. Carlsen-Smeets, Wijk aan Zee 2009: 11.♗d3 ♖c8 12.♘xd5 exd5 13.♘e5 ♗f6 14.♗f4 g6 15.♕b3 ♘a5 16.♕b4 ♗e6 17.♗h6 ♗g7 18.♗xg7 ♔xg7 19.h4 ♖e8 20.h5 f6 21.♘f3 b6 22.♗b5 ♖e7 23.♖e2 ♖cc7 24.♖ae1±.

For some reason, all of my opponents provoke me into a taking on c6, e.g. 10...♘f6 11.a3 a6 12.♗xc6 bxc6 13.♘a4 with a very comfortable edge (Benjamin-Herman U.S. Chess League 2013). The computer says it is equal, but don't believe it. The difference between this and analogous positions in the c3 Sicilian is the eternally hemmed in light-squared bishop.

7.♗c4 ♘c6 8.0-0 ♗e7 9.d4 0-0 10.♖e1

You see where we are headed. Now most players opt for 10...♘f6. White most often plays 11.♘e4, but 11.♗b3 is interesting, too. One game really impressed... and confused me a bit, but I really like the finish: 11.♗b3 ♘de7 12.♗f4!? ♗xd4 13.♘xd4 ♘xd4 14.♗c4 (at one time I would have thought Black won a pawn for nothing, but it isn't easy to complete his development) 14...♘ec6 15.♖c1 ♕f6 16.♗c7 e5? (the first real mistake. Now White is well on top) 17.♘d5 ♕g5 18.f4 exf4 19.♗xf4 ♕h4 20.♗g3 ♕d8 21.♘c7 ♖b8 22.♘b5 ♖a8 23.♗d6 ♖e8

24.♗xf7+ ♔xf7 25.♕h5+ g6 26.♕xh7+ ♔f6 27.♘xd4 ♘xd4 28.♕h4+ ♔f7 29.♖c7+ ♗d7 30.♕h7+ ♔f6 31.♖f1+ ♔e6 32.♕xg6+ ♔d5 33.♖c5 mate, Kramnik-Meier, Dortmund 2012. Black can also create a hanging pawns position with 10...♘xc3. This strategy is more effective with the bishop on c4, as it will almost always retreat to d3 after this exchange. Still, 11.bxc3 b6 12.♗d3 ♗b7 13.h4 offers White

good chances for an initiative, whether Black takes the pawn or not.

10...♘f6 11.a3 a6 12.♗a2 b5 13.d5 exd5 14.♘xd5 ♘xd5 15.♕xd5 ♗b7 16.♕h5 ♕d6 17.♗g5 ♖ad8

17...♗f6 18.♖ad1 ♘d4 19.♘xd4 ♕c5 20.♘e6+−.

18.♗xe7 ♘xe7 19.♘g5 ♕g6 20.♕xh7+ ♕xh7 21.♘xh7 ♔xh7 22.♖xe7

This time the technical phase went smoothly.

The story is a trilogy, with the final (though chronologically second) chapter taking a strange path. The first diagram was again reached, though not from a Caro-Kann. You might guess it was a semi-Tarrasch: 1.♘f3 ♘f6 2.c4 c5 3.♘c3 d5 4.cxd5 ♘xd5 5.e3 e6 6.♗c4 ♘c6 7.0-0 ♗e7 8.d4 cxd4 9.exd4 0-0 10.♖e1 ♘f6 11.a3 would be quite plausible (many of the grandmaster games seem to come from this move order). You would be right if you said Sicilian, but not the Alapin. Behold:

Joel Benjamin
Gennady Zaichik
Philadelphia 2001

1.e4 c5 2.♘f3 d6 3.♗c4 ♘f6 4.d3 ♘c6 5.c3 d5!?

I was unsure how to proceed here, but little by little I realized I could get to familiar ground!

6.exd5 ♘xd5 7.0-0 e6 8.d4 cxd4 9.cxd4 ♗e7 10.♘c3 0-0 11.♖e1 ♘f6 12.a3 b6

13.d5!?

This advance may not, objectively speaking, be the best continuation, because Black can survive with a few accurate moves: 13...♘a5! 14.♗a2 ♘xd5! (14...exd5 15.b4! with a big edge) 15.♘xd5 exd5 and now 16.♕xd5 ♗e6! is okay for Black, so White must be contented with a small edge after 16.♗xd5 ♗b7. The slow playing option looks quite pleasant for White: 13.♗a2 ♗b7 14.♗f4! (the more natural 14.♗g5 offers Black a chance to play ...♘f6-d5, perhaps right away) 14...♖c8 15.♕d3 (White can play these moves in different order).

Black lacks natural moves here. He would like to occupy d5, but he needs more control there. 15...♘a5 gets thrown back by 16.b4 ♘c6 17.d5. Meanwhile, White will complete his development with ♖a1-d1, and d4-d5 will hang heavy in the air.

13...exd5?! 14.♘xd5 ♘xd5 15.♕xd5 ♗b7 16.♕h5 ♕d6 17.♘g5

17.♗g5 might be even stronger here, as the a-pawn would be hanging at the end of the variation.

17...♕g6 18.♕xg6 hxg6 19.♗f4

White is still well on top, and I managed to win a nice endgame.

Joel Benjamin
Fabian Döttling
Boston US open 2001

1.e4 c6 2.d4 d5 3.exd5 cxd5 4.c4 ♘f6 5.♘c3 e6 6.♘f3 ♗e7 7.cxd5 ♘xd5 8.♗d3

This is quite a nice diagonal for the bishop as well. Setting up a battery on the b1-h7 diagonal is a key element of White's strategy.

8...♘c6 9.0-0 0-0 10.♖e1

10...♘f6

It strikes me now, how often my opponents have chosen to retreat the knight. Here fianchetto zeal pays a heavy price: 10...b6? 11.♘xd5 ♕xd5 (relatively better is 11...exd5 12.♗xh7+ ♔xh7 13.♕c2+ with an extra pawn) 12.♗e4 ♕d6 and now:

A) 13.♕c2 ♗d7 14.♗xh7+ is good but not yet decisive;

B) 13.♗g5!? is interesting, as Black really struggles after 13...♗xg5 14.♘xg5 h6 15.d5!;

C) 13.♘e5! ♗b7 14.♗f4 is decisive; Black can expect to lose material or get mated (14...♖fe8 15.♗xh7+).

Among more knowledgeable players you can expect 10...♗f6.

Fabian Döttling

In this case the d4-pawn is attacked; some players have tried 11.♘e4!? ♗xd4 12.♘xd4 ♘xd4 13.♘g5, but White can expect equality at best against several defenses of h7. 11.♗e4 exerts pressure on the long diagonal, and after 11...♘ce7 12.♕d3 (12.♘e5 is also frequently played) we have a crossroads.

Should Black defend with 12... g6 or 12...h6? In IQP positions Black normally wants to block the diagonal, because ...h7-h6 can be met by switching the queen to the front of the battery. But here the switch would be time-consuming, and 12...h6 prevents White from activating the second bishop. There is about an even split for the two moves in practice:

A) 12...h6 13.♘e5 ♘xc3 (if Black waits for ♕d3-g3 his kingside will come under fire) 14.♕xc3 ♘f5 15.♗e3. Black's position looks great, except he has trouble developing his queen's bishop;

B) 12...g6 13.♗h6 ♗g7 14.♗xg7 ♔xg7 15.♖ac1 ♗d7 (15...b6 16.♗xd5 ♘xd5 17.♘xd5 ♕xd5 18.♖c7±) 16.♗xd5 exd5 17.h3 with a small but pleasant edge for White

11.a3 b6 12.♗e3

I rejected 12.♗c2 because of 12...♗a6. 12.♗g5 is the most common choice The game Beliavsky-Karpov, Moscow tt 1986, was a classic confrontation representing plausible play: 12.♗g5 ♗b7 (12...h6 13.♗h4 ♗b7 14.♗c2 ♘h5 15.d5! exd5

16.♕d3 f5 17.♗xe7 ♘xe7 18.♕e3±, Tsereteli-Arabidze, Georgian Ch-W 2010) 13.♗c2 ♖c8 14.♕d3 g6 15.♖ad1 ♘d5 16.♗h6 ♖e8 17.♗a4 a6 18.♘xd5 ♕xd5 19.♕e3 ♘f6 20.♗b3 ♕d7 (20...♕d8 21.♘e5 ♗xe5 22.dxe5 and Black cannot move the queen to c6) 21.d5 exd5 22.♕xb6 ♖xe1+ 23.♖xe1 ♗xb2 24.♗xd5 ♗g7 25.♗xg7 ♔xg7 and now, instead of 26.h4, 26.♕b2+ ♔g8 27.♗a2 would have given White a powerful attack.

I think I was attracted to 12.♗e3 at the time because I had already known some success in analogous positions from the Alapin Sicilian.

12...♗b7 13.♕e2

White postpones setting up the battery, centralizing pieces while not encouraging exchanges.

13...♖c8 14.♖ad1

Here again it is premature to occupy d5: 14...♘d5 15.♘xd5 ♕xd5 16.♗c4 ♕h5 17.d5 ♘a5 18.♗a2 ♗xd5 19.♗xd5 exd5 20.♗xb6 ♘c6 21.♗xa7 ♗xa3 22.bxa3 ♘xa7 23.♕a2 and White won a pawn (Manca-Emms, Cappelle-la-Grande 1993 and Vogt-Grund, Germany Bundesliga 1998/99). Both of those games came out of the Alapin Sicilian.

14...♖c7 15.♗b1

15...♘a5 looks most natural, preparing to return the knight to d5: 16.♗g5 ♘d5 17.♕e4 g6 (17...♘f6 18.♕h4) 18.♕h4 (18.♗xe7 ♕xe7 19.♘xd5 ♕d8!=) 18...f6 19.♗h6 ♘xc3 20.bxc3 ♖f7 (20...♗xf3 21.gxf3 f5 22.♕g3 ♗d6 (22...♖f6 is better but White keeps an edge with 23.d5!) 23.f4±, Van Beers-Michel Yunis, Bled 2002) 21.♖xe6 ♖xc3 22.♕g3 ♔h8, Johannesson-Hoogendoorn, Gausdal 2003, and now instead of 23.h4 White could have won with 23.♘e5! fxe5 24.♕xe5+ ♔g8 25.♗xg6 hxg6 26.♖xg6+ ♔h7 27.♕h5. After the stronger 22...♕c7, White can claim an advantage in the complications after 23.♕g4 ♗f8 24.♗xg6 hxg6 25.d5!! e.g. 25...♗xh6 26.♕xg6+ ♗g7 27.♖de1!+−. Black can do better with 16...h6! (as usual the timing of this move is crucial) 17.♗h4 ♘d5 18.♕e4 ♘f6! is effective because the queen cannot swing to h4. If White doesn't want to accept a repetition he can try 18.♘xd5 ♗xd5 19.♗g3 with equality.

15...♖d7 16.♗a2

The bishop switches to cover the d5-square, which Black cannot 'win' with 16...♘d5 because his rook gets chased by 17.♘e5.

16...♖e8 17.♘e5 ♘xe5 18.dxe5 ♘d5 19.♗xd5 exd5

19...♗xd5 20.♕b5 is also better for White.

20.♕g4 ♗f8 21.♘e4 ♔h8

21...♖xe5 22.♘f6+ ♕xf6 23.♕xd7 ♖e7 24.♕a4 ♕xb2 25.♕xa7 is much better for White.

22.♗g5

I was on the fence with this decision. 22.♘g5! would have led to a decisive attack (and clear

first place in the tournament), e.g. 22...h6 23.e6 fxe6 24.♘xe6 and 22...♔g8 23.♕f5 g6 24.♕h3 h5 25.e6 are both crushing.

22...♕c8 23.♘f6 ♖c7 24.♕xc8 ♖exc8 25.♘xd5 ♖c2 26.♘e3 ♖2c5

Alas, I was not able to convert the extra pawn.

Joel Benjamin
Alexander Kaliksteyn
Saratoga 1996

1.e4 c5 2.c3

From a repertoire standpoint, we certainly need to meet the Sicilian. The Alapin fits in nicely with our Panov Attack in the Caro-Kann.

2...d5 3.exd5 ♕xd5 4.d4 ♘f6 5.♘f3 ♘c6 6.♗e3

This generally provokes a pawn trade that enables White to develop his second knight. It is worth noting the move 6...♗f5, which has seen some popularity in the last few years. A solid answer is 7.♘a3 cxd4 8.♗c4 ♕a5 9.♘xd4 ♘xd4 10.♗xd4 e5 11.♗b5+ ♗d7 12.♗xd7+ ♘xd7 13.♘c4 ♕d5 (13...♕c7 14.♕e2 0-0-0!?) 14.♕e2 f6 15.0-0 ♗e7 16.♖fe1 ♖c8 (Pap-Tadic, Kragujevac 2014) and now 17.♘e3 ♕e6 18.♕f3 with a pull, as 18...exd4? 19.cxd4! regains the piece with a large advantage.

6...cxd4 7.cxd4 e6 8.♘c3 ♕d6

Black can certainly retreat the queen to d8, leading into positions we just examined. In practice, Black usually avails himself of the 'free' developing

move. He will have an easier time connecting the rooks, but the differences are not all positive. The queen will be a target for attack in some lines, while the loss of contact with the g5-square is often a factor as well.

9.a3 ♗e7 10.♗d3 0-0 11.0-0 b6 12.♕e2 ♗b7 13.♖ad1 ♖ac8

This rook development is routine with the queen on d8, but here Black can bunch his rooks in the center, i.e. 13...♖ad8 14.♖fe1 ♖fe8 15.♗b1 ♕b8 16.♗g5 g6 17.♗a2 and now Black has tried three different moves of the same knight:

A) 17...♘h5 18.d5 exd5 19.♖xd5 ♗f8 20.♕d2 with a nice white advantage;

B) 17...♘g4 18.g3 (White has to be alert to tactics; 18.♗xe7? ♘xd4 19.♖xd4 ♖xd4 with a clear edge for Black) 18...♗xg5 19.♘xg5 ♘h6 20.♘ce4 ♔g7 21.♕f3 f5 (21...♘f5 22.g4 ♘cxd4 23.♖xd4 ♖xd4 24.gxf5±) 22.♘xe6+ ♖xe6 23.♗xe6 fxe4 24.♕c3+− Pavasovic-Chan, Bled ol 2002 and Pavasovic-J.Horvath, Austria Bundesliga B 2002/03;

C) 17...♘d5 18.♘xd5 (this will always be more pleasant for White, but 18.h4 is interesting) 18...exd5 19.♕d2=.

14.♖fe1 ♖fd8 15.♗g5 ♕b8

Alexander Kaliksteyn

Often dubious when the queen has to recapture, here 15...♘d5?? just loses after 16.♘xd5 ♕xd5 17.♗e4 ♕d6 18.d5.

15...h6 may be the critical move: 16.♗h4 (16.♗xf6 ♗xf6 17.d5 ♘d4=; 16.♗c1 ♗f8 17.♗b1 ♘e7 and Black's pieces are starting to coordinate well) 16...♕f4 (16...♘xd4? 17.♘xd4 ♕xd4 18.♗e4!+− Smith-Finegold, Lubbock 2010) 17.♗g3 ♕g4 18.h3 ♕h5 19.♕e3 ♗f8 with equality. This may suggest White is better off with the equally useful 15.♗b1.

16.d5!?

The thematic advance worked better than it should have here. The standard 16.♗b1 comes with a diabolical threat, e.g. 16...♕a8? 17.d5! exd5 18.♕d3+−. After 16...g6 17.♗a2 the black rooks look rather worse to me than on d8 and e8.

16...♘xd5

No choice here, in view of 16...exd5 17.♗f5 ♖c7 18.♗xf6 ♗xf6 19.♘xd5+−.

17.♘xd5 ♖xd5 18.♗xh7+ ♔xh7 19.♖xd5 exd5

19...f6 20.♕xe6 fxg5 21.♘xg5+ ♗xg5 22.♖xg5+−.

20.♗xe7 ♕f4?

In a later game, Sermek-P. Horvath, St Veit 2000, Black improved with 20...♘xe7 but still stood a lot worse. The right move is 20...♔g8!, the key point being that 21.♘g5 ♕e5! saves Black.

21.♕d3+

I played this game during my IBM days, so I took the opportunity

to feed it to DEEP BLUE. The analysis, which I published in Informant 67, is not earth-shattering by today's standards but is an interesting kind of historical document.

I took the 'bird in the hand' with this move, but DB showed I could have won with 21.♘g5+ ♔h6 (21...♔g6 22.♕d3+ ♕f5 23.♕g3 ♘xe7 24.♘e6+ ♔h6 25.♕xg7+ ♔h5 26.h3+−) and now:

A) 22.♘h3 ♕d4! (22...♕f5 23.g4 ♕g6 (23...♕d7 24.♕e3+ ♔h7 25.♘g5+ ♔g8 26.♕h3) 24.♕e3+ ♔h7 25.♘g5+ ♔g8 26.♗d8!!+−) 23.♗g5+ ♔h7 24.♕h5+ ♔g8 25.♗d8! ♖xd8 26.♘g5 ♕e5 27.♖xe5! (27.♕h7+ ♔f8 28.♕h8+ ♔e7 29.♕xg7 ♔d7! 30.♔h1 ♕xf2 31.♖xe5 ♖g8 and Black is okay) 27...♕xe5 28.♕h7+ ♔f8 29.♕h8+ ♔e7 30.♕xd8+ ♔xd8 31.♘xf7+ ♔e7 32.♘xe5 with an extra pawn for White but by no means a decisive edge.

B) 22.♘e6! fxe6 (22...♕f5 23.g4 and White wins the queen after 23...♕xe6 (23...♕g6 24.♕e3+ ♔h7 25.♘g5+ ♔g8 26.♗d8 again) 24.♕d2+) 23.♕xe6+ ♔h5 (23...g6 24.♗f6 ♕f5 25.♕f7 ♖g8 26.f4+−; 23...♔h7 24.♖e3) 24.♕h3+ ♔g6 25.♕d3+ ♔f7 26.♕xd5+ ♔g6 27.♕e6+ ♔h5 (27...♔h7 28.♖e3+−) 28.h3 is winning for White.

21...♔g8?

Black has to play 21...g6 22.♕xd5 and play a pawn down with 22...♘xe7 23.♕xb7 ♖c7 or

Benjamin Finegold

22...♖e8 23.♗g5 ♖xe1+ 24.♘xe1 ♕f5 25.♕xf5 gxf5.

22.♘g5 g6

Or 22...♕h4 23.♕xd5 ♕f4 (23...♕h5 24.♗d8+−) 24.♕d3 ♕h4 25.♕f3+−.

23.♕h3   **1-0**

23...♘xe7 24.♕h7+ ♔f8 25.♕h8+ ♘g8 26.♘h7# could be the finish.

**Joel Benjamin
Ralph Zimmer**
Parsippany tt 1998

1.e4 c5 2.♘f3 e6 3.c3 d5 4.exd5 ♕xd5 5.d4 ♘f6 6.♗e3 cxd4 7.cxd4 ♘c6 8.♘c3 ♕d6 9.a3 ♗e7 10.♗d3 0-0 11.♕c2

The battery usually does little with the bishop in front, but here it deters Black's preferred development of his pieces.

11...b6? 12.♘e4 ♘xe4 13.♗xe4 wins a pawn for White, so Black

will either have to commit himself on the kingside or renounce the fianchetto.

11...h6

This takes care of the threat to h7, and of ♗e3-g5 as well, but there are always potential problems with this placement.

Usually Black plays 11...♗d7; White's queen will usually slide to e2 later, but in return for the tempo, the bishop is posted less actively. I had a pleasant experience in this line: 12.♖d1 ♖ac8 13.0-0 a6 14.♖fe1 ♕b8 15.♘e5 ♖fd8 (the position was reached by a slightly different move order)

16.♘xd7! ♖xd7 17.d5 – the thematic advance gave White a nice advantage in Benjamin-Feldman, New York 1999.

11...g6 is perhaps an underrated approach, with the idea of 12.0-0 b6. White might try 12.♖c1 to force the bishop to d7.

12.0-0 b6 13.♖ad1 ♗b7 14.♖fe1 ♖ac8 15.♕c1!

This novelty has not been repeated, despite the fact that Black does not have any move to prevent ♗e3xh6 ! The standard approach should be okay for Black: 15.♕e2 ♖fd8 16.♗b1 ♗f8 17.♗c1 ♘e7 18.♘e5 and now not 18...♘ed5? 19.♘b5! and White will capture on a7 or f7, but 18...♘f5=.

15...♘d5

After 15...♘a5 16.♗xh6 Black has nothing better than 16...♘d5, transposing into the game.

16.♗xh6 ♘a5

After 16...♘xc3 17.bxc3 ♕xa3 18.♕f4 White's attack is decisive.

17.♗b1

Very possibly not the strongest. White can maintain an extra pawn with 17.♗g5 ♘xc3 18.♗xe7 ♕xe7 19.bxc3 ♗xf3 20.gxf3 or play for more with 17.♘e5.

17...♘xc3   18.bxc3   ♗xf3 19.gxf3 ♖fd8

19...♕d5? 20.♖e5 ♕b3 (20...♕xf3 21.♖d3) 21.♗xg7 ♖xc3 22.♕h6 ♕xd1+ 23.♖e1 ♕xe1+ 24.♔g2 and Black can

only put off checkmate for a few moves.

19...♘c4!? was a try though.

20.♗f4

It was stronger to press the attack with 20.♔h1.

20...♕xa3?

Black is okay after 20...♕d5.

21.♕c2   g6   22.♖xe6!   ♖c6 23.♗c1

White won the queen and the game.

While utilizing IQP positions for a 1.e4 repertoire was the main focus here, many of the positions we reached were of interest to those who open with 1.d4, 1.c4, or 1.♘f3. For instance, one who is happy playing IQP positions but opens with 1.d4 might consider entering the Rubinstein (4.e3) Nimzo-Indian.

In the coming installments, we will explore much more in IQP positions, like a different type of IQP structure, the IQP for Black, and strategies against the IQP.

The Traditional Start of the Year (Tata Steel)

by **Alexey Kuzmin**

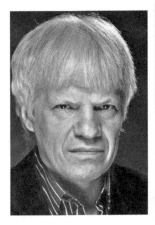

Experienced grandmaster Alexey Kuzmin, the former coach of Anatoly Karpov and Alexander Morozevich, probes the most recent top events for new tendencies in opening play.

By a long-established tradition the top-class chess year was opened by the tournament in Wijk aan Zee. In the fight for victory there turned out to be no intrigue. The World Champion proceeded confidently through the rounds to his already customary first place. But for the right to stand on the other steps of the podium there was a serious fight. In the end, finishing a whole point behind the winner, second and third places were shared by Fabiano Caruana and Ding Liren.

However, a description of the competitive course of the tournament does not come within my remit – I have gathered a harvest of opening ideas. And in this aspect of the chess battles in Wijk aan Zee, in particular one is struck by the rich arsenal of opening novelties by Fabiano Caruana and the original strategic experiments of Magnus Carlsen...

Canadian ploy

I don't remember when I first heard the phrase 'Canadian ploy'. Perhaps I read about it in reports on the first ice hockey World Championships, which reached us from Canada, with its winters similar to those in Russia? In the post-war years and even later, in the fifties and sixties, this is what it was called in the Soviet Union – 'Canadian hockey', in contrast to the more usual 'Russian' hockey, i.e. played with a ball.

No, of course, that was earlier...

Perhaps I heard about the 'Canadian ploy' in 1972?... That year the entire country, glued

Magnus Carlsen

to the television, followed the matches of the first and most famous Super Series. The USSR team played the Canadian team, made up of professional NHL players. Four matches across the ocean – in Canada, and four in Moscow. Even for adults this was an unprecedented spectacle, and I was just nine years old!

At that time, to us Russian boys the Canadian players seemed either like cowboys from 'westerns', or heroes of 'gangster movies', which, however, we had never seen – Hollywood films hardly ever reached the USSR. The captain and centre forward Phil Esposito, his brother Tony the goaltender, attackers Paul Henderson, Pete and Frank Mahovlich, Yvan Cournoyer ...

They were supermen! The Canadians played without helmets. During a match, irrespective of whether they were on the ice or were sitting flushed on the players' bench, their powerful jaws energetically masticated enormous sticks of chewing gum. Sometimes in vexation the Canadians colourfully spat these out directly onto the ice. This was entrancing! This provoked envy. In those years chewing gum was not produced in the USSR and at the school 'black market' one stick of Wrigley's Spearmint – not a pack of five, but one stick (!) – was worth as much as three school lunches, one black and white porno photo, or two portions of ice cream. What's more, the Canadians played with curved sticks, which could not be bought in the Soviet Union!

But the most important thing was that the Canadians fought! They fought recklessly, openly, with child-like daring, directly on the ice, discarding their gloves and throwing their sticks to one side, as though emphasizing that the fight would be fierce, but fair! Perhaps it was then that I heard the words 'Canadian ploy'. But more probably it was even earlier – from slightly older boys, when while still very young I played hockey in the yard, running across the ice simply in boots – without skates.

The 'Canadian ploy' is a kind of 'non-addressed pass' – when the puck is firmly struck into the zone close to the opponent's goal, and the attackers then rush after it.

I don't think that this 'clever manoeuvre' was called 'Canadian' on that side of the Atlantic or even in Europe. To be honest, it is also a long time since it was called this in Russia. But for my contemporaries – lads of the 1970s – knocking the puck into the opponent's zone, with the aim of initiating play there, remained the 'Canadian ploy'.

On 26 January 2016 the great Canadian ice-hockey player Wayne Gretzky celebrated his 55th birthday. That morning, digging about on the internet, I read several interesting articles about 'The

Great One' – that was what fans and journalists called him. And during the day, after comfortably settling in my armchair, as usual at the end of January, I logged on to the transmission of the current round from the Tata Steel tournament. I was still under the impression of the buzz of ice-hockey battles, when I noticed that in two identically developing games the white h-pawn, like a powerfully struck puck, was swiftly flying into the opponent's defensive zone...

1.e4 e5 2.♘f3 ♘c6 3.♗b5 ♘f6 4.d3 ♗c5 5.♗xc6 dxc6 6.♘bd2 0-0 7.♘c4 ♘d7 8.♕e2 ♖e8 9.♗d2 ♗d6 10.h4!N

In the first game the white pieces were commanded by the 'star boy' from China.

Wei Yi
David Navara
Wijk aan Zee 2016 (9)
10...c5 11.h5!

The puck has been struck into the opponent's zone. Is it possible to organize an attack?

11...h6 12.0-0-0 ♘b8?!
This defender should not have been moved away to the queenside. 12...♘f8 was correct. But probably Black's previous move was already a poor one.
13.♖dg1 ♘c6 14.g4 f6

15.g5!
The outstanding trainer and analyst Igor Zaitsev – the author of a well-known variation in the Ruy Lopez – wrote an excellent book (which, unfortunately, has not in fact been translated into English) called *Attack on a strong point*.

Of course, in the given instance the direction of the decisive breakthrough is fairly obvious, but at the board it is not so easy to realize that this breakthrough is indeed decisive!

Nevertheless, both the breakthrough itself, and the following piece sacrifice merely for the opening of attacking lines, are admirable!
15...fxg5 16.♘xg5! ♘d4 17.♕d1 hxg5 18.♗xg5 ♗e7 19.♗e3

The onslaught of White's pieces cannot be checked – his attack is irresistible!

In the other 'parallel' game Black erected a significantly better line of defence.

**Fabiano Caruana
Sergey Karjakin**
Wijk aan Zee 2016 (9)
10...♘f8 11.h5!

11...♘e6! 12.0-0-0 c5
As a matter of principle Sergey Karjakin does not advance his h-pawn, sensibly assuming that it is much less dangerous to allow the h5-h6 advance than to create a precedent for the opening of lines.
13.♕f1 f6 14.♘h4 ♘d4 15.c3 ♘c6

It is not easy to breach Black's defences – he has reasonable counterplay.

Their great predecessors
Fifty years ago, in 1966, the Chess Olympiad took place in the capital of Cuba – Havana. The United States team was led by Robert James Fischer; this

was his fourth Olympiad. In the match with Iceland the future World Champion was opposed by a future FIDE President.

**Robert Fischer
Fridrik Olafsson**
Havana 1966 (4)
**1.e4 e5 2.♘f3 ♘c6 3.♗b5 a6
4.♗a4 ♘f6 5.0-0 ♘xe4 6.d4 b5
7.♗b3 d5 8.dxe5 ♗e6 9.c3 ♗e7
10.♗c2!?**

Fischer liked this bishop retreat, which in those years also was much less popular than 10.♘bd2. He had already played this at the Piatigorsky Cup in Santa Monica just a few months earlier. In reply his opponent – the German grandmaster Wolfgang Unzicker – chose 10...0-0 and after 11.♘bd2 f5 12.♘b3 ♕d7 13.♘bd4 ♘xd4 14.♘xd4 c5 a position was reached from the first game of the Bogoljubow-Euwe match, which took place in Holland in 1928. Since then and until the 1966 Santa Monica tournament this variation had not occurred, and only after the Fischer-Unzicker game did it become popular.

Fischer was always very thoughtful about his choice of opening move orders. I think that by beginning with 10.♗c2, instead of the generally-adopted 10.♘bd2, he excluded the possibility of Black employing the plan with 10.♘bd2 ♘c5 11.♗c2 ♗g4, which was already known in 1966. Of course this is merely an assumption, but about the fact that, half a century later in the 2016

Tata Steel tournament, by playing 10.♗c2 against Wei Yi, Caruana avoided the topical variation 10.♘bd2 ♘c5 11.♗c2 d4, in which Black's stock is currently very high, I am absolutely sure.

But the first of the world champions to employ the move 10.♗c2 was Max Euwe. He played this back in 1941 at a tournament in Beverwijk against Sammelius. His opponent, like Unzicker in the game with Fischer, castled – 10...0-0. However, Euwe did not play 11.♘bd2, transposing into the 10.♘bd2 0-0 11.♗c2 variation, but preferred 11.♕e2. After 11... f5?! 12.exf6 ♖xf6 13.♘g5! the ex-World Champion gained an advantage. Euwe again employed 10.♗c2 in a game against Cortlever at a tournament in Amsterdam four years later, in 1945. In it his opponent responded with the more critical 10...♗g4. Now White cannot continue his development with 11.♘bd2, but must drive away the bishop. However, we will return to this position and the game slightly later.

I am convinced that already in 1966 Fischer took into account all these opening nuances.

It is interesting that nine years earlier, when in the New York Manhattan Club Max Euwe played a mini-match with the fourteen-year-old Fischer, in the second game the Open Variation was played. Bobby continued **10.♘bd2** and after 10...0-0 11.♕e2 ♘c5 12.♘d4 ♘xb3 13.♘2xb3 ♕d7 Euwe demonstrated to the young man that in this case Black has good play.

Perhaps it was then that, by an invisible baton, a virtual transference of opening ideas occurred between the past and future World Champions.
10...♗g4
Now also this move is considered, if not definitely the best, then at least definitely the most critical reply.

Incidentally, 10.♗c2 was also played by another World Champion. Anatoly Karpov continued in this way against Kortchnoi in their famous match in Baguio City in 1978. Viktor Lvovich replied **10...♘c5**, to which the World Champion responded with the solid, but rather slow **11.h3** 0-0 12.♖e1 ♕d7 13.♘d4. Bronstein acted far more energetically against Keres in a training match, played in the fashionable Voronovo Park Hotel in 1952 –

11.♘d4!

Why didn't Karpov play this?

I think that 9...♗e7 came as something of a surprise to him – in previous matches Kortchnoi had played 9...♗c5. In reply Karpov decided also to take his opponent slightly aback, by choosing not the main continuation 10.♘bd2, as he had played earlier, but 10.♗c2. But after the rare reply 10...♘c5 for the World Champion 'play at the board' began, and, in accordance with his style and the position in the match, he chose the most solid path.

11.h3

11...♗h5

In the game Euwe-Cortlever, Amsterdam 1945, the Dutch World Champion's opponent decided to exchange his bishop with 11...♗xf3, but after 12.gxf3 ♘c5 13.f4 0-0 14.b4 ♘a4 15.♖e1 White obtained a menacing position. Fridrik Olafsson's move is stronger.

12.g4 ♗g6

At this point, exploiting the fact that the queen's knight is not preventing a frontal attack on the d5-pawn, Fischer played 13.♗b3, and after 13...♘a5 14.♗xd5 ...

But I think that it is now time to move from tropical Havana 1966 to winter Wijk aan Zee 2016.

Fabiano Caruana
Wei Yi
Wijk aan Zee 2016 (10)

At this point, exploiting the fact that the queen's knight is not preventing a frontal attack on the d5-pawn, Fischer played 13.♗b3, and after 13...♘a5 14.♗xd5 c6 15.♗xe4 ♗xe4 16.♕xd8+ ♖xd8 17.♘bd2 ♗d5 18.♖e1 in the game Fischer-Olafsson, Havana 1966, he could have converted his minimal advantage. But first, subsequently Olafsson acted

Fridrik Olafsson

in clearly not the best way, and second, 13...♘c5! 14.♗xd5 ♕d7 was stronger, with excellent compensation for the pawn.

So Caruana could not simply 'follow Fischer', but he arrived at the board by no means empty-handed!

13.♘d4!?N

A very interesting idea.

As in the majority of cases in the Open Variation, an early ♘f3-d4 leads to an abrupt sharpening of the play.

13...♕d7

An alternative may be provided by 13...♘xd4 14.cxd4 h5 with an extremely complicated position.

14.f4

14...♘xd4?!

But Wei Yi committed an inaccuracy, which, however, is quite understandable. He should have slightly simplified the position, by exchanging the light-squared bishops with an original manoeuvre – 14...♘g3! 15.♖f3 ♗xc2 16.♕xc2 ♘e4.

But in this case it was necessary to assess accurately the consequences of the fearsome 15.f5!? ♘xf1 16.♕xf1. Objectively speaking, after 16...0-0, 16...♘xe5 or 16...♗c5 Black's chances are by no means worse, but to go in for such a position without preparatory analysis is an extremely risky business. Wei Yi decided to stabilize the position in the centre as far as possible, but in so doing it was precisely in the centre that he had to strengthen his opponent's position.

Fabiano Caruana

15.cxd4 f5 16.♗e3 0-0 17.♘c3
White has an enduring positional advantage. But apart from that, thanks to his opening novelty Caruana gained a big advantage on the clock, and after 'driving' his opponent into time-trouble he confidently won the game.

Three years before the Chess Olympiad in Havana, a match for the World Championship took place in Moscow. The encounter between Botvinnik and Petrosian was held in the Estrada Theatre in the very centre of the city. Later this enormous building on the Bolotny Island, created by a loop of the Moscow River, where the theatre was situated, would become known as 'The House on the Embankment' – from the name of a well-known story by the wonderful Soviet writer Yury Trifonov – incidentally, a great chess admirer.

When in the ninth game Mikhail Moiseevich Botvinnik made the move ...g7-g5, from the stalls to the last row of the dress circle a murmur of perplexity swept through the auditorium. This was hardly surprising! The chief strategist, the chief orthodox, the living classic with whose name in the Soviet Union the concept of 'chess' was altogether associated, suddenly, transgressing all the

dogmas, advanced his g-pawn away from his king!

Tigran Petrosian
Mikhail Botvinnik
Moscow 1963 (9)
1.c4 e6 2.g3 d5 3.♗g2 ♘f6 4.♘f3 ♗e7 5.0-0 0-0 6.d4 ♘bd7 7.♕c2 c6 8.♗f4 ♘e4 9.♘c3 g5!?

At that time, during the ninth game, the spectators – Muscovites and visitors to the capital who had arrived for the match – did not yet know that, for what was to be his last match for the world title, in the strict Queen's Gambit the World Champion had prepared an entire variation, beginning with the paradoxical move 7.g2-g4!. It would be first employed by Botvinnik in the twelfth game...
But in the present game, on encountering a surprise, Petrosian chose the most logical path – he first returned his bishop to its initial position – **10.♗c1** and after 10...f5 11.b3 he prepared to activate it on another diagonal. Botvinnik played 11...♗f6 12.♗b2 ♗g7, but he was unable to completely solve his opening problems. Probably he should not have spent two tempi on re-routing his king's bishop – he could also have concerned himself with its queenside colleague – 11...b6!? 12.♗b2 ♗b7.
It is interesting that many years later the sharp move **9...g5!?** was employed by another World Champion – in many respects the antipode of Mikhail Botvinnik – Boris Spassky. His opponent

retreated his bishop to e3. This was the 11th move, since with Spassky, thanks to the inclusion of a check on b4, the starting position arose a move later. Things took an analogous course in Carlsen's game...

Pavel Elianov
Magnus Carlsen
Wijk aan Zee 2016 (7)
1.d4 ♘f6 2.c4 e6 3.♘f3 d5 4.g3 ♗b4+ 5.♗d2 ♗e7 6.♗g2 0-0 7.0-0 ♘bd7 8.♕c2 ♘e4 9.♗f4 c6 10.♘c3 g5!? 11.♗e3

Here Spassky continued **11...f5 12.♖ad1 ♘d6** (Bernard-Spassky, Angers ch-FRA 1990) with an acceptable, although somewhat passive position. But such a development of events could in no way have surprised Elianov. At the tournament in Biel just six months earlier he had had this position with White, although he reached it via a completely different move order. In the game Elianov-Rapport, Biel 2015, there followed 13.b3 ♗f6?! 14.♗c1! ♖f7 15.♗a3 with an obvious advantage for White.
I think that in his preparation Carlsen took the existence of this game into account. In it after ...g7-g5 (in a different position) Elianov retreated his bishop to e3, and this was quite a good novelty, enabling him to win the opening part of the battle. Of course, in his memory he retained the positive image of that game, and this allowed Carlsen to hope that in the given concrete position Elianov

would again retreat his bishop to e3, although the 'Petrosian retreat' 11.♗c1 is objectively stronger.

11...♞d6!N

An excellent novelty by Carlsen, with a psychological undertone! This is an atypical manoeuvre for the Catalan Opening – the knight is switched with gain of tempo to f5, from where it very persistently harasses the white bishop. The quiet course of the game is unexpectedly disrupted, and it sharply switches to its calculating phase.

12.b3 ♞f5

It turned out that Elianov was not ready for such a swift change not even of scene, but of the tempo of the play – he makes a mistake.

13.g4?!

He should have decided on the gambit move 13.♗d2!?.

13...♞xe3 14.fxe3 b5!

By his energetic actions Magnus has seized the initiative. And after a not fully correct combination – **15.e4 b4 16.exd5 bxc3 17.dxc6 ♞b8**, his advantage acquired material embodiment. Carlsen confidently converted his advantage into a win.

More about the move ...g7-g5

Openings, variations, defences, attacks, gambits and counter-gambits all have their authors. There are inventors of brilliant ideas or memorable novelties. But sometimes it seems to me that individual moves can also have their authors. I do not have in mind concrete moves, with a number attached, even if this is number '1'. As, for example, the attack of the Swiss artist Henri Grob – **1.g4**, or the move **1.b4**, the consequences of which were studied by the Soviet master Alexey Sokolsky. I am talking about the absolute author's right to a move, irrespective of the number standing before it: first, eighth, fifteenth or twenty-first. Thus the capture **g2xf3** with a neighbouring pawn on e4 is for me 'Tal's move', the king manoeuvre ♚e1-e2 is 'Steinitz's move', and the pawn thrust ...**g7-g5** is 'Larsen's move'... Do you remember his fantastic, razor-sharp move?

Mark Taimanov
Bent Larsen
Vinkovci 1970 (13)

15...g7-g5!

In recent times the march of the g-pawn has also begun to be favoured by the present chess king – Magnus Carlsen. True,

Bent Larsen

Carlsen uses the move ...g7-g5 in combination with concrete leaps of the king's knight to e4 or h5. We have already discussed his game with Elianov. Here is an example from the recent past.

Maxime Vachier-Lagrave
Magnus Carlsen
Stavanger 2015 (7)

In the opening of this game it was not the move ...g7-g5 itself that was unexpected, but the knight leap associated with it. **1.d4 ♞f6 2.c4 e6 3.♞f3 d5 4.♞c3 c6 5.♗g5 h6 6.♗h4 g5 7.♗g3** and here there followed **7...♞e4!?**. This had not been played before in a serious game!

In the first round of the 2016 Tata Steel tournament Carlsen employed the plan with the sharp thrust of the g-pawn in the strict structure of the 'classical Carlsbad'.

David Navara
Magnus Carlsen
Wijk aan Zee 2016 (1)

1.d4 ♞f6 2.c4 e6 3.♞f3 d5 4.♞c3 ♞bd7 5.cxd5 exd5 6.♗g5 h6 7.♗h4 c6 8.e3

8...g5!?

An idea of Denis Khismatullin

José Raul Capablanca confidently defended the Carlsbad structure with the inclusion of the not very useful move ...a7-a6, he defended it with the pawn on h6, with the pawn on h7, with the move ...g7-g6 and without it. Sometimes the great Cuban's queen's bishop was transferred via d7 to e8, continuing to defend his backward pawn on c6. But on seeing the move ...g7-g5 I think that he would merely have sadly shaken his head!

However, what can be done – times change.

9.♗g3 ♘h5 10.♗d3 ♘xg3 11.hxg3 ♗g7!

The bishop occupies a place that is very unusual for it in the Queen's Gambit. Starting from the eighth move, this entire plan was introduced into tournament play by Denis Khismatullin. Last year he employed his new variation three times.

12.0-0

After 12.♕c2 ♘b6 Brodsky against Khismatullin (Sochi 2015) continued 13.0-0-0, but 13...♗e6 14.♔b1 ♕e7 led to a position with chances for both sides. Mozharov, again against Khismatullin (Moscow 2015), preferred to castle on the kingside – 13.0-0, but after 13...♗e6 14.a4 a5 15.♘e5 g4! Black even seized the initiative.

12...a5!N

An important refinement by Carlsen. In the blitz game Salem-Khismatullin, Berlin 2015, after

12...0-0 13.b4 ♘b6 14.♕c2 ♗e6 15.♘d2 White gained an initiative on the queenside, normal for the Carlsbad pawn structure.

But now Black will meet the 'minority' pawn attack with the forceful reply b7-b5.

13.a3 0-0 14.♕c2 ♖e8 15.b4 b5 16.♘a2 ♗b7 17.bxa5 ♖xa5

Black has a good game.

Bundle of novelties

Ruy Lopez

Fabiano Caruana
Ding Liren
Wijk aan Zee 2016 (7)

1.e4 e5 2.♘f3 ♘c6 3.♗b5 a6 4.♗a4 ♘f6 5.0-0 ♗e7 6.d3 b5 7.♗b3 d6 8.a3 ♘a5 9.♗a2 c5 10.♘c3 ♗e6

The latest word in fashion! Black saves a tempo on castling, in order to take control of the d5-square.

11.♘h4!?N

Only 11.♗xe6 and 11.♗g5 had previously occurred. The tactical justification of the knight manoeuvre is that Black cannot continue 11...♘xe4? 12.♘xe4 ♗xh4 because of 13.♗xe6 fxe6 14.♕h5+ with a decisive attack. And in the event of the preparatory exchange – 11...♗xa2 there follows 12.♘xa2 and again 12...♘xe4? is bad because of 13.♘f5.

11...c4

Consistent, but Black cannot retain control of the occupied space.

12.♘f5 ♗xf5 13.exf5 0-0 14.dxc4 ♘xc4 15.♗xc4 bxc4 16.♗g5

White's chances are preferable.

Petroff Defence

Fabiano Caruana
Hou Yifan
Wijk aan Zee 2016 (5)

1.e4 e5 2.♘f3 ♘f6 3.♘xe5 d6 4.♘f3 ♘xe4 5.♘c3 ♘xc3 6.dxc3 ♗e7 7.♗e3 ♘c6 8.♕d2 ♗e6 9.0-0-0 ♕d7 10.h4 h6 11.a3

11...♖g8!

White is intending to play 12.♘d4 and after the exchange either his bishop or his queen will end up on d4. The g7-pawn will be attacked, and in some cases also the a7-pawn. This latter factor may seriously hinder the possibility of queenside castling. The mysterious move of the black rook is the first of a series of preventive measures.

Earlier, 11...♗f6 and 11...f6 were tried, but they were not fully effective.

12.♘d4 ♘xd4 13.♕xd4 c5 14.♕f4 d5 15.♕g3 0-0-0 16.♗e2 g5 17.hxg5 hxg5

Black has a good game.

Sicilian Defence

Hou Yifan
Loek van Wely
Wijk aan Zee 2016 (8)

1.e4 c5 2.♘f3 d6 3.d4 cxd4 4.♘xd4 ♘f6 5.♘c3 a6 6.♗e3 e6 7.g4 h6 8.♕f3 ♘bd7 9.♕g2 g5

9...♘e5 10.♗e2 g5 11.h4 ♖g8 leads to the same position.
10.0-0-0 ♘e5 11.♗e2 b5 12.h4 ♖g8 13.hxg5 hxg5

14.♘f3!N
Previously 14.a3 and 14.f4 had occurred.
14...♘exg4
Hou Yifan's powerful novelty was obviously devised at the board. If the Chinese lady champion had analysed this position at home, now there would undoubtedly have followed **15.e5!** ♘xe3 16.fxe3 b4 17.♘d4 d5 18.♖df1!! with a very dangerous attack.
But in the game after **15.♗d4?!** ♗b7 16.♘e1 b4** Black seized the initiative.

Queen's Indian Defence

Ding Liren
Sergey Karjakin
Wijk aan Zee 2016 (5)
1.d4 ♘f6 2.c4 e6 3.♘f3 b6 4.g3 ♗a6 5.b3 ♗b4+ 6.♗d2 ♗e7 7.♘c3 c6 8.e4 d5 9.♗d3 dxe4 10.♘xe4 ♗b7 11.♕e2 ♘bd7

12.0-0-0!?N
A little risky, but very interesting! Previously Topalov against Leko tried 12.♖d1 and 12.♘xf6+ followed by kingside castling, but this did not bring him any particular benefits.
12...♘xe4 13.♗xe4 ♘f6 14.♗c2 a5 15.♖he1 b5 16.c5 b4 17.g4! ♗a6 18.♕e5 0-0 19.g5!

Now if 19...♘d5 there follows 20.h4! with a pawn storm, while if **19...♘h5**, as occurred in the game – **20.♕e4 g6 21.♕xc6**. Despite stubborn resistance, White converted his advantage.

Catalan Opening

Anish Giri
Shakhriyar Mamedyarov
Wijk aan Zee 2016 (6)
1.♘f3 ♘f6 2.c4 e6 3.g3 d5 4.d4 ♗b4+ 5.♗d2 ♗d6 6.♗g2 0-0 7.0-0 ♘bd7 8.b3

8...dxc4!N
The variation with the bishop retreat ...♗b4-d6 was always regarded as a modification of one of the classical systems in the Catalan Opening, in which Black avoids the capture on c4 and either immediately, or after the check on b4, plays ♗e7. In it ...c7-c6 is a fundamental move.
In the given version, as however also with the bishop on e7, Black more often plays ...c7-c6 on the seventh move, but also in the diagram position in practice only 8...c6 has occurred.
After the exchange on c4 the entire strategic picture is radically changed.
9.bxc4 c5 10.e3 ♕c7
10...b6!? deserved serious consideration, since in reply to 11.♘e5 Black gains a pawn and excellent positional compensation for the exchange – 11...♘xe5 12.♗xa8 ♘xc4.
11.♕c2 cxd4 12.♘xd4 a6 13.♖c1 ♖d8?!
13...♘c5 should have been played immediately, with a roughly equal game. But now, exploiting the threat of ♗d2-a5, with gain of tempo White prepares an important breakthrough.
14.♘b3! ♖b8 15.c5!
White has the initiative.

Hou Yifan

SURVEYS

FEATURING

28 Opening Variations

Sicilian Defence

Moscow Variation SI 1.3 (B51)

Explorers of New Routes

by Krzysztof Panczyk and Jacek Ilczuk

1.	e4	c5
2.	♘f3	d6
3.	♗b5+	♘d7
4.	0-0	♘f6
5.	♖e1	a6
6.	♗d3	b5
7.	c4	

With the Moscow Variation, White wants to avoid perfectly worked out main lines. He is more inclined towards manoeuvring play than in the typical Sicilian. Let's take a closer look from move 5.

5.♖e1 a6
The other move order, with 4...a6 instead of 4...♘gf6, is also possible. Then, after 5.♗d3 ♘f6, White can play 6.c3, followed by ♗c2 and d2-d4, which leads to another type of position.
Here a surprise occurs: White withdraws his bishop, not to the prepared f1-square but to d3.

6.♗d3
This place for the light-squared bishop looks a bit strange, but in some structures it is put there in connection with b2-b3, followed by ♗b2 or c2-c3 and ♗c2.

6...b5
Obviously, Black has other moves, e.g. 6...g6, but this move looks the most forcing.

7.c4
After this move, which has become popular lately, the initial position for our Survey arises. Here Black has a large selection of continuations.

Minor 7th Black Moves
Defending the b5-pawn with the rook, 7...♖b8, is met by 8.♘c3, with a slight but lasting advantage for White (Colovic-J. Christiansen, Reykjavik 2014). The position gets the same character after the queenside is closed with 7...b4 8.♗c2 e5 9.a3 bxa3 10.♖xa3 (Lagno-Ushenina, Khanty-Mansiysk 2014). In both cases Black has problems obtaining active play. Another solution is the not-so-popular but very simple 7...bxc4 8.♗xc4 ♘b6 9.♗b3 e5 10.d3 ♗e7, and now, after both 11.♘bd2, 11.h3 0-0 12.♘c3 (Lagno-Ushenina, Khanty-Mansiysk 2014) and 11.a4 ♖b8 (Safarli-Grandelius, Dubai 2015), White had problems achieving anything. Perhaps he could try 10.♘g5 ♖a7 11.♘c3.

The New 7...♘e5
A new idea is to exploit the fact that the d3-bishop is temporarily unprotected by going 7...♘e5. But White has a few good continuations at his disposal here. It is unclear if his position is better after capturing 8.♘xe5 dxe5 9.♗e2 b4 10.a3 e6 11.d3 ♗e7 12.axb4 cxb4 (Narayanan-Adhiban, Pune 2014), but withdrawing the bishop, followed by undermining Black's queenside with a2-a4, gives White a better game: 8.♗e2 ♘xc4 9.a4 (Goumas-Narayanan, Anogia 2014) or 8.♗f1 ♘xc4 (other moves do not change the assessment of the position) 9.a4 (Carlsen-Nakamura, Zurich 2014).

The Ultramodern 7...g5
Finally, there is the ultramodern and spectacular move 7...g5 (g2-g4 for White, e.g. in the Queen's Gambit, and ...g7-g5 for Black, e.g. in the French, have been quite fashionable lately). Now White has two responses. More popular (as far as we can talk about popularity after six games) is 8.cxb5 g4 9.e5 dxe5 10.♘g5 ♗g7 (10...e6 11.♘c3 gives White a slightly better game, Mamedov-Anand, Berlin rapid 2015), and now, after 11.♕e2 0-0 12.♘c3 ♘b6 (Bartel-Grischuk, Berlin rapid 2015), complicated positions with mutual chances arise. The more flexible move 11.♘c3 is more demanding for Black. Now Black should not immediately castle, as 11...0-0 (Mamedov-Grischuk, Berlin rapid 2015)

leads to a better game for White. According to Dave Smerdon, he should first play 11...♞b6. We think that after 12.♗f1 h6 Black should equalize. However, this line is one of the key positions in this variation and will have to be checked in tournament practice. In our opinion, the more straightforward 8.♞xg5 ♞e5 is better, and now, after both 9.♗f1 (Barski-Borovikov, Heusenstamm 2015) and 9.♗e2 bxc4 10.♞c3 (Carlsen-Grischuk,

London 2015), White has the better chances.

Conclusion

The move 6.♗d3 leads to very interesting play after 6...b5 7.c4. However, it is nearly untested in tournament practice, as there are only a few games in the database with some of the main lines, although they are by players from the very top of the chess hierarchy. In this situation it is difficult to give a definitive

assessment of the variation – we will have to wait for new games by grandmasters.

In our opinion, the extravagant move 7...g5 does not yield Black equality, but it does lead to extremely complicated positions. Perhaps Black should try to solve his problems by playing 7...bxc4 ? We should not be frightened by the unfavourable statistics (67% for White), as the number of games played with this line is quite small.

Minor 7th Black Moves

Aleksandar Colovic
Johan-Sebastian Christiansen
Reykjavik 2014 (2)

1.e4 c5 2.♞f3 d6 3.♗b5+ ♞d7 4.0-0 ♞gf6 5.♖e1 a6 6.♗d3 b5 7.c4 ♖b8 [7...♗b7 8.cxb5 axb5 9.♗xb5 ♗xe4 (9...♞xe4 10.♞c3 ♞ef6 11.d4+– Boruchovsky-Papp, Zalakaros 2015) 10.♞c3 ♗xf3 11.♕xf3 e6 12.♕g3±]

8.♞c3 [Black is a little behind in development, so opening the game may favour White: 8.cxb5 axb5 9.♕e2!? (9.a4 bxa4 10.♞c3 e6 11.♗b5 ♗e7 (Haslinger-Vereggen, Delft 2015) 12.d4=; 9.♗c2 e5 10.b4 ♗e7 (10...cxb4!? 11.d4 ♗e7 12.♗d2 d5 13.exd5 ♞xd5 14.dxe5 0-0=) 11.bxc5 (11.a3!?) 11...dxc5 12.a4 (Illingworth-Havasi, Budapest 2014) 12.♗b2!? ♕c7 13.♞c3=) 12...b4 13.d3 ♗a6 14.♞bd2 0-0=) 9...b4 (9...♗a6 10.b3 ♕c7 11.♞c3 c4 12.♗b1±; 9...c4 10.♗c2 e6 (10...♞c5 11.d4 cxd3 12.♗xd3 ♗xd3 13.♕xd3 ♗e6

14.♞a3±) 11.d4±] 10.a3 ♖a8 11.♗b5 e5 12.d3 ♗e7 13.♞bd2 0-0 14.♞c4±]
8...b4 9.♞d5 e6 10.♞xf6+ [10.♕a4 is very striking but not so effective: 10...♞g4! (10...exd5? 11.e5 ♗e7 (11... dxe5 12.♞xe5 ♗e7 13.♞c6 ♞b6 14.♕a5 ♕d6 15.♞xe7 ♔f8 16.cxd5±) 12.exf6+ (12.exd6+ ♔xd6 13.♞g5 ♞b6 14.♞xf7+ ♔c7 15.♕a5 ♕d7 16.♞xh8 ♗d6 17.a3 b3∞) 12...♔xf6 13.cxd5 g6 14.♗c4 ♗h6 15.♕c2 ♔g7 16.b3±) 11.h3 ♞ge5 12.♞xe5 dxe5 13.♞e3 ♗b7=] 10...♞xf6 11.♗c2 [11.e5 ♞d7 (11...dxe5 12.♞xe5 ♗e7 13.♗c2 ♗b7 (13...♕c7 14.d4±) 14.♗a4+ ♔f8 15.♕e2±) 12.exd6 ♗xd6=] 11...e5 12.♗a4+ ♞d7 13.a3 a5 14.axb4 [This capture is a little premature. The more flexible 14.d3 gave more chances of obtaining a small edge, e.g. 14...♗e7 15.♞d2 △ ♞f1-e3] 14...axb4 15.♗c6 [15.♗b5!?; 15.d3!?] 15...♕c7 16.♗d5 ♞b6 17.d3 ♗g4?! [The idea of exchanging the light-squared bishop is strategically unjustified. 17...♗e7=] 18.h3 [18.♗g5!?±] 18...♗xf3?! [It was not too late to withdraw the bishop, with equal chances, e.g. 18...♗d7 19.b3 ♗e7 20.♖e2 0-0=] 19.♕xf3 ♞xd5 20.cxd5 [In this position, White's bishop is much better than its counterpart] 20...♗e7 21.♗e3 [21.♕g4 0-0 22.♗h6 ♗f6 23.h4±] 21...0-0 22.♖a4 ♖a8 23.♖ea1 ♕b7 24.♕d1 ♖fc8 [24...f5!?] 25.♖1a2 h6 26.♕a1 ♖xa4 27.♖xa4 ♕b5 28.♖a7 ♗f8 [28...♗g5±] 29.♕a6 ♕xa6 30.♖xa6±   1-0 (70)

Kateryna Lagno
Anna Ushenina
Khanty-Mansiysk Wch rapid W 2014 (14)

1.e4 c5 2.♞f3 d6 3.♗b5+ ♞d7 4.0-0 a6 5.♗d3 ♞gf6 6.♖e1 b5 7.c4 b4 8.♗c2 [8.a3 bxa3 9.♖xa3 e5 10.♗c2 – 8.♗c2] 8...e5 [8...♗b7!? △ ...g7-g6, ...♗g7±]

9.a3 bxa3 10.♖xa3 [10.bxa3 g6 11.d3 ♗g7 12.♞c3 0-0 13.♗d2 ♞h5 14.♗g5 ♗f6 15.♗h6 ♗g7 16.♗g5 ♗f6 (Ghader Pour-Padmini, Tabriz 2014) 17.♗e3 △ ♖b1±] 10...♗e7 [10...g6 11.♗a4 (11.d3!? ♖b8 12.♞c3 ♗g7 13.♗g5±) 11...♗g7 (11...♗h6!?) 12.♗c6 ♖b8 13.♞c3 0-0 14.♞d5 (14. d3!?) 14...♞xd5 (Mahjoob-Tarlev, Rasht 2015) 15.cxd5±] 11.d3 [11.♞c3!? 0-0 12.d3 ♞b8 13.♗a4 h6 14.♗d2± Van den Doel-Goudriaan, Germany Bundesliga B 2014] 11...0-0 [11...♗b7 12.♗a4 0-0 13.♗xd7 (13.♞c3±) 13...♞xd7 14.♗d2 f5 (Kolodkin-Das, Leiden 2015) 15.♞c3±] 12.♗d2 ♕b6 [12...♞b8!? △ ♞c6±] 13.♗a5 [13.♞c3±] 13...♕b7 14.b4 [14.♗a4±] 14...♗d8 15.♕d2?! [15.

---

bxc5 ♗xa5 16.♖xa5 ♘xc5 17.d4 ♕c7 18.♖a3 exd4 19.♘xd4 ♗d7 20.♘c3±] **15...♗xa5 16.bxa5 ♘b8 17.♘c3 ♘c6 18.♖b1 ♕c7 19.♗d5 ♘xd5 20.cxd5 ♘a7** [20...♘b4!?=] **21.♗a4 ♗d7 22.♗xd7 ♕xd7 23.♖ab3 ♘b5 24.♘e1?** [24.♕e3 f5 25.♘d2=; 24.h3=] **24...♕c7?** [24...f5↑] **25.♘c2 c4?!** [25...f5∓] **26.dxc4 ♕xc4 27.♖b4 ♕c7?!** [27...♕c3 28.♕xc3 ♘xc3 29.♖e1 f5=] **28.♘e3 ♕xa5 29.♘f5 ♕d8 30.♘4b3 f6** [30...♔h8 31.♖g3 ♖g8 32.♖h3 ♕f6 33.♖f3♕!] **31.♖g3 ♖a7 32.♕h6** [32.h4!?] **32...♖ff7 33.♕h5 ♖fc7 34.♕g4?!** [34.h4♕] **34...♔h8 35.h4** [35.♖h3!?∓] **35...♖ab7** [35...g6!? 36.♘e3 ♖g7 △ ...♘d4, ...f6-f5∓] **36. h5♕ ♕c8 37.♔h2 ♕d8?!** [37...♘d4 38.♖xb7 ♖xb7 39.♘xd6 ♕xg4 40.♖xg4 ♖d7 41.♘c4=] **38.h6** [38.♖gb3!?±] **38...g6 39.♘g7 ♕e7?** [39...♘d4 40.♖xb7 ♖xb7 41.♘c3♕] **40.♖a3 f5?? **[40...♕b6±] **41.♖xa6+– ♕f8 42.♕h4 fxe4 43.♘e6 ♕f7 44.♖a8+** 1-0

Mladen Palac
Denis Kadric
Croatia tt 2014 (2)

1.e4 c5 2.♘f3 d6 3.♗b5+ ♘d7 4.0-0 a6 5.♗d3 ♘gf6 6.♖e1 b5 7.c4 bxc4 8.♗xc4 ♘b6 [With the idea to close the centre by 9...e5. Black's last move is necessary to be able to protect the vulnerable f-pawn with the a8-rook] **9.♗b3** [9.♗f1 e5 (9...g6!?) 10.b4 (10.a3 a5 11.♘c3 ♗e7 12.♗b5+ ♗d7 13.a4 0-0 14.d3 ♗e6=) 10...cxb4 11.d4 ♗b7 12.a3 (Van Kampen-Baron, Jerusalem Ech 2015) 12...♕xe4 13.♘bd2 ♘f6 14.dxe5 dxe5 15.♘xe5 ♗e7 16.♘dc4 ♕xd1 17.♖xd1 ♘xc4 18.♗xc4 0-0=] **9...e5**

10.d3 [10.d4? cxd4 11.♘g5 ♖a7 12.f4 ♗g4∓ Nakar-Oleksienko, Yerevan 2014; 10.♘g5!? ♖a7 (10...c4 11.♗a4+ ♗d7

12.♗xd7+ ♕xd7 13.♘c3 ♗e7 14.d4 cxd3 15.♕xd3±)] 11.♘c3 h6 12.♘f3 ♗e7 13.d3 0-0 14.h3±/=] **10...♗e7 11.h3** [11.♘bd2 0-0 12.♘c4 ♗g4 (12...♘xc4 13.♗xc4 ♗d7=) 13.h3 ♗h5 14.♗d2 (14.♘e3 △ ♗d2±) 14...♘xc4 15.♗xc4 ♘e8 16.b4 cxb4 17.♗xb4 a5 18.♗d2 ♗c7 19.♖b1± Markidis-Poulopoulos, Vrachati 2014; 11.♘c3!?] **11...0-0 12.♘c3 ♘e8 13.♘d5 ♘xd5 14.♗xd5 ♖b8 15.♗d2 ♗d7** [15...♗c7 16.♗c4 ♗e6=] **16.♖b1 a5 17.a3 a4 18.b4 axb3 19.♖xb3 ♘c7 20.♗a5** [20.♖xb8 ♕xb8 21.♗c4±] **20...♗e6?** [20...♕c8±] **21.♗xe6 fxe6 22.♕b1 ♖c8 23.♖b7 ♕d7 24.♘d2 ♕c6 25.♕b3 ♖f6?!** [25...♕g5!? 26.♘f3 ♗d8 27.♖xc7 c4 28.♖c1 ♖xc7 29.♖xc7 ♕xc7 30.♖xc4+–] **26.♘c4 ♗f8 27.♕b6 ♘a8 28.♕xc6 ♖xc6 29.♖b8 ♖a6 30.♗d8** [30.♖d8!] **30...♖f7 31.♖eb1 ♘c7** [31...♖fa7!?] **32.♖c8 ♘e8 33.♖bb8 ♘f6 34.♘xd6! ♘d7 35.♘xf7 ♘xb8 36.♘xe5** 1-0

Eltaj Safarli
Nils Grandelius
Dubai 2015 (8)

1.e4 c5 2.♘f3 d6 3.♗b5+ ♘d7 4.0-0 a6 5.♗d3 ♘gf6 6.♖e1 b5 7.c4 bxc4 8.♗xc4 ♘b6 9.♗b3 [9.e5 dxe5 (9...♘xc4 10.exf6 ♘e5 11.♘xe5 dxe5 12.fxe7 (12.♖xe5 ♕d4 13.fxg7 ♗xg7 14.♖e3 ♕d6 15.♘a3 ♗e6 16.d3 ♗d4 17.♖g3 h5♕) 12...♗xe7 13.♖xe5 0-0 14.d3±) 10.♘xe5 e6 (10...♘xc4 11.♕a4+ ♗d7 (11...♘d7 12.♘xc4 e6 13.d3 ♗e7 14.♕c6 ♖b8 15.♗f4 ♗b7 16.♕a4±) 12.♘xc4 e6 13.♘c3 ♗e7 14.d4 cxd4 15.♕xd4 0-0 16.♗g5±) 11.♗b3 ♗d6 12.d4 0-0 13.♘c3 ♗b7 14.♗g5 h6 15.♗h4 cxd4 16.♕xd4 ♗e7 17.♕e3 ♘bd5=; 9.d3!?] **9...e5 10.d3 ♗e7 11.a4**

11...♖b8 [11...a5 12.♗d2 0-0 13.♗c3 ♕c7 14.♕d2 (14.♘a3!? ♗b7 15.♘d2 g6 16.♘dc4±) 14...♗a7 (14...♗g4!?⇄) 15.♘a3 ♗d7 16.♕c2 ♘e8 17.♘d2± Ni-Zhao, Zhongshan 2015] **12.a5 ♘a8 13.♘a3 0-0 14.♘c4 ♘c7 15.♘b6 ♗e6 16.♗xe6 ♘xe6= 17.♗e3** [17.♗d2 ♘d7 18.♘c4 ♕c7=] **17...♘d7 18.♘c4 ♕c7** [18...f5!?⇄] **19.♕a4 ♕b7 20.♗d2 ♕b5** [20...f5!?⇄] **21.♕d1 ♖fe8?!** [21...f5!∓] **22.♗c3 ♘d4 23.♘fd2 ♕c6 24.♗e3 ♗g5 25.♘dc4 ♘f6** [25...♗xe3=] **26.♘b6 ♕b5 27.♗ec4 ♖bd8** [27...h5!?=] **28.♕f3 h5?!** [28...♗e6 29.g3 g6 30.h4 ♗h6 31.♘d5=] **29.♘d5 h4 30.♕f5 ♘h7 31.g3** [31.♘cb6 ♗e6 32.♕g4 ♕b7 33.f4 exf4 34.♘xf4 ♖h6±] **31...g6 32.♕g4 f5 33.♕f3?!** [33.♕h3±] **33...♕d7?!** [33...♖f8±] **34.♕g2** [34.♘cb6 △ exf5±] **34...hxg3 35.hxg3 ♗h6 36.♕h3 ♗g7 37.♔g2 ♕f7 38.♖h1?!** [38.♘cb6 fxe4 39.dxe4 ♘d4 40.♗xd4 exd4 41.♕g4±] **38...♕g5 39.♕h4 fxe4 40.♕xg5 ♗xd5 41.♘e3 ♕f3 42.dxe4 ♖f8 43.♘g4** [43.♖af1!? ♕f3+ 44.♔g1 ♕xe4 45.♖h4≅] **43...♕f3+ 44.♔g1 ♕xe4** [44...♖xc3 45.bxc3 ♕xe4 46.♕h4=] **45.♘h6+?!** [45.♕h4!? ♕xc3 46.bxc3 ♕e2 47.♕g5 ♕e4 48.♕h4=] **45...♗xh6 46.♖xh6 ♔g7 47.♖h4 ♕f5??** [47...♕f3 48.♕h6+ ♔f7 49.♕h7+ ♔e6 50.♕xg6+ ♖f6∓] **48.♕h6++– ♔f7 49.♖f4 exf4 50.♖e1** 1-0

S.L. Narayanan
Baskaran Adhiban
India tt 2014 (4)

1.e4 c5 2.♘f3 d6 3.♗b5+ ♘d7 4.0-0 ♘gf6 5.♖e1 a6 6.♗d3 b5 7.c4 ♘e5 8.♘xe5 dxe5 9.♗e2 b4 10.a3 [Although the centre is partly blocked and White has a bad light-squared bishop, Black must play very carefully as White wants to exchange pawns on b4, play d2-d3, check with the queen on a4 followed by ♕a5, and then push c4-c5, supported by ♗e3, with a possible d3-d4, reviving the e2-bishop. 10.d3 ♕c7 11.♗e3 e6 12.♘d2 ♗e7= Rosenthal-

Kadric, South Padre Island 2014] **10...e6 11.d3** [11.axb4 cxb4 12.d3 (12.♕a4+ ♗d7 13.♕a5 ♕xa5 14.♖xa5 ♗d6 15.d3 ♗c7 16.♖a2 a5=) 12...a5 13.♗e3 ♗e7 14.♕c2 (14.c5 ♕c7 15.♘d2 0-0 16.♖c1 ♗b7 17.♘c4 ♗c6∞) 14...0-0 15.c5∞]

11...♗e7?! [11...a5, preventing the exchange on b4 followed by the manoeuvre ♕a4+-a5, was better. Moreover, in that case Black's dark-squared bishop could have been developed to a more active position, e.g. c5 or d6: 12.♗e3 (12.♘d2 ♕c7 13.♘f3 ♗b7 14.axb4 cxb4=; 12.axb4 cxb4 13.♘d2 ♕b6 14.♘b3 (14.♖f1 ♗b7 15.♘f3 ♕c7=) 14...a4=) 12...♕c7 13.♘d2 ♘d7 14.♕c2 (14. axb4 cxb4 15.♘f3 ♗c5=) 14...♗b7 15.axb4 axb4 16.♖xa8+ ♗xa8 17.♖a1 ♗c6 18.♘b3 ♗e7=] **12.axb4 cxb4 13.♗e3** [13.♕a4+ ♗d7 14.♕a5 ♕b8 15.♗d2 0-0 16.c5±] **13...0-0** [13... a5 14.c5 ♕c7 15.♕c2 0-0 16.♖c1±] **14.♘d2?!** [14.♕a4 ♗d7 15.♕a5±] **14...♗d7** [14...a5 15.c5 ♗a6 16.♕c2 ♕c7=] **15.c5** [15.♘b3 a5 16.d4±] **15...♗b5 16.♕b3** [16.♘f3 △ d3-d4=] **16...a5 17.h3?** [17.♘c4!?=] **17...♘d7 18.♖ec1 ♖c8 19.♕a2** [19.♘c4∓] **19...a4 20.b3** [20.c6 ♘b8 21.♘c4 ♗xc6-+] **20...a3 21.♘f3 ♗xc5 22.♗xc5 ♘xc5 23.♘xe5 ♕d4 24.♘f3 ♕b2 25.♖d1 ♕xa2 26.♖xa2 ♘xb3 27.d4 ♘c1** 0-1

Georgios Goumas
Srinath Narayanan
Anogia 2014 (4)

1.e4 c5 2.♘f3 d6 3.♗b5+ ♗d7 4.0-0 a6 5.♗d3 ♘gf6 6.♖e1 b5 7.c4 ♘e5 8.♗e2 [This move allows 8...♘xf3+, which looks quite good for Black. In other lines there are no differences (playing ...♗g4 is not very realistic) in variations with ♗e2

and ♗f1] **8...♘xc4** [8...♘xf3+!? 9.♗xf3 e5 10.d3 ♗e7 11.♘c3 ♗d7 12.a3 ♖b8 13.♕c2 0-0=] **9.a4 ♗b7?** [9...♗d7 10.d4 cxd4 11.♘xd4 e5 12.axb5 exd4 13.♗xc4 transposes to the game Carlsen-Nakamura]

10.axb5 axb5 11.♖xa8 ♕xa8 [Black is completely underdeveloped] **12.b3?!** [12.♘c3! ♕a5 (12...♘e5 13.♗xb5+ ♘ed7 14.d4 cxd4 15.♕xd4 e5 16.♘xe5 dxe5 17.♕xe5+ ♗e7 18.♘d5+-; 12...♘c6 13.d4 ♘xe4 14.♘xe4 ♗xe4 15.b3 ♘b6 16.dxc5 dxc5 17.♗xb5+ ♗c6 18.♕d3 f6 (18...♘d7 19.♖d1 f6 20.♗c4+-) 19.♖e6 ♗xb5 20.♕xb5+ ♘d7 21.♕c4+-) 13.b3 b4 (13...♘a3 14.e5→) 14.♗xc4 bxc3 15.dxc3 e6 (15...♘xe4 16.♘g5 e6 (16...♘xg5 17.♕xd6 ♘e6 18.♕b8++-) 17.♕f3 ♘xg5 18.♕xb7 ♗e7 19.♗b2+-; 15...♗xe4 16.♗g5 ♕a8 17.♘e5 dxe5 18.♖xe4 ♘d7 19.♗b5+-) 16.e5 ♘e4 17.♖xe4 ♗xe4 18.exd6 ♗xf3 19.d7+ ♔d8 20.♕xf3+-] **12...♘b6** [12...♘e5?! 13.♘xe5 dxe5 14.♗xb5+ ♗c6 15.♕e2 ♗d7 16.♘c3 e6 17.♗b2 ♗e7 18.♖a1±] **13.♗xb5+ ♘fd7?!** [13...♘bd7 14.d4 cxd4 15.♘xd4 e5 16.♘f5 ♕a5 17.♗xd7+ ♘xd7 18.♗d2 ♕b6 19.♘c3±] **14. d4 cxd4** [14...♗c6 15.♘c3+-; 14...♗xe4 15.dxc5 ♗xf3 16.♕xd6 ♔d8 17.♕d3+-] **15.♕xd4 ♗c6 16.♗xc6?!** [16.♘a3!? ♗xb5 (16...e6 17.♗e3 f6 18.♕c3+-) 17.♘xb5+-] **16...♕xc6 17.♗e3 e5 18.♕d3** [18.♕c3 ♕xc3 19.♘xc3 ♗e7 20.♘b5 0-0 21.♖d1 ♖a8 22.g3 ♘c8 23.♘c7±] **18...♗e7 19.♖c1 ♕b7 20.♕b5 0-0 21.♘bd2 ♖b8 22.h3** [22.♖c6 ♗f8 23.g3±] **22...g6 23.♖c6 ♔g7 24.♘c4?!** [24.g3±] **24...♘xc4 25.♕xb7 ♖xb7 26.♖xc4?** [26. bxc4=] **26...f5∓** 0-1 (54)

Magnus Carlsen
Hikaru Nakamura
Zurich rapid 2014 (3)

1.e4 c5 2.♘f3 d6 3.♗b5+ ♘d7 4.0-0 a6 5.♗d3 ♘gf6 6.♖e1 b5 7.c4 ♘e5 8.♗f1 ♘xc4 [8...♗d7 9.♘xe5 dxe5 10.cxb5 (10.♘c3 b4 11.♘d5 e6 12.♘xf6+ ♕xf6 13.a3±) 10... axb5 11.d3 (11.♘c3!?±) 11...e6 12.♗e3 ♗d6 13.♘d2 0-0 (Brkic-Popilski, Bad Gleichenberg 2014) 14.h3=; 8...b4 9.a3 bxa3 10.♖xa3 ♘xf3+ 11.♕xf3 e5 12.d3±; 8...♘xf3+ 9.♕xf3 ♗d7 10.♘c3±] **9.a4** [9.♗xc4 bxc4 10.e5 (10.♘a3 e5 11.♘xc4 ♗e7 12.d3 0-0 13.♗d2 ♗e6=) 10...dxe5 11.♘xe5 e6 12.♘a3 ♗e7 13.♘axc4± Ni-Zhai, Wuxi 2014] **9...♗d7 10.d4 cxd4 11.♘xd4 e5** [11...g6?! 12.axb5 axb5 13.♖xa8 ♕xa8 14.♘c3 ♗g7 15.♘cxb5 ♕c8 16.♖e2 ♕b7 17.♖c2±]

12.axb5 exd4 [12...axb5?! 13.♖xa8 ♕xa8 14.♘xb5 (14.b3!↑ (Rozentalis) 14...exd4 15.bxc4 b4 16.♕xd4 ♗e7 17.♗d2 ♗b7 18.e5 dxe5 19.♖xe5±) 14...♗xb5 15.♘c3 ♗d7 16.♗xc4 ♗e7 17.♗g5±] **13.♗xc4 axb5 14.♖xa8 ♕xa8** [This apparently active move is not the best one] **15.♗b3?!** [15.♗f1 is better as the pressure on the b5-pawn is more important than the control over the a2-g8 diagonal. 15...♗e7 (15...♕a5 16.e5 dxe5 17.♖xe5+ ♗e7 18.♕xd4 ♕a1 19.♗f4 h6+; 19...♕xb1 20.♖xe7+! ♔xe7 21.♗d6+ ♔e8 22.♕a7 ♕c2 23.♗c5+-) 16.♕xd4 0-0 17.♘c3 ♕b7 18.b4 ♗c6 19.f3 ♖a8 20.♗f4±] **15...♗e7?!** [15...♕a7 was much better, as then White would have to put his knight on a less active position to regain the pawn: 16.♘a3 ♗e7 17.♘c2 0-0 18.♕xd4 ♕c5± (Rozentalis)] **16.♕xd4** [(White has obtained some advantage – Rozentalis)] **16...0-0 17.♘c3 b4** [17...♗c6 18.♗f4 ♖e8 19.f3 b4 20.♘d5 ♗xd5 21.exd5 ♗d7

(21...♗g5? 22.♖xe8+ ♕xe8 23.♔f2+− Balogh-Gajewski, Budapest 2014) 22.h3 (22.♕xb4 ♖b8 23.♕a3 ♕xa3 24.bxa3 ♗h4 25.g3 ♖xb3 26.gxh4 f6 27.♗xd6 ♖xf3 △ ...♖h3=) 22...♕a5 23.♔h2±] **18.♕xb4** [18.♘d5!? ♘xd5 19.♗xd5 ♕b8 20.♕c4±] **18...♖b8 19.♕c4 ♗e6 20.♘d5 ♗d8** [20...♘f8 21.♖d1 ♘xd5 22.exd5 ♗d7 23.♕d3 g6 24.♗c4±] **21.h3 h6 22.♗f4 ♕b7 23.♗c2** [23.♗a2!?±] **23...♗a5** [23...♗xd5!? 24.exd5 ♕b4 25.♕xb4 ♖xb4 26.♗c1 ♔f8±] **24.♖d1 ♗xd5 25.exd5 ♖c8 26.♕b3?!** [26.♕a4!?±] **26...♕xb3 27.♗xb3 ♖b8 28.♗c4 ♖xb2 29.♗xd6 ♗b6 30.♗e5** [30.♔h2 ♗xf2 31.♗e5±] **30...♖xf2 31.♔h2 ♖f5 32.♗g3 h5** [32...♘e4!? 33.♗b8 g5 34.d6 ♖c5 35.♗a6 f5 36.d7 ♗d8±] **33.d6** [33.♖b1!?±] **33...♖c5 34.♗e2 ♘e4 35.d7 ♗d8 36.♗b8 ♘f6** [36...h4±] **37.♗f3 ♔h7 38.♗f4 g5 39.♗e3 ♖b5 40.♗c6 ♖a5 41.♗d4 ♔g6 42.♔h1 ♖a6 43.♖c1 h4 44.♔g1 ♗e7 45.♗b5 ♖d6 46.♗c5 ♖xd7 47.♗xd7 ♗xc5+ 48.♖xc5 ♘xd7 49.♖c6+ f6 50.♔f2 ♘e5 51.♖c3 ♔f5 52.♔e3 ♘d7 53.♖b3 ♘f8 54.♖b5+ ♔g6 55.♔e4 ♘e6 56.♖b2 ♘f4 57.♖a2 ♘e6 58.♔d5 ♘f4+ 59.♔d6 g4= 60.hxg4 ♔g5 61.♔e7 ♘xg4 62.♔xf6 ♔g3 63.♔f5 ♘xg2 64.♖a3+ ♔f2 65.♔g4 ♘e3+ 66.♔h4 ♔f3 67.♖a4 ♘f5+ 68.♔g5 ♘e3 69.♖a3 ♔e4 70.♖xe3+ ♔xe3** ½-½

The Ultramodern 7...g5 8.cxb5

Rauf Mamedov
Viswanathan Anand
Berlin Wch rapid 2015 (8)

1.e4 c5 2.♘f3 d6 3.♗b5+ ♘d7 4.0-0 a6 5.♗d3 ♘gf6 6.♖e1 b5 7.c4 g5 8.cxb5 [By taking the other pawn, White avoids the opening of the g-file. The pawn structure is usually asymmetrical in these lines, with an advantage on the queenside for White against a mass of black pawns on the other side] **8...g4** [8...♖g8 9.♗e2 g4 (9...♘xe4 10.♘c3±) 10.♘h4 e6 11.♘c3±] **9.e5** [9.♘h4 e6 10.♘c3 ♗g7 11.g3 ♘e5 12.♗e2 axb5 13.d4 cxd4

14.♕xd4 0-0 15.♗xb5 ♗a6∞ Smerdon]
9...dxe5 10.♘g5 e6 [10...♘b6!?]

11.♘c3 [11.♘e4 h5 12.♘bc3 ♘d5 13.♗c4 ♘7b6 14.d3 ♗e7 15.a4±] **11...h5** [11...♗g7 (Smerdon)] **12.♕e2** [12.♕b3 ♘b6 13.♘ge4 ♘fd5 14.♘xd5 exd5 15.♕c3 ♕e7 16.♘g3 (16. bxa6 c4 17.♘g3 ♗g7 18.♗c2 ♖xa6 19.d4∞; 16.b3!? (Smerdon)) 16...♗g7 17.bxa6 c4! Smerdon; ∞] **12...♘d5?** [Black exposes his king to a strong attack. 12...♗g7 13.♗c4± Smerdon] **13.♘xe6 fxe6 14.♗g6+ ♔e7 15.d4 ♗h6 16.♘xd5+ exd5 17.dxc5 ♗f6** [17...♕c7 18.c6 ♘b6 19.f4 (→ Smerdon) 19...♕xf6 (19...axb5 20.b3 e4 21.♗xe4 dxe4 22.♕xe4+ ♔f7 23.♗b2 ♗g7 24.♗xg7 ♔xg7 25.♕d4+ ♔h7 26.♖e5+−) 20.♕d3 e4 21.♗xe4 dxe4 22.♕c3+ ♔g6 23.♕xh8 ♗f5 24.♕e5±] **18.♗c2 ♕e7** [18...♗xc1 19.♖axc1 axb5 20.c6+−] **19.c6** [19.♕d3!?+− Smerdon] **19...♗xc1 20.cxd7** [20.♖axc1! ♘b6 21.f4+− Smerdon] **20...♗xb2 21.dxc8♕ ♖axc8 22.♖ab1 ♗d4 23.bxa6** [(+− Smerdon)] **23...♕c5 24.♗b3 ♖hf8 25.♔h1 ♖c7** [25...♔g6 26.f3+−] **26.♕d2 ♔g6 27.♖ec1 ♗c3 28.♕xd5 ♕d4 29.♖c2 ♖d8 30.♕e6+ ♔g5 31.♖cc1** [31.h4+ gxh3 32.♔g1! h2 33.♖gc1!+− Smerdon] **31...♖d6 32.♕g8+ ♖g6 33.♕b8 ♖gg7 34.♖d1 ♕a7 35.♕d8+ ♖ce7 36.♕d3 ♖c7?** [36...♕c5+−] **37.♗c2 ♕xf2 38.♖f1** 1-0

Mateusz Bartel
Alexander Grischuk
Berlin Wch rapid 2015 (8)

1.e4 c5 2.♘f3 d6 3.♗b5+ ♘d7 4.0-0 a6 5.♗d3 ♘gf6 6.♖e1 b5 7.c4 g5 8.cxb5 g4 9.e5 dxe5 10.♘g5 ♗g7 11.♕e2 0-0

12.♘c3 [12.♘xh7?! ♘xh7 13.♗xh7+ ♔xh7 14.♕e4+ f5 15.♕xa8 axb5∞ Smerdon] **12...♘b6 13.bxa6 c4 14.♗c2** [14.♗xc4? ♘xc4 15.♕xc4 ♗xa6 △ ...♗d3 Smerdon; ∓; 14.♗b1 h6 15.♘ge4 ♘xe4 16.♗xe4 ♖xa6 ⇄ Smerdon] **14...♖xa6** [14...h6 15.♘ge4 ♘xe4 16.♕xe4 f5 17.♕e3 ♖xa6∞] **15.♕xe5 h6 16.♘ge4 ♘fd5 17.♕f5?!** [17.♕h5! e6 (17...♘b4 18.♗b1 ♗c8 (18...♘d3 19.♗xd3 cxd3 20.b3!± Smerdon) 19.♘g3 ♘d3 20.♗xd3 cxd3 21.♘f5±; 17...f5 18.d4 fxe4 19.♗xh6 ♖f7 20.♖xe4±) 18.d4! cxd3 19.♗b3 ♘f6 (19...♔h7 20.♗g5 f6 21.♗d2 ♗c4±) 20.♗xf6+ ♗xf6 21.♕xg4 (Smerdon) 21...♔h7 22.♖e4 ♘d7±] **17...♗c8** [17...e6 18.♕h5 f5 19.d4 (→ Smerdon) 19...fxe4 20.♕xg4 ♗xc3 21.♗xh6 ♕xd4 22.♗xg7 ♕xg7 23.♕xe6+ ♕f7 24.♕g4+ ♕g7 25.♕e6+ ♕f7=] **18.♕h5 ♘f4 19.♕c5 ♗d4** [19...f5!? 20.♘g3 ♗e6 21.♕b4 (21.♖xe6 ♗xe6 22.♗xf5 ♖xf5 23.♗xf5 ♗d7 24.♘xe7+ ♔f7 25.♕h5+ ♗xe7∓ Smerdon) 21...♘d4∓] **20.♕c6 ♗e6** [20...f5!? (Smerdon) 21.♕xh6 fxe4 22.♗xe4 ♖f7 23.♗g5+ ♔f8 24.d3 ♗xd3 25.♕h5∓] **21.♘c5 ♕d6?** [21...♘bd5 22.♖xe6 (22.♘xe6 fxe6 23.♖xe6 ♗xf2+ 24.♔h1 ♖c8 25.♗a6 ♘b4 26.♖g6+ ♔f7−+) 22...♖c8 23.♗b7 ♖xc6 24.♘xd8 ♖xe6 25.♖xe6 fxe6∓] **22.♕xd6 exd6 23.d3 ♘xg2 24.♖xe6?!** [24.♖xe6 fxe6=; 24.♗xg2 dxc5 25.♗b5 ♖fc8 26.♘xd4 cxd4 27.♗xh6 c3 28.bxc3 ♖xc3∞] **24...fxe6 25.♘xe6 ♗xc3 26.♘xf8 ♖e1 27.♗d1 ♗f6 28.♘e6?!** [28.♗xh6 ♗xb2 29.♖b1 ♘xd3∓] **28...♘xd3 29.♗xg4?** [29.♗xh6!? ♗xb2 30.♖b1 ♖xa2 31.♗xg4∓] **29...♖xc1 30.♖xc1 ♖xa2 31.♘c7 ♗xb2?** [31...♖xb2!? (Smerdon) 32.♗e6+ ♔h8−+] **32.♖c2 ♖a1+** [32...♗g7 33.♘e8+ ♔g6 34.♘xd6 c3∓] **33.♔g2 c3 34.♘b5**

♘a4 **35.♘xd6 ♖e1 36.♗e2 ♘c5** [36...♖c1!? 37.♖xc1 ♗xc1=] **37.♘b5 ♘e4 38.♗f3** [38.f3 ♘d2 39.♘xc3 ♗xc3 40.♔f2 ♘b1 41.♗c4+ ♔g7 42.♖xc3 ♘xc3 (42...♖h1 43.♖b3 ♖xh2+ 44.♔e3 ♘d2 45.♖b7+ ♔f6 46.♖b6+ ♔g7 47.♗d3 ♘xf3 48.♔xf3 Smerdon) 43.♔xe1 ♘a4= Smerdon; 38.♗d3 ♔g7 39.♘xc3 ♗xc3 40.♔xe4 ♖xe4 41.♖xc3=] **38...♗a1 39.♗xe4 ♖xe4 40.♔f3 ♖b4 41.♘d6 ♔h7 42.♔e3 ♔g6 43.f3 ♖b2 44.♖xc3**   ½-½

Rauf Mamedov
Alexander Grischuk
Berlin Wch rapid 2015 (15)

1.e4 c5 2.♘f3 d6 3.♗b5+ ♘d7 4.0-0 a6 5.♗d3 ♘gf6 6.♖e1 b5 7.c4 g5 8.cxb5 g4 9.e5 dxe5 10.♘g5 ♗g7 11.♘c3 [This move is more flexible than 11.♕e2. The queen can be developed both on e2 and c2]

11...0-0 [11...♘b6! (Smerdon) 12.♗f1 (12.♕e2 0-0 transposes to Bartel-Grischuk, Berlin rapid 2015) 12...0-0 (12...h6!? 13.♘ge4 ♘xe4 14.♘xe4 c4 15.bxa6 f5 16.♘c3 ♗xa6 17.b4 cxb3 18.♕xb3 ♗xf1 19.♖xf1 ♖a5 20.♘b5 ♕d7 21.♖b1 ♘d5= KP&JI) 13.♖xe5 (Smerdon) 13.bxa6 ♗xa6 14.♗xa6 ♖xa6 15.♖xe5 c4♙ Smerdon; 13.a4 c4!⇄; Smerdon 13...♘bd5!?) 13...axb5 14.♗xb5 ♗b7 15.♖e1 (15.♖xc5? h6!) 15...h6 16.♘ge4 ♘xe4 17.♘xe4 ♕d5 18.♗f1±] **12.bxa6** [12.a4 ♗b7 (12... e6 13.♕c2 h6 14.♘h7 ♘xh7 15.♗xh7+ ♔h8 16.♗e4 ♖a7 17.d3 f5 18.♗c6± Smerdon; 12...axb5 13.♗xb5 h6 14.♘ge4 ♘xe4 15.♘xe4 f5 16.♕b3+± Smerdon; 12...♘b6 13.♕c2! h6 14.♘h7! ♘xh7 15.♗xh7+ ♔h8 16.♗e4 ♖a7 17.a5!± Smerdon) 13.♕c2 h6 14.♘ge4 (14.♘h7 ♘xh7 15.♗xh7+ ♔h8♙ Smerdon; ±;

14.bxa6 ♗xa6 15.♗xa6 ♖xa6 16.♘ge4 ♘h5 17.d3 ♘f4∞) 14...♘xe4 15.♘xe4 f5 (15...e6 16.bxa6 ♗xa6 17.♗xa6 ♖xa6 18.♘xc5 ♘xc5 19.♕xc5± Smerdon) 16.♗c4+ ♔h8 17.♘g3 axb5 (17...e4 18.bxa6 ♗xa6 19.♗xa6 ♖xa6 20.d3 f4 21.♘xe4± Smerdon) 18.♗xb5 e6 19.♘h5 ♘f6 20.♘xg7 ♕d5 21.♗f1 ♔xg7±; 12.♕c2 axb5 (12...h6 13.♘h7 ♘xh7 14.♗xh7+ ♔h8 15.♗e4 ♖a7 16.a4 axb5 17.♗xb5 ♖a6 18.b3 △ ♗b2±) 13.♗xh7+ (13.♗xb5 ♖a6 14.♗xa6 ♖xa6 15.d3 (∓ Smerdon) 15...♕a8=) 13...♔h8 14.♗d3 c4 15.♗f1 ♘c5 16.♗xb5 (16.♖xe5 ♘b3 17.♘d5∞ Smerdon) 16...♘d3 17.♖e3! ♘d5 18.♕xc4 ♖xc1 19.♖xc1 ♘xe3 20.dxe3 ♕d2 21.♗c2 ♕d1 22.♘c7 ♖b8 (Smerdon) 23.h4 (23.b3↑ Smerdon) 23...♗f5 24.♖c1 ♕d2 25.♘xf7+ ♖xf7 26.♕xf7 ♕xc1 27.♘e8 ♗f6 28.e4 ♗c8 29.♘xf6 exf6 30.♕xf6+ ♔g8 31.♕g6+ ♔h8 32.♕h5+=) 23...♖b6 24.♕c5 ♕d6 25.♕xd6 ♖xd6=] **12... e6** [12...♘b6 13.♕c2 h6 14.♘h7 ♘xh7 15.♗xh7+ ♔h8 (Smerdon) 16.♗f5 ♖xa6 17.♗xc8 ♕xc8 18.b3±] **13.♘ge4?!** [13.♕e2 (Smerdon) 13...h6 14.♘ge4 (14.♘h7? ♘xh7 15.♗xh7+ ♔xh7 16.♕e4+ f5 17.♕xa8 ♕b6 18.a4 ♗xa6 19.a5 ♕d6 20.♘e4∓) 14...♘d5±; 13.♕c2!?] **13...♘xe4 14.♗xe4 ♖xa6** [(∓ Smerdon)] **15.♕e2** [15.♗d3 ♖d6 16.♗f1 f5 17.♘b5 ♖a6 18.a4 ♗b7 19.♕c2 h5∞] **15...f5 16.♗d3 ♖d6 17.♗c4?!** [17.♗b5 ♖a6 18.♗c4 ♘b6 19.d3 ♘xc4 20.dxc4 e4∓] **17...e4 18.d3?** [18.♗b5 ♘e5 (18...♖b6 19.♖d1 ♘e5 20.d3 f4 21.dxe4 ♗d7 22.♘a3 f3∓) 19.♘xd6 ♕xd6 (→ Smerdon) 20.♗b5 ♘d3 21.♗xd3 exd3 22.♕d1 ♗e5 23.♖xe5 ♕xe5∓] **18...♘e5** [−+ Smerdon] **19.dxe4 f4 20.♕f1 ♕h4 21.♗xf4 ♖xf4 22.♖ad1 ♖xd1** [22...♘f3+!?] **23.♖xd1 ♖f8**   0-1

Magnus Carlsen
Veselin Topalov
Saint Louis 2015 (1)

1.e4 c5 2.♘f3 d6 3.♗b5+ ♘d7 4.0-0 ♘gf6 5.♖e1 a6 6.♗d3 b5

7.c4 g5 [A move in ultra-modernist style, and a novelty found by Dave Smerdon. Black sacrifices a pawn (White can choose which one he wants to take), counting on the open g-file (if White takes on g5), his active light-squared bishop on the long diagonal and an extremely complicated, wild position] **8.♘xg5** [8.e5 ♘xe5 (8...dxe5!? 9.cxb5 (9.♘xg5 ♗b7 10.cxb5 ♘g8 11.bxa6 ♗xg2 12.♘xg2 ♖xg5+ 13.♔f1 e4⇄) 9...♗h6∞) 9.♘xe5 dxe5 10.♗f1 (10.♕e2 ♗g7 11.cxb5 (11.♕xe5 0-0 12.♗c2 h6♙) 11...0-0 12.♘c3 axb5 13.♗xb5 ♘d5♙) 10...b4 (10...♖b8!?) 11.d3 g4 (11...h6!?= 12.♖xe5?! ♕c7 13.♖e1 ♗g7 14.♗e2 0-0∓) 12.a3 e6 13.axb4 cxb4 14.♗g5 (14.♖xe5 ♕c7 15.♖e1 ♗d6 16.g3 ♗b7 17.d4∓) 14...♖g8 (Bartel-Bocharov, Berlin Wch rapid 2015) 15.♗h4±] **8...♘e5 9.♗e2** [The bishop retreat 9.♗f1!? deserves serious attention. It enables White to play 10.d4, as after 10...cxd3 the f1-bishop is not attacked: 9...bxc4

10.d4 (10.f4 ♘d3 11.♖xd3 cxd3 12.♕a4+ ♕d7 13.♕b3 d5 14.♕xd3 ♘xe4 15.♘c3 ♘xg5 16.fxg5 ♗b7∞; 10.♘f3 g4 11.♗e2 d3 12.♗xd3 cxd3 13.h3 ♘h5 14.♘c3 ♕d7 15.e5 dxe5 16.♖xe5 ♖g8=) 10...cxd3 11.f4 and now 11...♗g4 (11...♘c6 12.♗xd3 Barski-Borovikov, Heusenstamm 2015; 12.♘a3!?) 12...♗g7±) 12.♕d2 ♘c6 13.♕xd3 h6 14.♘f3 ♗b4 15.♕d1 ♗xf3 16.gxf3 ♖g8+ 17.♔h1± Smerdon] **9... bxc4 10.♘a3** [10.♘f3 ♘d3 (10...♘fg4 11.♘a3 ♘d3 12.♗xd3 cxd3 13.♕b3±) 11.♗xd3 cxd3 12.♕b3 (12.♘c3 ♖g8 13.e5 ♘g4 14.♕a4+ ♗d7 15.♕e4 ♘xe5 16.♘xe5 dxe5 17.♘d5 ♖b8∓) 12...♖g8 13.♕xd3 ♘h5 14.♕e3 e5 15.g3 ♗h3⇄] **10...♖g8**

11.♘xc4?! [11.d3 (or 11.d4) 11...cxd3 12.♗xd3 h6 13.♘f3 ♘xd3 14.♕xd3 d5=]

11...♘xc4 [11...♖xg5? 12.d4 ♘xc4 13.♗xg5 ♘xe4 (13...♘b6 14.dxc5 dxc5 15.♕c2 ♗e6 16.e5 ♘fd5 17.♗xh7+−; 13...♘a5 14.dxc5 dxc5 15.e5 ♕xd1 16.♖axd1 ♘g8 17.♗d3+−) 14.♗xc4 ♘xg5 15.♗d5 ♖b8 16.♕h5 ♘g7 17.♗xg5 ♗xd4 18.♕g8+ ♔d7 19.♕xf7+] **12.d4 ♘b6** [12...♘a5! 13.dxc5 ♘c6 14.cxd6 h6 15.dxe7 ♗xe7∓] **13.♗h5?!** [13.dxc5 dxc5 14.♗h5 ♘xh5 15.♕xh5 ♖g6 16.♖d1 ♕c7 17.♕xh7∓] **13...♘xh5 14.♕xh5 ♖g7?** [14...♖xg5! 15.♗xg5 cxd4 16.♕xh7 ♘d7∓] **15.♘xh7?!** [15.dxc5 ♘c4 16.♘xh7 ♘a5 17.♗f4 ♕xc5 18.♖xc5 dxc5 19.♘xf8 ♗xf8 20.b3 ♘a3 21.♖ac1=] **15...♕d7?!** [15...♖xh7 16.♗xh7 cxd4∓] **16.dxc5 dxc5 17.e5?** [17.♘xf8 ♕h3 18.♕xh3 ♘xh3 19.g3=] **17...♕c6 18.f3** [18.♗g5 ♗b7 19.♘f6+ ♔d8 20.♘e4 ♕g6 21.♕xg6 ♖xg6∓] **18...♕g6 19.♘f6+** [19.♕xg6 ♖xg6 20.♘xf8 ♔xf8∓] **19...♔d8 20.♕xg6 ♖xg6 21.♘e4**

♗b7 **22.h4 ♖c8** [22...♔e8!?∓] **23.h5 ♖g8 24.♗d2 ♘c4 25.♗c3?!** [25.♖ad1 ♘xd2 26.♖xd2+ ♔c7∓] **25...♗h6 26.♖ad1+ ♔e8 27.♖d3 ♗f4 28.♘f2 ♗c6 29.♘h3?** [29.g4!?−+] **29...♗g3 30.♖e2 ♗b5 31.♖d1 ♗c6** [31...♘b6−+] **32.♘f2** [32.♖d3 ♘b6−+] **32...♗xe5! 33.♘g4** [33.♗xe5 ♗xf3−+] **33...♗xc3 34.bxc3 ♔f8 35.♔f2 ♖h8 36.♘e5 ♗xe5 37.♖xe5 ♗e8 38.g4 f6 39.♖e6 ♗b5 40.♖de1 ♖c7** 0-1

Magnus Carlsen
Alexander Grischuk
London 2015 (9)

1.♘f3 c5 2.e4 d6 3.♗b5+ ♘d7 4.0-0 a6 5.♗d3 ♘gf6 6.♖e1 b5 7.c4 g5 8.♘xg5 ♘e5 9.♗e2 bxc4

10.♘c3 [Carlsen's improvement after his defeat on the hands of Topalov. White refrains from accepting the sacrifice and counts on his better development]

10...♖b8?! [This move does not contribute much. 10...♘g8 11.d3 (11. f4 ♘d3 12.♗xd3 cxd3 13.♕a4+ ♕d7 14.♕c4 ♖g7 15.♕xd3 h6 16.♘f3 ♘h5 17.♘e2 ♕g4 18.g3 ♘xf4=) 11...cxd3 12.♗xd3 h6 13.♘f3 ♗g4 14.♗e2 ♗xf3 15.♗xf3 ♖c8 16.♗f4 ♘xf3+ 17.♕xf3 ♕g4± ; 10...♕d7 11.♘f3 ♘fg4 12.♘xe5 ♘xe5 13.b3±] **11.♖f1?!** [11.f4! ♘d3 12.♗xd3 cxd3 13.♕a4+ ♕d7 14.♕c4±] **11...h6 12.♘f3 ♘d3** [12...♘xf3+ 13.♗xf3±] **13.♘e1** [13.♗xd3 cxd3 14.♘e1±/±] **13...♘xb2** [13...♘xc1 14.♖xc1 ♖xb2 15.♗xc4±] **14.♗xb2 ♖xb2 15.♗xc4 ♖b4 16.♕e2± ♗g7 17.♘c2 ♖b6 18.♖ab1 0-0 19.♖xb6 ♕xb6 20.♘e3 e6 21.f4 ♔h8 22.f5 a5 23.a4 ♕d8 24.h3 ♕e7 25.♗a6 ♗xa6 26.♕xa6 ♘h5 27.♖f3?!** [27.♘e2±; 27.♕xa5±] **27...♖g8 28.♘b5?!** [28.fxe6 fxe6 29.♕c4 ♗e5 30.♘e2±] **28...♗e5 29.♘g4 ♕h4 30.fxe6?** [30.♘xd6 ♗d4+ 31.♘e3 ♕e1+ 32.♕f1 ♕xd2 33.♘dc4 ♕c3 34.fxe6 fxe6 35.♕f2 ♘f6=] **30...fxe6?** [30...♖xg4! 31.hxg4 ♕h2+ 32.♔f2 ♗f4 33.♖g3 ♘xe6 34.♖f3 ♗g7∓] **31.♘xe5 dxe5 32.♕xe6 ♕e1+??** [32...♕g5 33.♖f2 (33.g4 ♘f4=) 33...♗f4 34.♕g4 ♕xg4 35.hxg4 ♖xg4=] **33.♔h2** [33.♖f1!+−] **33...♖xg2+ 34.♔xg2 ♕d2+?** [34...♕e2+ 35.♔g1 ♕xf3 36.♕xh6+ ♔g8 37.♕g5+ ♔f8 38.♕f5+ ♔xf5 39.exf5+−] **35.♔g1 ♕e1+ 36.♖f1 ♕e3+ 37.♖f2 ♕e1+ 38.♔g2** 1-0

Exercise 1

position after 10.♕d1-a4

Should Black accept the sacrifice with 10...exd5 ?
(solution on page 244)

Exercise 2

position after 20.♗d2-a5

What should Black play: 20...♗e6 to exchange White's active d5-bishop or 20...♕c8 to unpin his c7-knight?
(solution on page 244)

Exercise 3

position after 47.♖h6-h4

What should Black play: 47...♕f5 or 47...♕f3 ?
(solution on page 244)

Sicilian Defence

Najdorf Variation   SI 14.7 (B90)

Ignoring the 'Kinderangriff'

by Nikolay Ninov

1.	e4	c5
2.	♘f3	d6
3.	d4	cxd4
4.	♘xd4	♘f6
5.	♘c3	a6
6.	♗e3	♘g4
7.	♗g5	h6
8.	♗h4	g5
9.	♗g3	♗g7

Maxime Vachier-Lagrave was the hero of a Survey in Yearbook 116, based on his deep novelty and impressive win over Caruana in Wijk aan Zee, and he impressed again in the European team championship! Yet another stunning pawn sacrifice to eliminate the enemy dark-squared bishop, and again in one of the Najdorf branches.
In the 1990s, when Garry Kasparov started effectively using the knight sally 6...♘g4 in reply to the fashionable 6.♗e3, many players followed him, and some of the lines after the natural sequence 7.♗g5 h6 8.♗h4 g5 9.♗g3 ♗g7 were explored up to move 20 and beyond. This

is, however, not the case with 10.♗c4, which was Vallejo Pons's choice in our main game. The first official game with this move dates from 1994, and almost half of these nearly 70 tries are from the 20th century. It should be noted that a strong tactician like Topalov as Black made only one draw in three games here, losing his classical games against Anand and Ponomariov! Also, Azarov was twice victorious with 10.♗c4 against strong opposition. All of us are taught about the 'Kindermatt' on f7 in our childhood – can this accelerated 'Kinderangriff' against the f7-pawn create so much trouble? Black reacted in almost 75 per cent of the games with the natural 10...♘c6. Castling in anticipation of the move ♕d1-f3 is not to be recommended, but there are three other continuations:

Three Alternatives

10...♕a5 is the main alternative, with which Black has won all three games after 11.♗b3 ♘c6 12.♘e2 ♗e6. Essential is 11.0-0 ♕c5, when 12.♗e2 ♗xd4 13.♗xg4? did not save the piece in Kirillova-Dzagnidze. Instead, 13.♘a4 leads to immense complications in which White has to prove his compensation for the pawn. It is better for him to launch a counterattack on

Maxime Vachier-Lagrave

the knight with 12.♗e6, as in Azarov-Dydyshko.
10...♕b6 also has concrete intentions. In general this sortie in the ♘g4-variation is strongly met by 11.♘d5!, and this (as yet untried) jump is probably the most testing move. Apart from 11...♕xd4, Black once again has 11.. ♕c5!? at his disposal, but the unbalanced positions arising from this are far from easy to handle.
10...♘e5 deprives White's queen of the f3-square, but does not exert pressure on the long diagonal: 11.♗b3 ♘bc6 12.♘f5 ♗xf5 13.exf5 (V.Balogh-Tokmachev, 1999) is critical, and the assessment will probably depend on the strength of the move 13...♘d4!?.
All three above-mentioned alternatives to 10...♘c6 have been

tried in practice with satisfactory results; see the Game Section.

The Main Line: 10...♘c6

The established main line 10...♘c6 usually continues with 11.♘xc6 bxc6, strengthening Black's control over the central squares. On the other hand, it can be expected that Black's king will never castle and that this majority will gain in strength only in the endgame. White has to act vigorously, and 12.♕f3 ♖f8 13.♗b3 makes sense.

The most popular choice is 12.h4. It should be noted that White also has 10.h4, with the idea of transposing with 10...♘c6 11.♘xc6 bxc6 12.♗c4, avoiding the alternative 10...♕a5 – this was the exact move order used by Vallejo Pons. Did he have something up his sleeve after 12...♕a5 13.♕f3 ♗e6 from Ivanchuk-Dominguez Perez

(2013), or did he just want to go for the perpetual? Whatever the case, MVL came up with a surprising pawn sacrifice to obtain the bishop pair with 13...♘e5!?, winning in style. His compensation was never been in doubt, even after he offered a queen trade.

A similar idea was used successfully in another game from 2013 (Kenes-Li, which also featured the curious 12...♘e5!?), but here White took on f7 with the wrong piece. This also gave me pleasant memories – in one of my correspondence games with 6...♗g4 at the very end of the 20th century, my opponent was invited to take on f7 and in the end the bishop from g7 fully deserved to be called my 'extra piece'!

Conclusion

The line with 10.♗c4 ♘c6 11.♘xc6 bxc6 should not

worry Black, who can rely on his central preponderance. The expected double attack against the f7-pawn can be met by a timely ...♘g4-e5 or ...♗c8-e6. And if a defensive move like 12...♖f8 is not to his taste, Black can avoid the option of 12.♕f3 by going 10...♕a5 in reply to 10.♗c4.

12.h4 ♕a5 13.♕f3 ♗e6 leads to a draw by force – instead, Vachier-Lagrave's entertaining novelty 13...♘e5!? poses certain practical problems.

In the recent London Classics, Anand opted for another variation against MVL's Najdorf, and in the end the same piece once again had the decisive word, crowning an exciting tactical battle – a bitter present for Vishy's 46th birthday.

Nowadays the dark-squared bishop is a monster in Maxime's hands!

**Francisco Vallejo Pons
Maxime Vachier-Lagrave**

Reykjavik Ech-tt 2015 (5)

**1.e4 c5 2.♘f3 d6 3.d4 cxd4
4.♘xd4 ♘f6 5.♘c3 a6 6.♗e3 ♘g4
7.♗c1 ♘f6 8.♗e3 ♘g4 9.♗g5 h6
10.♗h4 g5 11.♗g3 ♗g7 12.h4
♘c6 13.♘xc6 bxc6 14.♗c4 ♕a5
15.♕f3**

15...♘e5!? [A highly unexpected novelty instead of the well-known 13...♗e6 – Black is simply ignoring the threat!] **16.♗xe5 ♕xe5 17.♗xf7+ ♔d8 18.hxg5** [18.♕e3 ♖b8 19.♗b3 ♖f8 can transpose to the text with 20.hxg5, avoiding the extra possibility for Black on move 19 in the game] **18...♖b8 19.♗b3** [The engines are incredible in discovering drawish lines – here is one by Stockfish: 19.♘d1 ♕xg5 20.♕h5 ♕xg2 21.♕a5+ ♔d7 22.♗e6+! ♔e8 23.♕h5+ ♔d8 24.♕a5+ ♔e8 25.♕h5+=] **19...♖f8** [One more original thought – being a pawn down Black does not mind the exchange of the queens! A notable alternative is 19...♕xg5!? with ample compensation for the pawn: 20.♖h5 (20.g3 ♖f8 (20...h5!? 21.♕e2 h4 △ 22.gxh4 ♕g2 23.0-0-0 ♗g4) 21.♕d3 ♗g4⩲ 22.f4 △ ♕c5; 20.♕h5 ♕xg2 21.♕a5+ ♔e8 22.♕h5+ does not force a repetition after 22...♔d7 23.0-0-0 ♕g5+∓; 20.♔f1 ♖f8 21.♕d3 h5⩱; 20.♖g1 ♖f8 21.♕e3 (21.♕d3?! ♖b4!) 21...♕xe3+

22.fxe3 ♖b4 23.♔d2 ♗xc3+ and White can still maintain the balance with 24.bxc3! ♖xe4 25.♖af1! ♖xf1 (25...♖f5 26.♖xf5 ♗xf5 27.♖f1 ♗g6 28.♖f4) 26.♖xf1 ♖g4 27.♖f8+ ♔d7 28.♖g8 ♖xg8 29.♗xg8) 20...♕g6 21.♗f7 ♕g4 22.♗b3 ♖b4!? (22...♕g6 23.♗f7 ♕g4=) 23.♔f1 ♗xc3 and the incredible 24.♗xc3!! ♕xh5 25.♕xb4! (25.♕xh8+?! ♔c7 26.♔g1 ♖xe4∓) 25...♕h1+ 26.♔e2 once again brings us into the wonderful world of the engines with various perpetuals, e.g. 26...♕xa1 (26...♗g4+ 27.♔d2 ♕xa1 28.♕b6+ ♔c8 29.♕xc6+ ♔b8 30.♕b6+ ♔c8 31.♕a6+ ♔b8 32.♕b6+ ♔c8=) 27.♕b6+ ♔e8 28.♕xc6+ ♔d8 29.♕b6+ ♔e8 (29...♔d7?? 30.e5!) 30.♕c7!? (30.♕c6+ ♔d8 31.♕b6+ ♔e8=) 30...♗g4+ 31.f3 ♕g1 32.fxg4 (32.♕b8+ ♔d7 33.♗a4+ ♔e6=) 32...♕xg2+ 33.♔e3 ♕g3+ 34.♔d2 ♕f2+ 35.♔d3 ♕f3+ 36.♔d2 ♕f2+=] **20.♕e3 ♕xg5 21.♕xg5 hxg5 22.f3?!** [The first important moment of the endgame. In order to defend his central pawn White would be forced to play the text move anyway, and he decided to execute it at once. But he had many more useful options at his disposal. First of all, a penetration by the rook must be considered: 22.♖h7 ♗d4 23.♘d1 ♖f4 24.f3 g4 25.c3 ♗e5 26.♔e2 a5 27.♔e3 ♖f6♒; or 22.♖h5 ♖b4!? 23.f3 g4 24.a3 gxf3 25.gxf3 ♖xb3!? (25...♖b8 △ ...c5-c4) 26.cxb3 ♖xf3♒. Then comes the immediate relocation of the knight by 22.♘d1 ♗e5 23.c3 (another sensible idea – now the bishop can support the e4-pawn) 23...♖f4 24.♗c2 (24.f3 g4 25.♔e2 a5 26.♔e3 ♖f8♒) 24...♗e6♒; White can also start with an activation of the king – 22.♔e2, though Black can try at once to disturb it, for instance 22...a5 23.f3 g4 24.♖ad1 gxf3+ 25.gxf3 c5 26.♖h7 ♗a6+ 27.♔d2 ♗e5 28.♘d5 ♗b7 29.f4 ♖xf4 30.♘xf4 ♗xf4+ 31.♔e1 ♗g3+ with one more beautiful perpetual] **22...g4 23.♔e2 a5 24.♘a4 ♗a6+ 25.c4?** [In my humble opinion, from this moment on there was no way back for White – Black's dark-squared bishop can operate without hindrance along the big diagonal until the end of the game, and the second rook got a nice outpost on b4 as well. The scope of these two pieces should have been limited as much as possible, and 25.♔e3 c5 26.c3 would have fulfilled that purpose. True, this set-up would have been a worse version of the aforementioned line with 22.♘d1 – exactly because of the stranded knight. However, Vallejo could have put up much more resistance in this case. Perhaps Vallejo did not like 26...♗e5 (26... gxf3 27.gxf3 ♗b5 28.f4 ♗xa4 29.♗xa4 ♖xb2 30.♖ab1 ♖xb1 31.♖xb1 ♔c7 and White can save himself with active play – 32.♗b3! ♗xc3 33.♗d5 ♗d4+ 34.♔f3 ♖b8 35.♖xb8 ♔xb8 36.a4=; 26... c4 27.♗c2 ♗b5 28.♖ab1 gxf3 29.gxf3 ♔c7 30.♖h7! (30.f4?! ♖h8 31.a3 ♗c6 32.♔f3 ♗f6 33.♖bg1 ♖bg8 34.♔f2 ♗d7 and Black, who is practically playing with an extra piece, will inevitably penetrate) 30...♗f6 31.f4 ♖h8 32.e5! dxe5 33.♘c5 (the knight is back and White can rely on a positive result due to the reduced material) 33...exf4+ 34.♔xf4 ♗b6 35.♖xh8 ♖xh8 36.♘e4 ♗g7 37.♖g1 ♗h6+ 38.♔e5 ♗e3 39.♖g6+ ♔c7 40.♗d1 ♖h2 41.♖g7⇄) 27.♖h7 ♗f4+ 28.♔f2 g3+, but actually he could avoid the loss of material with

29.♔e1 ♗b5 30.♖b1 (△ ♗c2) 30...♗d3?! 31.♖d1 c4 32.♘c5!] **25...♖b4 26.♖ac1 gxf3+ 27.gxf3 ♗d4 28.♖c2 c5 29.♖h2 ♗g8 30.♖c1 ♗c8 31.♘c3 ♗e6** [With his last moves Black was calmly improving his pieces – the bishop is not only attacking the c4-pawn, but is also working in the other direction. White had to be alert on both flanks and now he cracks under the pressure] **32.♔d3?** [The final mistake in a difficult position. Many sources pointed out 32.♖b1 as a chance for White to stay in the game, but in my view the position was beyond salvation for him ever since his 25.c4? move, especially when facing a super GM in a practical game. I would just like to mention a line like 32...♔d7 33.♘d5 ♗xd5 34.cxd5 c4 35.♗c2 ♗g1 (or 35...♗xb2) 36.a3 ♗xh2 37.axb4 ♖g2+ 38.♔d1 axb4 39.♗a4+ ♔d8 40.♖c1 ♖xb2 41.♖xc4 ♗f4 and refer the readers to the way in which MVL recently (Biel 2015) used a similar passed pawn in an opposite-coloured bishops ending to beat Navara] **32...♖g3–+ 33.♔e2** [33.♖f1 ♗h3 is hopeless too] **33...♗xc4+ 34.♔d2 ♖xf3 35.♗xc4 ♖xb2+** 0-1

Three Alternatives on Move 10

Sergei Azarov
Viacheslav Dydyshko
Minsk ch-BLR 2002 (9)

1.e4 c5 2.♘f3 d6 3.d4 cxd4 4.♘xd4 ♘f6 5.♘c3 a6 6.♗e3 ♘g4 7.♗g5 h6 8.♗h4 g5 9.♗g3 ♗g7 10.♗c4 ♕a5 [The main alternative to 10...♘c6 – the light-squared bishop is an extra target. It is not easy to recommend 10...♕b6

11.♘d5!. This is the typical and most challenging reaction to this queen sortie – in the two known practical games with 11.♘b3 Black did not experience serious problems. The text leads to complications, where Black not only has to find a way to capture the knight on a8, but also has to take constant care of his 'centralized' king: 11...♕xd4 (11...♕c5!? is worth a try, but 12.c3! ♕xc4 13.♘b6 ♕c5 14.♘xa8 b5 15.f3! is hard to meet – 15...♘e3 16.♕e2 ♕xd4 17.cxd4 ♘c2+ 18.♔d1! ♘xd4 19.♕d2 ♕a7 20.♘c7+ ♕xc7 21.♕xd4) 12.♕xd4 ♗xd4 13.♘c7+ ♔d8 14.♘xa8 b5 15.♗xf7, etc.] **11.0-0** [For 11.♗b3 ♘c6 12.♘de2 ♗e6 see the notes to Ivanchuk-Dominguez Perez] **11...♕c5!**

12.♗e6! [Nice, and practically the only move.

A) 12.♗e2?! ♗xd4 is playing with fire: 13.♘a4□ (saves the piece, but there is no clear way to equalize for White; 13.♗xg4 ♗xg4 14.♕xg4 h5 15.♕d1 (15.♕h3 g4–+) 15...♗xc3!. An accurate elimination of the potentially dangerous knight – Black remained a piece up and won effortlessly in Kirillova-Dzagnidze, Oropesa del Mar Wch U12 W 1999) 13...♘xf2 (also wins a pawn, and in a slightly better version – 13...♘e3 14.fxe3 ♗xe3+ and White can count on compensation after 15.♔h1 (15.♗f2 ♕a7 (15...♗xf2+ 16.♖xf2 ♕a5! transposes to 13...♘xf2 below) 16.♘c3 ♗e6) 15...♕d4 16.♘c3! (16.♗h5 ♗e6 17.♗f3 0-0 18.c3 ♕xa4 19.♗xe3 ♘d7 20.b3 ♕c6 21.♖ad1 f6) 16...♗e6 (16...♕xd1 17.♖axd1 ♗e6 18.♘d5 ♗xd5 19.exd5 ♘d7 20.♗h5) 17.♗d3 ♘d7 18.♘d5! (instead, 18.♕e2 enables Black to achieve a dream Sicilian set-up after 18...♗f4! 19.♗xf4 gxf4 20.♖xf4 ♘e5) 18...♗xd5 19.exd5 ♕xd5 20.♕e2 ♗f4 21.♗xf4 gxf4 22.♖xf4 ♘e5 △ 23.♗e4) 14.♗xf2 ♗xf2+ 15.♖xf2 and now:

A1) 15...♕e3?! 16.♘c3 ♗e6 (16...0-0 17.♘d5 ♕xe4 18.♗f3 ♕e5 19.♖e2 ♕xb2 20.♖b1 ♕xa2 21.♘xe7+ ♔g7 22.♘xc8 ♖xc8 23.♕d4+) 17.♘d5 ♕c5 18.b4 ♕c6 19.♕d4 △ b4-b5;

A2) 15...♕a7 16.e5! (instead, 16.♗c4 is a bit premature – 16...♗e6 (16...♖f8!? 17.♕h5 ♘d7!) 18.♗xf7+ ♔d8 19.c4 ♕e3 △ ...♘e5) 17.♗xe6 (17.♗e2?! ♘d7 18.♘c3 ♘e5) 17...fxe6 18.e5 ♘c6 19.exd6 0-0-0) 16...dxe5 17.♗c4! looks quite promising: 17...♖f8 (17...0-0 18.♕h5 ♔g7 19.h4 ♕e3 20.hxg5 hxg5 21.♔f1 ♗e6 (21...f6 22.♗d3 f5 23.♖e1 ♕g3 24.♖f3 ♕h4 25.♕xh4 gxh4 26.♖b6 ♖a7 27.♘xc8 ♖xc8 28.♖xe5) 22.♗xe6 fxe6 23.♖xf8 ♔xf8 24.♖d1 ♔g7 25.♕e8 ♕c6 26.♕xa8 ♕f4+ 27.♔g1 ♕xa8 28.♖e8! △ ♖f1→; 17...♗f5 18.♕f3 e6 19.g4! ♗g6 20.♗d3 f5 21.gxf5 0-0 22.♗c4) 18.♕f3 e6 19.♘c3 b5 20.♗b3 ♗b7 21.♘e4 ♗xe4 22.♕xe4 ♘d7 23.♕c6 ♗e7 (23...♖b8?! 24.♖d1 △ 25.♗xe6) 24.♖d1 ♘c5! △ 25.♕d6+ ♔e8 26.♕c6+ ♔e7=;

A3) 15...♕a5! is the best move, after which it is hard for White to stop the knight reaching the dominant e5-outpost: 16.♗c4 (16.♕d4 0-0! 17.♘b6 ♘c6 18.♕e3 ♖b8 19.h4 ♗e6 △ ...♘e5, △ ...f7-f6; 16.♘c3 ♗e6 17.♗g4 ♘c6 18.♗d5 ♘d5 19.exd5 ♘e5) 16...♖f8 (16...♕xa4? 17.♕d4!) 17.♗xf7+!? (17.♘c3 ♕c5) 17...♔xf7 18.♗xf7 ♕h5+ ♔g7 20.♖f1 ♗e6 21.♕e8 ♗c6 22.♕xa8 ♕xa4 23.♕f8+ ♔h7 24.♖f7+ ♔g6! (looks risky, but there is not even a perpetual in sight) 25.♖g7+ ♔h5 26.g4+ (26.♔f2 ♕xe4 27.h3 ♘e5 28.♖xe7 ♗xa2 29.b3 g4 30.♕g3 ♕d4+ 31.♔h2 ♗b1 32.c3 ♕e4 33.♖g7 b5 34.hxg4+ ♘xg4+ 35.♔h3 ♘e5) 26...♕xg4 27.h3+ ♔xh3 28.♕f3+ ♗h4 29.♖g6 ♕d4+ 30.♔h1 h5 31.♖xe6 ♗d2, etc.;

B) 12.♘e6?? fxe6 13.♕h5!? (13...♕xc4-+) 14.♕e2 ♗xc3 15.bxc3 h4-+ 16.♗xd6 exd6 17.♖ad1 ♘c6

18.♗b3 ♘e5 19.♕d2 h3 20.♕xd6 ♕xd6 21.♖xd6 ♔e7 22.♖fd1 ♗d7 23.g3 g4 24.c4 ♖ac8 25.c5 ♖xc5 0-1 Eydsteinsson-O.Berg, Faroe Islands 2013]

12...♗xe6?! [When choosing this move Black must have already been planning the tactical operation which would lead to disaster for him. Preserving the bishop seems to be the better option: 12...fxe6! 13.♘b3 ♗c4 14.♕xg4 ♗xc3! (a proper moment to part with the bishop – Azarov gives only 14...e5 15.♕h5+ ♕f7 16.♕xf7+ ♔xf7 17.♘d5±) 15.bxc3 e5! 16.♕h5+ ♔d8 with an acceptable position for Black: 17.h4 (17.f3 ♗e6 (or 17...♗d7 △ ...♗d7-e8-d7-e8) and White can hardly escape the coming repetition, e.g. 18.♕g6 ♗f7 19.♕g7 ♕g8 20.♕xh6 ♘d7 spells danger only for him; 17.♘d2 ♕xc3 and now the tricky 18.♕f7!? (18.♘f3 ♘c6 19.♘xg5 ♗c7 20.♗f7 ♖f8 21.♗xh6 ♗e6 and Black will soon regain the pawn with interest) seems to lead to a forced draw after 18...♕xd2 (or 18...♘c6 19.♖fd1 ♕e8 20.♕b3 ♕b5 21.♕f7 ♕e8=) 19.♗xe5 ♖e8 20.♖ad1 ♕xc2 21.♖xd6+ ♗d7 22.♖d4 ♘c6 23.♖xd7+ ♔xd7 24.♕d5+ ♔c8 25.♕e6+ ♔d8 26.♕d5+ ♔c8 27.♕e6+ ♔d8) 17...♕xe4 18.hxg5 ♕g4 19.♕h2 (safer is 19.♕xg4 ♗xg4 20.f4 exf4 21.♖xf4 ♗h5 22.gxh6 ♖xh6 23.♖f8+ ♗e8) 19...♘c6 20.f4 e4! 21.♘d4 (21.f5 ♗xf5 22.♗xd6 exd6 23.♕xd6+ ♔e8 and White can only hope for a perpetual after 24.♘d4 ♖d8 25.♕c5) 21...♖xd4 22.cxd4 ♗f5! and Black is ready to take over the initiative, for example: 23.♖fb1 ♔c7 24.gxh6 ♕g6 25.♕h4 ♖ae8 26.♕g5 ♖xh6 27.♕xg6 ♖xg6; 12...♗xd4?! 13.♗xc8 ♗xf2+ 14.♗xf2 ♕xc8 15.♘d5↑ – Azarov in his notes for Chess Informant] 13.♘xe6 fxe6 14.♕xg4 h5? [Consequent, but wrong. It was still not too late for 14...♗xc3, even though it is much easier to play with white, with so many targets in front of him. Here is a sample line: 15.bxc3 e5!? (15...♔d7 16.e5± Azarov) 16.h4 ♗c4 17.♖ab1 ♘d7 18.♗b4 ♘f6 19.♕f5 ♕c6 20.♕g6+! ♗d7 21.♖fb1 b5 22.a4 ♕xc3 23.axb5 axb5 24.♖xb5 ♖a1 25.♕f5+ ♔c7 26.♕e6 ♖xb1+ 27.♖xb1 ♖e8 28.f3 ♕xc2 29.♖a1↑] 15.♕xe6 ♗xc3 16.bxc3 ♘d7 [Unfortunately for Black, 16...h4 runs into 17.♕g6+!, when 17...♔f8 18.♖ad1 is hopeless for

him, while the other retreats are refuted by 18.♗xd6!] 17.h4± 0-0-0 18.♖ab1 gxh4 19.♗xh4 ♖h7 20.♖fd1 ♕e5 21.♕c4+ ♕c5 22.♕b3 ♕c7 [Allowing one more cunning blow, but White is clearly on top after 22...♕c6 as well – 23.♕e6! ♕xc3△ 24.♗xe7 ♖e8 25.♖b3! (25.♕d5 ♗exe7 26.♗xb7+ ♔d8 27.♖xd6+ Azarov) 25...♕c7 26.♕h3! ♖hxe7 27.♖c3+–] 23.♖xd6!+– exd6 24.♗xd8 ♗xd8 25.♕g8+ ♘f8 26.♕xf8+ ♔d7 27.♕f5+ ♗e8 28.♖d1 ♖h6 29.e5! dxe5 30.♖d5 1-0

Viktor Balogh
Gennady Tokmachev
Budapest 1999 (4)

1.e4 c5 2.♘f3 d6 3.d4 cxd4 4.♘xd4 ♘f6 5.♘c3 a6 6.♗e3 ♘g4 7.♗g5 h6 8.♗h4 g5 9.♗g3 ♗g7 10.♗c4 ♘e5 [Also possible. It stops any ideas with ♕d1-f3, but does not attack and restrict the knight on c3 as 10...♕a5 does] 11.♗b3 ♘bc6 12.♘f5 [A principled reply. In both games with 12.♘xc6 bxc6 13.h4 Black opted for 13...g4 and developed his queen only after 14.h5. However, 13...♕a5!? seems fully playable, e.g. 14.hxg5 hxg5 15.♖xh8+ ♗xh8 16.♕h5 ♘g6 17.0-0-0 ♗xc3 18.♕h7! ♔d8! 19.♕xf7 ♘e5 20.♕xg6 (20.♗xe5 ♘xe5 21.♕f8+ ♔c7 22.♕xe7+ ♔d7 23.♕xd6+ ♔b6∞) 20...♗xg3 21.fxg3 ♕e5♕] 12...♗xf5 13.exf5

13...♖c8?! [13...♘d4! is a quite typical trick for this kind of position and may well be the justification of his 10th move: 14.f4! (the preference of the engines. One more example of the thematic sacrifice of the f7-pawn can be seen after 14.0-0 ♘xf5 15.♗xe5 ♗xe5 16.♕h5 0-0! (16...♖h7 17.♘e4↑) 17.♕g6+ ♗g7 18.♕xh6 ♗xc3

19.bxc3 e6 20.f4 (20.♖ad1 ♖c8 21.♖d3 ♘f5 22.♕h5 ♔g7 23.f4 ♖h8 24.♕xg5+ ♕xg5 25.fxg5 ♔g6) 20...g4 21.f5 ♕b6+ 22.♔h1 exf5 23.♖ad1 ♖ae8 24.♖xd6 ♕f2 25.♖dd1 ♘e3 26.♔xe3 ♖xe3 27.♖d7 ♘e6! (≤ 27...♖xc3 28.♖xb7 ♖c5 29.♖b6 a5) △ 28.♖xb7 ♖d8⇄; 14.♕h5 ♘xb3 15.axb3 ♕c8! (xf5) △ 16.♘d5 (16.0-0 ♕xf5 17.f4 ♕g4; 16.0-0-0 ♕xf5 17.♖he1 ♖c8) 16...♕xc2 17.0-0 ♖c8), and now: 14...♘ec6!? (14...♕d7 does not solve all the problems – Black lacks a safe place for his king and must be extremely careful after 15.0-0!, e.g. 15...♖c8 (15...♕a5 16.fxg5 ♘xf5 17.♗xf7+! ♔xf7 18.♕h5+ ♔g8 19.♕g6→) 16.♗f2! (16.fxg5 hxg5 17.♕d2 ♕b6 18.♗f2 ♗e5 (18...♘xb3 19.axb3 ♕c6∞) 19.h3 ♖xh3!? (19...♕b4 △ 20.♕xg5? ♖xc3! 21.bxc3 ♘e2+ 22.♔h1 ♕e4−+) 20.♖fd1 ♘h2+ 21.♔f1 ♖hxc3 22.bxc3 ♕b5+ 23.c4 ♘xb3 24.cxb5 ♘xd2+ 25.♖xd2 ♗e5 26.♖b1 ♘f6 (26...a5!?) 27.♖e2 ♘d5 28.bxa6 bxa6 29.♖b7 ♘c3⇌) 16...♘xb3 17.axb3 gxf4 (17...♖g8 18.♕f3) 18.♘d5 ♘f6 (18...♗e5 19.♘h4!±) 19.♘xf4 ♕d7 20.♕d3 ♕c6 21.c3 (21.♖ae1 ♕xc2 22.♕xd6 0-0 23.♖xe7 ♕xf5=) 21...♕e4 22.♕xe4 ♘xe4 23.♗e3±; 14...gxf4 15.♗xf4 ♕b6!? is a tempting try to disturb the enemy king, but it has not yet received full computer approval on the basis of 16.♘d5 ♕c5 17.f6 ♗xf6 18.♗e3! ♕a5+ (a thorough analysis may reveal that Black has sufficient counterplay after 18...♘h4+ (!) 19.g3 ♘df3+ with immense complications) 19.c3 ♘xb3 20.♕xb3 ♘d3+ 21.♔d2 ♘c5 22.♘xf6+ exf6 23.♗xc5 dxc5 24.♖he1+ ♔f8 25.♕xb7 ♔g7 26.♕e4 ♖ab8 27.♔c2 with a pleasant edge for White) 15.0-0 ♘xf5 16.♕h5 ♘xg3! 17.♕xf7+ ♔d7 18.hxg3 (18.♗e6+ ♔c7 19.♘d5+ ♔b8 20.hxg3 ♗xb2 21.♖ab1 ♗d4+ 22.♔h1 ♗a7 23.c3 ♗c5) 18...♕b6+ 19.♔h2 ♗xc3! 20.bxc3 ♖af8 21.♕e6+ ♔c7 22.♘d5 ♖f6 23.♕e4 gxf4 24.gxf4 ♕c5! △ 25.♗xc6 ♕h5+ 26.♔g1 (26.♔g3?!) ♖g8+ 27.♔f2 ♕c5+ 28.♔e2 ♕xc6! 29.♕xe7+ ♔c8 30.♔d1 ♖xg2! 31.♕xf6?? ♕e4!−+) 26...♕c5+ 27.♔h1 (27.♖f2?! e5!) 27...♕h5+ 28.♔g1 ♕c5+=; 13...♕d7 has apparently been rejected because of 14.♘d5] **14.h4?!** [14.♕h5 would have been a real test for Black. After the text he comes up with an excellent counterattack

on the kingside] **14...♕d7! 15.hxg5 ♕xf5 16.gxh6 ♖xh6 17.♖xh6 ♗xh6 18.♔f1 ♗d7 19.♗d5 ♖h8 20.♗e4 ♕g5 21.♗xc6+ bxc6 22.♕d4 ♗g7 23.♖d1 ♖h1+ 24.♔e2 ♖xd1** [A surprising end. The preliminary check 24...♕h5+! would have won a pawn after 25.f3 ♖xd1 26.♘xd1 ♕g6] ½-½

Main Line
12.♕f3

Viswanathan Anand
Veselin Topalov
Monaco rapid 1998 (10)

1.e4 c5 2.♘f3 d6 3.d4 cxd4 4.♘xd4 ♘f6 5.♘c3 a6 6.♗e3 ♘g4 7.♗g5 h6 8.♗h4 g5 9.♗g3 ♗g7 10.♗c4 ♘c6 11.♘xc6 bxc6 12.♕f3 [An important alternative to 12.h4, to which] **12...♘f8** [has established itself as the most reliable reply] **13.♗b3** [A necessary retreat, as shown by 13.h4 ♘e5. He was fine after 14.♕e2 (14.♗xe5 ♗xe5 15.hxg5 hxg5 (even here 15...♗e6!? comes into consideration, e.g. 16.♗xe6 fxe6 17.♕h5+ ♔d7 18.gxh6 ♕b6 19.♘d1 ♗xb2 20.♖b1 (20.♘xb2? ♕xf2+ 21.♔d1 ♕d4+ 22.♔c1 ♖ab8−+) 20...♗c3+ 21.♘xc3 ♕xf2+ 22.♔d1 ♕d4+ 23.♔c1 ♕e3+=) 16.♖h7 ♗e6! (after 16...e6 17.0-0-0 ♕a5 18.♗b3 ♗d7 White, in H. Wu-Haessel, Vancouver 2000, unleashed the unexpected 19.♘b1!? and could have punished 19...c5? 20.♘a3 ♗b5 with 21.♗xe6!) 17.♗b3 (17.♗xe6 fxe6 18.♕e3 ♖b8↑) 17...♕a5 with comfortable play for Black) 14...♘xc4 15.♕xc4 ♕b6 as well – 16.0-0-0 ♖b8 17.b3 ♕b4 (17...♗e6 18.♕d3 ♕c5↑) 18.♕xb4 ♖xb4 19.a3 ♖b7 20.♘b2 f5 with a favourable ending in Szalanczy-Szeberenyi, Budapest 2010] **13...♘e5** [In combination with the next two moves, a solid and deservedly popular plan. 13...♕a5 seems not so effective here compared to the same sortie on the previous moves – 14.0-0 (on the theme of queenside castling we have already seen two games by Ni Hua with 14.h4 ♘e5) 14...♘e5 15.♕e2 ♗e6 16.♔h1 ♕c5 17.♖fe1 and here, instead of 17...a5 as in Cioara-Istratescu, Bucharest 1999, Black has 17...♘c4, inviting a repetition like 18.♘a4 ♕b5 19.♘c3

♕c5; 13...♕b6!?, taking control of the e3-square, was introduced in Cao Sang-Ruck, Kazincbarcika ch-HUN 2005. The game ended in a draw after 14.h4 ♘e5 15.♗xe5 (15.♕e2 △ 0-0-0 is much more natural) 15...♗xe5 16.hxg5 hxg5 17.0-0-0 g4 18.♕e2 a5?! (≥ 18...♗xc3 19.bxc3 a5 20.♕c4 ♗e6 21.♕d4 ♕xd4 22.cxd4 a4 23.♗xe6 fxe6 24.♖df1 ♗d7 25.♔d2 a3!? 26.♖b1! ♖xf2+ 27.♔e3 ♖af8 28.♗b7+ ♔d8 29.♖h7 ♔c8 30.♖hxe7 ♖xg2 31.♖ec7+ ♔d8 32.♖d7+=) 19.♘a4 ♕a7 20.♔b1?! (20.♖h7↑) 20...♖b8 21.♕d2 ♖b4 22.f4 gxf3 23.gxf3 ♖d4 24.♕c1 ♖xd1 25.♖xd1 ♖g8 26.f4 ♗d4 – in this final position the simplest reply to the forced 27.♕d2 is the familiar 27...♗e6] **14.♕e3 ♖b8 15.0-0** [15.h4 occurred in Ni Hua-Tatai, Budapest 1999, and White's success in this game had nothing to do with the opening. Black had a satisfactory position after 15...♕b6 16.♕xb6 ♖xb6 17.hxg5 hxg5 18.♖h7 ♗f6 (18...♖h8!?) 19.0-0-0 ♗e6 20.♗xe6 fxe6 21.b3 g4 22.♘e2 ♘f7 23.♖h5 ♖b5 24.♖dh1 ♖xh5 25.♖xh5 e5 26.♔d2 ♘g5 27.♔e3 ♘e6=] **15...♕b6** [Without the queens Black will not have to worry so much about his king] **16.♕e2**

16...♖h8! [A very nice idea, depriving White of any plan connected with the h5-square] **17.♔h1 h5 18.f4 gxf4 19.♗xf4 ♗g4 20.♕d2 ♗e6** [Black can be happy with the outcome of the opening] **21.♖ad1 ♕a5 22.♕e1 h4 23.h3 ♘c4 24.♗c1 ♔d7 25.♕f2 ♖b7 26.♘e2!** [A timely reaction to the increasing pressure, based on the insecure location of the rook on b7 and the black king] **26...♘xb2 27.♗xb2 ♗xb2 28.♖b1 ♕a3 29.♘f4 ♗xb3 30.axb3♕ ♗f6 31.♘d3 ♕a5 32.e5! ♗xe5 33.♕f5+ ♔c7 34.♖a1 ♕d5 35.♘xe5 ♕xe5 36.♕xe5** ½-½

Vasik Rajlich
Zeev Dub

Budapest 2000 (2)

1.e4 c5 2.♘f3 d6 3.d4 cxd4 4.♘xd4 ♘f6 5.♘c3 a6 6.♗e3 ♘g4 7.♗g5 h6 8.♗h4 g5 9.♗g3 ♗g7 10.♗c4 ♘c6 11.♘xc6 bxc6 12.h4 ♕b6 13.♗b3 [Perhaps it is only a matter of time before we will see 13.♕f3 in practice, especially since the b2-pawn seems to be poisoned. Thus, after the forced sequence 13...♕xb2 (?) 14.♗xf7+ ♔d8 15.♕xg7 ♕xa1+ 16.♔d2 ♕xh1 17.♕xh8+ ♔d7 the engines claim a decisive advantage for White with the help of the stunning 18.♕f8! ♘f6 19.♗xd6! ♔xd6 20.♕d8+ ♗d7 (20...♔c5 21.♘a4+! ♔xc4 22.♕d3+ ♔b4 23.a3+! ♔xa4 24.♕b3+ ♔a5 25.♕b4#; 20...♘d7 21.e5+! ♔c5 22.♗e6 ♕xg2 23.♕a5+ ♔d4 24.♘e2+ ♔e4 25.♕b4+ ♔xe5 26.♕xe7!) 21.♕xa8 ♕xg2 22.♕b8+ ♔c5 23.♘a4+, etc.]

13...♖f8! [An important subtlety.
A) 13...♗d7 seems to be a minor alternative: 14.hxg5 (14.♕d2 (!) 14...0-0-0 15.0-0-0 ♗e6?! (perhaps Black should opt for Anand's recommendation of 15...♗xc3!? in a similar position, without the h-pawns: 16.bxc3! (16.♕xc3 ♘xf2 17.♗xf2 ♕xf2 18.hxg5 ♕f4+ 19.♔b1 ♕xg5 20.♗c4 ♔c5 21.♗xa6+ ♔c7) 16...f6 17.f3 ♗e3 18.♕xe3 ♘xe3 19.♖dg1 d5 (19...f5?! 20.♔d2 f4 21.♗f2±) 20.♗f2 ♘c4 21.♗xc4 dxc4 22.♗c5↑) 16.♗xe6+ fxe6 17.hxg5 hxg5 18.♕xg5! ♗xc3 (18...♖xh1 19.♕xg7! ♖xd1+ 20.♘xd1 ♘e5 21.♕xe7 ♕d4 22.♕xe6+ ♔c7 23.f3±) 19.bxc3 ♘f6? (the best chance to resist lay in 19...♖xh1 20.♖xh1 ♘xf2 (20...♘f6 21.♘h4) 21.♖e1

d5 22.exd5 cxd5 23.♗xf2 ♕xf2 24.♖xe6 ♕f1+ 25.♔d2 ♕f2+ 26.♖e2 ♕f6 27.♕xf6 exf6 28.♖e6 ♗b7 29.♖xf6 ♖g8 30.♖f2 ♗g3) 20.♘xh8 ♖xh8 21.♗xd6! ♕xf2 22.♗xe7 ♘xe4 23.♕e5!+− ♕e3+ 24.♔b2 ♖e8 25.♕xe6+ ♔b8 26.♕xc6 ♖c8 27.♖d8 ♖xd8 28.♗xd8 ♘f2 29.♕b6+ 1-0 Rajlich-Blasko, Eger 2001) 14...0-0-0 15.♕d2! hxg5 16.♖xh8 ♖xh8 17.0-0-0 ♘e5?! (in his annotations Anand points out the correct idea – 17...♘e5! (the same manoeuvre is the best reaction in case of 14/15.♕f3 as well), when after 18.♘a4 (18.♕xg5 ♗xg3 19.fxg3 f6 20.♕g7 ♕d8♔ △ ...♕f8; 18.♗xf7 ♘xg3 19.fxg3 ♕e3♔; 18.♗xe5 ♘xe5 19.♕xg5 ♕xf2 20.♕xe7 ♗g4!⇄ are the tactical justifications) 18...♕a7! 19.♗xe5 ♘xe5 20.♕a5 ♔b7. White has a repetition with 21.♕b4+ ♔c7 22.♕a5+ ♔b7, but hardly more) 18.f3 ♕a5 19.♔b1 ♗f6 20.♕e3 ♗b7 (≤ 20...c5 21.♘d5) 21.♗f2↑ ♖b8 22.g3 ♗c8 23.♕e2 ♘g6 24.♗e1 ♕b6 25.♘a4 ♕b5 26.c4 ♕b7 27.♗a5. Anand severely criticized this natural move and even adorned it with two question marks! In his opinion 27.c5! would have led to a decisive advantage: 27...c5! 28.♘b6+ ♕xb6 29.♗xb6 ♖xb6 and with only two pieces for the queen, Black built an almost impregnable fortress in Anand-Topalov, Linares 1998;
B) The surprising 13...gxh4 14.♗xh4 h5 allowed Black to seize the initiative – 15.♕e2 (≥ 15.♕f3 ♗e6 16.0-0-0) 15...♘f6 16.♖h1 h4 17.♗f4 ♗d4! 18.♖f1 (18.f3 ♗f2+ 19.♔f1 ♗e3 20.♘a4 ♕a7 21.♗g3 ♗d4 22.♗f4 ♗e3 23.♗g3 ♗d4=), but 18...h3 19.gxh3 ♖xh3 was met by an excellent pawn sacrifice in order to complete development: 20.0-0-0! ♗xf2 21.♔b1!↑ and Black could not manage the defensive task after 21...♖b8? (21...♗d7□) 22.♘a4 ♕a7 23.♕c4 ♗e6 24.♕xc6+ ♗d7?! (24...♕d7 25.♕xa6±) 25.♕d5 ♗e6 26.♕g5!+− ♘e3 27.♗xe3 (27.♗xe6 fxe6 28.♕g8+ ♗d7 29.♖xd6+) 27...♗xe3 28.♕g7 ♗h6 29.♕h7 ♗f4 30.♕g8+ ♗d7 31.♗e6+ fxe6 32.♕g4 ♖a3 33.♕xf4 ♕c7 (33...♖xa4 34.♖xd6+) 34.e5 d5 35.♕d4 ♖b5 36.b3 a5 37.♖f7 ♖b4 38.♕c5 ♖bxa4 39.♖xe7+ 1-0 Azarov-Sutovsky, playchess.com 2004.]
14.hxg5 hxg5 15.♕d2 a5! [One more key move! In the splendid miniature

Ismagambetov-Wen Yang, Zaozhuang 2012, Black postponed this by one move: 15...♘f6 16.0-0-0 a5, which allowed the opponent to launch an attack by means of 17.e5!? ♘xe5 (17...♗xe5 was safer, e.g. 18.♕xg5 ♘xf2 (18...♗xg3 19.♗xf7+ ♔xf7 20.♖h8+ ♔d7 21.♕xg4+ ♔c7 22.♕xg3 ♖b8 23.b3 ♗xf2 24.♕g8∞) 19.♗xe5 ♘xd1 20.♖xd1 dxe5 21.♗xf7+ ♔xf7 22.♕g8+ ♔f8 23.♕g6+=) 18.♘e4 a4 19.♘xf6+ exf6 20.♗xf7+! ♔xf7 (≤ 20...♖xf7 21.♕xd6 ♕xb2+ 22.♔xb2 ♘c4+ 23.♔c3 ♘xd6 24.♖xd6) 21.♗xe5 (it was possible to start with 21.♖h7+ when 21...♗e8 is once again the only retreat: (21...♔g6? 22.♗xe5! ♖xh7 23.♕d3+ ♗g7 24.♖h1 ♗h3 25.♖xh3 ♖h8 26.♗xf6+ ♔xf6 27.♕xd6+ ♗g7 28.♕e5+ ♔g6 29.♖xh8 ♖xh8 30.♕xh8 ♕xf2 31.♕e8+ ♔g7 32.♕e4±) 22.♕xd6 ♖a7□ 23.♖xa7 (23.♗xe5 ♖xh7 24.♖e1 ♕xf2 25.♗g3+ ♕xe1+ 26.♗xe1 ♖h1⇄; 23.♗h6!?) 23...♕xa7 24.♗xe5 fxe5 25.♕xc6+ ♗e7 26.♖d5 ♗e6 27.♖xe5 ♖f6 with a probable draw) 21...dxe5 22.♖h7+ ♔g6? (allows an aesthetic mate; 22...♗e8□ 23.♕d7! ♖b8 24.b3 ♕b4 25.♕d3 (25.♔xb4 ♖xb4 26.♖d8+ ♔e7 27.♖xf8 ♔xf8 28.♖d8+ ♔e7 29.♖xc8 ♔d7) 25...f5 26.♖d8+ ♔f7□ (on 26...♔e7? 27.♖xf8 ♔xf8 28.♕d8+ ♔f7 29.♕c7+ (29.♖h1 wins) 27.♖xc8 ♕f4+ 28.♔b1 ♖bxc8 29.♕d7+ ♔g6 30.♖d6+ ♖f6 31.♖xf6+ ♔xf6 32.♕xc8 ♕xf2 33.♕xc6+ ♔e7 34.♕c7+ ♔e6=) 23.♕d3+ ♗f5 24.♖dh1!! ♗xd3 25.g4!! 1-0] **16.f3** [The stem game of 15...a5!, Van den Doel-Lutz, Bad Zwesten 2000, saw 16.♕xg5 ♗e5 17.♗h4?! (17.♕e2 was the lesser evil) 17...♗f6 18.♕d2 ♖h8 19.g3 ♗xc3! 20.bxc3 (20.♕xc3 ♕xf2+ 21.♔d1 ♘e5∓) 20...♘e5 21.0-0-0 a4 22.♕g5. His intuition did not betray the German GM – this thrilling game continued with 22...♕c7! (the situation after the recommended 22...♗b7 23.♖xd6 axb3 is in fact for from clear: 24.♕g7! (Lutz indicates only 24.♕xe5? f6−+; 24.♖hd1?! ♗g4! will cost White a lot of material: 25.♕g7 ♘g6 26.♖xg6 ♖f8 27.cxb3 (27.♗xe7 ♕xe7 28.♖xg4 bxa2 29.♔b2 a1♕+ 30.♖xa1 ♕b7+ 31.♔c1 ♖xa1+ 32.♔d2 ♕d7+; 27.♖xg4 bxa2) 27...♗xd1 – is always an enormous pleasure to see castling as a deciding move: 28.♖h6

0-0-0–+) 24...♖f8 (24...♘g6 25.♖xg6 ♖f8 26.♗g5! assures White of a draw at least) 25.♖hd1!! (the human line goes on with 25.♖d8+ ♔xd8 26.♕xf8+ ♔c7 27.♕xe7+ ♘d7 28.a3! and White has every chance to save the game) 25... exd6 (25...♘d7 26.♖e6! ♘f6 27.♖d8+ ♔xd8 28.♕xf8+ ♔c7 29.♕xe7+ with a perpetual to follow) 26.♕xe5+ ♗e6 27.♖xd6 b2+ 28.♔b1 ♖g8 29.c4! and the engines assess this amazing position as a positional draw!) 23.♕g7 ♖f8 24.f4 axb3 25.fxe5 bxc2 (here the contemporary engines give preference to the other two legal moves by this pawn, but the text is strong enough). Even with the relatively best move 26.♖xd6! (after 26.♖de1 ♕b6!. 27.♗xe7 ♕b1+ 28.♔d2 c1♕+ 29.♖xc1 ♖xa2+ 30.♔e3 ♕b6+ 31.♔f4 ♕f2+ 32.♔g5 ♖xg3+ 33.♔h6 ♖h2+ 34.♖xh2 ♕xh2+ 35.♔g5 Black did not reward his excellent play with 35...♔xe7 or 35...♖h8 and went for a perpetual) 26...♕b6! 27.♗xe7 ♕xe7 28.♕f6+ ♔e8 29.♔d2 ♖xa2 30.♖c1 ♖a4 White is just fighting to stay in the game, e.g. 31.♖xc6 ♕d8+ 32.♔xc2 ♗d7 33.♕xd8+ ♔xd8 34.♖d1 ♖a7 and the attempt to get rid of the last pawn by 35.e6 fxe6 36.♖xe6 ♔c8 will leave him a rook down. White has to pay more attention to the marching pawn – blockading it with 16.♘a4 seems reasonable: 16...♗b4 17.f3 (Black can react to 17.♕xb4 axb4 18.♖h7 in the spirit of the Paulsen/Kan: 18...♗d4!? 19.♖d1 ♗a7!, when 20.♖g7 ♖h8! △ 21.♖xf7 ♗a6! is yet another sacrifice of the f7-pawn!) 17...♗e5! with mutual chances] **16...a4! 17.♘xa4?!** [The awkward 17.fxg4 axb3 18.cxb3 was objectively better, but it was not easy to foresee the coming storm] **17...♖xa4 18.♗xa4 ♕xb2?** [The same goes for Black! What a pity – he missed an intermediate shot of exceptional beauty: 18...♖h8!! △ 19.♖xh8+ (19.♖f1?? ♕xb2–+ △ 20.♗xc6+ ♔f8) 19...♔xh8 20.♗xc6+ ♔f8 21.♗b5! ♕xb5 (21...♖xb2 22.♖b1 ♕g1+! 23.♗f1 ♗a6! 24.c4□ ♗xc4 25.♕xb2 ♕xf1+ 26.♔d2 ♕d3+ and Black has a perpetual and can try for more) 22.c3 (22.c4?! ♕c5) 22...♘e5 23.0-0-0 ♘c4↑] **19.♗xc6+ ♗d7 20.♗xd7+ ♔xd7 21.♔e2 ♖c8 22.♖ab1?!** [Touching the 'wrong' rook and thus returning the favour –

after 22.♖hb1! ♕xc2 23.♖b7+ ♔d8 (23...♔e6? 24.♖c1!+–) 24.♖d1 ♕a4 25.♕d5! ♖c2+ 26.♖d2 ♕a6+ 27.♖b5! ♘f6 28.♕b3 White preserves the a2-pawn and should win] **22...♕xa2 23.♖hc1 ♖c3!⇄ 24.fxg4** [Without the passer 24.♖b7+ ♔d8 25.♖b8+ ♗d7 (25...♔c7?? 26.♖b3!) 26.♕d5 ♖xc2+ 27.♖xc2 ♕xc2+ 28.♕d2 ♕c4+ 29.♕d3 ♕xd3+ 30.♔xd3 ♘e5+ the game is very close to a draw] **24...♕c4+ 25.♕d3?!** [25.♔d1 ♕xg3 26.♖b7+ ♔c8 27.♖cb1 ♕f1+ 28.♕e1 ♕xg2 and the perpetual is in the air – the most beautiful of them is forced by 29.♖c7+! ♔d8 30.♖b8+! ♗xc7 31.♕a5+ ♔b8 32.♕b6+ ♔c8 33.♕c6+ ♔d8 34.♕b6+ ♔d7 35.♕b7+=] **25...♖xd3 26.cxd3 ♕a2+ 27.♔f3 ♗d4 28.♖b7+** [28.♗e1 was necessary, but White forgot about his defence] **28...♗e6 29.♖cc7 ♕d2!–+ 30.♖xe7+ ♔f6 31.e5+ ♔g6 32.♔e4 ♕e3+ 33.♔d5 ♕xd3 34.exd6 ♗f6+ 35.♔c6 ♕c4+ 36.♔d7 ♕xg4+ 37.♔c6 ♕xg3 38.♖xf7 ♕xg2+ 39.♔c5 ♕c2+ 40.♔d5 ♕d3+ 41.♔c5 ♕d4+ 42.♔c6 ♕c4+ 43.♔b6 ♕xf7** 0-1

Vassily Ivanchuk
Leinier Dominguez Perez
Beijing blitz 2013 (7)

1.e4 c5 2.♘f3 d6 3.d4 cxd4 4.♘xd4 ♘f6 5.♘c3 a6 6.♗e3 ♘g4 7.♗g5 h6 8.♗h4 g5 9.♗g3 ♗g7 10.♗c4 ♘c6 11.♘xc6 [11.♘e6?? ♗xc3+ 12.bxc3 ♕a5! 13.0-0 ♘ge5! 14.♘g7+ ♔f8 15.♗b3 ♗xg7–+ 16.f4 gxf4 17.♗xf4 ♗g4 18.♕e1 ♗h5 19.♕g3+ ♗g6 20.♖ad1 ♕h7 21.♖d5 ♕b6+ 22.♗e3 ♕c7 23.h4 ♗h8 24.♕f4 ♕c8 25.♗d4 f6 26.h5 ♗xh5 27.♖xd6 ♕g4 28.♕xg4 ♗xg4 29.♗xe5 ♘xe5 30.♖b6 ♖g7 31.♔h2 ♗e2 32.♖f4 ♗c4 33.♖xb7 ♖ag8 0-1 Entem-Jolly, Fouesnant 2004; 11.♘de2 does not show big opening ambitions. Here is a lively example: 11...♗e6 12.♗b3 ♕a5 13.0-0 h5 (Black has the right to respond aggressively to his opponent's calm, somewhat passive play – see also 16...♖h8! from Anand-Topalov. Jobava and Bruzon played exactly in this manner and won the other two games with 11.♘de2 ♗e6 12.♗b3 ♕a5) 14.h4 ♗e5!? 15.♘d5 ♗xg3 16.♘xg3

gxh4 17.♘f5 ♗xf5 18.exf5 0-0-0 19.♕e1 ♕c5 20.♖d1 ♔b8 21.♗d3 e6! 22.fxe6 fxe6 23.♘f4 (23.♕xe6?! ♖he8! 24.♕f5△ ♖f8 25.♕h7 ♖xf2–+) 23...d5! 24.♘xe6?! (24.♕xe6 d4 △ ...♘ce5?) 24...♕d6 25.f4 ♖de8 26.♖xd5 ♕xe6 27.♖d8+ ♘xd8 28.♗xe6 ♖xe6 29.♕xh4 ♖e2 30.f5 ♖g8?! (30...♘f7∓) 31.♕e1? (31.♕g3+ ♔a8 32.♕d3⇄) 31...♖xc2 32.♕g3+ ♔a8 33.♕b3 ♖e8!–+ 34.♖d1 ♖ee2 35.♕xc2 ♖xc2 36.♖xd8+ ♔a7 37.g3 ♖xb2 38.♖h8 ♖xa2 39.♖xh5 ♖a5 40.♖g5 ♘e3 41.g4 ♖a4 42.f6 ♖f4 43.♖f5 ♖xg4+!? 44.♔f2 ♘xf5 45.f7 ♖f4+ and 0-1 in Szalanczy-Szeberenyi, Budapest 2012. Lots of fun till the very end!] **11...bxc6 12.h4 ♕a5 13.♕f3 ♗e6** [A good reply, which is equivalent to a draw offer. 13...♗f8 14.♗b3 ♘e5 appeared twice in junior games of Ni Hua: one year later he switched to 15.♕e3 (15.♕e2 ♕b4?! (Black could go for the more concrete 15...♘g6 16.♕c4 ♖b8! 17.hxg5 ♗e6! △ 18.♕xc6+? ♗d7 19.♕c4 ♗b5!–+) 16.hxg5 hxg5 17.f3 ♗e6 18.0-0-0 a5 19.♗f2 ♗c4 20.♕e3 ♖b8 21.♕xg5 ♗f6 22.♕d2 ♖g8 23.♗a7 ♖a8 24.♗e3 a4!? (Black is burning all the bridges – was this the idea behind his bizarre 15th move?) 25.a3 ♕b7 26.♗xa4 ♕a2!? (26...♗f1 was tricky too, forcing White to find 27.♘d5! ♗xg2 28.♘xf6+ exf6 29.♕xd3 ♔xh1 30.♕xf6!) 27.♗xa2? (and how many players could figure out 27.b3! ♘c4 28.♕d3 ♘xa3 29.e5!! ♗xe5 30.♕e4! ♖xa4 31.♕xa4+– ?) 27...♖xa4→ 28.♕d3 ♗c4? (28...♖c4! 29.♕a5 ♘d3+!–+ 30.♖xd3 ♕xb2+ 31.♔d2 ♕xc2+ 32.♔e1 ♕xd3 33.♕a8+ ♔d7 34.♕xg8 ♗c2!) 29.♗d4 ♗g5+ 30.♔b1 ♘xa3+ 31.♔a1 ♗b5 32.♕b3 ♕a6 33.c3 ♗d7 34.♔b1 ♖a8 35.♘b4 ♕b7?? (35...♖a1+ 36.♔c2 ♗c2 ♕a3+!–+) 36.♖h5! (36.♗f2±) 36...♖xd4 37.♖xd4 ♗f6? (37...♕b5! 38.c4 ♕xb6!) 38.e5!+– ♗g7 39.♕xf7 1-0 Ni Hua-Ruck, Gyula 2000. A real thriller, most probably in mutual time-trouble) 15...♗e6 16.hxg5 hxg5 17.0-0-0 ♘g4 18.♕d2 (18.♕e2!? ♗xb3 19.cxb3 ♗xc3 20.♕xg4) 18...♗xc3 19.♕xc3 ♕xc3 20.bxc3 a5 21.♗a4 ♖a6 22.♗b2 f6 23.♗a3 ♗d7 24.♖b1 ♔c7 25.♗b3 ♔d7 26.♗a4 ♔c7 27.♗b3 ♔d7 ½-½ Ni Hua-Xu Jun, HeiBei 2001] **14.♗xe6 fxe6**

15.♕xg4 [Black is okay in case of 15.hxg5 hxg5 (15...♖f8?! 16.♕xg4 ♗xc3+ does not force the perpetual – according to the engines White has the initiative after 17.♔f1 ♗xb2 18.♖b1! ♕xa2 19.♖d1 hxg5 20.♖h7!) 16.♖xh8+ (16.0-0-0!? ♖xh1 17.♖xh1 ♘e5 18.♕e2 ♖b8 19.♖h7 ♔f8 20.♕h5 ♔g8 21.♖xg7+ ♔xg7 22.♕xg5+ ♔f7 23.♕h5+=) 16...♖xh8 17.♔f1?! ♘e5 18.♕e2 ♔d7 19.♘d1 ♖b8 20.c3 ♕a4 (20...♕b5∓ makes sense – in an ending Black can rely on his pawn structure) 21.♗xe5 ♗xe5 22.g3 ♗f6 23.♔g2 a5 24.f3 c5 25.♘e3 ♔c7 26.♕d2 (26.♘c4) 26...♕b5 27.b3 a4 28.♖b1 axb3 29.♖xb3 ♕a4 30.♖xb8 ♔xb8 31.♘g4 ♔c7 32.e5 ♗xe5 33.♘xe5 dxe5 34.♕e2 ♔d6 35.c4 e4 36.♕xe4 ♕xa2+ 37.♔h3 ♕b2 (37...♕f2 38.♔g4 ♕g1 39.♕e2 ♕d4+ 40.♔xg5 ♕f6+ 41.♔h5 ♕f5+ 42.♔h4 ♕h7+ 43.♔g4 ♕f5+ 44.♔h4 ♕h7+=) 38.♔g4 ♕f2? (38...♕e5!? 39.♕xe5+ ♔xe5 40.♔xg5 ♔d4 41.♔h5 ♔xc4 42.g4 ♔d5 43.g5 c4 44.g6 c3 45.g7 c2 46.g8♕ c1♕ 47.♕d8+ ♔e5 48.♕h8+ ♔d5 49.♕d8+ ♔e5=) 39.f4! and White grabbed the sudden opportunity and won this endgame in Ponomariov-Topalov, Las Vegas 1999; 15.0-0-0 is hardly better, e.g. 15...♘e5 16.♕h5+ (16.♗xe5 ♗xe5 17.hxg5 transposes to the line with the suggested improvement 15...♗e6! from Kenes-Li) 16...♔d7 and Black is ready for actions along the b-file – also the c4-square is now accessible for his knight] **15...♗xc3+ 16.bxc3 ♕xc3+ 17.♔e2 ♕c4+ 18.♔d2 ♕d4+** ½-½

Aldiyar Kenes
William Xiang Wei Li
Al Ain Wch jr 2013 (10)

1.e4 c5 2.♘f3 d6 3.d4 ♘f6 4.♘c3 cxd4 5.♘xd4 a6 6.♗e3 ♘g4 7.♗g5 h6 8.♗h4 g5 9.♗g3 ♗g7 10.♗c4

♘c6 **11.♘xc6 bxc6 12.h4 ♘e5!? 13.♗xe5** [A very obliging decision by White. 13.♗b3 is preferable, transposing to 10...♘e5 11.♗b3 ♘bc6 12.♘xc6 bxc6 13.h4] **13...♗xe5 14.hxg5**

14...♕a5! [The key to Black's counterplay! White indeed has the initiative after 14...hxg5?! 15.♖xh8+ ♗xh8 16.♕h5 ♗xc3+ 17.bxc3 e6 18.e5! d5 (18... dxe5?! 19.♕h8+ ♔e7 20.♕xe5 f6 21.♕h2 ♕e8 22.0-0-0→) 19.0-0-0 ♕e7 20.♗e2 ♗b7 21.♖d3 0-0-0 22.♖g3] **15.♕f3 ♗g4!?** [Very attractive, but not the best option – in the search for maximum activity another pawn had to be invested: 15...♗e6! 16.♗xe6 fxe6 leads to the critical position, in which Black once again has rich play due to his powerful bishop: 17.gxh6 (17.♖xh6 ♖f8 18.♕h5+ ♔d7 19.♕h3 ♖ab8! 20.♔f1 ♖xb2! 21.♘d1 ♕b5+ 22.♔g1 ♖xc2 23.♖xe6 ♔d8 24.♕h7 (24.♖xe5 ♕xe5 25.♖b1 ♖e2!–+) 24...♖h8! 25.♕xe7+ ♔c8 26.♖h6 (26.♖xe5 ♕f1+!! 27.♔xf1 ♖h1#) 26...♖xh6 27.gxh6 ♗xa1–+; 17.0-0-0 ♖f8! (17...♖b8 18.♖d3 ♖f8 19.♕h5+ ♔d7 20.gxh6 ♖xb2 transposes to the above line with 17.gxh6) 18.♕d3 hxg5∓) 17...♖b8 18.0-0-0 ♖xb2 (18...♕b4 19.♖d3□ ♕xb2+ 20.♔d2 ♔d7 21.♕e3 c5⇄ 22.f4 c4 23.fxe5 cxd3 24.♕xd3 ♖bg8 25.g3) 19.♖d3 ♖f8 20.♕h5+ ♔d7 21.♔xb2 ♕b4+ 22.♔c1 ♗xc3 23.♖xc3 ♕xc3 24.♕h3 ♕a1+ 25.♔d2 ♔d7 (25...♖xf2+?? 26.♔e3 ♕f6 27.♕h4!+–) 26.♔c1 ♖xf2!? (26...♕a1+ 27.♔d2 ♕d4+=) 27.♕b3 ♕xg2 28.h7 ♖g1+ 29.♖xg1 ♕xg1+ 30.♔b2 ♕g7+ 31.e5 ♕xh7 32.♕b7+ ♔d8 33.♕b8+ ♔d7 34.♕b7+=] **16.♕xf7+??** [A grave mistake. Correct was 16.♗xf7+ ♔f8 17.♕xg4 ♗xc3+ 18.bxc3 ♕xc3+ 19.♔e2 ♔xf7 with better prospects for White, for example: 20.♕f4+ ♔g8 21.♕e3!? (or

21.♖ac1 △ 21...♖f8 22.♕e3 ♕xe3+ 23.♔xe3 hxg5 24.♖xh8+ ♔xh8 25.♖b1±) 21...♕xc2+ 22.♔f3 ♖f8+ 23.♔g3↑] **16...♔d7–+ 17.f3** [Loses at once. However, it is unlikely that White can survive in case of 17.0-0 hxg5] **17...♗xc3+ 18.♔e2 ♖af8 19.♕g6 ♕c5 20.♗d3 ♖fg8 21.♕f7 ♗e6 22.♕f4 hxg5 23.♕g3 ♗e5 24.♕e1 ♗f4 25.♕f2 ♕xf2+ 26.♔xf2 ♖xh1** 0-1

A Correspondence Game 10.♗e2

Sergey Grodzensky
Nicolay Ninov
cr 1996-2000

[The game Vallejo Pons-Vachier-Lagrave brought back some pleasant memories for me, as it closely resembles a game of my own. In the Antonio Lascurain Memorial I was twice victorious with the 6...♘g4-line on the way to my ICCF GM-norm and title. Even though the president of the Russian Federation, Sergey Grodzensky, did not opt for 10.♗c4, the opening stage is definitely of theoretical interest. Indeed, it was a great pleasure for me to go over the lines from one of the most significant games in my life again. I will recommend the impatient readers to hurry to moves 22-23 and compare the position there with the one after the alternative 19...♕xg5 in the main game for this Survey] **1.e4 c5 2.♘f3 d6 3.d4 cxd4 4.♘xd4 ♘f6 5.♘c3 a6 6.♗e3 ♘g4 7.♗g5 h6 8.♗h4 g5 9.♗g3 ♗g7 10.♗e2 h5 11.h4 ♘c6 12.♘xc6!?** [In general, 12.♘b3 is automatically played by the first player. Here is the course of my other game from the same tournament: 12...gxh4 13.♖xh4 ♗e6 14.♕d2 ♕b6 15.♗d5 ♗xd5 16.exd5 ♘ce5 17.0-0-0 ♗h6 18.f4 ♘g6 19.♖h3 ♕e3 20.♗xg4 ♕xd2+ 21.♘xd2 hxg4 22.♖h2! (a good novelty at that time, by ICCF GM Morozov) 22...♗g7 23.♖dh1 ♖xh2 24.♖xh2 ♔f7 25.♘c4 (25. f5 ♗e5) 25...♗d4 26.f5 ♘e5 27.♘xe5 dxe5 28.♖h7 ♖c8! 29.b3?! (the start of a dubious plan; ≥ 29.♘d2 ♗e3 30.♔d1 ♗xd2! (≤ 30...♖c5 31.♘e4! ♖xd5+ 32.♔e2) 31.♔xd2 f6=) 29...b5 30.♘a5?! ♗c3! (here comes our hero!) 31.♘c6 ♖f8 32.♖h6 f6 33.♖g6 ♔d6 34.♖xg4

♖a8! (my favourite move in this game, which most probably put my opponent off balance. I was not certain about my winning chances after the direct 34...♖h8 35.♔d1 e6, for example: 36.fxe6 ♗xd5 37.♘b4+ ♔xe6 (37...♗xb4 38.♖xb4 ♔xe6 39.a4) 38.♘xa6 ♖d8+ 39.♔e2 ♖d2+ 40.♔f3) 35.♖g7? (≥ 35.♖g3!? b4 36.♖g7 ♖h8 (36...e6?? 37.fxe6 ♗xd5 38.♘d8!+−) 37.♔d1 ♗xd5 38.♘xe7+ ♔d4) 35...e6!∓ 36.♘e7?! ♖h8 37.♔d1 exd5 38.♔e2 e4 39.♘g6 ♖h1−+ 40.a4 bxa4 41.♖a7 axb3 and White resigned in view of 42.♖xa6+ ♗c5 43.cxb3 ♖e1+ 44.♔f2 d4 45.♘f4 d3 46.♘e6+ ♗b4 47.♖a4+ ♔xb3 48.♘c5+ ♔c2 49.♘xe4 ♖xe4 50.♖xe4 d2 51.♖e2 ♗c1 52.♖xd2 ♗xd2] **12...bxc6 13.hxg5 ♖b8 14.♕c1 ♕a5** [For years on end I considered 14...♕b6 to be inaccurate in view of 15.♘d1. However, 15...h4! may justify the previous move (15...♕b4+? 16.♕d2! (16.c3? ♕xe4 17.f3 ♕d5!∞) 16...♕xe4 17.f3+−; we will see more of this motif) 16.♖xh4 ♖xh4 17.♗xh4 ♕b4+ 18.c3 (18.♕d2 ♕xe4) 18...♕xe4 19.f3 ♕h7 20.g3 ♘e5 21.♕e3 ♕c2≅] **15.♔f1!** [A strong and logical novelty. 15.0-0 was seen in the only over-the-board game, Ubayana-Mas, Singapore 1997. The natural 15...h4 16.♗f4 h3 would have created serious threats] **15...♕b4 16.♘d1 h4!** [Once again 16...♕xe4? drops a piece after 17.f3 ♕f5 18.♗d3+−] **17.♗f4!** [17.♗xg4?! ♗xg4 18.♖xh4 ♖xh4 19.♗xh4 ♗xd1! 20.♕d1 ♕xe4; 17.♗xh4 ♕xe4 18.f3 ♖xh4! (the point of 16...h4!) 19.♖xh4 ♘e3+ 20.♕xe3 ♕xh4 21.♕f2 ♕h8 22.c3 ♗e5 23.♗d3 a5↑] **17...h3 18.gxh3** [18.♖xh3 ♖xh3 19.gxh3 ♘h2+! 20.♔g1 ♕e1+ 21.♗xh2 ♕xe2 with plenty of counterplay − after 22.♕e3 ♕h5 23.♕g3 (Black is fine after both 23.♔g2 ♕h4! 24.♕g3 ♗xh3+ 25.♔h2 ♕xg3+ 26.♔xg3 ♗e6 27.c3 ♔d7 28.f3 a5≅; and 23.♕d3 ♗g4! 24.♖b1 ♔d7) 23...♕e2 White would be advised to settle for a repetition by 24.♕d3=] **18...♘e5 19.♕e3 ♘c4** [Aiming at an exchange of one of the bishops. White can meet 19...♖h4?! with the powerful 20.c3! ♕a4 21.b3! ♖xb3 22.♗g3! on the basis of 22...♖xh3 23.♖xh3 ♗xh3+ 24.♔g1 with advantage, e.g. 24...♘d7 (24...♘g6 25.♔h2 ♗e6 26.♕a7!; 24...♖b8 25.♗xe5 ♗xe5

26.♕xh3 ♕xe4 27.♗xa6; 24...♗c8 25.axb3 ♕a1 26.♗xe5 ♗xe5 27.f4 ♗g7 28.♕b6 e6 29.♕b8 ♔d7 30.e5! dxe5 31.♕a7+ ♗e8 32.♗h5 ♗d7 33.♕a8+ ♗e7 34.♕g8) 25.axb3 ♕xa1 26.e5! △ 26...dxe5 27.♕e4 f8 28.♕xc6 ♗g8 29.g6 fxg6? 30.♕d5+!] **20.♕f3** [20.♕d3 ♘xb2 21.♘xb2 ♕xb2 22.♖d1 ♖h4!? (an unusual deviation, recommended by the machines. ≤ 22...♗e5 23.♗c1! ♕xa2 24.f4 △ h3-h4; 22...♖b4!? 23.♔g2 c5 24.♖b1 ♕xa2 25.♖xb4 cxb4 26.h4 ♗b7∞) 23.♕g3 ♖h8. Now, White can deviate from the offered repetition in favour of the entertaining line 24.♔g2 ♕xc2 25.♗xd6! ♗xh3+ 26.♖xh3 ♖xh3 and now: 27.♕xh3 (27.♔xh3 ♕xe2 28.♗c5 ♖b5 29.♗c7 ♕h5+ 30.♔g2 ♕g4+ 31.♔h2 ♕h4+=) 27...exd6 28.♕e3 (28.♗h5 ♕xe4+ 29.♗f3 ♕f4 30.♗xc6+ ♔f8 31.♕g3 ♗e5 32.♕xf4 ♗xf4=) 28...♖b4 29.♖xd6 ♕xe4+ 30.♕f3 ♕xf3+ 31.♗xf3 ♖d4 32.♗xc6 ♖xa2 33.♗xa6 ♗d4⯑ 34.♗e2 ♖a3+ 35.♔g2 ♖a2 36.♖c4 (36.♗f3 ♖a3+=) 36...♖xe2 37.♖xd4 ♗f8 should result in a draw as well; 20.♕a7!? ♗xh3+ 21.♖xh3 ♖xh3 22.♗xc4 ♕xc4+ 23.♔g2 ♕xe4+ 24.♔xh3 ♖b4!⇄ and White has to repeat − 25.♕a8+ ♗d7 26.♕a7+ ♗c8 27.♕a8+=; 20.♗xc4 ♕xc4+ 21.♔g2 (21.♕d3 ♖b4! puts White in an unusual pin along the 4th rank: 22.f3 ♖xh3 (22...d5 23.♕xc4 ♖xc4) 23.♖xh3 ♗xh3+ 24.♔e2 d5 (24...♕xd3+ 25.♔xd3 ♗xb2 26.♘xb2 ♖xb2 27.♔c3 ♖b5) 25.♕xc4 ♖xc4 26.♘e3 ♖b4 27.♖h1 ♗e6 28.b3 dxe4) 21...♖b4! 22.f3 ♗xb2 23.♖b1 ♕xc2+ 24.♕d2 ♗xh3+! (24...♗xb1 25.♕xb4 ♕c2+ 26.♔g3 g7 27.♘e3 contains risks only for Black: 27...♕c3 (!) 28.♕xc3 ♗xc3 29.♘f5 d5 30.♖c1 d4 31.♗e5 ♖g8 32.♘xd4 ♖xg5+ 33.♔h2 ♖xe5 34.♖xc3 ♖h5 35.♖xc6 ♔d8=) 25.♖xh3 ♕xb1 26.♕xb4 ♖xh3 27.♕xh3 ♕xd1 and a draw by perpetual is the logical outcome after 28.♕b8+ (or 28.♕xb2 ♕xf3+ 29.♔g3 ♕h1+) 28...♔d7 29.♕b7+ ♔d8=; 20.♕b3?! ♘xb2 21.♖b1 ♕xe4! 22.♗f3 ♕xf4! 23.♗xc6+ ♔f8 24.♕xb8 ♕c4+ 25.♔g1 ♕xc6 26.♘xb2 ♗d4 27.♘d3 ♔g7 △ ...♗f5/...♕f3]

0-0 28.d7 ♗xd7 29.♗xb8 ♖xb8 30.♖b1 ♗e6 31.♘g4 ♔h8 32.♕g3 ♖d8 33.♘f6 ♗xf6 34.gxf6) 23.♗c1 e4 24.♕g3+−] **21.♗xd2 ♕xd2 22.♗c4** [The turning point of the game, which corresponds directly to the main theme of this Survey: Black sacrifices the f7-pawn, relying on the pair of bishops and the threats along the newly-opened file. Of course, it is very difficult to criticize the natural text move, but 22.♘e3! is objectively better, and now 22...♕a5 (the pin after 22...♗xb2? 23.♖b1 is more than unpleasant for Black: 23...♖b4 24.a3! ♗xa3 25.♖d1 ♕c3 26.♖d3 ♕a1+ 27.♔g2 ♖b1 28.♖xa3 ♗xh3+ 29.♕xh3 ♖xh3 30.♖xa1 ♖hxh1 31.♖xb1 ♖xb1 32.♗xa6) 23.h4 ♗e6 24.♖d1 ♗xb2 25.♗c4 ♗xc4+ 26.♘xc4 ♕xa2 (26...♕a4!? 27.♕d3 ♖b4⇄) 27.♕d3 ♖b4 and now the exciting fireworks with 28.♘xd6+!? exd6 29.c3! ♗xc3! 30.♕xc3 ♕c4+ 31.♕xc4 ♖xc4 32.f3 ♔e7 33.♗e2 a5 lead to a complex endgame with, probably, new simplifications and a draw]

22...♕xg5! 23.♕xf7+ ♔d8 24.h4 ♕e5 [24...♕g4!? 25.♗e2 ♕xe4 26.♗f3 ♕e5] **25.♕f3 ♖f8 26.♕e3 ♖f4** [A comparison with the main game of this Survey is already inevitable − in my case Black has a two-pawn deficit, but the queens are still on the board] **27.♗d3 c5 28.♖b1** [A rather unexpected decision to give up the central pawn. I expected a similar reaction to what Vallejo Pons played nearly two decades later: 28.f3 ♕f6 29.♔e2 ♗h6↑] **28...c4 29.♗e2** [29.♗xc4? loses to 29...♕xe4 30.♕d3 ♕e1+ 31.♔g2 ♗b7+ 32.f3 ♖xh1 33.♔xh1 ♕g3−+] **29...♖xe4 30.♕d2 ♗f6! 31.♗f3** [The point behind the last move is revealed after 31.♘c3 ♕xc3! 32.bxc3 ♖xb1+ 33.♔g2 ♗b7! 34.f3 ♖g4+ 35.♔f2 ♖xh1 36.fxg4

♗xh4+ 37.♔e3 ♗g5+] **31...♖f4! 32.♕d5 c3 33.♕xe5** [The main line from 1999 went something like 33.b3 ♖xf3! 34.♕xf3 ♗b7 35.♕h3 ♕e4 (35...♕b5+ 36.♔e1 ♕d5 37.♖g1 ♕d2+ 38.♔f1 ♕xc2 just transposes) 36.♖g1 ♕xc2 37.♖a1 ♗e4 38.♖g8+ ♔c7 39.♖g3 ♗f5! 40.♖xc3+ ♔d7 41.♕e3 ♗xc3 42.♘xc3 ♗d3+ 43.♘e2 ♖b5! (a refinement from 2015: the pin should decide the game, while 43...♖b4 44.♕a7+ ♔e6 45.♕e3+ ♔f7 46.♕f3+ leaves White with good chances to force a perpetual) 44.f4 ♖b4! (only now!) 45.♖e1 ♖e4 46.♕f3 ♔d8!. A strong waiting move. Stockfish promises a win

after the straightforward 46...e5 47.fxe5 ♖xe5!, but the text is much nicer: 47.h5 (47.♔f2 ♕c5+ 48.♔g2 (48.♔f1 ♖e3 49.♕f2 ♕d4! 50.h5 ♕e4!−+) 48...♖e3 49.b4 (49.♕f2 ♕d5+ 50.♔h2 ♕e6!−+) 49...♕b6 50.♕f2 ♗e4+ 51.♔g1 ♕xb4 52.♖d1 ♖h3 53.♘g3 ♗b7−+) 47...e5! 48.fxe5 ♗xe2+ 49.♖xe2 ♕c1+ 50.♔g2 ♕g5+. The point of the concrete 47...e5! − Black wins the queen, but has to do some more work to avoid theoretically drawish endgames] **33...♗xe5 34.♗e2 ♗f5 35.b3** [Also here White will lose material. In case of 35.♘e3 ♗e4 36.♖h3 cxb2, this passed pawn should decide the game, e.g. 37.h5 (37.♗xa6

♖a8 38.♗c4 ♗xc2 39.♘xc2 ♖xc4−+; 37.♗d3 ♗xd3+ 38.cxd3 ♖c8 39.♘c4 d5!−+) 37...♖c8! 38.♖g3 (38.♗d1 ♗h7 △ ...♖a4) 38...♖h4 39.♖g8+ ♔d7 40.♗g4+ e6 41.♖xc8 ♖h1+ 42.♔e2 ♖xb1−+] **35...♗xc2 36.♖c1 ♗e4 37.♖h3 c2 38.♘e3 ♖c8!−+ 39.♗c4 d5! 40.♘xd5** [Black remains a rook up after 40.♗xa6 ♖c6 41.♗b7 ♖c7 42.♗xd5 ♗b2 43.♗xe4 ♖xc1−+] **40...♗xd5 41.♖d3 ♖d4 42.♖xd4** [42.♗xa6 ♖a8 43.♖xd4 ♗xd4 44.♗d3 ♖xa2 with an extra piece − after 45.♗xc2, 45...♗xf2! is the simplest way to win] **42...♗xd4 43.♖xc2 ♗xc4+ 44.♖xc4 ♖xc4 45.bxc4 ♔d7** 0-1

Exercise 1

position after 15.♕d1-f3

White has just attacked the f7-pawn, realizing the idea behind 10.♗c4. How should Black react?
(solution on page 244)

Exercise 2

position after 16.f2-f3

In reply to 15...a5 White decided to chase the black knight. How can Black justify his last move?
(solution on page 244)

Exercise 3

position after 20...♕c5-e5

20...♕e5 was met by 21.♕c4+ ♕c5 22.♕b3, and here Black defended with 22...♕c7. Continue the attack!
(solution on page 244)

Sicilian Defence

Najdorf Variation   SI 14.12 (B50)

Great Attacking Chances with Fischer's 6.h3

by Jeroen Bosch

1.	e4	c5
2.	♘f3	d6
3.	d4	cxd4
4.	♘xd4	♘f6
5.	♘c3	a6
6.	h3	e6
7.	g4	b5

A respectable number of Najdorf Sicilians are countered by 6.h3 these days. If we take a look at the European Team Championship of November 2015 in Reykjavik (the Open Section), for example, we see that of the 16 games in which Black played the Najdorf, White replied 6.h3 five times. It was no coincidence, of course, that in Volumes 116 and 117, Peter Lukacs and Laszlo Hazai covered the popular 6...e5 7.♘de2 h5 – subjecting both 8.g3 and 8.♗g5 to scrutiny. In a recent SOS-column I looked at the weird (but interesting) 8.♘g1! instead. It is only natural that Najdorf players push their e-pawn two squares forward when confronted by the little rook-pawn move: what, after all,

was 5...a6 for if not to prepare ...e7-e5 ?

Wasting Time?
As an aside, many readers of the Yearbook series will probably also teach young children the fundamentals of chess: teaching them to develop pieces, play in the centre, not to waste vital tempi on moves like a2-a3 and h2-h3, and so on. Don't you find it interesting that at a 'higher level' we are so accustomed to playing 5...a6, not even spending a thought on the fact that a 'powerful' answer to this move, which does little to enhance Black's development, should be 6.h3 ?

Replies to 6.h3
Black is not forced to reply with the Najdorf-like 6...e5, of course. The Dragon approach 6...g6 has every right to exist, and so has the Scheveningen move 6...e6. The latter is actually the most common reply in the database. After the consistent 7.g4 Black has tried out quite a few moves. Indeed, 7...d5, 7...♗e7, 7...h6, 7...♘c6 and even the prophylactic 7...♘fd7 are all common replies. The strike in the centre, 7...d5, especially, was once thought to be a sufficient antidote to White's flank attack, but these days people are less convinced that

David Navara

8.exd5 ♘xd5 9.♘de2 (in YB 90 Kuzmin covered 9.♗d2, concluding that Black was fine) is such an easy equalizer for Black. Indeed, White's light-squared bishop will bear down on Black's queenside in much the same way as in the Catalan.

Logic Dictates that 5...a6 6.h3 Means 7.g4 b5 ?
This Survey will cover **1.e4 c5 2.♘f3 d6 3.d4 cxd4 4.♘xd4 ♘f6 5.♘c3 a6 6.h3 e6 7.g4**, and now **7...b5**, which is an eminently logical follow-up to 5...a6. Play continues **8.♗g2 ♗b7**, and of great importance now is Karjakin's 2008 discovery that White need not waste a tempo on 9.a3, but can play **9.0-0** instead, because 9...b4 is well-met by the sacrifice 10.♘d5!.

I refer loyal readers of the Yearbook series to Volume 89, in which Kuzmin covered all the relevant games – there have been no developments since then! This sacrifice was quite a blow to Black's case.

The unfortunate thing for Black is that the ♘d5 sacrifice looms in other lines as well, as are tactics involving e4-e5.

Indeed, here 9...♗e7?! is met by 10.e5, as is 9...♘c6?!. At the same time, 9...h6 only postpones the crucial decision because 10.♖e1 is a good reply – leaving ♘d5 and e4-e5 hanging in the air, so much so that Gelfand found himself forced to play 10...e5, when 11.♘f5 confirms White's edge (Carlsen-Gelfand, Monaco blindfold(!) 2008). As 9...♕c7 10.g5 ♘fd7 11.a4 is also no pleasure cruise, Black has come to prefer 9...♘fd7. This, then, is the real subject of this Survey. The idea of withdrawing the knight is that neither g4-g5 nor e4-e5 are now attacking it.

It All Favours White?

What we shouldn't forget, however, is that Black is playing twice with the same piece. White can (and should, as Steinitz has taught us) exploit such lackadaisical play by opening up the position. At present, all logical replies, 10.f4, 10.a4, and 10.♖e1, appear to promise White an advantage.

After 10.f4, a crucial game is the one between Nepomniachtchi

and Frolyanov, Olginka 2011, with the beautiful 12.f6! pawn sacrifice. In Skopje, David Navara (a specialist on both sides of the 6.h3 Najdorf!) told me in the post-mortem of our game that he was not pleased at all with Black's position, adding that the engines don't seem to understand these positions.

Anand and others have played 10.♖e1, when after 10...♗e7 White can once again start sacrificing with 11.e5. To make matters worse, White can also play the 'positional' 10.a4, attacking Black's queenside.

Conclusion

I hope I have enabled you to navigate confidently within the territory of 6.h3 e6 7.g4 b5. More specifically, we have looked at the position after 9...♘fd7, concluding that White has several tries that promise an advantage, rendering the entire line unattractive for Black at present. So, adapting the famous words from the bard, I end my soliloquy with how I could have started it: 'I come to bury 7...b5, not to praise it'.

SI 14.12
10.f4

Jeroen Bosch
David Navara

Skopje tt 2015 (1)

1.e4 c5 2.♘f3 d6 3.d4 cxd4 4.♘xd4 ♘f6 5.♘c3 a6 6.h3 e6 7.g4 b5 8.♗g2 ♗b7 9.0-0 ♘fd7 10.f4 ♘c6 11.♗e3 [11.f5] **11...♗e7** 12.e5 [12.f5 ♘xd4 13.♕xd4 e5 14.♕d2 h6! and Black controls important dark squares; 12.a4 b4 13.♘ce2 0-0 is fine for Black; 12.♕e1 ♘xd4 13.♗xd4 0-0 14.♖d1 ♕c7 15.♖d2 ♘b6 (15...b4 16.♘d1 e5∓) 16.♘e2 e5 (16...b4) 17.♗f2 exf4 18.♗d4∓ Gazik-Drori, Batumi 2014] **12...d5**

13.♘xc6 [13.f5!? ♘xd4 14.♗xd4 ♕c7 (14...0-0) 15.fxe6 fxe6 16.g5?! (16.♘e2!± △ 16...♘xe5 17.♘f4±) 16...♗c5 17.♔h1 0-0-0 18.♖f7 ♗xd4 19.♕xd4 ♕xe5 20.♕xe5 ♘xe5 21.♖xg7 ♖d7 (21...♖dg8 22.♖e7 ♖xg5∓ △ 23.♖xe6? ♖hg8−+) 22.♖xd7

♔xd7∓ Tejaswini-Varshini, Pune 2014]
13...♗xc6 14.♘e2 b4?! [14...0-0 15.a3!?; 15.♘d4 ♖c8 16.c3] **15.♘d4 ♗b5 16.♖e1 ♗c5 17.♕d2** [17.f5!± ♕b6 (17...♕e7 18.♗xd5!? (18.g5, planning 19.f6) 18...♘xd4 (18...exd5 19.f6!+− ♕f8 20.♘xb5 axb5 21.♕xd5 ♖a7 22.e6!; 18...0-0-0 19.♗g2 ♕xe5 20.c3→) 19.♗xd4 exd5 20.e6 0-0! 21.exd7 ♕xd7±; 17...♕xe5? 18.fxe6 f6 19.g5+−) 18.a4! bxa3 19.b4! ♗xd4 20.♗xd4±] **17...♕b6** [17...♖c8 18.f5±; 17...0-0 18.f5 ♗xe5 19.♘xe6 ♗xe3+ 20.♖xe3 ♗c4 21.♘xd8 ♗xd2 22.♘xf7! ♖xf7 23.♗xd5±] **18.♖ad1** [18.f5 ♖c8 19.a4 bxa3 20.♖xa3! ♗xa3 21.♘xe6 ♗c5 22.♘xc5 ♘xc5 23.b4⩲; best is perhaps 18.a4 bxa3

19.b4 ♗xd4 20.♗xd4± when Black has counterplay, but after 20...♕d8 21.♖xa3 ♘b6 22.♕f2 ♘c4 23.♖aa1 White must be better] **18...h5?!** [18...0-0∞] **19.g5** [As Navara pointed out after the game, it was better to play 19.f5! as 19...hxg4? (19...0-0-0 20.c3 bxc3 21.♕xc3 ♔b8 22.g5±) fails to 20.fxe6! fxe6 21.♘xe6! ♗xe3+ 22.♖xe3 ♕xe6 23.♗xd5+−] **19...g6 20.♔h1** [20.♔h2] **20...0-0 21.♕f2∞ a5 22.♗f3 ♖fe8** [I was more worried about 22...♔g7 as I had seen that the tempting 23.♗xd5? fails to 23...exd5 24.e6 fxe6 25.♘xe6+ ♕xe6 26.♗d4+ ♗xd4 27.♕xd4+ ♘e5! 28.♖xe5 ♕xh3+ and Black wins. So 23.f5!? is logical, but how to continue after 23...♔g8!?∞] **23.♖g1!? a4 24.♖d2** [Another preparatory move. 24.♗xh5 gxh5 25.g6 f6 (25...f5 26.♗g5!+− is very powerful, as Navara showed in the analysis afterwards) 26.♕h4 ♔g7 27.f5 ♘xe5 and Black can defend] **24...b3?!** [24...♔g7] **25.axb3 axb3 26.c3** [26.cxb3] **26...♖a2?** [Consistent, but now the sacrifice on h5 increases in strength. The rook is needed on the 8th rank. 26...♗c4; 26...♖e7!?] **27.♗xh5! gxh5 28.g6 f5 29.♕h4?!T** [Winning is 29.g7!. Somehow Black is helpless after this move. He cannot bring any defenders to the kingside: 29...♗xd4 (29...♖ea8 30.♕h4 ♖a1 31.♕xh5 ♖xg1+ 32.♗xg1+−) 30.♗xd4 ♕d8 31.♕g3+− (31.♖g5+−); 29.♖g5 (Navara) is also very dangerous for Black] **29...♔g7 30.♕xh5?!** [30.♖g5! was still a good attempt to win the game: 30...♖h8 31.♖xf5 exf5 32.♘xf5+ ♔g8 33.g7! (33.♗xc5 ♘xc5 34.g7 ♖a1+ 35.♔h2 ♖h7 36.♖g2 ♖a7 37.♘e7+ ♖xe7 38.♗xe7 ♕b8 39.♕xc5 ♖xg7 40.♕xd5+ ♔h8 41.♖xg7 ♔xg7 42.f5 ♕a7=) 33...♖h7 34.♕g5→] **30...♖h8□** [30...♘f8? 31.♗f2 (31.♖dg2+−) 31...♖a7 32.♗h4 ♔g8 33.♗f6 ♖g7 34.♗xg7 ♔xg7 35.♖dg2+− ♗xd4△ 36.♕h4 (36. cxd4 ♕c7 37.♕h4 ♕e7 38.♕f6+!) 36...♔g8 37.♕f6 ♕a7 38.♕f7+ ♔xf7 39.gxf7+ ♔xf7 40.♖g7#] **31.♘xf5+!** [31.♕g5 ♖xh3+ 32.♔h2 ♖xh2+ 33.♔xh2 ♖a8 34.♖g3 ♖h8+ 35.♖h3 ♖xh3+ 36.♔xh3 ♗d3=] **31...exf5**

32.♕xf5 ♖f8□ 33.♕h5 ♖h8 34.♕f5 ♖f8 35.♕h5 ♖h8 36.♕f5 ♖f8 37.♕h5 ♖h8 38.♕f5 ♖f8 39.♕h5 ♖h8 40.♕f5 ♖f8 ½-½

Ian Nepomniachtchi
Dmitry Frolyanov
Olginka tt 2011 (6)

1.e4 c5 2.♘f3 d6 3.d4 cxd4 4.♘xd4 ♘f6 5.♘c3 a6 6.h3 e6 7.g4 b5 8.♗g2 ♗b7 [8...♕c7 9.0-0 b4 10.♘a4 ♗b7 11.♖e1 ♗e7 12.a3!? A. Zhigalko-Sandipan, Moscow 2012] **9.0-0 ♘fd7** [9...♕c7 10.g5 ♘fd7 11.a4; 9...♗e7? 10.e5 ♗xg2 11.exf6 ♗xf1 12.fxe7 ♕xe7 13.♕xf1±; 9...♘c6?! 10.e5 dxe5 (10...♘xd4 11.♗xb7 dxe5 12.♘e4±) 11.♗xc6+ ♗xc6 12.♘xc6 ♕c7 13.♕f3 ♖c8 14.♘xe5 ♕xe5 15.♗b7±; 9...h6 10.♖e1] **10.f4 ♗e7 11.f5** [11.♗e3 0-0 12.♕d2 (12.a3 ♘b6 13.♕e2 ♘c4∓ Korpa-Zsirai, Budapest 2010) 12...♘b6 13.b3 ♘8d7 14.a4 (14. f5! e5 15.f6 ♘xf6 16.♘f5↑) 14...bxa4! 15.♘xa4 ♘xa4 16.bxa4?! (16.♖xa4∞) 16...♖c8 17.♗f2 ♘c5 18.♖fe1 d5∓ Adair-W.Jones, Canterbury 2010] **11... e5**

12.f6! [Clearing the f5-square for the knight! 12.♘de2?! h5! 13.♗f3 hxg4 14.hxg4 d5!? (14...♘b6) 15.♔g2 (15. exd5?? ♗c5+ 16.♔g2 ♕h4 mates) 15...d4 16.♘d5 ♘b6 17.♘xb6 ♗xb6∓ Golizadeh-Zhou, Guangzhou 2010] **12...♘xf6** [12...exd4 13.fxe7 ♕b6 (13...♕xe7 14.♕xd4) 14.♘d5 ♗xd5 15.exd5 ♘e5 16.♔h1 ♘bd7 17.♖f4 (17. b3! ♕xe7 18.♗b2±) 17...♖c8 18.♖xd4 ♕c7∓ ½-½ Van Melkebeke-Sarrau, Gent 2015; 12...♗xf6 13.♘f5 0-0 14.♕xd6± 13.♘f5 0-0 14.g5 ♘e8** [14...♘fd7 15.♕g4 g6 (15...♔h8 16.♗e3) 16.♗e3 ♔h8 17.♘h6 ♕e8 18.♖f2±] **15.♕g4∞**

♘d7 16.♗e3 ♖c8 [16...g6 17.♘h6+ ♔g7 18.♖ad1 (18.♖f2 b4 19.♖af1 (19.♘e2!) 19...bxc3 20.♗xf7+ ♖xf7 21.♖xf7+ ♔h8 22.♖f1 (22.♕e6 ♗g7 23.♕b3 ♗c6 24.♖f1 ♕b8 25.♘f7+ ♔g8 26.♘h6+=) 22...♔g7 23.♘f7+=) 18...b4 19.♘d5 ♗xd5 20.♖xd5±] **17.♖f2 d5?!** [17...♘c5 18.♖af1→] **18.exd5 ♘d6 19.♘xd6 ♗xd6 20.♘e4 ♘c5 21.♘f6+! ♔h8** [21...gxf6 22.gxf6+ ♔h8 23.♕g7#] **22.♕h5+− gxf6** [22...h6 23.♘g4 ♕g8 24.♖f6+−; 24.♘xh6+ gxh6 25.♖f6+−] **23.♖xf6 ♖g8** [23...♕e7 24.♖af1! ♔g8 25.♖h6 (25.b4+−) 25... f5 26.g6+−] **24.♖xf7 ♖g7 25.♖xg7 ♔xg7 26.g6! hxg6 27.♕h6+ ♔g8 28.♕xg6+ ♔h8 29.♖f1 ♗f8** [29...♔g8 30.♕xd6+−] **30.♖f7 ♕h4 31.♗g5** 1-0

Marco Codenotti
Milan Chovan
Porec Ech U18 2015 (2)

1.e4 c5 2.♘f3 d6 3.d4 cxd4 4.♘xd4 ♘f6 5.♘c3 a6 6.h3 e6 7.g4 b5 8.♗g2 ♗b7 9.0-0 ♘fd7 10.f4 b4

11.♘ce2 [Because of 10.f4 the knight sacrifice is not on: 11.♘d5? exd5 12.exd5 ♗e7 13.♘c6 ♘xc6 14.dxc6 ♗xc6! 15.♗xc6 ♕b6+!; 11.♘a4 ♗e7 (11...♘c5) 12.a3±] **11...♘c5 12.♘g3 ♗e7 13.g5** [13.a3±] **13...♘bd7** [13... g6 14.h4 (14.f5! e5 (14...♘xg5 15.fxe6 fxe6 16.c3!↑ △ 16...bxc3 17.b4) 15.f6 (15.♘f3) 15...♗f8 16.♘b3) 14...d5 15.f5↑ Vila Gazquez-Röder, Balaguer 2010] **14. h4 ♘b6** [14...0-0 15.f5 e5 [15...0-0 16.a3 bxa3 17.b4±] **16.f6! exd4** [16... gxf6 17.♘df5 ♗f8 (17...fxg5 18.♘xe7 ♕xe7 19.♘f5+−) 18.♘h5+−] **17. fxe7 ♕c7** [17...♕xe7 18.♘f5+−] **18.♕xd4+− ♘e6 19.♕f2 f6 20.gxf6 gxf6 21.♕xf6** 1-0

Sergey Fedorchuk
Sebastian Almagro Mazariegos
Navalmoral 2012 (3)

1.e4 c5 2.♘f3 d6 3.d4 cxd4
4.♘xd4 ♘f6 5.♘c3 a6 6.h3 e6
7.g4 b5 8.♗g2 ♗b7 9.0-0 ♘fd7
10.♖e1 ♗e7?!

11.e5! [11.a4 bxa4 12.♘xa4 0-0 (12...
h5?! 13.gxh5 ♕a5 14.h6! gxh6 15.♘c3
(15.♗d2 ♕e5 16.♘f5 ♖g8 17.♘xh6
♖xg2+ 18.♔xg2 ♗xe4+ 19.♔g1±)
15...♕e5 16.f4 ♕g7 17.♗e3 ♗h4? (Melia-
Guramishvili, Tbilisi 2009) 18.♘xe6!+−)
13.b3 ♕c7 14.♗b2 ♘c6= Xu-Ma, China
2015] **11...♗xg2?!** [For 11...d5 see
Anand-Volokitin; 11...dxe5? 12.♗xb7
exd4 13.♕xd4!+−] **12.exd6 ♗xd6**
[12...♗f6 13.♔xg2±] **13.♘xe6!+−
fxe6 14.♕xd6 ♗b7 15.♕xe6+ ♔f8
16.♗g5** [16...♕xg5 17.♕e8#; 16...♘f6
17.♗xf6 gxf6 18.♖ad1+−] **1-0**

Viswanathan Anand
Andrei Volokitin
Berlin rapid 2015 (7)

1.e4 c5 2.♘f3 d6 3.d4 cxd4
4.♘xd4 ♘f6 5.♘c3 a6 6.h3 e6
7.g4 b5 8.♗g2 ♗b7 9.0-0 ♘fd7
10.♖e1 ♗e7 11.e5!± d5□

12.a4! [12.♘xd5!? ♗xd5 (12...exd5
13.e6 ♘f6 (13...0-0 14.exd7±) 14.exf7+
♔xf7 15.♘f5 ♖e8 (15...♗c5 16.♗e3
♗xe3 17.♖xe3→ △ 17...♖e8 18.♖xe8
♘xe8 19.♕d4 ♘f6 20.♖e1 ♘c6
21.♕c5 ♘g8 22.♘d6+−; 15...♘c6
16.♗g5±) 16.g5!±) 13.♗xd5 exd5 14.e6
0-0 (14...♘f6 15.exf7+ ♔xf7 16.g5±)
15.exd7 ♕xd7 16.♗f4± ♗c5 17.♘f5
♘c6 18.♕d2 (18.♕f3±) 18...♖fe8
19.♖ad1 (19.♕c3 ♗f8 20.♖ad1 ♖e6=)
19...d4= 20.♗g3 g6 21.♕g5 ♗f8
22.♘h6+ ♔g7 23.♘f5+ ♔g8 24.♘h6+
♔g7 25.♘f5+ ♔g8 26.♘h6+ ♔g7 ½-½
Swiercz-Cerveny, Czechia tt 2015] **12...
b4** [12...bxa4 13.♘xd5 (13.♘xa4±)
13...♗xd5 14.♗xd5 exd5 15.e6 0-0
16.exd7 ♕xd7 17.c3±; 12...♘c6
13.♘xd5 (13.axb5 ♘xd4 (13...♘cxe5
14.f4 ♘g6 (14...♘c4 15.♘xd5+−)
15.f5+−) 14.♗xd4 axb5 15.♖xa8 ♕xa8
16.♘xb5 ♕a5 17.♘c3 0-0⨀) 13...exd5
(13...♘xd4?! 14.♘xe7 ♗xg2 15.♔xg2
♕b6 16.f3 (16.♗e3 ♕b7+ 17.♔g3)
16...♔xe7 (16...♘xc2? 17.♕xc2
♔xe7 18.♗g5++−) 17.♗e3±) 14.e6
♘xd4 15.exd7+ ♔xd7 16.♕xd4 0-0±]
13.♘xd5! ♗xd5 [13...exd5 14.e6
0-0 (14...♘f6 15.exf7+ ♔xf7 16.c4!
(this demonstrates the advantage of
interpolating 12.a4 b4: 16.♘f5) 16...bxc3
17.bxc3± △ 17...♖e8 18.♖b1 ♕c8
19.g5+−) 15.exd7±] **14.♗xd5 exd5
15.e6 0-0** [15...♘f6 16.exf7+ ♔xf7
17.g5±] **16.exd7 ♕xd7 17.♗f4±
♗f6** [17...♘c6!? 18.♘xc6 ♕xc6
19.♖xe7 ♕f6!±; 17...♖e8 18.♘f5]
18.♗e5 ♗xe5 19.♖xe5 ♘c6
[19...♖d8] **20.♘xc6 ♕xc6 21.♖xd5
♖ac8 22.♕d4! ♕xc2 23.♖xb4±
♖fe8** [23...f5 24.g5 ♖b8 25.♕d4
♕xb2 26.♕xb2 ♖xb2 27.♖d6±]
24.♖d2 ♕c6 25.♕d6 ♕f3
[25...♕c4] **26.♕d3 ♕f4 27.♖e2
♖xe2 28.♕xe2 h5?!** [28...♕c4]
29.♕xa6± ♖c2? [29...♖b8 30.♕e2
hxg4 31.hxg4 ♖b4 32.♔g2! ♖e4
(32...♖xa4?? 33.♕e8++−) 33.♕f3
♖xa4] **30.♕b6! ♕h7** [30...hxg4??
31.♕d8+ ♔h7 32.♕d3++−] **31.♕e3!
♕xe3 32.fxe3 ♖xb2 33.a5 hxg4
34.a6 ♖b8 35.a7 ♖a8 36.hxg4+−
♔g6 37.♔f2 f5 38.♔f3 fxg4+
39.♔xg4 ♔f6 40.♖a5 ♔e6 41.e4
♔d6 42.e5+ ♔c6 43.♔g5 ♔b6
44.♖a1** **1-0**

Lazaro Bruzon Batista
Bu Xiangzhi
Danzhou 2015 (3)

1.e4 c5 2.♘f3 d6 3.d4 cxd4
4.♘xd4 ♘f6 5.♘c3 a6 6.h3 e6
7.g4 b5 8.♗g2 ♗b7 9.0-0 ♘fd7
10.♖e1 ♘c6 11.e5

11...d5! [11...♘dxe5 12.f4 ♕b6!?
13.♗e3 ♘c4 14.♗f2 ♘xd4 (14...♘xb2
15.♕f3 ♘xd4 16.♕xb7 ♖xb7 17.♗xb7
♖b8 18.♗e4±) 15.♗xd4 ♕c7 16.♘d5
♗xd5 17.♗xd5⨀] **12.♘xc6 ♗xc6
13.♘e2 ♗b7** [13...b4 14.♘d4 ♗b7
(14...♗b5 15.a4 (15.♗xd5!? exd5
16.e6) 15...bxa3 16.b3 ♖c8 17.♗xd5!?
(17.♗xa3 ♖xa3 18.♖xa3 0-0=) 17...
exd5 18.e6→) 15.f4] **14.♘d4** [Note
the similarities (and differences!) with
Bosch-Navara] **14...♗c5 15.♗e3 0-0**
[15...♗xe3?? 16.♘xe6+−] **16.f4 ♕c7
17.c3 ♖ae8!?∞ 18.g5** [18.♕d2 f6?∓]
**18...♗b6 19.♔h1 ♘c5 20.♖g1!?
♖c8 21.♖c1 ♖fd8 22.h4 ♘e4⇄
23.♗f3 ♕e7 24.♖g2** [24.♘f5?! exf5
25.♗xb6 d4! 26.♗xd8 ♖xd8 (26...♘f2+?
27.♔g2+−) 27.♗xe4 ♗xe4+ 28.♔h2
dxc3 29.♕e2 c2 30.♖xc2 ♗xc2
31.♕xc2∓] **24...b4** [24...♗c5] **25.
cxb4** [25.♘f5 exf5 26.♗xb6 ♖d7
27.♗d4 ♖dc7⇄] **25...♖xc1 26.♕xc1
♕xb4 27.a3 ♕c4 28.♕d1
♗xd4!? 29.♗xd4 ♖c8= 30.♗e2
♕c1 31.♕xc1 ♖xc1+ 32.♔h2 g6
**[32...♖d2] **33.♗e3 ♖e1 34.♗d4 ♖c1
35.♗e3 ♖e1 36.♗d4 a5 37.♗b5
♖d1 38.♗e3 ♖e1 39.♗d4 ♖d1
40.♗e3 ♖e1 41.♗d4** **½-½**

Srinath Narayanan
S.P. Sethuraman
Ho Chi Minh City 2012 (1)

1.e4 c5 2.♘f3 d6 3.d4 cxd4
4.♘xd4 ♘f6 5.♘c3 a6 6.h3 e6

7.g4 b5 8.♗g2 ♗b7 9.0-0 ♘fd7
10.♖e1 ♘c6

11.a4 [11.♘xc6 ♗xc6 12.a4 ♗e7 (12...b4 13.♘d5 a5 transposes to the main game) 13.axb5 (13.♗f4 e5 14.axb5 axb5 15.♗e3 0-0 16.♕e2 b4 17.♘d5 ♗xd5 18.exd5 ♖xa1 19.♖xa1 ♗g5 20.♗xg5 ♕xg5 21.♕b5 ♘c5 22.♕xb4 f5± Gasik-Cerveny, Pardubice 2015) 13... axb5 14.♖xa8 ♕xa8 15.♕e2 ♕b7 16.♘d5± Barbosa-Delgado Ramirez, Florianopolis 2015) **11...b4** [11... bxa4 12.♖xa4 ♗e7 13.e5! (13.♗e3 ♘xd4 14.♗xd4 0-0 15.♕d2 ½-½ Litwak-Ringoir, Dortmund 2009) 13... d5 (13...♘dxe5 14.♖xe5 (14.f4±) 14...dxe5 15.♗xc6+ ♗xc6 16.♘xc6 ♕xd1+ 17.♘xd1±; 13...♘xd4 14.exd6 ♗xg2 15.dxe7±) 14.♘d5! exd5 15.e6±] **12.♘xc6 ♗xc6 13.♘d5 a5 14.♕d4?!** [14.♗d2∞] **14...♖c8 15.♘e3?! ♘c5 16.♘c4 e5** [16...♗xe4! 17.♗xe4 ♘xe4 18.♘b6 (18.♖xe4 d5∓) 18...♖c6∓] **17.♕d1 ♗e7∓ 18.b3** [18.♗e3] **18...0-0 19.f4?! ♘xe4** [19...♗h4∓] **20.♗b2 ♘c3?** [20...d5! 21.♘xe5 ♗c5+ 22.♗d4 (22.♔h2 ♕h4 23.♕d3 ♗f2∓) 22...♕b6 23.♗xc5 ♕xc5+ 24.♔h2 ♗b7∓] **21.♗xc3 ♗xg2 22.♔xg2 bxc3 23.fxe5 d5!** [23... dxe5 24.♕xd8 ♖fxd8 25.♖xe5±] **24.♘e3 ♗g5** [24...d4∞] **25.♕d3± d4 26.♘f5 ♕d5+ 27.♖e4 g6 28.♕xd4 ♖c5 29.♕xd5 ♖xd5 30.♘d4 ♖fd8 31.♘f3 ♗e7 32.♖ae1 ♗b4 33.g5 ♔g7 34.h4 ♖8d7 35.♖1e2 ♖d1 36.♖e1 ♖1d5 37.♖1e3 ♖d1 38.♖e1 ♖1d5** ½-½

SI 14.12
10.a4

Dariusz Swiercz
Martin Krämer
Germany Bundesliga 2014/15 (15)
1.e4 c5 2.♘f3 d6 3.d4 cxd4 4.♘xd4 ♘f6 5.♘c3 a6 6.h3 e6 7.g4 b5 8.♗g2 ♗b7 9.0-0 ♘fd7 10.a4 bxa4

11.♖xa4 [11.f4!? ♘c6 (11...♘c5 12.♘xa4± ♘xe4 (12...♘xa4 13.♖xa4±) 13.c4! d5 (13...♘c5? 14.♘xc5 ♗xg2 15.♘cxe6+−) 14.f5 e5 15.cxd5 ♗xd5 16.♕e2+) 12.f5 e5 13.♘f3 ♘b4 14.♗e3 ♖c8 15.♖xa4 a5 16.♖a1 ♘f6 17.♖f2! d5 (17...♘xe4? 18.♘xe4 ♖xe4 19.c3 ♘c6 20.♕a4+−; 17...♘xe4 18.♘xe4 (18.♖d2) 18...♘xe4 19.♖e2 ♘g3 20.♖d2 ♘e4 21.c3 ♘xd2 22.♕xd2±) 18.♘xe5 ♗d6 19.♘xf7! ♔xf7 20.g5! ♘xe4 21.♗xe4! (21.♘xe4 1-0 (32) Naer-Durarbayli, Plovdiv 2012) 21...dxe4 22.♕h5+ ♔g8 23.f6+−] **11...♗e7** [11...♘b6 12.♖a1 ♗e7 13.♕e2 (13.f4±) 13...0-0 14.♘b3 ♘c6 15.♗e3 ♕c7 16.f4 ♖fe8 17.g5± Ibrahimova-Varshini, Pune 2014] **12.♗e3** [12.♕e2 0-0 13.♖d1 (13.f4) 13...♘b6 14.♖a1 ♘8d7 15.♘b3 ♕c7 16.♘a5± Narayanan-Tzouganakis, Rethymno 2014] **12...♘c5 13.♖a2!?** ♘c6 **14.♘xc6 ♗xc6 15.♕a1** [15.♗xc5 dxc5 16.♕xd8+ ♔xd8 17.e5±] **15...♗b7 16.♖d1 ♘d7 17.♗f4± ♕b8 18.♖a5! 0-0 19.♕a3!** [xd6] **19...e5 20.♗e3 ♖c8 21.♖d2 ♗d8** [21...h6] **22.♖a4 ♘c5** [22...♗e7 23.♗f1±] **23.♖c4 ♗b6** [23...♘c6 24.♘d5] **24.♖b4! ♕c7?** [24...♗d8 25.♗f1 ♕c7 26.♘d5 ♗xd5 27.♖xd5±] **25.♖xb6! ♕xb6 26.b4+− a5**

27.bxc5 dxc5 28.♘d5 ♗xd5 29.exd5 a4 30.d6 ♗a6 31.♖d5 [31.♗xc5! ♕xc5 32.♕xc5 ♖xc5 33.d7+−] 31...♖d8 32.♗xc5 ♕b1+ 33.♔h2 ♕xc2 34.♕b4 ♖aa8? 35.♖d2 1-0

Stewart Haslinger
Markus Koch
Vlissingen 2010 (2)
1.e4 c5 2.♘f3 d6 3.d4 cxd4 4.♘xd4 ♘f6 5.♘c3 a6 6.h3 e6 7.g4 b5 8.♗g2 ♗b7 9.0-0 ♘fd7 10.a4 b4

11.♘a2 [11.♘d5 exd5 12.exd5 ♗e7 13.♘c6∞] **11...♘c5** [11...a5 12.c3±] **12.♖e1** [12.♘xb4! ♘xe4 (12...♗xe4 13.♖e1 ♗xg2 14.♔xg2 ♗e7 15.♕f3 d5 16.c4!) 13.♖e1 d5 14.♘xd5! exd5 15.f3 ♗c5 16.fxe4±] **12...♕b6** [12... e5 13.♘f5 ♘c6 14.c3 bxc3 15.♘xc3 (15.b4!?) 15...g6 16.♘e3 ♗g7 17.♘cd4⇄ Bajarani-Gordievsky, Moscow 2014] **13.c3!?** [13.a5! ♕xa5 14.c3! △ 14...bxc3? (14...b3 15.♘xb3±) 15.b4+−] **13...bxc3?! 14.b4! ♘cd7 15.♗e3± ♕d8 16.♘xc3 ♗e7 17.f4 0-0 18.♖c1 ♘b6 19.♕b3** [19.a5! ♘c4 20.♗f2 ♘c6 21.♘xc6 ♗xc6 22.♗f1±] **19...♘c6 20.♖ed1** [20.♘xc6 ♗xc6 21.♖ed1] **20...♘xd4 21.♗xd4 ♖c8 22.a5± ♘d7 23.♕b2 ♖c7? 24.♗xg7! ♔xg7 25.♘d5+ ♗f6 26.♘xf6 ♘xf6 27.♖xc7 ♕xc7 28.g5± e5 29.gxf6+ ♔xf6 30.♕f2 ♔g7 31.fxe5 dxe5 32.♕f5+− ♕e7 33.♖d7 ♕xb4 34.♕xe5+ ♔g8 35.♔h2! ♗c8 36.♖d3 f6 37.♕c7** 1-0
[Black probably lost on time; 37...♕b7 38.♖g3+ ♔h8 39.♕d6 ♕f7 40.e5+−]

Exercise 1

position after 9...♗f8-e7

White to move.
(solution on page 244)

Exercise 2

position after 12...♗e7xd6

White to move.
(solution on page 245)

Exercise 3

position after 15...♖h8-e8

White has sacrificed a piece. How does he retrieve it with interest?
(solution on page 245)

Looking for material from previous Yearbooks?

Visit our website *www.newinchess.com* and click on 'Yearbook'.
In this menu you can find games, contributors and other information from all our Yearbooks.
Surveys are indexed by opening, by author and by Yearbook.

Sicilian Defence

Scheveningen Variation   SI 24.11 (B85)

The Art of Waiting

by Istvan Almasi

1.	e4	c5
2.	♘f3	e6
3.	d4	cxd4
4.	♘xd4	♘c6
5.	♘c3	♕c7
6.	♗e2	a6
7.	0-0	♘f6
8.	♗e3	♗e7
9.	f4	d6
10.	♕e1	♘xd4
11.	♗xd4	b5
12.	a3	♗b7
13.	♕g3	0-0
14.	♔h1	♖ad8
15.	♖ae1	♖d7
16.	♗d3	♖e8

To do nothing at all is the most difficult thing in the world, the most difficult and the most intellectual. (Oscar Wilde)

In Yearbook 61 (2001), Tibor Fogarasi wrote an article on a Scheveningen set-up discovered by Hungarian grandmaster Jozsef Horvath, which was relatively new at that time. The point of Black's set-up is the following: he places his rooks on d7 and e8, and keeps his position flexible so he can react to White's kingside actions. I am not saying this set-up is the best, or even the only playable one against the solid 6.♗e2 system. Depending on what kind of Sicilian you play, there are many old and modern possibilities to face this system.

Being a regular Taimanov-player (where Black plays all three moves: ...♘c6, ...a7-a6 and ...♕c7), Jozsef Horvath developed a system that can arise from almost all types of Sicilian. Many experienced Taimanov players avoid the risky 8...♗b4, preferring to transpose to the Scheveningen. This is probably the reason why Jozsef Horvath's idea has gained in popularity in the past 20 years. It was taken up first by his Hungarian compatriots, but lately it has been adopted by some of the highest rated players as well.

In Yearbook 61, Fogarasi focused mainly on direct approaches like 17.e5 and 17.♕h3, but he also mentioned patient manoeuvring continuations like 17.♘d1 and 17.♖e3. Recently, the direct attempts have been replaced by clever waiting moves like 17.♖e3, 17.♖e2, 17.♖f3, 17.♖f2. If you want to understand White's ideas, you must first understand the position from Black's point of view. Youngsters of the modern

Wei Yi

era are usually satisfied if the engines assess the position as equal in almost all lines. If they see this, they simply close their laptops and go for their games with no worries at all. The problems begin when they reach the 'dead equal' positions after playing all the routine moves. Then they face a problem: everything is where it should be, there are no real threats from their opponent, but they still have to do something... And this is when they realize that 'doing nothing' is the most difficult thing! If you can no longer improve your position, you must be very careful not to make it worse! I think this is the key to understanding this solid opening system.

Playing this system with the black pieces is not an easy job. It's good to know the typical plans to neutralize White's initiative. One of them is playing ...g7-g6, followed by ...♘h5 and ...♗f6, to trade the powerful bishop on d4. This is what we can see after 17.♖e3 g6 18.♖ef3. Here White achieves one of his main goals: he more or less forces Black to play ...g7-g6, but in view of the temporarily unlucky placement of the e3-rook and d4-bishop, he must lose a tempo, allowing Black to realize his plan. 18...♕d8 or 18...♗d8 is refuted by a strong exchange sac: 18...♗d8 19.f5 exf5 20.exf5! (Navara-Maksimenko) and 18...♕d8 19.♕h3 ♗f8 20.f5 exf5 21.exf5! (Caruana-Sasikiran).

Another way to decrease the bishop's power is to play ...e6-e5 at some moment. In order to achieve this, you must find a place for your e7-bishop, since the e5-square is over-controlled by White's pieces for the moment. It is possible to transfer the dark-squared bishop to g7 via f8, but if Black wants to play ...g7-g6, he needs to protect the knight on f6 first. So this is the second possible approach: ...♗f8/♕d8/g7-g6(/♗g7), and of course ...e6-e5 in case of ♕h3. It looks a bit slow, so the modern way to treat this position is to send the e7-bishop directly to d8, and then play ...e6-e5. This is what Caruana suggests in case of 17.♖f3. It may be possible after 18.♖e3 as well, but this is untested as yet, and it also works after 18.♘d1. I discovered another continuation

which is still untested: 17.♖f3 ♕d8 18.♕h3 ♗f8!?.
However, 17.♖e2 eliminates this option and forces Black to play the traditional set-up ...♕d8/♗f8. The move also leaves open the possibility of doubling the rooks on the f-file. Here, in my opinion, 19.♖ef2 is an interesting improvement on the fashionable 19.a4. Compared to all other variations, it seems to me that this is the line in which White achieves the most: he prevents ...♗d8, as well as the ...♘h5/...♗f6 plan, and after 19...e5 20.♗e3 Black has no clear way to neutralize White's play. He is making quite illogical moves: back to e7 with the bishop, queen to c8, etc... The game Bok-Van Delft (2014) is worth studying. The coordination between the white pieces is better after 17.♖e2 than after 17.♖e3 or 17.♖f3. The rooks look more threatening on the third rank, but it is safer for White if he puts them on the second. White hopes for some pawn move on the kingside by Black, after which he has a target, and may still play ♖e3 later, even if he loses a tempo.
About the possible deviations: White can try to save the move ♔h1 (David-Negi, 2009), but sooner or later he will have to play it. In my opinion, omitting ♔h1 gives extra possibilities only for Black. However, it is worth noting that by delaying ♔h1, White can compel Black to play the ...♖ad8-♖d7 set-up, because leaving out ♔h1 can be good against other set-ups.

I was shocked to see that the engine includes 16...♖dd8!? among its first five suggestions (at level 35 it is actually the very first!) after 14...♖ad8 15.♖ae1 ♖d7 16.♗d3. And likewise: if Black begins with 15...♖fe8, the engine suggests 16...♖f8, or if he inserts 15...♗c6, then 16....♗b7. Strangely enough, Black's position remains so solid that there is no sudden and deadly punishment for giving away two tempi! The computer actually recommends a careful build-up for White with moves like 17.♖e2. I had the same experience while analysing Sethuraman-Van Wely (2013): I do not see how White can make use of the extra move...

Here I started to realize (although I had played this system with both colours for 10 years) that I had misunderstood what is going on all along! White's main goal is also to wait until Black misplaces a piece or two, or weakens his kingside. This is what we can see in the game Wei Yi-Bruzon, 2015 (19...♖e8?) or Meszaros-Antal, 2005 (18...♗f8?). These 'inaccuracies' were punished quickly and ruthlessly: the good old Scheveningen, renowned to be safe and reliable, led to a lost position in less than 25 moves.

Conclusion

Play in this line is very subtle and intricate. This is one of those types of position of which we can truly say that the best player will win – or perhaps that should be 'the most patient player'!

Sparing ♔h1
15.♗d3

Alberto David
Parimarjan Negi

Evry 2009 (3)

1.e4 c5 2.♘f3 e6 3.d4 cxd4 4.♘xd4 ♘c6 5.♘c3 ♕c7 6.♗e2 a6 7.0-0 ♘f6 8.♗e3 ♗e7 9.f4 d6 10.♕e1 ♘xd4 11.♗xd4 b5 12.a3 ♗b7 13.♕g3 0-0 14.♖ae1 ♖ad8 [14...♗c6

15.♗d3. Unfortunately for Black, in this move order (White sparing ♔h1), he can hardly play any other sub-systems, because White is already threatening e4-e5. And Black can parry this only by playing ...♖ad8 at some point, to preclude White taking back on e5 with the pawn: 15...♖ae8 (15...e5? 16.fxe5 ♘h5 17.exd6!! (17.♕f3 dxe5 18.♘d5! ♗xd5 19.exd5 exd4 20.♕e4! g6 21.♕xe7 ♕xe7 22.♖xe7± Heberla-Plischki, Teplice 2015) 17...♘xg3 18.dxc7 ♗xf1 19.♘d5!! ♗xd5 (19...♖fe8 20.♔xf1 ♖ac8 21.♘xe7+ ♖xe7 22.♗b6± Wang Z-Liang J, Beijing 1993) 20.exd5 ♗d6 (20...♘e3!? 21.♖xe3 ♗d6 22.♗e5 ♗c5 23.♔f2 ♖fe8 24.♗f3 ♗xe3 25.♔xe3 ♖xe5+ 26.♔d4 ♗e7 27.d6 ♖xc7□ 28.dxc7 ♖c8 29.♔c5 ♖xc7+ 30.♔b6+−) 21.♗e5! ♖fe8 22.♗xd6 ♖xe1 23.♔f2 ♖d1□ 24.♗c5 ♘xh2 25.♔g3 ♘f1+ 26.♔f4 1-0 Balinov-Kragelj, Bled 1999; 15...♗b7?! 16.e5! dxe5 17.fxe5 ♕d7 (17...♘d7 18.♗e4; ≤ 17...♘h5 18.♕h3 g6 19.♘e4± Hracek-Movsesian, Czechia tt 2001/02) 18.♗e3 ♘h5 19.♕h3 g6 20.♘e4 ♕xe4 21.♗xe4 ♖ac8 22.♗h1±) 16.e5!? ♘h5 (16...dxe5 17.fxe5! (this possibility arises from the fact that now the d4♗ is not attacked by the d8♖) 17...♘d7 18.♗f4! (18.♕h3 g6 19.♕h6 ♘c5?? (19...f5□ 20.exf6 ♗xf6⇄) 20.♖e3 1-0 Laznicka-L.Milov, Germany

Bundesliga 2005/06) 18...g6 (18...f5?? 19.exf6 ♗xf6 20.♖xf6!) 19.b4!?± Macieja-Vescovi, Bermuda 2005) 17.♕e3 (17.♕h3 Rytshagov-Lautier, Tallinn rapid 2002) 17...g6 18.g4 (≤ 18.♗e4 f5⇄; 18.♘e4 ♗xe4 19.♗xe4 ♘g7 Hracek-Movsesian, Germany Bundesliga 2001/02) 18...♘g7 19.♗e4 f5 20.exf6 ♗xf6 21.♗xc6 ♕xc6 22.♗xf6 ♖xf6 23.♘e4± Macieja-Lutz, Bled ol 2002] **15.♗d3**

15...e5!? [This move is not forced in any sense, as both 15...♖fe8 and 15...♗d7 are playable for Black. There is nothing better for White than to transpose with 16.♔h1 into the well-known positions. But if this move is possible (which it rarely is with the queen on g3), Black should take his chance and play it! 15...♖fe8 16.♔h1; 15...♖d7 16.♕h3 (16.♔h1; 16.e5 dxe5 17.♗xe5 ♕b6+ 18.♔h1 ♘h5 19.♕h3 g6 20.♘e4 (Recuero Guerra-Ortega Hermida, Mondariz 2006; 20.f5?! exf5 21.♗xf5 gxf5 22.♕xh5 ♕g6 23.♕h3 ♖d2 24.♗e2 ♖fd8∓) 20...f6 21.♗c3 ♗d5=) 16...e5 (16...h6?! 17.♗e3→; (△ ♖g3) 17.♕f3→; 16...g6?! 17.f5 e5 18.♗e3± (Osmanovic-Iotov, Nuremberg 2009) 18...d5 19.exd5 ♗xd5 (19...♘xd5? 20.♘xd5 ♗xd5 21.f6+−) 20.♔h1!± e4△ 21.♗f4) 17.♗f2 (17.fxe5 dxe5 18.♘d5 ♗xd5 19.exd5 ♗c5!=; 19...exd4 20.♖xf6 g6 is OK for Black too, but after 19...♗c5 it's much less of an effort for him) 17...♖dd8 18.♘d5 (18.♗h4 ♕c8) 18...♘xd5 (18...♗xd5!? 19.exd5 g6 20.♕f3 ♘h5 21.f5 (△ ♗e3) 21...♗g5!∞) 19.exd5 g6 20.f5 ♗xd5 21.♗h4⩱ (21.♗e3⩱); 15...d5!? This alternative central breakthrough shows that it is Black who profits if White omits ♔h1: 16.e5 (16.exd5 ♗c5! 17.♗xc5 ♕xc5+ 18.♔h1 ♘xd5=) 16...♘e4 17.♕e3∞ (△ ♗e2-c3)] **16.fxe5 dxe5!?N** [After 16...♘h5!? White

cannot pick up the exchange via 17.♕e3/f2 dxe5 18.♗b6 ♕c8, because Black has the nasty response 19...♗c5: 17.♕e3 dxe5 18.♗b6 ♕c8! 19.♘d5 (19.♗xd8?? ♗c5) 19...♗xd5 20.exd5 g6 (20...♖de8= Rojas Keim-Watanabe, Yerevan ol 1996) 21.♕xe5 ♗c5+ 22.♗xc5 ♕xc5+ 23.♕e3 ♕xd5= Salai-Dovzik, Slovakia tt 2003/04] **17.♗xe5**

17...♕c5+ [This is the difference between the moves 14...♗c6 and 14...♖ad8: on c6 the ♗ would block the way of the ♕ to c5. This pawn sacrifice is based on the temporary insecure placement of the e5♗, and Black needs the c5-square to exploit this] **18.♔h1** [18.♖f2!? ♘h5 19.b4□ ♘xg3 (19...♕xc3 20.♗xc3 ♘xg3 21.hxg3 ♗d6⩱) 20.bxc5 ♘h5 21.♗d6 ♗xd6 22.cxd6 ♖xd6=] **18...♘h5 19.♕e3** [19.♕h3 ♕xe5 20.♖f5 ♘g3+=] **19...♕xe5 20.♖f5 ♘g3+** [20...♕d4 21.♕xd4 ♖xd4 22.♖xh5 g6 23.♖h3 ♗g5⩱] **21.hxg3 ♕e6⩱ 22.♘d5 ♗d6** [22...♗xd5=] **23.♘f4 ♕h6+ 24.♖h5 ♗xf4 25.♕f3 ♕g6** [≥ 25...♕f6 26.gxf4 g6 (26...♕xb2 27.♕h3 h6 28.e5!±) 27.♖h3 ♕xb2 28.f5!] **26.gxf4± f5? 27.♕h3!± h6** [27...fxe4 28.f5!] **28.♖xf5 ♖fe8 29.♖h5 ♗xe4 30.♖xe4 ♖xe4 31.♖e5 ♖dd4 32.♗xe4 ♖xe4 33.♕d3** 1-0

Mixing Plans
16...♕d8 and 16...♖dd8

Wei Yi
Lazaro Bruzon Batista

Danzhou 2015 (2)

1.e4 c5 2.♘f3 e6 3.♘c3 a6 4.♗e2 ♘c6 5.d4 cxd4 6.♘xd4 ♕c7 7.0-0 ♘f6 8.♗e3 ♗e7 9.f4 d6 10.♔h1 0-0 11.♕e1 ♘xd4 12.♗xd4 b5 13.♕g3 ♗b7 14.a3 ♖ad8 [14...g6

This move is not part of the subject of this Survey. I just give it to demonstrate the difference to the text. If Black is going to play this structure (with 15.f5 e5) it is better to do without any preparation and hope for a fast ...d6-d5. The impotent pitter-patter of the black major pieces on the back rank just benefits White, if Black is going to follow this plan. 15.f5! (15.♘f3 is the other main move; 15.♗d3?! ♘h5 16.♕f2 (16.♕h3 ♘xf4 17.♖xf4 e5 18.♘d5 ♘xd5 19.exd5 exd4!) 16...♘xf4 17.♕xf4 e5 18.♕f2 exd4 19.♕xd4 ♕c5 20.♕xc5 dxc5∓ Yu R-Wang Y, China 2014) 15...e5 16.♗e3 d5 17.exd5 (17.♖h6!?) 17...♘xd5 18.♘xd5 ♗xd5] 15.♖ae1 ♖d7 [15...♕d7!? is another waiting move, but it is hard to see the idea behind it, and to guess Black's next moves] 16.♗d3

16...♕d8 [≥ 16...♖e8; 16...♖dd8!? This shocking move is recommended by Stockfish at a very deep level. 17.♖e2!? (17.e5 dxe5 18.♗xe5 ♕b6 19.♕h3 (19.f5 ♗d6 20.fxe6 fxe6∞; 19.♘e4 ♗xe4 20.♗xe4 g6 (△ ...♕d7/...♗f6)) 19...h5!? 20.♗xf6 ♗xf6 21.♕xh5 g6; 17.♕h3 e5 18.fxe5 dxe5 19.♘d5 ♗xd5 (19...♖xd5! 20.exd5 exd4 21.♖xf6 g6) 20.exd5 exd4 21.♖xf6 g6 and thanks to the opposite-coloured bishops Black has a good chance to hold this; 17.♗e3 g6 18.♖ef3 ♘h5)] 17.♕h3 g6?! [17...♖e8 18.♗e3 (18.♖f3 – Caruana-Sasikiran; 18...♗f8!?; 18.♖e2 – Negi-Adhiban) 18...g6 19.♖ef3 – Caruana-Sasikiran] 18.f5 e5 19.♗e3 ♖e8? [19...♘h5 is in harmony with 19...g6. However Black must sooner or later sacrifice a pawn with ...♘h5-f4. 20.♘d5 (20.♗h6 ♖e8 (≥ 20...♘f4) 21.a4 (21.fxg6 hxg6 22.♘d5± △ ♘xd5 23.exd5 ♘f4 24.♗xf4 exf4 25.♗xg6! fxg6 26.♕h6!+−) 21...♗f8 22.♗xf8 ♖xf8 23.axb5 axb5 (Kamsky-Stellwagen, Wijk

aan Zee 2009) 24.♗xb5±; 20.♖f3 ♗c6 (≥ 20...♘f4) 21.♗h6 ♖e8 22.♘d5±; 22.♕xh5?! (Bok-E.Hansen, Oslo 2013) 22...gxh5 23.♖g3+ ♔h8 24.♗g7+ ♔g8=) 20...♗xd5 21.exd5 ♘f6 22.g3±. Aimed against ...♘f4; 22.c3 ♘f4 23.♗xf4 exf4 24.♖xf4 ♖e7 25.♖fe4 ½-½ Lintchevski-Matlakov, St Petersburg 2013; 22.fxg6 fxg6 23.c3 ♖df7 24.g3 ♗g5= Lintchevski-Yakovenko, Tyumen 2012] 20.fxg6 hxg6 21.♘d5N ♘xd5? [≥ 21...♖xd5 22.exd5±]

22.♖xf7!! [Although 19...♖e8 was played several times, this refutation had never entered anyone's mind!] 22...♔xf7 [22...♘f6 23.♕e6+− (perhaps this move was overlooked by Bruzon) 23...♔h8 (23...♗f8 24.♗e7+) 24.♗g5] 23.♕h7+ ♔e6 [23...♘f6 24.exd5+− △ 25.♕xg6X; 25.♖f1X] 24.exd5+ ♔xd5 [24...♗xd5 25.♗xg6! ♕xg2+□ (25...♖f8 26.♕h3+ ♔f6 27.♖f1++−) 26.♔xg2 ♖f8 (26...d5 27.♗f7+ ♔d6 28.♕h6+ ♗f6 (28...♔c7 29.♗b6++−) 29.♗xe8+−) 27.♕h3+ ♔d5 28.♗b6!!+− ♕xb6 29.♗e4+ ♔c5 30.♕c3#] 25.♗e4+!! ♔xe4 [25...♔e6 26.♕xg6+ ♔f6 27.♕f5+ ♔f7 28.♕h7+ ♔f8 (28...♔e6 29.♗f5+ ♔d5 30.♗xd7+−) 29.♗h6+ ♖g7 (29...♗g7 30.♗xg7+ ♖xg7 31.♖f1+ ♔e7 32.♕xg7+ ♔e6 33.♕f7#) 30.♖f1+−] 26.♕f7 [26.c4 wins faster: 26...bxc4 (26...♗d3 27.♕xg6+ ♗e4 28.♖d1+ ♔c2 29.♕xe4++−; 26...♔f5 27.♕h3+ ♔f6 28.♖f1+ ♗g7 29.♕h6+ ♔g8 30.♕xg6+ ♔h8 31.♖f7+−) 27.♕xg6+ ♔d5 28.♕f7+ ♔e4 (28...♔c6 29.♕xc4#) 29.♕xc4+ ♔f5 30.♖f1+ ♔g6 31.♕f7#] 26...♗f6 27.♗d2+ ♔d4 28.♗e3+ ♔e4 29.♕b3! [△ 30.♕d3X] 29...♔f5 30.♖f1+ ♔g4 31.♕d3! [△ 32.♕xg6+; 32.♕e2+] 31...♕xg2+ [31...♖g7 32.h3+ ♔h4 33.♕e2 ♕d7 34.♔h2 ♗xg2 35.♕xg2 ♕f5 36.♖xf5 gxf5 37.♕f2+

♔h5 38.♕xf5+ ♗g5 39.♗xg5+−] 32.♔xg2 ♕a8+ 33.♔g1 ♗g5 34.♕e2+ ♔h4 35.♗f2+ ♔h3 36.♗e1! [An unbelievable game! The Chinese youngster played with extreme accuracy] 1-0

David Navara
Andrei Maksimenko
Wroclaw 2014 (6)

1.e4 c5 2.♘f3 d6 3.d4 cxd4 4.♘xd4 ♘f6 5.♘c3 a6 6.♗e2 e6 7.0-0 ♗e7 8.f4 ♕c7 9.♕e1 0-0 10.♕g3 ♘c6 11.♗e3 ♘xd4 12.♗xd4 b5 13.a3 ♗b7 14.♖ae1 ♖ad8 15.♔h1 ♖d7 16.♗d3 ♖e8 17.♖e3 g6 [17...♘h5?! 18.♕h3 ♗f6? (to execute this plan Black still needs the move ...g7-g6 18...g6 19.f5! △ 19...e5 20.fxg6 hxg6 21.♗b6!) 19.e5! (19.♗xf6 ♘xf6 20.e5 dxe5 21.fxe5 ♖xd3□ 22.cxd3±) 19...dxe5 20.♗xh7+! (20.fxe5 ♖xd4) 20...♔xh7 21.♕xh5+ ♔g8 22.♖h3 g6 23.♕h7+ ♔f8 24.fxe5+−; 17...♕d8?! 18.♕h3

18...g6□ (18...h6 19.♖g3 ♔h8□ 20.♘d5!± exd5 (20...♕g8 21.♘xe7 ♕xe7 22.e5 dxe5 23.♗xe5±) 21.e5! (♘e4?! 22.♗xe4 dxe4 23.e6+−; 18...♗f8? 19.♘d5!!N ♘xd5 (19...♘xe4 20.♗f6!+−; 19...exd5 20.♗xf6+−; 19...♘g4 20.♕xg4 exd5 21.e5 g6 22.f5 (22.e6+−) 22...dxe5 23.♗xe5 ♗g7 (Meszaros-Antal, Hungary tt 2005) 24.fxg6 fxg6 25.♗xg6 hxg6 26.♕xg6 d4□ 27.♗xg7 (27.♖h3 ♗e4!!) 27...♕xg2+ 28.♕xg2 ♖xg7 29.♖g3 ♖ee7 30.♖g1+−) 20.exd5 g6 21.dxe6+−) 19.♖ef3! (in YB/61, Tibor Fogarasi dealt with 19.♖g3 only. The text transposes to the game Caruana-Sasikiran) 19.♖g3 Z.Vukovic-Pe.Varga,

Neum 2000); 17...♗d8!?N (△ ...e6-e5, I.Almasi) 18.e5 (18.♖ef3 e5 19.fxe5 dxe5= Gusain-Konguvel, Aurangabad 2011; 18.♕h3 e5 19.♘d5 ♗xd5 20.exd5 g6.

The same position with the ♖ on e2 (instead of e3) would be fine for White, because now after 21.♗c3 ♘xd5 the ♖ on e2 would not be hanging!) 18... dxe5 19.♗xe5 ♕b6 (19...♕c5?! 20.b4! ♕b6 21.♕h3 g6 22.♖g3→) 20.♕h3 (20.f5 ♗c7! 21.fxe6 ♕xe6 22.♖xf6 (22.♗f4? ♕xe3!) 22...♕xe5□ 23.♖xe5 ♗xe5 24.♕e3 gxf6∓; 20.♗xh7+ ♔xh7 21.♕h4+ ♔g8 22.♖h3 ♗xg2+ 23.♔xg2 ♖d2+ 24.♔h1 ♕c6+ 25.♖ff3 ♔f8= 26.f5 ♗c7) 20...g6 21.♖g3 (△ ♕h4-♖h3) 21...♕c5 22.a4 (22.♕h4 ♕e7) 22...b4 23.♘d1↑) **18.♖ef3** [18.♖e2 d5 19.e5 ♘e4 20.♗xe4 dxe4 21.♕e3 ♕c4 22.♖d1 ½-½ Cigan-Antal, Hungary tt 2006; 18.e5 dxe5 19.♗xe5 ♕d8 (19...♘h5!? 20.♕h3 ♗d6↑ Ardelean-Dovzik, Berekfurdo 2007) 20.f5?! ♘h5 21.♕h3 exf5 22.♗xf5 ♖d2∓ Filippov-Adhiban, Barcelona 2013; 18.f5!? e5 19.♘d5□ ♗xd5 (19...♘xd5 20.exd5 ♗xd5 (20... exd4? 21.fxg6 fxg6 22.♗xg6+−) 21.fxg6 fxg6 22.♗xg6 ♗h4□ 23.♕g4 ♗g7 24.♗xh7+ ♔h8 25.♗g6 ♔g8∞) 20.exd5 exd4 21.fxg6 dxe3 (21...fxg6 22.♗xg6) 22.gxf7+ ♔xf7 (22...♔h8?? 23.♖xf6+−) 23.♗xh7 ♖h8 24.♕g6+ ♔f8 25.♕h6+ ♔f7 26.♕g6+=] **18...♗d8** [18...♕d8 19.♕h3 – Caruana-Sasikiran, 2009; 18...d5!? 19.e5 ♘e4 20.♕e1 (the e4♘ seems to be a very nice outpost for Black. Generally after such an achievement the position should be assessed as equal. All the same, White has a clear plan: ♘e2-c3-♖h3 or g2-g4 with attack on the kingside. Black must find some counterplay on the queenside) 20...b4 (20...♘xc3?! 21.bxc3!±; 20...f5

21.exf6 ♗xf6 22.♘e2±) 21.axb4 ♗xb4 22.♖h3 (22.♘xd5? ♗xd5 23.♕xb4 ♖b8 24.♕e1 ♘c5∓) 22...♕d8?! (prevents 23.♕h4, but after White's next move it turns out that the black ♕ is misplaced; if 22...♗c5 23.♘e2 (23.♗xc5 ♘xc5 24.♕h4 h5 25.♕g5 ♘xd3 26.cxd3 d4) 23...♗xd4 24.♘xd4 ♕b6 25.c3 ♕xb2 26.♕h4 h5∞) 23.♕e3± ♘xc3? (Areschenko-Ftacnik, Germany Bundesliga 2010/11; 23...♗f8 24.♖a1±; 24.♘d1± (△ ♘f2/c2-c3); ≥ 23...♕c7; 23...♗e7 (△ ...f7-f5) 24.♗b6!?↑ △ 24...♕c8 25.f5!! ♗g5 26.♘xe4 ♗xe3 27.♘f6+ ♔f8 28.♗xe3+−) 24.f5!! ♗f8 (24...♘e4 25.♕h6 f6 26.exf6 ♗f8 27.f7+ ♖xf7 28.♕xg6+ ♗g7 29.f6+−) 25.bxc3 exf5 26.♗xf5!+− (△ e5-e6) 26...♗g7 27.♖xh7! ♔xh7 28.♕h3+ ♔g8 29.♗xd7; 18...♘h5!?N is the latest development. I prefer it to the logical and typical 18...d5.

Black's plan is simple: he wants to exchange the dark-squared ♗s by 19...♗f6. This is also an unusual, but logical follow up on 17...g6. For example: 19.♕f2 (19.♕h3 ♗f6 20.♗xf6 ♘xf6= Firat-Potkin, Jerusalem Ech 2015) 19...♗f6 (19...♕d8!? 20.f5?! (≥ 20.♖h3) 20...exf5 (20...♗h4! (somehow, the author of 'The Most Flexible Sicilian' permanently 'forgets' about this nasty zwischenzug) 21.g3 (21.♕g1 exf5 22.exf5 ♗xf3 23.♖xf3 ♖e1−+) 21...exf5! 22.gxh4 fxe4) 21.exf5? (Delchev-C.Hecht, Wunsiedel 2015; 21.♖h3! ♗f6 22.♗xf6 ♕xf6 (22...♖xf6 23.exf5 g5) 23.exf5 ♕g5) 21...♗h4! 22.fxg6 hxg6 and now the white ♕ must abandon the defence of the f3♖, and Black can take the rook without worry) 20.♗xf6 ♘xf6 21.♕h3 d5 (21...♘g4!? 22.♕e2 (22.♕h4 f5) 22...♘f6 23.♕e1 ♘g4) 22.e5 ♘e4 23.♕h4 f5! 24.exf6 ♖f7=] **19.f5! exf5**

20.♖xf5?! [20.exf5! ♗xf3 (20...♘h5? (if Black wants to win the exchange, then it is better to keep the ♘ on f6, controlling the d5-square) 21.♕g4 ♗xf3 22.♕xf3± (△ ♘d5) 22...d5 23.g4 (23.♘xd5 ♖xd5 (23...♕d6 24.c4 ♘g7 25.fxg6 hxg6 26.♗f6±; 26.♗c3±) 24.♕xd5 ♘f4 25.♕f3 ♘xd3 26.cxd3±) 23...♘g7 24.♘xd5 ♕d6 25.c4± Pogonina-Kursova, Tromsø ol 2014) 21.♕xf3 ♖e5! 22.♕f4∞] **20...♘xe4 21.♗xe4?** [21.♘xe4 ♗xe4 22.♖h5 ♗xd3 23.cxd3 (23.♖xh7 ♖e5 24.♕h3 ♗f1 25.♖h8+ ♔g7 26.♕h6+ ♔f6-+) 23...f6∓; 21.♕f4 ♘c5!? 22.♕h6 f6∓ 23.♖xf6 ♗xf6 24.♗xf6 ♘xd3-+] **21...♗xe4 22.♖h5** [△ 23.♖xh7] **22...♕c4!-+ 23.♖d1 f5??** [23...♗xc2! 24.♖xh7 ♖e5 25.♗xe5 (25.♕h3 ♗xd1 (25...♕xd4-+) 26.♖h8+ ♔g7 27.♕h6+ ♔f6-+) 25...dxe5 26.♖h8+ ♔xh8 27.♕h3+ ♔g7 28.♕xd7 ♖xd1-+] **24.♖xh7!+− ♖xh7 25.♕xg6+ ♔f8 26.♕xh7 ♖e7 27.♕h8+ ♕g8 28.♕h6+ ♔e8 29.♘xe4 ♖xe4 30.♕xd6 ♕g4 31.♗c5 ♗e7 32.♕d7+ ♔f8 33.♖f1** 1-0

17.♖f3

**Fabiano Caruana
Krishnan Sasikiran**

Wijk aan Zee 2009 (11)

1.e4 c5 2.♘f3 d6 3.d4 cxd4 4.♘xd4 ♘f6 5.♘c3 a6 6.♗e2 e6 7.0-0 ♕c7 8.f4 ♗e7 9.♗e3 ♘c6 10.♔h1 0-0 11.♕e1 ♘xd4 12.♗xd4 b5 13.a3 ♗b7 14.♕g3 ♖ad8 15.♖ae1 [15.♗d3 ♖d7 16.♖f3N ♖e8 (16...♘e8? 17.♕h3± g6?) 18.♕xh7+ 1-0 Fedorchuk-Petre, Aix-les-Bains Ech 2011) 17.♖af1 ♗d8 (with a tricky move order – sparing the move

♖ae1 – White has managed to get this position with an extra tempo, compared to our game's 17th move, but the 'veteran' Dutch player solves the problem nicely. Funny thing is that it is not clear to me whether White can make use of his extra move. 18.e5?! (18.♕h3 e5 19.♗e3 (19.♗f2?! d5 20.fxe5 dxe4 and now White misses the same tactical motif which would be possible with 19.♗e3: the f2♗ blocks the f-file, therefore there is no 21.♘xe4 ♘xe4 22.e6: 21.♖e3=) 19...♕c8 (19... d5? 20.fxe5 dxe4 21.♘xe4 ♘xe4 22.e6!+−) 20.♖g3 ♕c7) 18...♘h5! (18... dxe5 19.♗xe5 ♕b6 20.♗xh7+ (20.♘e4 ♘h5 21.♕h3 g6 22.♕xh5 gxh5 23.♖g3+ ♔f8 24.♗g7+ ♔e7 25.♗f6+ ♔f8=) 20...♔xh7 21.♕h4+ ♔g8 22.♖h3= and we get the same position as in the notes to Navara-Maksimenko (17...♗d8)!) 19.♕g4 ♗xf3 20.♕xf3⩲ g6 21.g4 ♘g7 22.♘e4 (22.♗e4 (△ ♗c6) 22...d5 23.♗d3⩱ △ f4-f5) 22...dxe5 23.♗xe5 ♕b6⩱ Sethuraman-Van Wely, Canberra 2013]

15...♖d7 16.♗d3 ♖e8 17.♖f3!?
[This move was suggested to Caruana by Alexander Chernin, but it had been played one year earlier by Sergey Fedorchuk]

17...♕d8?! [Black gives up the control of the e5-square, so after 18.♕h3 he will not be able to cross White's plans with the usual ...e6-e5. 17...♘h5?! 18.♕h3 ♗f6? (≥ 18...g6 19.f5±) 19.e5 dxe5 20.♗xe5 ♗xe5 21.♗xh7+ ♔xh7 22.♕xh5+ ♔g8 23.♖h3 ♔f8 24.fxe5+−; 17...g6?! (contrary to after 17.♖e3, this move is not so great here: after 18.f5 e5 the d4♗ is not trapped in this case) 18.f5 e5 19.♗e3 (△ ♖ef1) 19...d5 (if Black is not able to execute this central break as soon as possible, he has to live with a clearly worse position, without any counterplay) 20.exd5 e4 21.♗f4!±; 17...♗d8! (△ ... e6-e5)

19.♗xf6 (19.♘d5?! ♘xd5 20.exd5 g6 21.dxe6 ♗xf3 (if the ♖s were placed on e3 and f1, as after 17.♖e3, now 21.dxe6 would win on the spot. However in the actual position the f3♖ would be hanging; 19.♖ef1 leads to a very similar position to the one in the game Giri-Grischuk – the ♕ was on g3 there) 19...♗xf6 20.♘d5 (20.e5 ♕h6 is not at all as tragic as the text was) 20...♕d8 (20...exd5? 21.e5! (21.♕xd7? ♖e7!) 21... h6 22.♕xd7+−; 20...♗xd5 21.exd5 h6 (21...♕h6 22.♕xh6 gxh6 23.f5±; 21...g6 22.f5!+−) 22.g4→ △ g4-g5) 21.e5 f5□ 22.exf6 gxf6∞ and the d7♖ finally does the job: defending the weakest point] **19.♖ef1 d5?** ['Sasikiran had clearly overlooked my next move. However, Black's defensive task is already unenviable' (Caruana). 19...♗f8 20.f5 exf5 (20...gxf5?? 21.♖g3+ ♔h8 22.♕h4 e5 (22...♘g7 23.♖xg7+−) 23.♗b6 ♕e7 24.♖xf5+− 1-0 Narayanan-

18.♕h3 (18.♘d1 e5! 19.♗c3 ♕c8! 20.♘f2 (20.fxe5 dxe5 21.♗xe5?? ♘h5−+) 20...♘h5 21.♕g4 ♘f6 22.♕g3 ♘h5 23.♕g4 ♘f6 (½-½ Mista-Kempinski, Czechia tt 2010/11) 24.♕f5 ♖de7 25.♕xc8 ♗xc8 26.♗b4 (Ni Hua-Hou Yifan, Xinghua ch-CHN 2010) 26...♖d7⩱ (△ ♗b6); 18.♖ef1 e5 (18... g6 – Navara-Maksimenko, 2014) 19.fxe5 dxe5 20.♗e3 ♘h5 21.♕g4 g6= is totally OK for Black – it is not necessary to enter into the labyrinth of 18...♘h5; 18.f5 e5 19.♗e3 d5 (19...♘h5!? 20.♕g4 (20.♕h3 ♘f4) 20...♘f6 21.♕g3 (21.♕h3 d5) 21...♘h5=) 20.♗h6 ♘h5 21.♕g4 ♖d6! 22.f6 g6 23.♕xh5 gxh5 24.♖g3+ ♔h8 25.♗g7+ ♔g8= Caruana) 18...e5 19.♗f2 (19.♘d5 ♗xd5 20.exd5 g6 21.♗c3 ♘xd5 22.fxe5 ♘xc3∓) 19...♕c8] **18.♕h3 g6** [18...♗f8N (△ ...e6-e5, I.Almasi). According to Caruana, with his previous move Black was preparing 18...♗f8. Then why didn't he play it?

19.♗xf6 (19.♘d5?! ♘xd5 20.exd5 g6 21.dxe6 ♗xf3 (if the ♖s were placed on

Mihok, Kecskemet 2011) 21.exf5! (by discovering this strong exchange sacrifice White practically refuted both set-ups with 18...♗d8 and 19...♗f8, connected with ...g7-g6) 21...g5 (21...♗xf3 22.fxg6 hxg6 23.♗xf6 ♕xf6 24.♕xd7+−) 22.♖g3! (≤ 22.♖e3 Fedorchuk-Jaracz, Dresden 2008) 22...h6 23.♘d1! ♗e4 (23...g7 24.♗xf6 ♕xf6 25.♘e3± Caruana) 24.♘e3 d5 25.♗xf6 ♕xf6 26.♘g4± Azarov-Lamoureux, Budva Ech 2009; 19...♘h5 20.f5! exf5 21.exf5! (21.♖xf5!? gxf5 22.♕xh5 ♗f6 23.♗xf6 ♕xf6 is not so clear) 21...♗xf3 22.♕xf3 ♗g5 (22...♗f8 23.♘d5+−) 23.♘d5 ♖e5! 24.g4 ♘g7 25.c4± Caruana]

20.f5! dxe4 21.fxg6 fxg6 [21... exf3? 22.♕xh7+!+−; 21...hxg6? 22.♖xf6! ♖xd4 23.♖xf7+−] **22.♖xf6! ♖xd4** [22...♗xf6 23.♗xf6 ♕a8 24.♗e2+−] **23.♖f7! ♗h4□ 24.♗e2** [24.♗xb5 axb5 25.♖xb7 ♖e7 26.♖xe7 (26.♖xb5? ♗f2⩲) 26...♕xe7 27.♕g4± Caruana] **24...♗c6** [24...♗a8 25.g3 Narayanan-Bukavshin, Kirishi 2009; 24...b4 25.axb4 ♖xb4 26.♘b5! axb5 27.♖xb7+−] **25. g3 e3+ 26.♔g1+− a5 27.gxh4 b4 28.axb4 axb4 29.♘d1 ♕d5 30.♘xe3 ♕c5 31.♗d3 b3 32.♕g3 bxc2 33.♗xc2 ♖d2 34.♖7f2 ♖ed8 35.♖xd2 ♖xd2 36.♖f2 ♖d4 37.♗xg6 hxg6 38.♕xg6+ ♔h8 39.♕h6+ ♔g8 40.♕xe6+ ♔h8 41.♕h6+ ♔g8 42.♕e6+ ♔h8 43.♕c8+ ♔g7 44.♖g2+** 1-0

17.♖e2

Parimarjan Negi
Baskaran Adhiban
Jalgaon 2013 (4)

1.e4 c5 2.♘f3 e6 3.d4 cxd4 4.♘xd4 ♘c6 5.♘c3 ♕c7 6.♗e2

a6 7.0-0 ♘f6 8.♗e3 ♗e7 9.f4 d6 10.♔h1 0-0 11.♕e1 ♘xd4 12.♗xd4 b5 13.♕g3 ♗b7 14.a3 ♖ad8 15.♖ae1 ♖d7 16.♗d3 ♖e8 17.♖e2!? [I do not see any benefits in 17.♖f2 compared to 17.♖e2. If we just look at the principles: it leaves the e1♖ undefended, which can hit back in some lines. If White plays ♖ef1 later, the game usually transposes to 17.♖e2 lines: 17...♕d8 18.♖ef1 ♗f8 19.♖f3!? (earlier, in the notes to Caruana-Sasikiran, I mentioned that White managed to get an extra tempo in the game Sethuraman-Van Wely compared to the regular 17.♖f3 lines. Now we witness another Dutch top player, Giri, demonstrate how to lose a tempo compared to the 17.♖f3 ♕d8 18.♕h3 g6 19.♖ef1 ♗f8 20.f5 line!) 19.♕h3 – 17.♖e2 ♕d8 18.♕h3 ♗f8 19.♖ef2) 19...g6?! (19...e5= Liang-Chandra, Doha 2014) 20.f5 exf5 (Giri-Grischuk, Beijing 2013) 21.exf5! Giri missed this very promising exchange sacrifice, which worked nicely in Caruana-Sasikiran. So it is hard to understand then why he was so precise about the nuances earlier, when he did not achieve his goal – however this idea was already known) 21...♘h5 22.♕g4 ♗xf3 23.♕xf3 ♗g7 24.f6 ♘xf6 25.♗xf6 ♕xf6 26.♕xf6 ♗xf6 27.♖xf6±]
17...♕d8 [Shockingly, instead of this move some engine strongly recommends 17...♖dd8 and 17...♖f8. Frankly speaking I do not see the big point behind 17...♕d8 either... 17...g6?! 18.f5 e5 19.♗e3± Di Berardino-Barbosa, Joao Pessoa ch-BRA 2013; 17...♗c6?! 18.♘d5! ♕d8 19.♗b6 ♕c8 20.♘xe7+ ♖dxe7 21.e5 dxe5 22.fxe5 ♘h5 23.♕g5 g6± Fedorchuk-Bocharov, Budva Ech 2009; 17...♖d8 18.♕h3 e5 19.♘d5 ♗xd5 (19...♕c8 20.♗c3±) 20.exd5 h6 (20...g6 21.♗c3 ♘xd5 22.fxe5± – contrary to the 17.♖f3 ♕d8 18.♕h3 e5 19.♘d5 line, here the pawn on e5 is not pinned after 22...♘xc3 and White can play 23.exd6!. With white rooks on e1 and f3, 23.exd6 is of course not a good idea. This small nuance is the difference between a better position for White or a slightly better one for Black) 21.♗c3±] **18.♕h3** [This is the critical position. White hopes that Black will now move one of his kingside pawns, when he will get an initiative. For 18.♖ef2 – see 17.♖f2 ♕d8 18.♖ef1]

18...♗f8 [18...g6?! 19.f5 e5 20.♗e3± d5 (20...♗c6 21.♖ef2 h5? 22.fxg6+– Kosteniuk-Khukhashvili, Antakya WCh W 2010) 21.exd5 ♘xd5 (21...♗xd5 22.♖ef2!±; 21...e4? 22.fxg6 hxg6 23.♘xe4 ♘h5 (Krivokapic-B.Ivanovic, Cetinje ch-MNE 2008) 24.♖xf7+–) 22.♘xd5 ♖xd5 (22...♗xd5 23.♗b6! ♕c8 (23...♕xb6 24.fxg6+–) 24.♖xe5±) 23.fxg6 hxg6 24.♖xf7! ♔xf7 25.♖f2+ ♔g8 (25...♗f6 26.♕h7+ ♗e6 27.♕xb7±) 26.♕e6+ ♔h8□ 27.♕xg6 ♖xd3□ 28.cxd3 ♗f8□ 29.♕h5+ ♔g8 30.♗h6±; 18...h6 19.♖e3! (19.♗g1!? (△ e4-e5) 19...e5 (Korneev-Matlakov, St Petersburg 2013) 20.a4!? bxa4 21.♖xa4 ♗f8 22.♘c3± △ 22...d5?! 23.♘xd5 ♘xd5 24.exd5 ♖xd5 25.♗c4±) 19...♗f8 20.♖g3 ♗h8 21.a4!? (21.♘d5 ♗xd5 22.exd5 e5 – this move saves Black's position, which is not possible in the line with 17.♗e3 ♕d8 18.♕h3 h6 19.♖g3 ♗h8 20.♘d5 ♗xd5 21.exd5, because the ♗ is still on e7 there!) 21...bxa4 (21...e5 22.fxe5 dxe5 23.♗e3± (△ ♖xf6; axb5) Alekseenko-Timofeev, Voronezh 2014; 21...b4 22.♘d5! ♗xd5 23.exd5 (23.♗xf6 ♕xf6 24.exd5± – weak a6-pawn) 23...e5 24.fxe5 dxe5 25.♖xf6 exd4 26.♖f1 ♖xd5 27.♗xa6±) 22.♘xa4 e5 23.fxe5 dxe5 (23...♘xe4!? 24.♕g4 (24.♖e3? dxe5 25.♗b6 ♘g5!) 24...dxe5 25.♗b6 ♘g5 (25...♖xd3!? 26.♕xd3 ♕d5∞ – I do not think Black has enough compensation here in the long run) 26.♕h4 ♕e7 27.♗c5± Danin-Simantsev, Prague 2015) 24.♗b6 ♕c8 (Motylev-Maletin, Taganrog 2014; 24...♕e7? 25.♗c5 ♕d8 26.♖xf6 ♖xd3 27.♖xh6+ gxh6 28.cxd3±) 25.♖xf6 ♖xd3□ 26.♖xh6+ gxh6 27.cxd3 ♕xh3! 28.♖xh3 ♗c6∞] **19.a4** [19.e5 dxe5 20.♗xe5 g6 21.f5 ♘h5 22.f6 ♗d6= Renet-Roser, Paris 2015; 19.♖ef2!?. I think we will see this plan more often in the future. If Black plays ...h7-h6 at some point, White lifts his ♖ to the 3rd rank.

19...e5 (19...h6?! 20.♖f3 e5 (this is not very consistent together with 19...h6, but what else? If 20...d5 21.♗xf6 ♕xf6 22.e5 ♕e7 23.f5±) 21.fxe5 dxe5 22.♗e3 ♘h7?! (22...♖d6=) 23.♕g4 (23.♖3f2±) 23...♘g5 Ni Hua-Li Shilong, Xinghua ch-CHN 2009 24.♖3f2 ♖e6 25.a4±) 20.♗e3 (≤ 20.fxe5 dxe5 21.♗e3 (21.♖xf6!? gxf6 22.♗e3≅ (△ ♖f3); 21.♗b6?? ♖xd3–+) 21...♗c8?! (Radjabov-Wang Yue, Beijing Blitz 2014; 21...♖d6=) 22.♖xf6! gxf6 23.♕h5!→) 20...♗e7 (20...♗c8 21.♖f3 ♗e7 (21...♖c7? 22.♕h4 ♗e7 23.♗b6; 21...♖b7 22.f5±; 22.♕h4 ♗e7) 22.♖g3→; 22.f5 d5!⇄) 21.♖f3 ♕c8 (Bok-Van Delft, Wijk aan Zee B 2014) 22.♖g3 ♔h8 (22...♖c7 23.f5 (△ ♗h6) 23...♔h8□ 24.♕h4± ♘xc3 (24...♗xe4 25.f6 ♘xg3+ 26.hxg3 g6 (26...e4 27.♘xe4+–) 27.fxe7+–) 25.bxc3 ♘xe4 26.f6 ♘xg3+ (26...♗xf6 27.♖xf6 ♘xg3+ 28.hxg3 e4 29.♗e2+–) 27.hxg3 e4 28.♗e2+–) 23.fxe5 (23.f5 (△ ♗g5-♕h4-♖h3) 23...d5) 23...dxe5 24.♗g5 ♕d8 25.♕h4 (25.a4 b4 26.♘d5 ♗xd5 27.exd5 e4) 25...♘g8] **19...e5 20.♗f2 b4** [≥ 20...bxa4 21.♖h4 ♗e7 22.♘xa4 exf4 23.♕f5 ♘xe4 24.♘b6 ♖c7 (24...♗xh4! 25.♕xd7 ♕xd7 26.♘xd7 ♗g5∞) 25.♖xe4 g6 26.♗xe7 ♖cxe7 (26...gxf5 27.♗xd8 fxe4 28.♗xc7 exd3 29.♗xd3 ♖e2 30.♖g1+–) 27.♖xe7 ♗xg2+ 28.♔xg2 gxf5 29.♖xe8+ ♕xe8 30.♘d5± Adhiban-Gopal, Sharjah Ach 2014] **21.♘d5 ♘xd5 22.exd5 g6 23.f5** [≥ 23.♗h4 ♗e7 (23...♕c7 24.♗f5±) 24.♗xe7 ♖exe7 25.f5 ♗xd5 26.♗xa6± P.Smirnov-Y.Geller, Samara 2012] **23...♗xd5 24.♖xa6 ♗c6∞ 25.♗c4** [25.♗b5 ♕c8 △ ...d6-d5] **25...♗xa4?!** [25...d5! 26.♗b3 g5⇄ (△ ...f7-f6; ...♗f6)] **26.♗d5≅ ♗g7?!** [26...♕c7⇄] **27.fxg6** [27.♖a1 ♗b5 28.♖e4±] **27...hxg6 28.♗h4 ♕c7 29.♕d3 ♗c6 30.♗e1 ♖b8 31.♖e4**

♗xd5 32.♕xd5 ♕c5 33.♕xc5 dxc5 34.♗f2 ♖d2 35.♗xc5 ♖xc2 36.♖xb4 ♖xb4 37.♗xb4 ♖xb2 38.♗c3 ♖c2 39.♗a1 f5 40.h3 e4 41.♔h2 ♖a2 42.♗xg7 ♔xg7 43.♖b1 g5 44.h4 gxh4 45.♖b6 ♖a3 46.♖e6 ♖g3 47.♖a6 ♖g3 48.♖a5 ♔f6 49.♖a8 ♖g4 50.♖e8 ♔g5 51.♖g8+ ♔f4 52.♖h8 e3 53.♖e8 ♖g7 54.♔h3 ♖g3+ 55.♔h2 h3   0-1

17.♘d1

Istvan Almasi
Jurij Dovzik
Paks 2006 (4)

1.e4 c5 2.♘f3 ♘c6 3.d4 cxd4 4.♘xd4 e6 5.♘c3 ♕c7 6.♗e2 a6 7.0-0 ♘f6 8.♔h1 ♗e7 9.♗e3 0-0 10.f4 d6 11.♕e1 ♘xd4 12.♗xd4 b5 13.a3 ♗b7 14.♕g3 ♖ad8 15.♖ae1 ♖d7 16.♗d3 ♖e8 17.♘d1
[At first sight, a quite mysterious move. Why does White willingly surrender the possibility of a later ♘d5? White is hoping to transfer his queen's ♘ to the kingside, helping the advance there. The other point of the text: in case of ...e6-e5 the d4♗ will be able to stay on the long diagonal (c3), preventing the push .... d6-d5 for a while. Usually the antidote to such manoeuvres is a fast central action by Black, although here this does not work. For a long time I thought that this was the most dangerous plan against the ...♖d7/...♖e8 set-up in the Scheveningen, but it is hard to tell where concretely the d1♘ is going. Exchanging it for the f6♘ (from g4) looks like a waste of time, but it is hard to see where else it can go] 17... g6 [I dislike this move. Black voluntarily weakens his kingside. However there is (still) no direct threat. 17...d5?! was suggested by Tibor Fogarasi in Yearbook 61: 18.♗xf6! (18.e5?! ♘e4⇄) 18...♗xf6 19.e5 ♗d8 20.♘e3 (20.f5?! exf5 21.♘e3 ♖xe5) 20...g6 21.f5±; 17...♘h5 18.♕h3 g6 (18...♘xf4 19.♖xf4 e5 20.♖f2 exd4 21.e5+−) 19.♘e3±; 17...♕d8 is the second most popular move. It has more sense than 17...g6: the ♕ defends the f6♘ and prepares ...♗f8/...g7-g6/...♗g7. 18.♕h3! (18.♘f2 ♘h5 (18...g6 (Ad.

Horvath-Dovzik, Kazincbarcika 2009) 19.♕h3! ♗f8) 19.♕g4 (19.♕f3?! ♘xf4!) 19...g6 20.f5 ♗f6) 18...g6 (≥ 18...♗f8 (Areschenko-Rublevsky, Khanty-Mansiysk World Cup 2009) 19.♗c3 (19.♘e3? ♘xe4) 19...e5 20.♘f2 ♕c8) 19.♘e3! (the ♘ is better placed here than on f2) 19.f5 e5 20.♗c3 and Black won't be able to play ...d6-d5 in the long run. However the c3♗ is misplaced as well: the ♗ belongs on the h4-d8 diagonal in this type of position) 19...♗f8 (Pokazanjev-P.Smirnov, Novokuznetsk 2008; 19...♘xe4? 20.♕g4 ♘f6 21.f5!+−) 20.f5 ♗g7∞; 17...♗d8! is the move I consider to be best.

18.♗c3 (this prophylactic move, known from the game Anand-Ivanchuk, Leon 2008, gives the best chances for White: 18.e5 dxe5 19.♗xe5 ♕c6 (19...♕c8 20.♘e3†) 20.♗e3 (20.f5? (Oleksienko-A. Vovk, Al Ain 2013) 20...♘h5!∓) 20... g6= △ 21.f5 exf5 22.♘xf5 ♖xe5! 23.♖xe5 ♗c7; 18.♘e3 e5 19.♘f5 g6 20.♗c3 ♘h5=) 18...♗c6 19.♕h3 e5 20.♘e3!? g6 21.♘g4 ♘xg4 22.♕xg4 f6∞] 18.♕h3! [18.♘f2 ♘h5 19.♕h3 (19.♕f3? e5 (19...f5∓) 20.fxe5 dxe5 21.♗e3 (21.♘g4 ♗f8) 21...f5∓ Bacrot-David, Paris blitz 2009) 19...♘xf4 20.♘g4! e5 21.♖xf4. In my analysis from 2006, I ended the line here with the assesment '+−', but now I see even here things are not so clear: 21...♗g5! (≤ 21... exf4 22.♕h6 f6 23.♕xf4 ♖f8 24.♖f1±) 22.♗b6 ♕xb6 23.♘h6+ ♗xh6 24.♕xd7 ♗xf4 25.♕xe8+ ♔g7♀; 18.♗c3!? ♘h5 19.♕h3 ♗f6 20.e5 dxe5 21.fxe5 (Anand-Ivanchuk, Leon rapid 2008) 21...♗e7 22.♗e2 (22.♘f2?? ♕f4−+) 22...♘g7 23.♘f2 (△ ♘g4) 23...h5!] 18...e5 19.♗c3 ♗d8 [≥ 19...♘h5 suits the line with 17...g6 better in my opinion: 20.fxe5 (20.f5 ♘f4 21.♕g4 ♗f8) 20... dxe5 21.♗xe5 ♖xd3!? 22.♗xc7 ♖xh3

23.gxh3 f5 24.♘c3 ♗c5♀] 20.f5 d5?! [I thought this should not work, but I reacted wrongly. 20...♗c6 21.♘f2 ♔h8 22.♖e3†; 20...♔h8!? △ ...♖g8] 21.♘f2?! [21.exd5 ♖xd5 (21...♗xd5 22.♘e3 ♗c6 23.♘g4 (23.♕h6!?→) 23...♘xg4 24.♕xg4±) 22.♘e3 ♗d6 23.♘g4 ♗xg4 24.♕xg4±] 21...dxe4 22.♘xe4 ♘xe4 23.♗xe4 ♗xe4 [Unfortunately for White, he had to exchange his d3♗ too, and without it there are much less threats to Black's kingside] 24.♖xe4 ♖d5= 25.♕f3 ♕d7 26.h3 gxf5 27.♕xf5 ♕xf5 28.♖xf5   ½-½

17.a4

Peter Leko
Wang Yue
Beijing rapid 2014 (6)

1.e4 c5 2.♘f3 e6 3.d4 cxd4 4.♘xd4 ♘c6 5.♘c3 ♕c7 6.♗e2 a6 7.0-0 ♘f6 8.♗e3 ♗e7 9.f4 d6 10.♕e1 0-0 11.♕g3 ♘xd4 12.♗xd4 b5 13.a3 ♗b7 14.♔h1 ♖ad8 15.♖ae1 ♖d7 16.♗d3 ♖e8 17.a4!? [The latest development: White is going to play on the queenside. As we saw in the notes to Negi-Adhiban, this a2-a4 plan comes into consideration after 17.♖e2 ♕d8 18.♕h3 ♗f8 too. 17.e5 dxe5 18.♗xe5.

18...♕d8 was the original idea of the inventor: Black prevents the ambitious move f4-f5. The importance of the ...♖d7/...♖e8 set-up lies rather in the option of ...♗e7-d8 and a quick ... e6-e5 nowadays. 19.♘e4 (19.f5 ♗d6! and Black has a comfortable game here, Haba-Ad. Horvath, Austria Bundesliga B 2003/04) 19...♘h5 (≤ 19...g6 20.♘xf6+ ♗xf6 21.♗xf6 ♕xf6 22.f5 ♕d4 (22...♕xb2?) 23.fxe6 fxe6 24.♖xe6!± R.Prasanna-A.

Sokolov, Metz 2010) 23.fxe6 fxe6 24.h4↑)
20.♕e3 (20.♕h3 g6 21.♖e3? (21.b4!?
△ ♘c5) 21...f5! 22.♘c3 ♗c5 23.♖ee1∓
Borocz-Jo.Horvath, Solymar rapid 1996) ≥
20...♕c8 (aimed against ♘c5, with the
idea of ...g7-g6 next) 20...♘f6? 21.♗xf6
♗xf6? (21...gxf6 22.f5±) 22.♘c5± Ni
Hua-Yakovenko, Nizhnij Novgorod 2007;
20...g6 21.♘c5 ♗xc5 22.♕xc5 ♘f6 and
although the position is equal, White has
the bishop pair and no weaknesses. Black
plays on the light squares, but still such a
position between human players would be
assessed as '±'; 22...♕h4!? A.Vovk-E.
Hansen, Hoogeveen 2014) 21.♗e2 (21.
b4!? f5 (21...g6=) 22.♘c5 ♗xc5 23.bxc5
♗d5⇄ Markovic-Iotov, Valjevo 2010)
21...♗xe4 22.♕xe4 ♘f6 23.♗xf6?!
(23.♕f3! △ 23...♕xc2 24.♖c1 ♕g6
25.♕c6⩲) 23...♗xf6∓ Andreev-
Maletin, Nizhnij Tagil 2008; 17.♕h3.
Not much happened in this line since
Tibor Fogarasi wrote his Survey: 17...e5
18.fxe5 (18.♗e3 ♗d8 (regarded as the
best move) 19.a4!?N (I.Almasi; 19.♘d5
♗xd5 20.exd5 e4) 19...bxa4 (19...b4
20.♘d5 ♗xd5 (20...♘xd5 21.exd5 g6
22.f5→) 21.exd5 – weak a6-pawn) 20.fxe5
(20.♘xa4?! exf4!) 20...dxe5 21.♘xa4)
18...dxe5 19.♘d5 ♗xd5□ (19...♕d6??
(Gaston-Antal, Paris 2000) 20.♗xe5!
♕xe5 21.♘xf6+ ♗xf6 22.♕xd7+−)
20.exd5 ♖xd5 (20...exd4? 21.♖xf6 g6
22.♖xf7!+−) 21.♗c3 ♗d8 (21...g6∓
Efimenko-Movsesian, St Petersburg rapid
2012) 22.♖f5 g6 23.♖g3 ♖e6 24.♗xe5
Paragua-Yakovenko, Tromsø 2013
24...♕c5! 25.♗xf6 ♖xe1+ 26.♕xe1
gxf5 27.♕g3+ ♔f8 28.♗c3 a5!] **17...b4**
[17...bxa4 is not too logical. The a6-pawn
becomes permanently weak, and if White
manages to consolidate the situation
in the centre (e.g. with c2-c4), he will
withdraw his ♘ to c3 and start his typical
kingside play. Also an unpleasant threat
is ...♘b6-c4. From this point of view the
only logical follow-up to 17...bxa4 is 18...
d5: 18.♘xa4 d5 19.e5 (19.exd5 ♗xd5
(19...♖xd5!? 20.♗e5 ♕d8 21.♘c3
♖d7 – 19...♗xd5 20.♗e5 ♕d8 21.♘c3
♗b7) 20.♗e5 (20.♘xa6? ♗xg2+ (△
...♖xd4)) 20...♕d8 21.♘c3 (21.f5!? ♗c6
22.♘c5 (22.fxe6 ♖xd3 23.exf7+ ♔xf7
24.cxd3 ♗xa4) 22...♘h5 23.♕f2 ♗xc5
24.♕xc5 ♕a8∞) 21...♗b7 22.♘e4
(△ ♗xf6-♘c5) 22.f5 ♗d6!=) 22...♘h5

(22...h6 23.♖e3→ ♘h5 24.♕h3; 22...
g6 23.♗xf6 ♗xf6 24.♘xf6+ (24.♘c5?
♗h4) 24...♕xf6 25.f5±) 23.♕e3 (with
the b5- and a2-pawns on the board,
Black should not worry here. But the
a6-pawn becomes weak, so it gives
chances for White) 23...♘f6 (23...♕a8
24.f5!; 23...g6 24.♘c5 ♗xc5 25.♕xc5)
24.♗xf6 gxf6 25.f5 ♔h8∞) 19...♘e4 (in
the annotations to Navara-Maksimenko
we could see a similar position already
after 17.♖e3 g6 18.♖ef3 d5 19.e5 ♘e4
20.♕e1, where Black played 20...b4
21.axb4 ♗xb4 in the game Areschenko-
Ftacnik, 2010. Compared to that game,
here White's queen and rook are better
placed. The e1 ♖ can press the a6-pawn
from a1) 20.♕e3± ♘c6 ((Asgarizadeh-
Shankland, Abu Dhabi 2015) 20...
f5? 21.exf6 ♗xf6 22.♗xe4 ♗xd4
23.♗xh7+±; 20...g6?! (Idani-Le Quang
Liem, Al Ain 2015) 21.♖a1 f5 22.exf6
♗xf6 23.c3±; 23.♗xe4?! ♗xd4 24.♕xd4
dxe4) 21.♖a1± △ c2-c3, b2-b4]

18.♘a2 [18.♘d1!? is an interesting
alternative here. The game is similar to the
one after 17.♘d1, but the insertion of the
moves a2-a4/b5-b4 rather profits White,
I think. He can fix the queenside with
b2-b3, keeping open a route for the retreat
of the d4♗. And later, the c4-square
can be a nice outpost for White's ♘ too.
Of course 18.♘a2 looks more logical
and forcing) 18...g6 Stukopin-Dragun,
Moscow 2014] **18...♕a5** [18...a5 19.c3
d5?! (19...bxc3 20.♘xc3± [b5]) 20.♗xf6
♗xf6 21.e5 ♗e7 22.f5± (Gao Rui-
Wang Yue, Zhongshan zt 2014); 18...d5
19.♗xf6 ♗xf6 20.e5 ♗d8 21.♘xb4 ♕a5
22.c3 d4 23.f5± (Alexeev-Stachowiak,
Wroclaw rapid 2014)] **19.♘c1** [19.
b3!?N d5?! (19...♗d8!? 20.♕e3 △
♕d2) 20.♗xf6 ♗xf6 21.e5 ♗d8 22.f5!
exf5 23.♗xf5 ♖de7 24.♕h3 (24.♕d3!

g6? (24...♔h8 25.e6) 25.e6!+−) 24...g6
25.♗d7 (25.e6) 25...♖f8 26.e6 f5⇄ (C.
Balogh-Yakovenko, Yerevan Ech 2014
26...♕c5!?∞)] **19...♕xa4** [19...♕h5
20.♘b3 ♕g6 (20...♖c8!? Schroeder-
Dragnev, Karpacz jr 2015) 21.♕h3 ♕g4
(21...♕h5 22.♕xh5 ♘xh5 23.♘a5±)
22.♕xg4 ♘xg4 23.♘a5± Giri-Hou Yifan,
Biel 2014] **20.♕h3 h6?!** [≥ 20...g6∞]
21.♘b3±

[In spite of his extra pawn, Black faces a
tough task here. White threatens e4-e5
sometimes, when he can take back with
the pawn on e5, since the b3♘ protects
the d4♗ now. Also White can play on both
wings: he can play ♖a1-♘a5-♘xb7 and
pick up the a6-pawn, and he can target the
h6-pawn via ♖f3-♖g3 as well] **21...♕c6**
[≥ 21...♗a8 22.e5 dxe5 23.fxe5 ♘h7
24.♖a1 ♕c6 25.♖xa6±] **22.♘a5 ♕c7
23.♘xb7 ♕xb7 24.♖e3!** [24.c3?! bxc3
25.bxc3 (△ 26.e5 dxe5 27.fxe5); 24.e5 dxe5
25.♗xe5⩲ △ f4-f5. In case of 20...g6, f4-f5
would be less of a threat to Black. 25.fxe5
♖xd4 26.exf6 ♗xf6 27.♖xf6 ♖xd3 28.cxd3
gxf6 29.♕xh6 ♕c7=] **24...♗d8?**
[24...♔h8 25.♖g3 (△ 26.f5 e5 27.♗e3;
26.♖ff3/27.♖xg7; 25.e5 dxe5 26.fxe5 ♘h7
(26...♖xd4?! 27.exf6±) 27.♖xf7 ♖xd4
(27...♘g5 28.♕h5 ♘xf7 29.♕xf7+−)
28.♕xh6 gxh6 29.♖xh7+ ♔g8 30.♖g3+
♔f8 31.♖hg7!! (31.♖h8+ ♔f7 32.♖h7+=)
31...♖h4 32.♖g8+ ♔e7 33.♖3g7+ ♔d8
34.♖xe8+ ♔xe8 35.♖xb7±) 25...♖g8
(25...♗f8?? 26.♗xf6 gxf6 27.♕g4+−)
26.♖ff3 △ ♖g5/♖fg3; 26.f5 e5□ 27.♗e3
♔h7] **25.♖g3** [25.e5 dxe5 26.fxe5 ♘h7
27.♕g4±] **25...♔h8?!** [25...♔f8
26.♖ff3 (△ ♖xg7; 26.e5 ♘e4!) 26...e5
27.fxe5 ♖xe5□ (27...dxe5 28.♗c5+ ♗e7
29.♖xg7 ♗xc5 30.♖xf6+−) 28.♗xe5±]
26.♖ff3? [△ 27.♖xg7; 26.f5! e5
27.♗e3 ♖g8 (27...♔h7 28.♖xg7+ ♔xg7
29.♕xh6+ ♔g8 30.♖f3+−; 27...♖g8

28.f6!! ♗xf6 29.♖xf6 ♘xf6 30.♗xh6+−)
28.♗xh6 gxh6 29.♕xh6+ ♔h7 30.f6 (△
♖g7; ♖h3) 30...♖g6 (30...♖xg3 31.hxg3
♗xf6 32.♖xf6 ♔g8 33.♖f5+−) 31.♕h5
♖xg3 32.hxg3 △ ♖f4] **26...e5□ 27.♗e3
♘h7** [27...♘g8!= (without 26.♖ff3 Black
would have had no time for this move,
because the g7-pawn is hanging and after
the insertion of 26.f5 e5 27.♗e3, 27...♘g8
is not possible either in view of 28.f6!!)
28.♗xa6?? ♕xa6 29.♕xd7 ♕a1+
30.♗g1 ♗b6 and the e8♖ is hanging,
but not with check, as would have been

the case after 27...♘h7] **28.♗xa6** [28.f5
f6!; 28...♗f6? 29.♗xh6!+−] **28...♕c6⇄
29.♗c4?!** ♗f6 [29...exf4! 30.♖xf4
(30.♗d5? ♕a4−+; 30.♗xf4? d5!∓)
30...♘g5! 31.♗d5□ ♕a4 32.♖f1 ♗xe3
33.♖xe3 ♘f6∓] **30.♗d5 ♕c8 31.♖f1
♖c7 32.♕xc8 ♖exc8 33.♗b3
exf4 34.♗xf4 ♗e5 35.♖xe5 dxe5
36.♖d3 ♘f6 37.♖e1 ♔g8 38.♔g1
♘d7 39.♖ed1 ♘c5 40.♖d8+
♖xd8 41.♖xd8+ ♔h7 42.♗d5
♘a4 43.♖b8 ♘xb2 44.♗b3 ♘d1
45.♖xb4 ♔g6 46.c4 ♘c3 47.♗c2**

♘e2+ 48.♔f2 ♘d4 49.♗a4 ♘e6
50.♔e3 ♔g5 51.g3 ♘c5 52.♗d1
♘e6 53.h4+ ♔f6 54.♗g4 ♘c5
55.♖b6+ ♔e7 56.♖b5 g6 57.♗d1
♔d6 58.♗c2 ♖b7 59.♔d2 ♖xb5
60.cxb5 ♘d7 61.♗b3 f6 62.♗f7
g5 63.♔e3 ♔c5 64.♗e8 ♘b6
65.♔f3 ♘c4 66.♔g4 ♘d6 67.♗c6
gxh4 68.gxh4 ♔b6 69.♔h5 f5
70.exf5 ♘xf5 71.♗d7 ♘g3+
72.♔xh6 e4 73.♔g6 e3 74.♗g4
♔xb5 75.♔g5 ♔c5 76.♔f4 e4
77.♗xe2 ♘xe2+   ½-½

Exercise 1

position after 24...h7xg6

White is clearly better, however the
presence of the opposite-coloured
bishops gives Black chances. Does
White have anything more here?
(solution on page 245)

Exercise 2

position after 18...♗e7-f8

Black looks fine, he has just played
18...♗f8. Is everything really OK
for Black?
(solution on page 245)

Exercise 3

position after 27...♘f6-g8

Black has played 27...♘g8,
preventing the ♗xh6 sacrifice. Is
his king safe now?
(solution on page 245)

Sicilian Defence

A Straightforward Option in the Rauzer

by Das Debashis and Mikheil Mchedlishvili

1.	e4	c5
2.	♘f3	♘c6
3.	d4	cxd4
4.	♘xd4	♘f6
5.	♘c3	d6
6.	♗g5	e6
7.	♕d2	a6
8.	♘xc6	

In the Rauzer Sicilian there are many extensively analysed lines. It's always good to surprise your opponent, which is why the line starting with 8.♘xc6 deserves attention. This move was already played by GMs Morozevich and Hovhannisyan, but I (Das Debashis) came to know about it when the Indian IM S.L Narayan played it in the Asian Continental. He told me that 8.♘xc6 was an interesting and less known variation. I decided to try the line later this

year in the Abu Dhabi Masters against my fellow-countryman Abhijeet Gupta. After my game against Abhijeet, Tigran Gharamian also played it.
It's hard to say at this point if this line is stronger or weaker than more popular lines, as there are not enough games with it. But it is definitely interesting. After 8...bxc6 9.0-0-0 Black is at a crossroads.

The most popular move 9...♗e7 may be not the best here. After taking on f6 and 10...gxf6, White follows a simple plan: play ♗c4-b3, f2-f4, ♖he1 to stop ...d6-d5, and then White will push f4-f5, which will be very unpleasant for Black. In all the games that we will see, the positions were complicated after taking on f6, but easier to play for White.

Lars Ootes

We consider 9...d5 to be probably the better choice, when both sides have lots of options to continue, but it's not yet clear what continuation is best. The positions are often similar to another Rauzer line: 8.0-0-0 h6 9.♘xc6 bxc6 10.♗f4, but an important point is that Black's position has not yet been weakened by the move ...h7-h6, which often creates a target for White's attack.

Conclusion
As a rule, we consider the 8.♘xc6 line very much worth trying, and we are expecting more games with it.

Robert Hovhannisyan
Ticia Gara

Doha 2014 (1)

1.e4 c5 2.♘f3 d6 3.d4 cxd4
4.♘xd4 ♘f6 5.♘c3 ♘c6 6.♗g5 e6
7.♕d2 a6 8.♘xc6 bxc6 9.0-0-0
♗e7 10.♗xf6 gxf6 11.♗c4 ♖b8!?
12.♗b3 ♛b6 [12...0-0!? is my
suggestion:

13.♖he1 (13.f4 d5 14.f5 ♔h8 (14...♗d6
15.fxe6 fxe6 16.exd5 cxd5 17.♘xd5 ♗e5
18.♕e2 exd5 19.♖xd5 ♗xb2+ 20.♔b1)
15.♖he1 a5 (15...♖g8 16.g3 a5 17.♔b1
♕c7 18.♕h6; 15...♗d6 16.♘a4 ♗e5
17.♘c5 a5 18.♗d3 ♗c7 19.g3 ♖g8
20.♔b1 e5 21.♕h6 ♖g7 22.g4 ♗b6
23.exd5 cxd5 24.g5 ♖xg5 25.♘xe5 fxe5
26.♖xd5 ♕g8 27.♖dxe5 ♗a6 28.a4±
♖g1) 16.♔b1 ♗d6∞) 13...♔h8 14.♖e3
♖g8 15.♖h3 ♖xg2 16.♕h6 ♖g7 17.♖dd3
♗d7 18.♖dg3 ♕g8∓.

White's bishop is doing absolutely
nothing; 12...d5 13.♖he1 0-0 (13...a5
14.exd5 cxd5 15.♕h6 ♗d7 16.♘xd5
exd5 17.♕xf6 ♖f8 (17...♖g8 18.♗xd5)
18.♖xd5) 14.♕h6 f5 15.f4 ♔h8 16.exf5
♗f6 17.♘e4 ♗g7 18.♕h5→; 12...♕a5
13.♖he1 ♗d7 14.f4 ♖g8 15.f5 ♕e5
16.g3 c5 17.♕h6±; 12...♖g8 13.f4 d5

14.f5 ♔f8 15.♕h6+ ♖g7 16.♖he1 ♗b7
17.fxe6 fxe6 18.exd5] 13.f4 c5 14.♕e2
[White is better and has the easier game
here] 14...a5

15.f5 h5 16.a4 ♔f8 17.♘b5 ♗d7
18.♗c4 ♗xb5 19.♗xb5 ♖h7
20.♖hf1 ♖d8 21.♗f3 d5 22.e5 fxe5
23.f6 e4 24.fxe7+ ♔xe7 25.♖f4 c4
26.♕e1 f6 27.♕h4 ♔f8 28.♖xe4
♖c8 29.♖xd5   1-0

Lars Ootes
Jelmer Jens

Netherlands tt 2014/15 (4)

1.e4 c5 2.♘f3 d6 3.d4 cxd4
4.♘xd4 ♘f6 5.♘c3 ♘c6 6.♗g5 e6
7.♕d2 a6 8.♘xc6 bxc6 9.0-0-0
♗e7 10.♗xf6 gxf6 11.♗c4 ♖b8
12.♖he1 ♕b6 13.♗b3 h5

14.♖e3?! [14.f4] 14...♗b7?! [14...d5
15.♘a4 ♕c7] 15.♕e2 ♕a5 16.f4
♔f8 17.♖h3 h4 18.g4 d5 19.♕e1
♕c7 20.♘e2 dxe4 21.♖xh4+ ♖g8
22.♕c3 ♖b5 23.♕h3 ♗d6 24.♔b1
♔e7 25.♖h8 ♖xh8 26.♕xh8 ♗d7
27.♕h6 c5 28.g5 fxg5 29.♕xg5+
♔e8 30.♕g8+ ♔e7 31.f5 ♗e5
32.fxe6 ♗xe6 33.♗xe6 ♖xb2+
34.♔c1 ♔xe6 35.♕e8+ ♔f6
36.♖f1+ ♔g5 37.♕g8+ ♔h6
38.♖xf7   1-0

S.L. Narayanan
Ishaq Saeed

Al Ain 2015 (8)

1.e4 c5 2.♘f3 d6 3.d4 cxd4
4.♘xd4 ♘f6 5.♘c3 ♘c6 6.♗g5 e6
7.♕d2 a6 8.♘xc6 bxc6 9.0-0-0
♗e7 10.♗xf6 gxf6 11.♗c4 h5
12.f4 ♕a5 13.♗b3 ♖b8

14.♖hf1 [14.♖he1] 14...♗d7?! [14...
f5 gives more chances for counterplay]
15.♔b1 ♖b7 16.f5 ♕e5 17.♕d3±
a5 18.g3 ♖g8 19.♖f4 ♖g4 20.fxe6
fxe6 21.♖a6 ♖c7 22.♘a4 ♕b5
23.♕a8+ ♖c8 24.♕a7 ♖b8
25.♘c5 ♗c8 26.a4 ♕b6 27.♕xb6
♖xb6 28.♗xe6 ♖xf4 29.gxf4
dxc5 30.♗xc8 c4 31.c3 ♗a3
32.♔a2 ♗c5 33.♗e6 ♖b7 34.♖e1
♖e7 35.f5 ♗d6 36.♖g1 ♔d8
37.h4 ♗e5 38.♔b1 ♔c7 39.♖g2
♔d6 40.♗xc4 ♗c5 41.♗e6 ♖e8
42.♔c2 ♖d8 43.♗f7 ♖d7 44.♗e6
♖d8 45.♖g6 ♖h8

46.♗g8 ♗f4 47.♔d3 ♗e5 48.♖g7
♗d6 49.♔e2 ♗e5 50.♔f3 ♗d6
51.♔e3 ♗e5 52.♖g2 ♗d6 53.♔f3
♗e5 54.♖g6 ♗h2 55.♔e2 ♗e5
56.♔d3 ♗f4 57.♔c2 ♗e5 58.♔b3
♗f4 59.♔a3 ♗c1 60.e5 fxe5 61.f6

♗h6 62.b4+ axb4+ 63.cxb4+ ♔b6
64.a5+ ♔c7 65.f7 ♗f8 66.♖e6
♗g7 67.♖e7+ ♔d6 68.♖e8 ♔c7
69.♔b3 e4 70.f8♕ ♗xf8 71.♖xf8
♖h6 72.♖e8 ♖g6 73.♗h7 ♖g3+
74.♔c2 e3 75.♔d3 c5 76.b5 ♖g7
77.b6+ ♔d6 78.♗e4 c4+ 79.♔xe3
♖g3+ 80.♔d4 ♖b3 81.b7 ♔d7
82.b8♕ ♖d3+ 83.♗xd3   1-0

Das Debashis
Abhijeet Gupta
Abu Dhabi 2015 (9)

**1.e4 c5 2.♘f3 d6 3.d4 cxd4
4.♘xd4 ♘f6 5.♘c3 ♘c6 6.♗g5 e6
7.♕d2 a6 8.♘xc6 bxc6 9.0-0-0
♗e7** [During my home analysis I didn't
consider 9...♕a5. After the round,
Abhijeet said maybe it was interesting.
I came up with 10.e5!? during the post
mortem, but 10.♗c4 is stronger:

10.♗c4! (10.e5!? dxe5 11.♗xf6 (11.♘e4
♕xd2+ 12.♖xd2 ♗e7 13.♘d6+ ♗xd6
14.♖xd6 ♗b7 15.f3 ♔e7 16.♖d2 c5;
16...♖hd8 17.♗d3) 11...gxf6 12.g4
(12.♗e2 h5 13.♔b1 ♗e7 14.♗f3 ♔f8
15.♗xc6 ♖b8↑) 12...♖b8 (12...♗e7
13.♗g2 0-0 14.♕h6) 13.♗g2 ♗e7
(13...♗a3 14.♘a4 ♕xd2+ 15.♖xd2
♗e7 16.♗xc6+ ♔f8∞) 14.♗xc6+ ♔f8
15.♕h6+ ♔g8 16.g5 f5 17.♕h5 ♗b7)
10...♗b7 (is not so logical as it blocks
the b-file: 10...d5 11.exd5→; 10...♗e7
11.♔b1 ♖b8 (11...d5? 12.♘xd5! ♕xd2
13.♘xf6+ ♗xf6 14.♖xd2+-; 11...0-0
12.♘d5) 12.♗b3± (12.♗f4, to provoke
12...e5, and then ♗g5/f2-f4/♗xf6/
f4-f5/♖he1-e3 is typical) 12...h6 13.♗f4
e5 14.♗e3) 11.♖he1 ♘d7 12.f4 ♕b4
13.♕e2 h6 14.♗h4 g5 15.fxg5 ♗e7
(15...♘e5 16.♗b3 hxg5 17.♗xg5 ♖xh2
18.♗f4 ♖h7 19.♕f2 (19.♗xe5 dxe5
20.a3 ♕c5 21.♔b1 ♖d8 22.♖xd8+ ♔xd8
23.♗c4 a5 24.♖d1+ ♔e8 25.♘a4 ♕e7

26.♕d2) 19...♕a5) 16.a3 ♕a5 17.♗g3
♕xg5+ 18.♔b1 ♘e5 19.♗b3 0-0
20.♕f1 ♖ad8 21.♗f4 ♕f6 22.♗e3 ♔g7
23.♘e2 ♖h8 24.♖g3+ ♔f8 25.♗xe5
♕xe5 26.♖f3 ♖h7 27.♘f4 ♔g8 28.♖g3+
♖g7 and ½-½ after 20 more moves,
Sarbok-Bu Xiangzhi, Reykjavik 2000.
When I analysed this game with my coach,
Mikheil Mchedlishvili, he suggested 9...
d5!. In the beginning I didn't really believe
in it, but after spending a long time on the
move I feel that it's really interesting and
deserves serious attention. Mchedlishvili
plays 1.e4 c5 2.♘f3 e6 3.d4 cxd4 4.♘xd4
♘c6 5.♘c3 a6 6.♘xc6 bxc6 on the
black side in many games. He said he
had studied this structure and he felt the
move 9...d5 is strong enough (it is also
played by Avrukh): 10.♕e3 (10.g4!? ♗e7
(10...♖b8 11.♗f4 ♖b4 12.f3 (12.exd5
cxd5 13.a3 ♖b6 14.g5 ♘d7 15.♖e1 ♗e7
16.h4 ♗b7 17.♘a4 ♖c6 18.♔b1 0-0
19.♖h3) 12...♕b6 13.♗e3 ♕b8 14.g5
♘d7 15.b3 a5 16.h4 a4 17.a3; 10...♗d6)
11.♖g1 (11.e5? ♕xg4 12.♗xe7 ♕xe7
13.♖g1 ♘xe5 14.♖xg7 ♘g6∓) 11...0-0-0∞;
10.e5 h6 11.♗h4 g5 12.♗g3

12...♘d7∞ (12...♘h5?! 13.♘e4! ♗e7
(13...♗xg3?! 14.♘f6+ ♔xf6 (14...♔e7
15.♕b4+) 15.exf6 ♘xh1 16.♗d3
♘xf2 17.♕xf2+-; 13...♖b8 14.♕c3)
14.♕c3±; too many square weaknesses)
13.h4 g4! (13...♗g7 14.♗e2! (a simple
developing move) 14.hxg5 hxg5 15.♗e2
♖xh1 (15...♗b7 16.♖xh8+ ♗xh8 17.♖h1
♗g7 18.♗h5 ♗xe5 19.♖h7 ♕f6 20.♕d4
♘d7 21.♕xf6 ♗xf6 22.♗h5 0-0-0 23.♗xf7
e5 24.♗e6 ♔c7 25.♗xd7 ♖xd7 26.♖h6!
(26.♖xd7+ ♔xd7) 26...♗g7 27.♖g6 ♔d8
28.♘a4± ; 15...♘xe5 16.♖xh8+ ♗xh8
17.♘e4 ♖b8 18.♖h1 ♗g7 19.♖h7+-)
16.♖xh1 ♘xe5 17.♕d4 (17.♖h7 ♕f6
18.♕d4 ♘g6 19.♕b6 ♗d7 20.♗b8 ♘f8
21.♖h5 ♕d8 22.♗c7 ♕f6) 17...♕f6

18.♕b6 ♕d8 19.♕xd8+ ♔xd8 20.♖h7
♗f6 21.♘a4 ♗d7 22.♘b6 ♖a7 23.♗xe5
♗xe5 24.♖xf7 ♘d4=; 14.♖e1 ♖b8 (14...
c5 15.hxg5 hxg5 16.♖xh8+ ♗xh8 17.f4
gxf4 18.♕xf4 ♕e7 (18...♗b7 19.♕h6)
19.♘xd5 exd5 20.♕h6 ♗xe5 (20...♕f8
21.♕c6+-) 21.♗xe5 ♘xe5 22.♕h8+
♔d7 23.♖xe5 ♔d6 24.♕e8+ ♔c7
25.♕xf7+ ♔c6 26.♕e7 ♗d7 27.♗b1!+-)
15.hxg5 hxg5 16.♖xh8+ ♗xh8 17.f4
♕b6 18.b3 gxf4 19.♕xf4 ♕b4 20.♕h6
♕f8 21.♕h5 ♗g7∞ 22.♗e2 (22.♗d3
♘c5) 22...♕h8) 14...♘xe5 (14...♗b7
15.hxg5 hxg5 16.♖xh8+ ♗xh8 17.♖h1
♗g7 18.♖h5 ♗f8 (18...♘xe5 19.♖h7
♕f6 (19...♗f6 20.♗h5) 20.♕d4 ♘d7
21.♕xf6 ♗xf6 22.♗h5 0-0-0 23.♖xf7
(though Black has a strong centre, his
pieces lack coordination. Easy play for
White) 23...♖f8 24.♖xf8+ ♘xf8 25.♗d6
♘d7 26.♗g4 e5 27.♘a4 ♔d8 28.f3±
Black must tread carefully here) 19.f4!→)
15.hxg5 (15.♕d4 ♕c7 16.♘a4 f5 17.hxg5
hxg5 18.♖xh8+ ♗xh8) 15...♕xg5 (15...
hxg5 16.♖xh8+ ♗xh8 17.♘e4) 16.♗f4
♕f5 17.g4 ♕g6 18.♕e3 ♘d7 19.♖h5
♘f6 20.♖h3↑; 20.♗d3 ♕xg4 21.♗e2
♕g6 22.♖hh1!? ♘d7 23.♖hg1 ♕f6 –
centre pawns!!) 14.♗e2 (14.♕e2 ♖g8
15.♕d3 ♖b8 16.♕h7 ♖g7 17.♕h8
(17.♕xh6 ♕a5→; in all the variations
I tried to keep the bishop on b3. Here
White's king is at risk) 17...♕a5 18.♖d3
d4 (18...c5!→) 19.♖xd4 ♖xb2 20.♔d2
♘b6 21.♗d3 ♕d5 22.♖c4 ♗b7 23.♖e1
♖b4 24.♖ee4 c5 25.a3 ♖xc4 26.♖xc4
♘b6∓ and 0-1 after 25 more moves in
Morozevich-Avrukh, Turin 2006; 14.f4 gxf3
15.gxf3 ♖b8; 14.♔b1 ♖b8 15.♔a1 ♕a5
and 16...♖xb2 is a threat) 14...♖b8!→;
(sacrificing the g4-pawn) 14...♖g8 15.♕d3
♗g7; 10.♗f4!? to control the b8-square;
10.♗e2) 10...♗e7 11.♕g3 (11.e5?
♘g4-+) 11...0-0 12.♗e2

12...a5 with the idea ...a5-a4-a3 and also ...♝a6 13.h4 ♔h8 14.h5 h6 15.♗f4 ♗a6]
10.♗xf6 gxf6 11.♗c4 [White's plan is very simple: ♗c4/♗b3/f2-f4/♖he1/f4-f5. One idea is to lift the rook to e3 for a kingside attack, or White can play ♖d3 to sac an exchange on d6 for positional compensation; ♘e2-d4 or ♘f4] **11...♕a5** [11...d5?? 12.♗b3 (12. exd5 cxd5 13.♘xd5 exd5 14.♗xd5 ♖a7 15.♗c6+ ♗d7 16.♕e3 ♕c8 (16...♕b8 17.♖xd7 ♖xd7 18.♖d1) 17.♖he1 ♗xc6 18.♕xa7 ♗b7 19.♖xe7+ ♔xe7 20.♕e3+ ♗e4 21.f3+−) 12...♗d7 13.f4 0-0 14.g4 ♔h8 15.♔b1 ♖g8 16.h3 a5 17.♗a4 ♖b8 18.b3 ♗b4 19.♕d3 ♖b7 20.f5 ♕b8 21.exd5 cxd5 22.♖xd7 ♖xd7 23.♘e4 ♕e5 24.♕d4 ♕xd4 25.♖xd4 ♔g7 26.c4 ♖gd8 27.fxe6 fxe6 28.cxd5 ♖xd5 29.♖xd5 ♖xd5= Jursevskis-Potter, Vancouver 1957; 11...♖b8 is analysed in the Hovhannisyan game] **12.♖he1** [I was playing all the moves very fast, and while he was thinking I felt 12...f5 interesting. White must be precise in his move order, otherwise Black's centre will be really strong, and it will be difficult to break through] **12...♖b8** [12...f5!? 13.♕h6 (13.♕f4 ♖g8 14.♔b1; 13.exf5 ♕xf5; 13.♕d4!?) 0-0!? (13...e5 14.♕d3 fxe4 15.♕xe4 ♕c7; 15...♗d7 16.f4 ♖b8 (16...♖c8; 16...f5 17.♕e3) 17.♔b3; 13...♖g8 14.exf5 ♕xf5 15.♗d3! ♕f6 (15...♕h5 16.♗xh7 ♖xg2 17.♗e4+−) 16.♕b6! ♗d7 17.g3 d5 18.f4 ♗d6? 19.♘xd5+−) 14.♕d3 e5 15.♕e3 f4 16.♕e2 ♔h8 17.g3 f5 18.gxf4 fxe4 13... f4 14.e5! d5 15.♔b3] **13.f4 h5** [13...f5 is also very risky: 14.♕d4 ♖g8 15.g3! ♗d7 (15...♗b4 16.exf5 ♕xb2+ 17.♔d2; 15...fxe4 16.♕xe4; 15...c5 16.♕d3 fxe4 17.♘xe4 ♗b6 18.♘c3 ♗f6 19.f5 ♕b4 20.♗b3 c4 21.fxe6 ♗xe6 22.♕xc4 ♕xc4 23.♗xc4 ♗xc3 24.bxc3 ♔e7 25.♖e4±) 16.exf5 ♕xf5 17.♕a7] **14.♗b3** [Up to here Black has made all the logical moves, but I think that White has easy play] **14...♕c5** [14...f5 15.exf5 (15.e5 d5) 15...♕xf5 16.♘e4 d5 17.♕c3 ♕xf4+ 18.♔b1 ♖g8 19.g3 (19.♕xc6+ ♗d7) 19...♕c7 20.♘f6+ ♗xf6 21.♕xf6→ with the idea c2-c4, opening the position. After 14...h4 a sample variation is 15.♔b1 ♖g8 16.f5 ♕e5 17.♕f2 ♖xh2 18.♕a7 ♖b7 19.♕xa6 ♖c7 20.♕b6 ♗d8 21.e5!+−]
15.f5 e5

16.♔b1?! [A careless move. 16.a3!± is a prophylactic move, with the idea ♔b1/♖e3/♖d3/♘a4 and c2-c4-c5: 16...d5 17.exd5 cxd5 18.♕xd5 ♕xd5 19.♘xd5. During the game I was considering 16.♖e3!?, but I felt that Black can somehow equalize: 16...♗f8 17.♘a4 ♕xe3 18.♕xe3 ♗h6 19.♕xh6 ♖xh6 20.♖d6 ♗b4! 21.♘c5 ♗b6 22.♗c4 ♗e7 23.♖d2 ♖h8 24.c3 ♖d8 25.♖xd8 ♔xd8 26.♗xf7 h4 27.b4 a5 28.a3 ♖b8 29.♗c4 ♔e7; 29...axb4 30.cxb4] **16...♖b4!** [My opponent played this move quite fast (like all the other moves) and to be honest I had missed the text. I didn't want to exchange my pair of rooks because my plans were very simple and deadly: ♖e3/♖ed3/♘a4 and c2-c4-c5] **17.♕e2** [17.♖e3 ♖d4 18.♖d3 ♖xd3 19.cxd3; 19.♕xd3] **17...♖d4 18.♘a4?!** [18.♖xd4!] (engine). During the game I felt that after exchanging one rook I would lose my initiative. But I was wrong: 18...exd4 (18...♕xd4 19.♖d1 ♕c5 20.♘a4 ♕a7 21.♕c4+−) 19.♘d1 ♕e5 (19...♕b5 20.♗c4 ♕e5 21.g3 h4 22.♕f2 hxg3 23.♕d3 ♕a5 24.hxg3 ♔f8 25.♕f2±) 20.♘c4 ♗xf5 21.♘xc6+ ♗d7 22.♕a6 0-0 23.g3±; 18.♖xd3 19.cxd3. I felt that this structure was quite interesting, but my main plan was not to exchange rooks; 18.♖c1!?] **18...♕b5** [18...♖xd1+? 19.♖xd1 ♕b5 20.c4 ♕b4 21.c5 dxc5 22.♘c3± h4 23.♗c4] **19. c4 ♕b4 20.♖c1** [Black's rook on d4 can't be attacked by the white knight. I should have found a way to trade off the d4-rook in favourable circumstances] **20...♗f8?!** [I didn't expect this move at all. After 20...♕d2! it's = only. Of course my opponent was ambitious that day. 21.♕f1 (21.♕xd2 ♖xd2 22.♖c2; 21.♕f3 ♕d3+ 22.♕xd3 ♖xd3 23.c5 dxc5 (23...d5 24.♘b6) 24.♘b6 (24.♘xc5

♖d2) 24...♗b7 25.♘c4 ♗d8 26.♖ed1 ♖xd1 (26...♖d4? 27.♖xd4+−) 27.♖xd1 ♗c7) 21...♕d3+ 22.♕xd3 ♖xd3 23.c5 dxc5 24.♗d1!! ♖d2 25.♗f3!± – sometimes a bad bishop also helps!]
21.♖ed1 h4 22.♖c3 ♖h6 23.♖cd3 c5 24.♘c3 ♗b7 25.♖h3 [25.♖xd4 cxd4 26.♘d5 ♗xd5 27.cxd5 ♔e7]
25...♗g5 26.g3 ♔e7 27.gxh4 ♗f4 [≥ 27...♖xh4 28.♖xh4 ♗xh4 29.♖xd4 cxd4 30.♘d5+ ♗xd5 31.cxd5± and only White can try for a win here] **28.h5 ♗h6 29.♗c2?** [29.a3! – I missed this move during the game. The idea is ♗a4 and ♔a2: 29...♕b6 30.♗a4 ♖b8 31.♔a2! (improving the king's position) 31...♗e3 32.b3 ♖g8 33.♕g3 ♕b8 34.♖xd4 cxd4 35.♘d5+ ♗xd5 36.cxd5 ♖c8 37.♗c6+] **29...♖c8?** [Simply 29...♕xc4! was good enough: 30.♗d3 (30.♕xc4 ♗xc4 31.♘d5+ (31.♗b3 ♗xe4+) 31...♗xd5 32.♖xd5. During the game I felt that due to the opposite-coloured bishops I would somehow equalize (my opponent also had the same thought), but we both didn't pay serious attention: 32...♖b4 33.♖b3 a5 and Black can try, but I believe White has enough resources to equalize: 30...♕b4 31.a3 ♕b3; 29...♖b8 30.♖xd4 (30.♗d3 ♗c6 31.♔a1 a5 32.♖b1 a4 33.a3 ♕b6 34.♖g3 ♕b3 35.h4 36.♘b5 ♗xc4 37.♗xc4 ♕xg3 38.♗xf7 30...cxd4 31.♘d5+ ♗xd5 32.♖b3 ♗xc4 33.♖xb4 ♗xe2 34.♖xb8 d3 35.♗a4 d5 36.♖e8+ ♗d6 37.♖d8+ ♗c7 38.♖d7+ ♗b6 39.♖xd5 ♗f3 40.♖xd3 ♗xe4 41.♗c2 ♗xd3 42.♗xd3 a5 43.♗c2 ♗c5 44.♔d1 ♗d4 45.♗e2 e4 46.♗b5 ♗e5 47.♗d7=] **30.♖xd4 cxd4 31.♘d5+ ♗xd5 32.cxd5±** [Now the position has been more or less simplified and White has easy play. **32...♔f8** [32...♖c3 33.a3 ♕b6 34.♖g3±] **33.a3 ♕c5 34.♖b3 a5 35.h4** [I wanted to control the g5-square (maybe sometime I could attack with ♖g3-♕g4)] **35...♕c7 36.♕d3 ♗e3 37.♖b5** [After the game Abhijeet said he had missed the ♖b5/♕b3 idea] **37...♖b8 38.♖xb8+ ♕xb8 39.♕a6 ♗d2 40.♗d3 ♔g7 41.♕b5 ♕h8 42.♗e2 ♕h6 43.♕d3 ♗e1 44.♔c2 ♕f4 45.♔b3 ♕c1 46.♕c2??** [I had less time on the clock, but not a lot less... I felt really bad after this game. But overall I had a great tournament.

46.♕d1! (I saw this move too... the idea was ♕d1 and then ♗d3. But I felt both moves amounted to the same, and in my overconfidence I played the text rather fast) 46...♕e3+ (46...♕xd1+? 47.♗xd1 ♗xh4 48.♔a4 ♗e1 49.b4+−) 47.♗d3±. Now the plan is so simple: my king goes to b5, then b2-b4, and I try to create a passed pawn and push it... so simple! 47...♔h6 (47...♔f8 48.♔a4 ♔e7 49.h6) 48.♔a4 ♗d2 49.♕e2 ♕f4 50.♔b5 (the d6-pawn is the problem) 50...♗c1 51.♔c6] **46...a4+**   0-1

Tigran Gharamian
Andrey Vovk
Germany Bundesliga 2015/16 (7)
1.e4 c5 2.♘f3 d6 3.d4 cxd4 4.♘xd4 ♘f6 5.♘c3 ♘c6 6.♗g5 e6 7.♕d2 a6 8.♘xc6 bxc6 9.0-0-0 ♗e7 10.♗xf6 gxf6 11.♗c4 ♕a5 12.♖he1 ♖b8 13.f4

13...♗d7 [1. With the idea ...0-0/...♕b6/ ...♖fc8 and ...c6-c5-c4; 2. When White's pawn is on g2, sometimes it is risky to play ...0-0 because White can transfer the rook to h3, via e3 or via d3] **14.♕d3** [14.f5!? ♕b6 (14...♕e5 15.♕f2!? (15.♕h6 a5 16.♗b3 ♖b4 17.♔b1 a4 18.fxe6 fxe6; 15.g3 0-0 16.♗b3 ♖fc8 17.♕e2 (17.♔b1 c5) 17...a5) 15...0-0!? (15...♕xh2) 16.♖d3 ♔h8 17.♖h3 ♖g8 18.♗xa6 ♕a5 (18...♖g7 19.♕a7 ♖d8 20.♗c8!±) 19.♗c4 ♕b4 20.♗b3 d5 21.a3 ♕a5 22.fxe6 ♗xe6 23.exd5 ♗xh3 24.♖xe7) 16.♗xa6 ♗d8 17.♖h1 ♕e5 18.♖h5 ♗c7 19.♕a7 d5 20.fxe6 ♕f4+ 21.♔b1 fxe6 22.♖f1 ♕g3] **14...♕b6** [≥ 14...♖g8 15.g3 ♔f8 16.♔b1 ♔g7 17.♗b3 ♔h8 18.f5 ♕b6 19.♘e2 a5→] **15.♗b3 ♕f2 16.♖f1** [16.f5 ♕xg2 17.♖e2 ♕g5+ 18.♔b1 with very strong compensation] **16...♕xg2 17.♖d2 ♕g4 18.♕xa6 f5 19.♕a7 ♖d8 20.♔b1**∞   ½-½

Exercise 1

position after 12...♘f6-h5

What is the best move in this position?
(solution on page 245)

Exercise 2

position after 15...e6-e5

What is White's best plan to prevent Black's counterplay?
(solution on page 245)

Exercise 3

position after 20.♖d1-c1

What is the best way for Black to reduce White's attacking chances?
(solution on page 245)

Sicilian Defence

A Comfortable Ending

by Sergey Kasparov

1.	e4	c5
2.	♘f3	g6
3.	c4	♘c6
4.	d4	cxd4
5.	♘xd4	♘f6
6.	♘c3	d6
7.	♗e2	♘xd4
8.	♕xd4	♗g7
9.	♗e3	0-0
10.	♕d2	a5
11.	0-0	a4

Hello everyone! We continue our search for an advantage in the Sicilian Defence. However, is there any opening where this is easy? Look at the starting position. The material is equal and the armies are symmetrically positioned. Why should White's position actually be better? The first-move advantage does not guarantee clear superiority and with adequate play by both opponents the normal outcome of any game is a DRAW. Let's start our Survey from this axiom and then you won't have anything to complain about the author or the variation.

1.e4 c5 2.♘f3 g6
This move might look strange, but it makes sense. There is a more natural continuation: 2...♘c6. However, in that case White can go for the currently quite popular Rossolimo Variation with 3.♗b5. The text deprives the opponent of this option.
3.c4
In this article we will consider the attempt by White to apply the 'Maroczy Bind'. The advance c2-c4 provides White with solid control of the centre – he should only prevent the counter-push ...e7-e5, equalizing the chances, as in that case the structure in the centre will be fixed.
3...♘c6 4.d4
White needs to hurry, while he still has sufficient control of the key point d4.
4...cxd4 5.♘xd4 ♘f6 6.♘c3 d6 7.♗e2 ♘xd4
In his turn, Black hastens to lure the white queen to d4. Otherwise the bishop will go out to e3 and White will be ready to play ♗e3xd4.
8.♕xd4 ♗g7 9.♗e3
However, White doesn't suffer too much from the queen's early exit to the centre as the opponent doesn't have time to harass this piece. The black knight's leaps are irrelevant because the g7-bishop is unprotected.
9...0-0 10.♕d2 a5 11.0-0 a4
This is the initial position of the line under discussion (see

the diagram above). Black has pushed the a-pawn as far as possible. The logic is the following:
1) The black queen will feel more comfortable on a5 under cover of the a-pawn, as the immediate b2-b4 is prevented.
2) In case of black pressure on the c4-pawn (...♗e6 and ...♖c8) it will be difficult for White to protect it. The natural b2-b3, after ...a4xb3 and a2xb3, will result in the opening of the a-file and the formation of a weak pawn on b3.
3) Black simply grabs space on the queenside.
White now has to choose a plan of action. There are several options.

A) The Pawn Is Put on f3
I usually apply an unsophisticated scheme: creating the pawn chain g2-f3-e4-d5. The pawn gets to d5 after the exchange of the knight (♘c3-d5 and c4xd5), which cannot be tolerated by Black on the d5 outpost. Otherwise White will have a space advantage and he will be permanently slightly better.
In a game played on the island of Bornholm (Denmark) you can observe an ending where both sides have exactly the same pieces (S.Kasparov-Svendsen). Conducting a boring defence turned out to be beyond Black's abilities.

Vassily Ivanchuk

In the Dutch Hoogeveen tournament, my opponent preferred to play with a knight and bishop against two bishops, which made sense in this case (S.Kasparov-J.Boersma). It was ostensibly easier to form a defence line on dark squares, as this way my light-squared bishop was of little use.

Nevertheless, there is a negative side to this: White can slowly reposition his pawns on dark squares, bring the king closer etc., before starting anything concrete. And it is unpleasant for any chess player to stand still without any counterplay, leaving the initiative to the opponent.

Meanwhile, in the Czech Open the author changed the pawn structure by the push c4-c5!? (S.Kasparov-Sadilek). And, although I did not play perfectly further on, all the same Black had to remain passive and keep the balance for a long time. In this game you can observe how White exerts pressure on the far advanced a4-pawn, which is fixed on a light square.

Now let's go over to examples of the creativity of strong grandmasters. In order to avoid general simplifications White can direct the knight on another

route – ♘c3-b5-d4. I won't say that this is very dangerous for Black, however the initiative is definitely in White's hands here. An unconventional structure (doubled pawns on c3 and c4) emerged in the encounter Malakhov-So. Despite the fact that the bastions of the American grandmaster looked very solid, Vladimir managed to break them down! The moral of this story: Black can't allow himself to relax for one moment during a long ending. Well, this speaks volumes for this variation, doesn't it?

The system has one more benefit: it is extremely difficult for an obvious Elo-favourite to obtain enough counterplay to win with black. The game Guttulsrud-Iturrizaga will prove this. No matter how hard the Latin-American grandmaster tried to complicate the struggle, White was the one who had the advantage during the largest part of the game. The eminent professional Itturizaga hardly managed to save a half-point.

Polish international master Warakomski applied a reasonable idea against Kanarek. Before bringing the knight forward he doubled rooks on the c-file. Here again, a boring and gloomy defence awaited Black.

B) The Bishop Goes to d4
This is another set-up that is less often used. We cannot exclude that it was an Israeli idea, as in the database I found two successful games by grandmasters from this country. The bishop goes to d4, 'threatening' the fianchettoed g7-bishop with a trade, and the f-pawn is used like a battering-ram, quickly running to f5. Black should tread carefully here, otherwise he will face real problems (Roiz-Boskovic).

Michael practically had a technically winning position by the 20th move.

In the Rodstein-Cabrera clash, the result of the opening appeared to be not so deplorable for Black. But all the same he ended up in an ending with a pawn down, and lost again.

Vassily Ivanchuk's treatment of the position with black against the great Vishy can be considered a model example for imitation. But the Indian grandmaster didn't push the f-pawn at all, which, probably, was a poor decision.

In the end I have added one extra game (Filippov-Al Modiahki) to remind you that in White's arsenal there is room for an additional nuance. From time to time, 11.♖d1 is used by White instead of the usual castling.

Why? Well, please read the notes inside the game. However, I would not exaggerate the value of this idea. Black gets a reasonable game, only he has to show some accuracy.

Conclusion
Either way, with adequate play from both sides White's initiative is not that big, but still it is there. And it is especially unpleasant for Black that he doesn't have free counterplay and has to defend passively, with good chances for a draw only.

Sergey Kasparov
Mads Svendsen

Bornholm 2007 (2)

1.e4 c5 2.♘f3 g6 3.c4 ♘c6 4.d4 cxd4 5.♘xd4 ♘f6 6.♘c3 d6 7.♗e2 ♘xd4 8.♕xd4 ♗g7 9.♗e3 0-0 10.♕d2 ♗e6 11.♖c1 a5 12.f3 a4 13.0-0 ♕a5 14.♘d5 ♕xd2 15.♗xd2 ♘xd5 16.cxd5 ♗d7 [In this game we will analyse an ending where each opponent has 2 rooks + 2 bishops with the already known pawn structure]

17.♗c3 [17.♗c7 is also possible, but I didn't like the intermediate 17...♗d4+, driving the king to the corner of the board: 18.♔h1 ♖fd8] **17...♖fc8 18.♗xg7 ♔xg7 19.♔f2** [Let's try to examine the situation. If we remove the rooks from the board, the a4-pawn is likely to be lost because the black king cannot protect it. It seems to me that in general his space advantage provides White with some chances of victory] **19...a3 20.b3 f5 21.exf5 ♗xf5 22.♔e3 ♔f6 23.♔d4** [The breakthrough ...f7-f5 hasn't improved Black's position. Now the d5-pawn constrains two black pawns at once. Meanwhile, the advance ...e7-e6(e5) may after d5xe6 in the future lead to the formation of an outside passed pawn for White on the kingside] **23...g5 24.♗d3** [Please pay attention! The disappearance of the e4-pawn from the board gives White the possibility to trade off his 'bad bishop'] **24...♗xd3 25.♔xd3 ♔e5** [What else?] **26.♖ce1+ ♔f6 27.♖e6+ ♔f7 28.f4 g4 29.♖fe1 ♖c7 30.♖h6 ♔g7 31.♖h4 ♖a5 32.♖xg4+ ♔f7 33.♖g5** [Now the mistakes begin, due to shortage of time] **33...h6?!** [33...♖ac5!?] **34.♖f5+ ♔g6?** [≥ 34...♔g7] **35.**

g4+– ♖ac5 36.♖e6+ ♔g7 37.g5? [37.♖h5!+–] **37...h5?!** 38.g6 ♖c3+ 39.♔e4 ♖xb3 40.♖f7+ ♔g8 41.♖exe7 ♖c4+ 42.♔f5 1-0

Sergey Kasparov
Jan Boersma

Hoogeveen 2014 (4)

1.e4 c5 2.♘f3 g6 3.c4 ♘c6 4.d4 cxd4 5.♘xd4 ♘f6 6.♘c3 d6 7.♗e2 ♘xd4 8.♕xd4 ♗g7 9.♗e3 0-0 10.♕d2 a5 11.0-0 a4 12.♖ac1 ♕a5 13.f3 ♗e6 14.♘d5 [Even straightforward play is sufficient to obtain some initiative] **14...♕xd2 15.♗xd2** [Let's consider the consequences of the zwischenschach 15.♘xe7+: 15...♔h8 16.♗xd2 ♖fe8 17.♘d5. Black will win the pawn back anyway because of the vulnerability of the bishop on e2: 17...♘xd5 (17...♗xd5? 18.cxd5 ♘xd5 19.♗b5 ♖e5 20.♗xa4±) 18.cxd5 ♘xd5 19.♗b5! ♖e5 20.♗xa4 (20.♖c7!?∞; 20.♗c3 ♖xa2 21.♗xe5 ♗xe5≅ Papp-Istratescu, Dubai 2015; 20.exd5?! ♖xd5 is weaker as both bishops are attacked now) 20...♗e6 (20...♗xa2 21.b3 b5 22.♖a1 bxa4 23.♖xa2 a3 looks like a draw) 21.♗b3 ♗xb3 22.axb3 ♖b5=] **15...♗xd5 16.cxd5 ♘d7**

17.♖c2 [17.♗e3!? is more interesting: 17...♗xb2 18.♖c7↑] **17...♗d4+ 18.♔h1 ♖fc8 19.♖fc1 ♖xc2 20.♖xc2 ♘c5** [It looks as if Black is very solid, whereas White's light-squared bishop is constrained by its own pawns on e2. But the thing is that White can gradually improve his position, while Black doesn't have any promising counterplay. And in the future the two-bishops advantage may tell] **21.♗c1** [A preventive measure against ...a4-a3] **21...h5 22.g3 ♔g7 23.♔g2 ♗f6 24.h4 a3** [My opponent doesn't want to remain passive, but this

doesn't bring any relief, and White's extra pawn will tell later] **25.bxa3 ♖a5 26.♗c4 ♗e5 27.♗e2 ♗f6 28.♖c4 ♖a4 29.♖b4 ♗c3 30.♖b1± ♗d4 31.♗b5 ♖a8 32.♖b4 ♗c3 33.♖c4** [The advantage has gradually increased] **33...♗f6 34.a4** [After f3-f4 and ♗c1-e3 the outpost on c5 may fall] **34...♘d3 35.♗e3 ♘b2 36.♖b4 ♘d1** [36...♖c8 37.♗e2±] **37.♗d2** [≥ 37.♗g1] **37...♘c3?** **38.♗d7±** [Now the b7-pawn perishes] **38...♘xa2** [38...♖b8 39.♗c6+–; 38...♖a7 39.f4+– e4-e5 is threatened] **39.♖xb7** [The rest is not very difficult] **39...♘c3 40.♗c6 ♖a6** [40...♖xa4 41.♖b4+–] **41.♖b4 ♖a7 42.♗e3 ♖a6 43.f4 e6 44.♔f3 exd5 45.exd5 ♘d1 46.♗b6 ♘b2 47.a5 ♘d3 48.♖b5 ♘c5 49.♗xc5 dxc5 50.♗b7 ♖a7 51.d6 c4 52.a6 ♔f8 53.♖c5 ♔e8 54.♔e4 ♗d7 55.♔d5 ♗d8 56.♖xc4 ♗b6 57.♖e4 ♗d8 58.♖e2 ♗f6 59.♔c5 ♗d8 60.♖e4** 1-0

Sergey Kasparov
Sadilek Peter

Teplice 2013 (4)

1.e4 c5 2.♘f3 g6 3.c4 ♘c6 4.d4 cxd4 5.♘xd4 ♘f6 6.♘c3 d6 7.♗e2 ♘xd4 8.♕xd4 ♗g7 9.♗e3 0-0 10.♕d2 a5 11.0-0 a4 12.f3 ♗d7 13.c5!? [If a chance to change the pawn structure turns up, why not try it?]

13...♘e8 [13...dxc5?! is unfavourable, as the control over the point e5 is lost and after 14.e5 the knight doesn't have a convenient retreat: 14...♘h5 (14...♘e8? is even worse due to 15.♖ad1+–) 15.f4 ♗c6 16.♕xd8 ♖fxd8 17.g4± and Black's compensation for the knight will be insufficient. It is possible to make another move with the bishop, although this is 'morally unpleasant'. Besides, an isolated pawn appears: 13...♗e6 14.cxd6 ♕xd6 15.♕xd6 exd6 16.♖fd1±] **14.♖fd1 ♗c6 15.cxd6?!** [To strengthen the pressure, optimal was 15.♖ac1 ♕a5 16.♘d5 ♗xd5 (16...♕xd2? 17.♘xe7+) 17.♕xa5 ♖xa5 18.♖xd5± and the two bishops provide White with a comfortable advantage in the ending] **15...♘xd6 16.♗d4** [16.♖ac1] **16...♗xd4+ 17.♕xd4 ♕a5 18.a3** [The situation has almost levelled out, however I hoped to exploit the weakness of the a4-pawn somewhere deep in the ending. It is far advanced and fixed on a light square, which is the colour of the bishops that remain] **18...♖fd8 19.♕e3 ♕e5 20.♕f2 ♕e6 21.♖d4 ♔g7 22.♖ad1 f6 23.♖1d2** [23.♗c4±] **23...♖a5 24.♗f1 ♖da8 25.♖b4 ♕e5 26.♖dd4** [See the comment to move 18. White's pieces gradually start to close in on the a4 outpost] **26...♕c5 27.♖d1 ♕xf2+ 28.♔xf2 ♖c5 29.♔e3 ♗f7 30.♖dd4 ♖h5 31.h3 ♖e5 32.♗c4+ ♔g7** [32...♘xc4+ is more persistent, although White keeps the initiative after 33.♖bxc4] **33.♔f2 f5 34.♗d5 fxe4 35.♗xe4 ♗xe4 36.♘xe4 ♘xe4+ 37.♖xe4 ♖xe4 38.♖xe4±** [After general simplifications a rook ending emerges where the play is for two results only. The presence of weaknesses on a4, b7 and e7 makes Black's defence extremely unpleasant] **38...♔f6 39.♖b4 ♖a7 40.♔e3 ♔e5 41.h4 ♔d5 42.h5** [Breaking up the pawn pair h7-g6. The rest is just a matter of technique] **42...♔c5** [42...gxh5!?] **43. hxg6 hxg6 44.♔f4 b5 45.♔g5 ♖a6 46.f4 ♖b6 47.♖e4 ♔d6 48.g4 ♔d7 49.♔h6 ♔d6 50.g5 ♔d7 51.♔g7 ♔e8 52.♖b4** 1-0

The Pawn Is Put on f3 ♘b5

Vladimir Malakhov
Wesley So

Khanty-Mansiysk 2009 (4)

1.♘f3 c5 2.c4 g6 3.d4 cxd4 4.♘xd4 ♘c6 5.e4 ♘f6 6.♘c3 d6 7.♗e2 ♘xd4 8.♕xd4 ♗g7 9.♗e3

0-0 **10.♕d2 a5 11.0-0 a4 12.f3 ♗e6 13.♖ac1 ♕a5 14.♖fd1 ♖fc8**

15.♘b5 [This knight leap to the queenside also makes sense; after all, now there will be no exchanges which change the pawn structure (like after ♘c3-d5)] **15...♘d7 16.♕xa5 ♖xa5 17.♘d4** [As a result of the knight pirouette ♘c3-b5-d4 the c4-pawn is protected (by the c1-rook)] **17...♘c5 18.♔f2 ♗d7 19.♖b1 ♘e6 20.♘b5 ♖aa8** [Probably 20...♗xb5 is acceptable, but with 21.cxb5 the diagonal for the e2-bishop is extended. It can try to move to c4, etc. The a4-pawn will be cut off from its friend (b7)] **21.♘c3!** [Very to the point. Vladimir is an expert in subtle endings, he is not to be confused by doubled pawns!] **21...♗xc3** [Otherwise the knight would go to d5 sooner or later] **22.bxc3 ♗c6 23.g4** [Black's position looks solid, however that always seems to be the case...] **23...f6 24.h4 ♔g7 25.g5 ♖f8 26.♔g3 f5 27.exf5 ♖xf5 28.f4 ♘c5 29.♔g4 ♘e4+ 30.♔h2 ♖af8** [Believe it or not, but I was also thinking of an exchange sacrifice after 28.f4. Black hopes to construct an impenetrable defence line on the light squares] **31.♖f1 e5?** [Why? Is it favourable to open files if the opponent has an extra exchange?] **32.♗xf5 ♖xf5 33.♖bc1 ♔f7 34.fxe5 dxe5 35.c5 ♔e6** [Here also, it is difficult to find a gateway for the penetration of the rooks into the enemy camp!] **36.c4 a3 37.♖ce1 ♗a4 38.h5 gxh5 39.♖xf5 ♔xf5 40.♖f1+ ♔g6 41.♖f8** [So, the Russian guy managed to invade to the 8th rank, and now he can harass the a3- and h7-pawns] **41...♗c6 42.♖g8+ ♔f5?** [42...♔f7 is more stubborn, keeping the h7-pawn alive] **43.♖g7** [Now the h7-pawn perishes, opening the way for the passed g-pawn] **43...♘c3 44.♖xh7 ♘xa2**

45.♗d2 [Alas, the knight is arrested on the edge of the board, which determines the outcome] **45...e4 46.♖f7+ ♔e6 47.♖f6+ ♔e5 48.♖f1** [Or 48.♗f4+ ♔d4 49.g6 ♘c3 50.g7 a2 51.♖e5+ ♔xe5 52.♖f1+−] **48...♔d4 49.♖a1 ♘c3 50.g6 ♗d7 51.g7 ♗e6 52.♗xc3+ ♔xc3 53.♖xa3+ ♔xc4 54.♖a7 e3 55.♖xb7** 1-0

Odd Martin Guttulsrud
Eduardo Iturrizaga

Basel 2015 (1)

1.e4 c5 2.♘f3 g6 3.d4 cxd4 4.♘xd4 ♘c6 5.c4 ♘f6 6.♘c3 d6 7.♗e2 ♘xd4 8.♕xd4 ♗g7 9.♗e3 0-0 10.♕d2 a5 11.0-0 a4 12.♖ac1 ♗e6 13.f3 ♘d7 14.♘b5 [The concrete 14.f4 is curious: 14...♕a5 15.f5 gxf5 16.exf5 ♗xf5 17.c5 ♗g6 18.cxd6 exd6 19.♕xd6 and White's position is slightly more pleasant due to the enemy isolated pawns on the kingside] **14...♘c5 15.♘d4 ♗d7 16.♖fd1 ♕b6 17.♗f1 ♖fc8 18.♖c2 h5** [The advance of this pawn in such structures seems doubtful to me because the benefits are unclear; it is just a weakening] **19.♕f2 ♕d8 20.♕d2 ♘h7 21.♗f2 ♕h8** [At least now we can see Black's idea. The queen has gone and occupied the corner, but what are the dividends of this?] **22.♕b4 ♖a6 23.♖cd2 ♗h6 24.♖c2 ♕d8 25.♘b5 ♖a5 26.♖c3 ♗g7 27.♖a3 ♖a6 28.♗h4** [Threatening to strike on d6. The players are manoeuvring without changing the pawn structure, and the assessment fluctuates around 'equality'] **28...♖ac6 29.♗e2** [It appears that the pawn is poisoned: 29.♘xd6? ♗e6 30.♗xe7 ♕xe7 31.♘xc8 ♖xc8∓] **29...♕b6 30.♗f2 ♕d8 31.♗h4 ♕h8?** [Here it is – the negative side of Black's piece arrangement. It is extremely difficult to obtain free counterplay. In search of a way to fight for a win the Venezuelan player goes too far] **32.♖b1?** [Playing for a draw. He could have made use of the opponent's negligence with the principled 32.♗xe7 ♗xb2 33.♘xd6 ♗xa3 34.♕xa3±] **32...♖b6 33.♔h1 ♗f6 34.♗f2 ♖a6 35.♕d2 ♘e6 36.♘c3 ♗d4 37.♗xd4** [There was no need for this exchange. The following exchange sacrifice was promising: 37.♗h4!? ♗c5 38.♘d5 ♗xa3 39.bxa3±. Dark-squared bishops are extremely strong in the given pawn set-up] **37...♕xd4 38.♕c2 ♘f4 39.♗f1 h4 40.♖d1 ♕f6 41.♕d2 ♗e6 42.♖xa4** [Better was 42.c5] **42...♖xa4 43.♘xa4 ♗xc4 44.♘b6** [Better was 44.♗xc4] **44...♗xf1 45.♖xf1 ♖c6 46.♘d5 ♘xd5 47.exd5 ♖c4** [After several inaccuracies by his opponent, the Latin-American grandmaster has managed to get some advantage, however it is rather difficult to convert this into a point] **48.h3 ♖d4 49.♕c3 ♕f4** [49...♖xd5 50.♕xf6 exf6 looks like a draw] **50.♕b3 ♕e5 51.♕xb7 ♖xd5 52.a4** [But now White stands not worse at all. I give the rest of the game without comments] **52...♖d2 53.b4 d5 54.a5 ♖a2 55.♖g1 ♕d6 56.♖d1 d4 57.♕e4 e5 58.f4 ♕xb4 59.fxe5 ♕e7 60.♕d5 ♖e2 61.♖f1 ♔g8 62.♕xd4 ♖xe5 63.a6 ♖a5 64.♖c1 ♔h7 65.♖a1 ♖xa1+ 66.♕xa1 ♕a7 67.♕f6 ♔g8 68.♕d6 ♔h7 69.♔h2 ♔g7 70.♕e5+ ♔g8 71.♕d6 ♔g7 72.♔h1 ♔h7 73.♕f6 ♔g8 74.♕d8+ ♔g7 75.♕a5 ♔g8 76.♕a1 ♔h7 77.♕a2 ♔g8 78.♕a4 ♔g7 79.♕a1+ ♔h7** ½-½

The Pawn Is Put on f3
Double Rooks on the c-File

Tomasz Warakomski
Marcel Kanarek
Poland tt 2015 (1)

1.e4 c5 2.♘f3 g6 3.d4 cxd4 4.♘xd4 ♘c6 5.c4 ♘f6 6.♘c3 ♘xd4 7.♕xd4 d6 8.♗e2 ♗g7 9.♗e3 0-0 10.♕d2 a5 11.0-0 a4 12.♖ac1 ♕a5

13.♖c2 ♗e6 14.♖fc1 [A curious idea. White doubles rooks on a file which

is still closed! But it might be opened in the future after ♘c3-d5 or c4-c5] **14...♖fc8 15.♕d1 ♘d7** [It turns out that the pawn is inviolable with the current placement of the white rooks: 15...♗xc4? 16.♘d5 ♘xd5 17.exd5 b5 (of course, also unsatisfactory is 17...♗xb2 18.♖xb2 ♕xd5 19.♗xc4 ♕xd1+ 20.♖xd1 ♖xc4 21.♖xb7+−) 18.b3+−] **16.♘b5** [It is perhaps more logical to jump to the centre: 16.♘d5, counting on 16...♗xd5 17.♕xd5 (or 17.cxd5) 17...♕xd5 18.cxd5± with a standard initiative for White] **16...♘c5 17.f3 a3 18.bxa3** [18.b3? fails to 18...♘xb3 19.axb3 (19.♖b1 ♘c5∓) 19...a2−+] **18...♗d7 19.♗g5 ♖e8 20.♔h1 ♘e6 21.♗d2 ♕a4 22.♗b4** ['Glueing together' the broken queenside pawns] **22...♗h6 23.♖b1 ♗xb5 24.cxb5 ♘d4** [A spectacular move, but still White gets the better position] **25.♖cb2 ♘xe2 26.♕xa4 ♖xa4 27.♖xe2 ♖c8 28.♔g1** [The immediate break in the centre was probably more accurate: 28.e5!? dxe5 29.♗xe7 ♗f8 30.♖xe5. However, this looks very much like a draw too as 'rook endings can't be won'] **28...♖c1+ 29.♖xc1 ♗xc1 30.e5** [30.♖c2 ♗xa3 31.♗xa3 ♖xa3 32.♖c7 ♔f8 is about equal] **30...♗xa3 31.♗xa3 ♖xa3 32.exd6 exd6 33.♖d2 ♖a5 34.a4 ♖xa4 35.♖xd6 ♖a2 36.♖d7 b6 37.♖b7 ♖b2 38.♖xb6** [As usual, Black has to defend himself, but in the end he manages to draw] **38...h5 39.h4 ♔g7 40.♔h2 ♖b4 41.♔g3 ♖b2 42.f4 ♔f8 43.♖b7 ♔g7 44.♔f3 ♔f6 45.b6 ♔e6 46.♖b8 ♔f5 47.♖e8** ½-½

The Bishop Goes to d4
f2-f4

Michael Roiz
Drasko Boskovic
Gibraltar 2011 (1)

1.♘f3 c5 2.c4 g6 3.d4 cxd4 4.♘xd4 ♘c6 5.e4 ♘f6 6.♘c3 ♘xd4 7.♕xd4 d6 8.♗e3 ♗g7 9.♕d2 0-0 10.♗e2 a5 11.0-0 a4 12.♖ad1 ♕a5 13.♗d4 [Establishing a counterbalance for the fianchettoed g7-bishop; the f-pawn doesn't go to f3, and is allowed to run further] **13...♗e6**

14.f4 ♕b4 15.a3 ♕a5 [It is risky to intrude into the enemy camp with 15...♕b3 as it might be pretty difficult to get back alive: 16.♖c1 ♖fc8 (16...♗xc4?? 17.♗d1+−) 17.♗f3 ♗g4 18.♖e3 ♗xe3 19.♘d5!+−] **16.f5 ♗d7** [The lesser of evils was to transfer to a slightly worse ending: 16...gxf5 17.exf5 ♗xf5 18.♗xf6. This blow may look strange, but it is applied from time to time in the given structure. There is a tactical justification: 18...♗xf6 19.♘d5 ♕xd2 20.♘xf6+ exf6 (20...♔g7?? 21.♘h5++−) 21.♖xd2± and the ruined pawn structure compels Black to a joyless struggle for a draw] **17. c5!** [Also typical. At the first opportunity White damages the enemy's pawn structure] **17...♗c6** [17...dxc5? 18.♗xf6 ♗xf6 19.♕xd7+−] **18.cxd6 exd6 19.♕f4±** [It becomes quite visible how well White has succeeded. His space advantage and harmoniously-placed pieces provide him with a strong initiative] **19...♖ad8 20.♕h4** [Now f5xg6 is in the offing, when the black knight will perish in the crossfire] **20...♘d7 21.f6** [The following line is even more accurate: 21.♗xg7 ♔xg7 22.f6+ ♔h8 23.♖d3+− with deadly threats] **21...♗h8 22.♖f3 ♖fe8 23.♗c4** [23.♖h3 is more precise: 23...♗f8 24.♗c4+−] **23...♘e5 24.♖h3 h5** [Somehow Black has dealt with the first surge of the attack] **25.♗e2** [Perhaps it was more logical to leave the bishop on the diagonal a2-g8: 25.♗a2 ♗d7 26.♗g3 ♔h7 27.♖f1+−, threatening ♗xe5, ♗xf7 etc.] **25...♘d7 26.♖f1** [26.g4!?] **26...♘e5 27.♔h1 ♖de8 28.♗xe5 ♕xe5 29.♖hf3 ♖e6 30.♗c4 ♖xf6 31.♕g3 ♕xg3 32.hxg3** [Now we can definitely conclude that the Israeli grandmaster was too sluggish with his attack and has let almost all of his advantage slip. He has to start all over again] **32...♔f8?!** [≥

32...♘e5] **33.♗b5 ♗xb5 34.♘xb5 ♔e7 35.♘c3 ♖xf3** [35...♘b6] **36. gxf3 ♘c5 37.♖d1 ♔e6 38.♔g2 ♗e5 39.♔f2 g5 40.♘b5 g4 41.f4 ♗xb2?** [The Serbian chess player misses an excellent opportunity to rock the boat: 41...♘xe4+! 42.♔e3 f5 43.fxe5 dxe5 and the situation gets out of control. The g3-pawn falls and the black avalanche might turn out to be not weaker than the rook] **42.♔e3 ♔e7 43.♖b1 ♗f6 44.♖h1 ♗b2 45.♖xh5 ♔d7 46.♖h1 ♘b3 47.♖b1 ♗g7 48.♖d1 ♔c6 49.♘xd6 b5 50.e5 b4 51.axb4 a3 52.♘c4** 1-0

Maxim Rodshtein
Alexis Cabrera

Andorra 2013 (4)

1.♘f3 ♘f6 2.c4 c5 3.♘c3 ♘c6 4.d4 cxd4 5.♘xd4 g6 6.e4 ♘xd4 7.♕xd4 d6 8.♗e2 ♗g7 9.♗e3 0-0 10.♕d2 a5 11.0-0 a4 12.♗d4 ♗e6 13.f4 ♕a5 14.♖ad1 ♖fc8
[The Spanish grandmaster attacks the pawn with the rook, which probably narrows down the opponent's options] **15.b3** [There is no alternative to be seen] **15...axb3 16.axb3** [Black has managed to open the a-file. Logically speaking, this should elate the a8-rook, however let's continue the analysis] **16...♕b4 17.f5!**

[Tactics serve strategy. White's pieces are as active as they can be, they don't even hurry to protect the weak b3-pawn. Activity on the kingside is more important] **17...♗d7 18.♗xf6 ♗xf6 19.♘d5 ♕xd2** [19...♕c5+ is useless: 20.♔h1 and the bishop cannot leave f6 because of the blow ♘d5xe7+] **20.♘xf6+ exf6 21.♖xd2±** [Skipping the middlegame, Maxim directs the opening into a pleasant ending] **21...♗c6**

22.fxg6 fxg6 23.♖xf6 ♖a1+ 24.♖f1 ♖xf1+ 25.♗xf1 ♖e8 26.b4 ♔f7 [26...♖e6? 27.c5± with the threat ♗f1-c4] **27.♖xd6 ♖xe4 28.♖d8 ♖e1 29.b5 ♗e4 30.♔f2 ♖c1 31.♖d7+ ♔e6 32.♖xh7 ♖c2+ 33.♔e3 ♗xg2 34.♗xg2 ♖xg2 35.♖xb7 ♖xh2 36.b6 ♔d6 37.♖c7** [The connected passed pawns can also advance without the aid of the white king] 1-0

**The Bishop Goes to d4
No f2-f4**

Viswanathan Anand
Vassily Ivanchuk

Wijk aan Zee 2010 (8)

1.e4 c5 2.♘f3 ♘c6 3.d4 cxd4 4.♘xd4 g6 5.c4 ♘f6 6.♘c3 d6 7.♗e2 ♘xd4 8.♕xd4 ♗g7 9.♗e3 0-0 10.♕d2 a5 11.0-0 a4 12.♗d4

12...♗d7!? [Vassily prefers to develop the bishop on c6, so now the c4-pawn can breathe a sigh of relief] **13.♖fe1** [Maybe it made sense to keep the rook on f1? 13.♕e3!? ♕a5 14.f4±] **13...♗c6 14.♕e3 ♘d7 15.♗xg7 ♔xg7 16.♘d5 e6 17.♘c3 ♕b6** [The d6-pawn is weakened by the move ...e7-e6 but if Black manages to protect it safely with the king, he will be alright] **18.♕d2** [I like 18.♕xb6 ♘xb6 19.♖ad1 better, with a micro-initiative. However, on a 2700-2800 Elo level, Black won't lose such a position] **18...♖fd8 19.♖ad1 ♘f6 20.♗f1 h5 21.♖e3 ♖d7 22.h3 ♖ad8 23.♕c2 ♔h7** [Demonstrating the invulnerability of his position to the opponent. 23...♕a5] **24.♖f3** [Indeed, the pawn would taste bad: 24.♘xa4? ♗xa4 25.♕xa4 ♕xb2↑] **24...♗g7 25.♖e3 ♔h7** ½-½

**An Additional Nuance
11.♖d1**

Anton Filippov
Mohamad Al Modiahki

Incheon 2013 (5)

1.e4 c5 2.♘f3 ♘c6 3.d4 cxd4 4.♘xd4 g6 5.c4 ♘f6 6.♘c3 ♘xd4 7.♕xd4 d6 8.♗e2 ♗g7 9.♗e3 0-0 10.♕d2 a5 11.♖d1!? [White's intentions are more than clear: he intensifies the pressure along the d-file. Should the opponent ignore the threat, then the unpleasant blow c4-c5 or e4-e5 can follow] **11...♗e6** [The principled 11...a4 is also acceptable: 12.c5 ♗e6 (12...♕a5?! is much weaker: 13.cxd6 exd6 14.0-0 a3 15.♗d4 ♗e6 1-0 (46), Stohl-Cebalo, Sibenik 2014. After simply 16.b3± White's pawn structure is obviously better) 13.cxd6 ♕xd6! 14.♕xd6 exd6 when Black's good piece play compensates for the weakness of the d6-pawn: 15.a3 ♖fd8 16.♗b6 ♖dc8 17.♗d4 (17.♖xd6?! ♘d7 18.♗d4 ♗f8 and White experiences problems with his rook) 17...♗b3 18.♖d2 ♖xe4! 19.♘xe4 ♖c1+ (½-½, Tomczak-Janaszak, Poronin 2014) 20.♗d1 ♖xd1+ 21.♖xd1 ♗xd1 22.♗xg7 ♗b3 23.♗f6 ♖e8 with a draw] **12.0-0 a4**

13.f4 [This is reasonable. White can play more aggressively than f2-f3] **13...♕c8 14.♕d3 ♘d7 15.♔h1** [15.f5?! doesn't win a piece because of the tempo-gain 15...♘e5. But 15.♗d4!? is interesting] **15...♘c5** [Suddenly it turns out that White has to give up the bishop, as the unpleasant ...♗g7xc3 and ...♘c5xe4 are threatened] **16.♗xc5 ♕xc5 17.f5** [I don't know how you feel, but such a massive weakening of the dark-square complex in the absence of the bishop seems shady to me] **17...♗d7 18.♘d5**

♖ae8 **19.b4 axb3 20.axb3 ♗c6 21.b4 ♕a7 22.♘e3 b6 23.♘g4?! ♕b7 24.♗f3 b5!∓ 25.c5 dxc5 26.bxc5 ♕c7 27.♕e3 ♖d8 28.♖de1 ♔h8 29.♕g5 ♗c3 30.♖e2** b4–+ [The c3-bishop protects the king against all troubles – Black's position is overwhelming] **31.e5 ♗b5 32.f6 e6 33.♖e3** [33.♕h6 is harmless: 33...♖g8, and there is nothing White can strengthen his attack with] **33...♗d2 34.♖fe1 ♕xc5 35.♗e4 ♗xe3 36.♘xe3 ♕c3 37.♖g1 ♗d3 38.♗xd3 ♖xd3 39.♘g4 ♕d2 40.♕h4 b3 41.♘h6 b2 42.h3 ♖d4 43.♘g4 ♕c1**   0-1

Exercise 1

position after 18.♘c3-d5

After the change of the pawn structure by the exchange on d5 White's position will be slightly better. What kind of advantage does he have?
(solution on page 245)

Exercise 2

position after 13.♗e3-d4

What is the idea of the bishop move to d4?
(solution on page 246)

Exercise 3

position after 15.♘c3-b5

Which object does White pursue by directing the knight on this route?
(solution on page 246)

Sicilian Defence

Karjakin Shows the Way

by Luis Rodi

1.	e4	c5
2.	♘f3	e6
3.	d4	cxd4
4.	♘xd4	♘f6
5.	♘c3	♘c6
6.	♘xc6	bxc6
7.	e5	♘d5
8.	♘e4	

Sergey Karjakin was the winner of the World Cup 2015 held in Baku, securing himself a place in the next Candidates' tournament. The key to this victory? An amazing recovery in his final match against Peter Svidler, his great technique in positions with a slight advantage, and, last but not least, a suitable selection of opening lines in the preparation for each match. A good example was the line he chose to face rising star Yu Yangyi. Knowing that the Chinese grandmaster had played the Sicilian Four Knights Variation to deviate from the hard-to-break Sveshnikov (two recent examples were a game against Karjakin himself in the World

Team Championship 2015 and one against Iordachescu in the first stage of this World Cup), the Russian player prepared the sharp continuation 6.♘xc6. This was a huge success, as you can see in our extensively annotated main game.

This game (Game 1, Karjakin-Yu Yangyi, Baku 2015) is also a good opportunity to check the latest developments in this highly complex and interesting line, which was discussed in excellent Surveys by René Olthof (Yearbook 25), Georgy Timoshenko (Yearbook 55) and A.C. van der Tak (Yearbook 92). As said, Black sometimes plays the Four Knights Variation in order to play a Sveshnikov, without the risk of being lured into secondary lines like 7.♘d5 or the very fashionable Rossolimo Variation 3.♗b5. But this happens only if White goes for the positional 6.♘db5, when Black can play 6...d6 (and if 7.♗f4 e5 8.♗g5 a6). White can circumvent this plan with the other main line, 6.♘xc6 (first played by Henry Bird in 1849), which leads to very complicated tactical play. In recent years, computers have shown that here, too, White can claim the famous 'opening advantage', and that Black's task is not easy. True, in a practical game the size of White's advantage is hard to assess, and treacherous

and dangerous complications are waiting around every corner. This is why the variation remains restricted to the repertoire of strong players. However, games like Karjakin-Yu Yangyi may show a way for White to get an advantage.

Secondary Lines

In the position that arises after 8.♘e4, which is the starting point of this Survey, by far the most common continuation is 8...♕c7, but Black has various alternatives. Some of them, like 8...f5 (which remains the second-most popular move, although without recent relevant games) or 8...♗a6, were no longer popular in the time of Timoshenko's Survey, and continue to be rarely used. An idea of Adorjan's, 8...♗b7, had its 15 minutes of fame when it was played by Peter Leko to draw against no less a player than Garry Kasparov in Linares 1999. But White has a logical way to get an advantage in the continuation 9.♗e2 c5 10.0-0 (Game 2, Shirov-Westerberg, Skopje tt 2015). The key move, against Westerberg's 15...♖fc8 or Leko's 15...♕d6, is 16.b3!, securing the better structure for White.

More solid and interesting is 8...♕a5+, when after 9.c3 Black has preferred 9...♕c7 in the last few years, a move that after 10.f4 ♕b6 transposes to the line 8...♕c7 9.f4 ♕a5+ – more on this later. Independent continuations are 9...f5 and especially 9...♗a6, which we will analyse in Game 3, Hefka-Soltau, cr 2010. In the critical position after 10.♗e2 ♗xe2 11.♕xe2 f5 12.exf6 ♘xf6 13.♘xf6+ gxf6, White has the better chances.

As mentioned, the main line starts with the move 8...♕c7, and after the logical continuation 9.f4 Black again has a choice to make.

Very interesting, but also very rarely played, is 9...f5!?, with the continuation 10.exf6 gxf6 (instead of 10...♘xf6, which is known to be good for White since Reggio-Marco, Monte Carlo 1903). A better way to fight for an advantage, I think, is Popilski's 11.♗d2. See my analysis in the commentaries to Game 4.

An important option (second in popularity in this position) is 9...♕a5+. Here, too, the best white plan involves the move 10.c3, when the main line goes 10...♗e7 (or 10...♕b6 11.♗d3 ♗e7) 11.♗d3 ♕b6 (11...f5 and other alternatives can be seen in Game 4, Grischuk-Andreikin, Moscow 2012), and now 12.♕e2.

This is one of the critical positions in the line with the exchange on c6 in the Four Knights Variation. With more space and better coordinated pieces, White has the upper hand, if my recommendations in the critical continuations 12...a5 and 12...♗b7 (played by Carlsen) are correct. You can see this in Game 5, Yu Yangyi-A. Muzychuk, Wijk aan Zee B 2014.

Since the 1990s, the move 9...♖b8!? has been popular with black players (Radjabov tested it, for example). The idea is to sacrifice a piece for the initiative with 10.c4 ♗b4+ 11.♔e2 0-0 12.cxd5 cxd5. In this position White has tried various ideas, but I think that Rombaldoni's continuation 13.♘g5 is the strongest and most critical one – Black has a hard time finding compensation for the material. More about this idea in Game 6, Kartikeyan-Borisenko, Pune 2015.

Main Line: the Check on b4

Historically, Black's main continuation is 9...♕b6, and after 10.c4, the check on b4: 10...♗b4+. Sometimes, checks are like sirens singing: tempting, but also problematic, if not downright dangerous. In this case, the result of this natural move is that – after 11.♔e2 – the white king loses the right to castle, while White's development is uncomfortable because the natural road to freedom for his light-squared bishop is closed. But Black is not only incapable of exploiting this circumstance, he has also committed his pieces and will find it more difficult to deploy them than White. This is evident, for example, in the previously popular line 11...♗a6 12.♔f3! f5 13.exf6 ♘xf6 14.c5! (Forcen Esteban-

Sergey Karjakin

Astasio Lopez, Elgoibar 2011, among others), which is now considered worse for Black. The critical continuation is 11...f5, after which White preferred 12.♘f2 for a while, but nowadays 12.exf6 is considered better. Although it reduces the pressure on d6, it is more common these days, as it allows White to secure the bishop pair.

Black can counter with 12...♘xf6 13.♗e3 and continue with 13...♕a5 (still more popular in the statistics), keeping the bishops. But this leads to other problems due to his weaknesses on his kingside. Game 7, Timofeev-Nikolaev, St Petersburg 2001, is a good example for White.

Black pins his hopes on 13...♕d8, a move that has recently been preferred by stronger players. After 14.♘d6+ ♗xd6 15.♕xd6 there are several factors that allow White to play for an advantage (bishop pair, better structure, space, dark-square weaknesses in Black's camp). We consider the less usual options in the comments to Game 8, Savchenko-Tregubov,

St Petersburg rapid 2015, which continued with the interesting new pawn sac 15...c5.

Against the more usual 15...♗b7 (introduced by Leko in 2001), the main reply has become the move 16.♖d1, with the continuation 16...♖c8 17.g4 (or 17.♖g1 c5 18.g4) 17...c5 18.♖g1, when 18...♖f8 can be considered of less value because of our main game Karjakin-Yu Yangyi. In correspondence chess Black has opted for more critical ideas like 18...♕b6, 18...♕c7 or 18...♖c6. We will analyse those in the comments to Game 9, Potrata-D. Fischer, cr 2014.

The New Option 10...♘e3

The problems in this line with the check on b4 have led black players to study the option of 10...♘e3, with interesting new ideas. This will be the subject of my next Survey.

Conclusion

White can expect to gain the initiative and a slightly better position in the lines discussed in this Survey. In the secondary lines, after 8...♕c7 9.f4, the most critical variations are 9...f5 10.exf6 gxf6 (very rarely played and therefore a good surprise weapon) and 9...♕a5+ 10.c3 ♗e7 11.♗d3 ♕b6

12.♕e2, and now 12...a5 or 12...♗b7.

In the main line with the check on b4, I think that theoretical improvements will be found in the line 13...♕d8 14.♘d6+ ♗xd6 15.♕xd6 ♗b7 16.♖d1, with special emphasis on the moves 18...♕c7, 18...♕b6 and 18...♖c6, for which more practical examples are needed. Some correspondence games, meanwhile, show evidence of a white advantage. In classical chess, this advantage is difficult to make concrete due to the tactical nature of the lines, but the statistics show that White has the upper hand.

| Main Game |
| 8...♕c7 |

Sergey Karjakin 1
Yu Yangyi

Baku 2015 (3)

1.e4 c5 2.♘f3 e6 3.d4 cxd4 4.♘xd4 ♘c6 5.♘c3 ♘f6 6.♘xc6 [In Karjakin's selection of this line two factors may be considered: a) the previous game between the same players in the World Teams 2015 in Armenia, where after 6.♘db5 d6 a Sveshnikov Variation ensued; b) the Chinese grandmaster had previous games with the position that appears after the check on b4, which undoubtedly facilitated the preparation of the white player] **6...bxc6 7.e5 ♘d5 8.♘e4 ♕c7** [A subtlety, forcing the next move to weaken the g1-a7 diagonal. The second option in the statistics – now out of fashion on the highest level – is 8...f5 when 9.exf6 ♘xf6 10.♘d6+ ♗xd6 11.♕xd6 leads to positions with a structure similar to the one in our game. An example is 11...♕b6 12.♗d3 c5 13.♗f4 ♗b7 14.0-0 ♖c8 15.c4 ♕xd6 16.♗xd6 ♖c6 17.♗e5± Santiago-Brito, Recife 2013] **9.f4 ♕b6 10.c4**

10...♗b4+ [This evident check is very tempting, and most of the black players give it as White loses the right to castle. For many years, the theoretical diagnosis was that the game was unclear, but more recently the computers have put this into question, showing ways for White to fight for an advantage. If this trend is confirmed, Black will search for equality with another logical idea, the second-most played move in this position: 10...♘e3. A sample game with the same white player is 11.♕d3 ♘xf1 (main alternatives are 11...♗b4+ and 11...♘f5) 12.♖xf1 c5 13.♗d2 ♗b7 14.0-0-0± Karjakin-Nepomniachtchi, Moscow ch-RUS playoff 2010] **11.♔e2 f5** [Instead, withdrawing the knight would allow 12.♗e3 with excellent play for White.

He can continue with c4-c5, and another detail is that the king now has the square f2 to go to, enabling him to coordinate his pieces by the development of the light bishop. The only real alternative to the text is 11...♗a6 – also out of fashion – which is answered by 12.♔f3 f5 when the en passant capture leads to an evident white advantage: his king is apparently more exposed, but Black cannot exploit this and the light-squared bishop is ready to act] **12.exf6** [With this capture White loses some pressure on d6, but if his knight retreats then Black can realize his defensive task without suffering serious consequences, because the c5-point isn't dominated by White. For example:

A) 12.♘g3 ♘c7 13.♗e3 ♗c5 14.♗xc5 ♕xc5 15.b3 0-0 is OK for Black, as in Blatov-Shkliar, Samara 2002;

B) 12.♘f2 is the most popular continuation in practice, but the position after 12...♗a6 13.♔f3 ♗e7 is not so clear, for instance 14.♗e3 ♗c5 15.♗xc5 ♕xc5 16.♕d6 ♕a5 17.♗e2 g5!? 18.♖hd1 ♖d8 19.g3 g4+ 20.♔g2 c5⇄ Areshchenko-Terrieux, Porticcio 2015] **12...♘xf6 13.♗e3 ♕d8** [The latest practical examples in this line show a preference for this retreat. After the alternatives, Black problems are evident] **14.♘d6+ ♗xd6** [Sadly for Black, the standard reply 14...♚e7 (Rmus-Rogozenco, Bucharest 2004) is not good in view of 15.c5!. At first sight Black doesn't seem to be in trouble, but White has a strong plan based on ideas like ♕d4 or f4-f5, for example 15...♘d5 16.♕d4 ♕f8 17.♚f2±. The exchange on d6 is the most usual continuation, but Black loses his better minor piece, and the resultant position can be considered somewhat better in practical games for the first player] **15.♕xd6** [White has the following advantages here: a) the bishop pair; b) the better structure: two solid islands against three with various weaknesses; c) more space; d) weaknesses in Black's dark-square complex. Whether White can turn these advantage into something concrete depends on his ability to coordinate his forces] **15...♗b7** [In practice this is the most common move, and the Chinese grandmaster had already used it. The idea is to continue with ...♖c8 and ...c6-c5, giving freedom to the restricted bishop. White can kill this plan with c4-c5, but this is at the high cost of granting the d5-square to the enemy knight. Instead, Karjakin develops a strong offensive on the kingside. Some alternatives for Black:

A) Logical is 15...♕e7, considering that White's queen is very strong on d6, although the exchange of queens reduces Black's control of the dark squares: 16.♗c5 ♕xd6 17.♗xd6 ♘e4 18.♗a3± Martin Gonzalez-Li Zunian, Biel 1985;

B) 15...♘e4 16.♕e5 ♕f6 (Frindt-Federic, Slovakia tt 2011) 17.♚e1!± with the idea of ♗d3;

C) A very recent try is 15...c5!?, giving a pawn for activity. More on this in game 8 of this Survey, Savchenko-Tregubov]

16.♖d1 [Maybe the most critical continuation, 16.♚d3, was played in Lu Shanglei-Yu Yangyi, China ch 2015, a game that may have formed the basis of Karjakin's preparation. After 16...c5 (16...♚f7!?) 17.♚c2 (17.♕xc5 ♗e4+ 18.♚d2 d6 19.♕b5+ ♚f7☒) 17...♖c8 18.♗d3 ♕b6 19.♕xb6 axb6 20.♖he1 ♗xg2 21.♖g1 ♗e4 22.♖xg7 ♗g6 Black has, at a minimum, an easy balance; 16.♚d1!? is another possibility (Svidler-Leko, Yerevan 2001, and other games)] **16...♖c8** [Very logical, planning to continue with ...c6-c5. Before this game this move was played only in correspondence games] **17.g4!** [White seizes the initiative with this move, which gains space and tries to drive out the ♘f6 and is also aimed against possible plans with ...♚f7. Note that the order 17.♖g1 c5 18.g4 is preferred in correspondence games] **17...c5** [It is not good to open the file for the ♖h1 with the risky 17...♘xg4 because of 18.♗c5! (18.♖g1 ♘xe3 19.♚xe3 g6 is less clear) 18...♘f6 (18... g6 19.♗h3+−) 19.♖g1 ♚f7 20.♖d3 and White's compensation is more than adequate] **18.♖g1 ♖f8?!** [I think this is wrong. In my view, critical are the options 18...♖c6, 18...♕c7 or the immediate 18...♕b6. More about these moves in the comments to the last game of this Survey] **19.f5!** [This break comes in time, when the exchange on f5 yields White absolute domination of the g-file. It is a novelty. A previous correspondence game continued 19.♗g2 ♗xg2 20.♖xg2 ♖f7 21.♚f1 ♕c7 22.♚g1 ♕xd6 23.♖xd6 h5 (Fabri-Troia, cr 2013). Now 24.g5 was perhaps the best way to continue, with some initiative for White] **19...♕b6** [After the coming exchange on e6, this move leaves Black with a highly deteriorated pawn formation: four islands, three of them consisting of isolated pawns. 19...♘e4 20.♕e5 ♕f6 is a better way to exchange queens, when 21.♕xf6 ♖xf6 22.♗g2 ♖c6 23.♖h1 exf5 24.gxf5 ♖f7 25.♗d3 offers the better chances to White] **20.fxe6 dxe6 21.g5!** [Now it is evident that White has won the strategic battle, forcing the queen exchange (due to the threat to d7) without connecting the black pawns on the queenside] **21...♘d5** [More resilient is 21...♕xd6 22.♖xd6 ♚e7 (22...♘g4?! 23.♗h3±) 23.♖xe6+ (the options 23.gxf6+ ♚xd6 24.fxg7 ♖g8 25.♗h3☒ and 23.♖d3!? deserve

consideration if you don't like the simplified position after the capture on e6) 23...♚xe6 24.♗h3+ ♚f7 25.♗xc8 ♖xc8 26.gxf6 gxf6 (26...♚xf6 27.♖g5±) 27.♖g3±. Despite the drawing tendencies of the opposite-coloured bishops, this position is better for the first player (structure, activity)] **22.♕xb6 ♘xb6 23.♚e1!±** [Another strong move by Karjakin, finally fully coordinating his army, as well as defending c4. Compared with our evaluation on the 15th move, here White has increased his advantages, especially those mentioned under a) and b). In the meantime, the road to this position was not easy, and neither is the next phase, where White tries to concretize his advantage] **23...♘d7 24.♗e2 ♚e7?!** [A move based on general principles, but it allows White to realize his plan freely. The more concrete 24...♘e5!? – directed against Karjakin's next reply – deserves consideration: 25.♖f1!? ♖f5 26.♗xf5 exf5 27.♚f2±] **25.♖d3!±** [Karjakin forges ahead with great energy. The rook is positioned actively on the third rank to start the attack on Black's structural weaknesses] **25...♗e4** [25...♘e5 26.♖a3 ♘f3+ 27.♗xf3 ♖xf3 28.♚e2±] **26.♖a3 ♖c7 27.♚d2** [Having a position with permanent advantages, the first player improves his pieces gradually. Meanwhile, Black's army lacks coordination and, consequently, the capacity to create the necessary counterplay] **27...e5** [I don't like this move – Black's pawns become more exposed –, but it is hard to show a constructive alternative. The main idea is to free the square e6 for the knight – which may later jump to d4 –, but this is not easy to realize, because this piece has the task of protecting c5] **28.♖f1** [This rook has done its duty on the g-file, and now tries to get exchanged for Black's more active rook on f8. Black doesn't accept, and as a result White ends up dominating the f-file. As we can see, Karjakin increases his advantage step by step with these strong little moves] **28...♖b8** [After 28...♖xf1 29.♗xf1 White preserves all his advantages, while threatening ♗h3. As mentioned, Black has problems if he tries to move the knight to d4: 29...♘f8 is met by 30.♖xa7! and if 29...♘b6 then 30.♖a5±] **29.♚c3 ♖b6** [Black finds new use for his e-pawn advance, but there isn't any target for him to attack] **30.♖d1** [A transformation of advantages. On the f-file this rook worked well, but there are no access points. In its new function the rook tries to exert pressure on d7 with the help of the move ♗g4] **30.♖bc6** [Freeing b6 for the knight, but not putting up any obstacles to White's plan. 30...♗f5 (aimed against ♗g4) is less cooperative – it can be met with 31.♖a5 (31.♗f3!?) 31...g6 32.♗f3±] **31.♗g4+–** ♘b6 [31...♖d6 32.♖xd6 ♗xd6 33.♖a6+ ♔c6 34.♖a5 ♗e4 35.♗xd7 ♖xd7 36.♖xc5+ ♔e6 37.♗xa7+–] **32.♖a5** [White continues to make progress, leaving Black's pieces tied up. Black is on the edge of zugzwang] **32... g6 33.b3** [33.♖e1!?, with a clear X-ray theme, was perhaps stronger] **33...♗f5 34.♗e2** [Obviously, White preserves the bishop pair – the exchange would concede Black a bit of counterplay] **34...♘d7 35.a3 ♗e6** [Black fights against a possible b3-b4 with the bishop on this diagonal, but now ...e5-e4 is not an option, and White ends up dominating the long light-squared diagonal] **36.h4 ♗f7** [36...♖b6 was more resilient, although 37.♗f3 would leave White with a strategically won position] **37.♗f3 ♖b6 38.♖xd7+!** [The beginning of the end. Now the capture with the rook loses material because of the check on c5] **38...♗xd7 39.♗xc5 e4** [A desperate try, based on 40.♗xe4 ♖e6. The rook has not square, for instance 39...♖e6 40.♗g4+–] **40.♗g4+** [Black resigned, since 40...♖e6 41.♗xb6 axb6 (41...♗xg4 42.♖xc7 is no better) 42.♖d5+ ♗e7 43.♖e5 ♖c6 44.♖xe4 leads to a pawn ending that is easily winning for White. An excellent technical demonstration by Karjakin!]   1-0

Secondary Lines
8...♗b7

Alexei Shirov   2
Jonathan Westerberg
Skopje tt 2015 (3)

1.e4 c5 2.♘f3 e6 3.d4 cxd4 4.♘xd4 ♘c6 5.♘c3 ♘f6 6.♘xc6 bxc6 7.e5 ♘d5 8.♘e4 ♗b7 9.♗e2 c5 10.0-0 ♕c7 11.♘d6+ [11.c4 is another popular option: 11...♘e3 12.♗xe3 ♗xe4⇄ Palac-Westerberg, Skopje tt 2015] **11...♗xd6 12.exd6 ♕c6** [12...♕b6 13.a3!? with the idea to continue with c2-c4] **13.f3! c4 14.♕d4 0-0 15.♗xc4**

15...♖fc8 [15...♕xd6 was played in the first game with 8...♗b7, Kasparov-Leko, Linares 1999. Garry played 16.♗b3, but better is 16.b3 (Anand's 16.♖d1 is also good) 16...♖fc8 with transposition to the game. Meanwhile, 16...♕b6 is met with 17.♕xb6 axb6 (Vavulin-Krapivin, Moscow 2012) 18.a4±] **16.b3 ♕xd6 17.♖d1 ♕b6 18.♕xb6 axb6 19.a4±** [White's structure is better, and so are his minor pieces] **19...♗c6** [19...♘b4 20.♖xd7 ♗c6 21.♖d2 b5 22.♗a3 bxc4 23.♗xb4 cxb3 24.cxb3± J.Geller-Lintchevski, Kazan 2015] **20.♗d2 ♘f6 21.♗f1 d5 22.♗e3 ♘d7 23.c4 ♘c5 24.♖ab1 ♘xb3 25.cxd5 ♗xd5 26.♖xd5 exd5 27.♖xb3 ♖xa4 28.♗xb6 ♖a2 29.♖b1 ♖cc2 30.♗d4 f6 31.h4 ♖d2 32.♗e3 ♖db2 33.♖d1±** [An interesting and difficult ending. Shirov starts the technical work by creating a second weakness on the enemy kingside] **33...♖a5 34.h5 ♔f7 35.h6 gxh6 36.♗xh6 ♖ba2 37.♖c1 ♖a1 38.♖c7+ ♔g6?** [The decisive mistake – the king is exposed here. 38...♔e6 was necessary] **39.♗c1+–** [White wins in a direct attack] **39...d4 40.♔f2 h5 41.♗d3+ f5 42.♖c6+ ♔f7 43.♗g5 ♖d1 44.♗c4+ ♔g7 45.♖c7+ ♔g6 46.f4 ♖d2+ 47.♔g3 ♖a3+ 48.♔h4 d3 49.♗g8**   1-0

Secondary Lines
8...♕a5+

Vladimír Hefka   3
Achim Soltau
cr 2010

1.e4 c5 2.♘f3 e6 3.d4 cxd4 4.♘xd4 ♘f6 5.♘c3 ♘c6 6.♘xc6 bxc6 7.e5 ♘d5 8.♘e4 ♕a5+ [Some players consider the schemes with ...♕a5 more solid for Black] **9.c3 ♗a6** [One of the classical tries. Nowadays 9...♕c7

---

is preferred, with great chances of a transposition to the line 8...♕c7 9.f4 ♕a5. Another old idea is 9...f5 10.exf6 ♘xf6 11.♘xf6+ gxf6. Now 12.♗e2 ♗a6 13.0-0 ♗xe2 14.♕xe2 transposes to the text, and 12.♗e3 is also good. An illustrative line is 12...♕d5 13.♕c2 f5 14.♗e2!? ♕xg2 15.♗h5+ ♔d8 16.0-0-0± with more than adequate compensation] **10.♗e2** [I think this is stronger than the alternatives, although 10.♗d3 deserves consideration, for instance 10...♗xd3 11.♕xd3 ♕b5!? 12.♕xb5 (12.♕g3!?, Walsh-Soltau, cr 2010) 12...cxb5 13.a4 bxa4 14.♖xa4 f6 15.exf6 gxf6 16.♖a5 f5 17.♘d2 with some white initiative, Wilczek-Soltau, cr 2010] **10...♗xe2** [10...♗e7!? 11.0-0 0-0 12.♗d2 ♗xe2 (12...♘b6 13.♗xa6 ♕xa6 14.b3±) 13.♕xe2 ♕c7 14.c4 (Biolek-Chladny, Ostrava 2006) 14...♘b6 15.♗f4!±] **11.♕xe2 f5 12.exf6 ♘xf6 13.♘xf6+ gxf6**

14.0-0± [A critical position for the evaluation of this line. White is a bit better because he has the better structure and development, as has been demonstrated in practice] **14...♕f5** [Some alternatives: A) 14...♖g8 15.♗e3 ♕d5 16.g3 h5 17.♖ad1 ♕f5 18.♖d4± Karjakin-Olenin, Nikolaev 2001; B) The most popular move is 14...♗d6, when 15.♗e3 ♕e5 16.f4 ♕f5 17.♖ad1 ♗e7 (Real de Azua-Salguero, Mendoza 2008) 18.♖d2± is somewhat better for White, with pressure against the black centre pawns] **15.♗e3 ♖g8 16.♖ad1 d5** [16...♖b8 17.g3 ♕b5 18.a4 ♕h5 (Nouro-Franssila, Finland tt 2004) 19.♕d3 ♖d5 20.♕c2±] **17.♖d4!±** [Control of the fourth rank is added to the mentioned white advantages, going for the initiative] **17...♗d6** [17...e5!? 18.♖a4±; 17...♗e7 18.♖h4 e5 19.♖h5 ♕e6 20.f4±] **18.♖h4 a5 19.g3 ♔f7 20.♖h5 ♕e4 21.f3 ♕g6 22.♖h6 ♕g7 23.♕d3**

♖h8 24.♔h1 ♗c5 25.♗c1 ♕g8
26.♕e2 ♗f8 27.♖h4 h5 28.f4 ♗d6
[28...♕h7 29.f5 e5 30.c4±] 29.♖e1
♔e7 30.♖xh5 ♖xh5 31.♕xh5 a4
32.♔g2 ♗d7 33.h4 [In correspondence
chess, this is a decisive advantage]
33...♕g7 34.♕e2 ♖e8 35.h5 e5
36.g4 e4 37.a3 ♖g8 38.♔h3 ♗e8
39.♗e3 ♕d7 40.♔h4   1-0

Secondary Lines
8...♕c7 9.f4 ♕a5+

Alexander Grischuk   4
Dmitry Andreikin

Moscow 2012 (7)

1.e4 c5 2.♘f3 e6 3.d4 cxd4
4.♘xd4 ♘f6 5.♘c3 ♘c6 6.♘xc6
bxc6 7.e5 ♘d5 8.♘e4 ♕c7 [This
is the way to reach the main line. Now,
after] 9.f4 [Black has some different
possibilities:] 9...♕a5+!? [This check
has some reputation. The most popular
moves, 9...♕b6 and 9...♖b8, will be
looked at later. Black also has 9...f5!? –
rarely played but not bad –, when 10.exf6
can be met with the interesting 10...gxf6
(10...♘xf6 11.♘xf6+ gxf6 12.♕h5+ ♔d8
13.♗d2 d5 was played in Reggio-Mieses,
Monte Carlo 1903. Now, best seems
14.♕h4!? ♕f7 15.♗c3 ♗e7 16.0-0-0±)

11.♗d2! (less clear is 11.♕h5+ ♔d8⇄)
11...♖b8 (11...♗e7!? can be met with
Roiz's idea 12.♕h5+ ♔d8 13.0-0-0. If
now 13...♘xf4 14.♕h6 with very good
compensation. Black can try instead 13...
♖b8, which isn't so clear, but earlier on
13.c4!? seems good for White) 12.c4
♘xf4 13.♕f3 (13.♕g4 is another way
to get compensation, as in Falomir-
Lyantsev, cr 2014) 13...♘g6 (13...e5
(Popilski-Baghdasaryan, Groningen 2014)
14.g3 ♘g6 15.♘xf6+ ♔d8 16.0-0-0±)

14.♘xf6+ ♔d8 15.0-0-0 ♗e7 16.g4!
♘e5 (16...c5 17.♖g1±; 16...h6!? 17.h4
♘e5 18.♕f2 should transpose) 17.♕f2!?
(better than 17.♕f4, Ivanovic-Lovakovic,
cr 2011) 17...♕b6 (17...♖f8 18.g5 h6
19.h4 ♘g4 20.♕e1 ♘xf6 21.gxf6 ♗xf6
22.♗a5 ♖b6 23.c5 ♕f4+ 24.♔d2 ♗xb2+
25.♔b1±) 18.♕xb6+ axb6 19.g5±] 10.
c3 [Some strong players (for example,
Michael Adams, Peter Svidler, Sergey
Fedorchuk) try the alternative 10.♗d2,
but the text move is considered more
critical] 10...♗e7 [10...♕b6 11.♗d3
♗e7 – see next game] 11.♗d3 f5
11...♕b6 is critical, transposing to the next
game; 11...♗a6!? 12.0-0 ♗xd3 13.♕xd3
f5 14.exf6 ♘xf6 15.♘xf6+ gxf6 16.♗e3±
Gschwendtner-Schmid, Germany tt 1995]

[12.exf6! [Less convincing is 12.♘f2
0-0 13.0-0 ♕c7 with good counterplay
in Gashimov-Radjabov, Wijk aan Zee
2012] 12...♘xf6 [12...gxf6!? 13.f5!↑]
13.♘xf6+ ♗xf6 14.0-0 ♗a6
[14...♕b6+ 15.♖f2 0-0 16.♕e2↑ with
the idea of ♗e3] 15.♗xa6 ♕xa6
16.♗e3± [The superior structure rules,
because Black's pieces aren't sufficiently
active] 16...♕b5 17.♖f2 [Going to d2,
with typical pressure against the black
pawns in this type of ...♕a5+ line] 17...
d5 [17...a5 18.a4 ♕f5 19.♕d6 ♕d5
20.♕c7 0-0 21.♖d2 ♘e4 22.♖e1±]
18.♕g4 [18.♕h5+!? g6 19.♕h3 ♔f7
20.♖e1± is another way] 18...♔f7
19.f5 e5□ 20.♕h5+ ♔e7 [20...♔g8!?
21.♗g5±] 21.b4± ♖hf8 22.♕xh7 [Of
course, also possible is 22.♗c5+ ♔d7
23.♗xf8 (23.♖c1±) 23...♖xf8 24.♕xh7
e4 25.♕h3±] 22...e4 23.♗c5+ ♔d7
24.♗d4 [24.♗xf8 ♖xf8 transposes to
22.♗c5+] 24...♖h8 [24...♗xd4 25.cxd4
♕xb4 26.f6±] 25.♕g6 ♖ae8 [A
desperate bid for counterplay] 26.♗xf6
gxf6 27.♕g7+ ♔c8 28.♕xf6 e3

[28...♖hf8 29.♕d6±] 29.♖f3+− ♕e2
[29...e2 30.♖e1+−] 30.♕xc6+ ♔b8
31.♕d6+ ♔c8 32.♕c6+ ♔b8
33.♕d6+ ♔c8 34.♖xd5 ♖hg8
35.♖f4 ♔b8 36.f6 ♖d8 37.f7
♖gf8 38.♕e5+ ♔b7 39.♖ff1 ♖d7
40.♖ae1 ♕xa2 41.♕b5+   1-0

Yu Yangyi   5
Anna Muzychuk

Wijk aan Zee B 2014 (11)

1.e4 c5 2.♘f3 e6 3.d4 cxd4
4.♘xd4 ♘f6 5.♘c3 ♘c6 6.♘xc6
bxc6 7.e5 ♘d5 8.♘e4 ♕c7 9.f4
♕a5+ 10.c3 ♗e7 11.♗d3 ♕b6!
[This is one of the critical positions (from
Black's viewpoint) in this Survey; White
has some problems trying to show an
advantage because the second player has
good control of the dark squares. White
will have to rely on his space surplus and
well-placed pieces] 12.♕e2! [Best. The
first player scores well with the alternative
12.c4, but after 12...f5 I see no reason
to complain for Black, because he has a
better version of the typical schemes in
this variation, for instance: 13.exf6 ♘xf6
14.♕c2 ♘xe4 15.♗xe4 ♗a6 16.♗d2
♗f6∓ Ye Jiangchuan-Ivanchuk, Manila
1992] 12...♖b8!? [Some other options
are:

A) 12...a5 is the most popular and,
perhaps, critical. I'm not satisfied with the
commonly played 13.a3, so we will look at

13.♗d2!? 0-0 (13...♕xb2? 14.♖b1 ♕xa2
15.0-0± and the black queen is in danger;
13...a4 14.c4 ♘b4 15.♗b1 ♗a6 16.♗e3
c5 17.0-0 ♘d5 18.♗c1 is a curious line.
It seems as if White has lost territory,
but his chances are actually preferable,
because he has the better structure, for
instance: 18...f5 19.exf6 ♘xf6 20.♘c3±)
14.c4 ♘b4 15.♗b1 ♗a6 16.♗e3 c5
(16...♕b8 17.a3 ♘d5 18.♕c2 f5 19.cxd5

fxe4 20.dxe6 ♗d3 21.♕c3±) 17.0-0 (17. b3 a4 with counterplay, for example: 18.♕h5 g6 19.♕h6 f5∞. Note that Black can refute White's attack with the advance of the h-pawn. How? Please go to Exercise 1) 17...♗d5 18.♗c1 (18.♕c2 f5 19.cxd5 ♗xf1 20.d6 ♗d8 21.♔xf1 fxe4 22.♕xe4 g6 23.♗d3⩲ deserves serious consideration) 18...f5 19.exf6 ♗xf6 (19...♘xf6 20.♗g5†) 20.♘xf6+ ♘xf6 21.♗d3 with initiative;

B) 12...♗b7 was Carlsen's choice:

13.a3 f5 (13...a5 14.c4 f5 (Fass-Ivanov, cr 2009) 15.♘f2!? ♘c7 16.♗e3†) 14.exf6 ♘xf6 (14...gxf6 (Tomczak-Koziak, Barlinek 2006) 15.c4 f5 16.cxd5 fxe4 17.♗e3 ♕c7 18.♕h5+ ♗d8 19.d6 ♗xd6 20.♗xe4±) 15.♗e3 c5 16.♘xf6+ gxf6 (Smeets-Carlsen, Schagen rapid 2005). Now it seems better to play 17.0-0-0± , when I prefer White because of his better coordinated army and better structure] **13. a3** [White needs to protect b4 to make c3-c4 effective. The immediate 13.c4 is (also here) well answered by 13...f5, but 13.g4!? – a Stockfish 6 idea – seems interesting. If 13...♗h4+ 14.♔f1 with a very complex position] **13...a5** [Black has also tried the standard 13...f5 (Kolomensky-Lobov, Nizhnij Tagil ch-RUS sf 2007), when 14.exf6 ♘xf6 15.b4 is a bit better for the first player, for instance: 15...♘xe4 16.♗e3 c5 17.♗xe4 g6 18.h4!?±]

14.c4 [According to plan. But also faithful to the a2-a3 idea is 14.b4!?, threatening 15.♗e3. After 14...axb4 (14...f5 15.exf6 gxf6 16.c4 f5 17.cxd5 fxe4 18.♗e3 is very good for the first player) 15.axb4 0-0 16.♗d2 c5 17.b5 the position seems a bit better for White, but Black's counterplay is also appreciable; 14.♖b1!? is another way to prepare a future ♗e3, and is perhaps the better choice. Now: 14...♗b7 15.c4 f5 and after 16.exf6 ♘xf6 17.♘xf6+ ♗xf6 White has 18.♗e3 c5 (18...♗d4 is no good because of 19.♕h5+±) 19.0-0±] **14...f5 15.exf6** [15.♘d6+!? ♗xd6 16.exd6 ♘f6 17.♗xf5 0-0 18.♗d3 (S.Villegas-Bertona, Cordoba 1993) and Black's compensation may not be sufficient; 15.♘f2 ♘c7 16.0-0 0-0, and perhaps White chances are better after 17.♗d2 a4 18.♗c3†] **15...♘xf6 16.♖b1** [16.♘xf6+ ♗xf6⇄] **16...♘xe4 17.♗xe4 ♕d4?!** [17...♗f6!, fighting for the dark squares, with good counterplay] **18.b3?!** [18.♗d3!†] **18...d5 19.♗d3 ♗f6?!** [19...0-0!?; 19...♗d6 20.♗e3 ♕c3+ 21.♗d2 ♕d4=] **20.♗e3** [Now Black has coordinating problems] **20...♕c3+ 21.♗d2 ♕d4 22.cxd5 ♗xd5** [22... cxd5 23.♗e3 ♕c3+ 24.♗f2±] **23.0-0** [Very logical, but 23.♗c4 ♗h4+ 24.♔f1± is also possible] **23...♖xb3 24.♖xb3 ♕xb3 25.f5!? ♕xa3** [Playing with fire. 25...0-0 26.♗c4 ♕xa3 27.fxe6 ♗e7= seemed necessary] **26.fxe6 ♕c5+ 27.♔h1 ♕e5 28.♗e4± ♗xe6?** [28...0-0? 29.♗xh7+ ♔xh7 30.♕xe5 ♗xe5 31.♖xf8+−; better is 28...♕b5 29.♕f3 0-0 30.♗xc6 ♕c5 31.♗d5±, although Black is not without counterplay] **29.♗xc6+ ♔e7 30.♕a6+−** [Black's exposed king is a great problem here] **30...♖d8** [30...♖c8 31.♖e1+−] **31.♗xa5 ♖c8 32.♖e1 ♕xa5 33.♕xa5 ♖xc6 34.♕a7+ ♔f8 35.h3 ♗c8 36.♕a8 ♖c7 37.♕d5 ♗b7 38.♕d6+** 1-0

Secondary Lines
8...♕c7 9.f4 ♖b8

Murali Karthikeyan   **6**
Viacheslav Borisenko
Pune 2014 (5)

1.e4 c5 2.♘f3 e6 3.d4 cxd4 4.♘xd4 ♘f6 5.♘c3 ♘c6 6.♘xc6 bxc6 7.e5 ♘d5 8.♘e4 ♕c7 9.f4 ♖b8 [First played in 1991, this move became popular

when it was used by no less a player than Radjabov. In the main line it involves a speculative sacrifice] **10.c4** [Accepting the challenge. I think this is the best way for White to deal with this scheme. In practice, meanwhile, more popular – and with some very good statistics – is the option 10.♗d3 as in Naiditsch-Radjabov, Dortmund 2003] **10...♗b4+** [10...♘b6 is not a good idea. White can get a clear advantage with many different moves, for example: 11.♘d6+ (11.♗e3±) 11...♗xd6 12.exd6 ♕d8 (Barlovic-Podravec, Croatia tt 2009) 13.♗e2±. The d6-pawn cuts the black position in two] **11.♔e2**

11...0-0!? [This is the crux of Black's idea – a brave move that has yielded excellent results in practice. The second player sacrifices the knight, hoping for compensation because of the exposed enemy king] **12.cxd5** [12.a3 ♗e7 13.cxd5 cxd5 (Perunovic-Pavlovic, Budva 2002). Now White can investigate 14.♘d6!?] **12...cxd5 13.♘g5!** [Strong. White has also played 13.♘f2 and 13.♘d6, but they are not as good as the text] **13...f6** [13... h6 14.♘f3 ♗c5 15.♕c2 d6 16.♗d2± Blike-Troia, cr 2010] **14.exf6 ♖xf6** [14...gxf6 15.♘f3 ♗b7 (15...♗c5 16.a3 ♕b6 17.♕c2 ♗a6+ 18.♗e1± Jensen-Troia, cr 2010) 16.♗e3 ♗d6 17.♕d2± Rombaldoni-Kanmazalp, Kemer 2007] **15.♕d3 g6 16.♗e3** [This move is not bad, but instead, ideas like 16.♔d1± or 16.g3 leave Black few possibilities; he simply runs out of compensation] **16...♗b7** [16...♖xf4!? 17.♗xf4 ♕xf4 18.♘f3 ♗c5 19.b3±] **17.♖c1± ♗c6 18.♘f3 ♗d6 19.♕d4 ♖f5 20.♔d1** [Why not 20.g3+− ?] **20...♗xf4 21.♗d3** [21.♖c2, protecting b2, is also good: 21...♗xe3 22.♕xe3 e5 23.♔c1±] **21...e5 22.♗xf4 ♖xf4 23.♕xe5 ♕xe5 24.♘xe5 ♖xb2 25.♘xc6?!** [It seems that 25.♖f1!± was necessary] **25... dxc6 26.♖f1** [26.♖xc6 ♖xa2 27.♖c2 ♖a1+ 28.♖c1 ♖a2⇄] **26...♖g4⇄** [Now the play is very complex, and after some adventures the game finished in a draw] **27.♖xc6 ♖gxg2 28.♔c1 ♖xa2 29.♖c7 ♖af2 30.♖e1 ♖f7 31.♖c2 ♖xc2+ 32.♗xc2 ♖f2 33.♖e7 ♖xh2 34.♗b3 ♔f8 35.♖xa7 d4 36.♖d7 ♖h3 37.♗e6 ♖e3 38.♗a2 d3 39.♖xh7 ♖e1+ 40.♔d2 ♖e2+ 41.♔xd3 ♖xa2 42.♔e3 ♔g8 43.♖b7 ♖a5 44.♔f4 ♖f5+ 45.♔g4 ♖f7 46.♖b5 ♔g7 47.♔g5 ♖f5+** ½-½

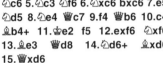

Main Line
Check on b4

Artyom Timofeev   **7**
Nikita Nikolaev
St Petersburg 2001 (1)

1.e4 c5 2.♘f3 e6 3.d4 cxd4 4.♘xd4 ♘f6 5.♘c3 ♘c6 6.♘xc6 bxc6 7.e5 ♘d5 8.♘e4 ♕c7 9.f4 ♕b6 [Finally we are in the main line] **10.c4 ♗b4+** [As mentioned in the introduction, some checks are like sirens singing. In this case, it is the most popular move, but maybe not the best, although proving this is of course very difficult. 10...♘e3 is the great alternative here. For more about this, see my next Survey] **11.♔e2 f5** [11...♗a6 was popular once, but not anymore. After 12.♔f3! White can coordinate his pieces in an effective way, for example: 12...f5 13.exf6 ♘xf6

14.c5! ♕a5 15.♘d6+ (also good is the most common move 15.♘xf6+ gxf6 16.♗xa6 ♕xa6 17.♕d4 ♕b5 18.♗e3 0-0-0 19.♖hd1± Yakovich-Kramnik, ch-URS qual 1988) 15...♔e7 (15...♔f8 16.♗xa6 ♕xa6 17.♗e3 ♘d5 18.♗d4±)

16.♗xa6 ♕xa6 17.♗e3 ♗a5 (17...♘d5 18.♕d4+– Forcen Esteban-Astasio Lopez, Elgoibar 2011) 18.f5±] **12.exf6 ♘xf6 13.♗e3**

13...♕a5 [This is the most popular move, but actually 13...♕d8 is the main continuation – see next games; 13...♕c7 14.♘xf6+ gxf6 15.c5 d6 16.♕xd6 ♕xd6 17.cxd6 ♗xd6 18.♖c1± Panchenko-Gorelov, Aktjubinsk ch-URS sf 1985] **14.♘xf6+ gxf6 15.a3** [15.♔f2± (Inarkiev-Galkin, Turkey tt 2011) is also good] **15...♗e7 16.♔f2±** [White's position is preferable, because he has the better structure and more space. Also, his pieces are well coordinated, while Black has some problems to activate his forces] **16...0-0** [16...c5 17.♕h5+ ♔d8 18.b4 (the immediate 18.♗e2± is even stronger) 18...♕c7 (Malec-Leniart, Warsaw 2012) 19.♗e2! ♗b7 20.♖hd1±] **17.b4 ♕d8 18.c5** [Threatening to put up an iron curtain over the dark squares. Black's reply is the only move from a strategic viewpoint:] **18...a5 19.b5** [19.♗c4 is interesting: 19...axb4 20.axb4 ♖xa1 21.♕g4+ ♔h8 22.♖xa1±] **19...cxb5 20.♗xb5 a4** [20...♕c7 21.♖c1±; 20...♖b8 21.a4±] **21.♖b1 ♕c7 22.♕d4 ♖d8 23.f5!?** [This was a rapid game, and in this type of game the initiative is very important, as well as the time control. The text move, guided by the principle of fighting for the initiative, is a bit impulsive, and allows Black to coordinate his pieces. 23.♖hc1±] **23...♔h8 24.♗d3 ♗b7 25.♖hc1 ♗c6∞** [Now both sides have chances] **26.♗e4 ♖g8?!** [26...exf5!? is better, with balanced play after 27.♗g5 ♗xe4 28.♗xf6+ ♗xf6 29.♕xf6+ ♔g8 30.♕g5+ ♔f7=] **27.♗xc6 ♕xc6** [27...dxc6 28.♕f4±] **28.g3** [White is again in the driver's seat] **28...exf5**

[28...e5 29.♕d3±] **29.♖b6± ♕e4 30.♖xf6! ♕xd4** [30...♔xf6 31.♕xf6+ ♖g7 32.♗d4 ♕g4 33.♕d6±] **31.♖xd4 ♗xf6 32.♗xf6+ ♖g7 33.♖d1+– ♖a6 34.♗xg7+ ♔xg7 35.♖xd7+ ♔g6 36.♔e3 ♖e6+ 37.♔d4 ♖e2 38.c6**   1-0

Boris Savchenko   **8**
Pavel Tregubov
St Petersburg rapid 2015 (10)

1.e4 c5 2.♘f3 e6 3.d4 cxd4 4.♘xd4 ♘c6 5.♘c3 ♘f6 6.♘xc6 bxc6 7.e5 ♘d5 8.♘e4 ♕c7 9.f4 ♕b6 10.c4 ♗b4+ 11.♔e2 f5 12.exf6 ♘xf6 13.♗e3 ♕d8 14.♘d6+ ♗xd6 15.♕xd6

15...c5!? [A very recent idea, trying to activate the queenside pieces at the expense of the c-pawn] **16.♖d1** [16.♕xc5 ♗b7, and now 17.♖d1 transposes to the text, but White has an independent option in 17.♖g1, for example: 17...♘e4 18.♕d4 0-0 19.g3 ♕e8 20.♗g2 ♕h5+ 21.♔e1 ♕a5+ 22.♔d1 d5 23.♗xe4 dxe4 24.♕e5 ♕d8+ 25.♔e1 ♕d3 26.♕c3 (perhaps somewhat better is 26.♕d4 ♕c2 27.♖d1±) 26...♕xc3+ 27.bxc3 (Pommerel-Troia, cr 2007). White is a bit better, but the opposite-coloured bishops and the now deteriorated white structure make any try for concretization of the advantage problematic] **16...♗b7 17.♕xc5 ♗e4** [Black continues playing active chess. Alternatives are:

A) In correspondence chess, Black tries 17...♗c6. Now, after 18.♖g1 ♕b8 19.♕a3!? (19.b3 ♘e4 20.♕d4 0-0⩲) 19...♔f7 (19...a5 20.♔d2 ♕b4+ 21.♕xb4 axb4 22.♗d4 ♖xa2 23.♗d3±; 19...♘g4 (Kaas-Troia, cr 2008) 20.g3 ♘xh2 21.♗g2 ♗b7 22.♗xc6 ♕xc6 23.♕c5 ♕f3+ 24.♔d2± with the idea ♔c1) 20.g3 (20.g4 ♖f8 21.♗g2 ♗xg2

22.♖xg2 ♔g8 23.♔f1±) 20...♕b7 21.♗d4± Black doesn't have any compensation for the pawn;

B) 17...♖c8!? is a new sacrifice: 18.♕xa7 (18.♕b4!? ♕c7 19.♔e1 e5 20.♗xa7±) 18...♗c6 19.♕b6 ♕e7 20.♗c5 ♕f7 21.♗b4 ♘e4 allows some activity to Black, but White emerges with an advantage after 22.♕d4 ♖g8 23.♔e1 (the safe way; also possible is 23.g3 ♘xg3+ 24.hxg3 ♗xh1 25.♔f2 when White's compensation is more than sufficient, because of the troubles of the black king and the passed pawns on the queenside) 23...♕xf4 24.♗d3 e5 25.g3 ♘xg3 26.♕xf4 exf4 27.♖g1±] **18.♖d4!?** [18.♖g1 ♖c8 19.♕d4 0-0 20.g4 d5∞ Burri-Gatineau, Avoine 2014; 18.♔e1, intending ♗e2 with immediate coordination, deserves serious attention: 18...♖c8 19.♕a3 ♗f7 20.♗e2 with the idea 20...♗xg2 21.♖g1 ♗e4 22.♗d4 (22.b4!?) 22...a5 23.♗xf6 gxf6 24.♕d6 ♖c7 25.♗g4±] **18...♕b8** [18...♖c8 19.♕a3 ♖c6 20.♔d1±] **19.b3±** [Like in similar positions in this variation, White is slightly better due to his better structure, more space and the superior cooperation of his minor pieces] **19...♔f7 20.♖g1 ♖c8?!** [≥ 20...d5 21.♔e1±] **21.♕e5± ♕b7 22.♖d6!?** [22.g4! d5 23.♔f2±] **22...♖c6** [22...♔g8 23.♔e1 (23.g4 ♗f3+ 24.♔f2 ♖f8 25.h3 ♘e4+ 26.♔xf3 ♘xd6+ 27.♔g3 ♘e4+ 28.♔h2±) 23...♘g4 24.♕d4 ♘xe3 25.♕xe3 ♕b4+ 26.♖d2±] **23.♔e1 ♕b4+** [23...♖xd6 24.♕xd6 ♗b1 25.g4±] **24.♖d2 ♗f5?** [24...d6 was necessary: 25.♕b2±] **25.♗e2 h5** [25...♘g4 26.♗xg4 ♗xg4 27.h3 ♗f5 28.g4 ♗d3 29.♔f2+−; 25...d6 26.♕b2±] **26.♗f3+− ♖ac8 27.♔f2 ♖c5 28.♕d6 a5 29.♖e1 ♗g4 30.♗xc5 ♖xc5 31.♖e5 ♖c8 32.♕xb4 axb4 33.♖b5** 1-0

Janko Potrata   9
Detlev Fischer
cr 2014

1.e4 c5 2.♘f3 e6 3.d4 cxd4 4.♘xd4 ♘f6 5.♘c3 ♘c6 6.♘xc6 bxc6 7.e5 ♘d5 8.♘e4 ♕c7 9.f4 ♕b6 10.c4 ♗b4+ 11.♔e2 f5 12.exf6 ♘xf6 13.♗e3 ♕d8 14.♘d6+ ♗xd6 15.♕xd6 ♗b7 16.♖d1 ♖c8 17.♖g1 c5 18.g4 [Today this is the critical

position of the main line with the check on b4. In our main game we have seen that Yu Yangyi's 18...♖f8 was not very accurate, while in this game we will see most of Black's critical continuations]

18...♕b6 [This move wins time compared to Yu Yangyi's plan. Alternatives are:

A) 18...♕e7 is a very logical continuation, but also logical is White's play in this case: 19.♗g2 ♗xg2 (19...♕xd6 20.♖xd6 ♔e7 21.♗xb7 ♖xd6 22.♖d1+ ♔e7 23.g5 ♘h5 24.♗xc8 ♖xc8 25.♖d3± Blauhut-Chiru, cr 2009. The bishop is stronger than the knight and the white rook, as in the main game, works well on the third rank) 20.♖xg2 ♕d5 21.♕a6 (21.♕xe7+ ♘xe7 22.♖d6 is another possibility, but here Black can complicate things with 22...h5 23.h3 hxg4 24.hxg4 ♖c7 25.b3 ♘c8 26.♖d3±) 21...♖c6 22.♕xa7 ♘xe3 23.♔xe3 ♖c8 24.♖gd2±;

B) 18...♕c7 19.g5 keeps the initiative in White's hands: 19...♘h5!? (19...♕xd6 20.♖xd6 transposes to the text) 20.♗h3 (20.♕xc7 ♖xc7 21.♗h3± is also possible) 20...♕xd6 21.♖xd6 ♖f8 22.♖f1 g6 (22...♔e7 23.♖fd1 ♖c7 24.f5 exf5 25.♗f2 (threatening 26.♗xc5 and 27.♖xd7+) 25...♖f7 26.♗f1 ♗e8 27.♗e2 g6 28.♗xh5 gxh5 29.♗f4±] 23.♗g4 ♘g7 24.♖fd1 ♖c7 25.♗d2 ♗c6 26.♖d3± and White's advantage is not easy to concretize;

C) 18...♖c6 19.♕e5 0-0 is another critical possibility. Now I think that better is 20.♗g2! (20.g5 ♘h5 21.♗h3 d6 22.♗xe6+ ♔h8 23.♕c3 ♘xf4+ 24.♗xf4 ♖xf4 25.♖df1. In this position the game Evans-Puzano, cr 2013, was agreed drawn; White preserves the initiative, but the concrete lines show that Black can more or less keep the balance, for instance: 25...♖e4+ 26.♔d1 ♖xe6 27.♖f7 ♖e5 28.♕f3 ♖e8 29.♖xb7 ♖b6 30.♖xb6

axb6 31.♔c2 ♖f8=) 20...♘xg4 (20...d5 21.cxd5 exd5 22.♗xd5+ ♘xd5 23.♕xd5+ ♕xd5 24.♖xd5 ♖e6 25.♖d7±) 21.♕c3 with good compensation, for instance: 21...d5 22.♖xd5 exd5 23.♗xd5+ ♔h8 24.♗xc6 ♗xc6 25.♖xg4 ♕d7 26.h3±. Here White has not only recovered the material, but also won a pawn. Meanwhile the concretization of his advantage is not easy, because of the opposite-coloured bishops and his exposed king] **19.g5** [The most logical try, but still possible was 19.♕xb6 axb6 20.♗g2 ♗xg2 21.♖xg2 ♔e7 22.♔f3 with some initiative] **19...♕xd6** [The alternative is 19...♘d5, when 20.♕xb6 ♘xb6 21.b3 is a bit better for the first player, for example: 21...♗e4 (21...d5 22.♗h3±) 22.♔f2 ♖c7 23.♗h3 0-0 24.♖d6 ♔f7 25.♗c1 ♖b8 26.♖e1 ♘c8 27.♖d2± Martin Sanchez-Soltau, cr 2013] **20.♖xd6 ♘e4** [20...♘g8!? 21.♗h3 (21.b3!? deserves attention, with the idea ♗h3, ♖gd1) 21...♘e7 22.♖gd1 Here the game Ivanov-Gromotka, cr 2011, was agreed a draw. I think that White can continue; at least in an over-the-board game he has good practical chances because of the already typical advantages of his position: bishop pair, structure, space... 22...♗c6 23.♗g4 (23.♗xc5 ♗a4⇄) 23...h6 24.gxh6 ♖xh6 25.h3 ♖f6 26.♖g1±] **21.♖d3** [As usual, the rook will be directed against the black weaknesses on the queenside] **21...d5 22.♖a3!** [Best. 22.♗g2 d4 23.♗c1 ♘d6⇄ and 22.cxd5 exd5 23.♖a3 a6∞ are good positions for Black] **22...d4** [22...a6 23.♗g2 d4 doesn't work here: 24.♔d3! ♘d6 25.♗xb7 ♘xb7 26.♗d2 a5 27.♖e1! ♔d7 28.♕e5±] **23.♖xa7 ♘d6 24.♗c1 0-0** [The second player has some compensation here because of his strong d-pawn, but is it sufficient? White's next move casts a shadow on Black's hopes:] **25.♗h3! ♖f7 26.b3! ♖e8 27.♖a5! ♘e4** [27...e5 28.f5 ♖c7 (28...♘xf5 29.♖f1 ♖c8 30.♗a3! ♘g3+ 31.hxg3 ♗xh3 32.♖xf7 ♔xf7 33.♗xc5±) 29.♗g4 (29.♖f1!?) 29...♘e4 (29...e4?! 30.♗f4±) 30.f6±] **28.♔e1 g6 29.♖f1 e5 30.f5 ♖c7 31.f6±** [White's chances are preferable, but Black isn't without counterplay because of the centre pawns. It is this type of position that is more difficult to play over the board, but in correspondence chess elements like the bishop pair and piece activity are a good feature from White's point of view] **31...♔f7** [Less logical is 31...♖a8 32.♖xa8+ ♗xa8 33.♗e6+ ♔f8 34.a4±] **32.♖g1 ♗c8?!** [32...♘d6 33.♔e2 (33.♗a3 ♖a8=) 33...♖a8 34.♗d2±] **33.♗xc8 ♖exc8 34.♔d1± ♘f2+ 35.♔e2 ♘e4 36.♖e1 ♖e8 37.h4 ♘d6 38.♔d1**

♘f5 **39.a4 h6** [39...e4 40.♗f4 ♖d7 (40...♖c6 41.♖a7+ ♔f8 42.♖xh7+−) 41.♖xc5±] **40.gxh6 ♘xh4 41.♖e4 g5** [41...♘f5 42.♗f4!+−] **42.♖g4 ♘f3** [42...♔g6 43.♖xg5+ ♔xf6 44.♖h5+−; 42...♔xf6 43.♖a6+ ♔f5 44.♖xg5+ ♔e4 45.♖f6+−] **43.♖a6 d3** [43...♖b7 44.♗xg5 ♖g8 45.h7+−] **44.♖d6 e4 45.♗xg5+−** [With the black pawns well

blocked on the dark squares, only White can make progress] **45...♖g8 46.h7 ♖h8 47.♗e3 ♖xh7 48.♔c1 ♘h4 49.♖xe4 ♘f5 50.♖xd3** [The rest is easy] 50...♖h1+ **51.♔b2 ♔xf6 52.♖f4 ♔g6 53.♖g4+ ♔f7 54.♗g1 ♖c8 55.♖d5 ♘e7 56.♖dg5 ♔f6 57.♗xc5 ♖h2+ 58.♔a3 ♘c6 59.a5 ♖h1 60.b4 ♖d1 61.♖g8** 1-0

Exercise 1

position after 19...f7-f5

This position arises in the line 9...♕a5+ 10.c3 ♗e7 11.♗d3 ♕b6 12.♕e2 a5 (see comments to game 5). How can Black refute the white plan starting with 20.h4 ?
(solution on page 246)

Exercise 2

position after 16...♘a6-c7

It is a good idea to play 17.c4 in this position?
(solution on page 246)

Exercise 3

position after 17.b2-b4

A position from the line with 9...♖b8. Black has more than enough compensation for the material, but how to continue now?
(solution on page 246)

Slaves of Habit

by Andras Adorjan

1.	e4	c5
2.	♘c3	♘c6
3.	g3	g6
4.	♗g2	♗g7
5.	d3	d6

Little kids already have peculiar habits of their own. Grown-ups are even tougher cases. Worst are us chess players. And in addition, we have superstitions, too.

Boris Spassky was a great champion, who regularly played the Closed Sicilian. You may say he made a habit of it – with good results. Of 61 games he won 26 (three against Geller!), lost seven and drew 28 (66-34 % in favour of White). I note, however, that in the MegaBase 2015 the statistics on B25 are 53-47% for Black! Life is complicated, it seems...

Spassky's overall result is overwhelming. But he also suffered painful losses in important games, twice against Portisch; in the Toluca Interzonal (1982) and in their Candidates' match (1980) in Mexico.

But why did Boris play such a dry and dull opening?

The handy answer could be that he avoided the Open Sicilian. Well, there the numbers show an even better result for him! That is, with 180 games he scored 70-30% with white. Still, someone could say that there might have been a lot of weak opponents playing Black.

I say, let's leave the numbers and statistics for those who religiously believe in them.

I daresay the Closed Sicilian is simply worse for White, but maybe this will not be printed on account of it being regarded as blasphemy. But what if I say

Boris Spassky

that to play this variation with black is more comfortable?

I always liked playing with black against the Closed, and with good results, viz.: +5, -2, =2 (one draw against Karpov). I had the honour of playing against Spassky himself, and getting a slightly better position...

My daughter says people don't read any text that exceeds five lines. Not even mine.

Seems that I blew it.

Martin Tabakov
Andras Adorjan

Varna jr 1969

1.e4 c5 2.♘c3 ♘c6 3.g3 g6 4.♗g2
♗g7 5.d3 d6 6.♘h3

6...h5?! [6...♘f6!?] 7.♘f4 h4 8.♗e3
♘f6 9.♕d2? [9.0-0] 9...♗d7
[9...♘g4∓] 10.♘fe2 [10.h3!? hxg3
11.fxg3 0-0 12.0-0-0 b5!] 10...♘g4!∓
11.0-0-0 ♕a5 12.♔b1 ♗e6!
13.d4 ♘xe3 14.fxe3 ♗g4 15.e5!?
0-0-0? [15...dxe5∓] 16.exd6 exd6
17.♖hf1 ♖d7 18.♖f4 [18.♗f3] 18...
f5 19.dxc5?? [19.♗f3 cxd4 20.♘xd4
♘xd4 21.♖xg4 (21.exd4 ♗h6∓)
21...♘c6 22.♗f3 hxg3 23.hxg3 ♗xc3
24.♕xc3 ♕xc3 25.bxc3 ♖h3 (25...♘e5)
26.♗xc6 bxc6 27.g4 fxg4 28.♖xg4 ♖h6∓]
19...♖xc3–+ 20.bxc3 [20.♘xc3
♗xd1 21.♕xd1 dxc5–+] 20...♕b5+
21.♔a1 ♕xe2 22.♕xe2 ♗xe2
23.♖d2 ♗h5 24.cxd6 hxg3
25.hxg3 ♖hd8 26.e4 ♗g4 27.exf5
gxf5 28.♗xc6 bxc6 29.♖fd4 ♗f3
30.♖2d3 ♗e4 31.♖d2 c5 32.♖c4
♖xd6 33.♖xc5+ ♔b7 34.♖xd6
♖xd6 35.♖e5 ♖g6 36.♖e7+ ♔b6
37.c4 ♖xg3 38.c5+ ♔xc5 39.♖xa7
♖g2 40.a4 ♔b4 41.c3+ ♔a3   0-1

Andras Ozsvath
Andras Adorjan

Hungary tt 1968

[To the memory of Andras Ozsvath (1929-
2015)... he was a 'master trainer' and his
famous middlegame book 'Harcászat 64
mezon' ('Fighting on 64 squares') was a
real masterpiece. He achieved the FIDE
master title and his attacking style was
very dangerous for everyone in his best
days. He even beat GM Lajos Portisch

once. He considered as his best game
the one against GM Smejkal, Warsaw
1970, which he won] 1.e4 c5 2.♘c3
g6 3.g3 ♗g7 4.♗g2 ♘c6 5.d3
d6 6.f4 e6 7.♘h3 ♘ge7 8.0-0 0-0
9.g4 f5 10.♘f2 ♖b8 11.♘e2 b5
12.c3 [12.a3!?] 12...b4∓ 13.♗e3
bxc3 14.bxc3 ♕a5 15.♕d2 ♕a3
[15...d5!?] 16.♖ac1 ♗d7 17.gxf5
exf5 18.♘d1 ♗e6 19.♖c2 ♖b1
20.♗f2 ♖a1 21.exf5 gxf5 22.♘c1
♖b8?! [22...♖f6!?] 23.♕e3?!
[23.♕e2 ♗f7 24.♘b3 ♖b1 25.♘d2‡]
23...♗f7 24.♕d2 ♖bb1 25.♘e3
♕a4 26.♗h4 ♘g6 27.♗g3 ♘ce7
28.h4 ♘f8 29.♗h3 ♗e6∓ 30.h5
♕e8 31.♕e2 ♗f7 32.♕f2 ♗xh5
33.♘c4 ♕g6 34.♗g2 d5 35.♘a3
♖b7 36.♗h4 ♘e6 37.♖e1 ♕f7
38.♗xe7 ♖xe7 39.♗xd5 ♕f6
40.♕e3 ♗f7 41.♖g2? [41.♘c4∓]
41...♘xf4!–+ [White has no chance
to save the game!] 42.♕xe7 ♕xe7
43.♖xe7 ♖xc1+ 44.♔f2 ♘xd5
45.♖xa7 ♗g6 46.♘c4 ♗xc3 47.a4
♘f4 48.♖h2 ♗d4+ 49.♔f3 ♘xd3
50.♘e3 ♘e5+ 51.♔f4 ♗xe3+
52.♔xe5 f4 53.♔e6 ♗d4 54.♖a8+
♔g7 55.♖a7+ ♔f8 56.♖a8+
♗e8 57.♖h4 ♖e1+ 58.♔d6 ♔g7
59.♖g4+ ♔g6 60.a5 f3 61.a6
f2 62.a7 f1♕ 63.♖g8+ ♔xg8
64.a8♕+ ♕f8+   0-1

Anatoly Karpov
Andras Adorjan

Groningen Ech-jr 1968 (6)

1.e4 c5 2.♘c3 ♘c6 3.g3 g6 4.♗g2
♗g7 5.d3 d6 6.♘ge2 e5 7.♘d5
♘ge7 8.♗g5

8...h6 9.♗f6 0-0 10.♘xe7+ ♘xe7
11.♗xg7 ♔xg7 12.♕d2 [12.0-0 d5
(½-½ Adorjon-Liptay, Budapest ch-HUN
1968; 12...♗g4)] 12...♗e6 13.f4 ♕d7

14.0-0 f6 15.♖f2 ♖ad8 16.♖af1 b6
[16...b6 17.b3 ♗g4 18.a3 ♘c6]   ½-½

Boris Spassky
Gyula Sax

Clermont-Ferrand 1989

1.e4 c5 2.♘c3 ♘c6 3.g3 g6 4.♗g2
♗g7 5.d3 d6 6.♘ge2 e6 7.a3 ♘ge7
8.0-0 [N 8.♖b1] 8...0-0 [8...b6 9.♖b1
♗b7 10.♗e3 ♘d4 11.♕d2 0-0 12.f4
♕d7 13.b4 ♖ac8 14.♗f2 ♖fd8∓] 9.♖b1
b6 10.b4 ♗b7 11.♗d2 ♕d7 12.f4
[12.♕c1 ♘d4 13.♗g5 ♖ac8∓] 12...♖ac8
13.bxc5 bxc5 [13...dxc5!? 14.e5 c4!
15.dxc4 ♘a5! 16.♗c1 ♕c7∓ Sax] 14.
g4 f5 15.♘g3 ♘d4 16.♖xb7?! [16.
h3 c4! 17.♔h1 cxd3 18.cxd3 ♗a6 19.exf5
exf5 20.♖e1 fxg4 21.♘d5 ♘xd5 22.♗xd5+
♔h8∓; 16.gxf5 exf5 17.♖xb7 ♕xb7 18.exf5
♕b2∓] 16...♕xb7 17.exf5 ♕b2
18.fxe6 ♘xc2! 19.♘ce2 [19.♘ce4 d5
20.♘g5 ♕d4+ 21.♔h1 ♕xd3 22.♖f3 ♕c4
23.♗f1 ♕a2 △ 24...♘d4∓ Sax] 19...
c4! 20.dxc4 ♘xa3 21.♗e3 ♘xc4
22.♖xa7 ♕a3 23.♗f2 ♘e3 24.♗xe3
♕xe3+ 25.♔h1 ♕xe6 26.f5 ♕e5
27.♘f4 [27.♖e1 d5 28.♕d2 ♖a8∓]
27...gxf5 28.♘d5 ♘xd5 29.♗xd5+
♔h8 30.♖e1? ♖c1! [31.♕xc1 ♕xd5+
32.♔g1 ♗d4+–+]   0-1

Boris Spassky
Efim Geller

Sukhumi 1968 (6)

[3 in 1 – not for the coffee, but for the
number of wins in the Closed Sicilian in the
same match! This encounter was the third
in a row, the two others will be mentioned
also] 1.e4 c5 2.♘c3 d6 3.g3 ♘c6
4.♗g2 g6 5.d3 ♗g7 6.f4 ♘f6?!

[This set-up is rare. In the 8th game of the match, Geller deviated from the previous games: 6...e6! 7.♘f3 ♘ge7 8.0-0 0-0 9.a3 ♗d7 10.♖b1 ♖c8 11.♗d2 ♘d4 12.♘e2 ♗a4 13.b3 ♗c6 14.c4 ♘xf3+ 15.♗xf3 d5 16.♗e3 d4 17.♗d2 ♕d7=/∓ Spassky-Geller, Sukhumi Candidates' 1968 (m/8)] **7.♘f3 0-0 8.0-0 ♖b8 9.h3** [9.♘h4 ♘d4 10.f5 b5 11.♗g5 b4 12.♘b1 ♘d7 13.♘d2 ♘e5 (Black is perfectly OK after the opening) 14.♔h1 a5 15.♖b1 a4 16.♘hf3 ♘exf3 17.♘xf3 ♗b5 18.♕d2 a3 19.bxa3 ♘xa3 20.♖be1 ♗c3 21.♕f2 ♗xe1 22.♖xe1 f6−+ (Black is more than OK in the middlegame) 23.♗h6 ♖f7 24.g4 e6 25.♘h4 g5 26.♘f3 exf5 27.gxf5 ♔h8∓ (Black is still OK) 28.h4 g4 29.♘h2 g3 (29...♕g8) 30.♕xg3 ♘xc2 31.♖g1 ♗b7? (31...♘d4) 32.♗f3 ♕d7 33.♗h5 ♖e7 34.♘g4 ♖g8 35.♕f2 ♘d4? 36.♘xf6 ♖xg1+ 37.♕xg1 1-0 Spassky-Geller, Sukhumi Candidates' 1968 (m/2)] **9...b5** [9...♘e8 10.♗d2 b5 11.♖b1 e6 12.♕e1 ♘d4 13.♘xd4! cxd4 14.♘e2 ♕b6 15.a3 with better play for White. Spassky-Benko, Palma de Mallorca 1968] **10.a3** [10.g4 b4 11.♘e2 c4! 12.♗e3 (12.dxc4? ♘xe4∓) 12...♗a6 1-0 (27) Smyslov-Taimanov, Moscow 1959] **10...a5 11.♗e3** [11. g4 b4 12.axb4 axb4 13.♘e2 c4 14.♗e3 cxd3 15.cxd3 ♗b7 16.♕d2 ♖a8 17.♘ed4 ♘xd4 18.♗xd4 ♗a6 19.f5! with more active play for White, Borngässer-Marjanovic, Dortmund 1978] **11...b4 12.axb4 axb4 13.♘e2 ♗b7** [≤ 13...♗d7 14.g4 ♘e8 15.♖b1 ♘c7 16.♕e1 ♘b5 17.♕f2 ♖a8 18.f5↑; ≤ 13...♘e8 14.♖b1 ♘c7 15.f5 ♘b5 16.♕d2 ♘bd4 17.♘h4 ♘xe2+ 18.♕xe2 ♘e5 19.♘f3 ♘xf3+ 20.♕xf3 ♗b7 21.h4∞ Reshevsky-Kortchnoi, Amsterdam Candidates' 1968] **14.b3!** [14.♕d2 ♖a8 15.♖ab1 ♗a5! 16.b3 d5! (e.g.: ≤ 16...♖fc8 17.f5 ♕b6 18.g4 ♖a2 19.♘c1 ♖a5 20.♕f2 ♕c7 21.♘e2 ♖a2 22.♖bc1 ♕d8 23.♘f4 ♕e8 24.♘g5 ♘d4∓ 1-0 (48) Spassky-Geller, Sukhumi Candidates' 1968 (m/4)] 17.e5 d4 18.♗f2 ♕d5∓] **14...♖a8 15.♖c1! ♖a2 16.g4 ♕a8** [16...♘a5 17.♕e1 ♕b5 18.♕f2 ♖fa8∓ and next 19...♘d7 and 20...♖a1; 16...e6 17.♕e1 ♕c7 18.♕h4 ♖e8∓] **17.♕e1 ♕a6** [17...d5 18.e5 (18.g5 ♗d7 19.exd5 ♘a5 20.d4 ♗xd4 21.dxc5 ♕b7∞) 18...♘d7 19.♕h4 e6 20.d4 ♗a6∓] **18.♕f2** [18.♕h4?? ♖xc2 (18...♘xe4−+ 19.dxe4 ♕xe2) 19.♖xc2

♕xd3−+] **18...♘a7** [18...d5 19.e5 d4 20.exf6 dxe3 21.♕xe3 ♗xf6 22.♕xc5 ♖c8 23.♕f2 ♘d8∓; 18...e6 19.e5 ♘d5 20.exd6 (20.♗d2 dxe5 21.fxe5 ♕b6∓) 20...♘xe3 21.♕xe3 ♘d4 22.♗xd4 cxd4 23.♗xb7 ♖xb7 24.♕d2 ♕b6∓] **19.f5 ♘b5 20.fxg6 hxg6 21.♘g5 ♘a3!?** [21...♖e8!? 22.♗xf7 ♔xf7 23.g5±] **22.♕h4 ♖c8 23.♖xf6! exf6 24.♕h7+ ♔f8 25.♘xf7!!** [25.♘f4+−] **25...♖xc2** [25...♗xf7 26.♗h6 ♖g8 27.♘f4 d5 (27...♖xc2 28.♖f1 g5 29.♗xg5! (29.♘h5 ♖xg2+ (29...♕xd3 30.♗xf6+−) 30.♔xg2 ♕xd3 31.♗xf6+−) 29... d5 (29...fxg5 30.♘d5+ ♗e8 31.♕xg8+ ♔d7 32.♖f7+ and 33.♖c7) 30.♘h5+−) 28.e5! fxe5 29.♘xd5+− Polugaevsky] **26.♗h6!+− ♖xc1+ 27.♘xc1 ♗xf7** [27...♗xh6 28.♘xh6 ♗e8 29.♘g8! ♖c7 (29...♗f8 30.♘e7 ♗e8 31.♘xg6) 30.♕xc7 ♗f8 31.♕d8+ ♗g7 32.♘xf6 ♗f7 33.♘h7 ♗g7 (33...♗e6 34.♕e8#) 34.♕d7+ ♗g8 35.♘f6+ ♗f8 36.♕e8+ ♗g7 37.♕e7+ ♗h6 (37...♗h8 38.♕f8#) 38.♘g8# Polugaevsky] **28.♕xg7+ ♗e8 29.g5!** [29.e5! d5 30.exf6 ♕e6 31.♕xb7+−] **29...f5** [29... fxg5 30.♗xg5+−] **30.♕xg6+ ♗d7 31.♕f7+ ♗c6 32.exf5+** [32...♗b6 33.♗xb7 ♕xb7 34.♕xb7+ ♗xb7 35.f6+−] **1-0**

Sarkis Bohosjan
Andras Adorjan
Varna 1972

1.e4 c5 2.♘c3 ♘c6 3.f4 g6 4.♘f3 ♗g7 5.g3 d6 6.♗g2 e6 7.0-0 ♘ge7 8.d3 0-0

9.h3?! [9.♗e3] **9...♖b8** [9...♕d7!? 10.♘e2 ♕b6 11.c3 e5∓] **10.g4 f5**

11.♕e1 ♘d4 12.♘xd4 cxd4 13.♘e2 ♗d7 [13...♕c7!? 14.c3 dxc3 15.bxc3 ♗d7∓] **14.♘g3** [14.c3 dxc3 (14...♘c6 15.cxd4 fxg4 16.hxg4 ♕b6 17.♗e3 ♘xd4 18.♘xd4 ♗xd4 19.♗xd4 ♕xd4+ 20.♕f2 ♕xd3=/∓) 15.bxc3 (15.♘xc3 ♕b6+ 16.♔h2 fxg4 17.hxg4 ♖bc8∓) 15...♗b5 16.♕g3 fxe4 17.♗xe4 ♗c6∓] **14...♖c8 15.♖f2 ♘c6** [15...fxg4!? 16.hxg4 ♗f7∓] **16.g5 fxe4 17.♗xe4 ♕b6 18.a3** [18.♗d2 ♗xb2 19.♖b1 ♕xa2 20.♖xb7 ♖f7∓/−+] **18...♘e7 19.h4 ♗e8!?** [19...♘d5!?∓] **20.h5 ♗f7** [20...d5!? 21.♗f3 ♗f7∓] **21.♖h2 ♖fe8 22.♕d2?** [≥ 22.♕b4 ♖xb4 23.axb4 d5 24.♗f3 a6∓] **22...♕f5?!** [22...♖xc2 23.b4 d5 (23...♕f5!?∓/−+) 24.♗f3 ♗a6 25.♕f1 ♖c3! 26.♗xc3 dxc3∓/−+] **23.hxg6 hxg6 24.♗a5!? ♕a6** [24...♕xb2 25.♖b1=] **25.♗b4 ♕b6 26.♖c1?** [26.♗a5 ♕b5 27.a4 ♕d7 28.♗f3 ♘e3∓] **26...♖xg3 27.♕xg3 a5∓/−+ 28.♗d2 d5 29.♗f3 ♕xb2 30.f5 exf5 31.♗f4 ♖e3 32.♖f1 ♕xa3 33.♗d6 ♖xf3 34.♖xf3 ♕c1+ 35.♔g2** [35.♖f1 ♕e3+ 36.♔hf2 ♕e8−+] **35...♖xc2+ 36.♖f2 ♖xf2+ 37.♔xf2 ♕d2+ 38.♔f1 ♕d1+ 39.♔g2 ♕e2+ 40.♔h3 ♕h5+ 41.♔g2 ♕e2+ 42.♔h3 ♕f1+! 43.♔h4** [43.♖g2 f4 (43...b5!?−+) 44.♗xf4 ♕h1+ 45.♕h2 ♗e6+ 46.♔g3 ♕e1+−+] **43...♕d1 44.♔h3 f4!−+ 45.♗xf4 ♗e6+ 46.♔g2 ♗f5 47.♗e3 ♕e2+ 48.♗f2 ♗e5** [49.♕h4 ♕xd3 50.♖h1 ♗e4+ 51.♔g1 ♕d1+ 52.♗e1 d3−+] **0-1**

Yury Balashov
Andras Adorjan
München 1979 (1)

1.e4 c5 2.♘c3 ♘c6 3.g3 g6 4.♗g2 ♗g7 5.d3 d6 6.f4 e6 7.♘f3 ♘ge7 8.0-0 0-0 9.♗d2 b6 [9...♖b8 10.♖b1 b5 11.a3 f5 (11...a5 12.a4 b4 13.♘b5 d5 14.c4 bxc3 15.bxc3 c4 16.♗e3 cxd3 17.e5 ♗a6 18.♕xd3 ♕d7 19.♖fd1 ♖fc8 20.♕d2 ♘f5 21.♗f2 h5 22.♗f1± Spassky-Larsen, Malmö Candidates' 1968 (m/3)] 12.♗e3 ♕c7 (12...♘d4) 13.♗f2 ♔h8 14.♖e1 b4 15.axb4 cxb4 16.♘e2 fxe4 (≥ 16...e5) 17.dxe4 e5 18.♕d2± Spassky-Larsen, Malmö Candidates' 1968 (m/7)] **10.♖b1** [10.♕e1N ♗b7 11.g4 f5 (≥ 11...♘d7) 12.exf5 exf5 13.♘g5 ♕d7?! (≥ 13...♗d4+ 14.♔h1 h6!? 15.♘e6 ♕d7 16.♘xf8 ♖xf8≅) 14.♕e6+ ♕xe6

15.♘xe6 ♖f7 (15...fxg4!? 16.♘xf8 ♖xf8 17.♖ae1 ♘f5±) 16.♘b5!± ♖d8 17.♘xg7 ♗xg2 18.♔xg2 ♖xg7 19.♗c3 ♘d5? (19...♖f7) 20.♗xg7 ♘e3+ 21.♔g1 ♘xf1 22.♗c3+− ♘e3 23.♖e1 ♘xg4 24.♖e8+ ♔f7 25.♘xd6# 1-0 Spassky-Beikert, Lyon 1991] **10...♗b7 11.a3 ♕d7 12.♘e2 ♘d4** [12...f5 13.♗c3 ♗xc3 (13...e5 14.b4 fxe4 15.dxe4 ♘d4 16.bxc5 bxc5 17.♕d3∞) 14.♘xc3 ♖ad8 15.♕d2 e5 16.exf5 ♘xf5 17.fxe5 ♘xe5 18.♘xe5 dxe5 19.♗xb7 (19.♖be1 c4 20.♗xb7 ♕xb7∓) 19...♕xb7 20.♕g5 ♘d4 21.♘e4 ♘xc2 22.♖xf8+ ♖xf8 23.♘f6+ ♔g7 24.♖f1 ♕b8 25.♘h5+ ♔g8 26.♘f6+ ♔g7=] **13.♘exd4 cxd4 14.♕e2 ♖ac8 15.♖bc1 a5 16.♕f2 e5 17.c4 f5 18.exf5 ♘xf5 19.fxe5 dxe5 20.♕e1 h6??** [A bad mistake. 20...♘d6!∓ 21.♘g5 (practically the only move which controls the important e4-square! 21.♘xe5 ♖xf1+ 22.♗xf1 ♕f5 (the knight on e5 is trapped!) 23.c5 (23.♗f4 g5−+) 23...bxc5 24.♘c4 ♕d5−+; 21.b4 e4! 22.dxe4 ♘xe4 23.bxa5 bxa5! (23...♘xd2 24.♕xd2 bxa5 25.♕d3!∓) 24.♗f4 (24.♗xa5 ♖ce8 25.♕d1 d3−+) 24...♖ce8 25.♕xa5 ♘c3 26.♔h1 ♖e2−+ 27.♕c7 ♕xc7 28.♗xc7 d3 29.♗f4 ♖f5∓/−+; 21.♕e2 e4 22.♘g5 (22.dxe4 ♘xe4 23.♕d3 ♘c5−+ with an overwhelming position for Black) 22...e3−+ 23.♗xb7 ♕xb7 24.♗e1 ♖xf1+ 25.♕xf1 ♖f8 26.♕e2 a4 27.♘e4 ♘c5 28.♘xc5 bxc5−+ and White's position is miserable) 21...♗xg2 22.♖xf8+ ♖xf8 23.♔xg2 ♗h6 (≤ 23...♕c6+ 24.♔g1 e4!? 25.♘xe4 ♖e8 26.♕f1 ♘xe4 27.dxe4 ♖xe4 28.♕d3=) 24.♕e2 ♗xg5 25.♗xg5 ♖f5∓] **21.♘xe5 ♗xe5 22.♗xb7 ♕xb7 23.♕xe5+−** [and White won on the 30th move] 1-0

Boris Spassky
Lajos Portisch
Mexico 1980 (1)

1.e4 c5 2.♘c3 d6 3.g3 ♘c6 4.♗g2 g6 5.d3 ♗g7 6.f4 e6 7.♘f3 ♘ge7 8.0-0 0-0 9.♖b1 b6 [9...♖b8 10.♘e2 (10.♗d2 b5 11.a3 f5 12.b4 cxb4 13.axb4 a5 14.♘a2 axb4 (14...a4!?∓) 15.♘xb4 ♘xb4 16.♗xb4 ♘c6 17.♗a3 b4 18.♗b2 e5 19.exf5 ♗xf5 20.♘d2 ♕d7 21.♘c4 (21.♕e2!?=) 21...♘g4 22.♕d2 exf4 23.♗xg7 ♔xg7 24.♖xf4 d5 25.♖xf8 ♖xf8 26.♘e3 ♗f3 27.♖f1 ♗xg2 28.♖xf8 ♔xf8 29.♕xg2= Karpov-Ribli, Hungary HUN-URS m 1969) 10...f5 11.♗e3 b5

12.e5 ♘d5 13.♗f2 dxe5 14.♗xc5 ♖e8 15.fxe5 ♘xe5 16.♘xe5 ♗xe5 17.c4?! (≥ 17.♗xa7 ♖a8 18.♗f2 ♖xa2 19.c3) 17...♕c7! 18.cxd5 ♕xc5+ 19.♔h1 (19.d4 ♕b6 20.♖c1 ♗b7∓) 19...♕d6 20.d4 ♗g7 21.dxe6 ♗xe6 22.d5 ♗f7 23.b3 ♖bd8 24.♘f4 ♗e5∓ Tears-Fischer, Oklahoma City 1956] **10.♗d2** [10.♖e1 ♗b7 11.♗d2 ♕d7 12.♘e2 d5 (12...f5) 13.e5 d4 14.g4 (14.a3 ♖ac8 15.b4 cxb4 16.axb4 ♘f5 17.b5 ♘ce7∓) 14...f6! (14...♘d5!?) 15.exf6 (15.♘g3!? seems to be somewhat better although after 15...fxe5 16.fxe5 ♘d5 Black can easily improve his position) 15...♖xf6 16.♘g3 ♘d5 17.♘g5 ♗xf4 (17...h6!? was probably more accurate) 18.♗xf4 ♖xf4 19.♘xe6 ♖f7 20.♘xg7 ♕xg7 21.♕e2 ♘b4 22.♗xb7 ♕xb7 23.♕e5+? (23.♖f1∓) 23...♕g8 24.♘e4 ♘xc2∓ Hazai-Adorjan, Hungary tt 1973; 10.♗e3 d5 11.♗d2 (11.♗f2 d4 12.♘e2 e5 13.h3 ♕d6 14.♕d2 ♗d7 15.g4 exf4 16.♘xf4 ♘e5∓ Kristiansen-Szekely, Zamardi 1980) 11...dxe4 12.dxe4 (12.♘xe4 ♘f5∓) 12...♗b7 13.♕e1 ♘d4 14.♖c1 ♕d7 15.♘xd4 (15.e5 ♘ef5 16.♘xd4 (16.g4 ♘xf3+ 17.♗xf3 ♗xf3 18.♖xf3 ♘d4 19.♖f2 f6∓) 16...cxd4 17.♘e4 h5∓) 15...cxd4 16.♘d1 ♖ac8 17.b3 ♖c7∓ Kristiansen-Pinter, Copenhagen 1985; 10.h3 ♖b8 11.g4?! (this 'attacking move', typical for the whole system, more often brings headaches than achievements...) 11...f5 12.♘h4 ♘d4 13.♘e2 d5 14.e5 ♘xe2+ 15.♕xe2 ♗b7 16.gxf5 ♘xf5 17.♘xf5 ♖xf5 18.b4 cxb4 19.d4 a5∓ Giam-Browne, Singapore 1969] **10...♗b7 11.♘e2 ♕d7** [11...♖c8 12.♗c3 e5 13.g4?! exf4 14.♗xg7 ♔xg7 15.♕d2 ♘e5 16.♕xf4 ♘7c6 17.g5 f6 18.♘xe5 dxe5 19.gxf6+ ♖xf6 20.♕xf6+ ♕xf6 21.♖xf6 ♔xf6 22.♖f1+ ♔e7 23.♔f2 ♘d4 24.c3 ♘e6 25.♔e3 ♖d8 26.♗h3 ♘g5 27.♗g2 ♖a6= Pester-Hort, Germany tt 1998] **12.g4**

12...f5! [The standard reaction] **13.gxf5 exf5 14.c4 ♘d8!** [Nice manoeuvre] **15.♘c3** [15.♗c3!? ♘e6 16.♗xg7 ♘xg7∓] **15...♘e6 16.♘g5 ♘xg5 17.fxg5 ♖f7** [17...♘d4+!? 18.♔h1 fxe4 19.dxe4 (19.♘xe4 d5∓) 19...♖xf1+ 20.♕xf1 ♖f8 21.♕d3 ♘c6∓] **18.♕f3 ♖af8 19.♕h3 ♕d8 20.exf5 ♗c8!** [White must have been surprised by this move!] **21.♘e4 ♗d4+ 22.♔h1 ♘xf5∓ 23.♘f6+ ♔h8 24.♗c3?** [24.♕g4≥ ♘g7 25.♖xf7 ♖xf7 26.♕g3 ♘f5∓] **24...♘e3−+** [White is lost already here] **25.♕h4 ♗xc3 26.bxc3 ♘xf1 27.♖xf1 ♗f5 28.d4 ♖xf6 29.gxf6 ♕xf6 30.♕xf6+ ♖xf6 31.a4 ♔g7 32.a5 ♗d3 33.♖xf6 ♔xf6 34.axb6 axb6 35.♗d5 ♔f5 36.dxc5 dxc5 37.♔g1 ♔f4 38.♔f2** 0-1

Main Line
Deviations on Move 10

Miodrag Todorcevic
Andras Adorjan
Lugano 1983

[The case is CLOSED] **1.e4 c5 2.♘c3 ♘c6 3.g3** [Sometimes everybody deviates from the main lines. But I could never understand what kind of fun the CLOSED Sicilian promises (I mean for White)] **3...g6 4.♗g2 ♗g7 5.d3 d6 6.f4 e6 7.♘f3 ♘ge7 8.0-0 0-0 9.♗e3 ♘d4**

10.♗f2 [It's been played a lot of times. I wonder what do they expect of this kind of set-ups?] **10...♘ec6** [10...♕b6] **11.♘d2** [Nothing came out of 11.♘xd4 ♘xd4 (11...cxd4 12.♘e2 e5 is not bad either) 12.♖b1 ♗d7 13.♘e2 ♕a5! 14.♘c1 (14.a3 ♗a4 15.b3 ♗c6∓ 14...♗a4 15.b3 (15.♘b3 ♘xb3 16.axb3 ♗c6=) 15...♗c6 16.♗e1 ♕a3 17.c3

♘b5 18.♘e2 f5!? (18...♕xa2 19.♖a1 ♕b2 20.♖b1=) 19.♕c2 ♖ae8 20.♖d1 ♖f7= (½-½ Spassky-Adorjan, Gjövik 1983) 21.c4 ♘d4 22.♘xd4 ♗xd4+ 23.♗f2 ♗g7 (23...e5!?⇄) 24.d4!? cxd4 25.♗xd4 ♗xd4+ 26.♖xd4 e5 27.fxe5 ♕c5 28.♕f2 ♖xe5 29.exf5 ♖exf5 30.♕d2 ♖xf1+ 31.♗xf1 ♕f5 32.♖f4 ♕c5+=. It's hard to believe, but Boris was very successful with the Closed Sicilian earlier – probably the only great player beating big sharks like himself! The 'Winning Weapon' is just the one you handle well. 11.e5!? is interesting: 11...dxe5 12.♘xe5 ♘xe5 13.fxe5 ♗xe5 14.♘e4 f5 (a bit strange-looking, but it proves to be right. 14...b6!? 15.c3 (15.♘xc5 ♖b8 16.♘b3 f5=; 15.♘f6+ ♗xf6 16.♗xa8 ♗d7 17.♗e4 ♗a4! 18.b3 ♗c6♔) 15...♘f5 16.♘f6+ ♗xf6 17.♗xa8 ♗a6 18.♗e4 ♘d6 19.♗f3 ♕d7♔) 15.♘xc5 ♕d6 16.b4 (16.♘a4 f4 17.gxf4 ♗xf4 18.h3 ♗d7♔) 16...♘b5 17.a4!? (≤ 17.♘xb7 ♗xb7 18.♗xb7 ♖ab8 19.♗f3 (19.♗c5 ♗d4+ 20.♔h1 ♗xc5 21.bxc5 ♕xc5 22.♗g2 ♘d4♔) 19...♕xb4 20.♖b1 ♕d6♔) 17...♘c3 18.♕e1∞] **11...♖b8** [11...b6!? 12.♘cb1 (this is the big returning point – a kind of hide-and-seek...) 12...♘e7 13.c3 ♘dc6 14.♘f3 e5 (14...♗a6 15.♖e1 ♕d7♔) 15.♘bd2 (15.d4? exd4 16.cxd4 ♗g4♔) 15...exf4 16.gxf4 d5♔) **12.♘cb1 b6!?** [Now it really gets strange. A few years later we saw 12...♘e7 13.c3 (13.♖e1 ♘ec6♔) 13...♘dc6 14.a4 (14.♘f3 e5 15.fxe5 ♘xe5 16.♘xe5 ♗xe5 17.d4 cxd4 18.♗xd4 (18.cxd4 ♗g7 19.♘c3 b5=) 18...♘c6=) 14...b6 15.♘f3 e5 16.♘bd2 ♗a6 17.♕e2 exf4 18.gxf4 ♖e8 19.♖fe1 ♘d5 20.♗g3 ♗h6 21.f5 ♘f4 22.♗xf4 ♗xf4♔ Todorcevic-Portisch, Szirak 1987] **13.c3 ♘b5 14.a4 ♘c7 15.♘a3 ♕d7 16.♘c2** [16.♘f3 e5 17.f5?!/!? (active but wrong! 17.♘c4 exf4 18.gxf4 ♖e8 19.♗g3 ♗a6 20.f5 ♗xc4 21.dxc4 ♘e5 (21...♖bd8!?) 22.♘xe5 ♗xe5=) 17...gxf5 18.♗h3 ♘e7 19.♘h4 ♕c6 20.♘xf5 ♘xf5 21.♗xf5 ♗xf5 22.exf5 d5♔] **16...♗a6 17.♘f3 f5! 18.♖e1 e5♔** [A kind of dream position] **19.exf5** [19.b4 cxb4 (19...fxe4!? 20.dxe4 exf4♔) 20.cxb4 ♗b7 21.b5 ♘e7 22.fxe5 dxe5♔] **19...♕xf5 20.♘e3 ♕d7** [20...♕xd3? 21.♘d2!+−] **21.♘g5** [21.fxe5 ♘xe5 22.♘xe5 ♗xe5♔] **21...exf4 22.gxf4 d5!?** [Nobody is perfect. It was a bit

silly of me that I almost never went for material (which is not a shame normally) but to sacrifice with both my hands. On the other hand, this attitude brought me 8 brilliancy prizes too – not only painful disappointments! To 'kill' my opponent? To try to create a masterpiece with the 'help' of his toughest opposition, that I can overcome! The world needs humble priests as well, not only 'Supermen'. 22...♖xf4 23.♗g3 ♖ff8 24.♘d5 ♘xd5 25.♕b3!? (25.♗xd5+?! ♔h8 26.♖f1 ♘e5 27.♗xe5 ♗xe5 28.♘f7+ ♔g7♔) 25...♘ce7 26.♗xd5+ ♘xd5 27.♕xd5+ ♔h8 28.♘e6 ♖f5 29.♕xd6 ♕xd6 30.♗xd6 ♖c8 31.♘xg7 ♔xg7 32.♖e7+ ♖f7=] **23.♗g3** [23.♕b3 ♗xd3 24.♗xd5+!? (24.♖ad1!? ♘a5 (24...c4 25.♘xc4! ♘d4 (25...dxc4 26.♕xc4+!! ♗xc4 27.♖xd7±/+−) 26.♘e5 ♗xe5 27.♗xd4 ♗xd4+ 28.cxd4 ♗f5 (28...c4 29.♕g3±) 29.♖e5=) 25.♕a2 c4 26.♘xd5 ♘xd5 27.♖xd3 cxd3 28.♕xd5+ ♕xd5 29.♗xd5+ ♔h8 30.♘f7+=) 24...♘xd5 25.♕xd5+ ♕xd5 26.♘xd5 ♖bd8♔] **23...♖be8 24.f5 d4! 25.♕b3+ ♔h8 26.fxg6 hxg6!?** [26...dxe3!? was not so bad either: 27.♘f7+ ♖xf7 28.gxf7 (28.♕xf7 ♖e7 29.♕f4 ♘e5 (29...♗xd3? 30.♕h4 ♗xg6 31.♗xc6+−) 30.♖e3 ♘d5 31.♗xd5 ♕xd5 32.♕e4 (32.♖ae1? ♗b7 33.♖e4 c4!♔/−+) 32...♕xe4 33.♖xe4 ♗b7 34.♖e5 ♗xe5 35.♖h4♔) 28...♖e7 29.♗h4 (29.♖f1 ♗f8 30.♗h4 ♖e6 31.♕d1∞) 29...♖xf7 30.♖e3 (30.♗xc6 ♕xc6 31.♕xf7 ♗b7−+) 30...♘a5 31.♕c2 ♗h6♔) 27.♗h3 [27.♗xc6 ♕xc6 28.♘f7+ ♖xf7 29.♕xf7 ♗b7−+; 27.♗xc7 dxe3♔] **27...♕e7! 28.♘d5 ♕xg5 29.♘xc7 ♖e3!!−+** [The whole combination is a kind of 'too nice to be true'. The difference is that this one is true too...] **30.♗g2** [30.♘xa6 ♖xg3+ 31.hxg3 ♕xg3+ 32.♗g2 ♗e5! 33.♖xe5 ♕xe5 34.♖f1 ♕xf1+ 35.♗xf1 ♘xd3 36.♔g1 ♕f2+ 37.♔h1 ♘f4 38.♗c6 ♘e2−+; 30.♘e6 ♖xg3+ 31.hxg3 ♕xg3+ 32.♗g2 ♖f2 33.♕d5 ♖f5!−+] **30...♖xg3 31.hxg3 ♕xg3** [Among other things, c7 is hanging!] **32.♕e6** [32.♘xa6 ♗e5 33.♖xe5 ♘xe5 34.♖f1 ♖xf1+ 35.♔xf1 ♘xd3!−+ See – previously!] **32...♗e5 33.♖xe5□ ♘xe5 34.♕h3+** [It's all the same: 34.♖f1 ♖xf1+ 35.♔xf1 ♘xd3+ 36.♔g1 ♘f3+ 37.♔h1 ♕h2#] **34...♕xh3 35.♗xh3 ♘xd3 36.cxd4**

♘f3+ 37.♔g2 ♘xd4 38.♗g4 ♖f7 39.♘e8 ♖e7 40.♘d6 ♔g7 41.a5 ♘c2 [Over!]   0-1

Anatoly Karpov
Mikhail Steinberg

Leningrad ch-URS jr 1969 (10)

[Mikhail Steinberg was born in Kharkiv in 1952. In 1966 he shared 1st place with Anatoly Karpov in the USSR Schoolboys' Championship. A few months later in the USSR Semi-final at Orel he obtained a master norm. Following this, at the end of 1966 at an international tournament in Groningen, the Netherlands, he won the European Junior Cup. After getting a mathematics degree at Kharkiv University he became seriously ill and passed away in Kharkiv at the age of twenty-four. He could be proud of this game] **1.e4 c5 2.♘c3 ♘c6 3.g3 g6 4.♗g2 ♗g7 5.d3 d6 6.f4 e6** [6...e5 7.♘f3 ♘ge7 8.0-0 0-0 9.♗e3 ♘d4 10.♕d2 ♘ec6 (10...♗g4!?) 11.♖ab1 ♗g4 12.♘d5 ♘e7 13.♘xe7+ ♕xe7 14.c3 exf4 15.♗xf4 ♘xf3+ 16.♗xf3 ♗e6 17.b3 ♖ae8 18.♖be1 b6 19.d4 cxd4 20.cxd4 ♕d7 21.♕b4 ♖d8 22.♗g2 ♖fe8 23.d5 ♗g4 24.♖c1± Karpov-Steinberg, Leningrad 1969] **7.♘f3 ♘ge7 8.0-0 0-0 9.♗e3 ♘d4 10.♕d2 b6** [10...♗d7!?]

11.♖ae1 [An unusual position arises after 11.♗xd4 cxd4 12.♘b5 e5 (12...a6 13.♘bxd4 e5 14.fxe5 dxe5 15.♘b3 with a pawn up) 13.♕b4 ♗d7 14.a4!? (14.♘xd6 ♘c6 15.♕d2 (15.♘c4 ♕e7! (15...♘a5 16.♕b4) 16.♘b5 exf4 17.gxf4 ♖ac8 with a very strong initiative for the pawn) 15...♗h6♔) 14...♘c8 15.♘d2∞] **11...♗b7 12.♗f2** [12.♗xd4 cxd4 13.♘b5 e5 14.♕b4 ♘c8 15.h3 a5 16.♕c4 (16.♕a3 ♗a6 17.♗xc8 ♗xb5 18.♗b7 ♖b8 19.♗d5 exf4 20.gxf4 ♖c8 21.♖f2=/♔) 16...exf4 17.♕c7 ♕xc7

18.♘xc7 ♖b8 with an approximately equal position] **12...♕d7 13.♘xd4 cxd4 14.♘e2 e5 15.c3 dxc3 16.♘xc3** [16.bxc3 ♖ae8 17.c4 f5∓] **16...♖ad8 17.♔h1?!** [Too slow, but it's hard to find a good plan for White: 17.d4?! ♗a6 18.♘e2 f5!∓] **17...d5! 18.exd5 exf4 19.♕xf4 ♘xd5 20.♕d2** [20.♕f3 ♗xc3! 21.bxc3 ♗a8 22.c4 (22.d4 ♖c8−+) 22...♘b4 23.♕f6 ♗xg2+ 24.♔xg2 ♕xd3∓] **20...♘xc3** [20...♘b4!?−+] **21. bxc3 ♗a6−+ 22.♗d4** [22.d4 ♗xf1 23.♖xf1 ♖fe8−+] **22...♗xd4 23.cxd4 ♕xd4 24.♖e7** [24.♖f3 ♖fe8−+] **24...♗xd3 25.♖d1 ♕f6 26.♖xa7 ♗e4** [26...♖fe8!−+] **27.♖d7 ♖xd7 28.♕xd7 ♗f5∓ 29.♕d4** [29.♕d6 ♕b2∓; 29.♕d2 ♖c8∓] **29...♕xd4 30.♖xd4 ♖c8 31.h4 ♖c3 32.♔h2 ♖a3 33.♗d5 ♖d3 34.♖xd3 ♗xd3 35.♔g2 ♔g7 36.♔f3 ♗f5 37.♔f4 ♔f6 38.g4?** [≥ 38.a3] **38...♗e6!−+ 39.g5+ ♔e7 40.♔e5 ♗xd5 41.♔xd5 f5! 42.♔e5** [42.gxf6+ ♔xf6 43.a4 g5 44.hxg5+ (44.♔e4 gxh4 45.♔f4 h3 46.♔g3 ♗e5−+) 44...♔xg5 45.♔e6 h5 46.♔xb6 h4 47.a5 h3 48.a6 h2−+] **42...♔d7 43.♔d5 ♔c7 44.♔e5 ♔c6 45.h5 gxh5 46.♔xf5 ♔d6** [Black won the endgame in his opponent's style]   0-1

Boris Spassky
Lajos Portisch

Toluca izt 1982 (9)

[Two years later, the old rivals met again in Spassky's favourite system] **1.e4 c5 2.♘c3 d6 3.g3 ♘c6 4.♗g2 g6 5.d3 ♗g7 6.f4 e6 7.♘f3 ♘ge7 8.0-0 0-0 9.♗e3** [A deviation from their previous game] **9...♘d4 10.♖b1 ♖b8** [10...b6 11.♘e2 ♘xf3+ 12.♗xf3 ♗b7 13.c3 f5 14.♕c2 ♕c7 15.c4 ♖ae8 16.♗f2 e5 (16...fxe4! 17.dxe4 (17.♗xe4 d5∓) 17...♘c6 18.♖bd1 (18.♕d2 ♘e5!∓) 18...e5 19.♗g2 ♕e7∓] 17.fxe5 ♗xe5 18.♘c3 ♕b8 (18...f4 19.♗g4 fxg3 20.♗e6+ ♔h8 21.♗xg3 ♘c6 22.♗d5=/∓) 19.♘d5 fxe4 20.♗xe4 ♘xd5 21.cxd5 ♕a8 22.♕c4 b5 23.♕xb5 ♗xd5 24.♗xd5+ ♕xd5 25.♕c4 ♕xc4 26.dxc4 ♖f3 27.b3 ♖ef8 28.♖be1 ♖d3 (28...a5) 29.♖e2 ♖f5?? (a blunder; 29...♗g7=) 30.♗xc5 ♖xf1+ (30...dxc5 31.♖xf5 ♗d4+ 32.♕f2 a5±) 31.♔xf1 ♖d1+ 32.♔g2 dxc5 33.♖xe5 ♖d2+ 34.♔h3 ♖xa2 35.♖xc5± Day-Adorjan, New York 1981] **11.♘e2 ♘xf3+**

12.♗xf3 b6 13.g4 [13.a3 ♗b7 14.c4 d5 15.b4 d4 16.♗d2 ♕d7 17.g4 f5 18.♕g3 ♗c6 19.b5 ♗b7 20.♕e2 ♖be8 21.♕g2 fxe4 (21...fxg4!? 22.♗xg4 ♘f5∓) 22.♗xe4 (22.♗xe4!?±) 22...♗xe4 23.♕xe4 ♘c8 24.♖be1± Bastian-Csom, Plovdiv Ech-tt 1983; 13.c3 ♗a6 (13...♗b7!? 14.b4 ♕d7) 14.♕c2 ♕d7 15.♖fd1 d5 16.♗f2 dxe4 (16...♖bd8!?) 17.dxe4 ♕c6 18.♔g2 ♗b7 19.♘g1 e5! 20.♗d2 ♗h6 (20...♕e6!?) 21.♗e3? (≥ 21.♘h3∓) 21...f5! 22.exf5 ♘xf5!∓ 23.♖e2 (23.♗xc6 ♘xe3+ 24.♔f2 ♘xc2 25.♗xb7 ♖xb7 26.♖xc2 exf4 27.g4 f3∓/−+) 23...♕c7−+ R.Ziska-Vogt, Leutersdorf 2003] **13...f5 14.♘g3** [14.h3 d5 15.♗g2 (15.gxf5 gxf5 16.e5 ♘g6∓) 15...d4 (15...fxe4!? 16.dxe4 ♗a6∓) 16.♗d2∓ Rouillon-Apicella, Avoine 1995] **14...♗b7 15.gxf5 exf5 16.c4** [16.h4?! fxe4 17.dxe4 d5 18.e5 ♘f5 19.♘xf5 ♖xf5 20.♕e1 d4 21.♗d2? (21.♗xb7 ♖xb7 22.♗d2∓) 21...♗xf3 22.♖xf3 ♗xe5−+ M.Lopez-Khenkin, Philadelphia 1994] **16...♕d7 17.♕d2 ♖be8 18.♖be1 ♘c6 19.♗g2** [19.exf5 ♘d4 20.♗xd4 ♗xd4+ 21.♔h1 ♖xe1 22.♕xe1 gxf5∓] **19...♘d4 20.♔h1 fxe4 21.dxe4 h5! 22.♕d3 h4 23.♗xd4** [The only move] **23...cxd4 24.♘e2 h3 25.♗f3 ♕e7 26.♕d2 g5! 27.♔g1** [27.fxg5? ♖xf3−+; 27.f5 g4 28.♗xg4 ♗xe4+ 29.♔g1 d3−+] **27...gxf4 28.♘xd4 ♕f6 29.♘b5 ♖d8 30.♘xa7** [30.b3 a6 31.♘c7 ♕d7 32.♘d5 ♕d4+∓] **30...♖a8 31.♘b5 ♖xa2 32.♕xd6** [32.♖b1!?∓] **32...♖xb2 33.♕xf6 ♖xf6 34.e5?!** [34.♖f2 ♖g6+ 35.♔f1 ♖xf2+ 36.♔xf2 ♗f8∓] **34...♖g6+ 35.♔h1 ♗xf3+ 36.♖xf3 ♗xe5! 37.♖xh3 f3! 38.♖f1?** [38.♖g1 ♗bg2 39.♖xg2 fxg2+ 40.♔g1 ♖g4 and it's not clear how Black wins in this almost 'zugzwang position' after 41.♖h5 or 41.♖h6] **38...♖bg2!−+ 39.♖d1 ♗f4 40.♘d4 f2 41.♘f3 ♗e3 42.♖d8+ ♔g7 43.♖d7+ ♔f6**   0-1

**Main Line
10...♕b6**

Boris Spassky
Jozsef Horvath

Rotterdam EU-Cup final 1988 (3)

1.e4 c5 2.♘c3 ♘c6 3.g3 g6 4.♗g2 ♗g7 5.d3 d6 6.f4 e6 7.♘f3

♘ge7 8.0-0 0-0 9.♗e3 ♘d4 10.e5 ♕b6!?N 11.♘e4

11...♘ef5 [11...dxe5!? (Adorjan) 12.♘xe5 (12.c3? exf4 13.♗xf4 ♘xf3+ 14.♕xf3 f5∓; 12.fxe5 ♘ef5 13.♗f4! (≤ 13.♗f2 ♕xb2 14.g4 ♘xf3+ 15.♗xf3 ♘d4 16.c3 ♘xf3+ 17.♕xf3♔) 13...♕xb2 14.♖f2 ♘xf3+ (14...♕b6 15.♖b1 ♘xf3+ 16.♗xf3 ♕c7 17.♕e1♔) 15.♗xf3 ♕a3 16.♖b1♔) 12...♘ef5 (12...♘d5 13.♗f2! (13.♗c1 ♘f5 14.♘c4 ♕c7 15.a4 b6∓) 13...♕xb2 14.♘xc5 ♘c3 (14...♘xc2 15.♕e2!+−) 15.♗xd4 ♗b4 16.♗xc3 ♗xc5+ 17.d4 ♗xc3 18.♖f3 ♕c7 19.♕d2 with approximately equal chances) 13.♗c1 (≥ 13.♗f2! ♕xb2 14.g4! (14.♘xc5 ♕xc2 15.♗xb7 ♕xd1 16.♖axd1 ♖b8 17.♖b1 (≤ 17.♘a5 ♖b2) 17...g5↑) 14...♗e7 15.♘xc5± 13...♖d8 14.c3 ♗b5 15.♕e2 ♘bd6 16.♔f2 ♘xe4 17.dxe4 ♘h6 18.h3 (18.♕e2!? ♕c7 19.a4±) 18...♕c7 19.♘f3 (≥ 19.♘c4!? b5 (19...♕d7 20.a4 f5 21.♘e5±) 20.e5 ♖b8 21.♘d6 ♘f5 22.♘e4±) 19...b6 20.g4 (20.f5!?↑) 20...♔h8?! (20...f6!?) 21.f5!± Kucera-Kohout, Karvina 1989] **12.♗f2 ♕xb2** [12...dxe5?! 13.♘xe5 (13.c3!? ♘xf3+ 14.♕xf3 exf4 (14...♕xb2?! 15.g4±) 15.♗xc5 ♕xb2 16.♗xf8 ♔xf8 17.♕xf4±) 13...♕xb2 14.c3 (14.g4! ♘e7 15.♘xc5±) 14...♘e2+ 15.♔h1 ♘xc3 16.♘xc3 ♕xc3 17.♖c1 ♕a5 18.♖xc5 ♕xa2 19.♘c4 ♘c3 20.g4 ♘e7 21.♗d4 ♗xd4 22.♖a5 ♕xa5 23.♘xa5 ♗d7∞ Liemann-Tolnai, Oberwart 1993] **13.♘xd4 cxd4 14.g4 ♘e3** [14...dxe5 15.gxf5 exf5 16.♘d6±] **15.♗xe3 dxe3 16.♘xd6 f6!** [16...g5!? 17.♖c1 (17.♕e2 gxf4 18.♘c4 ♘d4 19.♖ac1 ♖d8 (19...b5 20.c3 ♕d8 21.♗xa8 bxc4 22.d4 ♕g5±) 20.g5 b5! 21.♘a5 (21.c3 ♕xd3 22.♕xd3 ♖xd3 23.♘b2 ♖d2 24.♗xa8 ♖xb2∓) 21...♗d7 22.♗xa8 ♖xa8 23.♕f3 ♖c8∓) 17...♖b8 (17...gxf4 18.♘c4 ♕d4 19.c3

♕c5 20.♕e2 ♗d7 21.d4 ♕c7 22.♖b1 ♖ab8 23.g5±] 18.fxg5 ♕xe5 19.♘e4 b5 20.♕e2 ♗b7 21.♘xe3 ♕d4≅] **17.♕e2 fxe5 18.♘c4 ♕d4 19.fxe5 ♖f2 20.♕xe3 ♖xf1+ 21.♖xf1 ♗xe5 22.♕xd4 ♗xd4+ 23.♔h1 ♖b8 24.♖b1** [24...b6 25.♘a5 ♗d7 26.♘c6 ♗xc6 27.♖xc6 ♖c8 28.♗a4= Spassky, Adorjan] ½-½

Herbert Bastian
Olaf Müller
Germany Bundesliga 1988

1.e4 c5 2.♘c3 ♘c6 3.g3 g6 4.♗g2 ♗g7 5.d3 d6 6.f4 e6 7.♘f3 ♘ge7 8.0-0 0-0 9.♗e3 ♘d4 10.e5 ♕b6!? 11.♖b1 ♘ef5 12.♗f2 ♘xf3+ 13.♕xf3 dxe5 14.♘a4?! [14.fxe5 ♗xe5 15.♘e4 ♕c7 (15...♘d4 16.♕d1 f5 17.♘d2 ♕c7 (17...♗f6!? 18.c3 ♘c6 19.♕e2=) 18.c3 ♘b5 19.♘c4 (19.♕e2!?±) 19...♗g7 0-1 (42) Gvein-Reeh, Gausdal 1993) 16.♗xc5 ♖d8 17.c3=] **14...♕c7 15.fxe5** [15.♗xc5 ♗d7 16.♗xf8 ♖xf8 17.♘c3 ♗c6 18.♘e4 exf4 19.♕xf4 ♕b6+ 20.♖f2 (20.♔h1 ♘e3 21.♖f2 f5-+) 20...♘d4 21.c3 ♗e3 22.♕f3 ♖d8 23.d4 ♗xe4 24.♕xe4 ♗xf2+ 25.♔xf2 ♘xd4! 26.♕e3 (26. cxd4 ♖xd4 27.♕e3 ♘d2+ 28.♔f3 ♕c6+ 29.♕e4 ♖d3+ 30.♔f2 ♕c2+ 31.♕e2 ♖d2 32.♖e1 ♕xb2-+) 26...♘a5 27.♖d1 (27.cxd4 ♕f5+-+) 27...♘f5 28.♖xd8+ ♕xd8 29.♕e2 ♕b6+∓/-+; 15.♘xc5 ♘d4 16.♗xd4 exd4 17.♘b3 ♖b8 △ ...b7-b6, ...♗b7∓; 17...♕xc2?? 18.♖fc1+-] **15...♗xe5 16.♗xc5** [16.♘xc5 ♘d4! 17.♕e4 ♕xc5 18.c3 ♖d8 19.♖bc1 (19.♖be1 ♗g7∓) 19...f5 20.♕e3 ♕b5! (20...f4 21.♕e1 fxg3 22.hxg3 ♗xg3 23.cxd4 ♗xf2+ 24.♔xf2 ♕xd4 25.♖c7 ♕xf2+ 26.♖xf2 ♖d7 27.♖fc2 ♖xc7 28.♖xc7 e5 29.♖e7≅) 21.cxd4 ♗xd4 22.♕g5 (22.♕e2 ♕xb2 23.♕xb2 ♗xb2 24.♖c2 ♗g7∓) 22...♕b6∓] **16...♗d7!** [16...♖d8!? 17.♕f2 (17.b4? ♗d7 18.b5 b6 19.♕f2 ♕xc2 20.♕e4 ♗g7-+) 17...♗d7 18.♘c3 ♗c6 19.♕xc6 ♕xc6 20.♖be1 ♕xc5 21.♕xc5 ♗d4+ 22.♕xd4 ♘xd4∓] **17.♗xf8 ♖xf8 18.♘c3 ♗d4+** [18...♕b6+! 19.♔h1 (19.♖f2 ♗xc3-+) 19...♗c6! (19...♘e3 20.♖be1 (≤ 20.♖fe1 ♘xg2 21.♖xe5 ♗c6 22.♖e4 (22.♘e4 ♘e3-+) 22...♘e3 23.♘a4 ♕a5 24.♕xe3 ♕xa4-+) 20...♘xf1 21.♖xe5 ♘d2 22.♕xb7 ♕xb7 23.♗xb7 ♖b8

24.♖e2 ♗xb7 25.♖xd2 ♖xb2 26.♔g2 ♗g7 27.♔f3 f5∓] **19.♔h1** [19.♖f2 ♗c6 20.♘e4 ♗xe4! 21.dxe4 ♕xc2-+] **19...♘e3 20.♕e4?T** [20.♕xb7 ♕xb7 21.♗xb7 ♘xf1 22.♖xf1 ♖b8-+; 20.♖f2 ♘xg2 21.♖xg2 ♗c6 22.♕e2 ♗xc3 23.bxc3 ♗xg2+ (23...♕a5!?∓) 24.♔xg2 (24.♕xg2 ♕xc3 25.♖xb7 ♕a1+ 26.♕g1 ♕xa2∓) 24...♕xc3 25.♖b3 (25.♖xb7? ♕c6+ 26.♕f3 ♕xc2+-+) 25...♕c6+ 26.♔g1 b6∓; 20.♕f4 ♕b6! 21.♗e2□ ♗g7 22.c4 (22.♖fc1 ♘xg2 23.♖xg2 ♗xb2-+) 22...♘xf1 23.♕xf1 ♗c6∓] **20...♕b6 21.♖f4** [21.♕f4 f5∓] **21...e5-+ 22.♘e2 ♗c6 23.♘xd4 ♗xe4 24.♖xe4 exd4 25.♗f3 ♖c8 26.♖e7 ♕f6** 0-1

Main Line
10...♗d7

Liliana Burijovich
Zsuzsa Polgar
Novi Sad ol W 1990 (13)

1.e4 c5 2.♘c3 ♘c6 3.g3 g6 4.♗g2 ♗g7 5.d3 d6 6.f4 e6 7.♘f3 ♘ge7 8.0-0 0-0 9.♗e3 ♘d4 10.e5 ♗d7!?

11.♘e4 ♘ef5 [11...dxe5 12.fxe5 (12.♘xe5!? b6 13.c3 ♘dc6 14.♕e2 ♘xe5 15.fxe5 ♗c6 (15...♘xe5 16.♗h6 ♖c8 (16...♖e8? 17.♘xc5+-) 17.♗xf8 ♕xf8 18.♖ae1±) 16.♗f4 ♕c7±) 12...♘c6 13.♘xc5 ♘ef5 14.♗f2 ♕d5 15.♘e4 ♘xf3+ 16.♗xf3 ♕xe5 17.c3 ♕c7∓ (Meinhardt-Bogner, Germany 2009) 18.♗b6] **12.♗f2 ♘xf3+** [12... dxe5? 13.♘xe5± b6 14.g4! ♘e7 (14...♘h6 15.c3 ♘c6 16.g5 ♘f5 17.♘f6+ ♗xf6 18.gxf6 ♖c8 19.♕g4±) 15.♗h4! f6 16.♗xf6+- ♗xf6 17.♘xf6+ ♖xf6 18.♘xd7 ♕xd7 19.♗xa8 h5 20.c3 ♘b5 21.♗e4 1-0 Pavasovic-Appleberry,

Budapest 1994; 12...♗c6 13.c3 (13.♘fd2!?; 13.g4 ♘xf3+ 14.♗xf3 ♘d4 15.♗g2 dxe5 16.fxe5 ♗xe4 17.♗xe4 ♕e7 18.♖e1 ♖ac8 19.b4? (19.♗g2=) 19...♖fd8 (19...♗xe5-+) 20.bxc5? ♖xc5-+ 21.♖c1 ♖xe5 (21...♗xe5-+) 22.c3 ♘c6 23.♕f3 ♖a5 24.♖c2? (it's too much already...) 24...♘e5 25.♕g3 ♘xg4 0-1 Kroeze-Douven, Groningen 1993) 13...♘xf3+ 14.♗xf3 dxe5 (14...h5 15.exd6 b6 16.♗f6+ ♗xf6 17.♗xc6 ♖c8 18.♗b7 ♖b8 19.♗e4 ♕xd6 20.♕a4 ♕c7 21.♕a6 b5 0-1 (40) Sale-Sadler, Cannes 1995) 15.fxe5 ♗xe5 16.♘xc5 (16.♗xc5 ♖e8 17.♕e2 ♕c7 18.♗f2 h5 19.d4 ♗g7 20.♖fe1 e5 21.dxe5 ♖xe5 22.♕f1 ♖ae8 23.♖g2 ♕e7 24.♘d2 ♘e3 25.♖xe3 ♖xe3 26.♗xe3 ♕xe3+ 27.♕f2 ♕xf2+ (27...♖h6! 28.♗xc6 bxc6 29.♘f1 ♕e2∓/-+) 28.♔xf2 ♗a4 29.♘b3 b6=/∓ Ghita-A.Vovk, Arad 2014) 16...♕c7 17.d4 ♗g7 18.♘d3 ♖ad8 19.g4 ♘e7 20.♗g3 ♕b6 21.♕b3 ♗xf3 (21...♗b5!?=) 22.♕xb6 axb6 23.♖xf3± Schekachev-B.Vladimirov, Györ 1990, which was the very first game with 10...♗d7 according to the Megabase 2015, and was followed by another 257 games with the same move!] **13.♗xf3** [13.♕xf3 ♗c6∞ 14.c3 ♖c8! 15.exd6 ♗xd6 16.♕e2 b6= Lane-Sadler, London 1992] **13...dxe5 14.♘xc5 exf4 15.gxf4 ♗c6** [15...♗xb2 16.♖b1 ♗g7 (16...♗d4 17.♖xb7 ♖e8 18.♕e2 ♕d6 19.♘b3 (19.♘e4 ♕xf4 20.♖b4 ♗xf2+ 21.♕xf2 ♔h8∓) 19...♗xf2+ 20.♖xf2 ♗c6∓) 17.♖xb7 ♗e8 18.♘b3∞] **16.♗xc6 bxc6 17.c3** [17.♖b1 ♘h6 18.♕f3 ♕d6∓] **17...♕d5** [17...♕b8 18.♕d2 ♖d8 19.d4 ♗h6∓] **18.♕e2 ♖ab8 19.♖ab1 ♖fd8 20.a4 ♗f8 21.♘e4 ♕xd3 22.♕xd3 ♖xd3 23.a5** [23.♖xa7 ♖a8 24.♘c5 ♖xa4 25.♘f6+ ♔g7 26.♘e8+ (26.♗xf8+ ♔xf6+-) 26...♔h8 27.♘xf8 ♖a8 28.♗d1 ♖xd1 29.♖xd1 ♖xe8 30.♗b4 ♗g7∓] **23...a6 24.♗b6 ♗e7 25.♖bd1 ♖d5 26.c4 ♖xd1 27.♖xd1 ♖b7 28.♖d2 ♔f8 29.♔f2 ♔e8 30.♔e2 h5 31.b3 ♖d7** [31...♖b8!?] **32.♖xd7 ♔xd7 33.♔d3 ♗b4 34.♘f6+ ♔c8 35.♘e4 ♘d6 36.♘c5** [36.♗c5!? ♘xe4 37.♗xb4 f5 38.♗d4∓] **36...♗xc5 37.♗xc5 ♘b7 38.♗b6** [38.♗b4!? c5 39.♗e1 ♔d7 40.♔e4∓] **38...c5 39.♔c3 ♔d7 40.b4?!** [40.♔d3 was more advisable] **40...cxb4+ 41.♔xb4 ♘d8 42.♔c3** [42.♔c5? ♘c6 43.h4 f6Z] **42...♘c6 43.♔d3 e5!**—+ [White's position can't be defended] **44.♔e3 ♔e6 45.h3 exf4+ 46.♔xf4 ♘e5 47.c5 ♔d5 48.♔g5 ♘d7 49.♗a7 ♔c6 50.♔h6 ♘xc5 51.♔g7 g5 52.♔xf7 g4 53.h4 g3 54.♗b8 g2 55.♔h2 ♘e4 56.♔g6 ♘d2 57.♗g1 ♘f3 58.♗f2 ♘xh4+ 59.♔xh5 ♘f3 60.♔g4 g1♕+** [It was time to resign...] **61.♗xg1 ♘xg1 62.♔f4 ♔b5 63.♔e4 ♔xa5 64.♔d3 ♔b4 65.♔c2 a5 66.♔b2 ♘f3 67.♔a2 a4 68.♔b2 ♘d4 69.♔a2 a3** 0-1

Damien Vincent
Cyril Marzolo

Besancon 1998 (2)

1.e4 c5 2.♘c3 ♘c6 3.g3 g6 4.♗g2 ♗g7 5.d3 d6 6.f4 e6 7.♘f3 ♘ge7 8.0-0 0-0 9.♗e3 ♘d4 10.e5 ♗d7 11.♘xd4 cxd4 12.♗xd4 ♗c6 [12... dxe5 13.fxe5 (13.♗xe5??

13...♕b6+ (0-1 Kristensen-Feher, Aarhus 1992 – The very first game with the blunder where White resigned immediately, after which two others followed later: 14.♔h1 f6—+ 15.♘e4 fxe5 0-1 Angers-Khassanov, Montreal 1997) 14.d4 f6 15.♔h1 fxe5 16.dxe5 ♖ad8 17.♘e4 ♗b5 18.♘d6 ♗xf1 19.♕xf1 ♘f5 20.♘c4 ♕c7 21.b3 b5 22.♘a3 ♘e3 23.♕f2 ♘xg2 24.♕xg2 ♕c5 0-1 Aslan-Naroditsky, Kemer 2007) 13...♗c6 14.♗c5 (14.♗f2 ♗xg2 (14...♗xe5!? 15.d4 ♗g7 16.♘e4 ♗d5 17.b3 b5∓) 15.♔xg2 ♗xe5 16.d4 ♗g7 17.♕f3 (17.♘e4 ♖c8 18.c3 b6∓) 17...♘d5?! (≥ 17...♖c8 18.♖fd1 (18.♕xb7 ♖b8 19.♕f3 ♘f5∓) 18...♘f5 19.d5 ♕e7 20.a4 b6∓) 18.♘e4 (18.♘xd5 exd5 19.♖ae1 ♖c8 20.c3=) 18...♖c8 19.c3 b6 20.♖ad1 ♕d7 21.♖fe1 ♖fe8 (21...♗h6!?∓)

22.♖e2 h6 23.a3 ♖ed8= (½-½, 42) Turner-Dunnington, Hafnarfjordur 1996) 14...♗xg2 15.♔xg2 ♗xe5 16.♕f3 (16. d4!? ♗g7 17.♕f3 b6 18.♗a3 ♖c8 19.♖ad1 ♕d7=) 16...b6 17.♗a3 ♖c8 18.d4 ♗xd4 (18...♗d6 19.♗xd6 ♕xd6∓) 19.♖ad1 ♘f5 20.♗xf8 ♕xf8 21.♖d3 b5♔ (0-1, 49) Turner-Wilson, London 1995; 12...♘c6 13.♗e3 dxe5 14.fxe5 ♘xe5 15.♗xb7 (15.♗c5 ♖e8 16.♗xb7 (16.d4?! ♘c4; 16.♕e2 ♗c6∓) 16...♖b8 17.♗g2 (17.♗h1!? ♖xb2 18.d4 ♕a5 19.♘e4∓) 17...♖xb2 18.d4 ♕a5 19.♘e4 ♗c6∓) 15...♖b8 16.♗g2 ♖xb2 17.♘e4? (17.♗c5 ♖e8∓) 17...f5 18.♗f2 ♗a4—+ (0-1, 33) Novitzkij-Golubev, Minsk 1993] **13.♘e4 ♘f5 14.♗f2 dxe5 15.fxe5 ♗xe5 16.c3 ♖c8** [16...h5!? 17.♕e2 ♕c7∓; 16...♘d6 17.♘xd6 (17.♕e2!?=) 17...♕xd6 18.d4 ♗xg2 19.♔xg2 ♕c6+ 20.♔g1 (≥ 20.♕f3 ♕xf3+ 21.♔xf3) 20...♗g7 21.♗e3 ♖ad8 22.♕b3 (22.♕f3!? ♖d5=) 22...♖d5 23.♖ad1 b5 24.♖d2 ♕c7 (24...♖fd8!?) 25.♗f4 ♕d7=/∓ (0-1, 39) De Wiljes-Hofrichter, Oberhof 1999] **17.♕e2 b6 18.a4 h5 19.a5 bxa5 20.♗xa7 h4 21.d4 ♕c7 22.dxe5** [22.♗c5!? hxg3 23.dxe5 ♗xe4 24.♗xf8 ♕a7+ 25.♔h1 ♗xg2+ 26.♕xg2 ♘e3 (26...♖xf8 27.hxg3 ♘e3 28.♕f2 ♕a8+ 29.♔g1 ♘xf1 30.♖xf1 ♕b8∓) 27.♕xg3 ♘xf1 28.♖xf1 ♖xf8∓] **22...♕xa7+ 23.♕f2 ♕xf2+ 24.♔xf2 ♗xe4! 25.♗xe4 hxg3+ 26.hxg3 ♖c5 27.b4** [≥ 27.♗xf5 gxf5 28.♖fe1 ♖d8 29.b4 axb4 30.cxb4 ♖b5 31.g4!? (31.♖ab1 ♖d4∓) 31...♖d2+ 32.♔g3 ♖xb4 33.gxf5 exf5=/∓] **27... axb4 28.cxb4 ♖xe5 29.♗f3** [29.♖fe1 ♘d6∓] **29...♖b8 30.♖a8 ♖xa8 31.♗xa8 ♘d4 32.♖b1 ♖b5 33.♖b2?!** [≥ 33.♗e4∓] **33...♔f8 34.♗e4 ♔e7 35.♗d3 ♖b6∓/—+ 36.♔e3 e5 37.♔e4 ♔d6 38.g4?!** [38.b5 f5+ 39.♔e3 ♔d5 40.♗f1 g5 41.♗g2+ ♔d6 42.♗f1∓/—+] **38... f5+—+ 39.gxf5 gxf5+ 40.♔e3 ♔d5 41.b5 f4+ 42.♔f2 e4 43.♗f1 e3+** 0-1

Bernal Gonzalez Acosta
Leonardo Valdes

Antiguo ch-CRI 1999 (2)

1.f4 g6 2.♘f3 ♗g7 3.g3 c5 4.♗g2 ♘c6 5.d3 e6 6.e4 d6 7.0-0 ♘ge7 8.♘c3 0-0 9.♗e3 ♘d4 10.e5

♗d7 11.exd6 ♘ef5 12.♗f2 ♗c6 [12...♘xd6 13.♘e4 (13.♘xd4?! cxd4 14.♘e2 (14.♘e4 ♗c6∓) 14...♕b6 15.♖b1 ♗c6 16.♗xc6 bxc6 17.c3 ♘f5 (17...c5!? 18.b4 ♘f5 19.♕c1 ♖ac8∓) 18.♕a4 ♖ad8 19.♖fd1 (19.g4 ♘e3 20.♗xe3 dxe3 21.♕e4 ♖d7 22.♖f3 ♖fd8∓) 19...h5 20.h3 e5∓ 21.g4? (21. fxe5 ♗xe5∓) 21...hxg4 22.hxg4 ♘h6 23.g5 ♘g4—+ Dizdarevic-Degenhardt, Mannheim 1994; 13.♘e5!? ♖c8 14.a4 (14.♘e2 ♘c6!=) 14...♘c6!? (14...b6!? 15.♘e4 ♗e8=) 15.♘xc6 ♗xc6 16.♗xc5 ♗d4+ 17.♗xd4 ♘xd4♔) 13...♘xe4 14.dxe4 ♘xf3+ 15.♕xf3 (15.♗xf3 ♗b5 16.♕xd8 ♖fxd8 17.♖fd1 ♗c6 18.c3 (18.♗xc5 ♗xb2 19.♖ab1 ♗g7=) 18... b6=) 15...♗c6 16.♖fd1 ♕a5 17.♕b3 c4 18.♕xc4 ♗xb2 19.♖ab1 ♗a3 20.♖b3 ♖fc8 21.♕c3 ♗xc3 22.♖xc3 ♗e7= Blodig-Berndt, Bad Wörishofen 1995] **13.♘e5** [13.d7 ♘xf3+ (13...♕xd7 14.♘e5 ♗xe5 15.fxe5 ♗xg2 16.♔xg2 h5 17.h3=/±; 13...♗xf3 14.♗xf3 ♕xd7 15.♗g2 ♖ac8 16.♘e4 b6=) 14.♗xf3 ♗xf3 (14...♕xd7! 15.♗xc5 ♗d4+ 16.♗xd4 ♕xd4+ 17.♖f2 ♘e3 18.♕e2 ♗xf3 (18...♗xc2 19.♗xc6 ♖xa1 20.♗e4 ♖ac8 21.♕d1 ♖xc3 22.bxc3 ♗xc3 23.♗xb7 ♖d8=/∓) 19.♕xf3 ♗xc2 20.♖d1 (20.♖c1 ♘b4∓) 20...♖ad8∓) 15.♕xf3 b6 16.♗b7 ♕e7 17.a4 ♘d6 18.♕c6 ♖ad8 19.a5 ♕xd7 20.♕xd7 ♖xd7 21.axb6 axb6 22.♖a6 ♖b8 23.♖fa1= Veresagin-Vokarev, Podolsk 1993; 13.♘e4 ♖c8 14.c3 ♘xf3+ 15.♗xf3 b6 16.♕e2 ♘xd6= Ciruk-Kowalak, Krynica 1997] **13...♗xg2 14.♔xg2 ♘xd6 15.♘e4 b6 16.♗xd4 cxd4 17.♘xd6 ♕xd6 18.♘c4 ♕c7 19.a4 ♖fd8 20.♕f3 ♖ab8 21.♖f2 a6 22.♖e2 ♖d5 23.♖c1**∓ ½-½

**Main Line
Black Deviates on Move 9**

Boris Spassky
Suat Atalik

Tallinn rapid 1998 (7)

1.e4 c5 2.♘c3 ♘c6 3.g3 g6 4.♗g2 ♗g7 5.d3 d6 6.f4 e6 7.♘f3 ♘ge7 8.0-0 0-0 9.♗e3 b6!? [Another less frequently played, but decent possibility] **10.♗f2** [10.d4 ♘xd4 (10...♗b7 11.dxc5 bxc5 (11...dxc5 12.♕e2 ♕c8=) 12.e5?! (12.♘b5!±) 12...♘f5 13.♗f2 dxe5 14.♗xc5 (14.♕xd8 ♖fxd8 15.♘xe5 ♘xe5 16.♗xb7 ♖ab8 17.♖ad1 ♘d4∓) 14...exf4! 15.♗xf8 ♕b6+! 16.♔h1 ♖xf8∓ /−+; 10...♗a6 11.♖e1 ♖c8=) 11.♘xd4 cxd4 12.♗xd4 e5 13.♗e3 (13.fxe5 ♘c6) 13...exf4 14.♗xf4 ♗e5=] **10...♗a6** [10...♗b7 11.♕d2 ♕d7 12.♖ae1 ♘d4 13.♘h4 f5 14.♔h1 e5 (14...♖ae8!?) 15.♘d5 ♘xd5 16.exd5 ♖ae8 17.c3 ♘b5 18.♗e3 ♖f7 19.a4 ♘c7 20.c4 a5 21.b3 ♘a6 22.♘f3 ♖fe7 23.fxe5 dxe5 24.♗g5 ♖f7 25.♖e2 f4?? (anything else, but not this...) 26.gxf4+− h6 27.fxe5 ♖xf3

28.♖xf3 hxg5 29.♕xg5 1-0 Spassky-Krasenkow, Oviedo 1991]

11.♕d2   ♕d7   12.♖ae1   ♖ae8

13.g4 [13.a4!?] **13...f5 14.gxf5 exf5 15.♗h3 d5 16.e5** [16.exd5 ♘xd5 17.♘xd5 ♕xd5 18.♗g2 ♕d7∓] **16...♘d8 17.♘e2 d4 18.♗g2 ♘e6!** [An ideal square for the knight] **19.h4 ♗b7 20.♘g5** [20.c3 dxc3 21.bxc3 ♖d8 22.♖d1 ♗h6∓] **20...♗xg2 21.♔xg2 ♕d5+ 22.♔g3 ♘c6∓ 23.♘c1?** [23.♘xe6 ♖xe6 24.c4∓] **23...♘xg5 24.hxg5 ♗xe5!−+ 25.fxe5 f4+ 26.♔h2** [26.♔h3 ♕f3+ 27.♔h2 ♘xe5−+] **26...♖xe5 27.♗h4 ♘f3+ 28.♖xf3 ♕xf3 29.♕f2 ♕g4 30.♖e4 ♖xe4 31.dxe4 ♖e8 32.♕e1 h6 33.gxh6 g5**   **0-1**

Exercise 1

position after 19.d4xc5

White naively took on c5 on the previous move. What is the refutation?
(solution on page 246)

Exercise 2

position after 17.♘e4xc5

Black can win material in this position. How?
(solution on page 246)

Exercise 3

position after 49...f3-f2

Black threatens 50...f1♕, which is unavoidable... is there a solution to win the game with white?
(solution on page 246)

Pirc Defence

Stay on these Roads

by Alejo de Dovitiis

1.	e4	d6
2.	d4	♘f6
3.	f3	c5
4.	d5	e6
5.	♗b5+	

'Stay on these Roads' is the title of a song by a Norwegian band of the eighties, A-ha. In the ninth round of the Argentinean Championship 2015 my opponent was one of the best chess players of our country: grandmaster Fernando Peralta.

His chess level and his wisdom in opening theory forced me to explore less-trodden paths when preparing to face him. That is why I came to study the line we will deal with in this Survey.

After 5.♗b5+!? there are three moves (if we consider 5...♔e7 to be bad):

Worthy of Attention

5...♘fd7 does not have any games, but you can see a short analysis of this line in the first game (see Lapan-Leski).

Exchanging the bishops

5...♗d7 aims for a quick development of Black's forces. White must exchange the bishops and then can play on the light squares, first strengthening the d5-pawn (see the games Lapan-Leski, Kohlweyer-Movsziszian and Dokhoian-Agrest).

Black Goes for the Bishop Pair

5...♘bd7 followed by 6...a6 is an attempt to obtain the bishop pair, or a chance to mobilize his queenside. I think White should take on d7, since time is an important factor here, and try to exert to pressure on the d5- and e6-squares (see the games Murali Krisnan-Gagunashvili and De Dovitiis-Peralta).

Conclusion

Personally I would prefer 5...♘bd7 instead of 5...♗d7, because the former move forces White to make a decision to give his light-squared bishop or not at an early stage. Anyway, both moves are playable.

The final lesson is: Stay on these Roads (i.e. sideroads!) if you want to try and surprise a stronger opponent!

Exchanging the Bishops
5...♗d7

Dan Lapan
Marc Leski
Groningen EU-ch U20 1980 (2)

1.e4 d6 2.d4 ♘f6 3.f3 c5 4.d5 e6 5.♗b5+!? [5.c4 is the 'normal' move at this moment] **5...♗d7** [Currently the most popular reply. After 5...♘fd7 I do not see any refutation but White is slightly better: 6.♘h3 a6 7.♗e2 exd5 8.exd5 ♘f6 9.♘f2 ♗e7 10.0-0 0-0 11.♘c3±] **6.♗xd7+** [6.a4

exd5 7.exd5 ♗e7] **6...♘bxd7** [6...♕xd7 will be analysed further on] **7.♘e2** [7.dxe6 fxe6 8.♘h3 d5 and Black is OK, Dobrin-Hassan, Email 2001; 7.♘h3!? exd5 8.exd5 g6 (8...♕e7+ 9.♔f2) 9.0-0 followed by ♖e1+ is unpleasant] **7...exd5 8.exd5 g6 9.0-0 ♗g7 10.♘bc3 0-0 11.♗f4 ♕b6 12.♕d2 ♖fe8** [12...♕xb2? 13.♗xd6 ♖fe8 14.♖ab1] **13.♖ae1?!** [13.♖ab1] **13...♘h5 14.♗h6 ♗xh6 15.♕xh6 c4+ 16.♔h1 ♕xb2 17.♘e4 ♕e5 18.g4 ♘hf6 19.♘f4** [19.♘2g3 ♘xd5; 19.♘2c3!? ♘xe4

20.♘xe4 ♕xd5 21.♖d1] **19...♘xe4 20.♖xe4 ♕c3** [20...♕g7 21.♕xg7+ ♔xg7 22.♖xc4 ♖ac8 23.♖b4!] **21.♘h3 b5 22.♘g5 ♕g7 23.♕xg7+ ♔xg7 24.♖xe8 ♖xe8 25.♘e4 ♖e5 26.♖d1 ♘f6?!** [26...♘b6 27.♘xd6 a6−+] **27.♘xd6 a6 28.a4!** [Here we see the difference between 26...♘f6 and 26...♘b6] **28...♘xd5** [28...bxa4 29.♘xc4 ♖xd5 30.♖a1] **29.axb5 axb5 30.♘xb5 ♘e3 31.♖e1 ♘xg4!** [Anyway Black has a clear advantage] **32.♖xe5 ♘xe5 33.♔g2 ♔f6**

34.♔f2 ♔e6 35.♔e3 ♔d5 36.h3 ♔c5 37.♘c3 f5 38.♘e2 ♘c6 39.c3 ♔d5 40.♘f4+ ♔e5 41.♘e2 g5 42.f4+ gxf4+ 43.♔f3 ♘e7 44.♘xf4 ♘d5 45.♘e2 h6 46.h4 f4 [I prefer 46...h5 47.♔f2 (47.♘g3 ♘xc3 48.♘xh5 ♘d5 49.♘g3 c3 50.♘e2 c2 51.♘c1 f4 should win easily)] 47.♘d4 ♘xc3 48.♘c6+ ♔f5? [48...♔d5 49.♘a5 ♘b5 50.♘xc4 ♘d4+ 51.♔xf4 ♘xc4 52.♔e5 ♔d3 53.♔f6 ♘e4-+] 49.♘d4+ ♔g6 50.♔xf4 ♘h5 51.♘f5 ♘d5+ 52.♔e4 ♔g6 [52...♘b6 53.♘d4 ♔g6 54.♘d6 ♔f6 (54...♘h5 55.♘f5) 55.♘xc4 ♘xc4 56.♔xc4 ♔e5 57.♔d3 ♔f4 58.♔e2=] 53.h5+ [53...♔xh5 54.♔xd5 c3 55.♘e3 ♔g5 56.♔d4 ♔f4 57.♘d5+ ♔f3 58.♘xc3 h5 59.♘e4 h4 60.♘g5+ ♔g4 61.♘e4] ½-½

Bernd Kohlweyer
Karen Movsziszian

Llucmajor 2015 (6)

1.d4 d6 2.e4 ♘f6 3.f3 c5 4.d5 e6 5.♗b5+ ♗d7 6.♗xd7+ ♘bxd7 7.dxe6 [7.c4!?; 7.♘h3!?] 7...fxe6 8.♘c3 ♗e7 9.♘h3 [9.♗f4 ♕b6 10.♘ge2 could be interesting]

9...♘e5! 10.0-0 ♕d7 11.♕e2 [11.♘f4] 11...♘c6 [Going to d4] 12.♗e3 0-0 [12...♘d4 13.♕d2 e5 14.♘d1!?] 13.♖ad1 d5 14.exd5 exd5 15.♘xd5 ♘xd5 16.c4 ♘d4 17.♗xd4 cxd4 18.cxd5 [18.♖xd4?? ♗c5] 18...♗c5 19.♕c4 ♖ac8 20.♘f2 ♖fd8 21.♖fe1 ♗b6? [21...♔f8 looks strange, but after it Black will be able to capture on d5, since 22.♖e5 is bad: 22...♗d6!] 22.♕b3 ♕xd5?? [23.♖e8+ ♔f7 (23...♖xe8 24.♕xd5+) 24.♕xd5+ ♖xd5 25.♖xc8; necessary was 22...♕c7 in order to play 23...♕c4] 1-0

Yury Dokhoian
Evgenij Agrest

Münster 1993 (7)

1.d4 d6 2.e4 ♘f6 3.f3 c5 4.d5 e6 5.♗b5+ ♗d7 6.♗xd7+ ♕xd7 [The alternative is 6...♘bxd7] 7.c4

7...exd5 [7...b5 8.b3 exd5 9.exd5 ♕e7+ 10.♕e2 ♘bd7 11.♘a3 bxc4 12.bxc4 ♘b6 13.♗d2 0-0-0, Andreeva-Fominykh, Wch U18 W 2004] 8.cxd5 g6 9.♘e2 ♗g7 [9...b5!? 10.a4 b4 11.♘d2] 10.a4 0-0 11.♘a3 ♕e7 12.♘c4 ♘bd7 13.♗f4 ♘e8 [A standard Benoni scheme] 14.♖a3 ♘e5 15.♗xe5 ♗xe5 16.0-0 ♗g7 17.♖e3!? ♕d7 18.f4 ♘f6 19.h3 ♖ad8 [Black puts all his efforts in stopping e4-e5] 20.♘c3 h5 21.♕f3 [21.♕d3 △ ♖d1] 21...♘e8 22.e5! dxe5 23.fxe5 ♘c7 24.♖d1 ♕h7 25.♔h1 ♘a6 26.b3 ♘b4 27.♕e2 [27.♘e4 ♕f5 28.♕xf5 gxf5 29.♘ed6!?] 27...♕f5 28.♘d6 ♕d7 29.♘ce4 ♕e7 30.♘xc5? [30.♖f3 ♔g8 (30...♕xe5 31.♘xf7 ♖xf7 32.♖xf7 ♖e8 33.♘f6+) 31.♘f6+ ♗xf6 32.♖xf6+-] 30...b6 31.♘cb7 [31.♘ce4 ♕xe5] 31...♖d7 32.e6 ♖xd6 [32...♖xb7?? 33.♘xb7 ♕xb7 34.e7 ♖e8 35.d6+-] 33.♘xd6 ♕xd6 34.e7 ♖e8 35.♕b5 [35...♖xe7 36.♖xe7 ♕xe7 37.d6 ♕e4 38.d7 ♘c6 39.♕xc6 with a clear advantage. Perhaps White was suffering from time trouble] ½-½

Black Goes for the Bishop Pair: 5...♘bd7

B.T. Murali Krishnan
Murab Gagunashvili

Mumbai 2008 (4)

1.d4 d6 2.e4 ♘f6 3.f3 c5 4.d5 e6 5.♗b5+ ♘bd7 6.a4 [6.dxe6 is an option we will investigate in the next game; 6.♘c3 a6 7.♗xd7+ ♗xd7 is very comfortable for

Black] 6...a6 7.♗e2 exd5 8.exd5 g6 9.c4 ♗g7 10.♘h3 0-0 11.0-0

11...♖e8∓ [In my opinion Black has a better version of the Benoni here] 12.♘c3 ♘h5 [12...♖b8] 13.♗g5 [13.♔h1] 13...♗d4+ 14.♔h1 [14.♗xd4? cxd4 15.♗xd8 dxc3, winning] 14...♕b6 15.♕c2 ♘e5?! [15...♕c7] 16.g4!? [16.♘f2 f6 17.♗d2 f5] 16...♘g7 17.a5 ♕c7 18.♘e4! [White has the initiative] 18...♘d7 19.♗f4 ♗e5 20.♗xe5 dxe5 [20...♖xe5 21.f4 ♖e8 (21...♖xe4 22.♕xe4 ♘f6 23.♕g2+-) 22.f5!] 21.♗d3 ♖f8 22.♕d2 [22.♖g1] 22...f5 23.gxf5 ♘xf5 [23...gxf5 24.♘g3 ♕d6 25.♖g1→] 24.♕g5 b6 25.♘hf2 bxa5 26.♘g4 ♖b8 27.♖g1 ♔h8 28.♘h6 ♖xb2 [28...♖b3] 29.♘xf5 ♖xf5 30.♕e7! [The key] 30...♖h5 31.♖g2 ♖xg2 32.♔xg2 a4 [32...♖f5 33.♘g3 ♖f8 34.♘h5 ♖g8 35.♘f6] 33.♘d6 ♕a5 34.♖a2 ♕c3 35.♖f2 [35.♗e4 ♕e3 36.♕e8+ ♔g7 37.h4 ♕f4 38.♕xc8 ♖xh4 39.♕xd7+ ♔h6 and both kings are in trouble: 40.♘f7+ ♔h5 41.♔f1 ♕c1+ (41...♖h1+ 42.♔e2 ♖h2+ 43.♔d3 ♖xa2 44.♕h3+ ♕h4 45.♕xh4+ ♔xh4 46.d6 ♖b2 47.d7+-) 42.♔g2 ♕h1+ 43.♔g3 ♕g1+ 44.♖g2 ♕e1+ 45.♖f2 ♕g1+ 46.♖g2 ♕e1+ Draw.] 35...♕xd3? [Little time, many mistakes. The position is very difficult: 35...♕d4 36.h3 (36.♘xc8 ♖xh2+ 37.♔xh2 ♕xf2+) 36...♖xh3 37.♘e4 ♖h5 38.♕e8+ ♔g7 39.♗e2±] 36.♘e8! ♖g5+ 37.♕xg5 ♕f5 38.♕d8 ♘f8 39.♘d6 ♕f4 40.♕xc8 ♕g5+ 41.♕g4 1-0

Alejo de Dovitiis
Fernando Peralta

Buenos Aires ch-ARG 2015 (9)

1.e4 d6 2.d4 ♘f6 3.f3 c5 4.d5 e6 5.♗b5+ ♘bd7 6.dxe6 fxe6 7.♘c3 a6 8.♗xd7+ [A novelty. 8.♗e2 ♗e7

9.♗f4 ♘b8 10.e5 ♘h5 11.♗e3 dxe5 12.♕xd8+ ♔xd8 13.0-0-0+ ♔c7∓ Tinture-Guilloux, cr 1995] **8...♗xd7 9.♗f4 ♗c6** [9...e5 leaves a hole on d5: 10.♗g5±] **10.♘h3** [10.e5? ♘h5] **10...♗e7**

11.e5 [The right moment. After 11.♕d2 0-0 12.0-0-0 d5 I prefer Black] **11...♘d5 12.♘xd5** [12.exd6 ♗xd6 13.♗xd6 ♘xd6 14.♘e4 ♕e5 15.c3 ♘xc3 16.♕d6 (16.bxc3 ♗xe4 17.fxe4 ♕xc3+ 18.♔e2 ♖d8!) 16...♖xd6 17.♘xd6+ ♔e7 18.♘xb7 ♗xb7∓] **12...exd5 13.exd6 ♗xd6 14.♕e2+ ♔d7** [14...♗e7 15.♘g5 (15.♗g5 ♗f7) 15...♕d7 16.♔f2 0-0 17.♕e6+ ♔h8 18.♕xd7 ♗xd7 19.♖he1 with an equal game] **15.0-0-0 ♕f6 16.♕d2 ♔c7**

17.♗xd6+ ♕xd6 18.♘f4 d4 19.c3 [The only chance for White] **19...♖hf8 20.♘e2 ♕e6 21.cxd4 ♕xa2 22.♘c3 ♕c4** [22...♕a1+? 23.♔c2 ♗a4+ 24.b3+−] **23.♕g5 ♗b6 24.d5 ♗d7 25.♕xg7 ♗f5 26.d6 ♔a7 27.♖he1 ♖ad8 28.♕e5?** [28.♖e7 ♕b3 29.♖d2 ♖xd6 30.♘b5+! (the move that I missed) 30...♕xb5 (30...axb5 31.♖xb7+; 30...♔b6 31.♖xb7+ ♔a5 32.♕c7+ ♔a4 33.♘c3+) 31.♖xd6 ♕c4+ 32.♔d2] **28...♖d7 29.h4 ♗g6 30.h5 ♖e8** [30...♗f5 31.♕e4 ♖xe4 32.♘xe4 ♗f7 (32...♗xh5 33.g4; 32...♖xh5 33.♘f6) 33.g4] **31.♕g5 ♖xe1 32.♖xe1 ♗d3 33.♕f6** [33.♕e5] **33...♕d4** [33...♕b3 34.♔d2 ♕b6!] **34.♕xd4 cxd4 35.♘e4** [35.♖d1! ♗f1 36.♖xf1 (36.♖xd4 ♗xg2 37.♘e4) 36...dxc3 37.♖d1 cxb2+ 38.♔xb2 ♕b6 39.g4+−] **35...♗xe4 36.♖xe4 ♖xd6 37.♖e7 h6 38.♖g7 d3?** [38...♖c6+ 39.♔d2 ♖b6] **39.♖g6 ♖d5 40.♖xh6** [40.g4 is quicker] **40...♖c5+ 41.♔d1 ♖c2 42.♖g6 ♖xb2 43.h6 a5 44.♖g5??** [An incredible mistake: 44.♖g3 ♖b1+ 45.♔d2 ♖h1 46.♖h3 with an easy win] **44...♖b1+ 45.♔d2 ♖h1 46.♖xa5+ ♔b6 47.♖f5?** [47.♖a8 gives better chances to win: 47...♖xh6 48.♔xd3 ♔c5

(48...♔c7 49.g4 b5 50.g5 ♖c6 51.f4 b4 52.♔e4 (52.♖a4 ♖b6 53.♖a1 ♔d6 54.♔e4 b3 55.♔f5 ♔e7 56.g6 (56.♖a7+ ♔f8) 56...♖b5+ 57.♔g4 b2 58.♖b1 ♔f6=) 52...♖b6 53.♔f5 b3 54.♖a1 b2 55.♖b1 ♔d7) 49.g4 ♖g6 (49...♖h1 50.♔e4 b5 51.g5 ♖g1 52.f4 b4 53.♖c8+ ♔b5 54.♔f5 b3 55.♖b8+ ♔c4 56.g6 ♔c3 57.♔f6 b2 58.g7 ♔c2 59.f5+−) 50.♔e4 b5 51.♖c8+ ♔d6 52.♖b8 ♔c6 (52...♖g5 53.♔f4) 53.♔f5 ♖d6 54.g5+−; 47.♖a2 ♖xh6 48.♔xd3 ♔c5 49.g4 (49.♖c2+ ♔d5 50.♖b2 ♖h2 51.♔e3 b6 52.♔f4 ♔c5) 49...♖g6 (49...b5 50.g5 ♖h1 51.♖g2) 50.♔e4 b5 51.♔f5 ♖g8 52.g5 (52.f4 b4 53.g5 b3 54.♖a7 ♖f8+) 52...b4 53.f4 b3 54.♖b2 ♔c4 55.g6 ♔c3 56.♖xb3+ ♔xb3 57.♔f6 ♔c4 58.f5 ♔d5 59.♔f7 ♔b8 60.g7 ♔e5= - just in time] **47...♖xh6 48.♔xd3 ♔c6 49.g4 b5 50.g5 ♖h1 51.f4 ♖g1 52.♖f6+?** [The last mistake. 52.♔d4! ♖d1+ 53.♔e4 b4 54.♖f8; f5 is a critical square for the white king] **52...♔c5 53.g6 b4 54.♖f5+ ♔d6 55.♖b5 ♔e6!** [55...♔e7 56.♖b6 b3 57.f5 b2 58.f6+] **56.♔e4** [56.♖xb4 ♖xg6 57.♖b6+ ♔f5 58.♖xg6 ♔xg6 59.♔e4 ♔f6 is a draw] **56...♖e1+ 57.♔f3 ♖g1 58.♖b6+ ♔f5 59.♖b5+ ♔xg6 60.♖xb4** ½-½

Exercise 1

position after 10...c5-c4

Black's central pawns are weak. White to move.
(solution on page 247)

Exercise 2

position after 15.♕e2-d3

Black to move.
(solution on page 247)

Exercise 3

position after 18.♖h1-e1

Black to move. Can he keep the extra pawn?
(solution on page 247)

Petroff Defence

What's Up, Damiano? – Part II

by Piotr Wolochowicz

1.	e4	e5
2.	♘f3	♘f6
3.	♘xe5	♘xe4
4.	♕e2	♕e7
5.	♕xe4	d6
6.	d4	dxe5
7.	dxe5	

In Part I of this Survey, in Yearbook 117, we started our update of the Damiano Variation with an investigation of the

Friedrich-Karl Volkmann

minor lines with 6.f4 (line A) and 6.d4 dxe5 7.♕xe5 (line B1). In this Part we will see what is going on in:

The Main Line

B2) After 6.d4 dxe5 7.dxe5 Black plays 7...♘c6, threatening to take back the pawn.

White has four principally different ways to continue here. We will consider them below:

B21) The strategic idea of 8.f4 is to keep the pawn, signalling to Black that he really cannot do White any harm. This very interesting line was presented in all three previous publications: SOS 10 (game Grinkevich-Afromeev); Yearbook 107 (games Short-Ipatov and Ipatov-Ilmaz); and Yearbook 109 (Forum Section, game Kalhorn-Wolochowicz). We think this is enough for now, even though the topic is not closed yet – this is probably the only area in which White can fight for more than just a slight advantage.

B22) 8.♗f4 also tries to keep the pawn, but in fact White is ready to return it here, getting some slight advantage. This line was dealt with in SOS 10 (game Baron-Cohen) and in Yearbook 107 (Ye Jiangchuan-Ni Hua). We will extend this by showing the game Saim-Cherrad;

B23) 8.♗b5 is a very important idea. By deploying this bishop White transforms the battle scene. After the natural and only reply 8...♗d7 White faces another choice:

B231) Yearbook 107 only showed one game with 9.0-0 here (Dolzhikova-Andrenko), which featured a rare sub-line. In fact, after 9...0-0-0 there is a lot to discover. White can play at least three serious lines: 10.♗xc6, 10.♗f4, and 10.♘c3. We will summarize these lines in the games Ozimek-Wolochowicz, Plachetka-Volkmann and Zaitsev-Novikov. White gets no more than a slight advantage here.

B232) We will regard 9.♘c3 as the main move. Now there are two ways for Black: first there is the 'old-fashioned' reaction 9...0-0-0, which was investigated in Yearbook 107 (game Papp-Volkmann) and 109 (Forum section, game Pazuzu-Wolochowicz). Black faces some real challenges here; after 10.♗f4 g5 11.♗g3, for example, we reach a crucial point: after many difficulties black players found the strong move 11...♖e8, but 11...a6 has also been reinstated recently. So here there is a lot going on, as we will show in the games Eiben-Remis and Vyskocil-Volkmann.

The alternative, more modern reaction is Volkmann's 9...♕b4 – several games with this line have already been presented in both SOS 10 (Shaw-Volkmann) and Yearbook 107 (Nedev-Volkmann; Naiditsch-Volkmann; Savchenko-Ipatov). We will add the important game Maffei-Wolochowicz, which also contains a few subtle and crucial moments.

The Critical Moment

B24) We could call 8.♘c3 the main line. The critical moment comes after 8...♕xe5 9.♕xe5+ ♘xe5.

Black has got the pawn back, but White has a tempo and the possibility to gain the initiative.

In order to do so he can play in two different ways:

B241) 10.♗f4 is a classical line. Black's basic reply here is 10...♗d6, with the threat of 11...♘d3+, followed by ...♗xf4. In 1975, GM Vasiukov introduced 11.♗g3! here. White wants to go ♘e4 or ♘b5, followed by ♘xd6, spoiling Black's pawn structure and getting the advantage of the two bishops. The traditional reply was 11...♗d7 (see the game Sivuk-Ipatov in Yearbook 107), but in 1990 FM Charles Hertan proposed 11...f6, which was not widely noticed; IM Volkmann found it independently and played it only in 2004. Two games with that line were already given: in SOS 10 (Nisipeanu-Varga) and in the Forum Section of Yearbook 109 (Lanzani-Wolochowicz). We will describe the actual challenges of 11...♗d7 in Perrin-Wolochowicz and those of 11...f6 in Szczepankiewicz-Remis. But that is not all! There is another alternative, 10...f6, played by Volkmann quite a few times, with good results. This line is given in the game Buchnicek-Volkmann.

B242) 10.♘b5 is White's modern idea. Black has to go 10...♗b4+, and now, if White chooses 11.♗d2, the play continues 11...♗xd2+ 12.♔xd2 ♔d8. About this line, sufficient material was shown in Yearbook 107 (game Lehner-Volkmann) and in the Forum Section of Yearbook 109 (Kuosmanen-Wolochowicz). In general Black holds on. But here we have added a game Jovanovic-Doric, which features a second line, 11.c3, in which Black defends c7 with 11...♗a5. Anyway, here too, Black retains a quite good position.

Conclusion

So to Bugs Bunny's question 'What's Up?', in the Damiano Variation the answer is: 'We're OK!'. White gets at best a minimal advantage, if any at all, in all lines. Especially correspondence games from recent years, played with computer support, show that Black is generally able to hold the draw here. Also, IM Volkmann has shown in many classical games how to keep the balance, and his contribution to this variation cannot be overestimated (he published his own analysis on his webpage www.volki.at). So I would risk the opinion that the ball is in White's court, and he will have to find something new to damage Black's position.

The variation lives on, and in classical, rapid, blitz and correspondence chess there are still new games (on January 1, 2016, there were 723 games in my database, a lot of which from recent years). So this might be a good weapon, not only if you want just to surprise your opponent (as I guess GM Shakhriyar Mamedyarov did against GM Sergey Fedorchuk in the 6th Rabat Blitz Marathon in May 2015, producing the novelty 6.d4 dxe5 7.♕xe5 ♗e6), but especially if a black player is lower rated and a draw is a good result for him. He puts White in a difficult position: to either agree to an equal or only symbolically better position (and one in which Black knows exactly how to continue) or to start fighting hard for a win, with realistic risks of losing. A good example of the latter is the game Zwardon-Skockova (Part I), in which the much more lowly rated black player (1799) got a better position and almost won against a 2399 IM.

Main Line
8.♗f4

Mohamed Saim
Mustapha Cherrad
Algiers 2015 (2)

1.e4 e5 2.♘f3 ♘f6 3.♘xe5 ♘xe4
4.♕e2 ♕e7 5.♕xe4 d6 6.d4 dxe5
7.dxe5 ♘c6 8.♗f4

8...g5 9.♗d2 [9.♗g3?? f5–+
10.♕e2 f4 11.♕h5+ ♕f7 12.♕xg5
fxg3 13.hxg3 ♗c5–+ Nagaitzcev-
Yaroslavtzev, Iwanowo 1971] **9...
f5!** [9...♗g7? 10.♘c3+ ♕xe5
(10...♗xe5?? 11.♘d5+–) 11.♕xe5+
♗xe5 12.♘xg5±] **10.♕e2!** [10.♕e3
is weaker – White loses a tempo after
10...f4!. Last example: 11.♕e4 ♗g7!
(better than 11...♕xe5 12.♕xe5+ ♘xe5
13.h4±) 12.♗b5 0-0± (M Spornberger-A
Meier, Austria Bundesliga B 2014). With
12...♕xe5! 13.♕xe5+ ♗xe5 Black is OK]
10...g4?!N [Not a good idea. 10...♗g7
Ye Jiangchuan-Ni Hua, YB 107/109. Best
is 10...♗e6!= 11.♕h5+ ♕f7 12.♕xg5
♕xe5+ 13.♕e3 (Hernandez-Garcia,
Pamplona 1995) 13...0-0-0 14.♕xe5 ♘xe5
15.♗c3 ♗d6 16.f4 ♘g4 17.♗xh8 ♖xh8
18.♘c3 ♖e8+ 19.♗e2 ♘e3 20.♔f2 ♗c5
21.♘a4 ♘g4+ 22.♔f1 ♘e3+ 23.♔f2=,
Ipatov in YB 107/109; 10...♖g8 was
introduced in Baron-Cohen, SOS 10/126;
but lately there was an important novelty:
11.h4!N (White was better after Baron
played 11.♗c3) 11...♘d4 12.♕h5+ ♕f7
13.♕xf7+ ♔xf7 14.♗d3 g4 15.♗f4±
Almarza-Baroin, cr 2015] **11.♗c3?!**
[11.♘c3 ♗e6 12.0-0-0 0-0-0 13.f4! gxf3
14.gxf3±] **11...♗g7?** [11...♗e6=]
**12.♘a3± ♗xe5 13.♗xe5 ♕xe5
14.♘b5 ♕xe2+? 15.♗xe2+–
♔d8 16.0-0-0+ ♗d7 17.h3 ♘e5
18.♘d4?** [With two weak moves White
gives back his entire advantage and

the game ends in a draw. 18.♖d4 h5
19.hxg4 fxg4 20.♖d5+–] **18...♗e7+
19.♖he1?!** [19.hxg4 ♘xg4 20.♗f3
♘xf2 21.♖de1+ ♘e4 22.♗xe4 fxe4
23.♖xe4+ ♔d8 24.♖d1±] **19...♗f6±
20.f4 ♘g6 21.hxg4 fxg4 22.♘b3
♗f5 23.♘d4 ♘xf4 24.♘xf5 ♘xe2+
25.♖xe2 ♔xf5 26.♖e7 ♔f4**   ½-½

Main Line
9.0-0

Piotr Ozimek
Piotr Wolochowicz
cr 1986

1.e4 e5 2.♘f3 ♘f6 3.♘xe5 ♘xe4
4.♕e2 ♕e7 5.♕xe4 d6 6.d4 dxe5
7.dxe5 ♘c6 8.♗b5 ♗d7 9.0-0
0-0-0 [9...a6 (Cohen) 10.♗a4 0-0-0
11.♘c3 b5 12.♗b3 ♕xe5 13.♗xf7 ♕xe4
14.♘xe4 ♗f5 15.f3 ♗c5+ 16.♔h1±
J.Rasmussen-S.Nielsen, Copenhagen
2008]

10.♗xc6 [10.♗f4 g5 (Hertan:
10...♘xe5?? 11.♕xe5 ♕xe5
12.♗xd7++–; 10...f6!?) 11.♗d2
(11.♗xc6 ♗xc6 12.♕f5+ ♔b8 13.♗xg5
♖g8 14.h4 h6 15.♕h7 ♖xg5 16.hxg5
♕xg5 17.g3 ♗c5 0-1 J. Rodriguez-P.
Blanco, Villa de Gijon 2012) 11...
f5 12.♕a4 a6 13.e6? (13.♗xa6 bxa6
14.♕xa6+ ♔b8 15.♕b5+ ♔c8=)
13...♕xe6 14.♗c4?! (14.♗xa6 bxa6
15.♕xa6+ ♔b8 16.♕b5+ ♔a8 17.♗xg5
♖b8 18.♕a6+ ♘a7∓) 14...♕g6?!∓
(Alvarez Nistal-Remis, Autonomico
Equipos 2013; 14...♕h6∓); 10.♖e1 ♘xe5
11.♗xd7+ ♖xd7 12.♗d2 f6= Boricsev-
Marzano, Krakow 2014; 10.♗e3 ♘xe5
11.♘c3 ♗xb5 12.♘xb5 ♘c6 13.♕a4
a6 14.♖ad1 ♕b4?? 15.♗a7+!+– ♖xa7
16.♖xd8+ ♔xd8 17.♖d1+ 1-0 Marek-
Vizner, Ostrava 2011; 10.e6? Dolzhikova-

Andrenko, YB 107/109; 10.♘c3 see the
game Plachetka-Volkmann] **10...♗xc6
11.♕g4+** [11.♕f5+ ♔b8 12.♘c3 ♕d7
13.♕xd7 ♖xd7 14.♗e3 ♗b4± Lobov-
Enderov, Satka 2012; 11.♕e3 ♔b8
12.♘c3 g5?! (12...♕e6=) 13.♖e1?!
(13.♘e2±) 13...h6= Nowicki-Chmiel,
Jastrzebia Gora 2014] **11...♔b8
12.♕g3 h5**

13.♗g5?? [Now we have a critical
moment. White did not find 13.h4□ ♖d4≌]
13...f6–+ [Now Black is easily winning,
using the power of the bishops] **14.exf6**
[14.♗d2 h4 15.♕c3 fxe5–+; 14.♗f4 h4
15.♕c3 fxe5 16.♗e3 (16.♕xe5 ♕f7!
17.♕e3 b6 18.♕c1 ♗c5–+) 16...h3–+]
14...gxf6 15.♗h4 ♗b5 [Even stronger
was 15...♗h6! with ...♖hg8 next] **16.♖c1
♗h6 17.f4 ♖hg8 18.♖e1 ♖xg3
19.♖xe7 ♖d1+ 20.♔f2 ♖g8 21.♗xf6
♖f1+**   0-1

Jan Plachetka
Friedrich-Karl Volkmann
Vienna 2014

1.e4 e5 2.♘f3 ♘f6 3.♘xe5 ♘xe4
4.♕e2 ♕e7 5.♕xe4 d6 6.d4 dxe5
7.dxe5 ♘c6 8.♗b5 ♗d7 9.0-0
0-0-0 10.♘c3 ♘xe5 [For 10...a6 see
the game Zaitsev-Novikov; 10...♕xe5??
11.♗xc6+– Blackman-Sun, cr 2004]

11.♗e3 [11.♗f4 ♘g6 12.♗xd7+ ♖xd7= Slagter-Le.Ootes, Enschede 2008; 11.♖e1 ♘g6 12.♕xe7 ♗xe7= Espin-Briceno, cr 2006; 11.♗xd7+ ♖xd7 (11...♘xd7 12.♕a4 (12.♕xe7 ♗xe7= Stambulia-Maiorov, Anapa 2008; 12.♗f4 ♕xe4 13.♘xe4= Bakutin-Moiseev, Tula 2011) 12...a6 (12...♘b8 13.♗f4 ♗b6 14.♕b3 ♕f6 15.♗g3± Yakimkin-Bezvitelnov, Dimtrovgrad 2010) 13.♘d5 ♕c5 14.c4 ♘b6 15.♘xb6+ ♔xb6 16.♕c2 ♗c5 ½-½ Nuding-Stabernack, Schwäbisch Gmünd 2013) 12.♗e3 ♘c6 13.♕f3 (13.♕a4 ♕b4= Rabinovich-Yaroslavtzev, Rostov-on-Don 1972) 13...♕h4 14.h3 ♗b4= Zuykov-Maneluk, Nizhnij Novgorod 2008; 11.a4 ♘c6 12.♗f4 a6 (12...♘e5?? 13.♗xc6 ♕xf4 14.♗xd7+ 1-0 Atanasov-Wolochowicz, Wroclaw 1987; 12...♘b4!?; 12...f6!? with ...g7-g5 next) 13.♗e3 f6 14.♖fd1 ♕e5= Miller-Porat, Petach Tikva 2007; 11.♕a4?! a6 12.♗xd7+ ♕xd7∓]

11...♗xb5 [11...♗c6 12.♕f5+ ♕e6 13.♕xe6+ fxe6 14.♗xc6 ♘xc6 15.♘e4 ♗e7± Divirny-Stips, Montecatini Terme 2011; 11...♘c6 12.♕a4 ♕b4 13.♖ad1 ♕xa4 14.♗xa4 ♗b4 15.♘d5 ♗d6= Pogonina-Krestianova, Moscow 2008; 11...a6?! 12.♗xa6 (12.♘d5 ♕e6 (12...♕e8 13.♗xd7+ ♘xd7 14.♕c4 ♗d6 15.♗a7 ♕f8 16.♖fe1 ♖e8 17.♗d4 f6 18.a4 ♔b8 19.a5 ♕f7 20.♘b6 ♕xc4 21.♘xc4= Engelhardt-Viksna. cr 2002) 13.♗f4 f5?? (13...♕f6±) 14.♘xe6 fxe4 15.♘xd8 ♗xb5 16.♖fd1+= Kruchem-K.Adamski, cr 1990; 12.♗xd7+ ♖xd7 13.♖fd1 ♖xd1+ 14.♖xd1 ♘c6 15.♕g4+ ♕e6 16.♕xe6+ fxe6± Rossmann-Wolochowicz, Frankfurt/Oder 1985) 12...♘c6 13.♕f5+ ♗d7 14.♕e4 ♗c6 15.♕f5+ ♗d7 0,5-0,5 Nardykhanov-Koniushkov, Sochi 1996] **12.♘xb5 a6** [12...♘c6 13.♘xa7+ ♘xa7 14.♕a4 ♘c6 15.♕a8+ ♔d7? (Kholmov: 15...♘b8 16.♗a7 ♕e4! 17.♖fe1 (17.♕xb8+?? ♔d7-+) 17...♕c6 18.♖ad1 ♗d6= and now we have two different propositions: GM Pachmann – 19.♖xd6 ♕xd6 20.♕xb8+ ♔d7 21.♕xb7∞; or GM Wolchok: 19.♖e7 ♗xh2+ 20.♔xh2 ♕h6+ 21.♔g3 ♕g5+ 22.♔f3 ♕f6+ 23.♔g3=) 16.♖ad1+ ♔e8? 17.♕xb7+- Kholmov-Belousov, Gorki 1974] **13.♘c3** [13.♕f5+ ♖d7 (13...♕e6 14.♕xe6+ fxe6 15.♘d4 ♗d6 16.♗f4 ♖xd4 17.♗xe5 ♖d7= Gano-Bito, cr 2009) 14.♗d4 (14.♗f4 ♗c5 15.♕xe5 ♕xe5 16.♘a7+ ♔b8 17.♗xe5 f6 18.♘c6+ bxc6

19.♗c3± Plat-Plecha, Marianske Lazne 2012) 14...♘c6 15.♖ae1 ♕d8 16.♘a7+ ♘xa7 17.♗xa7 g6= Oldrati-Giesemann, cr 2012; 13.♘d4 g6 (13...♘c4!? IM Morris) 14.♘f3 (½-½ Morris-Hertan, New York 1981; 14.b4 ♗g7 15.b5 ♕d6 16.♖ab1 f5 17.♕f4 ♘c4 18.bxa6 ♕xf4?? (18...♗xd4!∓) 19.axb7++- Lin Yi-Huang Yicheng, Suzhou 2001); 13.a4 ♘c6 14.♕f3 axb5? 15.axb5 ♘b8 16.♖a7 c6 17.♗f4? (17.♗b6+!) 17...♕c5 18.♖a8 ♗d6 19.bxc6 ♕xc6∓ Kallgren-Almstrom, Växjö 1992] **13...♘c6 14.♕c4** [14.♕g4+ ♕d7 15.♕xd7+ ♖xd7 16.♖ad1 ♖xd1 17.♖xd1 ♗d6 18.♘e4 ♗e7 19.♔f1 ♖e8= Mazur-Volkmann, Wiener Neustadt 2011] **14...♘e5 15.♕e4** [15.♕f4 ♘g6 (15...♕e6=) 16.♕f3 ♘e5 17.♕f5+ ♕e6 18.♕xe6+ fxe6 19.♘e4 ♘c4= Tiviakov-Cherrad, Algiers 2015] **15...♘c6 16.♕c4 ♘e5 17.♕e2** [White refuses to repeat moves and tries to get an advantage, but Black defends well] **17...g6 18.♖ad1 ♗g7 19.♗f4 ♖xd1 20.♖xd1 ♖e8 21.h3 ♘c6 22.♕xe7** [22...♖xe7 23.♘d5 ♖d7∓ (23...♖e2 24.♗d2=) 24.♗xc7 ♗d4 (24...♖xd5 25.♖xd5 ♗xc7∓) 25.c4 ♖xc7 26.♘xc7 ♔xc7 27.b3 ♔d6 28.g3 ♔c5∓; 22.♕c4 ♕e6 23.♘d5 ♕e2∓] ½-½

Alexander Zaitsev
Maxim Novikov
Suvorov 2012 (3)

1.e4 e5 2.♘f3 ♘f6 3.♘xe5 ♘xe4 4.♕e2 ♕e7 5.♕xe4 d6 6.d4 dxe5 7.dxe5 ♘c6 8.♗b5 ♗d7 9.♘c3
[A game between two IM's in May 2015 continued: 9.e6? ♕xe6 10.♕xe6+ ♗xe6N (10...fxe6?! 11.0-0 ♗c5 12.♘d2 0-0-0= Berrocal-Navarro Diaz, Mislata 2009) 11.0-0 ♗c5?! (better is 11...0-0-0 and White must go 12.♗xc6 bxc6∓ since Black gets an advantage after 12.♘c3 ♘b4 13.♗a4 ♗f5∓) 12.♘c3 0-0-0= Galic-Biti, Sibenik 2015] **9...0-0-0 10.0-0** [A transposition: the usual order is 9.0-0 0-0-0 10.♘c3. By the way: 10.♗d2 ♘xe5?! (10...a6 11.♗a4 ♘xe5=) 11.♗xd7+?! (11.0-0-0±) 11...♖xd7 12.♕e2? ♘c4∓ 13.0-0 ♕b4?? (13...♕xe2 14.♘xe2 ♗c5∓) 14.♕e8+ ♖d8 15.♕xd8+ ♔xd8 16.♗g5+ 1-0 Siwirski-Wolochowicz, cr ch-Warsaw 1985] **10...a6!?**

11.♗a4 [11.♗xc6 ♗xc6 12.♕g4+ ♔b8 13.♗g5 (13.♗f4 g5 14.♗e3 ♕xe5 15.♖fe1= Hutchings-Mollekens, Buenos Aires ol 1978) 13...f6 14.exf6 gxf6 15.♗h4∞ Sibarevic-Kos, Bled 2000. In such positions, often the move 11.a4!? must be considered, and now best looks 11...f6 (11...♘xe5 12.♖d1 ♘c6±; 11...axb5?? 12.axb5 ♘b8 13.♗a7+-) 12.♗f4 (12.♗xc6 ♗xc6 13.♕g4+ ♔b8 14.e6 ♕b4!=) 12...fxe5 (12...g5 13.♗xc6 ♗xc6 14.♕f5+ ♗d7 15.exf6 ♗xf5 16.fxe7 ♗xe7 17.♖fe1 gxf4 18.♖xe7 ♖d2=) 13.♗e3 ♕b4=] **11...♘xe5 12.♗xd7+ ♖xd7 13.♗e3 ♘c6 14.♕f3** ½-½

Main Line
9.♘c3 0-0-0

Pavel Eiben
Jesus Julio Remis Fernandez
cr 2014

1.e4 e5 2.♘f3 ♘f6 3.♘xe5 ♘xe4 4.♕e2 ♕e7 5.♕xe4 d6 6.d4 dxe5 7.dxe5 ♘c6 8.♗b5 ♗d7 9.♘c3 0-0-0 10.♗f4 [10.♗e3 a6 11.♗a4 ♘xe5 12.0-0-0 ♖xa4 13.♘xa4± Mahdy-Volkmann, Vienna 2012; 10.f4 ♕h4+! 11.g3 ♕h3 12.♗f1?= (Schmoll-Mühlenhaus, Niederrhein 1996 12.♗e3±)]

10...g5 [For 10...♕b4 see the game Vyskocil-Volkmann] **11.♗g3** [11.♗xc6 ♗xc6 12.♕f5+ ♗d7 13.♕xd7+ ♖xd7 14.♗xg5 ♖g8 15.♗d2? (15.h4 h6 16.♗e3 ♖xg2 17.♔e2 ♖e7 18.♖hg1 ♖xg1 19.♖xg1 ♖xe5 20.♖g8 ♖e8=) 15...♖xg2 16.0-0-0 ♖xf2∓ Portilla-Sarabia, Madrid 2007] **11...a6!?** [IM Remis and GM Cruzado have lately restored this move, and used it several times in correspondence games, with good results. 11...♖e8!? was Pazuzu-Wolochowicz, YB 109/ 13; 11...f5? 12.exf6 ♕xf6 13.0-0-0+−; 11...h5? 12.h4!+− a6 13.♗a4 ♗h6 14.hxg5 ♗xg5 15.f4 f5 16.♕e3+− Pacheco-Sarabia, cr 2007; 11...♗g7? 12.0-0-0+−♖he8 13.♖he1 ♘xe5 14.♕xh7! ♗xb5 15.♕xg7!+−; 15.♘xb5?? ♘d3+!!=] **12.♗c4** [12.♗a4 ♖e8 13.♕e3 (13.f4 gxf4 14.♗xf4 ♘xe5 15.0-0-0 ♗xa4 16.♕xa4± Blazeka-Pejic, Sv. Filip i Jakov 2011; 13.0-0-0 f5 14.♕d3 f4 15.♘d5 ♕e6 16.♘xf4 gxf4 17.♗xf4 ♗h6 18.♗xh6 ♕xh6+−+ Dianov-Izbranov, Krasnoyarsk 2011) 13...f5 14.f4 gxf4 15.♗xf4 ♘xe5 16.0-0-0 ♗xa4 17.♘xa4 ♘c6± 18.♕d3 (18.♕xe7 ♘xe7 19.♖de1 ♗g7 20.♘c5 ♘g6 21.♗d2= Begliy-Remis, cr 2012) 18...♗f7 19.♘c3 Neto-Cruzado, cr 2012] **12...♗e6** [12...♖e8N] ½-½

Neklan Vyskocil
Friedrich-Karl Volkmann

Vienna 2015

1.e4 e5 2.♘f3 ♘f6 3.♘xe5 ♘xe4 4.♕e2 ♕e7 5.♕xe4 d6 6.d4 dxe5 7.dxe5 ♘c6 8.♗b5 ♗d7 9.♘c3 0-0-0 10.♗f4 ♕b4 11.0-0-0 ♕xe4 12.♘xe4 ♘xe5 13.♗xd7+ ♘xd7 14.♘g5 [14.♖he1?! ♗b4 15.c3 ♗e7 16.♘g5 ♗xg5 17.♗xg5 ♖de8± Szakolczai-Volkmann, Austria 2005]

10.♗c4 [10.♕f4 a6 (10...0-0-0 11.0-0 ♕xf4 (11...a6 Cohen) 12.♗xf4 ♖e8 13.♖fe1 ♗b4 14.♗d3 g5?! 15.♗xg5 ♘xe5 16.♖xe5 ♖xe5 17.♗f6 ♖ee8 18.♗xh8 ♖xh8 19.♘d5± Osmanodja-Stabernack, Nuremberg 2012) 11.♗d3 ♕a5 12.♗e4 0-0-0 13.♕xf7 ♗b4 14.0-0 ♕xc3 15.bxc3 ♕xe5∓ Antoniewski-Volkmann, Graz 2009; 10.♕d5 0-0-0 11.♕xf7 ♘xe5 12.♗xd7+ ♖xd7?? (12...♔b8!±)

14...♗e7! [IM Volkmann: 14...♗c5? 15.♘xf7 ♖df8 16.♘xh8 ♖xf4 17.♖he1 ♔d8 18.♖e5+− Hotting-Mes, cr 1988] **15.♘xf7** [15.♖he1 Papp-Volkmann, YB 107/110; 15.h4?! ♗c5 16.♖xd8+ ♖xd8 17.♖e1 ♗f6 18.b3 ♖d5 19.g3 h6 20.♘xf7 ♖f5 21.♖e8+ ½-½ Ilyasov-Rashitov, cr 2012] **15...♖df8 16.♘xh8 ♖xf4 17.♖he1 ♔d8 18.♖e6** [GM Ipatov: 18.♖d3!? ♖f8 19.♖g3 (19.♖de3?? ♗g5) 19...♖f6 20.♘g6 hxg6 21.♖xg6+] **18...♖f8 19.♘g6 hxg6 20.♖xg6±** **♖f7N** [20...♗f6 21.c3 ♖e8 22.♖g3 ♗e5 23.♖f3 ♗d6 24.♔c2 ♗e4 25.♖fd3 ♔e7 26.h3 ♘c5 27.♖d4 ♖e2+ 28.♖4d2 ♖e4 29.b4 ♘a4 30.♔d3 ♖h4 31.♖e1+ ♗f6± Csonka-Volkmann, Austria 2014] **21.♖g4 ♗d6 22.h3 ♗f4+ 23.♔b1 ♔e7 24.g3 ♗e5 25.♖d2 ♘c5 26.a3 b6 27.♖c4 ♖f3 28.♖g4** ½-½

```
     Main Line
    9.♘c3 ♕b4
```

Umberto Maffei
Piotr Wolochowicz

cr 2005

1.e4 e5 2.♘f3 ♘f6 3.♘xe5 ♘xe4 4.♕e2 ♕e7 5.♕xe4 d6 6.d4 dxe5 7.dxe5 ♘c6 8.♗b5 ♗d7 9.♘c3 ♕b4

13.♕e8+ 1-0 Mohankrishanan-Krett, cr 2010; 10.♗d2 Savchenko-Ipatov, YB 107/110] **10...0-0-0 11.a3** [11.♗xf7?! ♕xe4+ 12.♘xe4 ♘xe5 13.♗b3 ♗b4+ (13...♗c6?! 14.f3 ♗xe4 15.fxe4± Mahjoob-Volkmann, Calvia ol 2004) 14.♗d2 ♗xd2+ 15.♘xd2 ♖he8= Tishin-Afromeev, Tula 2006] **11...♕a5 12.♗xf7** [12.0-0 ♕xe5 13.♗xf7 ♕xf7 (13...♗f5? 14.♕xe5 ♘xe5 15.♗b3± Jäger-Kahl, cr BDF 2008) 14.♘xe4 ♗f5 15.f3 ♗d4 16.c3 ♘e2+ 17.♔h1 ♘xc1 18.♖axc1 ♗e7 (18...g6 19.♘ce1 ♗h6 20.g4 ♗xe4 21.fxe4 ♗g5 22.♖e2 ½-½ Lange-Giesemann, cr BDF 2011) 19.♖fe1 ♖hf8 20.♗b3 (20.♗h5 ♗xe4 21.♖xe4 ♗f6± Firnhaber-Giesemann, cr BDF 2012) 20...♗xe4 21.♖xe4 ♗g5± Vielsack-Giesemann, cr BDF 2011; 12.♗f4 Nedev-Volkmann, YB 107/109] **12...♘xe5 13.b4 ♗xb4 14.♕xb4 ♕xb4 15.axb4 ♘xf7 16.♖xa7 ♔b8** [16...♖he8+ Najditsch-Volkmann, YB 107/110; 16...♗f5 17.♖a2 ♖d4 18.0-0 ♖hd8 19.♖e1 ♖xb4 20.♖e7 ♔b8 21.h3 (21.♖xf7? ♗b1!−+) 21...♗d7 22.♖e8+ ♖d8 23.♖e7 ♖d7 24.♖e3 h5= Solak-Volkmann, Istanbul Ech 2003] **17.♗e3 b6** [17...♘e5!? Cohen] **18.♖a1 ♗f5** [18...♘d6 19.0-0 ♗f5 20.♖fc1 ♖he8 21.♗f4 ♔b7 22.f3± Warzecha-Langheld, cr BDF 2012] **19.♘b5** [19.0-0 Shaw-Volkmann, SOS 10/130; 19.♖c1 ♘e5 20.0-0 ♘c6 21.♗f4 ♔b7 22.♘b5 ♘d4 23.♘xd4 ♖xd4 24.♗e5 ♖xb4 25.♗xg7= Mahdy-Volkmann, Wiener Neustadt 2005] **19...♘d6** [19...♖xc2 20.♘xc7 ♔xc7 21.♖c1 ♗c6 22.♖xc2+ ♔b5 23.♖c7±] **20.♘d4 ♗e4 21.0-0 ♘f5 22.c3** [22.♘xf5 ♗xf5 23.c3 ♔b7 24.♗d4 ♗d7 25.♖fe1 ♖hd8 26.f3 h5 27.♖a2 g6 28.♔f2 ♖a8 29.♖xa8 ♔xa8± Ivanovic-Wolochowicz, cr 2007] **22...♘xd4** [Here Volkmann proposes 22...♘xe3!? 23.fxe3 ♖d7≅] **23.♗xd4 ♖d7** [23...♗d5 24.♗xg7? ♖hg8 25.♖fd1 ♖xg7 26.c4 ♖xg2+ 27.♔h1 ♖xf2+ 28.♖xd5 ♖xd5 29.cxd5 ♖d2∓; 23...♖he8!? (Volkmann) 24.f3 (24.♗xg7 ♖g8 25.f3 ♗d3 26.♗f6 ♖xf1 27.♖xd8 (27.♖xf1 ♖d6=) 27...♖xg2= Volkmann) 24...♗d3 25.♖f2 (25.♖fd1 ♗e2) 25...g6 26.♖fa2 ♗b7 27.♔f2 ♗c4 28.♖a7+ ♔c6 29.g4± Volkmann] **24.♖fe1 ♗g6 25.f4 ♖f8** [25...♖e8 26.♗e5 ♔b7 27.g4 ♗d3] **26.g3 ♖e8 27.♖xe8+ ♗xe8**

28.Ze1 &g6 [28...&h5 29.h3 &f3 30.f5 &b7 31.g4 &d5 32.Ze8±] **29. g4 &c2 30.f5±** [White is much better, and in an excellent way he converts his advantage to victory. I don't see where I could have played better from here, so this position is probably technically won. Black has to seek an improvement earlier on – maybe the above-mentioned idea by Cohen, 17...&e5, is a solution?] **30...&b7** [30...h5 31.h3 hxg4 32.hxg4 Zf7 33.Ze6 &c8 34.Zg6+–; 30...Zf7 31.Ze8+ &b7 32.&g2 &b3 33.&g3 &c6 34.Zh8 g6 35.f6+–] **31.&g2 &c6 32.&g3 Zf7** [32...&b5 33.Ze5+ &c4 34.Ze8 c5 35.bxc5 bxc5 36.Zc8+–] **33.Ze2 &b3 34.Ze8 &d7 35.Zh8 g6 36.f6 &e6 37.g5 &f5 38.h4 &e6 39.&f4 &c4** [39...&d5 40.Ze8+ &d6 41.Zd8+ &e6 42.&e5 &b3 43.b5 &c4 44.Zc8 &xb5 45.Zxc7+–] **40.&e5 &d7** [40...&d5 41.Zd8 (41. h5? gxh5 42.Zxh7?? Zxh7 43.g6 Zd7 44.f7 &e7–+) 41...&c4 42.Zc8 &d5 43.b5! &c4 44.Zxc7 &xb5 45.Zxf7 &xf7 46.&c7+–; 40...b5 41.&d4 c6 42.&c5 &b3 43.Zd8 &d7 44.Ze8+ &f7 45.Zh8 &e6 46.&e7+–] **41.&e3 &e6** [41...c5 42.bxc5 bxc5 43.&e4 &e6 44.Ze8+ &d7 45.Zb8+–] **42.&g3 &f5 43.Ze8 b5** [43...&e6 44.b5 h6 45.c4 hxg5 (45...&xc4 46.gxh6) 46.hxg5 Zh7 (46...&xc4 47.Ze5+ &g4 48.Ze4+ &xg3 49.Zxc4+–) 47.Ze7 Zxe7 48.fxe7 &f7 49.&xc7+–] **44.&d4 &e6** [44...&g4 45.&e1 &f5 46.&f2 &g4 47.&c5+–] **45.&h2 Zd7+** [45... c6 46.&c5 &d5 47.&d6 h5 48.&e5+ &g4 49.Zxd5! cxd5 50.&e6+–] **46.&c5 Zf7 47.Zd8 &c4 48.Zd4 h6** [48...&e6 49.&c6 h6 50.gxh6 &xf6 51.&xc7+–] **49.Zf4+ &e6 50.Ze4+ &f5 51.Ze5+ &g4 52.gxh6** 1-0

**The Critical Moment
10.&f4**

**Richard Perrin
Piotr Wolochowicz**
cr 2005

1.e4 e5 2.&f3 &f6 3.&xe5 &xe4 4.&e2 &e7 5.&xe4 d6 6.d4 dxe5 7.dxe5 &c6 8.&c3 &xe5 9.&xe5+ &xe5 10.&f4 &d6 11.&g3!

11...&d7 [For 11...f6 see the game Szczepankiewicz-Remis; 11...&f5?! 12.&b5+N (12.0-0-0 f6; 12...0-0?? 13.Zd5+–; 12...0-0-0?? 13.Zd5+–) 12...c6? (12...&c6 13.&xd6 cxd6 14.0-0-0 0-0-0±) 13.0-0-0± Kudriashov-Volkov, Nizhnij Novgorod 2013] **12.&e4! &c6 13.&xd6+ cxd6 14.0-0-0 0-0-0 15.f3 Zhe8** [15... h5 16.Zd4 (16.h4 Zh6 17.Zd2 (17.&f2 Sivuk-Ipatov, YB 107/111) 17...Zg6 18.&f2 b6 19.&d4 f6± Yu Yangyi-Ipatov, Dubai Wch blitz 2014) 16...&c7 (16...Zh6!?) 17.&e2 g5 18.h4 g4? (18...Zdg8±; 18...f6±) 19.fxg4 hxg4 20.Zf1+ Les Ellis-Trebizan, cr 2012] **16.Zd4** [16.&e2 &g4?! (16...&c7!) 17.Zd2 &e3?! (17...&e5±) 18.&d3± Heinz Offenborn-Karl Kahl, cr BDF 2008] **16...&c7** [16...f5N 17.h4 h5 18.a4 Ze6 19.b3± Sosnin-Izbranov, Krasnoyarsk 2013] **17.a4 f5 18.h4 h5!** [This move is the key for Black to hold the position. If 18...g6?! 19.&f4 Zd7 20.b4 Zde7 21.&b2 a6 22.a5 d5 23.h5+ Vasiukov-Chekhov, Kishinev 1975] **19.b4 Ze6 20.b5 &d7 21.&f4 Zg6 22.&g5 Ze8 23.&b2** [23.f4 &f7 (23...&g4 24.&c4 &e6 25.Ze1 &d7 26.b6 a6 27.&d2±) 24.&d2 Zge6 25.&d3 &xg5 26.hxg5 g6=] **23...&f7 24.&f4 &e5 25.&g5** [25.c4 b6 26.&c3 &e6±; 25.&c3 a6 26.Zd2 axb5 27.&xb5 &xb5 28.axb5 Zc8 29.&b3 &b6±; 25.Zd2 &e6 26.&c3 &f7 27.a5 &d7±] **25...&f7 26.&f4** [White found nothing better than the move repetition] ½-½

**Dariusz Szczepankiewicz
Jesus Julio Remis Fernandez**
cr 2013

1.e4 e5 2.&f3 &f6 3.&xe5 &xe4 4.&e2 &e7 5.&xe4 d6 6.d4 dxe5 7.dxe5 &c6 8.&c3 &xe5

9.&xe5+ &xe5 10.&f4 &d6 11.&g3 f6!

12.0-0-0 &d7 [12...a6?! Nisipeanu-Varga, SOS 10/129] **13.f4N** [13.&b5 &xb5 14.&xb5+ &f7 15.Zhe1 (15.&a4 g6 16.&b3+ &g7 17.Zhe1 Zhe8 18.&d5 Zab8 19.f3 b6 20.Zd2 &f7 21.Zxe8 Zxe8 22.&xf7 &xf7 23.&xd6 Ze1+ ½-½ Luhrig-Wolochowicz, cr 1989; 15.f4 &c6 16.&c4+ g6 Lanzani-Wolochowicz, YB 109/14; 15.f3 Zhd8 16.&f2 c6± Szabo-Varga, Budapest 2009) 15...a6N (15...Zad8 16.c3 c6 17.&e2 Zhe8 18.&c2 &c7 19.Zd8 (19.f4!? &g6 20.&c4+ &f8 21.f5 &e5 22.&e6 Zxd1 23.Zxd1±) 19...Zxd8± Chuiko-Afromeev, Tula 2006) 16.&a4 g5 17.&b3+ &g7 18.Zf1 Zad8 19.f4 gxf4 20.&xf4 h5 21.Ze4 Zhe8 22.&h4 &g6 23.Zhd4 &c6 24.Z4d3 &xg3 25.Zxg3+ &h6 26.&d5 &b4 27.&c4 Zxd1+ 28.&xd1 Zd8+ 29.&c1 &d4 30.&f7 &f4 31.Zh3 &g7 32.&b3 &f5+ Fagerstrom-Cruzado, cr 2013; we have shown more moves from this game in order to illustrate the character of the position. 13.&e4 &e7 14.&xe5 (14.&e2 0-0-0 15.f3 &e6 16.b3 &a3+ ½-½ Dubois-Wolochowicz, cr 1989) 14...fxe5 15.&d5 &f6 16.&xf6+ gxf6 17.f3 0-0-0= Zielinski-Wolochowicz, cr sf ch-POL 1987] **13...&f7** [Even though a computer program assesses the position as +–, Black demonstrates that he is in fact OK] **14.&c4 h5 15.Zhe1+ &f8 16.&xf6 &xf7 17.f5 Zhe8 18.Zf1 &c6 19.&xd6 cxd6 20.Zxd6 &xg2 21.Zd7+ &e7 22.Zxe7+ &xe7 23.Zg1 &c6 24.Zxg7+ &d6 25.Zh7 Zg8 26.Zxh5 Zg2 27.b4 &e5 28.Zh3 a6 29.a4 &d7 30.Ze3+ &xf5 31.b5 &e6 32.h3 axb5 33.axb5 b6 34.&a4 &c4 35.&xb6 &xb5** ½-½

Petr Buchnicek
Friedrich-Karl Volkmann

St Veit an der Glan 2013

1.e4 e5 2.♘f3 ♘f6 3.♘xe5 ♘xe4 4.♕e2 ♕e7 5.♕xe4 d6 6.d4 dxe5 7.dxe5 ♘c6 8.♘c3 ♕xe5 9.♕xe5+ ♘xe5 10.♗f4 f6!? [A move developed by IM Volkmann]

11.0-0-0 ♗d7 [11...♗d6 12.♗g3?! ♔f7? (12...♗f5 13.f4 ♘c6 14.♘b5 0-0-0 15.♘xd6+ ♖xd6 16.♖xd6 cxd6±) 13.♘b5± Will-Stabernack, Hofheim 2013; 11...♗c5 12.♘e4 ♗e7 13.♗b5+ ♔f7 14.♖he1 (14.♘g5+ ♔g6 15.♖he1 ♗d6 16.♗g3 a6 17.♗f1 ♔xg5 18.f4+ ♔f5 19.fxe5 fxe5 20.♗d3+ ♔f6± Garbarino-Grushka, Pehuajo 1983) 14...♗g4 15.f3 ♗e6 16.♘g5+ fxg5 17.♗xe5 c6 18.♗d3 ♗f6= Srienz-Volkmann, Austria Bundesliga B 2004] **12.♘b5 ♗xb5 13.♗xb5+ c6 14.♗a4** [14.♗xe5 fxe5 15.♗c4 ♖d8 16.♖de1 ♗d6 17.f4 ♖f8 18.fxe5 ♗c7 19.♖e2 ♗e7 20.♖he1 ♖f4 21.♗d3 ♖df8 22.c3 Ja.Broekmeulen-Volkmann, Fügen 2006; 14.♗e2 ♗c5 15.♗g3 0-0 16.c3± Collins-Vidoniak, Gausdal 2008] **14...♗c5!** [14...♖d8? 15.♗e3± a6 16.♗b3 ♖d6?! (16...♗e7±) 17.♖he1 (17.♖de1!+−) 17...♔d8?? 18.♗b6+ ♔c8 19.f4 ♘g6 20.♖e8+ ♔d7 21.♖d8+ 1-0 Lehner-Volkmann, Austria Bundesliga 2005/2006] **15.♖he1** [15.♗b3 ♖d8 16.♖he1 ♗xf2 17.♖e2 ♗b6 18.♗xe5 ♖xd1+ 19.♖xd1 fxe5 20.♖xe5+ ♔d7 21.♖f5 ½-½ Grötz-Volkmann, Austria Bundesliga 2007] **15...♖d8 16.♗xe5 ♖xd1+ 17.♔xd1 fxe5**

18.♖xe5+ ♗e7 [When opting for 10...f6, Black has to reckon with getting this position. The general idea is that a pawn does not matter very much when we have opposite-coloured bishops] **19.c3 ♖f8 20.♔e2 ♔d7 21.♗c2 h6 22.g3** [22.♗f5+ ♔d8 23.♗e4 ♗d6 24.♖e6 ♖f6 25.♖xf6 gxf6± Kreisl-Volkmann, Graz 2009] **22...♗f6** [The further moves show that Black can hold the draw quite easily] **23.♖a5 ♖e8+ 24.♔d2 a6 25.f4 ♔d6 26.♗g6 ♖e6 27.♗f5 ♖e8 28.♗g6 ♖e6 29.♗f5 ♖e8 30.♗g4 ♗d8 31.♖f5 ♗f6 32.♖a5 ♗d8 33.♖a3 ♗b6 34.♖b3 ♗e3+ 35.♔c2 ♔c7 36.c4 ♗g1 37.h3 ♖e3 38.♖xe3 ♗xe3 39.♗f3 ♗f2 40.g4 ♗g3 41.f5 a5 42.♔d3 ♔d6 43.♔e4 ♗h4 44.b3** ½-½

The Critical Moment
10.♘b5

Zoran Jovanovic
Nenad Doric

Pula 2014 (6)

1.e4 e5 2.♘f3 ♘f6 3.♘xe5 ♘xe4 4.♕e2 ♕e7 5.♕xe4 d6 6.d4 dxe5 7.dxe5 ♘c6 8.♘c3 ♕xe5 9.♕xe5+ ♘xe5 10.♘b5 ♗b4+ 11.c3!? [11.♗d2 Lehner-Volkmann, YB 107/111, and Kuosmanen-Wolochowicz, YB 109/14] **11...♗a5 12.♗f4 f6**

13.♗xe5 [13.♗e2 0-0 (13...♗d7 14.a4 ♗xb5 15.axb5 ♗b6 16.♖d1 ♖d8± Krum Georgiev-Trifunov, Pernik 1983) 14.0-0

a6?! (14...♗e6=) 15.♘d4± Faibisovich-Marzano, Bad Wiessee 2013; 13.0-0-0 ♗e6 14.♔b1 0-0 15.♘d4 ♗f7 16.♗e2 ♖ad8= Yehuda Shlam-Or Cohen, Givataim 2008; 13.♘a3 ♗f5 14.0-0-0 ♖d8?? (14...♗b6=) 15.♖xd8+? (15.♖e1!+−) 15...♔xd8= Saltaev-Kotrba, Budapest 1989] **13...fxe5 14.♘a3** [14.0-0-0 ♔e7 15.f3 ♗e6 16.♔b1 ♖hd8∓ Pallas-K. Schröder, Magdeburg 2014; 14.♗c4 ♗d7 15.0-0-0 a6 16.♘a3 0-0-0 17.♖d5 ♗b6 18.♖hd1 ♗c6? (18...♖he8=) 19.♖xd8+ ♖xd8 20.♗e6+ ♔d7 21.♖xd7 ♖xd7 22.♘c4 ♗d8 23.♗xd7 ♔xd7 24.♘xe5+± Schmakel-Arond, USA 2011] **14...c6 15.0-0-0** [15.♘c4 ♗c7 16.♘e3 ♗e6= 17.♗c4 ♗xc4 18.♘xc4 0-0-0= Filipenko-Zybura, Kamena Vourla WCh sen 2012] **15...0-0 16.f3 ♖d8 17.♗c4+ ♔f8 18.♖de1 ♗c7 19.♗b3 ♗f5 20.♗c2 ♗xc2 21.♔xc2 ♖d5 22.♖e2 ♖e8 23.♘c4 b5 24.♘d2 a6 25.h4 h5 26.a4 ♗d8 27.axb5 axb5 28.♘e4 ♔f7 29.♖ee1 ♗f6 30.♖a1 ♔g6 31.♖a7 ♖e7 32.♖a8 ♖dd7??** [A terrible mistake! 32...♖c7 was still okay: 33.g3 (33.♖h8 ♖d8) 33...♖d8 34.♖ha1 ♖xa8 35.♖xa8 ♗e7±] **33.♗a6??** [And White does not seize his chance! After 33.♖h8! ♖d5 34.g4! he would have been winning!] **33...♖c7 34.♖d1 ♗xh4 35.♖d6+ ♔f6 36.♖dxc6 ♖xc6 37.♖xc6 ♖b7 38.♔d3** [38.g4 hxg4 (38...h4 39.g5 h3 40.gxf6 h2 41.f7+ ♔xf7 42.♘f2 b4 43.♖c8 bxc3 44.♔xc3 ♖b6 45.♖h8 ♖h6 46.♖xh6 gxh6 47.♔d3+−) 39.fxg4 ♖a7□ (39...♔f7 40.♘d6+; 39...♔h7 40.♘xf6+ gxf6 41.♖xf6+−) 40.♖b6+ (40.g5? ♗f5=)] **38...h4** [Again we see that White has a slight advantage, but is not able to get more than a draw] **39.♔e3 ♖b8 40.♔f2 ♔f5 41.♔g1 ♗e7 42.♔h2 b4 43.♖c7 bxc3 44.bxc3 ♔e6 45.c4 ♖b1 46.c5 ♖c1 47.♖c8 ♔d7 48.♖g8 ♗f6 49.♖a8 ♗e7 50.♖a6 ♗xc5 51.♖g6 ♗e3 52.♖xg7+ ♔e6 53.♔h3 ♖h1+ 54.♔g4 ♖h2 55.♖g6+ ♔d5 56.♔f5 ♗f4 57.♖g8 ♔d4** ½-½

Exercise 1

position after 20...♚c8-b8

White chose 21.h3 here. Why not 21.♖xf7 ?
(solution on page 247)

Exercise 2

position after 13.0-0-0

Black considered here the positional 13...♕xe2 but finally decided to attack with 13...♕b4. Was this a good choice?
(solution on page 247)

Exercise 3

position after 12.0-0-0

Which side should Black castle?
(solution on page 247)

Looking for material from previous Yearbooks?

Visit our website *www.newinchess.com* and click on 'Yearbook'.
In this menu you can find games, contributors and other information from all our Yearbooks.
Surveys are indexed by opening, by author and by Yearbook.

Ruy Lopez

Hunting for Small Advantages in the Marshall

by Peter Lukacs and Laszlo Hazai (special contribution by Peter Svidler)

1.	e4	e5
2.	♘f3	♘c6
3.	♗b5	a6
4.	♗a4	♘f6
5.	0-0	♗e7
6.	♖e1	b5
7.	♗b3	0-0
8.	c3	d5
9.	exd5	♘xd5
10.	♘xe5	♘xe5
11.	♖xe5	c6
12.	d3	♗d6
13.	♖e1	♗f5

The 12.d3 variation in the Marshall Attack of the Ruy Lopez is regarded as a quiet, practical choice in comparison to the main line 12.d4. If White doesn't want to be drawn into a morass of long and complicated variations, and still wants to accept the pawn sacrifice, this remains his best option.

True, the lines beginning with the other main continuation 13...♕h4 may lead to more complicated positions, but you still cannot compare them to the complexity of the 12.d4 main lines.

In our Survey we will deal with the quieter 13...♗f5, when Black is usually happy with simple equalization, and can only rarely start a devastating attack on the kingside.

This quiet developing move allows the double attack with 14.♕f3, and now Black is at a crossroads.

Slightly Better for White

The simple defence by 14...♕d7 allows White to liquidate to a slightly better endgame with a good knight versus bad bishop and an isolated pawn on d5. There follows 15.♗xd5! cxd5 16.♗f4 ♗xf4 17.♕xf4 ♗xd3, and White has neutralized Black's bishop pair.

In the game Am.Rodriguez-L. Vajda, Canberra 2012, White chose the precise move 19.♘f3! after 18.♘d2 ♖fe8.

The knight ideally blockades the vital d4-square, and all black pawns on the queenside are on the colour of the bishop. In

Viswanathan Anand

the endgames with an isolated pawn it is advisable for White to keep the rooks on the board, double them on the d-file, and try the force the enemy ones into passive positions, defending the vulnerable isolani on d5. However, in the game White deliberately exchanged both rook pairs on the e-file, and the game ended in a quick draw. Here we can already see the special feature of this variation: in many cases a technical endgame arises immediately from the opening.

The Rare 14...♗g6

In Anand-Carlsen, Shamkir 2015, Black went for the rare 14...♗g6 and after 15.♗xd5 cxd5 16.♗f4 it looked as if White would again get his small but durable advantage, as in the previous encounter. However, the World Champion didn't take on f4 and d3, but played 16...d4!, temporarily sacrificing the pawn, but creating weak white passers on the d-file. After 17.cxd4 ♗b4 18.♘c3 ♕xd4 19.♗e5 the improvement 19...♕xd3! 20.♖e3 ♕c4 21.♘d5 ♖ad8 solves Black's problems. Better for White seems to be 19.♗e3 ♕xd3 20.♖ed1 ♕f5 21.♕xf5 ♗xf5 22.♘d5 ♗d6 23.♘f6+ gxf6 24.♖xd6

with a small, but durable advantage in the endgame. Beware that, although opposite-coloured bishop endgames and rook endgames tend to have a drawish character, with both rooks and bishops on the board the chances for a win are much higher!

More Active

14...♕f6 is a more active approach, when again White can create a weakness on d5 by 15.♗xd5 cxd5. Now, in Vallejo Pons-Atalik, Bangkok 2014, White opted for 16.♗e3. After 16...♕e5 17.g3 ♗xd3 18.♘d2 ♖fe8 Black had kept his strong bishop pair, which fully compensates for the weakness on d5. As an improvement to the game we suggest 19.♗d4 ♕f5 20.♕xf5 ♗xf5, but without exchanging the dark-squared bishops White has no real chances to get an advantage.

Accepting the pawn sacrifice with 16.♕xd5? may lead to problems after 16...♕g6. The more positional 16.♗f4 is again met by the typical 16...♗xf4 17.♕xf4 d4!, and the ensuing rook ending after 18.cxd4 ♖ad8 19.♘c3 ♖xd4 20.♘e4 ♗xe4 21.♕xf6 gxf6 22.dxe4 ♖d2 or 22.♖xe4 ♖xd3 gives excellent drawing chances for Black.

If White wants more than a simple draw, he can opt for 15.♘d2 ♕g6 16.♗d1 ♗xd3 17.♘e4, forcing Black to give up the bishop pair with 17...♗xe4. Now, 18.♕xe4 f5 is more in the spirit of the Marshall Attack than immediately exchanging the queens. However, even here White can simplify the position with 19.♕e6+ ♕xe6 20.♖xe6 ♖ae8 21.♖xe8 ♖xe8 22.♔f1 with only a microscopic advantage.

In the game Caruana-Kasimdzhanov, Thessaloniki 2014, Black exchanged the queens, and after 18...♕xe4 19.♖xe4 ♖fe8 20.♖xe8+ ♖xe8 21.♔f1 ♗e5 22.♗d2 b4 23.♖c1 bxc3 24.bxc3 ♗f4 25.♗xf4 ♘xf4 26.♗f3 the white bishop looked a bit better than the black knight, but this was not sufficient for success. 22.♗f3...

... can be met by 22...♘xc3!, and now, after 23.♗d2 ♘d5, the subtle rook manoeuvre 24.♖e1 ♖e6 25.♗g4 ♖e7 26.♖c1 finally wins back the pawn, with a very small advantage for White.

However, even this line can be improved on by Black with the straightforward 21...♗f4!, immediately liquidating the pair of bishops. In Anand-Svidler, Khanty-Mansiysk 2014, 22.♗f3 was seen, but after 22...♗xc1 23.♖xc1 ♔f8 White had nothing substantial in his hands. Perhaps 22.♗xf4 ♘xf4 23.♗f3 ♖e6 deserves attention, with a microscopic advantage for White.

The Main Line

However, the main line is 14...♕h4, and after 15.g3 ♕h3

16.♘d2 was seen in Radjabov-Aronian, Wijk aan Zee 2015. Now, after 16...♖ae8 17.♘e4 ♗g4 18.♕g2, Black is forced to exchange queens with 18...♕xg2+ 19.♔xg2, and now he cannot win the piece with 19...f5 due to 20.h3. In the game Radjabov reached an endgame with only slightly better chances due to the weak pawns on the queenside and a slightly better bishop versus the knight. However, Aronian defended well and got the draw. If White wants to complicate matters, he can try 21.g4 fxg4 22.hxg4 ♗xg4 23.a4, but Black has nothing to fear here.

White can 'simply' win a pawn with 16.♗xd5 cxd5 17.♕xd5, and after 17...♖ad8 18.♕g2 ♕xg2+ 19.♔xg2 ♗xd3 we reach another tabiya position, which was seen in Karjakin-Inarkiev, Nizhnij Novgorod 2013.

White is a healthy pawn up, but Black's strong bishop pair and active pieces simply give enough compensation in the endgame. This position is very important from the point of view of endgame theory. We can state a general rule: 3 pawns versus 3 on the kingside and 3 versus 2 on the queenside without significant weaknesses and with a bishop and a knight is not enough for a win against an active bishop pair. Sooner or later, the rooks will be exchanged and the white king will not be able to penetrate, because the bishops cover all the important squares. In several cases, Black can exchange his bishop for the knight and go for a totally drawish endgame with opposite-coloured bishops. In most top-level games, Black did achieve the draw.

However, from a practical point of view the situation is not so simple. In top-level tournaments, matches, Olympiads, etc., a draw with black against a world-class player is not a bad achievement. In open tournaments you will desperately need a win with black as well, and to aim for a position like this against a lower-rated player is not very clever. So the tournament situation may decide whether you go for this variation either with white or with black.

16.♗e3 looks like a simple developing move, giving back the pawn without a fight, but there is a bit more venom under the surface.

In So-Al.Onischuk, Saint Louis ch-USA 2015, 16...♗xd3 17.♘d2 ♗f5 occurred, and after 18.♗d4 ♖fe8 19.c4 ♗g4 20.♕g2 ♕xg2+ 21.♔xg2 ♘b4 22.♘e4 ♗f8 23.cxb5 Black missed the beautiful intermediate move 23...♗e6! and got into trouble. 19.a4 is considered to be a bit better for White after 19...♗g4 20.♕g2 ♕h5 21.f3.

18.♗xd5 cxd5 19.♕xd5 ♖fd8 20.♕g2 ♕xg2+ 21.♔xg2 leads to similar positions to the ones discussed before.

More precise seems to be 17...♕f5. After 18.♗d4, 18...♖ae8 was played in the game Vachier-Lagrave-Adams, Biel 2015. Now, after 19.♔g2 h6 20.a4 ♕xf3+ 21.♔xf3 ♖e6 22.axb5 axb5 White had some threats on the a-file.

The flexible 18...♖fe8 looks more logical, and after 19.a4 h6 20.♔g2 the sophisticated 20...♔f8 was seen in Caruana-Aronian, Zurich 2014. Now, after 21.♖xe8+ ♖xe8 22.axb5 axb5, White, according to Caruana, missed the difficult manoeuvre 23.♖a6! ♘e7 24.♗d1! ♕g6 25.♕g4!, with slightly better chances for White.

Black can improve on his play with 20...♕xf3+! and after

21.♘xf3 ♖ac8 22.axb5 axb5 White has no direct plan for an advance. Or 21.♔xf3 ♖xe1 22.♖xe1 ♗f5 23.♘e4 ♗f8, with good chances for a successful defence.

Another Active Plan

Black has another active plan: 14...♖e8, when his queen will penetrate to the first rank. Play continues 15.♖xe8+ ♕xe8 16.♘d2 ♕e1+ 17.♘f1, and now 17...♗g6 is regarded as best.

In Sevian-Naroditsky, Saint Louis ch-USA 2015, White took the pawn by 18.♗xd5 cxd5 19.♕xd5, and now after 19...♖d8! 20.♗g5 ♕xa1 21.♗xd8 ♗f8! a complicated endgame arose. In spite of White's material advantage, Black has enough compensation due to the weakness of White's back rank.

White's best option is 18.g3!, avoiding the troubles on the first rank. Now, after 18...b4!, 19.h4?! was an unsuccessful novelty in our Illustrative Game Ivanchuk-Svidler, Reykjavik Ech-tt 2015. Black replied 19...h5, and after 20.c4 ♘f6 Svidler recommends 21.d4!, but the insertion of 19.h4 h5 clearly favours Black.

19.c4! is the theoretical main line. Here, after 19...♘f6, White made a mistake with 20.♗d1? in Stellwagen-Gustafsson, Germany Bundesliga 2007/08, after which Black got good chances and won the battle.

The correct way is paved with difficult computer moves, and theoretical knowledge is of great importance. Play may continue: 20.♕xc6! ♖d8 21.♕b6! ♖d7 22.♗c2! ♘g4! 23.♖b1! ♕e2! 24.♗d2 ♗c7 25.♕c5 ♘e5 26.♕e3 ♕xe3 27.♗xe3 ♘xc4 28.dxc4 ♗xc2 29.♖c1 ♗e4

with some compensation for the pawn. But these lines need very deep analytical work with the help of engines.

Conclusion
All in all, this variation requires good endgame skills and diligent homework for both colours. We believe there will be many new top games with this line in the near future.

Amador Rodriguez
Levente Vajda
Canberra 2012 (4)

1.e4 e5 2.♘f3 ♘c6 3.♗b5 a6 4.♗a4 ♘f6 5.0-0 ♗e7 6.♖e1 b5 7.♗b3 0-0 8.c3 d5 9.exd5 ♘xd5 10.♘xe5 ♘xe5 11.♖xe5 c6 12.d3 ♗d6 13.♖e1 ♗f5 14.♕f3 ♕d7≤ 15.♗xd5! cxd5 16.♗f4 ♗xf4 [16...♖fe8 17.♗d2 ♗xf4 18.♕xf4 ♗xd3] **17.♕xf4 ♗xd3 18.♘d2 ♖fe8** [18...♖ae8 19.♘b3!± (19.♖e3 ♖xe3 20.♕xe3 ♗g6 21.♘b3; 21.♖e1?! b4! (21...h6?! 22.♘b3 ♖c8 23.a3 ♕c7 24.♘d4± Smagin-Geller, Moscow 1989) 22.cxb4 d4♔ Smagin; 19.♘f3±); 18... a5 19.a3 ♖a6 20.♖e3 ♗g6 21.♖ae1 ♖e6 22.♖e5 (22.♘b3 ♖xe3 23.♖xe3±) 22...♖fe8 (22...♖xe5 23.♖xe5 f6 24.♕d4 ♖e8 25.♖xe6+±) 23.♖xe6 (23.♕d4 (Damjanovic-Brujic, Belgrade 2007) 23...h6∞) 23...fxe6 24.♘b3±] **19.♘f3!** [19.♖e3 ♗e2 20.♘b3 ♖xe3 21.♕xe3 ♖e8 22.♕d2 ♕h5 23.f3 f6 24.♖d1 ♗f7 25.♘d4± Zagrebelny-Barcenilla, Asia tt 1993; 19.h3 h6 20.♕d4 ♗g6 21.♘b3 ♕c6 22.♘c5 (22.♕d2 ♕c4 23.♖xe8+ ♖xe8 24.♘d4 b4 25.cxb4 ♖e4 26.♖d1 ♕xa2) 22...a5 23.a3 a4 24.♖ad1 ♖ac8 25.♖xe8+ ♖xe8∞ Anand-Adams, Paris rapid 1992; 19.♘b3 ♕c6 (19...♗c4!? 20.♘d4 ♖xe1+ 21.♕xe1 ♖e8 (21...♗xa2? 22.b3±) 22.♖a1) 20.♕d2 ♗g6 21.♘d4 ♕d6 22.f3± (22.♖ad1!?; 22.♖e3; 22.h3 h6 23.♖e2 ♖e4 24.♖ae1 ♖ae8= Fressinet-Hamdouchi, Belfort 2003 YB86/119); 19.♕d4!? ♗c2 (19...♗e2 Finkel) 20.♘f1 ♗e4 21.♖ad1 ♕g4

22.♘g3 ♕g6 23.♖e2± A.Vovk-Voynov, Lviv 2005; 19.a3 a5 20.♘b3 ♗c4 21.♘d4 a4 22.f3 f6 23.♔f2± Efimenko-Leontiev, Sevastopol 2000] **19...♗e4** [19...♗g6 20.♘e5 ♕e7 21.♗e3±; 19...f6 20.♘d4 ♗g6 21.f3± (21.♕d2 ♖ac8 22.♖xe8+ ♖xe8 23.♖e1 ♗f7 24.h3 g6 25.♕f4 ♔g7 26.♖e3 ♖e8 27.a3 ♖xe3 28.♕xe3 ♕d6 29.♘f3 ♗e6 30.♕f1 ♗f5 31.♘d4± Givon-Zanan, Jerusalem Ech 2015)] **20.♘d4 a5 21.f3 ♗g6 22.♕d2** [22.a3±] **22...h6 23.♖xe8+?!** [23. a3] **23...♖xe8 24.♖e1?** [24.a3] **24...♖xe1+ 25.♕xe1 b4! 26.cxb4 ♕a7 27.♕c3 axb4 28.♕xb4 ♕xa2 29.♔f2** ½-½

Viswanathan Anand
Magnus Carlsen
Shamkir 2015 (1)

1.e4 e5 2.♘f3 ♘c6 3.♗b5 a6 4.♗a4 ♘f6 5.0-0 ♗e7 6.♖e1 b5 7.♗b3 0-0 8.c3 d5 9.exd5 ♘xd5 10.♘xe5 ♘xe5 11.♖xe5 c6 12.d3 ♗d6 13.♖e1 ♗f5 14.♕f3 ♗g6 15.♗xd5 [15.♘d2 ♘f4! (15...♖e8 16.♖xe8+ ♕xe8 17.♘e4 f5 18.♘g3 ♕e1+ 19.♘f1 ♗f7 20.h3 ♖e8 21.♗d1 g6 22.♗d2) 16.d4 ♕d7 17.♘e4 ♗h5 18.♕e3 ♖ae8∞; 15.g3 ♖e8 16.♖xe8+ ♕xe8 17.♗d2 ♘f6♔; 15.♘a3!? (I.Sokolov) 15...♕c7 (≤ 15...♗xa3 16.bxa3 ♘xc3 17.♗b2 (17.♕xc6 ♕xd3 18.♗b2 ♖fc8) 17...♕d5 18.♖ac1 ♖c8 (18...♕d6 19.h4±) 19.♖c5±; 15...♕d7 16.♗xd5 cxd5 17.♘c2 ♕f5 18.♕xf5 ♗xf5 19.♖d1 ♖fe8 20.♗e3±) 16.g3

♗xa3 17.bxa3 ♘xc3 18.♗b2 ♘d5 19.♖ac1±] **15...cxd5 16.♗f4** [≤ 16.♗e3 ♗xd3 17.♘d2 ♗g6 (17...b4 18.cxb4 ♗xb4 19.a3 ♗e7 20.♗d4 ♗g6) 18.g3 (18.♗d4 b4) 18...♗e5 19.♘b3 ♖e8 20.♘c5 ♗e4 21.♕d1 ♗d6]

16...d4! 17.cxd4 ♗b4 18.♘c3 ♕xd4 19.♗e5 [19.♗e3!? ♕d7 (19...♕xd3 20.♖ed1 ♕f5 21.♕xf5 ♗xf5 22.♘d5 ♗d6 (22...a5 23.a3 ♗d6 24.♘f6+ gxf6 25.♖xd6 ♗e6 26.♖ad1±) 23.♘f6+ gxf6 24.♖xd6 ♗e6 25.a3±) 20.♖ed1 (20.d4 ♖ac8 21.♖ac1 ♖fe8∞) 20...♖ad8 (20...♖fd8 21.a3 (21.♗b6 ♖e8 22.♘d5 ♗d6) 21...♘xc3 22.bxc3 ♖ac8 23.♗d4± 21.a3 ♗e7 22.♗b6 ♖c8 23.d4 ♖fe8 24.♗c5±] **19...♕d7?!** [≥ 19...♕xd3 (I.Sokolov) 20.♗e3 ♕c4 21.♘d5 ♖ad8 22.♘xb4 (22.♘f6+? ♔h8!) 22...♕xb4=] **20.♘d5 f6** [20...♗xe1?? 21.♘f6++-] **21.♘xb4 fxe5 22.♕d5+ ♕xd5 23.♘xd5 ♗xd3 24.♖xe5 ♖fe8 25.♖xe8+ ♖xe8 26.♘e3** [≤ 26.♘c7 ♖e2 27.b4 ♗c4 28.a3 a5 29.bxa5 ♖e6 30.♘a6 ♖a7 31.♘b4 ♖xa5; 26.♘b4!? ♗c4 27.b3 a5 28.♘c6 ♗d5 29.♘xa5 ♖a8 30.f3±] **26...♖c8 27.a3** [27.f3] **27... a5 28.h4 ♗g6** [28...♔f7 29.♖d1 ♖d8 30.g4±] **29.♖d1 b4 30.axb4 axb4**

31.g4 b3 32.h5 ♗f7 33.♔g2 ♔f8
34.♔g3 ♖a8 35.♖d2 h6 36.♘f5 [36.
f4] 36...♗e6 37.♘d4 ♗f7 38.f3 ♖c8
39.♔f4 ♖c1 40.♘f5 ♔g8 41.♖d8+
♔h7 42.♖d7 ♔g8 43.♖d8+?
[43.♘h4! ♖c6 44.♔g3 ♗e6 45.♖b7
♗f7 46.f4 ♖c2 47.♖b8+ ♔h7 48.f5
♖e2 (48...♖xb2? 49.♘g6 ♗g8 50.f6+−)
49.♘g6 ♔e8 50.♖b7±] 43...♔h7
44.♖d7 ♔g8 45.♘d6 ♗e6 46.♖e7
♗d5 47.♔f5? [47.♖e3 ♔h7] 47...♖c6!
48.♔e5 ♗xf3 49.♘f5 g5 50.♖g7+
♔h8 51.♖g6 ♔h7 52.♖g7+ ♔h8
53.♖g6 ♔h7   ½-½

More Active
14...♕f6

Fransisco Vallejo Pons
Suat Atalik
Bangkok 2014 (6)

1.e4 e5 2.♘f3 ♘c6 3.♗b5 a6
4.♗a4 ♘f6 5.0-0 ♗e7 6.♖e1 b5
7.♗b3 0-0 8.c3 d5 9.exd5 ♘xd5
10.♘xe5 ♘xe5 11.♖xe5 c6 12.d3
♗d6 13.♖e1 ♗f5 14.♕f3 ♕f6
15.♗xd5 cxd5

16.♗e3 [16.♕xd5? ♕g6 17.♘d2
(17.♗e3 ♖ad8⇌) 17...♖ad8 18.♕f3
♗xd3 19.♘b3 (19.♕e3? f6 20.♕h3??
♖fe8 21.♘f3 ♗f5 22.♕h4 ♗g4!−+;
22...♖xe1+ 23.♘xe1 ♖e8 24.♗f4 ♖e4−+
Wang Yue-A.Muzychuk, Batumi 2012)
19...♖fe8⇌; 16.♗f4 ♗xf4 17.♕xf4 d4!
18.cxd4 (18.♕xd4 ♕xd4 19.cxd4 ♖ad8
20.♖e5 ♗xd3 21.♘c3 ♖xd4=A.Feher-B.
Csonka, Budapest 2012) 18...♖ad8
19.♘c3 (19.♕e5 ♖xd4 20.♕xf6 gxf6
21.♘c3 ½-½ Vallejo Pons-Gustafsson,
Pattaya 2011; 19.♖e5 ♗xd3 20.♕e3
♕d6 21.♘c3 ♕xd4= S.Solomon-
Illingworth, Melbourne 2011) 19...♖xd4
20.♘e4 ♗xe4 21.♕xf6 gxf6 22.♖xe4
(22.dxe4 ♖d2 23.b3 ♖c8 24.♖ed1 ♖b2⇌
Zelic-Brkic, Sibenik 2015) 22...♖xd3 23.a4
(23.♖g4+ Shirov-Tomashevsky, Saratov
2011; 23.♔f1 Perez Candelario-Adhiban,
Linares 2014) 23...♖fd8= J.Polgar-
Aronian, London 2012] 16...♕e5
[16...♗xd3 17.♕xf6 gxf6 18.♘d2 ♖fe8
19.♘b3 ±/=] 17.g3 ♗xd3 18.♘d2
♖fe8 19.♔g2 [≥ 19.♗d4!? ♕f5
(19...♕xe1+!? 20.♖xe1 ♖xe1+ 21.♔g2
♗g6 (21...♗e4? 22.♘xe4 dxe4 23.♕f5
♗f8 24.♕d7±) 22.♕xd5 ♖d8 23.♕c6
♗f8 24.♕xa6 ♖d1 25.♕a5 (25.♘f1
♗e4+ 26.f3 ♗d3) 25...♖e8⇄) 20.♕xf5
♗xf5=] 19...♗e4?! [19...♗f8?! 20.♗d4
♕f5 21.♕xf5 ♗xf5±/=; ≥ 19...♕e6!
20.♗f4 ♗e2! 21.♕e3 ♕f5 22.♕d4
♗xf4 23.♕xf4 ♕c2!↑] 20.♘xe4 dxe4
21.♕e2 ♗f8 [21...♗c5?! 22.♖ad1±;
21...♕e6 22.a4 b4 23.c4 b3 24.c5 ♗e5=]
22.♖ad1 [22.a4! ♕f5 (22...b4 23.c4±;
22...bxa4 23.♖xa4 ♕b5 24.♖a2±)
23.♖ed1 h5 24.h3±] 22...♕e6 23.a3
[23.b3 ♖ac8 24.♗d4 ♕c7=] 23...♖ad8
24.♖xd8 ♖xd8 25.♖d1 [25.♗d4
f5=] 25...♖xd1! [25...♖d5 26.a4!]
26.♕xd1 f6?! [26...♗e7 27.a4 h6=]
27.a4! ♕c4?! [27...♕c6 28.a5
(28.♕b3+ ♕c4 29.♕xc4+ bxc4 30.g4
♔f7 31.f3 exf3+ 32.♔xf3 ♗e6 33.♔e4
♗d6 34.h3 ♗c7=; 28.axb5 axb5 29.♕d4
♗d6 30.♕a7 ♗e5) 28...♗d6 29.♕g4
♗b8=] 28.a5 b4?? 29.b3? [29.cxb4
♗xb4 30.♕a4 h6 31.♔g1!+− (31.♗d2
e3 32.♗xb4)] 29...♕b5?T [29...♕xc3?
30.♕d5+ ♔h8 31.♕a8 ♗g8 32.♕xa6
♕xb3 33.♕b7 ♗a3 34.a6 b3 35.a7
b2 36.♕d5+ ♔h8 37.a8♕+−;
29...♕c6? 30.cxb4 ♗xb4 31.♕d8+ ♔f7
32.♕b6+−; 29...♕e6? 30.cxb4 ♗xb4
31.♕d8+ ♔f7 32.♕b6 ♗e7 33.b4+−;
29...♕d3! 30.♕xd3 exd3 31.c4 (31.♗d2
bxc3 32.♗xc3 ♔f7 33.♔f3 ♗e6 34.♔e4
f5+ 35.♔xd3 (35.♔d4 ♗d6) 35...♔d5
36.b4 g6⇔) 31...f5 32.♔f1 ♔f7 33.♔e1
♔e6 34.♔d2 g6 35.♔xd3 ♗d6 36.♗b6
♗g7 37.h3 h5 38.f3 ♗e5 39.g4 ♗f6=]
30.c4 ♕xa5 31.c5 ♕c7 32.♕d5+
♕f7 33.♕xe4 f5! [33...♕xb3? 34.c6
♕f7 35.♗f4+−] 34.♕xb4 [34.♕c2 f4
35.gxf4 g6 36.c6 ♗d6 37.♕d3+−] 34...
g5?!T [≥ 34...♕d5+ 35.f3 g5] 35.h3!
f4? [≥ 35...♕d5+ 36.♔h2 f4 37.gxf4 gxf4
38.♗d4 (≤ 38.♕xf4 ♗xc5±)] 36.gxf4
gxf4 37.♕xf4 ♕xf4 38.♗xf4 ♗xc5
39.♗e3 ♗b4 40.♔f3 ♔f7 41.♔e4

♔e6 42.f4 ♗c3 43.♗d4 ♗e1
44.♗e5 h5 45.f5+ ♔f7 46.♔d3
♔e7 47.♔c4 ♔d7 48.♗c3 ♗f2
49.♔d5 ♗h4 50.f6 ♗g5 51.♔e5
♗h6 52.♗b4   1-0

Fabiano Caruana
Rustam Kasimdzhanov
Thessaloniki 2013 (4)

1.e4 e5 2.♘f3 ♘c6 3.♗b5 a6
4.♗a4 ♘f6 5.0-0 ♗e7 6.♖e1 b5
7.♗b3 0-0 8.c3 d5 9.exd5 ♘xd5
10.♘xe5 ♘xe5 11.♖xe5 c6 12.d3
♗d6 13.♖e1 ♗f5 14.♕f3 ♕f6

15.♘d2 ♕g6 16.♗d1 ♗xd3
17.♘e4 ♗xe4 18.♕xe4 [18.♖xe4
♖fe8] 18...♕xe4 [18...f5!? 19.♕e6+
(19.♕d4 ♖ae8 20.♖xe8 ♖xe8 21.♗d2
♗c7 22.♗b3 ♔h8 23.♗xd5 cxd5=;
19.♕f3 ♖ae8 20.♖xe8 ♖xe8 21.♗d2
♗f4 (21...♕h6 22.♕h5! ♕e6 (22...♗xh5
23.♗xh5 ♕e6 24.g3±) 23.g3±) 22.♗b3!
♗xd2 23.♗xd5+ cxd5 24.♕xd5+ ♕e6
25.♕xd2 ♕e2 26.♕xe2 (26.♕d5+ ♔h8
27.♖f1 ♕xb2 28.♕c6 ♖b8 29.♕xa6
♕xc3=) 26...♕xe2 27.♖b1 ♔f7♕; 27...
g5♕) 19...♕xe6 20.♖xe6 ♖ae8 21.♖xe8
♖xe8 22.♔f1 ♔f7 23.♗h5+ g6 24.♗f3
a5 25.♗d2 (25.a4 b4 26.cxb4 ♗xb4
27.♗g5) 25...a4 26.♖c1 ♗e6 27.b3
axb3 28.axb3 ♖a8 29.c4 bxc4 30.bxc4
♘e7 31.g3 ♗c5= Kraft-Svilponis, cr
2014] 19.♖xe4 ♖fe8 20.♖xe8+
♖xe8 21.♔f1 ♗e5 [≥ 21...♗f4=
Anand-Svidler, Khanty-Mansiysk 2014]
22.♗d2 [22.♗f3 ♘xc3! (22...♖d8?!
23.♗d2; ±/= 23.g3 (Karjakin-Nguyen
Ngoc Truong Son, Berlin blitz 2015) 23...
b4 24.cxb4 ♘xb4 25.a3 ♘d3=) 23.♗d2
(23.bxc3? ♗xc3; 23.♗xc6 ♖e6 24.♗f3
♘a4 25.♖b1 h6 26.g3 ♗e7 27.b3 ♘c3
28.♖b2 ♗c7 29.♗e3 ♘d1=) 23...♘d5
24.♖e1 (24.♖c1 ♗f4 25.♗xf4 ♘xf4
26.♖xc6 ♘d3 27.♗e2 ♘f4 28.♗g4

♘d3=) 24...♖e6 25.♗g4 ♖e7 26.♖c1 h5 27.♗xh5 ♗f4 28.♗c2 ♗xd2 29.♖xd2∓/=]
22...b4 [22...♘b6 23.♗b3] **23.♖c1 bxc3 24.bxc3 ♗f4 25.♗xf4 ♘xf4 26.♗f3 ♘d5** [26...♘d3 27.♖b1] **27.c4 ♘b4** [27...♘e7 28.♖b1] **28.♖b1** [28.a3! ♘d3 29.♗xc6 ♘xc1 30.♗xe8] **28...c5 29.a3 ♘c2 30.♗d5 ♔f8 31.g3 ♘xa3 32.♖b2 g6 33.h4 h5 34.♖b7 ♖e7 35.♖b8+ ♖e8 36.♖b2 ♖e7 37.♔g2 ♔g7 38.♗f3 f5 39.♖a2 ♘b1 40.♖xa6 ♘d2+ 41.♔g2 ♘b3= 42.♖c6 ♔h6 43.♖c8 ♔g7 44.♗f3 ♖a7 45.♗c6 ♘c1 46.♖d8 ♖c7 47.♖d6 ♖e7 48.♗b5 ♘b3 49.♖d5 ♖a7 50.♖d6 ♖e7 51.♖c6 ♖a7 52.♖c8 ♘d2 53.♖e8 ♘e4 54.♗c6 ♘f6 55.♖e5 ♘g4 56.♖e2 ♔f6 57.♗d5 ♖e7 58.♖a2 ♔g7 59.♗f3 ♘e5+ 60.♔g2 ♘g4 61.♖b2 ♔h7 62.♗f3 ♘e5 63.♖e2 ♔g7 64.♗d5 ♔f6 65.♖a2 ♔g7 66.♖a6 ♔h7 67.♖d6 ♔g7 68.♖a6 ♔h7 69.♖a8 ♘g4 70.♗f3 ♘e5+ 71.♔g2 ♘g4 72.♖a2 ♔g7 73.♖d2 ♘e5 74.♖e2 ♘c6 75.♖d2 ♘e5 76.♖a2** ½-½

Viswanathan Anand
Peter Svidler
Khanty-Mansiysk 2014 (14)
1.e4 e5 2.♘f3 ♘c6 3.♗b5 a6 4.♗a4 ♘f6 5.0-0 ♗e7 6.♖e1 b5 7.♗b3 0-0 8.c3 d5 9.exd5 ♘xd5 10.♘xe5 ♘xe5 11.♖xe5 c6 12.d3 ♗d6 13.♖e1 ♗f5 14.♕f3 ♕f6 15.♕d2 ♕g6 16.♗d1 ♖xd3 17.♘e4 ♗xe4 18.♕xe4 ♕xe4 19.♖xe4 ♖ae8 20.♖xe8 ♖xe8 21.♔f1

21...♗f4 22.♗f3 [≥ 22.♗xf4 ♘xf4 23.♗f3 ♖e6 24.g3± (24.♖e1±)]
22...♖xc1 23.♖xc1 ♔f8 24.a3 [24.c4 ♘b4=; 24.b3 ♖e6 25.c4 ♘b6 26.cxb5 cxb5 27.a4 (27.a3 ♘d3 28.♖d1 ♘e5 29.♗e2 ♗e7=) 27...bxa4 28.bxa4

♘d3 29.♖b1 ♘c5 30.a5 ♖e5 31.♗e2 ♘e6 ½-½ Shirov-Nybäck, Helsinki 2014]
24...♖d8 25.c4 ♘f4 26.♗xc6 ♘d3 27.♖c2 bxc4 28.♖xc4 [28.♗e4 ♖d4 29.f3 ♘c5 30.♔e2 ♘xe4 31.♔e3 ♖d3+ 32.♔xe4 ♘e7 33.♖xc4 ♖d2 34.♖c7+ ♔e8=] **28...♘xb2 29.♖c2 ♖c8 30.♔e2 ♗e7 31.♗e4 ♖xc2+ 32.♗xc2 ♘c4 33.♗d3 ♘xa3 34.♗xa6** ½-½

The Main Line
14...♕h4

Teimour Radjabov
Levon Aronian
Wijk aan Zee 2015 (10)
1.e4 e5 2.♘f3 ♘c6 3.♗b5 a6 4.♗a4 ♘f6 5.0-0 ♗e7 6.♖e1 b5 7.♗b3 0-0 8.c3 d5 9.exd5 ♘xd5 10.♘xe5 ♘xe5 11.♖xe5 c6 12.d3 ♗d6 13.♖e1 ♗f5 14.♕f3 ♕h4 15.g3 ♕h3 16.♘d2

16...♖ae8 17.♘e4 [≤ 17.♖xe8 (Wolff) 17...♖xe8 18.♘e4 ♗g4 (18...♗xe4? 19.dxe4 f5 20.♗xd5+! cxd5 21.e5!±) 19.♕g2 f5 20.♕xh3 ♗xh3 21.f3 fxe4 22.fxe4 a5 23.a3 a4 24.♗a2 ♗c5+ 25.d4 ♗xd4+ 26.cxd4 ♖xe4∓]
17...♗g4 18.♕g2 ♕xg2+ [18...f5? 19.♕xh3 ♗xh3 20.♗d2 fxe4 21.dxe4 ♗c5 (21...♖e6 22.exd5 ♗xd5 23.♖xe8 ♖xe8 24.♗e3± Pariente Lopez-Rubio Doblas, Malaga 1995) 22.♗e3 (+– Kasimdzhanov) 22...♖xe4 23.♗xc5 ♖fe8 24.♖xe4 ♖xe4 25.♗e3! ♔f8 26.♗xd5! (26.♖e1± Kotronias-Nakamura, Port Erin 2004) 26...cxd5 27.♖e1 ♔f7 28.f3 ♖e8 29.♔f2±] **19.♔xg2 f5 20.h3** [20.♗f4 ♗xf4 21.gxf4 fxe4 (21...♔h8? 22.♗xd5 cxd5 23.♘c5±) 22.dxe4 ♗f3+! (½-½ Külaots-Nybäck, Heraklio Ech-tt 2007) 23.♔xf3 ♗xf4+ 24.♔g3

♖fxe4 25.♖xe4 ♖xe4= J.Polgar-Svidler, San Luis 2005 YB86/118] **20...♗h5** [20...fxe4? (Mikhalevski) 21.hxg4 exd3 22.♖xe8 ♖xe8 23.♗e3! ♖e5 24.♖d1 ♔f8 25.♗d4±] **21.♗f4** [21.g4 fxg4 (21...fxe4 22.gxh5 exd3 23.♖xe8 ♖xe8 24.♗e3 ♖e5 (Kotronias-Nybäck, Turin 2006) 25.h6 gxh6 26.♖d1±/=) 22.hxg4 ♗xg4 23.a4 ♗f3+ (23...♗b8 24.axb5 axb5 25.♖a6 ♗d7 26.♗d2 and now 26...♖e6 (Agopov-Gustafsson, Heraklio Ech-tt 2007) or 26...♔h8 (S.Hansen-Gyimesi, Turin 2006 YB86/118); 23...b4 24.c4 ♘f4+ 25.♗xf4 ♗xf4 26.c5+ ♔h8 ½-½ Kotronias-Asrian, Kemer 2007) 24.♔f1 ♖e5 25.♗e3 (Kotronias-Vescovi, Turin 2006 YB86/118) 25...♗b8! (25...♗e7 26.axb5 axb5 27.♘f6+! ♗xf6 28.♖xf3±) 26.axb5 axb5 27.♖a6 ♔h8=] **21...♗xf4 22.gxf4 fxe4 23.dxe4 ♗f3+! 24.♔xf3 ♖xf4+ 25.♔g3 ♖fxe4 26.♖xe4 ♖xe4 27.f3 ♖e5** [27...♖e2 28.c4 bxc4 29.♗xc4 ♖xb2 30.♗xa6 g5 31.a4 (31.♗c4 ♔f7 32.a4 h5 33.f4 gxf4+ 34.♔f3 ♔e6 35.♗b7 ♖a7=) 31...♔g7 32.a5 ♘f4 33.♗f1 ♔g6 34.h4 ♔f5 35.a6 ♘h5+ ½-½ Nakamura-Aronian, Gibraltar 2005] **28.c4 bxc4 29.♗xc4±/= a5 30.♖c1 ♖g5+ 31.♔f2 ♔f8 32.♗d3** [32.♗f1 ♘e7 33.♖c4 ♖d5 34.♖a4 ♖e8 35.♗c4 ♖d2+ 36.♔g3 (36.♔e3 ♖xb2 37.♖xa5 ♔d7= J.Polgar-Aronian, Wijk aan Zee 2008 YB86/118) 36...♖xb2 37.♖xa5 ♔d7 38.a4±/=] **32...♘b4 33.♗xh7 g6 34.♖d1 ♘xa2 35.♖a1 ♘b4 36.h4 ♖h5 37.♗xg6 ♖xh4 38.♔g3 ♖d4 39.♖xa5 ♖d2 40.b3 ♖b2 41.♖a3 ♔g7 42.♗e4 ♔f6 43.♔f4 ♔e6 44.♔e3 ♘c2+ 45.♗xc2 ♖xc2 46.♔d4 ♖d2+ 47.♔c5** [47.♔e4 ♖e2+ 48.♔f4 ♖b2 49.♔g5 c5=] **47...♖c2+ 48.♔b6 ♖c3 49.f4 ♔d6 50.f5 ♖f3 51.f6 ♖xf6 52.b4 ♔d5 53.♖a5+ ♔c4 54.♖c5+ ♔xb4 55.♖xc6 ♖xc6+ 56.♔xc6** ½-½

Sergey Karjakin
Ernesto Inarkiev
Nizhnij Novgorod 2013 (4)
1.e4 e5 2.♘f3 ♘c6 3.♗b5 a6 4.♗a4 ♘f6 5.0-0 ♗e7 6.♖e1 b5 7.♗b3 0-0 8.c3 d5 9.exd5 ♘xd5 10.♘xe5 ♘xe5 11.♖xe5 c6 12.d3 ♗d6 13.♖e1 ♗f5 14.♕f3 ♕h4 15.g3 ♕h3 16.♗xd5 cxd5 17.♕xd5
[17.♗f4?! ♗g4! 18.♕g2 ♗xf4 19.♕xh3

(19.gxf4 d4 20.♕g3?! (20.♕xh3 ♗xh3 –
19.♕h3) 20...♖ad8 21.c4?! ♗d6! 22.♖e5
f5–+ Kotronias-Grischuk, Tripoli Wch
2004 YB73/105) 19...♗xh3 20.gxf4 d4
21.♘d2 (21.♘a3 dxc3 22.bxc3 ♖fd8∓;
21.a4 (Grischuk) 21...♖ae8; 21.cxd4
♖ad8 (21...♖fd8 22.♖e3 ♗f5 23.a4
b4 24.♘d2 ♖xd4 25.♘e4 ♖c8!? (25...
g6 Grischuk-Tkachiev, Prague rapid
2002) 26.♘g3 (26.♖ae1 f6∓) 26...♖xf4
27.♘xf5 ♖xf5 28.♖ae1 ♔f8∓ Naiditsch)
22.♘c3 ♖xd4 23.♖e3 ♗f5 24.♘e4
♖c8 25.♘g3 ½-½ Solodovnichenko-
Miton, Germany Bundesliga B 2006/07
YB86/117) 21...♖ac8 (21...dxc3 22.bxc3
♖fd8 23.♖e3 ♗f5 24.♘e4 Bauer-Adams,
Senat 2003) 22.c4 ♖c6♔; 17.♗e3 ♗xd3
18.♕xd5 ♖ad8 19.♖f3!? (19.♕xd3?
♗xg3! 20.♕e4 ♗xh2+ 21.♔h1 ♗b8+
22.♔g1 ♖d6–+; 19.♖g2 ♕h5
20.♘d2 ♗f5 (≤ 20...♕g6 21.♗d4 b4;
≤ 21...♗f5 (Vocaturo-Ubilava, Benasque
2015) 22.♕c6!) 21.♕c6! (21.♗d4
♗e6 22.♖f3 ♕g6 23.♕e4 ♕h5
24.♖f3 ♕g6 25.♕e4 ♕h5 26.♕f3
½-½ Wang Hao-Jakovenko, Nizhnij
Novgorod 2007) 21...♗e6 (21...♗h3
22.a4 (22.♗d4 Smeets-Khalifman,
Amsterdam 2007) 22...♗b8 23.axb5
(23.♕xa6?? ♖xd2!–+) 23...axb5
24.♖a5 ♗d7 25.♕c5± Stellwagen-
Pashikian, Yerevan 2007) 22.♕xa6
♕d5 23.♕b6 ♖fe8!? (23...♗h3 24.f3
(Shirov-Jakovenko, Khanty-Mansiysk
m/1 2007) 24...♖fe8!) 24.f3) 19...♗c4!?
(19...♕f5 20.♖xf5 ♗xf5 21.♘d2 ♖fe8
22.♗d4 f6 23.f3!? b4 (23...♗f7 24.♔f2
h5 25.♘e4 ♗f8 26.♖e2± Naiditsch)
24.♘e4 ♗c7 25.♔f2 bxc3 26.bxc3
♖b8 27.♖e2 ♗f7 28.♖d1 h5 29.♗c5
♔g6 30.♗d4 ½-½ Carlsen-Anand,
Leon rapid 2005 YB86/117) 20.♘d2
♗e6 21.♗d4 ♗b8!?♔ (Bacrot-Aronian,
Khanty-Mansiysk m/1 2005 YB86/117
21...♗e7 22.♕g2 ♕h5 23.♖e5 ♕g6
24.♘e4 ♖d7 25.♘c5 ♗xc5 26.♖xc5
♖fd8 27.♕f3 h6 (Naiditsch-Ivanchuk,
Cesme 2004) 28.♘c6!? ♕c2 29.♖xa6
♕xb2 30.♖e1 b4 31.♕e3± Naiditsch);
17.a4 ♖ae8 18.♗d2 ♗g4 19.♕xd5 ♖d8
20.axb5 (20.d4 b4 21.♗e3 (21.♕g2 ♕h5
22.♖e3) 21...bxc3 22.bxc3 (22.♘xc3?!
♗a3!∓) 22...♕xg3= Nakamura-Adams,
London 2010) 20...axb5 (20...♗xg3?
21.♕g2!+–) 21.♕c6 (21.♕g2 ♕h5♔)
21...♖c8 22.♕g2 ♕h5 23.♖e3]

17...♖ad8 [17...♖fe8? 18.♖xe8+ ♖xe8
19.♗e3 ♖d8 20.♘d2±] 18.♕g2
♕xg2+ [18...♗g4 19.♗e3 ♗xd3
20.♗b6 ♖de8 21.♘d2±; 18...♕h5
19.♗e3 ♗xd3 (19...♗h3!? 20.♕h1
(20.♕c6?! ♗e6 21.♘d2 ♗d5 22.♕xa6
♕h3 (22...f5♔) 23.♘e4 f5 24.♕xb5
♗c7♔) 20...f5 21.♗b6 (21.f4 ♗c7 (21...
g5 22.♕d5+!±) 22.♘d2 ♖xd3 23.♘b3
♗g4 24.♕g2 ♗f3 25.♕f2 ♗a8 26.♘c5
♖d6 27.♗d4 ♕f7 28.h4± Shirov-
Jakovenko, Dagomys 2008) 21...♖d7 (21...
f4 ! 22.♖xd8 f3 ↑ 23.♗b6! ♗g2 24.♕xg2
fxg2 25.♘d2 ♕g6 26.♗d4 ♕xd3
27.♖ad1± Naiditsch) 22.♕d5+ ♔h8
23.♘d2 ♗xg3 24.♕xd7 ♗f4 25.♕d5!?
(Finkel) 25...♗xd2 26.♕d6 (26.♗d4!?
♗xe1 (26...♗g4? 27.♖e7+–) 27.♖xe1
♖e8 28.♖xe8+ ♕xe8 29.♗e5±) 26...♖g8
27.♕g3 f4 28.♖e5! ♕xe5 29.♕xh3±)
20.♘d2 b4!? (20...♗f5) 21.♕f3 (21.♗d4
bxc3 22.♗xc3 ♗e2 23.♘e4 ♗f3 24.♕f1
(Lizarzaburu-Almiron, cr 2008) 24...♗b8!
25.♘d2 (25.♕xa6 ♕h3 26.♕f1 ♕f5♔)
25...♗c6♔) 21...♕xf3 22.♘xf3 bxc3
23.bxc3 ♗a3 24.♖ad1 f6 25.♗b6 ♖d6
26.♗d4 ♗c2 27.♖d2 ♗a4♔ Maliangkay-
Almiron, cr 2007] 19.♔xg2 ♗xd3
20.♗e3 f6 [20...♗e4+ 21.f3 (21.♔f1
♗c6 22.♘d2 f6 23.♗d4 ♖fe8 24.♖e2
♔f7 25.♖ae1 ♖xe2 26.♔xe2 ♖e8+
27.♔d1 ♖xe1+ 28.♔xe1 g5 29.♘e2 ±/=
Karjakin-Kobalia, Al Ain 2008) 21...♗c6
22.♘d2 ♖fe8 23.♘b3 (23.♗d4 h5
(23...♖xe1 24.♖xe1 f6 and now: 25.♔f2,
Leko-Naiditsch, Dortmund 2008, or 25.♘f1,
Bacrot-Sargissian, Evry 2008) 24.♔f2 f6
25.♖xe8+ ♖xe8 26.♘f1 ♔f7 27.♘e3
Leko-Aronian, Yerevan m/1 rapid 2008
27...♗b8± ∆ ...h5-h4) 23...f6 24.♔f2
(24.♘d4 ♗b7 25.g4 ♗c5 26.b4 ♗xd4
27.♗xd4 ♖xe1 28.♖xe1 ♔f7 29.♗c5
♖d7 30.h4 ♗d5 31.a3 ♗e6 32.♗d4
♗c4♔ Naiditsch-Bacrot, Dortmund 2009;
24.♗b6 ♖xe1 25.♖xe1 ♖d7 26.♖d1

♔f7 27.♗c5± Bacrot-Aronian, Kallithea
2008; 27.♘c5 ♗xc5 28.♖xd7+ ♗xd7
29.♗xc5= B.Socko-Sargissian, Antwerp
2009) 24...♗c7 25.♘d4 ♗d7 26.♖ad1
♔f7 27.♖d2 ♗c8 28.♖ed1 h5 29.♘e2
♖d2 30.♖xd2 ♗e6 (30...h4±/=) 31.b3
g5 32.♗c5±/= Leko-Sargissian, Yerevan
m/2 rapid 2008] 21.♘d2 b4 [21...♖fe8
22.♗b6 ♖b8±/=] 22.♗d4 bxc3
23.♗xc3 ♖fe8 24.f3 ♔f7 25.♖ac1
♖xe1 26.♖xe1 ♗e7 27.g4?! [27.
h4 Stellwagen; 27.♘e4!? (Finkel) 27...h5
(27...f5 28.♘f2 ♗c4 29.b3 ♗e6 30.♖d1
±/=) 28.♔f2 (28.♖d1? ♗xe4 29.♖xd8
♗xf3+ 30.♔xf3 ♖xd8=) 28...f5 29.♘d2
g5 30.♘b3±/=] 27...h5! 28.h3 g6
[28...hxg4 29.hxg4 ♖b5 30.♘b3 (30.♘e4
(Stellwagen) 30...♗c6 31.♘e2 g6±/=)
30...c4! 31.♖e4 ♖c8 32.♖d4 ♖c7
33.♘d2!? ♗xa2 34.♖a4 ♗e6 35.♖xa6
f5 36.gxf5 ♗xf5 37.♘g3 g6 38.♘e4±/
= Stellwagen-Harikrishna, Wijk aan Zee
2008 YB86/116] 29.♘b3 ♖d7 30.♘d4
♗c4 31.♘c6 ♗d5 32.♘xe7 ♖xe7=
33.♖d1 ♗xa2 34.gxh5 gxh5
35.♖d4 ♖e6 36.♔g3 ♖c6 37.♔h4
♔g6 38.♖d1 ♗f7 39.♖d4 ♖c4
40.♖xc4 ♗xc4 41.f4   ½-½

Wesley So
Alexander Onischuk
Saint Louis ch-USA 2015 (7)

1.e4 e5 2.♘f3 ♘c6 3.♗b5 a6
4.♗a4 ♘f6 5.0-0 ♗e7 6.♖e1 b5
7.♗b3 0-0 8.c3 d5 9.exd5 ♘xd5
10.♘xe5 ♘xe5 11.♖xe5 c6 12.♖e1
♗d6 13.d3 ♗f5 14.♕f3 ♕h4 15.g3
♕h3 16.♗e3 ♗xd3 17.♘d2 ♗f5
[≥ 17...♕f5, see next games!] 18.♗d4
[18.♗xd5 cxd5 19.♕xd5 ♖fd8 20.♕g2
♕xg2+ 21.♔xg2±/=] 18...♖fe8
[18...♖ad8!? 19.a4]

19.c4 [≥ 19.a4 ♗g4 20.♕g2 ♕h5
21.f3 ♖xe1+ 22.♖xe1 ♗e6] 19...♗g4

20.♕g2 ♕xg2+ [20...♕h6 21.f3 ♗h3 22.♕f2] **21.♔xg2 ♘b4** [21...♘c7 22.cxb5 axb5 23.♖xe8+ ♖xe8 24.♖c1] **22.♘e4 ♗f8 23.cxb5** [≤ 23.c5 ♖ed8 24.♘d6 ♗xd6 25.cxd6 c5 (25...♗xd6? 26.♗c5) 26.♗xc5 ♘d3 27.♗d5 ♗xc5 28.♗xa8 ♖xa8∓/=] **23...cxb5?!** [23...♗e6!= I.Sokolov] **24.♘g5** [24.a3 ♘c6 (24...♖ed8 25.♗c3 ♘d3 26.♗e3±) 25.♘g5 ♗h5 26.♗c3±] **24...♗h5 25.g4!?** [25.f3 ♘d3] **25...♗g6 26.f4 ♘c2** [26...h6 (I.Sokolov) 27.f5 ♗h5! 28.gxh5 hxg5 29.♖xe8 ♖xe8 30.♖c1±] **27.♖xe8 ♖xe8 28.♖d1?** [28.f5! ♘xd4 (28...♖e2+ 29.♔f1 ♘xa1 30.fxg6) 29.fxg6 ♖e2+ 30.♔f1 ♖xh2 31.gxf7+ ♔h8 32.♔g1 ♖d2 33.♖e1±] **28...♘xd4** [28...h6 29.f5 ♗h5! 30.gxh5 hxg5=] **29.♖xd4 ♗e7** [29...♗c5 30.♖d5±] **30.♘f3 ♗b1?** [30...h5 31.f5 hxg4 32.fxg6 gxf3+ 33.♔xf3 ♔f8 34.gxf7 ♖d8 35.♖xd8+ ♗xd8 36.♗e6 a5=] **31.♖d2+− ♗f6 32.♖d7 ♗e4+ 33.♘xe4 ♖xe4 34.♗xf7 ♖e2+ 35.♔f3 ♖xb2 36.♗e6** 1-0

Maxime Vachier-Lagrave
Michael Adams

Biel 2015 (8)

1.e4 e5 2.♘f3 ♘c6 3.♗b5 a6 4.♗a4 ♘f6 5.0-0 ♗e7 6.♖e1 b5 7.♗b3 0-0 8.c3 d5 9.exd5 ♘xd5 10.♘xe5 ♘xe5 11.♖xe5 c6 12.d3 ♗d6 13.♖e1 ♗f5 14.♕f3 ♕h4 15.g3 ♕h3 16.♗e3 ♗xd3 17.♘d2

17...♕f5 18.♗d4 [18.♕xf5 ♗xf5 19.♗d4 ♖fd8 20.a4 (20.♘e4 ♗f8 21.a4 – 20.a4) 20...♗f8= Ivanchuk-Aronian, Nice blindfold 2008; 18.♖ad1 ♖fe8 19.♕xf5 ♗xf5 20.♗xd5 cxd5 21.♘b3 ♗e4= (21...♗e6 22.♗c5 ♗c7 23.♘d4 J. Polgar-Leko, Wijk aan Zee 2008 YB86/117)] **18...♖ae8** [18...♖fe8 – Caruana-Aronian, Zurich 2014] **19.♔g2** [19.a4 h6 20.♔g2 – 19.♔g2; 20.axb5 axb5 21.♔g2 (21.♕xf5

♗xf5 22.♖xe8 ♖xe8 23.♖a6 ♖e2⇄) 21...♕xf3+ 22.♔xf3 ♖e6 – 19.♔g2] **19...h6** [19...♕xf3+ (Milanovic) 20.♔xf3 (△ a2-a4, ♘e4); 20.♘xf3?! ♗e4] **20.a4 ♕xf3+ 21.♔xf3 ♖e6 22.axb5 axb5 23.♔g2** [23.♖xe6 (Milanovic) 23...fxe6+ 24.♔g2 c5 25.♖a6 ♖d8 26.♗xc5 ♗xc5 27.♖xe6 ♗c2! 28.♗xc2 ♗e3+! 29.♖xe3 (29.♔h3 ♗xd2 30.♗b3 ♘f1 31.♖e1+ (31.♖e5+ ♔h7 32.♖xc5 ♗xf2 33.♖xb5 g5 34.♖b7+ ♔g6=) 31...♔f8 32.♖xf1 ♖xb2=) 29...♗xe3 30.♘f3∞] **23...♖fe8 24.♖xe6 ♖xe6 25.c4** [25.♖a6 ♗e7=] **25...bxc4 26.♘xc4 ♗e4+?** [26...♗c7 (Milanovic) 27.♘e3 ♗e5 28.♗xd5 cxd5 29.♖a8+ ♔h7 30.♗xe5 ♖xe5=] **27.f3 ♗d3** [27...♗g6 28.♘d6 ♖xd6 29.♖a8+ ♔h7 30.♗c5±] **28.♘xd6 ♖xd6 29.♔f2 ♖d7 30.♖a3 ♘c7 31.♗e3 ♘d5 32.♗c5± f6 33.♗a4 ♗b5 34.♗c2 ♘c7 35.♗g6 ♗a6** [35...♖d2+ 36.♔e1 ♖e2+ 37.♔d1 ♘a6] **36.♗e3 ♖d8 37.♗e7 ♖c8** [≥ 37...♖d2+ 38.♔e1 ♖xh2 (38...♖xb2? 39.♗a3) 39.♗d6±] **38.b4 c5?** [38...♘c7 39.♗d6 ♘d5 40.♖a3±] **39.♗f5 ♖c6 40.♗d7 cxb4 41.♗xc6 ♗xc6 42.♖e6** 1-0

Fabiano Caruana
Levon Aronian

Zurich 2014 (5)

1.e4 e5 2.♘f3 ♘c6 3.♗b5 a6 4.♗a4 ♘f6 5.0-0 ♗e7 6.♖e1 b5 7.♗b3 0-0 8.c3 d5 9.exd5 ♘xd5 10.♘xe5 ♘xe5 11.♖xe5 c6 12.d3 ♗d6 13.♖e1 ♗f5 14.♕f3 ♕h4 15.g3 ♕h3 16.♗e3 ♗xd3 17.♘d2 ♕f5 18.♗d4

18...♖fe8 19.a4 h6 [19...♕xf3?! 20.♘xf3] **20.♔g2 ♔f8** [20...b4 21.c4 c5 22.♗xd5 ♕xd5+ 23.cxd5 cxd4 24.♘c4 ♗xc4 25.♗xc4± ; 20...♖xe1 21.♖xe1 ♔f8 22.♕xf5 ♗xf5 23.♘e4 ♖e4+ 24.♖xe4 ♖b8 25.axb5 axb5 26.♖e1 ♘b6 27.♖d1

♗e7 28.♗c2± Naiditsch-Caruana, Baden-Baden 2015; ≥ 20...♕xf3+ 21.♘xf3 (21.♔xf3 ♖xe1 22.♖xe1 ♗f5 (22...bxa4 23.♖xa4 c5 24.♗e5 ♗f8 Vachier-Lagrave-Tomashevsky, Baku 2015) 23.♘e4 ♗f8 24.♘c5 (24.g4 ♗e6 25.axb5 axb5 26.♘c5 ♗xc5 27.♗xc5 ♘f4 28.♗c2 g5⇄) 24...♘b6 25.g4 (25.a5 ♘c4 26.♗xc4 bxc4 27.g4 ♗xc5 28.♗xc5 ♗e6) 25...♘d7 26.gxf5 ♗xc5 27.♗xc5 ♗xc5 28.♖d1 ♗f8 29.♖d7 ♖a7 30.♖xa7 ♗xa7 31.axb5 ½-½ Adams-Aronian, Tromsø 2014] 21...♖ac8 22.axb5 axb5 23.♔g1= (Leko-Svidler, Reykjavik Ech-tt 2015); 23.♗e5 ♗xe5 24.♖xe5 ♖xe5 25.♗xe5 ♘b6 26.♗d4 ♘c4 27.♖a7 ♗e4+ 28.♔h3 ♗d5=)]

21.♖xe8+ ♖xe8 22.axb5 axb5 23.♕xf5 [23.♖a6! ♗e7 24.♗d1! (24.♖a7 c5) 24...♗g6 25.♕g4! (25. Caruana) 25...♕xg4 26.♗xg4 ♖d8 27.♘b3±] **23...♗xf5 24.♗xd5 cxd5 25.♖a6 ♗e7** [25...♖e2! 26.♗xd6 (26.♗e3 ♗e7 27.♖a1; 26.♘f3 ♔e7 27.♗xg7 ♗e4) 26...♖xd2 27.b4 ♗e4+ 28.♔h3 f5!! 29.♖g6 (29.♖b6 g5 30.♖xh6 ♗d3 31.♔g2 ♗e4+; 29.♖d8+ ♗e7 30.♖h8 ♔f7 31.♖h7 ♖xd4 32.cxd4 ♔g8) 29...♖d1! (29...f4 30.♖b6) 30.♖b6 g5= Caruana] **26.♘f1** [≥ 26.♖b6 ♗g5 27.♘f3 ♗e4 28.♖xb5±] **26...b4 27.♘e3 ♗d3** [27...♗e6 28.f4±] **28.♖a5 bxc3 29.bxc3 ♗d8 30.♖a8 f6 31.f3 ♗e7 32.♖a7** [32.♖xe8+ ♔xe8 33.♘xd5 ♗d6♔; 32.♖a5 ♖b8 – 32.♖a7] **32...♗d6** [32...♖d8 33.♔f2 (33.♖a5 ♖b8 34.♘xd5 ♗b2+)] **33.♖d7 ♗a3 34.♖xd5 ♔g8 35.h4 ♗c1 36.♘g4** [36.♔f2 ♗xe3+ 37.♔xe3 ♗c4 38.♖c5±] **36...♗c4 37.♖c5 ♗e6?!** [37...♖e2+ 38.♘f2 (38.♔f1 ♗a6) 38...♗e6 39.h5 (39.♖a5 ♖c2♔) 39...♖a2♔] **38.♘f2 ♖a8 39.g4 ♖a2?** [39...♗f4! 40.♘d3 ♖a2+ 41.♔f2 ♗e3 42.♘c6 (42.♘c7 ♖d2=) 42...♗d7 43.♖c7 ♖d2 44.♖xd7 ♗xf2 45.♔h3 ♗e3⇄ Caruana] **40.♔g3 ♖a6 41.♖c7 ♗d2** [41...♖a3 42.♗c5 ♗b2 43.♗b4!±] **42.♘e4 ♗e1+ 43.♗f2 ♗xf2+ 44.♔xf2 ♖a2+?!** [44...f5 45.♘c5 ♖d6 46.♘xe6 (46.g5 hxg5 47.hxg5 f4) 46...♖xe6 47.gxf5 ♖e5 48.f6 (±; 48.c4) 48...gxf6 49.c4 h5 50.c5 ♔f8 51.c6 ♗e8 52.♖h7 ♗d8 53.♖f7 ♖e6 54.c7+ ♔c8 55.f4 ♖a6 56.♔f3 ♖a4 57.♔f6 ♔xc7 58.♖f5 ♔d7

59.♖xh5 ♔e6=] **45.♔g3 ♖c2** [45...
f5 46.♘c5+−] **46.♔f4 ♖a2 47.h5
♖a5 48.♘c5 ♗d5 49.♖c8+ ♔f7**
[49...♔h7 50.♘d7 g5+ 51.♔e3 (51.
hxg6+ ♔xg6 52.♖c7) 51...♔g7 52.♖c7
Caruana] **50.c4+− ♗a8** [50...♗xc4
51.♘b7+−] **51.♖c7+ ♔g8 52.♘e6
♖a3 53.♖xg7+ ♔h8 54.♔f5
♗xf3 55.♖g6 ♗e2 56.♖xh6+
♔g8 57.♖g6+ ♔h8 58.♖xf6
♖f3+ 59.♘f4 ♗xc4 60.♔g5 ♔g8
61.♔h6 ♖a3 62.g5 ♖a7 63.g6
♖c7 64.♘h3 ♖c8 65.♘g5 ♖d8
66.♘h7** 1-0

Another Active Plan: 14...♖e8

Samuel Sevian
Daniel Naroditsky
Saint Louis ch-USA 2015 (4)

**1.e4 e5 2.♘f3 ♘c6 3.♗b5 a6
4.♗a4 ♘f6 5.0-0 ♗e7 6.♖e1 b5
7.♗b3 0-0 8.c3 d5 9.exd5 ♘xd5
10.♘xe5 ♘xe5 11.♖xe5 c6 12.d3
♗d6 13.♖e1 ♗f5 14.♕f3 ♖e8
15.♖xe8+ ♕xe8 16.♘d2** [16.♗d2
♕e6!? (16...♕d7!?) 17.♘a3 ♖e8
18.♘c2 ♗g4 19.♕e4 ♕d7 20.♕d4
♖e5∞ Sieber-Winterberg, Hamburg 2015]
16...♕e1+ [16...♕e5? 17.♘f1 ♗g6
(Kotronias-Pavlovic, Vrnjacka Banja 2005
YB86/119); 17...♖e8 18.♗d2 ♘f4 19.d4
♕e4 20.♕xe4 ♗xe4 21.♗xf4 ♗xf4
22.g3± Smagin-Blatny, Naleczow 1985)
18.♗d2!± (Finkel) 18...♘h5?! 19.g4
♗g6 20.♖e1+−; 16...♕e6 17.h3 ♖e8
18.♘e4 ♗xe4 19.dxe4 (19.♕xe4??
♕d7) 19...♕xe4 (19...♕e5? 20.♔f1
♗c5 (20...♕h2 21.g4! ♗c5 22.♗xd5
(22.exd5? ♗xf2!) 22...cxd5 23.♗f4 dxe4
24.♖e1! ♖d8! 25.♔g3 ♕xg3 26.♗xg3±)
21.♗d2 ♕h2 22.♔e2 ♖e6 23.♔d3
♖f6 24.♔g3 ♕xg3+ 25.fxg3± Shirov-
Onischuk, Poikovsky 2008) 20.♕xe4
♖xe4 21.♘f1±] **17.♘f1 ♗g6** [17...♘e7
18.♗f4!±; 17...♗e6 18.♕d1!±; 17...
g6 18.g4 ♗e6 19.♔g2! ♖e8 20.♘g3
♗f8 (20...♗f4 21.♗xf4 ♕xa1 22.♘e4;
22.♗h6) 21.♘e4 ♗g7 22.h3±]
18.♗xd5 [18.♗c2?? ♘xc3!−+;
18.♗d1? ♗xh2+ 19.♔xh2 ♕xf1; 18.h4
♘f6 19.♕xc6 ♗xd3! 20.♕xa8+ ♗f8
21.♔h2 ♕xf1 22.♗e3 ♕xa1 23.♗c5
♘d7 24.♗xf7+! ♔xf7 25.♕d5+ ♔e8

26.♕a8+ ♔f7 27.♕d5+=; 18.h3 ♖e8
19.♗d1 ♘xc3!? (19...♗h2+ 20.♔xh2
♕xf1 21.♗d2 ♕xd3 22.♕xd3 ♗xd3
23.a4 f6 24.axb5 axb5 25.♔g4 f5 26.♗h5
g6 27.♗f3 ♗e4 28.♗d1!?±; 28.♔g3
f4+!= Dolmatov-Khalifman, Moscow 1990)
20.bxc3 ♕xc3 21.♖b1 ♖e1 22.♗f4!±
Kotronias-M.Pavlovic, Vrnjacka Banja
2005] **18...cxd5 19.♕xd5**

19...♖d8! [19...♗f8?! 20.♕xa8 ♗xd3
21.h3 ♕xf1+ 22.♔h2 ♕xf2 23.♗g5±]
20.♗g5 [20.♕g5? ♖e8 21.♕d2 ♗f4!
22.♕c2 ♖d8! 23.♖b1 ♗xd3 24.♗xf4
♕xb1] **20...♕xa1 21.♗xd8 ♗f8!**
[21...♗xh2+ 22.♔xh2 ♕xf1 23.♗h4
(23.♕a8 h6 24.d4 ♕e2=) 23...h6 24.d4
♕b1 25.♕b3± (25.♕a8+ ♔h7 26.♕xa6
♕xb2 27.d5 ♕xc3= Stellwagen-l'Ami,
Schagen rapid 2005 YB86/119); 21...♕b1
22.♕xd6 ♗xd3 23.h3 ♕xf1+ 24.♔h2
♗e4 25.♕g3 h6 26.♗f6 ♗g6 27.♗d4±
Karasek-Likhachev, cr 2001] **22.h4** [22.f4
♕xb2 23.f5 (23.g4? ♕e2! 24.f5 (24.♕g2
♗xd3∓) 24...♕xg4+ 25.♘g3 ♕d1+
26.♔g2 ♕h5∓ Naiditsch) 23...♗h5 24.f6
(24.♕a8 ♕a3) 24...♕e2! (Naiditsch)
25.fxg7 ♕xg7 26.♗a5 h6 27.♕a8+ ♔h7
28.♕e4+ ♗xe4 29.dxe4 ♗g6=; 22.h3
♕xb2! (22...♕e1? 23.♗b6+−; 22...
h6?! 23.f4 ♕xb2 24.f5 ♗h7 25.♗a5!±
b4 (25...♕a3 26.♕d8+−) 26.♗xb4
♗xb4 27.cxb4 ♕xb4 28.d4±) 23.♗b6
(23.♗a5 ♕b1 24.♕a8 ♗xd3 25.♗b4
h6 26.♕xf8+ ♔h7 27.♕xf7 ♗xf1)
23...♕b1 24.♕a8 ♗xd3 25.♗c5 h6=]
22...h6 [22...♕b1?! 23.♕a8 ♗xd3
24.♗e7 h5 25.♕xf8+ ♔h7 26.♕xf7
♕xf1+ 27.♔h2±; 22...h5 23.f4±]
23.h5 [23.♕a8? ♗xd3−+; 23.♗b6!
♕xb2! 24.h5 ♗h7 25.♕a8 (25.♗d8
♕b1 26.♗c5 ♗xd3 27.♕xf8+ ♔h7=)
25...♗xd3! 26.♗c5 ♕c1 27.♕xf8+ ♔h7
28.♕xf7 ♕xf1+=] **23...♗h7 24.f4
♕xb2 25.♗a5 ♕a3 26.♕d8 ♕d6**

27.♕e8 ♕e6 [28.♕d8 ♕d6 29.♕e8
♕e6 30.♕d8] ½-½

Vassily Ivanchuk
Peter Svidler
Reykjavik Ech-tt 2015 (4)

**1.e4 e5 2.♘f3 ♘c6 3.♗b5 a6
4.♗a4 ♘f6 5.0-0 ♗e7 6.♖e1 b5
7.♗b3 0-0 8.c3 d5 9.exd5 ♘xd5
10.♘xe5 ♘xe5 11.♖xe5 c6 12.d3
♗d6 13.♖e1 ♗f5 14.♕f3 ♖e8
15.♖xe8+ ♕xe8 16.♘d2 ♕e1+
17.♘f1 ♗g6 18.g3** [18.♗c2?? ♘xc3!
(18...b4?? 19.c4 b3 20.♗d1 ♘b4 21.♗d2
♕e5 22.♗c3 ♕c5 23.♗xb4 ♕xb4
24.♗xb3± Karjakin-Svidler, Baku m/9
rapid 2015)] **18...b4**

19.h4 h5 20.c4 [20.♗xd5 cxd5 21.♕xd5
♖e8!? (21...♖d8 22.♗g5 ♕xa1 23.♗xd8
bxc3 24.bxc3 ♕d1) 22.♕xd6 ♕d1!
23.♕d4 ♖e1 24.♗h6 ♖xf1+ 25.♔g2
♖g1+ 26.♔h2 ♖h1+ 27.♔g2 ♖g1+=
Svidler] **20...♘f6 21.♗d1** [21.d4! ♘g4
22.c5 ♗xc5! (22...♗e7 23.♗e3 (23.♗d2!?
♕xa1 24.♕xc6 ♗f8 25.♕xg6 ♕xb2
26.♕d3 ♗f6 27.d5 ♗d4) 23...♕xa1
24.♕xc6 ♗d3! 25.♕xa8+ ♔h7 26.♕g2 f5
27.c6 ♗d6 28.♗d2 ♕xb2 29.♕d5 ♘f6!=
Svidler) 23.dxc5 ♖e8 24.a3 (24.♗d2 ♕xa1
25.♕xc6 ♘f6; 24.♗c4 ♘e5 25.♕e2
♘xc4 26.♕xc4 ♕d1) 24...bxa3 25.bxa3
♖e2 26.♗f4 ♕xf2+ 27.♕xf2 ♘xf2
28.♔h2 ♘d3+ 29.♔g1 ♘f2= Svidler]
21...♖e8 22.♗d2? [22.d4! c5= (Svidler
22...♕e6)] **22...♕e5 23.♖c1** [23.♖b1
♗c5∓ Svidler] **23...♗c5 24.a3?!**
[24.♕xc6! ♗xd3 25.♗f3 ♖e6 (25...♗xf1
26.♖xf1 ♕xg3+ 27.♔g2 ♗d4 28.♗g5
♕b8) 26.♕c8+! (26.♕a8+ ♔h7 27.♖e1
♕xb2) 26...♔h7 27.♖e1 ♕f5 28.♖xe6
fxe6 29.♗f4! ♗d4 30.♕d8 e5 31.♘e3
♗xe3 32.♗xe3 ♗xc4∓ Svidler] **24...a5**
[24...♘g4! 25.axb4 ♗xf2+ 26.♔g2 ♗d4!
27.♖c2 ♕d6!−+ Svidler] **25.axb4 axb4**

26.♖c2 [26.♕xc6 ♗xd3 27.♗f3 ♖e6 28.♕c8+ (28.♕b5 ♗e4! 29.♗xe4 ♘xe4 30.♗e3 ♖xe3 31.♘xe3 ♖xb2 32.♖f1 ♕e2!) 28...♔h7 29.♖e1 ♕f5 30.♖xe6 ♗xf2+! 31.♔xf2 ♘g4+ 32.♔g2 ♗xf1+ 33.♔xf1 ♕xf3+ 34.♔e1 ♕xg3+ 35.♔d1 fxe6 36.♕xe6 ♕f3+! 37.♔c1 b3!–+ Svidler] **26...♘g4 27.♘e3** [27.♗f4 ♕d4] **27...♕d6!** [27...♕d4 28.♕xc6 ♖xe3? (28...♖e5–+) 29.♗xe3 ♘xe3 30.♕e8+ ♔h7 31.♕xe3± Svidler] **28.♘xg4 hxg4 29.♕xg4 ♗h5 30.♕xh5 ♕xg3+ 31.♔h1 ♕xf2**   0-1
Svidler M/15-8-21

Daniel Stellwagen
Jan Gustafsson
Hamburg 2008 (10)

1.e4 e5 2.♘f3 ♘c6 3.♗b5 a6 4.♗a4 ♘f6 5.0-0 ♗e7 6.♖e1 b5 7.♗b3 0-0 8.c3 d5 9.exd5 ♘xd5 10.♘xe5 ♘xe5 11.♖xe5 c6 12.d3 ♗d6 13.♖e1 ♗f5 14.♕f3 ♖e8 15.♖xe8+ ♕xe8 16.♘d2 ♕e1+ 17.♘f1 ♗g6 18.g3! b4!
[≤ 18...♘xc3? 19.bxc3 ♕xc3 20.♖b1 ♕xd3 21.♗xf7+! ♔f8 22.♗e3! ♗xf7 23.♖d1+–; 18...♖e8 19.♗d1!] **19.c4** [19.h4?! – Ivanchuk-Svidler, Reykjavik m/9 rapid 2015; 19.♗xd5?! cxd5 20.♕xd5 ♖d8! 21.♗g5 (21.♕d4!?

♗e7! (21...f6!? 22.cxb4!±) 22.♕e3 (22.♗h6 ♕xf1+ 23.♖xf1 ♖xd4 24.cxd4 gxh6∓) 22...♕xe3 23.♗xe3 bxc3! 24.bxc3 ♖xd3! 25.♗d4 ♗a3!= Nataf] 21...♕xa1 22.♗xd8 ♗f8 23.♗a5 ♕b1! (23...bxc3? 24.♗xc3 ♕d1 25.♕e5!!±) 24.♗g2 ♗xd3 25.♘d2 ♕c2 26.♕a8 (26.♕g5 h6 27.♕e3 ♗c5 28.♕e1 ♕xb2 29.♗xb4 ♗xb4 30.cxb4 ♕xa2= Vouldis-Gustafsson, Greece tt 2005) 26...♕xd2 27.♗xb4 h5!= Team Ojjeh-Team Nataf, cr 2003] **19...♘f6!?** [19...♘c7 (Radjabov) 20.d4 (20.♗d1 ♘e6 21.♗d2 ♕e5 22.♕xc6 ♖d8 23.♗g4) 20...♖e8 21.♗d1±; 21.♕d1 ♖e2 22.♗e3 ♕xd1 23.♖xd1 ♖xb2 24.f3 ♘e6 25.c5±]

20.♗d1? [20.d4?! ♗h5!! (20...♖d8 21.c5) 21.♕xc6 (21.♕e3 ♗e2) 21...♖e8 22.c5 ♗f8∞; ≥ 20.♕xc6!

♖d8 21.♕b6! ♖d7 22.♗c2! (22.♗a4?! ♗xd3–+; 22.♕e3 ♗e7 23.♕xe1 ♖xe1 24.♗c2 ♘g4 25.♖b1 ♗c5∞) 22...♘g4! 23.♖b1! (23.h3? ♗c7 24.♕c5 ♘e5 25.♕e3 ♗e7 26.♖b1 ♘xc4! 27.♕xe1 ♖xe1; 23.♗f4? ♕xa1 24.♗xd6 h5–+) 23...♕e2! (23...♗c7 24.♕c5! ♕e2 25.♗d2! ♗d6 26.♖e1+) 24.♗d2 ♗c7 (24...♘e5?! 25.♕e3 ♕h5! 26.♗d1! (26.d4? ♘f3+! 27.♔g2 ♗xc2! 28.♕e8+ ♗f8 29.♗xb4 h6 30.♖c1 ♘g5!–+) 26...♕f5! 27.♗e2 f6 (27...♖f8± (Nataf) 28.♖e1) 28.♕e4 (28.b3 ♗c5= Hauenstein-Suto, cr 2010; Novak-Chopin, cr 2008) 28...♕xe4 29.dxe4 ♗xe4 30.♖e1 ♘f3+ 31.♗xf3 ♗xf3 (Dolgov-Simmelink, cr 2010) 32.b3±] 25.♕c5 ♘e5 26.♕e3 ♕xe3 27.♗xe3 ♘xc4 28.dxc4 ♗xc2 29.♖c1 ♗e4⨀] **20...♖e8** [20...♖d8 21.♕e2 ♕xe2 22.♗xe2 ♗e7 23.♗f4 ♗xd3=] **21.♗d2 ♕e5 22.♕xc6?** [22.♖b1 ♗c5 23.♗a4 ♖d8 24.♗f4 ♕e7 25.♗e3=] **22...♗f8** [22...♕xb2 23.♖c1 ♗e5] **23.♗b3?!** [23.♗f3 ♕xb2∓] **23...♗xd3 24.c5** [24.♗e3 ♗e4∓] **24...♗e4** [24...♗xc5 25.♗e3 ♕xb2∓] **25.♕xa6 ♕f5 26.♕e2 ♗c6** [26...♗xc5∓] **27.♘e3 ♗e4 28.f3 ♕d4 29.♖c1 ♗xc5 30.♖c4 ♕e5 31.♖xc5 ♕xc5 32.♕c4** [32.♕f2 ♘d7–+] **32...♕xc4 33.♘xc4 ♗xf3 34.♗xb4 ♖e2 35.♘d2 ♗b7**   0-1

Exercise 1

position after 22...h7-h6

Is it favourable for White to exchange rooks in an isolani endgame?
(solution on page 247)

Exercise 2

position after 26...♖f8-e8

How can White liquidate to a much better endgame?
(solution on page 247)

Exercise 3

position after 23.c4xb5

Here Black simply took back on b5, missing a nice zwischenzug!
(solution on page 248)

The Main Line in the Open Variation

by Alexey Kuzmin

1.	e4	e5	
2.	♘f3	♘c6	
3.	♗b5	a6	
4.	♗a4	♘f6	
5.	0-0	♘xe4	
6.	d4	b5	
7.	♗b3	d5	
8.	dxe5	♗e6	
9.	♘bd2		

For already twenty years, if not more, the plan beginning with 9.♘bd2 has been White's main reply to the Open Variation of the Ruy Lopez. It is the one which struck the most appreciable blow against the image and popularity of this variation. For a long time Black was unable to find acceptable ways of creating counterplay or a sufficiently sound way of holding the position. And devotees of the bold capture of the e4-pawn merely sighed gloomily, remembering that at one time Kortchnoi and then Anand upheld their favourite variation even in matches for the World Championship.

But in very recent years the situation has radically changed. In what used to be considered a rather dubious line, involving the advance of the d-pawn, a number of new ideas have been discovered. Thanks to them the Open Variation of the Ruy Lopez has again become a frequent guest in games at elite tournaments.

9...♘c5 10.c3 ♗e7 11.♗c2 d4

It is this version of the central breakthrough that is currently the main direction of Black's counterplay. The position is regularly upheld by Shakhriyar Mamedyarov, periodically he is assisted by Giri, Nakamura and Wei Yi, and a number of important games with respect to the opening have been played by Humpy Koneru.

An examination of the possibilities of the two sides, beginning from this position, is what this Survey is about.

It should be immediately mentioned that the black player

Shakhriyar Mamedyarov

must be prepared to defend his position in two different types of endgame, which if desired by White can be reached by force. The first of these arises after **12.cxd4 ♘xd4 13.♘xd4 ♕xd4 14.♘f3 ♕xd1 15.♖xd1 0-0**.

And the second after **12.♘b3 d3 13.♘xc5 dxc2 14.♕xd8+ ♖xd8 15.♘xe6 fxe6 16.♗e3 ♖d5 17.♖fc1 ♘xe5 18.♘xe5 ♖xe5 19.♖xc2**.

The white rook can be either on a1 or f1 – this depends on White's 17th move.

Of course, in both of these endgame positions one cannot speak of any marked advantage for White. But nevertheless Black is the one who has to play the more accurately.

The main theme of our discussion is the principal variation **12.♘b3 d3 13.♗b1 ♘xb3 14.axb3 ♗f5**.

The initial position, from which a very interesting strategic battle begins.

White has tried four continuations: 15.♖e1, 15.b4, 15.♗e3 and 15.♗f4.

It should be mentioned that often in this variation different move orders lead to one and the same position.

Talking about White's general strategic plan, two directions can be singled out.

The first is the attempt to eliminate the d3-pawn as quickly as possible. This can be achieved by a direct attack –

15.♗f4 0-0 16.♘e1, or by using the idea of blocking on d4 – 15.♗e3 0-0 16.♗d4 or 16.♘d4. Often White includes the move 16.♖e1 ♕d5 and then plays 17.♗d4. Practice has shown that in exchange for the d-pawn Black is able to pick up the b3-pawn and obtain reasonable play. Here I would mention the games Sengupta-Wei Yi and especially Abdumalik-Koneru, Chengdu 2015.

The second strategic direction is more dangerous for Black. White does not rush to attack the d3-pawn, but after playing h2-h3 and b3-b4 he combines the ideas of driving back the black bishop with g2-g4, the e5-e6 breakthrough, and the inclusion of his bishop in the action via ♗b1-a2.

15.♖e1 ♕d7 16.b4 0-0 17.h3 ♖fd8

This position is currently the subject of topical discussions.

In the game Svidler-Mamedyarov (Reykjavik 2015) White played **18.♗f4** immediately, trying to exploit the nuance that after 18... a5 19.bxa5 ♖xa5 20.♖xa5 ♘xa5 21.♘d4 the white knight, apart from blocking the d-file, is also attacking the opponent's bishop on f5. Mamedyarov responded very accurately, and after a few moves of sharp play a draw was agreed.

18.g4 is more often played. Now 18...♗e6?! is bad, since

after 19.♗f4 by transposition of moves a position is reached from the game Caruana-Mamedyarov, Baku 2015, in which Fabiano accurately demonstrated the defects of the bishop's position on e6. The other retreat is correct – **18...♗g6**.

After this, Caruana against Giri (Stavanger 2015) continued 19.♗f4, while Shirov in a game with Mamedyarov (Reykjavik 2015) preferred to activate his other bishop – 19.♗a2. Both continuations led to sharp and very complicated play with chances for both sides.

Conclusion

In the main and most critical variations, Black's plan with the ...d5-d4 break on the 11th move leads to a very interesting game. The play in them is deeply strategic in character, but at the same time it is full of sharp tactical possibilities. It is too early to produce any evaluative verdict – the discussion is in full swing. For the present Black is successfully parrying attempts by his opponent to demonstrate his opening superiority. Moreover, the character of the play is such that Black can have real chances of seizing the initiative. Of course, his actions must be extremely accurate – a slight mistake or an incorrect move order can lead to serious problems.

A certain drawback to the variation – from the standpoint of employing it not at the highest level or in a game with an opponent of inferior class – is the fact that White has two possibilities of immediately taking the game into a slightly favourable endgame. However, in this case his chances of success are minimal – with accurate play Black should be able to equalize.

Endgame
12.cxd4

Twan Burg
Steven Geirnaert

Skopje tt 2015 (4)

1.e4 e5 2.♘f3 ♘c6 3.♗b5 a6
4.♗a4 ♘f6 5.0-0 ♘xe4 6.d4 b5
7.♗b3 d5 8.dxe5 ♗e6 9.♘bd2
♘c5 10.c3 ♗e7 11.♗c2 d4
12.cxd4 ♘xd4 13.♘xd4 ♛xd4
14.♘f3 ♛xd1 15.♖xd1 0-0
16.♗e3 ♖fd8 17.♘d4 [17.♖dc1 h6
18.♘d4 (18.♗xc5 ♗xc5 19.♗e4 ♗d5
20.♖xc5 ♗xe4 21.♖xc7 ♗xf3 22.gxf3
♖d2 23.b3 ♖e8= Saric-Nielsen, Aix-
les-Bains Ech 2011) 18...♗d5 19.f4
♘e6 20.♘xe6 (20.♘e2 c5=) 20...fxe6
21.♗g6 ♖ac8 22.♗c5 ♗f8 23.♗xe7+
♔xe7 24.♖c5 ♗c4 25.b3 ♗d3 26.♗xd3
♖xd3 27.♖ac1 ♔d7= Hou Yifan-Koneru,
Beijing 2012] 17...♗d5

18.♖ac1 [18.♖dc1 ♗f8 (18...g6!?)
19.♘e2 ♘e6 20.f4 c5= 21.f5 ♘d4
22.♘xd4 cxd4 23.♗xd4 ♗xg2 24.♔xg2
♖xd4 25.♗b3 (Leko-Johannessen,
Tromsø 2013) 25...♖d2+ 26.♔f3 ♖ad8=]
18...♘e6 [18...g6!? 19.♗b1 ♘e6
20.♘e2 f6=] 19.♘f5 ♗f8 20.♗b1!?
[20.a3 ♗d7 (20...a5!? 21.♘g3 b4⇌)
21.♘d6 c6 22.♘e4 ♖ad8 23.f4 c5!
24.f5 ♘d4 25.♘xc5 ♗xc5 26.♗xd4
♗f3! 27.♗xc5 ♖xd1+ 28.♗xd1 ♖xd1+
29.♖xd1 ♗xd1= Vachier-Lagrave-Wei
Yi, Leon 2015] 20...♗b7!? [20...♖d7
21.♘d6 c6 22.♘e4 ♖ad8 23.f4± ♗xe4
24.♖xd7 ♖xd7 25.♗xe4± Brkic-Bosiocic,
Sibenik 2015; 20...♖ab8 21.♘g3 c5
22.f4 c4 23.♘e4 ♗xe4 24.♗xe4 ♗c5
25.♔f2±] 21.♘g3 [21.f4!? g6 22.♘g3
♖xd1+ 23.♖xd1 ♖h6 24.♘e2 ♗g7⇌]
21...♖xd1+ 22.♖xd1 ♖d8 23.♖xd8
♘xd8 24.♘e4 ♗e7 [24...♘c6! 25.f4

♘b4 26.a3 ♘d5 27.♗d2 f6⇌] 25.f4± f6
[25...g6 26.g4±] 26.exf6 gxf6 27.♘c5
♗c8 28.f5 ♗d6?! [28...h5!?±]
29.♗e4 ♗f7 30.g4 ♔e7 31.♔g2
♘f7 32.b3 ♘e5 33.h3 ♘d7?!
[33...a5!?±] 34.♘d3! a5 35.h4!
♘e5 36.♘xe5 ♗xe5 37.g5 ♔d6?
[37...♔f7] 38.♔f3 c5 39.♔g4+−
♗b2 40.♗f4+ ♔e7 41.♔h5 fxg5
42.hxg5 ♗g7 43.♗e3 c4 44.bxc4
bxc4 45.♗c5+ ♔e8 46.f6 1-0

Tigran Gharamian
Dennis Wagner

Biel 2015 (7)

1.e4 e5 2.♘f3 ♘c6 3.♗b5 a6
4.♗a4 ♘f6 5.0-0 ♘xe4 6.d4
b5 7.♗b3 d5 8.dxe5 ♗e6 9.c3
♗e7 10.♘bd2 ♘c5 11.♗c2 d4
12.cxd4 ♘xd4 13.♘xd4 ♛xd4
14.♘f3 [14.♛e2 ♖d8=] 14...♛xd1
15.♖xd1 0-0 16.♘d4 [16.♘g5 h6
17.♗h7+ ♔h8 18.♘xe6 ♘xe6 19.♗e4
♖ad8 20.♗e3 g5 21.♗xg5 hxg5=
Efimenko-Caruana, Poikovsky 2011;
16.♗g5 ♗xg5 17.♘xg5 h6 18.♗h7+
♔h8 19.♘xe6 ♘xe6 20.♗e4 ♖ad8 21.g3
♖fe8= Svidler-Kramnik, Dortmund 2004]
16...♖fd8 17.♗e3 [17.b4 ♘a4 18.♘c6
♖xd1+ 19.♗xd1 ♗f8 20.♗f3 ♖e8 21.a3
♘b6= Hou Yifan-Koneru, Tirana Wch-W
2011 m-5] 17...♗d5 18.♘f5 [18.h4
♘e6 19.♘f5 ♗f8 20.f3 a5 (20...♖d7!?
21.♘d6△!? ♗xf3) 21.♘g3 a4 22.♗e4
c6= Lopez Martinez-Delorme, Barcelona
2015; 18.♖ac1 and 18.♖dc1 see the
game Burg-Geirnaert, Skopje tt 2015]
18...♗f8

19.♘d6 [19.♗g5 ♖d7 20.♘e7+ ♔xe7
21.♗xe7 ♘e6 22.♗e4 c6 23.♗xd5
♖xd5 24.♖xd5 cxd5 25.♖c1 h5 26.f3
♔h7= Svidler-Caruana, Amsterdam
2009] 19...♗xg2 20.♘xf7 ♖xd1+

21.♖xd1 ♗f3 22.♖d4 ♘e6 23.♗b3
♘xd4 24.♘h6+ ♔h8 25.♘f7+ ♔g8
26.♘h6+ ♔h8 27.♘f7+   ½-½

Endgame
12.♘b3/♘e4

Jure Borisek
Matej Sebenik

Slovenia tt 2014 (4)

1.e4 e5 2.♘f3 ♘c6 3.♗b5 a6
4.♗a4 ♘f6 5.0-0 ♘xe4 6.d4 b5
7.♗b3 d5 8.dxe5 ♗e6 9.c3 ♗e7
10.♘bd2 ♘c5 11.♗c2 d4 12.♘b3
d3 13.♘xc5 dxc2 14.♛xd8+ ♖xd8
15.♘xe6 fxe6 16.♗e3 ♖d5 17.♖fc1
[17.♖ac1 ♖xe5 18.♘xe5 ♖xe5 19.♖xc2
(19.c4 ♗c5 20.♗xc5 ♖xc5 21.♖xc2 ♔e7
22.♖fc1 ♖d8= Anand-Mamedyarov, Berlin
Wch blitz 2015) 19...♔f7 20.♖d2 ♖d5
21.♖fd1 ♖hd8= Sevian-Radjabov, Baku
2015] 17...♘xe5 18.♘xe5 ♖xe5
19.♖xc2 ♔f7 [for 19...0-0 see the
game Bologan-Giri, Germany Bundesliga
2012/13] 20.c4 [20.a4 ♖d8=; 20.g3 ♖d8
21.a4 ♖ed5 22.♔g2 ♗c5 23.♗xc5 ♖xc5
24.axb5 axb5 25.♖e2 Klovans-Kortchnoi,
Arvier Wch sen 2006]

20...b4 21.♖d1 ♖d8 22.♖xd8
♗xd8 23.♔f1 [23.♖d2 ♘e8 24.♔f1
♗g5= Kosintseva-Koneru, Kazan 2012]
23...♗g5 24.♔e2= [24.♗a7!? h5
(24...♗e7 25.♖e2 ♗f5 26.♗e3 h5
27.g3 (Sutovsky-Sorokin, Sochi tt 2005)
27...♗c5 28.♗f4 ♗d6=) 25.♗b8 ♖c5
26.♔e2 ♗f4 27.g3 ♗d6 28.f4 (Sutovsky-
Haba, Austria Bundesliga 2015/16)
28...e5 29.fxe5 ♖xe5+=; 24.♗d4 ♖f5
(24...♖a5 25.b3 (Potkin-Amin, Abu Dhabi
2006) 25...e5!? 26.♗a7 ♗e6) 25.b3 h5=]
24...♗xe3 25.fxe3 ♔e7 26.b3 a5
27.a4 bxa3 28.♖a2 ♖g5 29.♔f3
♖f5+ 30.♔e2 ♖g5 31.♔f3   ½-½

Viktor Bologan
Anish Giri

Germany Bundesliga 2012/13 (7)

1.e4 e5 2.♘f3 ♘c6 3.♗b5 a6 4.♗a4 ♘f6 5.0-0 ♘xe4 6.d4 b5 7.♗b3 d5 8.dxe5 ♗e6 9.♘bd2 ♗e7 10.c3 ♘c5 11.♗c2 d4 12.♘e4 d3 13.♘xc5 dxc2 14.♕xd8+ ♖xd8 15.♘xe6 fxe6 16.♗e3 ♖d5 17.♖fc1
[17.♖ac1 ♘xe5 18.♘xe5 ♖xe5 19.♖xc2 (19.c4 ♗c5 20.♗xc5 ♖xc5 21.♖xc2 ♔e7 22.♖fc1 ♖d8= Anand-Mamedyarov, Berlin Wch blitz 2015) 19...♔f7 (for the plan with ...♔f7, see the game Borisek-Sebenik, Slovenia tt 2014) 19...0-0 20.c4 b4 21.♖d1 ♖d8); 17.c4?! bxc4 18.♗ac1 (18.♖fc1 ♗b4 (18...c3 19.bxc3 ♗c5=) 19.♘d2 ♔d7 20.♘xc4 ♖xa2 21.♖xc2 ♘b4 22.♖d2 ♖b8= Buessing-Anderson, Email 2011) 18...♘b4 19.♗d2 (19.a3 ♘d3 20.♖xc2 ♔d7= Hou Yifan-Koneru, Tirana Wch-W 2011 m-4) 19...♘d3 20.♖xc2 ♔d7 21.♖xc4 ♘xb2 22.♖g4 g6= Ehlvest-Mikhalevski, Philadelphia 2004] **17...♘xe5 18.♘xe5 ♖xe5 19.♖xc2** [19.♗d4 ♖g5 (19...♖e2 20.♔f1 ♖d2 21.♗e3) 20.♖xc2 ♔f7 (20...0-0?! 21.♖e2±) 21.♗e3 ♖e5 22.a4 ♖d8=] **19...0-0** [again, for 19...♔f7 See the game Borisek-Sebenik, Slovenia tt 2014] **20.a4** [20.g3!? ♗c5 21.♗f4 ♖ef5 22.♖e1 g5 Sutovsky-Krasenkow, Shenyang 1999; 20.c4 ♗c5 21.cxb5 ♗xe3 22.fxe3 axb5 23.♖xc7 ♖xe3 24.♖d1 h5⇄]

20...bxa4! [20...♗c5] **21.♖xa4 ♗c5! 22.♖e2 ♖d8 23.♔f1** [23.h3 ♖d6=] **23...♖d1+ 24.♖e1 ♖xe1+ 25.♔xe1 ♗xe3 26.fxe3 a5!** [26...♖xe3+?! 27.♔d2 ♖e5 28.♖xa6±] **27.♔d2 ♖b5 28.♔c2 ♖c5= 29.♔b3 ♖b5+ 30.♔a3 ♖c5 31.♖e4 ♔f7 32.♔a4 h5 33.h3 ♔e7**   ½-½

Deep Sengupta
Wei Yi

Tsaghkadzor Wch-tt 2015 (9)

1.e4 e5 2.♘f3 ♘c6 3.♗b5 a6 4.♗a4 ♘f6 5.0-0 ♘xe4 6.d4 b5 7.♗b3 d5 8.dxe5 ♗e6 9.c3 ♗e7 10.♘bd2 ♘c5 11.♗c2 d4 12.♘b3 d3 13.♗b1 ♘xb3 14.axb3 ♗f5 15.♗f4 0-0 [15...♕d5?! 16.♖e1 0-0 17.b4±] **16.♘e1N** [16.♖e1 ♕d7] **16...♕d5 17.♗xd3 ♗xd3 18.♕xd3** [18.♘xd3? ♖fd8∓] **18...♕xb3 19.♕f3?!** [19.♘f3! ♖fd8 20.♕e4 ♕e6=] **19...♕e6 20.♘d3 ♖fd8 21.♖ad1?!** [21.♖fd1]

21...♖d7!∓ 22.♖de1?! [22.♘b4 ♗xb4 23.♖xd7 ♕xd7 24.♖d1 ♕e8 25.cxb4 ♘xb4∓] **22...♖ad8 23.♘c1 ♘a5↑ 24.♘e2 ♘b3 25.♕g3?!** [25.h3] **25...c5∓ 26.♔h1 ♘d2 27.♗xd2 ♖xd2 28.♘f4** [28.f4 ♕f5! 29.♕f3∓] **28...♕f5 29.b3 c4?!** [29...h6! 30.f3 ♖c2∓] **30.bxc4 bxc4 31.h4?!** [31.♘e2! ♗c5 32.♕h4] **31...a5 32.h5?** [32.♖a1∓] **32...a4!-+ 33.h6 ♗g5 34.♘h3 ♖2d3 35.f3 ♗xh6 36.♕h4 ♗d2 37.♖e2 ♗xc3 38.e6 fxe6 39.♕xc4 a3 40.♘f2 ♖d2 41.♖fe1 ♖xe2 42.♖xe2 ♗e5 43.♕b3 ♖b8**   0-1

Zhansaya Abdumalik
Humpy Koneru

Chengdu Wch-tt W 2015 (1)

1.e4 e5 2.♘f3 ♘c6 3.♗b5 a6 4.♗a4 ♘f6 5.0-0 ♘xe4 6.d4 b5 7.♗b3 d5 8.dxe5 ♗e6 9.♘bd2 ♘c5 10.c3 ♗e7 11.♗c2 d4 12.♘b3 d3 13.♗b1 ♘xb3 14.axb3 ♗f5 15.♖e1 [15.♗e3 0-0 16.♖e1] **15...0-0 16.♗e3** [for 16.h3 ♕d7 17.b4 see 16.b4] **16...♕d5 17.♗d4**

17...♖fd8! [17...d2 18.♗e2 ♗xb1 19.♖xb1 ♘xd4 20.♘xd4 ♗g5 21.g3± Caruana-l'Ami, Reykjavik 2012] **18.♗xd3** [18.♖e3 ♘xd4 19.♘xd4 (19.cxd4 c5 20.♗xd3 cxd4 21.♖e2 ♕e6 22.h3 ♖ac8!⇄ 23.♘e1 ♖c6 24.♕b1 (24.♗xf5 ♕xf5 25.♘d3 h5∞) 24...♗xd3 25.♕xd3 h6= Svidler-Motylev, Moscow ch-RUS 2004) 19...♗g6 20.b4 (20.e6!? ♗g5 21.♖xd3 c5 22.exf7+ ♔xf7 23.♘c6 ♗xd3 24.♘xd8 ♖xd8 25.♗xd3 c4♕) 20...c5 (20...a5!? 21.bxa5 c5 22.♘xb5 ♖ab8♕) 21.bxc5 ♗xc5 22.♗a2 ♕b7= Kosteniuk-Koneru, Beijing rapid 2012] **18...♗xd3 19.♕xd3 ♕xb3 20.e6** [20.h3 ♕e6=] **20...fxe6 21.♕e4 ♕c4 22.♕xe6+ ♕xe6 23.♖xe6 ♗d6=** [23...♘xd4 24.♘xd4 ♗f6=] **24.♖e4 a5 25.♖g4 ♖d7 26.♖g5 b4 27.♔f1?!** [27.♖a4=] **27...a4∓ 28.♖g4 a3 29.cxb4 ♗xb4 30.♗c3 ♗xc3 31.bxc3 a2** [31...♘e7!?∓] **32.♖e4 ♖e7 33.♖e2 ♔f7**   ½-½

Dmitry Frolyanov
Sergey Vokarev

Khanty-Mansiysk 2011 (4)

1.e4 e5 2.♘f3 ♘c6 3.♗b5 a6 4.♗a4 ♘f6 5.0-0 ♘xe4 6.d4 b5 7.♗b3 d5 8.dxe5 ♗e6 9.♘bd2 ♘c5 10.c3 ♗e7 11.♗c2 d4 12.♘b3 d3 13.♗b1 ♘xb3 14.axb3 ♗f5 15.♗e3 0-0 16.♗d4 [16.♘d4 ♘xd4 17.cxd4 c5 18.♗xd3 (18.dxc5 ♕d5=) 18...cxd4 19.♗xd4 ♕xd4 20.♗xf5 ♕xb2= Ganguly-Naer, Moscow 2005] **16...♕d5 17.♗xd3** [for 17.♖e1 see the game Abdumalik-Koneru, Chengdu 2015] **17...♗xd3 18.♕xd3 ♕xb3= 19.♕e4 ♕e6** [19...♕c4!?] **20.♗e3 f5 21.♕f4 a5= 22.♖fd1 ♖fd8 23.h4 ♖xd1+ 24.♖xd1 ♖d8 25.♖e1 ♖d5 26.♗c1 ♖d8 27.♗e3 ♖d5 28.♗c1**   ½-½

White Does Not Rush to Eliminate the d3-Pawn: No g4

Peter Svidler
Shakhriyar Mamedyarov
Reykjavik 2015 (5)

1.e4 e5 2.♘f3 ♘c6 3.♗b5 a6
4.♗a4 ♘f6 5.0-0 ♘xe4 6.d4 b5
7.♗b3 d5 8.dxe5 ♗e6 9.♘bd2
♘c5 10.c3 ♗e7 11.♗c2 d4
12.♘b3 d3 13.♗b1 ♘xb3 14.axb3
♗f5 15.♖e1 0-0 16.h3 ♕d7 17.b4
♖fd8 18.♗f4 a5! [18...♕c8?! 19.♗g3
(19.♗a2!?; 19.e6!? ♗xe6 20.♗xd3 ♗c4
21.♖e3±) 19...♕d7= (Karjakin-Wei Yi,
Heixiazi 2015) 20.♖e3!?] 19.bxa5N [19.
g4 ♗g6] 19...♖xa5 20.♖xa5 ♘xa5
21.♘d4

21...g5!= [21...c5 22.e6 fxe6 23.♘xf5
exf5 24.♕xd3 ♕xd3 25.♗xd3 ♖xd3
26.♖xe7±] 22.b4 [22.♗e3 c5]
22...♘c4 23.♗c1 d2! 24.♗xf5
dxe1♕+ 25.♕xe1 ♕d5 26.e6
[26.♗e4 ♕xe5 27.♘c6 ♕e6 28.♗xd8
♗xd8=] 26...♕e5! 27.exf7+
♔xf7 28.♗e4 [28.♕xe5?! ♘xe5
29.♗xh7 ♘c6↑] 28...♖e8= 29.♘f3
♕e6 30.♘d4 ♕e5 31.♘f3 ♕e6
32.♘d4   ½-½

White Does Not Rush to Eliminate the d3-Pawn: g2-g4!

Fabiano Caruana
Shakhriyar Mamedyarov
Baku World Cup 2015 (4)

1.e4 e5 2.♘f3 ♘c6 3.♗b5 a6
4.♗a4 ♘f6 5.0-0 ♘xe4 6.d4 b5
7.♗b3 d5 8.dxe5 ♗e6 9.♘bd2
♘c5 10.c3 ♗e7 11.♗c2 d4 12.♘b3
d3 13.♗b1 ♘xb3 14.axb3 ♗f5
15.♖e1 0-0 16.♗e3 ♕d5 17.b4
♕d7N [17...a5? 18.bxa5 ♖xa5 19.♖xa5

♘xa5 20.♘d4± Cheparinov-Jussupow,
Amsterdam 2008; 17...♖fd8 18.♗a2 (18.
h3 ♕d7 – see the games Timofeev-Reshef
and Giri-Caruana. 18...♕e6!?; 18.♗f4
♕d7 19.h3 a5 – see the game Svidler-
Mamedyarov, Reykjavik 2015) 18...♕d7
19.♗g5 (19.♘d4 ♘xd4 20.♗xd4 ♗xb4
21.e6 ♗xe6 22.♖xe6 fxe6 23.♕g4 ♔h8
24.♗xe6 ♗e7 25.cxb4 ♖xd4= Robson-
Ernst ½-½, Hoogeveen 2008) 19...h6
20.♗xe7 ♕xe7 21.♘d2 ♗e6= Smirnov-
Iordachescu, Khanty-Mansiysk 2008] 18.
h3 ♖fd8 19.g4

19...♗e6?! [≥ 19...♗g6 20.♗f4
– see Caruana-Giri] 20.♗f4 h5
21.♖e3!± ♗xg4 [21...hxg4 22.hxg4
♗xg4 23.♕xd3 ♕xd3 24.♗xd3± ♗e6
25.♘g5 ♗d5 26.♗h7+ ♔f8 27.♗c2
♔g8 28.e6!± Krakalovich-Haag, Email
2010] 22.♕xd3 [22.♖xd3!? ♕e6
23.hxg4 ♕xg4+ 24.♔g3 h4 25.♕c2 g6
26.♔g2! hxg3 27.fxg3±] 22...♕xd3
23.♗xd3 ♗e6 [23...♖xd3 24.♖xd3
♗xh3 25.♘d4 ♘xd4 26.cxd4±]
24.♔h2?! [24.♘g5 ♗d5 25.♗h7+
♔f8 26.e6!±] 24...♗d5± 25.♖g1 [≥
25.♗e2!?] 25...a5!⇄ 26.♗xb5 axb4
27.e6 fxe6 28.♗xc6 ♗xc6 29.♘e5
♗d6= 30.♖eg3 ♖d7 31.♘xd7
♗xf4 32.♘f6+ ♔f7 33.♘xh5
♗xg3+ 34.♖xg3 g6 35.♘f4 ♖a1
36.♖g5 bxc3 37.bxc3 ♗e4 38.♖e5
♖h1+ 39.♔g3 ♖g1+ 40.♔h2
♖h1+   ½-½

Artyom Timofeev
Omer Reshef
Jerusalem Ech 2015 (8)

1.e4 e5 2.♘f3 ♘c6 3.♗b5 a6
4.♗a4 ♘f6 5.0-0 ♘xe4 6.d4 b5
7.♗b3 d5 8.dxe5 ♗e6 9.♘bd2
♘c5 10.c3 ♗e7 11.♗c2 d4 12.♘b3
d3 13.♗b1 ♘xb3 14.axb3 ♗f5
15.b4 0-0 16.♖e1 ♕d7 17.h3 ♖fd8

18.♗f4 a5! 19.g4 [For 19.bxa5 see
the game Svidler-Mamedyarov, Reykjavik
2015] 19...♗g6 20.bxa5 [20.♗a2
♕c8!∞] 20...♖xa5 21.♖xa5 [For
21.♗a2 ♖f8∞ see the game Caruana-
Giri, Stavanger 2015] 21...♘xa5

22.e6 fxe6 23.♘e5 ♕d5 24.♘xg6
hxg6 25.♗xc7 d2!⇄ 26.♖f1
♘c4 [26...♖a8!?⇄] 27.♗xd8 ♗xb2
28.♗xe7!? [28.♕c2 ♗xd8 29.♕xb2
d1♕=] 28...♘xd1 29.♖xd1 ♕b3
30.♖xd2 ♕xb1+ 31.♔g2 ♕e1
[31...♕e4+ 32.f3 ♕e3 33.♖d8+ ♔f7
34.♗b4=] 32.♖d3!= ♔f7 33.♗d6
♕e4+ 34.♖f3+ ♔e8 35.♔g3 g5
36.♖e3 ♕d5 37.♗e5 ♔f7 38.♔h2
♔g6 39.♔g1 ♔f7 40.♔h2 ♔g6
41.♔g1 ♔f7 42.♔h2 ♔g6   ½-½

Fabiano Caruana
Anish Giri
Stavanger 2015 (9)

1.e4 e5 2.♘f3 ♘c6 3.♗b5 a6
4.♗a4 ♘f6 5.0-0 ♘xe4 6.d4 b5
7.♗b3 d5 8.dxe5 ♗e6 9.♘bd2
♘c5 10.c3 ♗e7 11.♗c2 d4
12.♘b3 d3 13.♗b1 ♘xb3 14.axb3
♗f5 15.♖e1 0-0 16.b4 ♕d7 17.h3
[17.♗g5 ♗xg5! (17...♖fd8 18.♗xe7
♕xe7 19.♖e3 a5 (Safarli-Nakamura,
Tromsø 2013) 20.h3!) 18.♗xg5 h6 19.♘f3
♖fd8=] 17...♖fd8 [17...♗g6?! 18.♗g5!
♗xg5 19.♘xg5 a5 20.e6! fxe6 21.♘xe6
♖fe8 22.♘c5± Caruana-Nakamura,
Shamkir 2014] 18.g4 ♗g6 19.♗f4 a5
20.bxa5 [20.♗a2 ♕c8!∞] 20...♖xa5
21.♗a2 ♖f8!∞ [21...♖da8?! 22.e6 ♕d8
23.exf7+ ♔h8 24.♘g5↑ ♖xa2 25.♖xa2
♖xa2 26.♕f3! ♗a6 27.♘e6↑] 22.b4
[22.e6!? ♕d8 23.exf7+ ♔h8 24.♕d2
♕a8⇄] 22...♖a4 23.♕d2?! [23.e6∞]
23...♘d8!∓ 24.♗g5?! [24.♗b3 ♖xa1
25.♖xa1 ♘e6∓] 24...c5! 25.♗xe7
♕xe7 26.bxc5 ♕xc5 27.♘h4?!

♘e6 [27...♕a7!?∓] **28.♗b3** [28.♘xg6 ♖fa8!! (28...hxg6 29.♗b3) 29.♘h4 b4! 30.cxb4 ♕c2!∓] **28...♖xa1 29.♖xa1 ♕xe5?** [29...♘e4! 30.♖e1 ♗a8!→] **30.♘xg6 hxg6 31.♗xe6 fxe6 32.♕xd3=** b4 33.♖c1 ♕f4 34.♖f1 b3 35.♕xg6! ♕c4 36.♖e1 ♖f6 37.♕e8+ ♔h7 38.♕h5+ ♖h6 39.♕e5 ♖xh3 40.♕xe6 ♕xe6 41.♖xe6 ♖xc3 42.♖b6 ♖c4 43.♖xb3 ♖xg4+   ½-½

Alexei Shirov
Shakhriyar Mamedyarov
Reykjavik Ech-tt 2015 (7)

1.e4 e5 2.♘f3 ♘c6 3.♗b5 a6 4.♗a4 ♘f6 5.0-0 ♘xe4 6.d4 b5 7.♗b3 d5 8.dxe5 ♗e6 9.♘bd2 ♘c5 10.c3 ♗e7 11.♗c2 d4 12.♘b3 d3 13.♗b1 ♘xb3 14.axb3 ♗f5 15.♖e1 0-0 16.b4 ♕d7 17.h3 ♖fd8 18.g4 ♗g6

19.♗a2 ♕c8 [19...♔h8!? 20.♗f4 ♖f8!∞ 21.e6!? (21.♕d2 a5 22.e6 ♕d8 (22...fxe6 23.♗xe6 ♕d8∞) 23.exf7 (23. bxa5 ♘xa5 24.♘e5 ♘c4!⇄) 23...axb4∞ 24.♘g5! (24.♗g5? (Bulmaga-Olsarova, Braila 2014) 24...♗f6!∓) 24...♗xg5 25.♗xg5 ♕d6 26.♕e3!⇄) 21...fxe6 22.♗xe6 ♕d8 23.♕d2 a5!∞ 24.bxa5 ♘xa5 25.♘d4 (25.♘e5 ♗h4⇄) 25... c5! 26.♘xb5 ♗a6∞ (26...♗h4∞)] **20.e6** [20.♗g5!? a5! 21.bxa5 (21.♗xe7 ♘xe7 22.bxa5 c5⇔) 21...♗xg5 22.♘xg5 ♘xa5 23.e6 (23.♗xf7+ ♗xf7 24.♘xf7 ♔xf7 25.e6+ ♔g8 26.e7 ♖e8 27.♕xd3 ♘b7 28.♖xa8 ♕xa8 29.♕xb5 ♘d6 30.♕c5 ♕b7= Robson-Hartl, Lechenicher SchachServer 2010) 23...♘c4 24.exf7+ ♗xf7 25.♘xf7 ♔xf7∓] **20...f6 21.♘h4** [21.♗f4 a5 22.bxa5 ♘xa5 23.b4 ♘c4 24.♗xc4 bxc4 25.♖xa8 ♕xa8 26.♗xc7 ♖e8⇔] **21...a5 22.bxa5 ♖xa5∞ 23.b4 ♖a6 24.♗f4 ♕a8 25.♕d2** [25.♘xg6 hxg6 26.♗xc7 ♖c8 27.♗a5 ♘xa5 28.♕xd3! ♘c4 29.♕xg6 ♖xa2 30.♕f7+=] **25...♕a7∞ 26.♖e3?** [26.♗e3 ♕b7 27.f4∞; 26.♘xg6 hxg6 27.♖e3 ♔h7!∓] **26...♖a8?** [26...♗e8!! 27.♘f5 ♖a8 28.♖xd3 ♖xa2 29.♖xa2 ♕xa2 30.♕xa2 ♖xa2 31.♗xc7 ♔f8−+] **27.♘xg6 hxg6 28.♕xd3 ♖xa2 29.♖xa2 ♕xa2 30.♕xg6⇄ ♕d5 31.♖e1 ♔h8 32.♗xc7 ♖f8 33.♗f4 ♘e5 34.♗xe5 fxe5 35.♕h5+ ♔g8 36.♕xe5 ♕c6 37.♖e3 ♗h4**

38.f3?! [38.♕e4! ♗xf2+ 39.♔g2 ♕xe4+ 40.♖xe4 ♗h4 41.♖e5=] **38...♗f6 39.♕h5?** [39.♕e4 ♕xe4 40.♖xe4 ♗xc3∓] **39...♕d6** [39...♕b6! 40.♔f2 ♕d6 41.e7 ♗xe7 42.♕e5 ♕d2+ 43.♖e2 ♗h4+ 44.♔g2 ♕d7∓] **40.e7 ♗xe7 41.♕e5 ♖a8 42.♕xd6 ♗xd6∓ 43.♖d3 ♗e5 44.♖d5 ♗xc3 45.♖xb5 ♖a2 46.h4 ♖b2 47.♖f5 ♗xb4 48.h5 ♖c2 49.♔f1 ♗e7 50.♔e1 ♖h2 51.♔d1 ♔h7 52.♔e1 ♔h6 53.♔f1 ♗h4 54.♖f4 ♗g3 55.♖f5 ♖f2+ 56.♔g1 ♖e2 57.♔f1 ♖h2 58.♔g1 ♖f2 59.♖f7 ♖e2 60.♖f5 ♖c2 61.♔f1 ♗f2 62.♖d5 ♗e3 63.♖f5 ♗a7 64.♖f7 ♗e3 65.♖f5 ♖c5 66.♖f7 ♗d4 67.♔e2 ♔g5 68.♔d3 ♗b2 69.♔e3 ♗h4 70.♔f4 ♖b5 71.♖d7 ♗f6 72.♖f7 ♗g5+ 73.♔e4 ♗h6 74.♖f5 ♖b3 75.♔d5 ♖b6 76.♔e4 ♖a6 77.♖f7 ♖a5 78.♖f5 ♖a7 79.♖d5 ♖a3 80.♖d3 ♖a1 81.♖d5 ♖a8 82.♖f5 ♖a3 83.♔d5 ♖e3 84.♔d4 ♖e7 85.♔d5 ♗c1 86.♔d6 ♗a3+ 87.♔d5 ♔g3∓ 88.g5?? ** [88.♔d4; 88.♔c6] **88...♗h4−+ 89.g6 ♖a7 90.♔e6 ♗c1 91.f4 ♔g4??** [91...♖a6+! 92.♔f7 ♔g4!−+] **92.♖f7 ♖a6+ 93.♔d5!∓ ♗b2 94.h6 gxh6 95.f5??** [95.♖b7!! ♗c3 96.g7 ♖a8 97.♔e6 ♖g8 98.♖c7=] **95...♔g5−+ 96.♔e4 ♖a8 97.♔f3 ♗f6 98.♖h7 ♖g8**   0-1

Exercise 1

position after 27.♘e1-f3

Find the best continuation.
(solution on page 248)

Exercise 2

position after 24.♗f4-g5

Can Black get more than an 'unclear position'?
(solution on page 248)

Exercise 3

position after 29.♖e1xa1

Find the best continuation.
(solution on page 248)

Trying to Choke the Antoshin Part I

by Tibor Karolyi

1.	e4	e5
2.	♘f3	d6
3.	d4	exd4
4.	♘xd4	♘f6
5.	♘c3	♗e7
6.	g3	

Richard Rapport surprised Maxime Vachier-Lagrave somewhat with the Antoshin Variation in Biel 2015. There are some sharp lines for White after 5...♗e7, but the very strong French grandmaster opted for the somewhat slow 6.g3. Michiel Abeln examined this line in 2006, and I will have a look at the games that have been played since. You will find MVL's game in Part II. The only move I will not discuss is 6...d5, with which Black tries to liberate his position at once. According to Vachier-Lagrave, this is slightly better for White, and White's plus score backs the grandmaster's words.

The point of developing the bishop to g2 is that it aims to defend the e4-pawn, a possible target in this line. The bishop tries to stop Black neutralizing White's space advantage with ...d6-d5. On the other hand, the bishop no longer covers the c4-square. White often gains space on the kingside with his pawns in this line.

Minor 6th Moves
6...h5 doesn't seem to cause enough problems for White. In the game Gara-Vajda, Black played 6...♗d7 to prepare 7...♘c6; this preparatory move takes the sting out of the possible ♘xc6 capture. White obtained a small edge with two bishops.

The Immediate 6...♗g4
Attacking the queen with 6...♗g4 is much more popular. In the game Tomczak-Berzinsh, 2012, White castled queenside, which doesn't happen often, and obtained a nice position. In other games, White got a small edge. E.Hansen drew with Khenkin, while Kovchan was able to win against Bytensky. White usually meets 6...♗g4 with 7.f3, after which Black usually withdraws the bishop to d7. Giving up the bishop pair with 7...♗e6 did not work well for Black in Stukopin-Fedoseev, 2012. Black gets nothing for the bishop pair. After 7...♗d7 White has several ways to try and exploit Black having avoided the exchange on d4 with 9.♘de2. Later he transferred the knight to f4 and got some

advantage. I like his idea. After 9.0-0 Bu took on d4 and did not equalize, but got a position which allowed him to outplay his opponent. It's interesting to note that Krivobodorov faced this line twice as White. In the first game he developed the c1-bishop to b2, the second time he went for the e3-square. Both ideas yielded him a slight edge. White can also play a completely different idea: castling queenside and launching a pawn storm with g3-g4. In the game Burg-Fridman, White started the plan with 9.♗f4, Ivanisevic opted for 9.♗e3, and Wojtaszek chose 9.g4. So far, no one has been able to demonstrate how to equalize. However, Black doesn't score badly against queenside castling.

More Popular: 6...♘c6
6...♘c6 is more popular than 6...♗g4. White's main move is 7.♗g2, but White's very good score here justifies a closer look at 7.♘xc6. After 7...bxc6 8.♗g2 Black can castle, but 8...♖b8 and 8...♗a6 have been tried as well. Against the first move Lagno obtained an edge against Stojanovic. Bu improved on Black's play and got a reasonable game, but I think White could have got a small edge. In the game Schneider-Zude, Black tried the interesting 8...♗a6, meeting 9.e5 with 9...dxe5, which did not look great.

Instead, 9...♞d7!? would have been very interesting. After 8...0-0 9.0-0 both 10...♝g4 and 10...♞d7 do not score well. Objectively it looks okay for Black, but the ensuing positions look easier to play with white. Bu, who regularly plays the Antoshin, lost only two games with it. Both losses happened in this line, one against Brkic and one against Judit Polgar.

The Positional 7.♞de2

7.♞de2 has a positional point: with more space it is logical to keep as many pieces on the board as possible. The move is obviously somewhat slow, so it raises the question of what Black can do with this extra time. Pogonina tried 7...h5, but I don't think this creates enough play in compensation for the weakened kingside. Black has another aggressive attempt: 7...d5, temporarily sacrificing a pawn to open the centre. Sadler, against Haslinger, gave back the pawn under favourable conditions. Black could have played better, but that would only have reduced his disadvantage somewhat.

In the game Volokitin-Predojevic Black tried 7...♞e5, and after 8.♝g2 c6 White concentrated on the kingside. This game ended in a draw in 19 moves. There are moves for White that may give him hope for a slight edge. Gopal, however,

stopped ...b7-b5 with 9.a4, and only then started focusing on the kingside. He went on to beat Roktim. Hickl tried 7...a5 against Glek, and did all right, but one attempt is not enough to draw conclusions here. In the game between Zoltan Almasi and Vassallo Barroche, Black tried the interesting 7...♜b8. The idea behind this is to gain space on the queenside. My fellow-countryman won the game, but not because of the opening. Black's simplest move is 7...0-0. After 8.♝g2 there are several plans. 8...♜b8 worked well in Korneev-Kabanov. Korneev stopped ...b7-b5 with 9.a4. It is not clear yet what White should do against the ...♜b8-b5 plan. One way or the other, Black will gain space on the queenside. I think White will be able to get a slight edge.

Allowing the Knight Swap: 7.♝g2

White's most common choice is 7.♝g2. This allows Black to swap the d4-knight, but Black can insert 7...♝g4, or he can just bring his king to safety with 7...0-0. After 7...♝g4 I think 8.♞xc6 offers no more than a balanced position, but both 8.f3 and 8.♞de2 are promising for White. After playing the former move, Nadev and Zufic castled queenside and got pleasant positions. Two other strong players, Maksimenko and Haslinger, chose the slower

Vladimir Antoshin

8.♞de2. It seems that this move gives White an edge, as it is hard for Black to create counterplay against White's kingside pawns. Black can also play 7...♞xd4 8.♕xd4 0-0 9.0-0. At this point Black has several plans. 9...♝e6 worked well in the game Strikovic-Berkovich, but White should try to put pressure on d6 somehow. Black can settle for a slightly worse position with 9...♝d7 and ...♝c6. After 9...c6 White has several ways to put pressure on d6, but none of them is really convincing. Interestingly, Solak allowed the queen swap and still managed to grind down Bogosavljevic.

In **Part II** of this Survey, in **Yearbook 119**, we will investigate Black's most common move, which is 6...0-0.

The Immediate 6...♝g4

Alexander Kovchan
Igor Bitensky
Wijk aan Zee 2013 (4)

1.e4 e5 2.♞f3 d6 3.d4 exd4 4.♞xd4 ♞f6 5.♞c3 ♝e7 6.g3 ♝g4 [6...h5 7.h3 h4 8.g4 d5 (8...♞c6 9.f4 0-0 10.♝g2±) 9.e5 ♞e4 (9...♞fd7 10.e6±) 10.♞xe4 dxe4 11.♝g2 ♕d5 12.0-0 ♕xe5 13.♜e1 0-0 14.♜xe4 ♕d6 15.♝f4 ♕d8 16.♞b5 ♞a6 17.♜d4 ♕e8 18.♞xc7 ♞xc7 19.♝xc7 ♕b5 (Marrero Lopez-Puntier Andujar, Havana 2006) 20.b3±; 6...♝d7 7.♝g2 ♞c6 8.0-0 (8.h3 0-0 9.♝e3 ♜e8 10.♕d2

♞xd4 11.♝xd4 c5 12.♝e3 ♝c6=; 8.♝e3 ♞g4 9.♝f4 ♞xd4 10.♕xd4 ♝f6 11.♕d3 (11.♕d2 g5=) 11...♞e5=) 8...♞xd4 9.♕xd4 ♝c6 10.♝f4 0-0 11.♜ad1 ♞d7 12.♞d5 ♝f6 (12...♜e8 13.♜fe1 h6 14.c4±) 13.♞xf6+ ♕xf6 14.♕xf6 gxf6 (14...♞xf6 15.e5±) 15.♜fe1 ♜fe8 16.♝d2 ♜e7 17.♝c3 ♜ae8 18.f3 ♔g7 19.♔f2± Gara-S.

Vajda, Zalakaros 2014] **7.♕d3** [7.♕d2 c5 8.♘f5 ♗xf5 9.exf5 ♘c6 10.♗g2 0-0 11.h3 ♗d7 12.g4 h6 (12...♖ad8 13.0-0 h6 14.♘d5 ♗xd5 15.♕xd5 ♗b4 16.♕d1 d5=) 13.0-0 ♖fe8 14.b3 ♖ad8 15.♖d1 d5 16.♗b2 d4 17.♘e2 ♗d6 18.♔h1 ♗c7∓ White-Conquest, Great Yarmouth 2007] **7...♘bd7** [7...0-0 8.h3 ♗d7 9.♗g2 ♘c6 10.♗e3 ♖e8 11.0-0-0 ♘e5 (11...♘xd4 12.♗xd4 c5 13.♗e3±) 12.♕e2 c5 13.♘f5 ♗xf5 14.exf5 ♕a5 15.♕b5± ♕d8? 16.f4 a6 (Tomczak-Berzinsh, Warsaw 2012) 17.♕xb7+−] **8.♗g2 0-0** [8...♘c5 9.♕e3 0-0 10.0-0 ♗d7 (10...c6 11.h3 ♗d7 12.b4 ♘a6±) 11.f3 ♗h3 12.♗xh3 ♘xh3 13.♘f5 ♖fe8 (Kollen-Schütte, Germany tt 2014) 14.g4 g6 15.♗xe7+ ♖xe7 16.♕f4±] **9.h3** [9.0-0-0 ♘e5 10.♕e3 ♘c4 11.♕f4 ♖e8 12.♘f5 ♗f8 13.h3 (13.♘h6+ gxh6 14.♘d5±) 13...♗h5 14.♕h4 c6 15.♗g5 ♗g6 16.b3 ♘a3 ½-½ E.Hansen-Khenkin, Ortisei 2013] **9...♘e5**

10.♕e3 ♗d7 11.0-0 ♖e8 12.g4 h6 13.♘f5 [13.b3 ♗f8 14.f4 ♘c6 15.♗b2 d5 16.e5 ♗c5 17.♘xd5 ♘xd5 18.♗xd5 h5 19.♔h2 hxg4 20.♘xc6 ♗xe3 21.♘xd8 ♖axd8 22.♗xb7 ♗b5 23.c4±] **13...♗f8 14.♕g3 c6 15.f4 ♘g6 16.♗e3 d5 17.e5 ♗xf5 18.gxf5 ♘e7 19.♗f2± ♘xf5 20.♕d3 ♘e4 21.♘xe4 dxe4 22.♕xe4 g6 23.♖fd1 ♕c7 24.♖d3 ♖ad8 25.♖ad1 h5 26.♕c4 ♗h6 27.♗e4 ♖xd3 28.♖xd3 ♖d8 29.♗xf5 gxf5 30.♖g3+ ♔h7 31.♕e2 h4 32.♖d3 ♖xd3 33.♕xd3 ♔g6 34.♕d4 ♕e7 35.♔g2 b6 36.♘f3 ♗f8 37.a4 ♕b7 38.c4 ♗e7 39.♔e2 ♕c8 40.♔f3 ♕e6 41.b3 ♕c8 42.a5 ♕d8 43.♕xd8 ♗xd8 44.♔e2 ♔g7 45.♔d3 ♗f8 46.♔c3 ♔e8 47.♔b6 ♗xb6 48.axb6 axb6 49.c5 b5 50.♔b4 ♔d7 51.♔a5 ♔e6 52.♔b6 ♔d5 53.b4 ♗e4 54.♔xc6 ♔xf4 55.♔d5 ♔g3 56.c6**

f4 57.c7 f3 58.c8♕ f2 59.♕g4+ ♔h2 60.♕f3 ♔g1 61.♕xf7 ♔h1 62.e6   1-0

Andrey Stukopin
Vladimir Fedoseev
Sochi jr 2012 (7)

1.e4 e5 2.♘f3 d6 3.d4 exd4 4.♘xd4 ♘f6 5.♘c3 ♗e7 6.g3 ♗g4 7.f3

7...♗e6?! [7...♘c8 8.♗g2 0-0 9.0-0 c6 10.a4 a5 11.h3 (11.♗e3 ♘a6 12.♕d2 ♖e8 13.♖ad1 ♗f8 14.♖fe1 ♕c7 15.♗f4 ♘b4 16.♘b1 h6 17.♘a3±) 11...♘a6 12.f4 ♘c5 13.♗e3 ♖e8 14.♗f2 ♗f8 15.♖e1 g6 16.♕d2 ♕c7 17.♖ad1 ♗d7 18.g4± Kulovana-Moser, Heraklio 2007] **8.♘xe6 fxe6 9.♗h3 ♕d7 10.♘d5 ♗d8?** [10...♘a6 11.♘f4 ♘c5 12.b4±] **11.♘f4 g5 12.♗xe6 ♕e7 13.♗c8 gxf4 14.♗xb7 fxg3 15.hxg3 c6 16.♗xa8 ♗b6 17.♗f4+− ♗c5 18.c3 0-0 19.♕b3+ ♔h8 20.0-0-0 ♘fd7 21.♕b7 ♕e6 22.♖h6 ♕xa2 23.♖dh1**   1-0

Radoslaw Wojtaszek
Mateusz Bartel
Poznan 2014 (3)

1.e4 e5 2.♘f3 d6 3.♘c3 ♘f6 4.d4 exd4 5.♘xd4 ♗e7 6.g3 ♗g4 7.f3 ♗d7

8.g4 [8.♗g2 ♘c6 9.0-0 (9.♘de2 ♕c8 10.♘f4 ♘e5 11.♕e2 c6 12.a4 0-0 13.0-0 ♘e8 14.b3 ♘c7 15.♗a3 ♖d8 16.♖ad1 ♘e8 17.♖d2 ♗f8 18.♖fd1± Sevillano-Barclay, Indianapolis 2009) 9...♘xd4 10.♕xd4 0-0 11.♗e3 (11.b3 c6 12.♗b2 ♕b6 13.♕xb6 axb6 14.a4 ♘e8 (14...d5 15.exd5 ♘xd5 16.♘xd5 ♗c5+ 17.♔h1 cxd5 18.f4±) 15.f4 f5 16.♗h3 ♖d8 (Krivoborodov-Jovanovic, Schwarzach 2008) 17.♖ad1±) 11...♗c6 (11...♖e8 12.♖ad1 c5 13.♕d2 ♕b6 14.g4 ♗c6 15.g5 ♘d7 (Weinzettl-Okhotnik, Vienna 2012) 16.b3±) 12.♖ad1 ♖e8 (12...♗d7 13.♘d5 ♗f6 14.♘xf6+ ♕xf6 15.♗xf6 ♘xf6 16.♗d4 ♖fe8 17.♖fe1± Krivoborodov-Persson, Vienna 2013) 13.♔h1 a5 14.♖fe1 ♗d7 15.♘d5 ♗f6 (15...♘e5 16.f4±) 16.♘xf6+ ♕xf6 (Tazbir-Bu Xiangzhi, Guimaraes 2012) 17.♕xf6 ♘xf6 18.♗d4±; 8.f4 ♘c6 9.♕d2 ♘e5 10.♗e2 (10.0-0-0 0-0 (10...c5 11.♘db5±) 11.g4 c5 12.♘f5±) 10...a6 11.g4 b5

12.0-0-0 (12.a3 c5 (12...g6 13.0-0-0 c5 14.♘b3 ♖c8 15.♗h6±) 13.♘f5 ♗xf5 14.exf5 ♘c6 15.0-0-0 ♘d4 16.♗e3 b4 17.axb4 ♘xe2+ 18.♘xe2± P.Papp-Szieberth, Hungary tt 2014) 12...g6 (12...b4 13.♘d5 ♘xd5 14.exd5 a5 15.g5±) 13.♕e3 ♕b8 (13...b4 14.♗xe5 dxe5 15.♘c6±) 14.♘d5 (14.♗h6±) 14...♘xd5 15.exd5 0-0 16.♗xe5 dxe5 17.♕xe5 ♗d6∓ Burg-R.Fridman, Netherlands tt 2010/11; 8.♗e3 ♘c6 (8...a6 9.g4 h6 10.♕d2 ♘c6 11.0-0-0 (11.♘f5 0-0 12.0-0-0±) 11...♘e5 12.h3 c5 13.♘f5 ♗xf5 14.exf5 ♘xf3 15.♕f2 ♘d4 16.♗xd4 cxd4 17.♕xd4± B.Savchenko-Sirotine, St Petersburg 2006; 8...0-0 9.♕d2 a6 (9...♖e8 10.0-0-0 c5? 11.♘db5 ♗xb5 12.♘xb5 ♘c6 13.♘xd6 ♗xd6 14.♕xd6 ♕a5 15.♕xc5+− Collins-Wall, Bunratty 2008) 10.g4 b5 11.0-0-0 b4 12.♘ce2 c5 13.♘f5 ♗xf5 14.gxf5 ♘c6 (Glantz-Heimrath, Pardubice 2014) 15.♘f4 ♗e5 16.♖g2±) 9.♕d2 (9.♕e2 0-0 10.0-0-0 ♘xd4 11.♗xd4 b5 12.♘xb5 ♖b8 13.c4 (13.♘c3 c6 14.e5±) 13...c6 14.♘c3 c5 (14...♖e8 15.♗xa7±) 15.♗e3 ♕a5 16.g4 ♗c6 17.h4 ♗b7 (Roa Alonso-Garcia Fernandez, San Sebastian 2008) 18.♕c2±) 9...0-0 10.0-0-0 a6 (10...♘xd4 11.♗xd4 ♗e6 12.f4 (12.♔b1!?) 12...c5 13.♗e3 ♕a5 14.♘d5 ♕xd2+ 15.♖xd2 ♘xd5 16.exd5 ♗f5= Stojic-Sriram, Parramatta 2009) 11.g4 ♘xd4 12.♗xd4 b5 13.♔b1 (13.g5 ♘h5 14.♗e3±) 13... b4 14.♘e2 c5 15.♗e3 ♗c6 16.♘g3 g6 17.♗h6 ♘d7 (17...♖e8 18.♘f5±) 18.♗xf8 ♕xf8 19.♗c4± Ivanisevic-Tadic, Ulcinj 2014) **8...♘c6 9.♗e3 0-0 10.♕d2** [10.g5 ♘h5 11.f4 g6 12.♘e2 ♘g7 13.h4±] **10...♘xd4 11.♗xd4 c5 12.♗e3 ♗c6 13.0-0-0 ♘d7 14.g5 ♘b6** [14...♕a5 15.♔b1 (15.h4!? f5) 15...♖ae8 16.♘d5 ♕xd2 17.♖xd2±] **15. h4 ♕e8 16.h5 ♖d8 17.♘d5 ♗xd5 18.exd5 ♕a4 19.♔b1** [19.h6±] **19...♘c4 20.♗xc4 ♕xc4 21.g6± ♗f6 22.gxh7+ ♔xh7 23.♗g5 ♖de8 24.h6 ♖e2 25.hxg7+ ♔xg7 26.♗h6+ ♔g6 27.♖dg1+ ♔f5 28.♖g5+ ♗xg5 29.♕xg5#** 1-0

Ante Brkic
Bu Xiangzhi
Biel 2011 (10)

1.e4 e5 2.♘f3 d6 3.d4 exd4 4.♘xd4 ♘f6 5.♘c3 ♗e7 6.g3 ♘c6 7.♘xc6 [7.♘ce2 ♖b8 (7...♘xe4 8.♗g2 d5∓) 8.a4 a6 9.a5 ♘b4 10.♗g2 c5 11.♗d2 ½-½ Lastin-Kabanov, Voronezh 2007; 7.♗b5 ♗d7 8.0-0 (8.♗f4 0-0 9.♕d2? ♘xe4 10.♘xe4 ♘xd4∓) 8...0-0 9.♗f4 ♘xd4 10.♕xd4 ♗xb5 11.♘xb5 ♕d7 12.a4 ♖fe8 13.f3 ♘h5 14.♗e3 c6 15.♘c3 ♗f6 16.♕d3 ♗e5 17.♗d4 ♕c7 18.♖ad1 ♖ad8= Heinrich-Ciron, playchess.com 2006] **7...bxc6 8.♗g2 0-0** [8...♖b8 9.0-0 (9.e5 dxe5 10.♗xc6+ ♗d7 11.♗xd7+ ♕xd7 12.♕xd7+ ♔xd7=) 9...0-0 10.b3 (10.♘e2 c5 11.c4 ♘d7 12.f4 ♗f6 13.♖b1 ♖e8 14.♕c2 ♗b7∓ 15.g4? ♕e7 16.♘g3 ♘d4+ 17.♔h1 ♘f6 Osmanodja-Zude, Nuremberg 2013)

10...♘d7 (10...c5 11.♗f4 ♗e6 12.♕e2 (12.♖e1) ♘g4 13.♘d5 ♖e8 14.♕e2 ♕d7 15.♖ad1 ♖d8 16.♗c1±) 12...♘d7 13.♖ad1 ♗f6 14.♘d5 ♗xd5 (14...♖e8 15.♘xf6+ ♕xf6 16.♗c1±) 15.♖xd5 ♕e7 (15...♗d4 16.♗d2 g6 17.c3 ♗g7 18.f4±) 16.♕a6 ♗e5 17.c3 c6 18.♕dd1± Lagno-Stojanovic, Plovdiv Ech-W 2008) 11.♗e3 ♘f6 12.♕d2 c5 13.♖ad1 ♖e8 (13...♘b6 14.f4 ♗b7 15.e5±) 14.♘d5 ♗b7 15.♘xf6+ (15.♕a5±) 15...♕xf6 (15...♘xf6 16.f3±) 16.f3 ♗e6 17.♖fe1 (Thorhallsson-Bu Xiangzhi, Reykjavik 2013) 17...♘e5=; 8...♗a6

9.e5 dxe5 (9...♘d7 10.exd6 (10.♗xc6 0-0 11.f4 ♖b8☖) 10...♗xd6 11.♕d4 (11.♗xc6 0-0 12.♗e3 ♘e5∓) 11...0-0 12.♗e3=) 10.♗xc6+ ♘f8 11.♕xd8+ (11.♗e3!? g6 12.♕f3 ♖b8 13.♖d1 ♕c8 14.b3±) 11...♖xd8 12.♗e3 g6 13.♖d1 (13.a3 ♔g7 14.♗xa7±) 13...♔g7 14.♗xa7 ♗b4 15.a3 ♗xc3+ 16.bxc3 ♗c4 17.♗c5 (Schneider-Zude, Germany 2013) 17...♘d5=] **9.0-0 ♘d7** [9...♘g4 10.♕d2 (10.♕d3 ♕c8 11.♖e1 ♘d7 12.f3 ♗e6 13.f4 ♖b8 14.b3 ♘b6 (14...♖e8 15.♗e3 ♕b7=) 15.a4 a5 16.♗d2 ♘h3 17.♘e2 ♗xg2 18.♔xg2 ♖a8 19.♘d4 ♕d7 20.♘f5± Zelcic-Jovanovic, Plitvicka Jezera 2013) 10...♕c8 11.♖e1 ♖b8 12.b3 ♗h3 13.♗h1 ♘d7 14.♗b2 ♗f6 15.♘d1 ♕d8 (15...♖e8=) 16.f4 ♗xb2 17.♘xb2 ♖e8 18.♘d3 ♕f6 19.♘f2± Klundt-Zaragatski, Nuremberg 2012] **10.b3** [10.h3 ♖b8 (10...♗f6 11.♖b1 ♖b8 12.♗e3 c5 13.♕e2 ♗xc3 14.bxc3 ♘b6=) 11.b3 ♗b7 12.♗b2 ♗f6 13.♕d2 ♘b6 14.♖ad1 c5 15.♖fe1 ♗c6 (15...♘d4=) 16.♗a1 (16.e5±) 16...♗d4 17.♘h2 (17.♘d5 ♗xa1 18.♖xa1 ♖e8 19.♗e3±) 17...♗b7 18.a4 ♖e8 19.f4 ♘d7 (Nestorovic-D. Popovic, playchess.com 2007) 20.♘d5±] **10...♗f6 11.♗b2 ♖b8** [11...♗b7

12.♖e1 ♖b8 13.♕d2 c5 14.♖ad1 ♖e8 15.♗c1 ♗c6 (15...g6 16.♘d5 ♗d4 17.♕a5 ♗xd5 18.exd5 ♕f6⇄) 16.♘d5 ♗e5 17.♕a5 ♘b6 18.♗d2 (18.♗f4 ♗xf4 19.♘xf4 ♖e5 20.♘d5 ♖a8 21.c4±) 18...♖a8 19.c3 g6 20.c4± Salgado Lopez-Deviatkin, Cappelle-la-Grande 2008; 11...♘b6 12.♕d2 (12.f4 ♖b8 13.♕d3 d5 14.e5 ♗e7 15.♘e2±) 12...♖b8 13.♖ab1 c5 14.♗a1 ♖e8 15.♖fe1 ♘d7 16.♘d5 ♗xa1 17.♖xa1 ♗c6 18.c4 h6 19.h4 ♘d7 20.♕a5± Gao Rui-Wen Yang, Hefei rapid 2011] **12.f4** [12.♕d2 ♖e8 13.♖ad1 c5 14.♗c1 ♘b6 15.♖fe1 ♘g4 (15...h5!?) 16.♘e2 a5 17.h3 (17.a4 c4=) 17...♗xe2 18.♖xe2 a4 19.♔h2 ♘c8 20.f4 axb3 21.cxb3 (J. Polgar-Bu Xiangzhi, Khanty-Mansiysk ol 2010) 21...♗d4=] **12... c5** [12...♘b6 13.e5 dxe5 14.♘e4 ♗c2 (Kovchan-I.Jensen, Copenhagen 2010) 15.♕xd8 ♗xd8 16.♗c1±]

13.e5 dxe5 14.♘e4 exf4 15.♘xf6+ ♘xf6 16.♖xf4 ♕xd1+ [16...♖b8 17.♕xd8 ♖xd8 18.♗xf6 gxf6 19.♖xf6 ♗e6 20.♖e1 c4± Klek-Zude, Nuremberg 2013; 16...♗e6 17.♕f1 (17.♗xf6 ♕xd1+ (17...gxf6 18.♕h5±) 18.♖xd1 gxf6 19.♖a4 ♖bd8 20.♖e1±) 17...♗d5 (17...♖b8 18.♖xf6 gxf6 19.♖d1 ♖d4 20.♗xd4 cxd4 21.♕a6±) 18.♗xf6± Perunovic-Jovanovic, Hungary tt 2012/13] **17.♖xd1 ♗e6 18.♖a4 ♖fd8 19.♖xd8+ ♖xd8 20.♖xa7 ♖d1+ 21.♔f2 h5 22.♔f3± ♘g4+ 23.♔e2 ♖b1 24.♗c3 ♗f5 25.h3 ♘h2 26.♗xh5 f6 27.♖c7 ♖c1 28.g4 ♖xc2+ 29.♗d2 ♗e4 30.♔e3 ♔h7 31.♔xe4 ♖xd2 32.a4 ♖d4+ 33.♔e3 ♘f1+ 34.♔f2 ♖f4+ 35.♔e1 ♘h2 36.♗f7 ♘f3+ 37.♔d1 ♖d4+ 38.♔c2 ♖d2+ 39.♔c3 ♖h2 40.♖xc5 ♘e5 41.♗c4 ♖xh3 42.♔b4 ♖h1 43.a5 ♖a1 44.♗b5 ♘xg4 45.a6 ♘e5 46.♖xe5 fxe5 47.♗a4** 1-0

The Positional 7.♘de2

Zoltan Almasi
Mauricio Vassallo Barroche
Spain tt 2014 (5)

1.e4 d6 2.d4 ♞f6 3.♞c3 e5 4.♞f3 exd4 5.♞xd4 ♝e7 6.g3 ♞c6 7.♞de2

7...♜b8 [A] 7...h5 8.h3 ♝e6 9.♝g2 ♕d7 (9...0-0 10.0-0 ♕d7 11.♞f4 ♝c4 12.♜e1 h4 13.b3 ♝a6 14.g4 ♜ae8 15.♝b2 ♞e5 16.♞cd5 ♝d8 17.♞b4 ♝b5 18.c4 c5 Pantani-Ciron, playchess.com 2006 19.cxb5 cxb4 20.a4±) 10.♞f4 ♝c4 11.♝e3 (11.b3 ♝a6 12.h4 0-0 13.♝b2 (13.♞xh5 ♞xh5 14.♕xh5 ♝b4♔) 13...♞e5 (13...g6 14.♞cd5±) 14.♞xh5 ♜ae8 15.f4±) 11...♞e5 12.♞cd5 (12.b3 ♝a6 13.♞cd5 0-0-0 14.♝xa7 ♜de8 15.♝e3±) 12...♞xd5 13.♞xd5 ♝xd5 (13...h4 14.g4 0-0 15.f4±) 14.♕xd5 ♞c6 15.♕xc6+ ♞xc6 16.h4 (16.f4±) 16...♞f6 17.0-0-0 0-0-0 18.f4± Forsaa-Pogonina, Gibraltar 2011;

B) 7...d5 8.exd5 ♞b4 9.♝g2 ♝f5

10.♞d4 (10.0-0 ♞xc2 11.♞d4 (11.♜b1 ♞b4=) 11...♞xd4 12.♕xd4 0-0 13.♝f4 ♝d6 (13...a6 14.♞d1 (14.♞a4 ♝d6 15.♞c5 ♜b8 16.♜fe1 ♜e8 17.b4±) 14...♝d6 15.♞e3 ♕d7 16.♜ac1 ♜ac8 17.♞c4 ♝xf4 18.♕xf4 ♞g6 (18...♝h3 19.♝xh3 ♕xh3 20.♞e3 ♕d7 21.♜fd1

♜fe8 22.♞c4±) 19.♜fd1± Blehm-Zivanic, Washington DC 2006) 14.♜ac1 a6 15.♞a4 ♕d7 16.♜fd1 (16.b4 ♜e8 (16...b6 17.♜c6±) 17.♞c5±) 16...b5 17.♞c3 ♜e8 18.♝xd6 cxd6 19.♕f4 ♕f6 ½-½ Brkic-Jovanovic, Bosnjaci 2006) 10...♝g4 11.♕d2 (11.♞ce2 ♞bxd5 12.h3 ♝xe2 13.♕xe2 0-0 14.0-0±) 11...♞bxd5 12.♞xd5 ♞xd5 13.0-0 0-0 14.c4 ♝b4?! (14...♞b6 15.♝xb7 ♜f6 16.♞c6 ♕xd2 17.♝xd2 ♞xc4 18.♝b4±) 15.♕c2 ♞e7 16.♝e3 (16.♕e4 ♕d7 17.♕xb7±) 16...♕d7 17.c5 c6 18.♞b3 a5 19.a3 a4 20.axb4 axb3 21.♕xb3± Sadler-Haslinger, Haarlem 2011;

C) 7...♞e5 8.♝g2 c6 9.a4 (9.f4 ♞g6 10.h3 0-0 (10...♞b6 11.b3 0-0 12.♕d3 ♝d7 13.♝e3 ♕a5 14.0-0±) 11.0-0 (11.♝e3 ♜e8 (11...♞c7 12.♞d4±; 12.♕d2 b5⇄) 12.♕d3 ♕c7 13.♞d4±) 11...♜e8 12.♝e3 ♝f8 13.♕d2 (13.a4 d5⇄) 13...b5 14.a3 a5 15.e5 (15.♞d4±) 15...dxe5 16.♕xd8 ♜xd8 17.♝xc6 ♝xh3 18.♝xa8 ♝xf1 19.♜xf1 ♞g4 ½-½ Volokitin-Predojevic, Sarajevo 2005) 9...♝g4

10.f4 ♞g6 11.h3 ♝d7 12.♝e3 h5? (12...0-0 13.♕d3 c5 14.0-0-0 ♕a5 15.g4 ♞h4 16.♝f1±) 13.♝d4 (13.♞d4±) 13...♕c8 14.♕d3 ♞f8?! (14...♕c7±) 15.0-0-0 ♞e6 16.e5 dxe5 17.♝xe5 ♞d5 18.♝xd5 cxd5 19.♜xd5+- Gopal-Roktim, Chennai 2008;

D) 7...a5 8.♝g2 0-0 9.0-0 ♜e8 10.h3 ♝f8 11.g4 (11.♝e3 ♝d7 12.b3 g6 (12...♜b8 13.♕d2 b6 14.♞f4±) 13.♕d2 ♞c5 14.♜ad1±) 11...♝d7 12.♝e3 ♜b8 13.♕d2 b6 14.♞g3 ♞ce5 15.b3 ♞c5 16.♜ad1 ♝b7 17.♞d5 ♞ed7 18.♝g5 ♕c8 19.♜fe1 (19.a4!?) 19...c6 20.♞c3 b5∞ Glek-Hickl, Switzerland 2009;

E) 7...0-0 8.♝g2 ♜e8 (8...♜b8 9.a4 a6 10.a5 (10.♞f4 b5 11.axb5 axb5 12.0-0±) 10...♞b4 11.0-0 c5 12.h3 (12...♞c6 (12...♜e8 13.b3 ♝f8

14.♝b2 ♞c6 15.♕d2 ♕xa5 16.♞cd5 ♞xd5 17.exd5♔) 13.♞cd5±) 12...♞c6 13.f4 ♞xa5 14.e5 ♞e8 15.♞d5 ♞c6 16.♞xe7+ ♕xe7 17.exd6 ♞xd6 18.♞c3 ♜d8 19.♞d5 ♕f8♔ Korneev-Kabanov, Voronezh 2007; 8...♞e5 9.0-0 (9.f4 ♞g6 10.♕d3 c6 11.a4 ♕c7 (11...♕a5 12.♝d2 ♜e8 13.0-0-0 ♞g4 14.♝e1±) 12.♝d2 ♜e8 13.0-0 ♝f8 14.♔h1 ♝d7 15.b4 (15.♝e3 a5 16.♝d4±) 15...♜ad8 16.a5 c5 17.b5 ♞c8 18.♞g1 c4∞ Hector-Seel, Germany Bundesliga 2009/10) 9...c6 10.a4 ♜e8 11.b3 (11.a5!?) 11...♞g6 12.♝b2 ♕a5 13.h3 ♝d7 14.f4 ♜ad8 15.♕e1 (15.♞d4 ♝f8 16.♕d3 ♕h5 17.g4 ♕a5 18.♜ad1±) 15...♕h5 (15...♝c8 16.♜d1 ♕c5+ 17.♞d4±) 16.f5 d5 17.fxg6 ♝c5+ 18.♔h1 hxg6 19.♜xf6 gxf6 20.♕f1± Howell-Berkovich, La Massana 2008; 8...♝e6 9.0-0 ♞d7 10.♞d5 ♝f6 11.♞xf6+ (11.♝ef4 ♝e5 12.c3 g6 13.♝e3 ♝g7 14.♞xe6 fxe6 15.♞f4±) 11...♕xf6 12.h3 ♞b6 13.f4 ♝c4 14.♝f2 ♜fe8 15.♞c3 ♜ad8 16.♝d2 a5 (16...d5 17.e5 ♕e7 18.b3 d4 19.♞e4 ♝d5=) 17.b3 ♝a6 18.g4± Cherniaev-Wade, London 2008) 9.0-0 (9.h3 ♜b8 10.♝e3 ♝f8 11.g4 b5 12.g5 (12.a3) 12...♞d7 13.♕d2 a5 14.b3 ♞c5 15.♞g3 b4 16.♞d5 ♞e5 17.f4 ♞g6 (17...♞ed7 18.♝f2 c6 19.♝e3 a4=) 18.0-0-0 ♝a6 (A.Ivanov-Kaufman, Tulsa 2008) 19.h4±) 9...♝f8 (9...♞d7 10.h3 ♞c5 11.♝e3 ♝e6 12.♕d2; ½-½ Sedlak-Bogosavljevic, Vrsac 2008 12.♞d5!?) 10.h3 ♞e5

11.g4 (11.f4 ♞g6 12.♔h2 ♝d7 13.♕d3 c5 ½-½ Sharapov-Okhotnik, Mukachevo 2013) 11...c6 12.♞g3 ♞c4 13.b3 ♞b6 (13...♕a5 14.♞ce2 ♞e5 15.g5 ♞fd7 16.♝b2 ♞g6 17.f4 ♞h4 18.♝h1±) 14.g5 ♞fd7 15.♝e3 ♕c7 16.♕d2 ♞e5 (Prenzler-Schnitzspan, Bad Homburg 2011) 17.f4±] **8.♝g2 b5 9.0-0** [9.a3 0-0 10.0-0 ♜e8 11.h3 ♝f8 12.g4 a5 13.♞g3 ♝a6 14.g5 (14.♜e1 g6

15.♗g5 h6 16.♗e3 ♘e5 17.♕c1 ♔h7 18.f4 ♘c4 19.♗f2=) 14...♘d7 15.♘d5 ♘e7 16.♘xe7+ ♗xe7 17.f4 ♘c5 18.b3 ♗f8 19.♗b2 ♗b7 20.♕d4 ♘e6= Bobras-Seel, Germany Bundesliga 2009/10] **9...0-0 10.h3 a5 11.♖e1 ♖e8 12.a3** [12.♘d5!? ♘xd5 (12...a4 13.♗e3 ♘e5 14.b3 b4 15.♘d4 axb3 16.axb3 ♗b7 17.♘f5±) 13.exd5 ♘e5 14.♘d4±] **12...♗d7 13.♘f4 ♗f8 14.b3** [14.♘cd5 ♘e5 15.♗d2 ♘xd5 16.♘xd5 ♘c4=] **14...g6 15.♗b2 ♗g7 16.♖b1** [16.a4 b4 17.♘b5 ♘e5 18.c4 bxc3 19.♗xc3±] **16...b4 17.axb4 axb4 18.♘cd5 ♘xd5 19.♘xd5 ♗xb2 20.♖xb2 ♗e6= 21.♘e3 ♕f6 22.♖a2 ♕c3 23.♕a1 ♕xa1 24.♖exa1 ♘d4 25.♖a7 ♘b5 26.♖7a5 f6 27.e5 fxe5 28.♗c6 ♘d4 29.♗xe8 ♖xe8 30.♖a8 ♔f8 31.g4 h5 32.♔g2 ♗d7 33.♖xe8+ ♔xe8 34.gxh5 gxh5 35.♔g3 ♗c6 36.♔h4 ♗f3 37.♖a4 c5 38.♖a7 ♗e4 39.♔xh5** 1-0

Allowing the Knight Swap 7.♗g2

Dragan Solak
Boban Bogosavljevic
Kragujevac ch-SRB 2010 (6)
1.e4 e5 2.♘f3 d6 3.d4 exd4 4.♘xd4 ♘f6 5.♘c3 ♗e7 6.g3 ♘c6 7.♗g2

7...♘xd4 [7...♗g4 8.♘de2 (8.♘xc6 bxc6 9.f3 ♗e6 10.0-0 h5 (10...0-0 11.♗e3 ♖b8 12.b3 c5 13.♘e2 c6 14.♘f4 ♗c8=) 11.h3 ♖b8 12.b3 d5 13.e5 ♘d7 14.f4 ♗f5 15.♘e2 ♘c5+ 16.♔h2 ♗g4 17.♕d3± Roganovic-Nadj Hedjesi, Subotica 2008; 8.f3 ♗xd4 9.♕xd4 ♗d7 10.♗e3 (10.g4 0-0 11.♗e3 ♗e6 12.g5 (12.0-0-0±) 12...♘h5 13.f4 (13.♕d2±) 13...f6 14.f5 ♗f7 15.g6 hxg6 16.0-0-0 c6 17.fxg6 ♗xg6 18.♖hg1± Nedev-Voiska, Plovdiv 2013) 10...b5 11.g4 c5 12.♕d2

b4 13.♘e2 ♗c6 (13...♗b5 14.0-0-0 0-0 15.♘g3 g6 16.♗h6 ♖e8 17.♘f5±) 14.♘g3 g6 15.0-0-0 ♕a5 16.♔b1 0-0-0 17.g5± ½-½ Zufic-Stojanovic, Zadar 2009) 8...♕d7 (8...♘e5 9.f4 ♘g6 10.h3 ♗xe2 11.♕xe2 c6 12.♗e3 ♕a5 13.0-0-0 0-0 14.g4 (14.♔b1 ♖fe8 15.h4 h5 16.♗f3±) 14...♘d7 (14...♘h4 15.g5±) 15.h4 ♖fe8 (15...b5 16.h5 b4 17.hxg6 bxc3 18.gxf7+ ♖xf7 19.♔b1±) 16.g5 b5 17.h5± Maksimenko-Krivec, Rogaska Slatina 2009; 8...♗c8 9.h3 ♗d7 10.♗e3 (10.g4 h6 11.♘g3 0-0 12.♘f5 ♖e8 13.♘xe7+ ♖xe7 14.g5±) 10...♘e5 11.g4 ♘g6 12.♘d4 (12.g5 ♘h4 13.♘f4 ♘xg2+ 14.♘xg2 ♘g8 15.♕d4±) 12...0-0 13.♕e2 (13.g5 ♘h4 14.♗f1 ♘e8 15.♕h5±) 13...♘h4 14.♗f1 c5 15.♘f3 ♘xf3+ 16.♕xf3 ♗c6= 17.g5? ♘xe4 18.♘xe4 ♕e6 19.♗g2 d5∓ Zelcic-Galic, Sibenik 2012) 9.h3 ♗e6 10.♗e3 (10.♘f4±) 10...0-0 11.g4 ♖ad8 (11...h6 12.b3 a5 13.♕d2±) 12.♘d5 ♔h8 (12...♘e5 13.b3 ♘g6 14.0-0 ♘h4 15.♘g3 ♘xg2 16.♔xg2=) 13.♘g3 ♘e5 14.b3 ♘g6 15.0-0 ♘h4 16.♗h1 ♘xd5 17.exd5 h6 18.♕d4± Haslinger-Abergel, Benidorm 2008] **8.♕xd4 0-0** [8...c6 9.♗f4 0-0 (9...♘h5 10.♗e3 ♘f6 11.h3 0-0 12.0-0-0±) 10.0-0-0 ♗e6 11.♗xd6 ♗xd6 12.♕xd6 ♕b6 13.♕d4±] **9.0-0** [9.♗f4!?] **9...c6** [9...♗e6

10.f4 (10.♗f4!?) 10...c5 (10...♕c8 11.♗e3 ♗h3 12.♖ad1 ♗xg2 13.♔xg2 ♘g4 (13...♖e8 14.♔g1 ♕e6 15.♖fe1 a6=) 14.♘d5 ♘xe3+ 15.♕xe3 ♖e8 16.f5 ♕d8 (16...♖d8 17.f6 ♕g4∞) 17.f6 ♗xf6 18.♘xf6+ gxf6 19.♖f4± Swinkels-Kindermann, Germany Bundesliga 2008/09) 11.♕d3 ♕b6 12.h3?! (12.f5 ♗d7=) 12...d5 13.♕e2 dxe4 14.f5 ♗d7 15.g4 h6 16.h4 Strikovic-Berkovich, La Massana 2008 16...♗c6∓; 9...♗d7 10.h3 (10.♗f4 ♗c6 11.♖ad1 ♘d7 12.♘d5 ♗f6 13.♘xf6+

♕xf6 14.♕xf6 gxf6 15.♖fe1 ♖fe8 16.♗d2 ♖e7 17.♗c3 ♖ae8 18.f3 ♗g7 19.♔f2 Gara-Vajda, Zalakaros 2014; 10.b3 c5 11.♕d2 ♗c6 12.♗b2 ♘d7 (12...♖e8±) 13.♘d5 ♗g5 14.f4 ♗h6 15.♖fd1± Pilavov-Mukabenov, Bolshoy Tsaryn 2011) 10...♗c6 11.b3 ♗d7 12.♘d5 ♗f6 13.♘xf6+ ♕xf6 14.♗b2 ♖fe8 15.♖fe1 a5 16.a4 ♕xd4± ½-½ Schmittdiel-Arnaudov, Augsburg 2013] **10.h3** [10.♗f4 ♕b6 11.♖ad1 ♖d8 12.♔xb6 axb6 13.a4 (13.♖d3 ♗e6 14.♖fd1 ♘e8 Meier-D.Popovic, playchess.com 2005 15.a4±) 13...♗e6 14.♖d2 d5 15.exd5 cxd5 (15...♘xd5 16.♘xd5 cxd5 17.♖fd1±) 16.♗c7 ♖dc8 17.♗xb6 ♗b4 18.♗d4 ♗xc3 19.♗xc3 ♖xa4 20.♗xf6 ½-½ Meszaros-Stevic, Austria 2006; 10.a4 ♘d7 (10...♕a5 11.♗f4 ♖d8 12.h3 ♗e6 13.♕d2 ♕c7 14.♖fe1 ♕d7 15.♔h2 d5 ½-½ Palkövi-Jovanovic, Budapest 2005) 11.♗f4 ♕c7 12.♕d2 ♘e5 13.b3 a5 14.♘e2 f5 15.exf5 ♗xf5 16.♘d4 Bodnaruk-Pogonina, Moscow 2011 16...♕d7∓; 10.b3 ♕a5 (10...♖e8 11.♗b2 ♗f8 12.h3 ♕a5 13.♖ad1 ♗e6 14.♕d3 ♖ad8 15.♘e2 (15.♖fe1 ♗e7 16.a3±) 15...♘d7 16.♗c3 (16.♘f4 ♘e5 17.♕e3 ♕xa2 18.♗d4±) 16...♕a3 17.♘f4 ♘c5 (J. Wang-D.Wang, China 2014) 18.♕d4±) 11.♗b2 ♕h5 12.h4 (12.♘d1 ♗h3 13.♘e3 ♖fe8 14.♖ad1±) 12...♖fe8 13.♖ae1 ♗f8 14.♘d1 ♕a5 15.♘e3 ♗e6 16.a3 ♕e5 17.♖d1 ♘g4 18.♗xg4 ♗xg4 19.f3 ♗e6 (Anisimov-Karasev, St Petersburg 2006) 20.f4±] **10...♕b6 11.♗e3 ♕xd4 12.♗xd4 ♗e6 13.f4 ♖fd8 14.b3 d5 15.e5 ♘e4** [15...♘e8 16.g4 ♘c7±] **16.♘xe4 dxe4 17.♗e3 f5 18.exf6 ♗xf6± 19.♖ad1 h5 20.♖xd8+ ♖xd8 21.f5 ♗c8 22.g4 hxg4 23.hxg4 g6 24.fxg6 ♔g7 25.♗xe4 ♗xg4 26.♗h6+ ♔xh6 27.♖xf6 ♗h5 28.♔f2 ♖d7 29.♗e3 a5 30.♖f8 ♔g7 31.♖f5 ♔h6 32.♖f8 ♔g7 33.♖f4 ♖e7 34.♔d4 b6 35.♗d3 ♗e2 36.♗e4 ♖h5 37.c4 ♗xg6 38.♗xc6 ♖e2 39.a4 ♖d2+ 40.♔e5 ♖d3 41.♖g4 ♖e3+ 42.♗e4** 1-0

Eric Hansen
Aleksander Delchev
Spain tt 2014 (5)
1.e4 e5 2.♘f3 d6 3.d4 exd4 4.♘xd4 ♘f6 5.♘c3 ♗e7 6.g3 ♘c6 7.♗g2 0-0 8.h3 [8.♘de2 ♘e5 (8...♖e8 9.0-0 (9.h3 ♖b8 10.♗e3 ♗f8 11.g4 b5 12.g5

♘d7 (12...b4 13.gxf6 bxc3 14.fxg7 ♗xg7 15.bxc3 ♕h4⇄) 13.♕d2 a5 14.b3 ♘c5 15.♘g3 b4 16.♘d5 ♘e5 17.f4 A.Ivanov-Kaufman, Tulsa 2008 17...♘ed7 18.♗f2 c6 19.♘e3 a4⇄) 9...♗f8 (9...♘d7 10.h3 ♘c5 11.♗e3 ♗e6 12.♕d2 ½-½ Sedlak-Bogosavljevic, Vrsac 2008) 10.h3 ♘e5 (10...♖b8 11.g4 b5 12.♘g3 b4 13.♘d5 ♘xd5 14.exd5 ♘e5 15.f4 ♘d7 (15...♘c4 16.♕d4 ♘b6 17.g5 h6 18.b3±) 16.g5 ♗a6 (16...a5 17.b3 h6 18.♕d4 ♘c5=) 17.♖f2 ♕e7 18.♗d2 (Motylev-Kovchan, Taganrog 2014) 18...g6=) 11.b3 (11.g4 c6 12.♘g3 h6 13.b3 ♕a5 14.♗b2 ♘g6 15.♕d2 ♘h4 16.♖ad1 ♗h7 17.f4 b5∞; 11.f4 ♘g6 12.♘h2 ♗d7 13.♕d3 c5 (½-½ Sharapov-Okhotnik, Mukachevo 2013) 14.a4 a6 15.♘d5±) 11...c6 12.♗e3 ♘g6 13.♕d2 ♗d7 14.♖ad1 b5 15.a3 a5 16.f3 b4 17.axb4 axb4 18.♘a4 c5∓ (Abergel-Kazhgaleyev, Paris 2009); 8...♖b8 9.a4 (9.0-0 ♗d7 10.a4 ♖e8 11.b3 ♗b4 12.♗b2 ♗f8 13.♘f4 (13.♕d2 c6 14.♘d1 ♘a6 15.♘ec3 ♕e7 16.♖e1 d5 17.♖e2±) 13...a6 14.♕d2 g6 15.♘cd5 ♘bxd5 16.♘xd5 (16.exd5 ♗g7 17.♖ae1 ♗f5 18.♗d4 ♖xe1 19.♖xe1 ♕f8=) 16...♗g7 17.♗xf6 ♗xf6 18.♘xf6+ ♕xf6 19.♖fe1 ♗c6= Verheyden-Berry, Leuven 2011) 9...a6 10.a5 ♘b4 11.0-0 c5 12.h3 (12.♘f4 ♗g4 13.♕d2 ♖e8 14.b3 h6 15.♗b2 ♗f8 16.f3 ♗d7 17.♘a4±) 12...♘c6 13.f4 ♘xa5 14.e5 ♘e8 15.♘d5 ♘c6 16.♗xe7+ (16.♘ec3 dxe5 17.♘xe7+ ♕xe7 18.fxe5 ♘c7=) 16...♕xe7 17.exd6 ♕xd6 18.♘c3 ♖d8 19.♘d5 ♕f8 20.c3 ♗e6∓ Kornev-Kabanov, Voronezh 2007; 8...♗e6 9.0-0 (9.h3 ♘d7 10.0-0 ♗f6 11.♘d5 ♗xd5

12.exd5 ♘ce5 (Van Delft-Ree, Netherlands tt 2010) 13.♘d4 ♖e8 14.b3 ♘c5 15.♗b2 ♕d7 16.♖e1±) 9...♘d7 10.♘d5 ♗f6 (10...♘f6 11.♘ef4±) 11.♗xf6+ (11.♘ef4 ♗e5 12.c3 ♗xf4 13.♘xf4 ♕f6 14.♗e3 ♖fe8 15.♕e2±) 11...♕xf6 12.h3 ♘b6 13.f4 ♗c4 14.♖f2 ♖fe8 15.♘c3 ♖ad8 16.♗d2 (Cherniaev-Wade, London 2008) 16...d5=) 9.f4 (9.0-0 c6 10.a4 ♖e8 11.b3 ♘g6 12.♗b2 ♕a5 13.h3 ♗d7 14.f4 ♖ad8 15.♕e1 ♕h5? (15...h5 16.♖d1 a6∞) 16.f5 d5 17.fxg6 ♗c5+ 18.♔h1 hxg6 19.♖xf6 gxf6 20.♕f1± Howell-Berkovich, La Massana 2008; 9.h3 c6 10.a4 d5 11.exd5 cxd5 12.0-0 ♘c6 13.♗g5 h6 14.♗xf6 ♗xf6 15.♕d2 ♗xc3 (15...d4 16.♘d5 ♗e5=) 16.♕xc3 ♗e6 17.♘f4 ♖c8 18.♖ad1± Van den Doel-Dahm, Germany Bundesliga B 2011/12) 9...♘g6 10.0-0 (10.♕d3 c6 11.a4 ♕c7 12.♗d2 ♖e8 13.0-0 ♗f8 14.♔h1 ♗d7 15.b4 ♖ad8 16.a5 c5 17.b5 ♕c8 18.♘g1 (Hector-Seel, Germany Bundesliga 2009/10) 18...d5 19.♘xd5 ♘xd5 20.exd5 c4 21.♕c3 ♗xb5∓) 10...c6 11.♘d4 ♖e8 12.h3 ♖b8 13.a4 d5 14.exd5 (14.e5 ♘d7 15.a5 ♗b4 16.a6 ♕c7 17.axb7 ♗xb7 18.♘a4±) 14...cxd5 15.♔h2 (Gaponenko-Benderac, Zlatibor 2006) 15...♗b4=]
8...♗xd4 9.♕xd4 c6 10.0-0 [10.♗f4 ♕b6 (10...♕a5 11.0-0-0 ♗e6 12.♖he1 ♖fd8 13.♔b1 d5 14.exd5 ♘xd5 15.♘xd5 ♗xd5 16.♗xd5 ♖xd5 17.♕e3 ♗f8=) 11.0-0-0 ♕xd4 12.♖xd4 ♖d8 13.a4 ♗e6 14.♖hd1 ♖e8 15.g4 ♗d7 16.♗g3 ♖ad8 17.♘d5 ♗xd5 18.exd5 c5 19.♗e4 ♗f6 20.f4± Jones-Jovanovic, Dresden ol 2008] **10...♗e6 11.♗e3 ♕c8** [11...♕c7 12.f4 (12.♖ad1 b6 13.♖fe1 ♖ad8 14.♕d2 ♖fe8

15.f4 d5 16.exd5 ♗xd5 17.♗xd5 cxd5= Lukovic-D.Popovic, Kragujevac tt 2013) 12...♖fd8 13.♖ad1 (13.f5 ♗c8 14.♘e2 ♘d7 15.c4 ♗f6 16.♕d2 ♗e5 17.♖ac1 b6 18.g4 ♗a6 19.♖f2= Swinkels-D.Popovic, Zurich 2010) 13...d5 (13...b5 14.b3 c5 15.♕d3 b4 16.♘a4 ♖ab8=) 14.e5 c5 15.♕a4 d4 16.exf6 ♗xf6 17.♘b5 ♕b6 18.♗d2 ♗d7 19.♗a5 ♕xb5= Brandenburg-Zaragatski, Germany Bundesliga 2011/12]

12.g4 [12.♔h2 ♖d8 13.♖ad1 d5 14.exd5 ♘xd5 15.♘xd5 ♗xd5 16.♗xd5 ♖xd5 17.♕e4 ♕e6 18.♕xe6 fxe6= Kudrin-Benjamin, ICC 2008] **12...♖d8 13.♖fd1 d5 14.exd5 ♘xd5 15.♘xd5 ♗xd5 16.♗xd5 ♖xd5= 17.♕e4 ♗f6 18.c3 ♖e5 19.♕f3 ♕e6 20.♖d2 ♖e8 21.♔g2 h5 22.♗f4 ♖e4 23.gxh5 ♕c4 24.♗g3 b5 25.♕f5 ♖e2 26.♖ad1 ♖xd2 27.♖xd2 ♕xa2 28.♕f3 ♕c4 29.♖d6 ♖e6 30.♖d1 a5 31.h6 gxh6 32.♖d2 ♕e4 33.♕xe4 ♖xe4 34.♔f3 ♖c4 35.♖d6 ♔g7 36.♗f4 ♗g5 37.♗e5+ f6 38.b3 ♖c5 39.♗d4 ♖f5+ 40.♔g4 ♔g6 41.♖xc6 b4 42.♔g3 ♗f4+** ½-½

Exercise 1

position after 10...♗e7-f6

White to move.
(solution on page 248)

Exercise 2

position after 15...♕a5-h5

White to move.
(solution on page 248)

Exercise 3

position after 14...♘f6-e8

How can White keep an edge?
(solution on page 248)

Fegatello +−

by Marc Schroeder

1.	e4	e5
2.	♘f3	♘c6
3.	♗c4	♘f6
4.	♘g5	d5
5.	exd5	♘xd5
6.	♘xf7	♔xf7
7.	♕f3+	♔e6
8.	♘c3	♘b4

In Yearbook 75, Maarten de Zeeuw considered the game Polerio-Fra Domenico ('Rome, around 1600') as 'probably the oldest game still relevant to opening theory'. Recently I discovered Peter Monté's The Classical Era of Modern Chess (McFarland 2014). A phone and an e-mail conversation later, Monté mailed me the following facts.

In 1575, Polerio stayed at the Spanish Court in Madrid, where he watched games being played between Italian and Spanish players. Shortly thereafter he mentioned Fegatello variations, but did not relate them to players. Had he picked up the opening as a spectator? However

this may be, Polerio-Giovanni Domenico d'Arminio must have been a real game, played before 1606 (Polerio's last sign of life). It may be the oldest known Fegatello encounter.

The term 'fegatello' (piece of liver, bait) is used for the first time in the lost *Doazan Manuscript* (written between 1610 and 1612), copied by Von der Lasa. 8...♘e7 is known as the Polerio Defence, in spite of d'Arminio being Black in the stem game. Well, the move appeared in Polerio's writings as early as in 1575. 8...♘b4 is first mentioned in the (anonymous) *Elegantia Manuscripts*, written shortly after 1580. The oldest notation of a Fegatello Attack is found in the *German Manuscript*, written between 1550 and 1575: the last moves being 7...♕f6 8.♗xd5+ ♔e8 9.♗xc6+ ♕xc6.

Details about the quoted manuscripts can be found in Monté's book.

Let us move on to New In Chess. In his above-mentioned Survey, De Zeeuw concluded that 6.♘xf7 is insufficient for equality, based (with three ∓'s of disapproval) on the variation 9.0-0∓ c6 10.d4 ♕f6∓ 11.♕e2 ♔e7 12.dxe5 ♕g6∓.

In the FORUM section of YB/110, Moody & Rodriguez ('M&R') believed that with the innovations addressed in their

Marc Schroeder

article, 5...♘xd5 had not been refuted and that the assessment of 6.♘xf7 was still unclear.

One innovation was 9.0-0 c6 10.d4 ♕f6 11.♕d1!!. The closest Black could get to equality was after 11...♔e7 12.♖e1±. Apparently not many moves are needed to prove that 5...♘xd5 does hold for Black.

Another innovation was 9.♗b3, a move that De Zeeuw had not covered. According to Moody, White usually gets three pawns for the piece, but whether this is sufficient for a plus is somewhat unclear. With optimal play White would get at least an equal position. As Black's main defence M&R gave 9...c6 10.a3 ♘a6 11.♘xd5 cxd5 12.d4 ♔d6, analysed to =. A subline ended in ≅, at which point Rodriguez stated that Black can maintain the balance but that he would prefer to be White. I wonder what he had in mind against 13.dxe5+ ♔c7 14.♗f4!N±, Game 10.

In 2014, the International Correspondence Chess Federation held a thematic tournament (WSTT/1/14) with the 'Fegatello' theme, played in two stages. Both the variations 9.0-0 and 9.♗b3 were heavily tested here.

Variation 9.0-0

After 9...c6 10.d4, king moves are bad (Game 1). Correct is 10...♕f6!. White then has the strong 11.♕d1!. Insufficient is 11...exd4? (Games 2, 3), Black must play 11...♗e7. After 12.♖e1 the move 12...h6 (Game 4) looks suspect, but might just hold. Black's toughest is 12...♕g6! 13.♖xe5+

♔d8 14.a3 ♞xc3 15.bxc3 ♞d5 16.♗g5+. By the way, White should not trade knights on d5 himself (Game 5). After 16...♔c7? (Games 6, 7) Black seems to lose by force, but with 16...♗e7 (Games 8, 9) he can reach a draw. Game 9 gave me many hours of correspondence fun/trouble. At moves 22 and 24 Elison missed his only opportunities to equalize. At move 36, I was seduced into a rook ending three pawns up, only to find out to my dismay that the endgame is (probably) drawn. At move 51 Black had to solve a remarkable endgame study before he could decide to leave pawn c2 untouched.

Variation 9.♗b3

I basically claim that 9.♗b3 refutes 5...♞xd5. Game 10 shows that after 9...c6 10.a3

♞a6 11.♞xd5 cxd5 12.d4 Black loses after 12...♞d7, 12...♞d6 and 12...exd4. 12...♞c7 (Game 11) loses too. In the remaining games Black played 12...♗e7, but this did not help him either. Game 12 shows that White should not omit c2-c4.

At this moment I do not have an antidote against 9.♗b3, and I became a victim of it myself in my game with Elison (Game 17), who won the thematic tournament by a full point. Congratulations!

Conclusion

After 9.0-0 Black may hold his own, but he will have problems. The computer move 11.♕d1! is hot. The bone-crusher, however, is the variation 9.♗b3, which looks like it is winning. It looks like the Fegatello Attack (6.♞xf7) is +−.

**Variation 9.0-0
King Move Is Bad**

Marc Schroeder   **1**
Igor Yasakov
cr 2014

1.e4 e5 2.♞f3 ♞c6 3.♗c4 ♞f6 4.♞g5 d5 5.exd5 ♞xd5 6.♞xf7 ♔xf7 7.♕f3+ ♔e6 8.♞c3 ♞cb4 9.0-0 c6 10.d4

10...♔d7 [The old main line 10...♔d6? of Estrin is refuted by 11.♗g5!+−] **11. a3 ♞xc3 12.axb4 ♞d5 13.♖xd5 cxd5 14.♖a5 ♔c7 15.♖xd5 ♕f6 16.♕g3 ♕g6** [16...b6   17.♗g5

♕c6 (17...♕g6 18.♖d8+− Haller-Sabbatini, cr 2014) 18.♖xe5 ♗d6 19.♗f4 ♖f8 (19...♗xe5 20.♕xg7++−; 19...♗b7 20.b5+−) 20.♕xg7+ ♕d7 (20...♗d7 21.b5 △ ♕b7?) 22.♖c5+ bxc5 23.♗xd6++−; 20...♔b8 21.♕xf8+−) 21.♖e7 ♖xf4 22.♖xd7+ ♗xd7 23.c3+−] **17.♗g5 ♗xb4 18.c3 ♕c6** [18...♔c6 19.cxb4 ♖e8 20.♖c1+ and mate in 9 moves] **19.♖xe5 ♗d6 20.♗f4 ♖f8 21.♕xg7+ ♗d7** [21...♔b6 22.♖c5+−; 21...♕d7 22.♖c5+−] **22.♖c5+− ♖xf4** [22...♗xf4 23.♖xc6+ bxc6 24.g3 ♗d6 25.♕xh7 ♖f5 26.b4 ♖af8 27.♖a1+− Naeter-Yasakov, cr 2014] **23.♖xc6+ ♔xc6 24.g3 ♖f5 25.♕xh7 ♖e8 26.c4 ♖e2** [26...b6 27.♕h6 a5 28.♖d1 ♖ef8 29.c5 ♖8f6 30.♕h4 bxc5 31.dxc5 ♔xc5 32.♕h8 ♗c6 33.♕d8 ♗f3 34.♖d3 ♗c6 35.g4 ♖xg4 36.♖c3+ ♗c5 37.♕d4 ♖f7 38.♕xg4 ♔b6 39.♕g8 ♗xf2+ 40.♔g2 ♗c5 41.♕b8+ ♔c6 42.♕a8+ ♔b6 43.h4 ♖f8 44.♕e4 ♖8f7 45.♔h3 ♖5f6 46.♕d5 ♗b4 47.♖e3 ♔c7 48.♕c4+ ♔d8 49.h5 ♖e7 50.♕d4+ ♔c7 51.♕xf6 ♖xe3+ 52.♔g4 ♗d6 53.h6 ♖e4+ 54.♔h5 1-0 Haller-Yasakov, cr

2014] **27.c5 ♗e7 28.b4 a6 29.h4 ♖d5 30.♕d3 ♖e6 31.♕f3 ♗f6 32.h5 ♗h8 33.♖b1 ♖e7 34.b5+ axb5 35.♕b3 ♗c8 36.♕xb5+ ♔c7 37.♕b3 ♖ed7 38.c6 bxc6 39.♕b6+ ♔d6 40.♕b8+ ♖c7 41.♕b4+ ♔e6 42.♖e1+ ♔f7 43.♕b8 ♖dd7 44.♕b3+ ♔f8 45.♕e3 ♖e7 46.♕f4+ ♔g8 47.♖e3**   1-0

**Variation 9.0-0
11...exd4?**

Igor Yasakov   **2**
A. N. Burumcekci
cr 2014

1.e4 e5 2.♞f3 ♞c6 3.♗c4 ♞f6 4.♞g5 d5 5.exd5 ♞xd5 6.♞xf7 ♔xf7 7.♕f3+ ♔e6 8.♞c3 ♞cb4 9.0-0 c6 10.d4 ♕f6 [Best according to De Zeeuw in Yearbook 75: in his opinion, White had to play 11.♕e2 and struggle for survival] **11.♕d1!!** [By 2014 the chess engines started to realize that 11.♕e2 is not forced. Suddenly it

is not White but Black who is in trouble]
11...exd4?

12.♘e4± **♕f5** [12...♕g6 13.c3
♔f7 (13...♔d7 14.♖e1± YB/110-24
M&R) 14.♕xd4 ♘c2 15.♗xd5+ cxd5
16.♕xd5+ ♔e8 17.♗g5+–] **13.c3
dxc3** [13...♔f7 14.♘g5+ ♔g8 15.cxb4±;
13...♘a6 14.♗d3 ♔e7 15.♖e1+– ♔d8
16.♗g5+ ♔c7 17.♗h4 ♖f4 18.♗g3 g5
19.♗xa6 ♖g7 20.cxd4 bxa6 21.♖c1 ♖e8
22.♖c5 ♕xe4 23.♖xe4 ♖xe4 24.♖xg5
♗f6 25.♖c5 ♔d7 26.♕d2 1-0, Elison-
Brunner, cr 2014] **14.bxc3 b5** [14...♔d7
15.♖e1+– YB/110-23] **15.♗b3 ♔d7**
[15...♔f7+– Game 3]

16.cxb4 **♕xe4** **17.♖e1** **♕f5**
18.♗xd5 **cxd5** [18...♕xd5?
19.♗f4! ♗d6 20.♕e2+–] **19.♕d4**
♗b7 20.♗f4 ♕f6 21.♗e5 ♕b6
22.♕g4+ ♔e6 [22...♔d8 23.♗xg7
♕g6 (23...♖g8 24.♕g5+ ♔c7 25.♕f4+
♔d8 26.♗f6+ ♔d7 27.♕f5+ ♔c7
28.♕xh7+ ♖g7 29.♗xg7+–) 24.♕h4+
♔d7 25.♕h3+ ♔d8 26.♗xh8+–]
23.♕xe6+ ♗xe6 24.♗xg7+ ♔d7
25.♗xh8 ♗xb4 26.♖eb1 ♗c5 [26...
a5 27.♗d4 ♗c6 28.♖b3 ♖e8 29.♖h3
♖e7 30.g3 a4 31.a3 ♗d6 32.♖h6 1-0
Schroeder-Haas, cr 2014] **27.♖xb5**
♔c6 28.♖ab1 ♗a6 29.♖b8 ♖xb8
30.♖xb8 d4 31.♗g7 ♗c4 32.a4 a5
33.♖c8+ ♔d5 34.♖d8+ ♔e4 35.f3+

♔d3 36.♔f2 ♗c3 37.f4 ♗b3 38.f5
♗xa4 39.♖c8 ♔b4 40.f6   1-0

Marc Schroeder 3
Philipp Haller
cr 2014

**1.e4 e5 2.♘f3 ♘c6 3.♗c4 ♘f6
4.♘g5 d5 5.exd5 ♘xd5 6.♘xf7
♔xf7 7.♕f3+ ♔e6 8.♘c3 ♘cb4
9.0-0 c6 10.d4 ♕f6 11.♕d1 exd4?
12.♘e4 ♕f5 13.c3 dxc3 14.bxc3
b5 15.♗b3 ♔f7**

16.♘g5+ **♔g8** **17.cxb4** **♗xb4**
[17...♗b7 18.a4+–] **18.a4 h6 19.♘f3**
♗c3 **20.♘d4** **♕g4** . [20...♗xd4
21.♕xd4 bxa4 22.♗b2!+–] **21.♘xc6**
♕xd1 22.♖xd1 ♗xa1 23.♗xd5+
♔h7 **24.♘e7** **♗g4 25.f3 ♗f6**
26.♗e4+ **g6** **27.♖d6** **♖ae8**
[27...♗xe7 28.♖xg6 ♗f5 29.♗xf5 ♖hf8
30.♗e4 ♖ad8 31.♔f2+–] **28.♗xg6+**
♔g7 29.♗xe8 ♖xe8 30.♗xh6+
♔f7 [30...♔xh6 31.♖xf6+ ♔g7 32.♖g6+
♔f7 33.♖xg4 ♖xe7 34.axb5+–]
31.♘c6 **♗xf3** [31...♖e6 32.♖xe6
♗xe6 33.axb5 ♗d7 34.♗e3 a6 35.bxa6
♗xc6+–] **32.gxf3 bxa4 33.f4 a5**
[33...♖e2 34.♗d7+ ♔g6 35.♗f8 ♖e4
36.♔g2+–] **34.♘e5+ ♗xe5 35.fxe5
♖xe5 36.♖d4**   1-0

Variation 9.0-0
12...h6

Kari Elison 4
Igor Yasakov
cr 2014

**1.e4 e5 2.♘f3 ♘c6 3.♗c4 ♘f6
4.♘g5 d5 5.exd5 ♘xd5 6.♘xf7
♔xf7 7.♕f3+ ♔e6 8.♘c3 ♘cb4
9.0-0 c6 10.d4 ♕f6 11.♕d1 ♔e7
12.♖e1 h6** [12...♘xc3? 13.bxc3 ♘d5
14.♗g5!+–; 12...♕g6 Games 5-9]

13.♘e4 [13.♖xe5+ ♔d8 14.♘e4 ♕g6
15.a3 (15.c3 ♗f5 16.♕f3 (16.♘g3 ♗d3!∓)
16...♕xe4 17.♖xe4 ♘c2 18.♖b1 ♗f6
19.♗d3±) 15...♗f5 (15...♘xc2 16.♕xc2
♗d6 17.f3±) 16.♘g3 ♗xc2 17.♕f3 ♗d3
18.♖f5 ♔c7 19.♗xd3 ♗xd3 20.♕xd3
♖e8 21.♗d2±] **13...♕g6 14.c3 ♘b6**
[14...♘a6 15.dxe5 ♔f7 16.♖e3 ♘ac7
17.♖f3+ ♔g8 18.♗d3 (≤ 18.♘f6+ gxf6
19.♖g3 ♕xg3 20.hxg3±) 18...♗e6 19.c4
♘b4 20.♗b1±; 14...♗f5 15.♘c5 ♘c2
16.♖xe5+ ♔d8 17.♗xf5 ♕xf5 18.♗d3 ♕f7
19.♕xc2 ♗xc5 20.dxc5 ♗c7±] **15.♗f1**
♘a6 [15...♘4d5 16.dxe5 ♔f7 17.c4 ♗c7
18.♘d6+ ♔g8 19.♗d3±] **16.dxe5 ♔f7**
17.♗d3 ♗g4 18.f3 ♗e6 19.f4 ♔g8
**20.♗e3 ♕g4 21.♕c2 ♘d5 22.f5
♘ac7 23.♗d4 ♘f4 24.♖f1 ♘cd5**
**25.♖f3 ♖h7 26.♖af1 ♔h8 27.e6
♘xd3 28.♕xd3 ♕h5 29.c4**   1-0

Variation 9.0-0
12...♕g6!

Timofey Denisov 5
Marc Schroeder
cr 2014

**1.e4 e5 2.♘f3 ♘c6 3.♗c4 ♘f6
4.♘g5 d5 5.exd5 ♘xd5 6.♘xf7
♔xf7 7.♕f3+ ♔e6 8.♘c3 ♘cb4
9.0-0 c6 10.d4 ♕f6 11.♕d1 ♔e7
12.♖e1 ♕g6 13.♖xe5+ ♔d8**

14.♘xd5 [White keeps his pawn chain intact, but denies himself an open b-file; a pawn on c3 would also keep the knight away from d4. I prefer 14.a3] **14...♘xd5** [14...cxd5? 15.♗e2 ♕f7 16.c4± Denisov-Gagliardi, cr 2014. The position was reached via a different move order] **15.♗g5+ ♗e7** [15...♔c7 16.♕f3 h6 17.♕g3 ♕d6 18.♗d2 b6 19.♖ae1 ♗d7 20.♗a6±] **16.♗xe7+ ♘xe7 17.d5 c5 18.d6 ♘c6 19.♖xc5** [19.♖e3 ♗f8 20.♕d5 (20.d7? ♗xd7 21.♗e6 ♘d4! 22.♗xd7 ♕xc2∓) 20...♕xc2=] **19...♗d7 20.c3 ♖c8 21.♖d5 ♘b4** [21...♖e8=; 21...♖f8 22.♗b3 ♖e8=] **22.♖d4 ♘c6 23.♖f4** [23.♖d5 ♘b4= repetition] **23...♘e5 24.♗f1=** [The position is equal. Black did not suffer much pressure in this game, so White should prefer 14.a3. The remainder of the game is not relevant to the theory] **24...♖e8 25.♕d4 b6 26.♖d1 ♖c5 27.b4 ♘c6 28.♕d2 ♖ce5 29.g3 ♕e6 30.b5 ♘a5 31.c4 g5 32.♖d4 ♔c8 33.f4 gxf4 34.♖xf4 ♘b7 35.♗g2 ♘c5 36.♔d4 ♖f5 37.♗c6 ♖xf4 38.♕xf4 ♕e2 39.♕d4 ♖f8 40.♗g2 ♗g4 41.♗f1 ♖xf1+ 42.♗xf1 ♕e4 43.♕f6 ♕e3+ 44.♔g2 ♕e6 45.♕h8+ ♔d7 46.♕xh7+ ♔xd6 47.♕b1 ♕e4+ 48.♕xe4 ♘xe4 49.h3 ♗e6 50.♗e2 ♔e5 51.h4 ♘c3 52.♗f1 ♗g4 53.♔f2 ♔d4 54.♗g2 ♘e4+** 0-1

Marc Schroeder 6
Timofey Denisov
cr 2014

1.e4 e5 2.♘f3 ♘c6 3.♗c4 ♘f6 4.♘g5 d5 5.exd5 ♘xd5 6.♘xf7 ♔xf7 7.♕f3+ ♔e6 8.♘c3 ♘cb4 9.0-0 c6 10.d4 ♕f6 11.♕d1 ♔e7 12.♖e1 ♕g6 13.♖xe5+ ♔d8 14.a3 ♘xc3 15.bxc3 ♘d5 16.♗g5+ ♔c7? [16...♗e7 Games 8, 9]

17.♕f3 h6 [17...♗d6?? 18.♗d3+−] **18.♕g3 ♕d6** [18...♗d6?? 19.♗d8++−] **19.♗d2 b6 20.a4 ♗d7** [20...♔b7 21.a5 ♗d7 (21...g5 22.♗xd5+−) 22.a6+ ♔c7 23.♗xd5 cxd5 24.c4 dxc4 25.♗f4 g5 26.♕f3 ♗c6 27.♖e7+ ♗xe7 28.♗xd6+ ♗xd6 29.♕f7++−] **21.♗a6 ♔d8** [21...g5 22.c4 ♘f4 23.c5 ♕xd4 24.♗c3 ♘h5 25.♗xd4 ♘xg3 26.♖ee1 ♗xc5 27.♗e5+ ♗d6 28.♖xh8 ♖xh8 29.hxg3±; 21...♖e8? 22.c4 ♖xe5 (22...♘b4 23.♗xb4 ♕xb4 24.♖xe8+ ♗d6 25.♖e5+−) 23.dxe5 ♕e6 24.cxd5+−] **22.c4 ♘e7** [22...♘c7 23.c5± Game 7; 22...♘f6 23.♗f4+−]

23.c5 ♘f5 [23...♕xd4 24.♗c3± ♕g4 25.♕d3 ♕g6 (25...♕g6 26.♖e4 ♕f5 (26...♕f4 27.♖xf4 ♕xf4 28.♖d1 ♕g4 29.♗b7 ♖c8 30.cxb6 ♗c5 31.h3 ♕xd1+ 32.♕xd1 axb6 33.♗xc8 ♔xc8+−) 27.g4 ♘f4 28.gxf5 ♖xd3 29.cxb6 ♘b4 30.b7 ♖b8 31.♖xb4 ♗xb4 32.♗xb4 c5 33.♗a5+ ♔e7 34.♖e1++−) 26.♕c4 1-0 Schroeder-Gagliardi, cr 2014. An appropriate finish could have been 26...♘d5 27.♖d1 ♘xc3 28.♕xc3 ♗xc5 29.♖xc5 bxc5 30.♕a5+ ♔e8 31.♖e1+ ♔e6 32.♗c4+−] **24.cxd6 ♘xg3 25.hxg3 ♗xd6 26.♖e3 ♖e8** [26...♔c7 27.c4± ♖he8 28.c5 ♗e7 29.♖f3 (29.♖xe7!? ♖xe7 30.♗f4+ ♔d8 31.♗b7±) 29...♗e6 30.♗f4+ ♔d7 31.♖c3 ♗d5 32.♖d1 ♗f8 33.♗b7 ♖ad8 34.cxb6 ♗b4 35.♖c2 axb6 36.♖b2 ♗a5 37.♗a6 g5 38.♗e5 h5 39.♗e2 g4 40.f4 gxf3 41.♗xf3 ♖g8 42.♗xd5 cxd5 43.♖b5 ♗c6 44.♔h2 ♖gf8 45.♖c1+ ♔b7 46.♖cc5 ♔a6 47.♖xd5 ♖de8 48.♖d7 ♖f1 49.♖h7 ♖a1 50.♖xh5 ♖xa4 51.♖b3 ♖g8 52.d5 ♖a2 53.♗f4 ♖c2 54.♖d3 ♖c3 55.♖d1 ♖c5 56.♔h3 1-0 Elison-Denisov, cr 2014] **27.♖f3 ♖b8 28.♗d3 ♖e7 29.c4 c5 30.d5 ♔c7 31.♗f5 ♗xf5 32.♖xf5 ♖be8 33.♔f1 ♔c8 34.a5**

♗e5 35.♖b1 ♗c7 36.♗f4 ♖d7 37.f3 bxa5 38.♖a1 ♖d8 39.♗e5 ♖xe5 40.♗xe5 h5 41.♗c3 ♖b7 42.♔e2 g6 43.♔d2 ♖b3 44.♖a2 ♖b1 45.♗xa5 ♗f6 46.♗c3 ♖g1 47.♔d3 ♖xc3 48.♔xc3 ♔b7 49.♖a5 ♖xg2 50.♖b5+ ♔a6 [50...♔c7 51.♖xc5+ ♔b6 52.d6+−] **51.d6 ♖xg3** [51...♖g1 52.♖xc5 ♖d1 53.♖c6+ ♔a5 (53...♔b7 54.♖c7+ ♔b8 55.c5 g5 56.♔c4 g4 57.♖h7+−) 54.f4+−] **52.♖xc5 ♖xf3+ 53.♔d4** 1-0

Marc Schroeder 7
Burkhard Naeter
cr 2014

1.e4 e5 2.♘f3 ♘c6 3.♗c4 ♘f6 4.♘g5 d5 5.exd5 ♘xd5 6.♘xf7 ♔xf7 7.♕f3+ ♔e6 8.♘c3 ♘cb4 9.0-0 c6 10.d4 ♕f6 11.♕d1 ♔e7 12.♖e1 ♕g6 13.a3 ♘xc3 14.bxc3 ♘d5 15.♖xe5+ ♔d8 16.♗g5+ ♔c7? 17.♕f3 h6 18.♕g3 ♕d6 19.♗d2 b6 20.a4 ♗d7 21.♗a6 ♔d8 22.c4 ♘c7 23.c5

23...♕f6 [23...♕xd4?? 24.♗g5+ hxg5 25.♕xg5+ ♗e7 26.♕xe7#] **24.♖a3 ♘xa6 25.♖f3 ♗e7 26.h4 ♘c7 27.♖xf6 ♗xf6 28.♖e1! ♖e8 29.♖d1 ♘e6** [29...♖c8 30.♗f4 ♗xh4 31.♕xg7±] **30.♗c3 ♔c8 31.a5 bxc5 32.dxc5 ♘xc5 33.♕xc3 ♖b8** [33...a6 34.f4±] **34.a6 ♖f8** [34...♖e7 35.♕e5±; 34...♖b5 35.♕g3+−] **35.♕e5 ♖f6 36.f4 ♘d8** [36...♖b8 37.f5 ♘f8 38.♕e1+−; 36...♘xf4?? 37.♕e7 ♘d5 38.♕xg7 ♖e6 39.c4 ♖e6 (39...♘f6 40.♖xd7 ♖e1+ 41.♗f2+−) 40.♕xh6+−; 36...♖xf4?? 37.♖xd7 ♖b1+ 38.♔h2 ♖xh4+ 39.♔g3 ♖xd7 40.♕d6+ ♔e8 41.♕xe6++−] **37.h5 ♘e6 38.c4 ♘d8** [Black tries in vain to achieve

a fortress] **39.f5 ♖f7** [39...♗xf5??
40.♕e8+– is mate in 6 moves;
39...♖xf5?? 40.♕xg7 ♖f7 41.♕xh6+–]
40.♕d6 ♖b2 41.g4 ♖b4 42.♔f2
♘e6 [42...♖xc4?? 43.♖b1+–] **43.♖e1**
♘g5 44.♖e7 ♖xe7 45.♕xe7 ♖xc4
46.♕xg7 ♖xg4 47.♕xh6 ♘f7
48.♕f8+ ♘d8 49.f6 ♖f4+ 50.♔e3
♖h4 51.f7   1-0

Variation 9.0-0
16...♗e7!

Philipp Haller   **8**
Kari Elison
cr 2014

1.e4 e5 2.♘f3 ♘c6 3.♗c4 ♘f6
4.♘g5 d5 5.exd5 ♘xd5 6.♘xf7
♔xf7 7.♕f3+ ♔e6 8.♘c3 ♘cb4
9.0-0 c6 10.d4 ♕f6 11.♕d1
♔e7 12.♖e1 ♕g6 13.♖xe5+
♔d8 14.a3 ♘xc3 15.bxc3 ♘d5
16.♗g5+ ♗e7

17.♗xe7+ ♖xe7 18.d5 c5 19.d6
♘c6 20.♖xc5 [20.♖e3! Game 9]
20...♗d7 21.♗b5 ♖c8 22.♖b1
[22.♖d5 ♖e8 23.♖b1 b6∓] **22...b6**
23.♖d5 ♘b8∓ [Black is already better.
This game is given to support the view
that 20.♖e3 is stronger than 20.♖xc5]
24.♖d3 ♖e8 25.♖g3 ♕h6 26.a4
♖e6 27.♕f3 ♖xd6 28.♕b7 ♘c6
29.♗xc6 ♖dxc6 30.a5 ♖6c7
31.♕d5 ♖c5 32.♕g8+ ♔c7
33.axb6+ axb6 34.♕xg7 ♕xg7
35.♖xg7 h5 36.♖d1 ♖d8 37.♖d3
♔c8 38.h4 ♗c6 39.♖g5 ♖xd3
40.cxd3 ♖xc3 41.♖xh5 b5 42.♖e5
b4 43.h5 ♖xd3 44.h6 ♔c7 45.f3
b3 46.♔f2 ♖d8 47.♖h5 ♗d5
48.♖h1 ♔f7 49.♖c1+ ♔b6 50.♖b1
♖h8   0-1

Marc Schroeder   **9**
Kari Elison
cr 2014

1.e4 e5 2.♘f3 ♘c6 3.♗c4 ♘f6
4.♘g5 d5 5.exd5 ♘xd5 6.♘xf7
♔xf7 7.♕f3+ ♔e6 8.♘c3 ♘cb4
9.0-0 c6 10.d4 ♕f6 11.♕d1 ♔e7
12.♖e1 ♕g6 13.a3 ♘xc3 14.bxc3
♘d5 15.♖xe5+ ♔d8 16.♗g5+ ♗e7
17.♗xe7+ ♘xe7 18.d5 c5 19.d6
♘c6

20.♖e3! ♗d7 [20...♘f8?, like in
Game 5, is not possible here. There
would follow 21.d7! ♗xd7 22.♗e6 ♘d4
23.♗xd7 ♖xc2 (23...♔xd7 24.cxd4+–)
24.♕e1 ♔xd7 25.♖e7+ ♔d8 26.cxd4
♕xf2+ 27.♕xf2 ♖xf2 28.♖xg7 ♖f8
29.dxc5+–] **21.♕d5 ♕f5 22.♕d2**
h6?! [22...♘e5!= 23.♗d5 ♕f6 24.♕e2
(24.♗xb7? ♖b8∓) 24...♘c6 25.♖e1
(25.♖d1 ♖e8 26.♖xe8+ ♗xe8=; 25.♗f3
♖c8=) 25...a6=] **23.♖ae1 ♖b8 24.a4**
a6 [24...♕g5 25.f4 ♕f6=; 24...♖e8
25.h3 ♖e5=] **25.h3 ♖e8** [25...♔c8
26.♕d1±; 25...♕g5 26.h4! ♕xh4
27.♕d5 ♔c8 28.♕xc5 ♖f8 29.♖e4+–]
26.g4! ♕f6 27.♕d5 ♖f8 28.♖1e2
g6 [28...b6 29.♖e7 ♘xe7 30.dxe7+ ♔c7
31.exf8♕ ♖xf8 32.♗xa6 ♗c6 33.♕d3±]
29.♕xc5 b6 30.♕d5 h5 31.♖e6!
♕f4□ [31...♗xe6?? 32.♕xc6+–;
31...♕f3?? 32.♕g5++–; 31...♕xc3??
32.♕g5++–] **32.♖xg6 hxg4**
33.h4± [33.hxg4? ♘a5=; 33.♖g8?
♕c1+ 34.♔h2 ♕f4+ 35.♔g2 gxh3+
36.♔h1□=] **33...g3 34.f3!** [34.fxg3??
♕f1+ 35.♔h2 ♕h3+ 36.♔g1 ♖f1#;
34.♖xg3 ♘a5! 35.♖g8 ♘xc4 36.♕xc4
(36.♕g5+?? ♕xg5+–+ with check)
36...♕xc4 37.♖xf8+ ♗e8 38.♖exe8+
♔d7 39.♖xb8=] **34...♖a8** [34...♘a5??
35.♖g8 ♘xc4 36.♕g5+ ♕xg5 (without
check) 37.♖xf8+ ♗e8 38.hxg5+–] **35.**
h5! ♖a7 36.h6? [36.♖g8! ♔c8□

37.♗d3!!** (37.♖xf8+ ♕xf8 38.♕g8
(38.♔g2) 38...♕xg8 39.♗xg8±)
37...♖d8 (37...♖xg8 38.♕xg8+ ♘d8
39.♕c4+ ♔xc4 40.♗xc4 ♗h3 (40...
b5 41.♖e7! ♗b7 42.axb5 axb5 43.h6
♗f5 44.♗d5△ ♗e4+–) 41.♖e7!+–;
37...♘d8 38.♖xf8 ♕xf8 39.♖e7+–;
37...b7 38.♖xf8 ♕xf8 39.♔g2+–)
38.♖xd8+ ♘xd8 39.♖e7+–] **36...b5**
[36...♘a5 37.♕d3 ♗c6 38.♕g5+ ♕xg5
39.♖xg5+–] **37.♕d3□ bxa4 38.♕e4**
♕xe4 39.♗xe4 ♗e8 40.♖xg3
♔d7□ [40...a3 41.h7 a2 42.♖e1 ♖b7
43.♖g8 ♖b1 44.♔f2 ♖xe1 45.♖xf8
a1♕ 46.♖e8+ ♔d7 47.♗xc6+ ♔xc6
48.h8♕+–] **41.♖g7+ ♔f7 42.♗xc6+**
♔xc6 43.♖e7 ♖xe7 44.dxe7 ♖e8
45.♖xf7 [During the remainder of the
game I kept cursing myself for not having
played 36.♖g8. Three pawns up and still
not winning, or am I missing something?]
45...a3 46.♖f6+ ♔b7□ 47.♖f4
♖xe7 [47...♔c6? 48.h7+–] **48.♖b4+**
♔a7 49.♖a4 ♗e6 50.♖xa3 ♖xh6
51.♔f2 ♔b6 [After 51...♖h2+ 52.♔e3!
♖xc2 White wins with a crazy series
of forced moves: 53.f4□ ♔b6 54.f5□
♖h2 55.♔f4 (or 55.♖b3+–=) 55...a5
56.♔g3□ ♖h8 57.♔g4□ ♔b5 58.f6□
♖a1□ 59.♖a1 ♖c8 60.♖b1+□ ♔a5 61.♖c1□
a3 62.♔f5□ ♖c7 63.♔g6 ♖c6 64.♔g7
♖c4 65.f7□ ♖g4+ 66.♔h6 ♖f4 67.♔g6
♖f2 68.♖a1 ♔a4 69.♖b1 ♖g2+
70.♔h5 ♖h2+ 71.♔g4 ♖h8 72.♖b7
73.♖a7+□ ♔b3 74.♔g5□ ♖c8 75.♔g6
♔b2 76.♔g7 a1♕ 77.♖xa1□ ♔xa1
78.f8♕+–] **52.♔e3** [52.♔g3 ♖c6
53.♔g4 ♖c7 54.f4 ♔d7 55.f5 ♔e8
56.♔g5 ♔f7 57.♖b3 a5=] **52...a5!**
53.c4!? ♖h5 [53...♖h8? 54.c5+! ♔b5
55.c6 ♖c8 56.♖c3 ♔b4 57.♖b3+ ♔c4
58.♔d2 ♖c7 59.♖c3+ ♔b4 60.♔d3 a4
61.♖c4+ ♔b5 62.♔c3 a3 63.♖b4+ ♔a5
64.♔b3 ♖xc6 65.♖a4+ ♔b5 66.♖xa3+–]
54.♖b3+ [I will not bore you with a full-
blown analysis tree here: a draw is the
outcome, if you believe me – which you
shouldn't!] **54...♔a6 55.♖b1** [Last trick]
55...a4! 56.♔d3 ♖f5 57.♖f1 ♔a5
58.♔c3 ♖f4□ 59.♖f2 ♖f8 60.f4
♖b8 61.♖e2 [61.♖d2 a3 62.♖d5+
♔a4 63.♖d7 ♖a8 64.f5 a2 65.♔b2 ♔b4
66.♔a1 ♖f8 67.♖d5 ♖xc4= attacks the
rook] **61...a3 62.♖e5+ ♔a4??** [Only
this is the losing move; 62...♔a6□=]
63.♖e7+– ♖a8 [63...♔a5 64.♖a7+

144

♔b6 65.♖xa3 ♖f8 66.♖a4!+−] **64.f5□**
[64.♖b7? a2 65.♔b2 a1♕+ 66.♔xa1=]
64...♖a6 [64...a2 65.♔b2 ♔b4 66.♔a1
♖f8 (66...♖a5 67.♖b7+ ♔xc4 68.f6□
♖f5 69.f7□ ♖f2 70.♔xa2□ ♖xc2+
71.♖b2□+−) 67.♖e5 ♔xc4 does
not attack the rook: 68.♔xa2□+−]
65.♖b7 1-0

Variation 9.♗b3
Alternatives on Move 12

Kari Elison 10
Philipp Haller
cr 2014

**1.e4 e5 2.♘f3 ♘c6 3.♗c4 ♘f6
4.♘g5 d5 5.exd5 ♘xd5 6.♘xf7
♔xf7 7.♕f3+ ♔e6 8.♘c3 ♘cb4
9.♗b3 c6 10.a3 ♘a6 11.♘xd5
cxd5 12.d4**

12...♔d7? [12...♔d6? (M&R in YB/110
FORUM) 13.dxe5+ ♔c7 14.♗f4!N
transposes to the main line; 12...exd4?
13.♗f4+− Sabbatini-Tanti, cr 2014;
12...♘c7 Game 11; 12...♗e7 Games
12-17] **13.dxe5 ♔c7** [13...♗e7
14.♗f4!±] **14.♗f4!N** [14.♗xd5?
♗g4!=] **14...g5** [14...♘c5 15.♖d1 ♘e6
(15...♘xb3?? 16.♖xd5+−) 16.♗xd5
♘xf4 17.♕xf4±] **15.♗g3 ♗e6
16.♖d1 ♕e8** [16...g4 17.♕c3+ ♗c5
(17...♔b6 18.f4±) 18.♗xd5 ♗xd5 19.0-0
b6 20.♕e1 b5 21.b3 ♗b7 22.c4 bxc4
23.bxc4 ♗e6 24.♖xd8 ♖axd8 25.♕b1+
♗b6 26.a4+− Denisov-Korman, cr 2014]
**17.♗xd5 ♖d8 18.0-0 ♘c5 19.c4 h5
20.h4 gxh4 21.♗h2** [21.♗xh4?! ♗e7
22.♗f6 ♖f8 23.♕g3± Calio-Burumcekci,
2014] **21...h3 22.b4 hxg2 23.♖fe1
♖g8 24.bxc5 ♗xc5 25.♗xe6 ♖xd1
26.♖xd1 ♕xe6 27.♕d5 ♕xd5
28.cxd5 ♔d8 29.♖d3 h4 30.♖f3
♖g5 31.d6 ♔e8 32.e6 ♖d5 33.d7+**

♔e7 34.♗c7 ♗b6 35.d8♕+
♖xd8 36.♗xd8+ ♔xd8 37.♖f7
h3 38.♖d7+ ♔e8 39.♖xb7 h2+
40.♔xh2 1-0

Igor Yasakov 11
Mario Filippo Calio
cr 2014

**1.e4 e5 2.♘f3 ♘c6 3.♗c4 ♘f6
4.♘g5 d5 5.exd5 ♘xd5 6.♘xf7
♔xf7 7.♕f3+ ♔e6 8.♘c3 ♘cb4
9.♗b3 c6 10.a3 ♘a6 11.♘xd5
cxd5 12.d4 ♘c7**

13.c4 exd4 [13...♘f6 14.cxd5+ ♔d7
15.♕g4+ ♔e8 16.♕h5+ g6 (16...♕g6
17.♕xg6+ hxg6 18.dxe5±) 17.♕xe5+±]
**14.cxd5+ ♔d7 15.♕g4+ ♔e8
16.♕h5+ g6 17.♕e5+ ♕e7
18.♗f4 ♘a6 19.0-0** [19.d6 ♕xe5+
20.♗xe5 ♘c5 21.♗c4 ♖g8 22.♗xg8
♘d3+ 23.♔f1 ♘xe5 24.♖e1 ♗xd6
25.f4±] **19...♕xe5 20.♗xe5 ♘c5
21.♗c4 ♖g8 22.♖fe1 ♗f5 23.b4?±**
[23.♗xd4+ ♔d7 24.♗b5+ ♔d6 25.♗e5+
♔e7 26.♖ac1 ♗f7 27.♖c3±] **23...♗d3
24.♗xd4+ ♔d7 25.♗a2 ♘e4
26.♖e3 ♗c2 27.d6 ♗xd6 28.♗xg8
♖xg8= 29.♖c1 ♗c8 30.♖e2 ♗d3
31.♖xc8 ♔xc8 32.♖e3 ♗b1 33.f3
♗g5 34.♗xa7 ♔d7 35.♖e2 b5
36.♖d2 ♔e6 37.♔f2 h5 38.g3 ♗f5
39.♔e3** ½-½

Variation 9.♗b3
12...♗e7

Bernhard Haas 12
Marc Schroeder
cr 2014

**1.e4 e5 2.♘f3 ♘c6 3.♗c4 ♘f6
4.♘g5 d5 5.exd5 ♘xd5 6.♘xf7**

♔xf7 7.♕f3+ ♔e6 8.♘c3 ♘cb4
9.♗b3 c6 10.a3 ♘a6 11.♘xd5
cxd5 12.d4 ♗e7

13.0-0? [White must open up the
centre with 13.c4!] **13...♖f8 14.♕e3**
[14.♕e4 ♕d6 15.dxe5 (15.♕xh7
exd4=) 15...♕xe5= 16.♗xd5+ ♔d6
17.♗xb7 ♗xb7 18.♕xb7 ♘c5□=
(18...♘c7?? 19.♗d2+− Watson-
Maurer, cr 2006); 14.♕g3 ♔f7 (M&R in
YB/110-25 prefer 14...♖f5=) 15.♕xe5=
see below] **14...♔f7** [14...♕d6?
15.c4+−] **15.♕xe5 ♔g8 16.♗xd5+
♔h8 17.♗e4 ♕e8 18.c3** [18.♖e1
♗f6 (18...♕f7=) 19.♕xe8 ♖xe8
20.c3 ♗f5 21.f3 ♖e7 22.♖e3 g6
23.♗xf5 ♖xe3 24.♗xe3 gxf5 25.♗f4
♔g7 26.♔f2 ♖c8 27.♖e1= Sabbatini-
Brunner, cr 2014] **18...♘b8 19.♖e1
♘d7 20.♕g3 ♘f6** [20...♕f7 21.♗d5
♕xd5 (21...♘d6!? 22.♗xf7 ♗xg3
23.hxg3 ♖xf7∞; 21...♘h4 22.♗xf7
♗xg3=) 22.♖xe7 ♖f7 23.♖e8+ ♘f8=
(23...♖f8 24.♖e7 ♕f7=)] **21.♗b1
b6!?** [21...♕d7 22.♗f4 b6 23.♗c2=]
22.♕h4 ♕f7 [22...♕d7?! 23.♗xh7
♘d5 24.♖e7 (24.♕h5 ♘f6 25.♕h4=
repetition) 24...♕xe7 25.♗g5 ♖f4
26.♗xe7 ♖xh4 27.♗xh4 ♔xh7±]
23.♗xh7 [23.♗a2 ♘g8 24.♕g3
♗d6!? 25.♗xf7 ♗xg3 26.hxg3 ♖xf7=]
**23...♘e4!! 24.♕f4 ♗xf4 25.♗xf4
♘xc3 26.♖xe7 ♗xh7□ 27.♗e5
♘e2+□ 28.♔f1 ♗a6 29.♖xg7+?!**
[29.g4= ♘f4+ 30.♔g1 ♘d3 31.♖g7
♖fe8 (31...♖xf2!? 32.♖d1 ♗g6 33.♖xd3
♖f7 34.♖xf7 ♔xf7 35.♖c3 ♗xg7=)
32.♖c7 ♖ec8 33.♖d7 ♖d8 34.♖e7
♖e8= △ 35.♖f7?? ♗g6∓] **29...♔h6∓**
[I hope I have convinced you that without
c2-c4 White does not win] **30.g4
♘f4+ 31.♔g1 ♘d3 32.g5+ ♔h5
33.♗f6 ♔g4 34.b4 ♗c4 35.♖f1
♔f3 36.♖e7 ♖ae8 37.♖e3+**

♖xe3 38.fxe3+ ♔xe3 39.h3 ♘f4
40.♖e1+ ♔e2 41.h4 ♖e8 42.♖c1
♖e4 43.♖c7 ♘d5 0-1

Timofey Denisov 13
Bernhard Haas
cr 2014

1.e4 e5 2.♘f3 ♘c6 3.♗c4 ♘f6
4.♘g5 d5 5.exd5 ♘xd5 6.♘xf7
♔xf7 7.♕f3+ ♔e6 8.♘c3 ♘cb4
9.♗b3 c6 10.a3 ♘a6 11.♘xd5
cxd5 12.d4 ♗e7 13.c4

13...♖f8 [13...♔d7 was investigated
by M&R in YB/110 FORUM: 14.♕xd5+
(14.0-0 e4 15.♕g4+ ♔c6 16.♕xg7 ♖g8
17.♕h6+ ♔g6 18.♕xh7 ♗f5 19.♕f7
♖f6 (19...♔f8 20.♕xd5+ ♔c7 21.♗f4+
♗d6 22.♗xd6+ ♖xd6 23.♕a5+ b6
24.♕xa6 ♖g6 25.g3 ♘h3 26.♗d1 ♗xf1
27.♔xf1= Naeter-Denisov, cr 2014)
20.cxd5+ ♔b6 21.♕h5≅ M&R) 14...♔e8
15.♕xe5 ♔f8 16.0-0 ♗f6 17.♕g3
♕xd4 18.♖e1!± M&R; 13...exd4 Game
14; 13...♕d6 Games 15-17] 14.cxd5+±
♔d7 15.♕h3+ ♔c7 16.♕c3+
♔b8 17.dxe5 ♘c5 18.0-0 ♘xb3
19.♕xb3 ♕b6 20.♕c3 ♕c5
21.♕d3 ♗f5 22.♕g3 b6 23.d6
♗d8 24.♕xg7 ♖e8 25.♗f4 ♕d5
26.d7 ♖e6 27.♕f8 ♗d3 28.♖ad1
♖g6 29.♗g3 ♗b7 30.♖fe1 ♗g5
31.♕b4 ♖d8 32.h4 1-0

Kari Elison 14
Philipp Haller
cr 2014

1.e4 e5 2.♘f3 ♘c6 3.♗c4 ♘f6
4.♘g5 d5 5.exd5 ♘xd5 6.♘xf7
♔xf7 7.♕f3+ ♔e6 8.♘c3 ♘cb4
9.♗b3 c6 10.a3 ♘a6 11.♘xd5
cxd5 12.d4 ♗e7 13.c4 exd4
14.0-0 ♔d7

15.♗f4+− ♘c5 16.♖fe1 ♖f8
[16...♗xb3 17.♕xb3 ♕b6 18.♕f3 ♖f8
19.♕xd5+ ♗d6 20.♗g5 ♔c7 21.c5
1-0 Elison-Tanti, cr 2014] 17.♕xd5+
♔e8 18.♖xc5 ♖xf4 19.♕h5+ g6
20.♕xh7 ♕d6 21.c5 ♕f6 22.♕g8+
♔d7 23.♖ad1 a6 24.g3 ♖f5 25.♖e6
♕f8 26.♕h7 ♖f7 27.♕xg6 ♗xc5
28.♖c1 ♖xf2 29.♖e5 ♖f6 30.♕h7+
♔c6 31.♖exc5+ ♔b6 32.♖c7
♕d8 33.♕c2 ♖f5 34.♖xc8 ♖xc8
35.♕xc8 1-0

Kari Elison 15
Burkhard Naeter
cr 2014

1.e4 e5 2.♘f3 ♘c6 3.♗c4 ♘f6
4.♘g5 d5 5.exd5 ♘xd5 6.♘xf7
♔xf7 7.♕f3+ ♔e6 8.♘c3 ♘cb4
9.♗b3 c6 10.a3 ♘a6 11.♘xd5
cxd5 12.d4 ♗e7 13.c4 ♕d6 14.0-0
e4

15.♕h5! g6 [15...♖f8 16.c5 ♕c6
17.♕e5+ ♔d7 18.♗xd5 ♕f6
19.♕xe4±; 15...♘c7 16.c5 ♕c6 17.♗f4
♔d7 18.♗xc7 ♔xc7 19.♕e5+ ♔d8
20.♗xd5±] 16.♕h6 [16.cxd5+ ♔f7
17.♕h6± see below] 16...♔f7 [16...♗f6
17.♗e3+−] 17.cxd5 ♗f6 [17...g5
Games 16, 17] 18.♗f4 ♕f8 19.d6+
♔e8 20.♖ae1 ♗f5 21.♗a4+ ♔d8
22.♗g5 ♕xd6 [22...♕xh6? 23.♗xf6+

♔c8 24.♖c1+ ♘c5 25.♗xh8+−] 23.
f3 e3 24.♖xe3 ♗xg5 25.♕xg5+
♔c7 26.♖c1+ ♔b8 27.♕e7 ♕xe7
28.♖xe7 ♖c8 29.♖xc8+ ♗xc8
30.♖xh7 ♘c7 31.♗c2 g5 32.♖h8
♘b5 33.f4 gxf4 34.h4 ♘xd4 35.h5
a5 36.h6 ♖a6 37.♗d3 ♖d6 38.h7
♖h6 39.♖d8 1-0

Igor Yasakov 16
Marc Schroeder
cr 2014

1.e4 e5 2.♘f3 ♘c6 3.♗c4 ♘f6
4.♘g5 d5 5.exd5 ♘xd5 6.♘xf7
♔xf7 7.♕f3+ ♔e6 8.♘c3 ♘cb4
9.♗b3 c6 10.a3 ♘a6 11.♘xd5
cxd5 12.d4 ♗e7 13.c4 ♕d6
14.0-0 e4 15.♕h5 g6 16.♕h6 ♔f7
17.cxd5

17...g5 18.♕h5+ ♔g7 19.♗xg5
♗xg5 20.♕xg5+ ♕g6 21.♕e5+
♕f6 22.f3± [22.♖ae1!± Elison-
Schroeder (Game 17)] 22...e3 23.♖fe1
♗d7 [23...♗f5 24.g4 ♗g6 25.♖xe3 ♖he8
26.g5+−] 24.♕g3+ ♕g6 25.♖xe3
♖ae8 26.♖e5 ♕xg3 27.hxg3 ♘c7
28.♖ae1 ♖b5 29.♗a4 ♖hf8 30.♔f2
[30.d6 a6 31.♔f2±] 30...♖d8 31.♖e7+
♖f7 32.♖xd7 ♖fxd7 33.♗xb5
♖xd5 34.♖e7+ ♔f6 35.♖xb7 ♖xd4
36.♔g1 [36.♗e3 ♖d2 37.♖xh7 ♖xb2
38.♗c6 ♖b3+ 39.♔f4 ♖xa3 40.g4±]
36...♖d1+ 37.♔h2 h5 38.♖xa7
[38.♖h7 ♖b1 39.♖xh5 ♖dd1 40.g4 ♖h1+
41.♔g3 ♖xh5 42.gxh5 ♖xb2=] 38...♖b1
39.f4 [39.b4?? ♖dd1 40.g4 h4−+;
39.♖d7 ♖xd7 40.♗xd7=; 39.♖a6+
♔g7 40.♗a4 ♖d2 41.♖a7+ ♔f8=]
39...♖dd1 40.g4 hxg4 41.♗e2
♖d4 42.♔g3 ♖xb2 43.♗xg4 ♖b3+
44.♗f3 ♖c3 45.♖a6+ [45.a4 ♖cc4
46.a5 ♖xf4=] 45...♔g7 46.a4 ♖cc4
47.a5 ½-½

Kari Elison   **17**
Marc Schroeder
cr 2014

1.e4 e5 2.♘f3 ♘c6 3.♗c4 ♘f6
4.♘g5 d5 5.exd5 ♘xd5 6.♘xf7
♔xf7 7.♕f3+ ♔e6 8.♘c3 ♘cb4
9.♗b3 c6 10.a3 ♘a6 11.♘xd5
cxd5 12.d4 ♗e7 13.c4 ♕d6
14.0-0 e4 15.♕h5 g6 16.♕h6
♔f7 17.cxd5 g5 18.♕h5+ ♔g7
19.♗xg5 ♗xg5 20.♕xg5+ ♕g6
21.♕e5+ ♕f6

22.♖ae1! **♗d7** [22...♕xe5 23.dxe5
♘c5 24.♗a2 ♗f5 25.e6 a5 26.f3 ♗g6
27.d6 ♖ad8 28.♖d1 ♘d3 29.fxe4 ♖xd6
30.♖f3 ♗xe4 31.♖e3 ♗g6 32.♗b1
♖e8 33.♗xd3 ♖exe6 34.♖xe6 ♖xe6
35.♗c4±; 22...♗f5 23.f3 ♕xe5 24.dxe5
♘c5 25.fxe4 ♗xe4 26.♗a2±] **23.♖e3**
♖hf8 [23...♕xe5 24.dxe5 ♘c5 25.♗c4
♗f5 26.f3 exf3 27.♖fxf3 ♗g6 28.b4±]
24.f3 ♗b5 25.♖c1 exf3 [25...♕xe5
26.dxe5 ♖ac8 27.♖ec3 ♖xc3 28.♖xc3
b6 29.a4 ♗e8 30.fxe4 ♘c5 31.♗c2
a5 32.e6 ♗g6 33.e7 ♖h8 34.d6±]
26.♖xf3 ♕xe5 27.dxe5 ♖ac8
28.♖g3+ ♔h6 29.♖d1 ♘c5 30.e6
♗e2 [30...♘e4 31.♖h3+ ♔g7 32.a4
♗c4 (32...♗e2 33.♖e1 ♘d6 34.♖g3+
♔h8 35.e7 ♖f6 36.♖e3 h5 37.♖e6
♖xe6 38.♖xe6 ♖c1+ 39.♔f2 ♖b1
40.♖xd6 ♖xb2+ 41.♔g3 ♖xb3+ 42.♔h4
♗f7 43.♖d8+ ♔g7 44.g4+−) 33.e7
♖fe8 34.♗xc4 ♖xc4 35.b3 ♖c7 36.d6±]
31.e7 ♖fe8 [31...♖f6 32.♖e1 ♘d3

33.♗d1 ♘xe1 34.♗xe2 ♘c2 35.♖d3
♖d6 36.♖h3+ ♔g7 37.♗h5 ♘d4
38.e8♕ ♖xe8 39.♗xe8±]

32.♖e3□ ♗xd1 33.♗xd1 ♖c7
[33...b5 34.♗g4 ♖b8 35.d6 ♔g5
36.♖e5+ ♔xg4 37.♖xc5±] **34.**
d6 ♖d7 35.♖h3+ ♔g5 36.♗h5
♖dxe7 37.dxe7 ♖xe7 38.♔f1
♘d3 39.♖xd3 ♔xh5 40.♔f2 ♔g6
41.h4 ♖c7 42.♖d6+ ♔g7 43.♔f3
b6 44.♔e4   1-0

Exercise 1

position after 23.♗xh7

How does Black save himself?
(solution on page 248)

Exercise 2

position after 52...♖xc2

Black could have forced White into
this position. White wins.
(solution on page 248)

Exercise 3

position after 64...♖a6

After White's next move Black
resigned. What did White play?
(solution on page 249)

Fame or Foolhardiness?

by Ufuk Tuncer

1.	d4	♘f6
2.	c4	e5
3.	dxe5	♘g4
4.	♗f4	g5

The prudent embark when the sea is calm – the rash when the sea is stormy (Maori proverb)

When Baadur Jobava beat Radoslaw Wojtaszek in Wijk aan Zee 2014 with 4...g5, he found many followers and caused confusion among the commentators. In his 'Chess Improver' blog, Nigel Davies celebrated this 'Budapest Revival' and advised players with white to try '4.e3, followed by ♘h3', or to avoid the dangerous gambit altogether with 2.♘f3.

However, in the sober light of analysis it soon becomes clear that the trendy and aggressive 4...g5 causes serious weaknesses, which White can exploit by advancing his h-pawn.

The undisputed main line is the prudent 4...♘c6 5.♘f3 ♗b4+ 6.♘bd2 ♕e7 7.e3, of course. I will not discuss it in this article, but refer you to Viktor Moskalenko's letter in Yearbook 114.

5.♗g3!

Pavel Elianov has played 5.♗d2, but I will analyse only the stronger text-move.

After 5.♗g3! Jobava played the tricky move order 5...♘c6!? 6.♘f3 ♗g7 in the above-mentioned game, which transposes to 5...♗g7 6.♘f3 ♘c6 below, while avoiding the sharper 6.h4!.

Therefore, after 5...♘c6 I suggest 6.♘c3! ♘gxe5 7.♘d5 and only then h2-h4, exploiting the temporary weakness of the d5-square.

This finesse is not mentioned in the (German) book *Tennison-Gambit/Budapester-Gambit* by Uwe Bekemann (2015), which helped my research.

5...♗g7

And here White has a choice between 6.h4 and 6.♘f3.

The Most Principled Move 6.h4!

This move demands a far-reaching decision from Black, because it is not yet clear that the knight must go to f3.

6...♘xe5

The moves 6...h5?!, 6...♗xe5?! and 6...♘c6?! are inferior, but it is quite possible that 6...h6!? is the lesser evil. Still, after 7.♘f3 ♘c6 8.hxg5 hxg5 9.♖xh8+ ♗xh8 10.♘c3±, followed by ♕c2 and 0-0-0, the open h-file and better development gave White the advantage in Girones Barrios-Mendez Fortes, Havana 2014.

7.hxg5 ♘xc4

Budapest expert B.Fister tried 7...d6 without success here. It was met by the astonishing 8.♗xe5!? ♗xe5 9.♕d2! ♗e6 10.f4± in Pellen-Fister, cr 2015.

8.♘c3 c6

8...♘xb2? loses to 9.♕c2 ♘a4 10.♘d5!, and 8...♕xg5?! is horrible after 9.♖c1± or the creative 9.♖h4!?.

9.♕c2 d5 10.e3! ♕a5

Although Black has managed to occupy the centre and is

threatening 11...♘xb2, White has a clear advantage after both 11.♘e2±, winning pawn h7 (Dunlop-Maitre, cr 2012), and 11.♗xc4 dxc4 12.♔f1±, Kolanek-Vasquez Nigro, Lechenicher SchachServer 2012.

The Most Common Move 6.♘f3 ♘c6 7.♘c3 ♘gxe5 8.♘xe5 ♘xe5 9.h4!

Black has succeeded in exchanging a pair of knights, but

he is still far from equalizing. Even the moderate 9.e3 d6 10.h4± led to a comfortable advantage in Kotanjian-Movsisyan, Jermuk 2014.

9...g4

The move 9...h6!? would lead to the variation 6.h4 h6 mentioned above.
9...♘xc4?! 10.♕c2± is not advisable and 9...d6?! 10.hxg5 ♕xg5 11.e3 (Rojicek-Svoboda, Kouty nad Desnou 2010) leads to a situation from which White has won many miniatures (Exercise 3) because of the powerful ♘c3-d5.

10.h5!

White played the listless 10.e3 d6 11.♗e2 ♗e6 in Wojtaszek-Jobava, Wijk aan Zee 2014, and after 12.♖c1?!=, forfeiting the right to castle queenside, not a scintilla of a white advantage is left.

10...d6 11.h6! ♗f6

In the game Dronavalli-Zwardon, Pardubice 2012, White won after 12.c5±, but stronger was 12.♕c2!±, intending to castle queenside, as demonstrated in several computer games.

Conclusion

I think that 4...g5?! is a dubious move that only invites White to attack with his h-pawn. After 6.h4! the rare 6...h6!? offers Black some slight chance to resist.
As against his, there are plenty of resources in the other main line 4.♗f4 ♗b4+ (4...♘c6), and it is hard to understand why black players try to avoid it at all cost. I am looking forward to seeing the developments in this direction.

The Most Principled Move 6.h4!

Gordon Dunlop
Fabien Maitre
cr 2012

1.d4 ♘f6 2.c4 e5 3.dxe5 ♘g4 4.♗f4 g5 5.♗g3! [5.♗d2 ♘xe5 6.♘f3 ♘bc6± Elianov-R.Mamedov, Shamkir 2014] 5...♗g7 [5...♘c6!? – Jobava's tricky move order is consistently met by 6.♘c3! (instead of 6.♘f3 ♗g7± – 5...♗g7 6.♘f3 ♘c6) 6...♘gxe5 7.♘d5

7...d6 (7...♗g7 8.h4 g4 (8...d6 9.e3± – 7...d6) 9.h5± △ h6/♗h4) 8.e3 ♗g7 9.h4 g4 (9...h6 10.hxg5 hxg5 11.♖xh8+ ♗xh8

12.♕h5 ♗g7 13.♗e2 ♗f5 14.♘h3±) 10.h5± and Black cannot prevent both h5-h6 and ♗h4] **6.h4!** [See the diagram in the introduction. 6.♘f3±; 6.♘c3 ♘xe5 7.h4± – 6.h4] **6...♘xe5** [6...h6!? is probably no worse than the main line: 7.♘f3 ♘c6 8.hxg5 (8.♘c3 ♘gxe5 9.♘xe5 ♘xe5 10.e3 (10.hxg5 hxg5 11.♖xh8+ ♗xh8 – 8.hxg5; 10.♕c2 d6 11.hxg5 hxg5 12.♖xh8+ ♗xh8 – 10.hxg5) 10...d6 11.c5 ♗e6 12.hxg5 hxg5 13.♖xh8+ ♗xh8 is also comfortably better for White as given by Bekemann: 14.♕c2±; 14.♕h5±) 8...hxg5 9.♖xh8+ ♗xh8 10.♘c3 (10.♕c2 ♘gxe5 11.♘xe5 ♘xe5 12.♘c3 – 10.♘c3) 10...♘gxe5 11.♘xe5 ♘xe5 12.♕c2, looking at h7.

12...♔f8! (△ 13.♕h7 ♗g7) 12...♘g6 13.0-0-0 d6 (13...♔f8 14.c5 ♘e5 15.e3±) 14.c5 ♗e5?! (14...♗e6 15.e3±) 15.♗xe5 ♘xe5 16.g3+– Mootamri-Jimena Bonillo, cr 2008; 12...d6 13.♕h7! (13.c5 ♗e6 14.♖d1 ♔f8 15.e3 ♕e7 16.cxd6 cxd6 (Maximus-Smallmaster, Infinity Chess 2014) 17.♗e2±) 13...♗f6 14.♕g8+ ♗e7 (14...♔d7 15.♘d5 ♗e6 – 14... ♔e7) 15.♘d5+ ♗e6 16.♘xf6 ♕xf6 17.♗xe5 ♕xe5 18.0-0-0 ♗e7 19.♖d3 ♗f5 (19...♕f4+ 20.♖e3+ ♔f6 21.g4 ♗xg4 22.♖xa8 ♕xf2 23.♔d2 ♕xf1 24.♕xb7 ♕f4 25.♕xa7+) 20.♕xg5+ ♕f6 (Varnatiger-Kikoursus, gameknot.com 2013) 21.♖e3+! ♗e6 22.♕xf6+ ♔xf6 23.♖f3+ ♔g6 24.e3±) 13.0-0-0 d6 14.c5 (14.e4!? ♗e6 15.♗b1±; 14.e3 ♗e6 15.♘b5 (15.c5!±) 15...a6 16.♘d4 ♗d7 (Girones Barrios-Mendez Fortes, Havana 2014) 17.c5! ♖c8 18.♕b3 dxc5 19.♘f3 ♘xf3 20.gxf3 ♕e8 21.♕xb7 ♗c6 22.♕a7±) 14...♗e6 15.e4 (15.e3!?± – 14.e3) 15...♕e7 16.♘d5 ♗xd5 17.♖xd5 (17.cxd6! cxd6 18.♖xd5 ♖d8 19.f3±) 17...♖d8 18.♕c3± Topmagic-Temp, www.bestlogic.ru 2012; 6...h5?! 7.♘f3 ♕e7?! (7...♘c6 8.♘c3 ♘gxe5

9.♘xg5 ♞xc4 10.♖c1±) 8.♘c3 ♞xe5
9.♘d5+− Bier-Lauer, Lechenicher
SchachServer 2013; 6...♗xe5?! 7.♗xe5
♞xe5 8.♘f3 ♞bc6 9.hxg5 d6 (9...♞xf3+
10.gxf3 ♕xg5 11.♘c3±) 10.♘xe5 dxe5
(10...♞xe5 11.f4+−) 11.♕xd8+ ♖xd8
12.♘d2±; 6...♞c6?! 7.hxg5! (7.♘f3± –
6.♘f3 ♞c6 7.h4) 7...♕xg5 (7...♞gxe5
8.e3 ♕xg5± – 6...♞xe5 7.hxg5 ♕xg5
8.e3 ♞bc6) 8.♘c3! ♗xe5 9.♘xe5 ♞cxe5
10.♘d5?! (10.e3!! ♕f5 11.♕d2 d6 12.f3
♞f6 13.e4 ♕g6 14.0-0-0+−; 10.♘f3±)
10...♕d8 11.♘f3± Haluschka-Herzog,
cr 2005] 7.hxg5 [7.♘c3 d6 (7...g4!?
8.h5 d6 9.h6 ♗f6 10.♕c2± Bekemann)
8.hxg5 ♞bc6 9.e3 ♞e6 10.♘d5±
Khairullin-Mamedyarov, Khanty-Mansiysk
blitz 2013] 7...♞xc4 [7...d6 (the latest
attempt)

8.♗xe5 (8.♘c3?! ♗e6± is also good for
White after any of 9.e3, 9.♗xe5 or 9.f4)
8...♞xe5□ 9.♕d2! (a multi-purpose
square for the queen. f2-f4 will kick the
bishop with tempo) 9...♗e6 10.f4 ♗g7
11.e4 ♕e7 12.♗e2 (12.♘f3+ △ ♘c3,
0-0-0) 12...f6 13.gxf6 ♗xf6 14.♘c3
♞d7 15.♗h5+ ♔f7 16.e5! with the idea
x♘d5 16...♞xe5□ 17.fxe5 ♗h4+ 18.g3
♗xg3+ 19.♔d1 0-0-0 20.♕e2 dxe5+
21.♔c2±; later Black forfeited on time
in a hopeless position, Pellen-Fister,
cr 2015; 7...♕xg5?! 8.e3 (8.♘c3 ♞a6
(8...♞xc4± – 7...♞xc4 8.♘c3 ♕xg5; 8...
d6 9.e3± △ ♘h3, ♘d5 Bekemann) 9.e3
(9.♘h3 ♕h6 10.e3 d6± – 9.e3) 9...d6
(9...♞c6 10.♘d5 ♗xb2 11.♖b1 ♕g7
12.♗xc7 ♞c3+ 13.♔e2±) 10.♘h3 ♕h6
(10...♗xh3 11.♖xh3 ♕f5 12.♖h5±)
11.♗e2 ♞c6 12.♘d5 (12.♕d2± ♞c5?
13.♘d5+− ♞e4 14.♗f4 ♕g6 15.♕c2)
12...♗xb2 13.c5 (13.♖b1!?±) 13...0-0
14.cxd6 cxd6 15.♖b1 ♗e5 16.f4 ♗g7
17.♗xa6 bxa6 18.♖c1± Hugodave-
Jamwan, Engine Room 2012) 8...♞bc6

9.♘c3 d6 10.♘d5 ♕d8 (10...♗g4?!
11.♗e2 0-0-0 12.f4 ♕g6 13.fxe5 ♗f5
14.♗f2+− Morbier-Kikoursus, gameknot.
com 2009) 11.♗h4 f6 12.♕h5+ ♔f8
13.♗e2± Petzold-Anders, freechess.de
2014] 8.♘c3 c6 [△ ...d7-d5 8...♕xg5?!
9.♖c1!! (- simply compare the activity
of all the rooks on the board! 9.♖h4!?
♗xc3+ (9...b5?! 10.e3+− Wagner-
Alozy, Email 2005; 9...♗xb2?? 10.♘e4+
♔d8 11.♕c2+−) 10.bxc3 d5 11.e4±
Mkchess-Reksal, gameknot. com 2013)
9...c6 (9...♗xb2 10.♕c2 ♞c4 11.e3
♕c5 (11...d5 12.♘f3 ♕f5 13.♗d3+−)
12.♘xc4 ♕xc4 13.♕d2 ♗xc3
(13...♞a6 14.♖h4+− Zagor Almanah-
Alexander3, Engine Room 2011)
14.♖xc3 ♕b5 15.♗xc7+− Sawiniec-
Fister, cr 2012) 10.♘f3 (White goes
for the h7-pawn instead of preventing
...d7-d5; 10.e4 d5 11.exd5 ♞e5 12.♘h3
♕h6 13.♗e2±) 10...♕a5 11.♕d3
d5 12.♖xh7 ♗xc3+ 13.♖xc3+−
1-0 Sabbatini-Herzog, Lechenicher
SchachServer 2013; 8...♞c6 (Bizovi-
Vekemans, Avoine 2014) 9.e4! ♞b6
(9...♗xb2?? 10.♕c1+−; 9...♗xc3+
10.bxc3 ♞b6 11.e5±) 10.♕d2 d6
11.0-0-0±; 8...♗xb2? 9.♕c2 ♞a4
10.♘d5!+− (Ling-Bitmanis, Email 2010)
and here after 10...♗xa1, 11.♘e4+!
is even stronger than 11.♕xa4 ♞a6
12.e3+−, e.g. 11...♔f8 12.♗xc7+−]
9.♕c2 [△ ♕e4+] 9...d5 10.e3! [10.
e4 gives Black more counterplay than
he deserves: 10...♞xb2?! (10...♞a6!
11.exd5 ♕e7+ 12.♗e2 ♕xe2+
13.♗xe2 ♗xb2 14.♘e4±) 11.♗xb2
♕a5 12.e5 (12.♖c1! d4 13.♕b3 dxc3
14.♗c4 0-0 15.♘f3±) 12...d4 13.♘ge2
dxc3 14.♗xc3 ♕xc3+ 15.♘xc3 ♗f5
16.♘d1 (16.0-0-0= Mareco-Santiago,
Mar del Plata 2014) 16...♗g6 17.♘e3±]
10...♕a5 [△ ♞xb2, see the diagram in
the introduction] 11.♘ge2 [11.♗xc4!?
deserves attention too: 11...dxc4 12.♔f1
♗f5 13.e4 ♗e6 14.e5 ♞d7 15.♖xh7
(15.f4 0-0-0 16.♘f3 ♞c5 17.f5 ♗d5
18.f6 ♗f8 19.♖xh7 ♞e4 20.♘xd5±
Kolanek-Vasquez Nigro, Lechenicher
SchachServer 2012) 15...♖xh7 16.♕xh7
♗xe5 17.♗xe5 ♕xe5 18.♘f3 ♕f5
19.♕h8+ ♔f8 20.♖d1 ♕h7 21.♕e5
♞d7 22.♕c7+− Stalhandske-Osclopez,
gameknot.com 2013] 11...♕b4
12.♖b1 ♞d7 13.♖xh7 ♖g8

[13...♖xh7 14.♕xh7 ♔f8 15.♘d4 ♞db6
16.♗e2 ♕e7 17.♗f4+− Meissner-
Fels, cr 2009] 14.a3 ♕c5 15.♖c1
♞f8 16.♖h1± ♕g6 17.♗f4 ♞xf4
18.♗xf4 ♗e6 19.b4 ♕e7 20.♗xc4
dxc4 21.♘e4 ♖d8 22.♖h7 ♔f8
23.♘c5 ♗d5 24.e4 b6 25.♔f1
♗e6 26.♗e3 ♗c8 27.♕xc4 ♕d6
28.f4 ♔e8 29.e5 ♕g6 30.♖xg7
♖xg7 31.♘e4 ♗a6 32.♘f6+ ♔f6
33.exf6 ♗xc4+ 34.♖xc4 ♖h7
35.♔f2 ♖d5 36.♖e4+ ♖d8 37.♖e7
♖d7 38.♖xd7+ ♔xd7 39.f5 ♖h5
40.g4 ♖h2+ 41.♔g3 ♖h8 42.g6
fxg6 43.fxg6 ♔e6 44.f7   1-0

Ildar Khairullin
Shakhriyar Mamedyarov
Khanty-Mansiysk 2013 (2)

1.d4 ♞f6 2.c4 e5 3.dxe5 ♞g4
4.♗f4 g5 5.♗g3 ♗g7 6.h4± ♞xe5

7.♘c3 [7.hxg5!±] 7...d6 [7...g4 8.h5
h6 (8...d6 9.♘h4 ♞f6 10.♕c2 ♗e6
11.e3±) 9.h4 ♗f6 10.♗xf6 ♕xf6
11.♘d5±] 8.hxg5 ♞bc6 9.e3
♗e6 10.♘d5 ♞a5? [10...♕d7
11.♕d2±] 11.b3!? [11.♕a4+!
♞ac6 12.♘f3 ♞xf3+ (12...♞d7
13.♕c2+−) 13.gxf3+−] 11...♞d7
[11...♞ac6 12.♘e2 ♕d7 13.♘ec3+−]
12.♖c1+− c6 13.♘f4 ♕xg5
14.♘xe6 fxe6 15.♖h5 ♕d8
16.♕xd6 ♔f7 17.♘f3 h6 18.b4
[18.♗h4!+−] 18...b5 19.bxa5
♖c8 20.♗e2 ♕xa5+ 21.♕d2
♕xd2+ 22.♘xd2 b4 23.♘e4 ♗f8
24.♖a5   1-0

Jacek Stopa
Andrzej Migala
Figueira da Foz 2015 (7)

1.d4 ♞f6 2.c4 e5 3.dxe5 ♞g4
4.♗f4 g5 5.♗g3 ♗g7 6.h4 h6
7.hxg5 hxg5 8.♖xh8+ ♗xh8

9.e3 [9.♘c3 ♗xe5 10.♘xe5 ♘xe5
11.♘f3 d6 12.♘xe5 dxe5 13.♕b3±]
9...♘xe5 [9...♗xe5 10.♘xe5 ♘xe5
11.♘c3 d6 12.♘f3 g4 13.♗e2±]
10.♘c3 d6 11.♕h5± ♗g7
[11...♘f6 12.♘h3 ♗g4 13.♕h7 ♘bd7
14.♘e4 ♘g6 (14...♗xh3 15.♕xh3 ♘c5
16.♘xc5 dxc5 17.♕h7±) 15.♕g8+
♔e7! (15...♘df8 16.c5!+−) 16.♕xd8+
♖xd8 17.♘hxg5±] **12.♘h3 ♗xh3
13.♕xh3** [13.gxh3! ♘bc6 14.0-0-0
♘g6 15.♘e4±] **13...♘bc6** [13...♘bd7!
14.♘e4 (14.♗e2 ♘g6 15.♘e4 ♕e7
16.♕f5 ♗xb2 17.♖b1 ♗e5 18.♗xe5
♕xe5 19.♕xe5+ ♘gxe5 20.♖xb7 ♔d8
21.♖xg5 ♘c5 22.♖b5±] 14...♕e7
15.♕h7 f6 16.♗xe5 ♘xe5 17.♘g3 ♕f7
18.♗e2 (18.♕f5 ♕g6 19.♗e2 ♕xf5
20.♘xf5 ♔f7 21.♖h5+ ♔g8 22.0-0-0±]
18...0-0-0 19.♘f5 ♗f8 20.♕xf7
♘xf7 21.0-0-0±] **14.0-0-0± ♕d7
15.♕xd7+!?** [15.♕h7! ♗f8 16.♗e2
♖e8 17.c5±] **15...♘xd7 16.♘d5±
0-0-0 17.♗d3± ♔b8 18.f4** [18.♖h1!
♗e5 19.f4 gxf4 20.exf4 ♖h8 21.♖xh8+
♗xh8 22.b3±] **18...gxf4 19.exf4
♘c5** [19...♖h8 20.♗f5 ♘c5 21.♗f2
a5=] **20.♗b1 ♖e8= 21.♖e1 ♖xe1+**
[21...♖g8! 22.♗f2 a5=] **22.♗xe1 ♘d4
23.g3 c6 24.♘e7 ♔c7 25.b3 ♗e2+
26.♔c2 ♘d4+** [26...♔d7! 27.♘f5
♗f6 28.♔d2 ♘c3=] **27.♔d1 ♔d7
28.♘f5 ♘xf5 29.♗xf5+± ♔e7
30.♔e2 ♘e6 31.♔d3 ♘d4 32.♗c8
b6** [32...♘e6 33.b4±] **33.b4** [33.♗h3
♘e6 34.♗g2 c5 35.♗e4±] **33...c5
34.b5=** [34.bxc5 dxc5 35.g4 ♔d8
36.♗b7 (36.♗a6 f5 37.gxf5 (37.♗h4+
♔c7 38.gxf5 ♘xf5=) 37...♘f6=) 36...
f5 37.g5 ♗f8=; 34.g4 ♘f3 35.♗f2 cxb4
36.♗b7 ♘h2 37.g5 ♗b2 38.♗g3 ♘f1
39.♗h4 c3 40.♗f2=] **34...♗d8?**
[34...d5! 35.♗d2 (35.♗f2 dxc4+ 36.♗xc4
♔d6=) 35...♘f3 36.cxd5 (36.♗e3
♘e1+ 37.♔e2 ♘c2 38.cxd5 ♔d6=)

36...♘xd2 37.♔xd2 ♔d6=] **35.♗b7±
f5 36.a4 ♔c7?** [36...♗f6 37.♗g2 ♔e7
38.♗h3 ♔e6 39.g4 d5 40.gxf5+ ♔d6
41.cxd5 ♔xd5 42.♗g2+ ♔d6 43.♗e4±]
37.♗g2 ♔d7 38.a5!? [38.♗h3! ♔e6
(38...♗f6 39.g4 fxg4 40.♗xg4+ ♔e7
41.♗d1±) 39.g4 fxg4 40.♗xg4+ ♔e7
41.♗d1! (41.♗e4 ♘c2 42.♗d2 ♘b4
43.♗d1±) 41...♘e6 (41...d5 42.cxd5
♘f5 43.♗g4 ♘d6 44.♗e6±) 42.♔e4
♘c7 43.♗h4+ ♗f6 44.♗f2 ♗f8 (44...
d5+ 45.cxd5 ♘e8 46.♔f5+−) 45.♔f5
♔e7 46.♗f3±] **38...♗f6 39.a6 ♗d8
40.♗c3 ♗f6 41.♗c6+** [41.♗h3! ♔e6
42.g4±] **41...♗e6 42.♗b7** [42.♗d5+
♔d7 43.♗g2 ♗e6 44.♗h3 d5=]
**42...♔d7 43.♗g2 ♔e6 44.♗d5+
♔d7 45.♗g8 ♗g7 46.♗h7 ♔e6
47.♗g6 ♗f6** [47...d5! 48.cxd5+ ♔xd5
49.♗xd4 c4+ 50.♔e2 ♗xd4 51.♗xf5
♔c5 52.♗d7 ♔d4 53.g4 ♔e4=]
48.♗h5 ♗b3?? [48...d5! 49.cxd5+
♔xd5 50.♗f7+ ♔d6 51.♗c4 ♔d7=]
49.♗e1± d5 [49...♘c1+ 50.♔e3 ♘a2
51.g4 ♘b4 52.gxf5+ ♔xf5 53.♔f3±;
49...♘d4 50.g4±] **50.cxd5+**   1-0

The Most Common Move
6.♘f3

Alina l'Ami
Orkhan Eminov
Malatya 2015 (8)

**1.d4 ♘f6 2.c4 e5 3.dxe5 ♘g4
4.♗f4 g5 5.♗g3 ♗g7 6.♘f3 ♘c6
7.h4 ♘gxe5**

**8.hxg5 ♘xf3+ 9.gxf3 ♗xb2
10.♘d2 ♕xg5 11.♗xc7 ♕f6** [11...
d6] **12.♖b1± d6 13.♗xd6 ♗f5
14.e4** [14.c5! ♗xb1 15.♕xb1 ♖d8
16.♘e4 ♕d4 (16...♗c3+ 17.♔d1 ♕d4+
18.♔c2 ♗a1 (18...♘b4+ 19.♔c1+−)
19.e3 ♕a4+ 20.♔c1! (20.♕b3 ♕xb3+

21.axb3 ♗e5 22.♖h5 ♗xd6 23.cxd6±)
20...♕a3+ 21.♔d2 ♕a5+ 22.♔d1
♕a4+ 23.♔e1 ♕a5+ 24.♘d2 ♖xd6
25.cxd6 ♗c3 26.♕xb7 ♗xd2+ 27.♔d1
♕d5 28.♗c4 ♕xd6 29.♕xf7+ ♔d8
30.♔e2 ♗c3 31.♖d1 ♘d4+ 32.♗f1+−)
17.e3 ♗b4+ 18.♔e2 ♕c4+ 19.♔d1
♕a4+ 20.♕c2 ♕xc2+ 21.♔xc2 ♗e5
22.♗c4±] **14...♕xd6 15.♖xb2 0-0-0
16.♖h5?** [16.♕b3! ♕e7 17.♖h5 ♗e6
18.♖c5 ♕c7 19.f4 ♖hg8 20.f5 ♗d7
21.♖d5±] **16...♗e6♙ 17.♖hb5 ♖d7
18.♕a4?** [18.♖d5! ♕c7 19.♖xd7
♕xd7♙=] **18...♖hd8 19.c5?** [19.♗e2
♖g8 20.♖d5 ♖g1+ 21.♘f1 ♕e7∓]
19...♕xd2+ [19...♕e5! 20.♖xb7 ♖xb7
21.♕xc6+ ♕c7∓] **20.♖xd2 ♖xd2
21.♖b1??** [21.♗c4! ♖d1+ 22.♔e2 ♖c1
23.♗xe6+ fxe6 24.f4 (24.♔e3?? ♖e1+
25.♔f4 e5+ 26.♔f5 ♖g1−+) 24...♘d4+
25.♔d2 (25.♔e3?? ♖c3+ 26.♔d2
♘xb5+−+) 25...♘b3+ 26.♔e2 ♘d4+
27.♔d2=] **21...♘e5 22.♗e2 ♖xa2??**
[22...♗c4!! 23.♗xc4 ♘xf3+ 24.♔f1
♖g8−+] **23.♕b5?? [23.♕b4 ♖d1
24.♔c3+−] 23...♖xe2+−+ 24.♔f1
♖e1+ 25.♔xe1 ♘xf3+ 26.♔f1
♗c4+**   0-1

Dronavalli Harika
Vojtech Zwardon
Pardubice 2012 (3)

**1.d4 ♘f6 2.c4 e5 3.dxe5 ♘g4
4.♗f4 g5 5.♗g3 ♗g7 6.♘f3 ♘c6**
[6...d6 7.h4 dxe5 (7...gxh4?! 8.♗xh4
♕d7 9.♘c3± Bekemann) 8.♕xd8+
♔xd8 9.♘c3±] **7.♘c3** [7.h4 ♘gxe5
(7...h6± − 6.h4 h6 7.♘f3 ♘c6) 8.hxg5!?
(8.♘xe5 ♘xe5 9.♘c3± − 7.♘c3;
8.♘c3± − 7.♘c3) 8...♘xf3+! (the human
solution is trickier than the computer's, but
objectively it is not enough for equality:
8...♘xc4 9.♘c3 d6 10.e4 (10.♖c1 ♘b6
(10...♗e6 11.e4± − 10.e4)) 11.♕d5
♗e6 12.♖xh7±) 10...♗e6 11.♖c1 ♘xb2
12.♕c2 ♘c4 13.♘d5 ♘b6 14.♗b5
♔f8 15.♘f4± With Love-AmOs 4EvEr,
Engine Room 2011) 9.gxf3 ♗xb2 10.♘d2
♕xg5 11.♗xc7 d6! (11...♕f6? (A.l'Ami-
Eminov, Malatya 2015) 12.♖c1!± ♗xc1
13.♕xc1+−) 12.♘e4 ♕g7 (12...♗xa1
13.♕xa1 ♕e5 14.♕c1+−) 13.♖c1
0-0 14.♕h5 h6 15.♗xd6±] **7...♘gxe5**
[7...♘cxe5?! 8.h4 h6 (8...♘xc4 9.♗xg4
♘xb2 (9...♘d6 10.hxg5+−) 10.♕e4+
♕e7 11.♕xe7+ ♔xe7 12.♘d5+ ♔f8

13.罩c1+− Serjant-Harijs, www.bestlogic. ru 2012) 9.豐c2 (9.公xe5 公xe5 – 6.h4 h6!? 7.公f3 公c6 8.公c3 公gxe5 9.公xe5 公xe5) 9...d6 10.0-0-0 (10.hxg5 hxg5 11.罩xh8+ 魚xh8 12.0-0-0 魚e6 (12... f5 13.e3 c6 14.魚e2 豐f6 15.公e1±) 13.c5± Victorious-Oops, playchess.com 2013) 10...f5 11.e3 f4 (11...c6 12.魚d3 豐f6 (12...罩f8 13.魚e2+−) 13.魚e2±) 12.exf4 gxf4 13.魚xf4 0-0 14.魚xe5 公xe5 (14...魚xe5 15.公xe5 公xe5 16.豐d2 豐f6 17.公d5 豐xf2 18.罩xc7±) 15.公xe5 魚xe5 16.豐g6+ 魚g7 17.魚d3 罩f6 18.豐h7+ 含f8 19.罩d2±] 8.公xe5 [8.h4 公xc4? (8...h6± – 6.h4 h6!? 7.公f3 公c6 8.公c3 公gxe5; 8...d6 9.公xe5 公xe5± – 8.公xe5 公xe5 9.h4 d6; 8...g4 9.公xe5 公xe5±; - 8.公xe5 公xe5 9.h4 g4 9...魚xe5 10.公xe5 公xe5± – 8.公xe5 公xe5 9.魚xe5 公xe5 10.h4 g4) 9.e3!± (9.hxg5± – 7.h4 公gxe5 8.hxg5 公xc4 9.公c3) 9...公xb2 △ 10.豐c1] 8...公xe5 [8...魚xe5 9.魚xe5 公xe5 10.h4 (10.豐d4 d6 11.h4 魚e6 (11...g4 – 10.h4) 12.c5 g4 13.0-0-0 0-0 14.g3±) 10...g4 (10...gxh4 11.豐d4 d6 12.f4 公g6 13.0-0-0±) 11.豐d4 d6 12.f4 gxf3 13.exf3 罩g8 14.0-0-0± De Blois Figueredo-Roth, cr 2007] 9.h4! [See the diagram in the introduction. The position after 9.e3 d6 (9...公g6 10.c5 0-0 11.豐h5↑) 10.h4 g4 △ ...h7-h5 11.h5 h6 has occurred numerous times in human practice, and it is good enough for a solid advantage too (≤ 11...魚e6 12.h6 魚f6 13.公d5± Moiseenko-Scerbin, Olginka 2011): 12.魚h4± 魚f6 13.魚xf6 豐xf6 14.公d5 豐d8 15.豐d4 c6 16.公c3 c5 17.豐f4 魚e6 18.0-0-0 豐e7 19.公b5±, and White won a pawn in Kotanjian-Movsisyan, Jermuk 2014. Bekemann's innovation 9.e4?! is not so strong because it blocks the diagonal b1-h7 and restricts the 公c3: 9...公g6!?N (no more h2-h4!) 10.c5 0-0⇄ △ ...b7-b6) 9...g4 [△ ...h7-h5 9...h6± – 6.h4 h6!? 7.公f3 公c6 8.公c3 公gxe5 9.公xe5 公xe5; 9...gxh4? 10.魚xh4 f6 11.e4+−; 9...c6?! 10.e3!± 豐a5?! 11.豐c2!! g4 (Raznikov-Efroimski, Rishon Le Ziyyon 2015) 12.0-0-0!+−; 9...公xc4?! 10.豐c2 d5 (10...公e5 11.公b5 c6 12.公d6+ 含f8 13.0-0-0+− Narkun-Lauer, Lechenicher SchachServer 2014; 10...公b6 11.公b5+−; 11.hxg5 a6 12.罩xh7+− Krallmann-Raimann, Germany tt 2015) 11.e4 公e5 12.0-0-0 d4 13.公b5 0-0 14.公xd4 豐e7 15.hxg5±; ≤

9...d6 10.hxg5! (10.e3± – 9.e3) 10...豐xg5 (10...魚e6 11.e3 公xc4? (11...豐xg5 – 10...豐xg5; 11...c6 12.豐c2 (12.豐a4±) 12...豐xg5 13.0-0-0±) 12.魚xc4 魚xc3+ (12...魚xc4 13.豐a4+ b5 14.魚xb5+−) 13.bxc3 魚xc4 14.豐d4+− Serna Lara-J. Diaz, Albacete 2005) 11.e3±.

Black is in trouble because of 公c3-d5, for example: 11...魚g4! (11...豐g4? (Kasantsev-Tkachenko, Voronezh 2010) 12.公d5 豐d8 13.h4 f6 14.魚e2 公e5 15.魚h5++−; 11...h5? 12.魚h4 豐g6 (12...豐h6 13.公d5+−) 13.公d5+− Rach-Jimena Bonillo, cr 2007; 11...0-0?! 12.魚f4 豐g6 13.公d5+− wins at least a pawn, Smuts-Joubert, Email 2010; 11...魚e6?! 12.公d5 豐d8 (12...0-0-0?? 13.罩h5 1-0 Riazantsev-Tjurin, Voronezh 2004. There is no escape: 13...豐g4 14.魚e2 豐e4 15.f3+−; 12...魚xd5 13.cxd5 0-0-0 (13...0-0 14.罩c1 c5 (Perunovic-Saheb, Algiers 2015) 15.dxc6 bxc6 16.魚e2 豐g6 17.罩h4±) 14.罩c1 公g6 (14...豐e7 15.罩h4+−) 15.豐c2 豐e7 (Dziuba-Kepeschuk, Polanica Zdroj 2005) 16.魚h4! f6 (16...公xh4 17.罩xh4+−) 17.魚d3±) 13.魚h4 f6 (13...豐d7 14.魚f6±) 14.豐h5+ 含f8 (14...魚d7 15.魚e2 c6 16.魚f4 豐e8 (16...魚f7!? 17.豐f5+ 含c7 18.公e6+ 魚xe6 19.豐xe6±) 17.豐xe8+ 罩axe8 (17...罩hxe8 18.公h5 罩g8 19.公xg7 罩xg7 20.魚xf6+−) 18.公h5+− 1-0 Gavin Roche-Diaz Fernandez, Oropesa del Mar 1996) 15.魚e2 c6 16.魚f4 魚f7 17.豐f5± Wong-Toth Katona, Budapest 2015) 12.豐d2! (12.豐b3 豐d8 (Rojicek-Svoboda, Kouty nad Desnou 2010; 12...公g6! 13.魚xb7 0-0 14.魚d3 豐a5 15.罩c1 罩ab8 16.豐d5 豐xd5 17.公xd5 罩xb2 18.公xc7±) 13.f3 魚e6 14.0-0-0±) 12...豐d8 (12...公g6 13.公d5± △ 13...0-0-0?? 14.豐a5+−) 13.豐c2± △ f2-f3, 罩xh7] 10.h5! [△ h5-h6 10.e3 d6 (10...h5 11.豐a4!± prevents ...d7-

d6) 11.魚e2 (11.h5!± – 9.e3) 11...魚e6 12.罩c1?! (Wojtaszek-Jobava, Wijk aan Zee 2014) 12...c6!?⇄ Vuckovic] 10...d6 [10...公xc4? 11.公d5 魚e5 12.罩c1 魚xg3 13.fxg3 c6 14.豐d4+−; 10...f5?! 11.e3 (11.公d5!? c6 12.h6 魚f6 13.魚xf6+ 豐xf6 14.e3±) 11...d6 (11...h6 12.魚h4 魚f6 13.豐d4±) 12.h6 魚f6 13.公d5 c6 (13...0-0 14.豐c2±) 14.公xf6+ 豐xf6 15.豐d2+ Guseva-Kashlinskaya, Khanty-Mansiysk 2014. The alternative is to stop the advance of the h-pawn: 10...h6!? 11.魚h4 魚f6 (11... f6?! 12.f4 公xc4 (12...gxf3 13.gxf3+−) 13.豐d3 公b6 (13...d5 14.0-0-0 魚e6 15.e4 d4 16.公b5+−) 14.豐g6+ 含f8 15.e4 豐e8 (J. de Jong-Kuzmicz, Haarlem 2014) 16.公b5! 豐xg6 17.hxg6+− △ 17...c6 18.公d6) 12.魚xf6 豐xf6 13.公d5 豐d6 (≥ 13...豐d8 14.豐d4 (14.f4 gxf3 15.exf3±) 14...d6 15.0-0-0! (15.f4 gxf3 16.gxf3±) 15...魚e6 16.f4 gxf3 17.exf3 魚xd5 (17... c5 18.豐f4 魚xd5 19.罩xd5 豐e7 20.魚d3 0-0-0 21.魚e4±) 18.cxd5 f6 (18...0-0 19.罩h3 豐f6 (19...f5 20.f4) 20.含b1 罩fe8 (20...罩ae8 21.豐xa7) 21.魚d3±) 19.含b1 公d7 20.豐a4 豐d8 21.魚d3 公c5 22.豐c2 公xd3 23.罩xd3 罩e8 24.罩c1 罩c8 25.罩b3 b6 26.罩c3 罩e7 27.g4±) 14.f4 gxf3 15.exf3 c6 16.公e3 魚b4+ (Visloguzov-Vasquez Nigro, Email 2011; 16...豐f6 17.豐d2 0-0 (17...d6 18.0-0-0 0-0 (18...魚d7 19.豐xd6 豐f4 20.豐d4 豐xd4 21.罩xd4±) 19.豐xd6 (19.魚e2!N – 17...0-0) 19...魚e6 20.豐d4 罩fd8 21.豐h4 罩xd1+ 22.公xd1 含g7 23.b3± Kurowski-Vasquez Nigro, Lechenicher SchachServer 2012) 18.魚e2 d6 (Akjoltoy-Kikoursus, gameknot.com 2012) 19.0-0-0! 罩e8 20.罩hf1 豐f4 21.g3 公d3+ 22.魚xd3 豐xe3 23.豐xe3 罩xe3 24.魚e4±) 17.含f2!N d6 (17...魚xb2+ 18.魚e2 f6 19.罩e1±; 17...公c5 18.豐d2±) 18.魚e2±] 11.h6! [11.e3± – 9.e3 10.h4 g4 11.h5; ≤ 11.魚h4 魚f6= Sarkar-Sipos, Kecskemet 2014] 11...魚f6

12.c5 [More powerful was 12.♕c2!, intending to castle queenside: 12...♗e6 13.e3 ♘d7 (13...♘xc4 14.♖h5 ♘e5 15.0-0-0±) 14.♘d5 ♗e5 (14...♘xd5 15.cxd5 ♘e5 16.♗h4 ♗f6 17.♗xf6 ♕xf6 18.♗b5±) 15.♗h4 f6 16.♘f4 ♗f7 (16...♗xf4 17.exf4 a5 18.0-0-0 ♘c5 19.f5 ♗f7 (19...♘d7 20.♗e2+−) 20.♕c3+−) 17.♗e2 c6 (17...♗xf4 18.exf4 ♕e7 (18...♗g6 19.♕c3+−) 19.0-0-0-0-0 20.c5 (20.♗xg4 ♖hg8 21.f3±) 20...♗g6 21.f5 ♗f7 (21...♗xf5 22.cxd6 ♗xc2 23.dxe7 ♖de8 24.♗xg4+−) 22.c6+−) 18.0-0-0 ♘a5 19.a3 ♘c5 (19...f5 20.♗d3+−) 20.♗xg4 b5 21.♘d3 (21.♘h5 b4 22.♘xf6+ ♔f8 23.axb4 ♕xb4 24.♘d7+ ♖xd7 25.♗xd7 ♖b8 26.♖d2±) 21...♘xd3+ (21...♗g6 22.f4 ♗xb2+ 23.♔xb2 (23.♔xb2?? ♖b8‼) 24.♔a2 bxc4 25.♔xc4 ♖b3∓) 23...♗xd3 24.♗xf6 ♖g8 25.♖h5+−) 22.♖xd3+ Robotman-Kohl3178, Engine Room 2012] **12...♗e6** [12...0-0 13.e3 ♗e6± – 12...♗e6] **13.e3 d5??** [13...0-0±] **14.♖h5!+− ♘d7 15.♘xd5 ♗xb2 16.♖b1 ♗xd5 17.♖xd5 ♗c3+ 18.♔e2 ♕e7 19.♕d3 ♗f6 20.♖xb7 ♖c8 21.♗xc7 ♕e6 22.♗d6 a6 23.♖b4 ♗e5 24.♗xe5 ♖xc5 25.♖xc5 ♘xc5 26.♖b8+** 1-0

Jan Willem de Jong
Krystian Kuzmicz
Haarlem 2014 (1)

1.d4 ♘f6 2.c4 e5 3.dxe5 ♘g4 4.♗f4 g5 5.♗g3 ♗g7 6.♘c3 ♘xe5 7.♘f3 ♘bc6 8.♘xe5 ♘xe5 9.h4 g4

10.h5 h6 11.♗h4± f6 [11...♗f6 12.♗xf6 ♕xf6 13.♘d5±] **12.f4 ♘xc4** [12...gxf3 13.gxf3+−; 12...♘c6 13.e4±] **13.♕d3 ♘b6** [13...d5 14.0-0-0 c6 15.♕g6+ ♔f8 16.e4+−] **14.♕g6++− ♔f8 15.e4 ♕e8** [15...d5 16.e5 ♕e8 17.♕xe8+ ♔xe8 18.exf6 ♗f8 19.♗d3+−] 16.♕xg4 [As mentioned in the notes to the previous game, here 16.♘b5! ♕xg6 17.hxg6+− was winning] **16...d5** [16...d6 17.f5 ♗d7 18.0-0-0+−; 16...♘d5 17.f5 ♘xc3 18.bxc3 d5 19.♗d3+−] **17.f5 d4** [17...dxe4 18.0-0-0 ♗d7 19.♗g3 ♕c8 20.♘xe4 ♗xf5 21.♕f4+−] **18.♘b5 ♕d5** [18...♕e5 19.0-0-0 ♗d7 20.♘xd4+−] **19.♘xd4 c5** [19...♘e3 20.♕f3 ♘xf1 21.♖xf1 ♗d7 22.0-0-0+−] **20.♘e6+ ♗xe6 21.fxe6**

♘e3 22.♕e2 ♘xf1 23.♖xf1 ♕xe6 24.e5 ♖e8 25.♗xf6?? [25.0-0-0‼ ♕xe5 (25...♔g8 26.♕e4 ♕xe5 27.♕g6 f5 28.♗f6 ♕xf6 29.♕xe8++−) 26.♕xe5 ♖xe5 27.♖xf6+ ♗xf6 28.♗xf6+−] **25...♗xf6= 26.♖xf6+ ♕xf6 27.exf6 ♔f7 28.♖d1 ♖xe2+ 29.♔xe2 ♖e8+?!** [29...♔xf6! 30.♖d7 ♖b8 31.♖c7 b6 32.♖xa7 ♔g5=] **30.♔f3 ♔xf6 31.g4** [31.♖d7! ♖e5 (31...♖e7?? 32.♖xe7 ♔xe7 33.♔e4 ♔d6 (33...♔e6 34.a4! b6 35.g4 a6 36.b3! b5 37.a5!+−) 34.♔f5+−) 32.♖xb7 ♖f5+ 33.♔g3 ♖g5+ 34.♔f2 ♖xh5 35.♖xa7±] **31...♖e6= 32.♖d7 ♖e7 33.♖d5 ♖e5 34.♖d7 ♖e7 35.♖d8 ♔e5** [35...♔g5 36.♖d5+ ♔h4 37.♖xc5 ♖d7=] **36.g5** [36.♖c8 b6 37.♖h8 ♖f7+ 38.♔g3 ♖f6=] **36...♖f7+= 37.♔g3** [37.♔g4 ♖f4+ 38.♔g3 hxg5 39.♖e8+ ♔f6 40.♖f8+ ♔e5=] **37...hxg5 38.♔g4 ♔f6 39.♖d6+ ♔g7 40.♔xg5 ♖c7 41.a4 c4 42.♔f5 b5 43.axb5 ♖c5+ 44.♔e4 ♖xb5 45.♖d2 ♖xh5 46.♖f2 ♖h1 47.♔d4 ♖c1 48.♔c5 ♔g6 49.♔b4 ♔g7 50.♖f3 ♖c2 51.♔a3 ♖c1 52.♖f5 ♔g6 53.♖c5 ♔f6 54.♔b4 ♖c2 55.♖xc4 ♖xb2+ 56.♔a5 ♔e6 57.♖a4 ♖b6 58.♖h4 ♔d6 59.♖h7 ♖b1 60.♖xa7 ♖a1+ 61.♔b6 ♖b1+ 62.♔a5 ♖a1+ 63.♔b6 ♖xa7 64.♔xa7** ½-½

Exercise 1

position after 8...c7-c6

Black seems OK, preparing ...d7-d5 and ...♕a5/...♘xb2. What should White do?
(solution on page 249)

Exercise 2

position after 8...g5-g4

Black has kept the h-file closed. How does White proceed?
(solution on page 249)

Exercise 3

position after 12...0-0-0

Black's last move 12...0-0-0 was a blunder. Deliver the final blow!
(solution on page 249)

1...e6 and 2...b6:
Is It Really Playable? – Part I

by Laszlo Gonda

1.	d4	e6
2.	c4	b6
3.	e4	♗b4+

During its entire existence, chess theory has always regarded this line as suspect. Although no one has ever been able to show a winning line against it, there have been problems for Black recently.

After 1.d4 e6 2.c4 b6, 3.e4 is probably the strongest option from White's point of view, and most repertoire books analyse it in detail. In the first game of this article, I will demonstrate the problems which cause chess theory to regard this opening as dubious. 3...♗b4+ is my recommendation, which might be playable.

Of course, White can just play 4.♘c3, but this line does not cause any harm and is just a transposition, so no problem. I may write about it in a future edition.

Another main line starts with 3.a3 ♗b7 4.♘c3 f5, and now

5.d5. This may also be the subject of a future Survey.

In the first part I will examine the most critical line of the variation. In recent years I have played this line successfully against good grandmasters in classical as well as rapid and blitz games. I always got the upper hand, even against highly-rated opponents.

History

I introduced and analysed this line against Jiri Jirka in 2012 in Pardubice. There were already a couple of games with 3...♗b4+. Against GM Tratar in 2015, I tried a new idea with 4.♗d2 ♗xd2+ 5.♕xd2 d5 6.cxd5 exd5 7.exd5 ♘e7. Before my game against Jirka, I had tried all the possible alternatives. To tell you the truth, I was afraid of the main line(s), so I had no choice but to find a playable alternative. The variation with 3...♗b7 4.♗d3 ♗b4 5.♔f1 was not as well-known then as it is now, but I have to admit I was afraid of it. Then I realised that after 3...♗b4+ White could not play 4.♔f1 and that this might merit further analysis. The problem was that I did not find equality in the line 4.♗d2 ♗xd2+ 5.♕xd2 ♘e7 or 5...d6, and this helped me to find the move 5...d5. My pupils and I frequently play this line, with good results. A good friend of mine, GM David

Jonas Lampert

Berczes, also used this idea successfully in 2015 against GM Alex Lenderman – he equalized without problems.

Conclusion

The critical test of 3...♗b4+ is very likely the line that starts with 9.♕e3. If White keeps playing the best moves, this might be slightly better for him, but the position is playable for Black. This is the maximum that White can achieve. As this is still completely unexplored territory, it is very likely that this article will generate some games in this variation.

One drawback of the repertoire with 1...e6-2...b6 is that White can just go for the French Defence. However, in my experience only very few 1.d4 players do this. Of course, Black has to be ready for this scenario, too. This system also offers some wild and interesting complications,

and due to the fact that it is still completely unexplored, it might catch several white players

completely off-guard. I believe that 3...♗b4+ is a perfectly playable alternative!

Postponing 3...♗b4+

Wesley So
Baadur Jobava
Bergamo 2014 (6)

1.d4 e6 2.c4 b6 3.e4 ♗b7 4.♗d3 ♗b4+ [A] 4...♘c6 5.♘e2 ♘b4 (although Black gets the bishop pair, the closed position and his strong centre rather favours White. 5...g6 (unfortunately this continuation leads to a very passive position with no counterplay) 6.♘bc3 ♗g7 7.♗e3 ♘ge7 8.♕d2 d5 9.cxd5 exd5 10.e5 ♕d7 11.♗h6 ♗xh6 12.♕xh6 0-0-0 13.0-0 ♖df8 (Plischki-Gonda, Pardubice 2012) 14.♕e3±) 6.♘bc3 (6.0-0 g6 7.♘bc3 ♘xd3 8.♕xd3 ♗g7 9.♗e3 ♘e7 10.♕d2 d5∞ Juhasz-Gonda, Zalakaros 2011) 6...♘xd3+ 7.♕xd3 g6 8.h4! h5 9.♗g5 ♗e7 10.♕e3 d6 11.0-0-0 ♕d7 12.♔b1 a6 13.♔a1 b5 14.c5± Gonda-Czebe, Balatonlelle 2009;

B) There are many repertoire books that analyse the move 4...f5 from White's point of view, and therefore it is pretty risky to play it nowadays. Previously it offered wild complications and even strong players would lose control. It is also true that many players avoid the 3.e4 line because they do not want to allow such a sharp position. There can follow: 5.exf5 ♗b4+ (5...♕xg2?! 6.♕h5+) 6.♔f1 ♘f6 7.a3 ♗e7 (theory considers 7...♗d6 better than 7...♗e7, but it also does not promise sufficient counterplay for the sacrificed material) 8.♘c3 0-0 9.♘f3 ♕e8 10.♕e2 ♕h5 11.d5?! (11.fxe6!±) 11...exd5! (this is a nice example of how sharp and dangerous the position miay become) 12.♕xe7 ♖e8 13.♕b4 ♘a6 14.♕b3 ♘c5 15.♕c2 d4 16.♘d5 ♘xd5 17.cxd5 ♘xd3 18.♕xd3 ♗xd5 19.♘xd4 (19.h3 c5 20.g4 ♕f7♔) 19...b5! 20.♘xb5 ♕xf5 21.♕c3 ♕e4♔ Beliavsky-Czebe, Hungary tt 1999/00;

C) 4...g6 5.♘c3 ♗g7 6.♘ge2 (6.♘f3) 6...d6 7.h4 h6 8.♗e3 ♘e7 9.♕d2 ♘d7 10.0-0-0 a6 11.g4± Erdös-Ianov, Paks 2005] **5.♔f1!**

[The latest fashion, which is considered to be the most annoying line against this set-up. White wants to fully develop and later plans to castle by hand. Black has to solve the placement of the b4-bishop and he is struggling in the centre, too. 5.♘c3 transposes; 5.♗d2 is the older move, which does not cause any problems for Black: 5...♗xd2+ 6.♘xd2 (6.♕xd2 f5) 6...d6; 6...♘h6!?; 6...♕f6!?] **5...♗e7** [Maybe I would go for 5...e5, but Black still has to show that he has enough compensation for the missing material: 6.a3 (6.d5 a5 7.♘f3 d6 8.g3 ♗e7 9.h4 (Berczes-Bukal, Zadar 2011) 9...♗c8! 10.♔g2 0-0∞; 6.dxe5 ♘c6 (6...d6 7.a3 ♗c5 8.exd6 ♕xd6 9.♘c3 ♘c6 (Ragger-Hamitevici, Bilbao tt 2014) 10.♘d5±) 7.♘f3! (7.f4 d6 8.a3 ♗c5 9.exd6 ♕xd6 10.♘c3 0-0-0 11.♘d5 (1-0 (34) Holt-Berczes, Dallas 2013) 11...f5 (11...b5!? 12.b4 ♗d4 13.♖b1 ♘f6∞) 12.e5 ♕d7⯑) 7...f6 (7...d6 8.a3 ♗c5 9.b4 ♗d4 10.♘xd4 ♘xd4 11.exd6 ♕xd6 12.♘c3 0-0-0 13.♘d5±) 8.a3 ♗e7 9.exf6 ♗xf6 10.♘c3 ♗d6 (10...0-0 11.e5 ♘g4 12.♗e4±) 11.g3 0-0 12.♔g2 ♘e5 13.♘xe5 ♗xe5 14.♘d5±) 6...♗d6 (6...♗e7 7.dxe5 is worse compared to the 6.dxe5 line as the black bishop could go to c5 after a2-a3 in the aforementioned line 7.d5!?) 7.d5 a5 8.♘c3 ♘a6 9.g3 ♘e7 10.♔g2 0-0 11.♘f3± **6.♘c3 d6 7.♘f3 ♘f6 8.g3 0-0 9.♔g2 ♘bd7 10.♕e2±** [White has a solid edge] **10...c5 11.d5 ♖e8 12.♖d1 ♘f8 13.dxe6 fxe6 14.♗c2 a6 15.♗f4 ♕c7 16.♖d2 ♘e5 17.♖ad1 ♗c6 18.♗xe5 dxe5 19.♗a4 ♗xa4 20.♘xa4 b5**

21.cxb5 axb5 22.♕xb5 c4 23.♖c2 ♖ec8 24.b3 ♕b8 25.♕xb8 ♖axb8 26.bxc4 ♘xe4 27.♘xe5 ♖b4 28.♘b2 ♗c5 29.f4 ♗e7 30.♘bd3 ♖a4 31.♘xc5 ♖xc5 32.♖b1 ♖c8 33.c5 g5 34.c6 ♗d6 35.♘d7 gxf4 36.♘b6 f3+ 37.♔f2 1-0

Analysis 5.♘xd2

1.d4 e6 2.c4 b6 3.e4 ♗b4+ 4.♗d2 ♗xd2+ 5.♘xd2 [It is more logical to take back with the queen and develop the knight to c3, but this is also a sound alternative. However Black can easily be worse if he does not play the proper plan] **5...♘e7** [If we compare this position to the 3...♗b7 line, the difference is that Black should not develop his bishop to b7 here as he can play a kind of Bogo-Indian with ...d7-d6 and ...e7-e5 next. 5...d6!?] **6.♗d3** [6.f4 d5 7.cxd5 exd5 8.e5 c5∞; 6.♘gf3 0-0 (6...d6!? 7.♗d3 e5!? 8.d5 (8.c5 dxc5 9.d5 ♘g6; 8.0-0 ♘g6; 8.dxe5 dxe5 9.♕a4+ (9.♘xe5? f6 10.♕h5+ g6 11.♘xg6 ♘xg6∓) 9...♗d7 10.♕a3 ♘g6∞) 8...0-0 9.0-0 – 6.. .0-0) 7.♗d3 (7.♗e2 d6 8.0-0 ♘g6 9.g3 e5 10.d5 a5 (10...f5!?) 11.b3 (11.a3 a4) 11...♘a6 12.a3 f5 13.exf5 ♗xf5↑) 7...d6 8.0-0 (8.e5 ♗b7 9.♕c2 ♘g6∞) 8...e5 9.d5 a5. A pleasant position for Black. He can hold the queenside and then start to advance on the other flank with ...f7-f5: 10.b3 (10.a3 ♘g6 11.g3 (11.b4 ♘f4 12.♕c2 ♗g4↑) 11...♗h3 (11...a4!? 12.♗c2 ♗d7= 13.♘b1 (13.♘e1 b5 14.cxb5 ♗xb5 15.♗d3 ♗d7 16.♘c2 ♘a6∞) 13...♗g4 (13...♕e8 14.♘c3 ♖a5 15.♘d2 ♘a6 16.b4 axb3 17.♘xb3±) 14.♘bd2 (14.♘c3 ♘d7 15.♘xa4 f5→) 14...♘d7=) 12.♖e1 ♘a6∞) 10...♘a6∞] **6...d6 7.♘e2** [7.f4 e5 8.fxe5 (8.♘e2 exd4 9.♘xd4 0-0 10.0-0 ♗b7∞) 8...dxe5 9.d5 ♘d7∞] **7...e5 8.0-0** [8.d5 ♘g6 9.0-0 a5∞; 8.f4 ♗g4 9.fxe5 dxe5 10.d5 0-0 11.0-0] **8...0-0** [8...♘g6 9.f4 exd4 (9...exf4 10.♘xf4 0-0 11.♘xg6 hxg6

12.♘f3 ♕e7 (12...c5 13.e5) 13.♕d2 ♘d7 (13...c5 14.e5) 14.♖ae1 ♗b7 15.♕f4±] 10.♘xd4 0-0 11.♕e2 (11.♘b1?! ♕f6∞) 11...♗b7 12.♘b1! ♘c6 13.♘xc6 ♗xc6 14.♘c3±] **9.f4** [The structure after 9.d5 is not dangerous for Black as here the white knight is not well placed on d2. I believe that the line starting with 9.f4 is the most dangerous here. If White plays, for example, 9.d5, there can follow 9...a5 (9...♘g6 10.b4 a5 11.a3 ♕g5) 10.♘c3 (10.f4 exf4 11.♘xf4 ♘d7 12.♘f3 ♘g6 13.♘xg6 hxg6 14.♗c2 (14.♕d2 ♕e7=) 14...♕e7 15.♕d2 ♘e5∞) 10...♘a6 11.a3 ♘g6 12.g3 ♕g5∞] **9...♗g4!** [A strong move; now Black can fully develop with ease. After 9...exd4 Black would be slightly worse because of his space disadvantage: 10.♘xd4 ♘ec6 (10...♗b7 11.♘b1 ♘d7 12.♘c3↑) 11.♘b5 ♘d7 12.♗c2 ♘c5 13.a3 a6 14.♘c3±] **10.♘f3** [10.fxe5 dxe5 11.d5 ♘d7 12.h3 ♗xe2 13.♗xe2 a5∞]

10...exf4 [10...♘g6?! 11.f5 ♘h4 12.♘e1↑; 10...c5!? 11.fxe5 cxd4 12.exd6 ♕xd6 13.e5 ♕h6 14.♘exd4 ♘bc6 15.♕e1! ♖ad8 16.♘xc6 ♘xc6 17.♗e4 ♖fe8] **11.♘xf4 ♘d7** [11...c5 12.e5 g6 13.dxc5 dxc5 14.♗e4 ♘bc6∞] **12.♕e1 ♘g6 13.♕g3 ♗xf3 14.♖xf3** [14.gxf3 ♕f6 15.♘e2 c5∓] **14...♘xf4 15.♕xf4** [15.♖xf4 c5] **15...♕f6 16.♕e3 ♕e6=** [△ ...c7-c5]

5.♕xd2

Jiri Jirka
Laszlo Gonda

Pardubice 2012

1.d4 e6 2.c4 b6 3.e4 ♗b4+ 4.♗d2 [4.♘c3!? ♗b7 (4...c5?! just transposes: 5.d5 (5.dxc5 ♘f6 6.♗d3 (6.♗d2 ♘c6

7.cxb6 ♕xb6) 6...♗b7 7.cxb6 ♗xc3+ 8.bxc3 axb6∞; 5.a3 ♗xc3+ 6.bxc3 ♘c6∞; 5.♘ge2!? cxd4 6.♘xd4±) 5...♗xc3+ 6.bxc3 d6 7.♗d3 ♘d7 (7...♘f6 8.♘e2) 8.f4±)] **4...♗xd2+ 5.♕xd2 d5**

6.cxd5 exd5 7.e5 [An ambitious move, which looks promising at first sight. If we delve more deeply into the position we may realize that the advanced e5-pawn does not hamper Black's play in any way. Black's plan is easy: ...♘e7, ...c7-c5, ...♘bc6 and ...♗g4 in order to tear White's centre apart] **7...♘e7 8.♘c3** [8.♗b5+ c6 9.♗a4 White gains some additional time to finish his development. The bishop stands quite useful on a4, hindering Black's plan of ...c7-c5 and ...♘bc6, and it can also retreat to c2: 9...0-0 10.♘e2 f6 (10...c5!? 11.0-0 ♘bc6 (11...♗a6 12.♖d1∞) 12.♘bc3 ♗a6 (12...cxd4 13.♘xd4 ♘xe5 14.♖fe1≅) 13.♗xc6 ♘xc6 14.♖fd1∞) 11.exf6 (11.0-0 fxe5 12.dxe5 c5∞ – I would prefer to play this with black) 11...♖xf6 12.0-0 (Lenderman-Berczes, Las Vegas 2015) 12...♗a6 13.♖e1 ♕d6 14.♘bc3 ♘d7∞] **8...0-0 9.f4** [There is no time for this, as Black is faster. If 9.♗d3 c5 10.♘ge2 ♘bc6↑; 9.♖d1 c5 10.dxc5 ♘bc6 11.♘xd5 bxc5≅; 9.♘f3 c5 10.♗e2 ♘bc6 11.dxc5 bxc5 12.0-0 ♖b8∞] **9...c5 10.♘f3 ♘bc6** [10...♗g4 11.♗e2 ♘bc6 12.dxc5 bxc5 13.0-0 ♖b8∞] **11.♗b5** [11.dxc5 bxc5 12.♗e2 ♖b8 13.b3 ♕a5 14.0-0 ♖d8↑] **11...♗g4** [White is unable to hold his centre together] **12.dxc5 ♗xf3! 13.gxf3 bxc5 14.♗xc6 ♘xc6 15.0-0** [15.0-0-0 ♘d4 16.♘e2 ♘xe2+ 17.♕xe2 c4∓; 15.♕xd5 ♕h4+−+] **15...♘d4 16.♘a4 f6 17.exf6** [17.♔h1! fxe5 18.fxe5 ♖xf3 19.♘xc5 ♕f8 20.♖xf3 ♕xf3+ 21.♕g2 ♖c8∓] **17...♕xf6 18.♘xc5 ♖ae8 19.♖ae1** [19.♖f2??

♖e2!−+] **19...♖xe1 20.♕xe1 ♕xf4 21.♘e6** [21.♔h1!? ♕d6 22.♘d3 ♘xf3 23.♕g3 ♕h4∓] **21...♕xf3! 22.♘xd4 ♕g4+ 23.♔h1 ♖xf1+ 24.♕xf1 ♕xd4 25.♕b5 h6 26.a4 ♕e4+ 27.♔g1 d4 28.♕b8+ ♔h7 29.♕xa7 d3?!** [29...♕b1+! 30.♔f2 ♕xb2+ 31.♔g3 ♕b3+ 32.♔f2 ♕e3+ 33.♔g2 ♕e2+ 34.♔g3 ♕e5+ 35.♔f3 h5−+] **30.♕f2! ♕g4+ 31.♔f1 ♕d1+ 32.♕e1 ♕f3+ 33.♔g1 ♕g4+ 34.♔f1 ♕f4+** [34...♕xa4! 35.b4 ♕c6 36.♔f2 and White has some practical drawing chances] **35.♔g2 ♕g4+** [35...♕xa4 36.♔f3!] ½-½

Marko Tratar
Laszlo Gonda

Croatia tt 2015 (9)

1.d4 e6 2.c4 b6 3.e4 ♗b4+ 4.♗d2 ♗xd2+ 5.♕xd2 d5 6.cxd5 [6.♘c3 dxe4 7.♘xe4 (7.f3 is slightly romantic, but let's have a look at it! 7...exf3 (7...e5 8.d5 (8.dxe5 ♕xd2+ 9.♔xd2 ♗b7 10.♖e1 (10.♘d5 exf3 11.♘xc7+ ♔d8 12.♘d5 ♘e7=) 10...♘d7 11.♘xe4 ♘xe5=) 8...f5 9.fxe4 fxe4 10.♘ge2 (10.♕e3 ♘f6 11.♘xe4 ♘xe4 12.♕xe4 0-0 13.♘f3 ♕d6∓) 10...♘f6 11.♘g3∞) 8.♘xf3 ♗b7 9.0-0-0 ♘f6 10.♔b1 ♘bd7 11.♗d3 0-0 (11...♕e7 12.♖he1 0-0-0 13.d5 ♔b8 14.♗c2) 12.♕f4 a6→ ...b6-b5 is coming soon) 7...♗b7 8.♘c3 ♘e7 (8...♘a6 9.0-0-0 ♘f6 10.♘f3) 9.0-0-0 0-0 10.♔b1 ♘d7 11.♘f3 a6! 12.♗d3 b5∞] **6... exd5 7.exd5 ♘e7** [Black has to play precisely to gain back the d5-pawn and finish his development. With 7...♕xd5? I found a couple of games in the database, but it is hardly playable: 8.♘c3 ♕e6+ 9.♗e2 ♗a6 10.0-0-0±]

8.♗b5+ [8.♗c4 ♗b7 9.♘c3 0-0 10.♘f3 ♘xd5=] **8...♘d7** [8...♗d7 9.♗c4±] **9. d6** [White chooses the simplest way to achieve equality. If 9.♘c3 0-0 10.♘f3 ♗b7 11.♗c4 ♘f6 12.♘e5 ♘fxd5 13.0-0 f6 14.♘d3 ♕d6= (14...♔h8=); 9.♗c6 gives White an extra pawn for the time being, but Black can get good play with 9...♖b8 10.♘e2 0-0 11.♘bc3 ♘f6 12.0-0 ♘fxd5 13.♗a4 ♗b7∞] **9...cxd6 10.♘e2 0-0 11.0-0 ♘f6 12.♘bc3 ♗b7 13.♖fe1 ♘ed5 14.♖ac1 ♖c8** [14...a6 15.♗d3 b5 16.♘xd5 ♘xd5 17.♘c3 ♕b6 18.♗e4=] **15.a3 g6 16.h3 a6 17.♗d3 ♖e8 18.♘xd5 ♘xd5 19.♖xc8 ♕xc8 20.♘c3 ♖xe1+ 21.♕xe1 ♘xc3 22.♕xc3 ♕xc3 23.bxc3** [Draw after 39 moves]   ½-½

Jonas Lampert
Balazs Szabo

Budapest 2015 (4)

1.d4 e6 2.c4 b6 3.e4 ♗b4+ 4.♗d2 ♗xd2+ 5.♕xd2 d5 6.♗d3 [In my opinion this is a good reaction for White, as he keeps the tension in the centre. If 6.cxd5 exd5 7.♗d3 dxe4! (7...♘e7 8.♘f3 0-0 9.♘c3 (9.0-0 ♘bc6) 9...♖e8?! 10.0-0 ♘bc6 11.♖ac1 ♗b7 12.e5± Krstulovic-Balint, Budapest 2015; 7...♗b7 8.e5±) 8.♘xe4 c6 9.♘f3 (9.d5 ♘f6 10.♘f3 0-0) 9...♘f6 10.♗c2 0-0 11.0-0 ♖e8 12.♘c3 ♗g4 13.♘h4 (13.♘e5 ♖xe5) 13...♘bd7=] **6...dxc4** [6...♗b7?! 7.cxd5 exd5 8.e5± and Black cannot develop the bishop to g4 as it is already standing on b7! A huge difference. 6...♘c6 7.cxd5 (7.♘f3 dxe4 8.♘xe4 ♗b7 9.♘c3 (9.0-0) 9...♘f6 10.♗xc6+ ♗xc6 11.♘e5! ♗b7 12.0-0 0-0 13.♖fe1 ♘d7 14.♖ad1±) 7...exd5 8.exd5 ♕xd4 9.♘c3 ♘f6 10.0-0-0→; 6...♘e7 7.♘c3±; 6...♗a6!? 7.cxd5 (7.♘a3 ♘f6 8.e5 dxc4 9.♘xc4 ♘d5∞) 7...♗xd3 8.♕xd3 exd5 9.♘f3 (9.e5 ♘e7 10.♘e2 0-0 11.♘bc3 c5 12.0-0 (12.♖d1 ♘bc6) 12...♘bc6 13.♖ad1 cxd4 14.♘xd4 ♘xe5 15.♕g3 ♗c4 16.♖fe1∞) 9...♘e7 10.0-0 0-0 11.♘c3 ♘bc6 (11...dxe4 12.♕xe4 ♘d7 13.♖fe1 ♖e8±) 12.a3 ♕d7 13.♖fe1 dxe4 14.♕xe4 ♖ad8 15.♖ac1±] **7.♗xc4 ♗b7 8.♘c3 ♘f6** [The viability of Black's position depends on whether he can carry out his plan with ...c7-c5! **9.♗d3** [9.f3 strengthens the centre, and this might look better for White... 9...0-0 10.♘ge2 c5! (10...♘e8 11.0-0 ♘d6 12.♗d3 ♘c6 13.♖ac1 e5 14.d5 ♘b4 15.♘b5 ♘xd3

16.♕xd3 ♗a6 17.a4; 10...♘c6 11.♖d1 (11.0-0-0 ♕e7 12.e5 ♘d7 13.♔b1 ♖fd8∞) 11...♘e8 (11...e5 12.0-0; 12.d5 ♘e7 13.0-0 ♕d6 14.♕e3 a6 15.♘c1) 12.0-0 ♘d6 13.♗d3 e5 14.d5 ♘b4 15.♘c1 ♖xd3 16.♘xd3 ♕e7 17.♖c1±; 10...♘bd7 11.e5 ♘d5 12.♘xd5 exd5 13.♗d3 c5 14.0-0 ♕e7 15.f4±).

Although Black will have a weakness on c5, the misplaced bishop on c4 guarantees him good play: 11.dxc5 (11.♖d1 ♕e7 (11...♘c6 12.dxc5; 11...cxd4!? 12.♘xd4 ♕c8 13.♗e2 ♖d8 14.♕e3 ♘c6 15.♘db5 ♖xd1+ 16.♗xd1 ♕d8) 12.0-0 (12.d5 ♘xd5 13.♗xd5 exd5 14.♘xd5 ♕xd5 15.exd5 (15.♕xd5 ♘a6=) 15...♖e8=) 12...cxd4 13.♕xd4 ♘c6=; 11.d5 exd5 12.exd5 ♘e8=) 11...bxc5 12.♕e3 (12.b3 ♘bd7 13.0-0 ♘e5=; 12.♕xd8 ♖xd8 13.♖d1 ♘bd7=) 12...♘c6 13.0-0 (13.♕xc5 ♘d7 14.♕e3 ♘de5 15.♗b3 ♘d3+ 16.♔f1 ♗a6⇄ 17.♖d1; 13.♖d1 ♕a5 14.0-0 ♘e5 15.♗b5 a6 16.♗a4 ♖fd8=) 13...♕a5= (13...♕e7 14.♘a4 ♗a5 15.♖ac1 ♖fc8)] **9...0-0 10.♘f3 c5 11.dxc5 bxc5?!** [11...♘bd7! 12.c6 (12.cxb6 ♘c5∓) 12...♗xc6=] **12.♖d1 ♕a5 13.0-0± ♘fd7 14.♕f4 ♘c6 15.e5 ♘d4 16.♘xd4 cxd4 17.♘b5 ♗a6 18.♘xd4 ♗xd3 19.♖xd3 ♕xe5 20.♕d2 ♘f6 21.♖e1 ♕d5 22.♘xe6 fxe6 23.♖xd5 exd5 24.♖e7 ♖f7 25.♖xf7 ♔xf7 26.♕d4 ♔g8 27.g4 ♖d8 28.g5 ♘e4 29.b4 ♖d7 30.♔g2**   1-0

Analysis
The Critical Line: 9.♕e3

1.d4 e6 2.c4 b6 3.e4 ♗b4+ 4.♗d2 ♗xd2+ 5.♕xd2 d5 6.♗d3 dxc4 7.♗xc4 ♗b7 8.♘c3 ♘f6 9.♕e3

9...♘bd7 [9...0-0 10.♘f3 ♘bd7 11.e5 transposes] **10.♘f3** [10.e5?! ♗xg2 11.exf6 ♗xh1 12.fxg7 ♖g8∓; 10.♘ge2 c5 (10...0-0?! 11.e5 ♘d5 12.♘xd5 ♗xd5 13.♗xd5 exd5 14.0-0±. e2 is a very good square for the knight, the plan is f4-f5) 11.e5 (11.d5 exd5 12.exd5+ ♕e7=; 11.dxc5 bxc5 12.0-0 0-0) 11...♘g4! 12.♕g3 cxd4! 13.♕xg4 (13.♘xd4 ♘gxe5 14.♕xg7 ♕f6↑) 13...dxc3! 14.♕xg7 cxb2 15.♕xh8+ ♔e7 16.♕xd8+ ♖xd8 17.♖b1 ♘xe5∓] **10...0-0** [10...♕e7 11.e5 ♘g4 12.♕f4 ♗b4 13.♗b3 ♘h6 14.0-0-0→; 10...c5!? 11.e5 (11.d5 exd5 12.exd5+ ♕e7 13.0-0 ♕xe3 14.fxe3 a6) 11...♘d5 (11...♘g4 12.♕f4 ♗xf3 13.gxf3 cxd4 14.♕xg4 dxc3 15.♕xg7 ♘e6 16.0-0-0→) 12.♘xd5 ♗xd5 13.♗xd5 exd5 14.0-0 0-0 15.♖ad1 – 10...0-0] **11.e5** [11.0-0 c5 12.♖fd1 (12.dxc5 ♕c7!=) 12...♕e7 13.h3 cxd4 14.♖xd4 e5 15.♖d2 ♖ac8 (15...♘c5 16.♘d5) 16.♗d5 ♗xd5 17.♘xd5 ♗xd5 18.♖xd5 f6 19.♖ad1 ♖c7=; 11.h3 c5 12.e5 ♘d5 13.♘xd5 cxd4 (13...exd5 14.♗d3 cxd4 15.♕xd4 (15.♘xd4 ♘xe5) 15...♘c5 16.0-0 ♖c8=) 14.♘xd4 ♖c8 15.♗b3 ♖c5 16.f4 ♗xd5 17.0-0 ♕a8=] **11...♘d5** [11...♘g4 12.♕f4 ♘h6 13.0-0-0! (13.♘e4 ♕e7 14.0-0 ♖fd8; 13.0-0 ♗xf3 14.♕xf3 c5=) 13...a6 (13...♗xf3 14.gxf3 c5=) 14.♘g5→] **12.♘xd5**

12...exd5 [It looks ugly to close the diagonal of the bishop, but without the bishops White would have a clear edge: 12...♗xd5 13.♗xd5 exd5 14.0-0 (14.♖d1 ♖e8 15.0-0 – 14.0-0) 14...♖e8 (14...♕e7 15.♖fd1 (15.♖ad1) 15...♖fd8 16.g3 ♘f8 17.♘h4 g6 18.f4 c5 19.f5 cxd4 20.♖xd4±; 14...c5 15.♖ad1 c4 16.g3 b5 17.♘h4→) 15.♖ad1! (in the long term White will advance with ♘e1 and f2-f4-f5. 15.♖ac1 c5 16.♖fd1 c4 (16...♖c8 17.g3 f6 18.dxc5 ♘xe5 19.♕b3 ♗xf3+ 20.♕xf3 ♖e5 21.b4) 17.♘d2 (17.g3 f6 18.♔g2 ♕c7 19.♖e1 ♖e6∞) 17...♘f8 (17...b5 18.♘f1 b4 19.f4 a5 20.f5 – I do not like his for Black) 18.f4 f5 19.♘f1 ♕d7 20.♕f3 ♘g6 21.♘e3 ♗e7 22.h3 b5∞) 15...♖c8 (15...c5 16.dxc5 ♘xc5 17.♕d2±; 15...♘f8 16.g3 ♘g6 17.♘e1 c5 18.f4±) 16.♘e1 (16.g3!?) 16...c5 17.f4 f5 (17...♘f8 18.f5→) 18.♕f3 ♘f8 19.♘c2±] **13.♗d3 c5** [13...f6 14.0-0 (14.e6 ♖e8 15.0-0 ♘f8) 14...fxe5 15.♘g5 (15.dxe5 ♘c5 16.♗c2 ♘e6) 15...e4 16.♘e6 ♕f6 17.♘xf8 ♘xf8 18.♗e2 ♘e6 19.♖ac1 c6 20.♖fd1±; 13...♖e8 14.0-0 ♘f8 15.b4±] **14.0-0** [14.♘g5 h6 15.e6 cxd4∓] **14...♕e7** [14...♖e8 would be very risky due to 15.♘g5! (15.♖ac1 ♖c8 (15...♕e7 16.♖fe1 cxd4 17.♘xd4±; 15...cxd4 16.♕f4) 16.♘g5 (16.♗f5 ♖c7 17.♘g5 (17.♗xd7 ♖xd7) 17...♘f8 18.f4 g6 19.♗d3 cxd4 20.♕f2 ♖xc1 21.♖xc1 ♕e7=; 16.♖fe1 ♖c7; 16...h6 17.♗b1 a5 (17...♖c7) 18.♕d3 ♘f8 19.g3; 16...♕e7 17.♗f5) 16...

cxd4 (16...♘f8 17.f4 cxd4 18.♕h3 h6 19.♘f3±) 17.♕f4 ♘xe5 18.♗xh7+ ♔f8∞; 15.♖fe1 cxd4 (15...♖c8 16.♘g5 ♘f8 17.f4 cxd4 18.♕g3) 16.♕f4 ♘f8 17.♘xd4 ♘e6 18.♕g4 ♘xd4 19.♕xd4 ♖c8 20.f4 ♕c7, and if Black can trade off the queens he cannot have any problems; 15.♗f5!? ♕e7 (15...cxd4 16.♕f4 ♘f8 17.♘xd4±) 16.♖fe1 (16.♗xd7 ♕xd7 17.dxc5 d4 18.♘xd4 (18.♕xd4 ♕xd4 19.♘xd4 bxc5 20.♘b3 ♖xe5 21.f4 ♖f5 22.♖ac1 ♗a6 23.♖f2 c4=) 18...bxc5 19.♘f3 ♗xf3 20.♕xf3 ♖ab8 21.b3 ♖xe5=) 16...♘f8 17.♖ac1 c4 18.♘d2 g6 19.♗c2 b5 20.f4 f5∞; 15.♖ad1 ♕e7 16.♖fe1 ♘f8∞) 15...cxd4 (15...♘f8 16.f4 ♕e7 17.♗b5 ♖ec8 18.f5 cxd4 19.♕g3!→; 15...h6 16.♗h7+ ♔f8 17.♘xf7! ♔xf7 18.♕f4+ ♘f6 19.♖ac1 ♖c8 20.♕f5±) 16.♗xh7+ (for 16.♕f4 ♘xe5 17.♗xh7+ ♔f8 – see 16.♗xh7+; 16.♕h3 ♕xg5 17.f4 ♕d8 18.♕xh7+ ♔f8 19.♖ae1 ♖e6 20.♕h8+ ♔e7 21.♕h4+=) 16...♔f8 17.♕f4 ♘xe5 18.♕h4 (18.♖fe1!? ♕f6 19.♕h4; 18...♕h4 19.♗f5 ♔g8) 18...♕f6 (18...♗a6!? and Black survives easily; it is better to start with 18.♖fe1: 19.f4 (19.♖fe1 f6 20.♕xd4 ♕d7 21.f4 ♘c6 22.♕a4 fxg5 23.♕xa6 gxf4) 19...♗xf1 20.♖xf1 ♘c4 21.♗d3 (21.♗g6 ♘e3 22.♖c1 ♖c8 23.♖xc8 ♕xc8 24.♘h7+ ♔g8 25.♘f6+ ♔f8=) 21...♔e7!! (see diagram). According to the computer this is equal, but I am certain that human beings would be scared here)

19.♖fe1 (19.♗c2 ♔g8 20.♕h7+ ♔f8 21.♕h5 (21.f4 ♘c4) 21...♔g8 22.♗a4 (22.♗h7+ ♔f8; 22.f4 ♕h6 23.♕xh6 gxh6 24.fxe5 hxg5 25.♖f5 g4 26.♗a4 ♖e7 27.♖d1 ♖d8 28.♖xd4 ♗c8=) 22...♘c6 (22...♖ec8 23.♕h7+ ♔f8 24.f4 ♘c4 25.♖fe1 ♘e3 26.♕h8+ ♔e7 27.♕h3→) 23.♕h7+ ♔f8 24.♗xc6 ♘xc6 25.♖ac1 ♖ac8 26.f4 ♕h6 27.♕f5 ♕g6 28.♕h3 ♔g8=; 19.♗d3 ♔g8 20.♕h7+ ♔f8 21.♕h5 ♔g8) 19...♕h6 20.♕g3 ♕f6 21.♖ac1 ♘c4 22.♗d3 ♔g8 23.♕h3 g6 24.♕h7+ ♔f8 25.g3→] **15.♖fe1** [For 15.♗f5 ♖fe8, see 14...♖e8] **15...♖fd8** [15...♖fe8 16.♗b5] **16.♖ac1** [16.e6 fxe6 17.♕xe6+ ♕xe6 18.♖xe6 ♖e8 19.♖ae1 ♖xe6 20.♖xe6 cxd4 21.♘xd4 (21.♖e7 ♘c5 22.♗f5 ♘f8 23.♖c7 d3 24.b4 ♖e8 (24...d4 25.bxc5 ♗xf3 26.♗xd3 ♗d5 27.f3 bxc5 28.a3 h6 29.♖xc5 ♗e6 30.♖a5±) 25.h3 ♖e1+ 26.♔h2 d4 27.bxc5 ♗xf3 28.♗xd3 ♗e4=; 21.b4 ♖c8 22.♔f1 ♖c3 23.♔e2 ♘f6=) 21...♘c5 22.♖e3] **16...♖ac8 17.♗f5 g6** [Perhaps Black is slightly worse but the position remains playable]

Exercise 1

position after 11.d4xc5

Find the best continuation.
(solution on page 249)

Exercise 2

position after 11.e4-e5

Is 11...♘d5 the only move here?
(solution on page 249)

Exercise 3

position after 11.♘g1-f3

Find the strongest plan for Black.
(solution on page 249)

Tomashevsky's New Attacking Idea

by Viacheslav Ikonnikov (special contribution by Evgeny Tomashevsky)

1.	d4	d5
2.	c4	e6
3.	♘c3	♘f6
4.	♗g5	♘bd7
5.	e3	c6
6.	♘f3	♕a5
7.	cxd5	♘xd5
8.	♖c1	♘xc3
9.	bxc3	♗a3
10.	♖c2	b6

This way to develop the light-squared bishop, which is unusual for the Cambridge Springs Variation, was introduced by Bart Michiels in his game against Vadim Malakhatko in 2011. Since that time, this method of defence for Black has become more popular.

Obviously, the main idea is to simplify the position by exchanging the light-squared bishops, something that White, incidentally, cannot avoid.

In the diagram position White has a choice of where he wants to make his bishop swap: on d3 (after 11.♗d3) or on e2 (after 11.♗e2). Independently from

the position of his queen, White has two plans:

1) The active plan on the kingside connected with e4-e5 and ♘f3-d2-e4;

2) The positional plan with c3-c4, ♗f4 (preventing ...e6-e5), ♖d1 (or ♖b1).

Black, on his part, will have to organize counterplay in the centre with ...♖c8 and ...c6-c5.

White Queen on d3

11.♗d3 looks the most logical. However, in practice the queen is quite unstable on d3, especially with regard to the plan e4-e5 (as witness Gelfand-Carlsen; it favours White to meet Black's ...c6-c5 break with d4-d5, but with the queen on d3 Black can always reply ...c5-c4!). More reliable looks the 'positional plan' with c3-c4, ♗f4, ♖b1, with pressure on the queenside. The big specialist of this plan is Alexander Moiseenko – he is one of a minority of high-level players who still support the move 11.♗d3.

White Queen on e2: More Options

The modest 11.♗e2 is more popular these days. In this line the queen is situated on e2, where it is safer than on d3 when the fight in the centre starts. Better than on d3, the queen on e2 supports the active plan with e4-e5, which was

Natalia Pogonina

invented by Carlsen against Mamedyarov. In this game, after 11.♗e2 ♗a6 12.0-0 ♗xe2 13.♕xe2 0-0 14.e4, Black's inaccurate move 14...♖ac8 cost him a point. In the later game Kosteniuk-Pogonina, Black improved the position with 14...♖fe8!, controlling the important square e6 against White's central break with d4-d5 and e5-e6. Also, the 'positional plan' is supported by ♕e2 as well as ♕d3, so this gives White more options.

Black's Defence 14...♕a4

Besides the 'normal' defensive plan with ...♖c8 and ...c6-c5, a quite interesting-looking idea is to play an early ...♕a4. After 11.♗e2 ♗a6 12.0-0 ♗xe2 13.♕xe2 h6 14.♗h4, 14...♕a4 is a multifunctional move:

1) It attacks the 'weakness' in White's position – ♖c2 – thereby preventing White's plan of e4-e5 and ♘f3-d2-e4;

2) It adds strength to the threat of ...♖c8, ...c6-c5, ...cxd4;

3) After ...c6-c5, the knight on d7 will be protected in case of complications in the centre;

4) Black exerts pressure on c4, and after ...c6-c5 and ...b6-b5 Black achieves quite comfortable positions, as we can see from the games.

Tomashevsky's Novelty

A very interesting idea after 11.♗e2 ♗a6 12.0-0 ♗xe2 is for White to take with 13.♖xe2!. Obviously, taking with the rook only supports White's 'active plan', but it strengthens this plan considerably with the 'extra rook'. In general White's plan is:

1) e3-e4-e5
2) ♘f3-d2-e4
3) ♖g3 (-h3; -f3)

In his comments on his game against Ipatov, Evgeny writes: 'White dominates in the centre, which he would like to use for play against his opponent's king; capturing on e2 with the queen leaves the rook on the c-file, which will probably soon be opened, which favours exchanges and does not assist the attack.' Exactly! The big problem of White's attacking plan (with e4-e5) is his 'handicapped rook' on c2, which will be placed in a better position, even at the cost of a pawn. On the other hand, White already has to be prepared to sacrifice a pawn if he chooses the 7.cxd5 line in the Cambridge Springs.

As we can see in the game Tomashevsky-Ipatov, the most important factor is White's e-pawn. If White is able to move this pawn to e5, his attack may become unstoppable.

The future evaluation of the ♖xe2 line will depend on the question of whether Black can prevent e4-e5 by playing ...e6-e5 himself.

Conclusion

Since the 'positional plan' with pressure on the queenside with c3-c4 does not yield White much, I expect that future investigations will focus on the kingside attack starting with e4-e5. From this point of view, the line with 13.♖xe2 may radically change the evaluation of the position: from 'balanced' today, to 'better for White' in the future.

White Queen on d3 11.♗d3

Boris Gelfand
Magnus Carlsen

London 2013 (3)

1.d4 ♘f6 2.c4 e6 3.♘f3 d5 4.♘c3 ♘bd7 5.♗g5 c6 6.e3 ♕a5 7.cxd5 ♘xd5 8.♖c1 ♘xc3 9.bxc3 ♗a3 10.♖c2 b6 11.♗d3 ♗a6 12.0-0 ♗xd3 13.♕xd3

13...0-0 [13...h6 14.♗h4 0-0 15.c4 ♖fe8 16.e4 (16.♖b1!?) 16...e5 17.d5 ♘c5 (17...♖ac8 18.d6 f6 19.♗xf6 ♘xf6 20.d7 ♘xd7 21.♕xd7 ♕a4 22.♖d2 ♖a8 23.♕g4⩱) 18.♕e2 ♕a4! 19.♖c3

♖ac8 20.♗g3 cxd5 21.cxd5 (21.exd5 ♘d7 22.♖b1 ♗c5⇄) 21...♘xe4 22.♖xc8 ♖xc8 23.♘xe5 ♘xg3 24.hxg3 ♕e8= Malakhatko-Michiels, Antwerp ch-BEL 2011] **14.e4 ♖fe8**

15.e5?! h6 16.♗h4 c5 17.♘d2 cxd4 [17...b5 18.f4 cxd4 19.cxd4 ♖ac8 20.f5∞] **18.cxd4 ♖ac8 19.♘c4 ♕b5** [19...♕a6? 20.♕xa3+−] **20.f4** [20. f3!? ♗b2 21.♗f2 ♖ed8⇄] **20...♕c7 21.♕xa3 ♖xc4 22.♖xc4 ♕xc4 23.♗f2 ♕c7** [23...a5 24.♖c1 ♕d5 25.h3 (25.♕d6!?) 25...♘f8 26.♖c7∞] **24.♖c1 ♕b7 25.♕d6** [25.♕f3!? ♕xf3 26.gxf3 ♘f8 27.♖c7 ♘g6 28.f5 ♘f4 29.fxe6 fxe6 30.♖xa7 ♖c8⩲]

25...♘f8 26.g3 [26.♕c7 ♕a6=] **26...♖c8 27.♖xc8 ♕xc8 28.d5 exd5 29.♕xd5 g6 30.♔g2 ♘e6 31.♕f3 ♗g7 32.a3 h5 33.h4 ♕c2 34.♕b7 ♕a4 35.♕f3 b5 36.f5 gxf5 37.♕xf5 ♕xa3 38.♕xh5 a5 39.♕g4+ ♗f8 40.h5?** [40.♕h5! ♔e8 (40...♗e7 41.♕h8) 41.♕h8+ ♕f8 (41...♔d7 42.♕a8⇄) 42.♕f6 a4 43.h5⇄] **40...♕c1 41.♕e4 b4 42.♗e3 ♕c7 43.♕a8+** [43.h6 ♔g8 44.♕a8+ ♕d8 45.♕f3 ♕d3∓] **43...♔g7 44.h6+ ♔h7 45.♕e4+ ♔g8 46.♕a8+ ♕d8 47.♕xd8+ ♘xd8 48.♔f3 a4 49.♔e4 ♘c6 50.♗c1 ♘a5 51.♗d2 b3 52.♔d3 ♘c4 53.♗c3 a3 54.g4 ♔h7 55.g5 ♔g6 56.♗d4 b2 57.♔c2 ♘d2** 0-1

Alexander Moiseenko
Evgeny Agrest

Berlin Wch rapid 2015 (11)

1.d4 d5 2.c4 c6 3.♘c3 ♘f6 4.♘f3 e6 5.♗g5 ♘bd7 6.e3 ♕a5 7.cxd5 ♘xd5 8.♖c1 ♘xc3 9.bxc3 ♗a3 10.♖c2 b6 11.♗d3 ♗a6 12.0-0 ♗xd3 13.♕xd3 0-0 [13...h6 14.♗h4 0-0 15.♗g3 ♖fd8 16.c4 e5?! 17.♕f5?!

(17.♗xe5!? ♘xe5 18.♘xe5 ♕xe5
19.♕xa3 ♕e4 20.♕c3±) 17...g6
18.♕h3!? (18.♕e4! exd4 19.♘xd4±)
18...♘a4 19.♖c3 (19.♖d2!±) 19...exd4
20.exd4 ♗f8 21.♗c7 ♖xa2 (21...♖e8
22.♕xd7 ♗e7 23.♕d6 ♖c8 24.♗xb6
axb6 25.♕a3 ♖a8≋) 22.♗xd8 ♖xd8
23.♘e5? (23.♕g3±) 23...♘xe5 24.dxe5
♗c5⇄ Moiseenko-Navara, Wroclaw Ech
blitz 2014]

14.♖b1 ♖fe8 15.c4 [15.♗h4 ♖ac8
16.c4 ♗d6 (16...h6 17.♗g3∞) 17.♘g5
(17.c5!? ♗c7 (17...♗e7 18.♗xe7
♖xe7 19.cxb6 axb6 20.♘d2±) 18.♘g5
♘f6 19.f4↑) 17...♕f5 (17...♘f6 18.e4
h6 19.♘f3 ♗d7 20.e5±) 18.♕xf5
(18.♘e4 c5 19.♖d1 ♗b8∞) 18...exf5
19.♗g3 ♗xg3 20.hxg3 c5 21.♘f3
♘f6 22.♕f1 ♗e4 23.d5 ♘d6 24.♔e2
f6 25.♘d2 ♔f7 26.a4± Moiseenko-
Dreev, Jakarta 2013] **15...♗f8** [15...
e5!? 16.♕f5 ♗e6 17.dxe5 ♗d6 18.♗f4
♘xe5 19.♘d4 ♗c5 20.♕e4 ♖ee8
21.♘b3 ♕b4 22.♗xe5 ♗xe5 23.♕xc6
♖ac8≋] **16.♗h4 h6 17.♗g3 ♖ad8
18.♕b3 ♖c8 19.h3 ♘f6 20.♗h4
♘d7 21.♖d1 ♕h5?!** [21...♗d6
22.e4 ♗c7∞] **22.♕a4 a5 23.♗g3
♕f5 24.♖cc1 ♖ed8 25.♘d2
♗b4 26.♕c2 ♕h5** [26...♕xc2
27.♖xc2 ♘f6 28.f3 c5⇄] **27.♘e4
♗a3** [27...♕f5 28.c5±] **28.♖b1 ♕g6
29.♗h4 ♖e8 30.♕d3** [30.c5!? bxc5
31.♖b7 ♗f8 32.♖b3 ♗b4 33.dxc5 ♘xc5
34.f3 ♗e7 35.♗xe7 ♖xe7 36.♖bd3
c5 37.♕c3±] **30...♗f8 31.♗g3
c5** [31...e5 32.dxe5 ♘xe5 33.♗xe5
♖xe5 34.♘c3 ♕xd3 35.♖xd3 ♖b8≋]
**32.dxc5 ♘xc5 33.♘xc5 ♗xc5
34.♕xg6 fxg6 35.♖d7 ♖ed8
36.♖bd1 ♗e7 37.♔f1 ♖xd7?**
[37...♔f8 38.♖xd8+ ♗xd8 39.♖d7
g5 40.♗d6+ ♔e8 41.♖xg7 ♖xc4∞]
38.♖xd7 ♗f6 39.♖c7 ♖d8 40.♔e2

♗c3 41.♖c6 ♖d2+ 42.♔f3 ♖xa2
43.♖xb6 ♖c2 44.c5 ♗e1 45.c6 e5
46.♗xe5 ♖xf2+ 47.♔e4   1-0

Anton Smirnov
Surya Shekhar Ganguly
Canberra 2015 (7)
**1.♘f3 d5 2.d4 ♘f6 3.c4 e6 4.♘c3
c6 5.♗g5 ♘bd7 6.e3 ♕a5 7.cxd5
♘xd5 8.♖c1 b6 9.♗d3 h6 10.♗h4
♘xc3 11.bxc3 ♗a6 12.0-0 ♗a3
13.♖c2 ♗xd3 14.♕xd3 0-0**

15.♘d2 ♖fe8 16.c4 ♗f8 [16...♗e7
17.♗xe7 ♖xe7 18.c5 bxc5 (18...♕a4
19.♘b3 ♘f6=) 19.♘b3 ♕a4= Cmilyte-
Gurevich, Turkey tt 2012] **17.♗g3 ♖ad8
18.♘b3 ♕a4 19.♗h4 ♖c8 20.♖d1
c5! 21.♗g3 b5** [21...cxd4 22.exd4 e5
23.d5 ♗d6=] **22.♖dc1?!** [22.♖cc1 ♘b6
23.♘xc5 ♗xc5 24.dxc5 ♘xc4 25.♕d7∞]
22...♘b6 23.♘xc5 [23.♘d2 cxd4
24.cxb5 (24.exd4? ♗a3–+) 24...dxe3
25.fxe3 ♖xc2 26.♖xc2 ♖d8 27.♕b3
♕g4∓] **23...♗xc5 24.dxc5 ♘xc4**
[24...♖ed8!? 25.♕b3 ♘xc5∓] **25.♕b3
♕a5 26.♗d6 ♖ed8 27.h3 ♖c6
28.♗e7** [28.♖xc4! bxc4 29.♖xc4 ♕e1+
30.♔h2 ♕xf2 31.♖f4 ♕d2 32.♕b7∞]
**28...♖d7 29.a4 ♖xe7 30.axb5
♖xc5 31.♖xc4 ♕xb5 32.♕a3
♖xc4 33.♖xc4 ♕xc4 34.♕xe7
♕a4 35.h4 a5 36.g3 ♕d1+ 37.♔g2
♕d5+ 38.♔g1 ♕a8 39.♕a3 a4
40.h5 ♕a5 41.g4 ♕a8**   0-1

White Queen on e2
More Options

Magnus Carlsen
Shakhriyar Mamedyarov
Shamkir 2014 (1)
**1.d4 d5 2.c4 c6 3.♘f3 ♘f6 4.♘c3
e6 5.♗g5 ♘bd7 6.e3 ♕a5 7.cxd5**

♘xd5 8.♖c1 ♘xc3 9.bxc3 ♗a3
10.♖c2 b6 11.♗e2 ♗a6 12.0-0
♗xe2 13.♕xe2 0-0 14.e4

14...♖ac8?! [14...♖fe8! 15.♖d1 (15.
e5 c5⇄) 15...♖ac8 16.e5 (16.♗f4
c5 17.♘d2 b5 18.dxc5 (18.♘b3
♕a4 19.dxc5 ♘xc5 20.♖d4 ♕a6∞)
18...♘xc5 19.♖b1 e5 20.♗g3 a6 21.c4
b4 22.♖d5 ♕a4 23.f3 (23.♖xa3 ♕xa3
24.f3 b3⇄) 23...b3 24.axb3 ♕xb3
25.♘xa3 ♕xa3 26.♗f2 ♘e6 27.g3
♖c6 28.♔g2 f6 29.c5± Cmilyte-Dreev,
Gibraltar 2014) 16...♗f8 (16...c5!?
17.d5 exd5 18.♖xd5 ♕a4!? 19.♖cd2
♗f8 20.♖d1 ♕g6=) 17.c4 (17.♘d2 h6
18.♗e3 ♖ed8 19.♘e4 ♕g6∞) 17...h6
18.♗e3 ♘g6 19.h4 ♕a4 20.h5 ♘e7
21.♘h4 c5!? (21...♖ed8=) 22.d5 exd5
23.cxd5 ♘xd5 24.♖c4 ♕c6 25.♗xh6
(25.♘f5 ♖xe5 26.♕g4 ♕xf5 27.♕xf5
♘xe3 28.fxe3 ♗b2⇄) 25...♘xh6
26.♖xd5 ♕e6 27.♕d1 ♗b2∓
Kosteniuk-Pogonina, Bilbao Ech-tt W
2014] **15.e5 ♕a4** [15...c5 16.d5!
♖fe8 (16...exd5? 17.e6 ♘f6 (17...fxe6?
18.♕xe6+ ♔f7 19.♘e5+–) 18.♗xf6
gxf6 19.e7+–) 17.d6 h6 18.♗e7±]
**16.c4 ♖fe8 17.♖d1 c5 18.d5
exd5 19.♖xd5 ♗f8** [19...♘b8!?] **20.
h4 h6 21.♗e3 ♘g6?!** [21...♖cd8
22.♕d3 ♖d7∞] **22.♕d3 ♖e6
23.h5 ♘e7 24.♖d6 ♗b4** [24...♖e8
25.♖xe6 fxe6 26.♘h4±] **25.♖c1 ♖e8**
[25...♗f8 26.♖d8±] **26.♖xe6 fxe6
27.♘h4 ♕c6 28.a3 ♗a5 29.♖d1
♕c7 30.♘g6** [30.f4 a6 31.♕d6±]
**30...♘xg6 31.♕xg6 ♕f7 32.♖d3
a6 33.a4 ♖f8 34.g4 ♕e8 35.♖d6
♕xa4** [35...♕xg6 36.hxg6 ♖e8
37.♖d7 ♗c3 38.f4+–] **36.♕xe6+
♔h8 37.♗xh6 ♕a1+ 38.♔g2
♖xf2+ 39.♔xf2 ♕e1+ 40.♔g2
♕e4+ 41.♔h3 ♕h1+ 42.♔g3
♕e1+ 43.♔f4 ♗d2+ 44.♖xd2**

♕xd2+ 45.♔f5 gxh6 46.♕e8+ ♔g7 47.♕e7+ 1-0

Petar Drenchev
Levente Vajda
Albena 2014 (8)

1.d4 ♘f6 2.c4 e6 3.♘f3 d5 4.♘c3 ♘bd7 5.♗g5 c6 6.e3 ♕a5 7.cxd5 ♘xd5 8.♖c1 ♘xc3 9.bxc3 ♗a3 10.♖c2 b6 11.♗e2 ♗a6 12.0-0 ♗xe2 13.♕xe2 0-0 14.e4 e5

15.♖d1 [15.dxe5 ♘xe5 16.♘xe5 ♕xe5 17.f4 ♕c5+ 18.♔h1 f6 19.♗h4 ♖ae8⇄] 15...♖fe8 16.♗h4 ♖ac8 [16...♗e7!? 17.♗g3 (17.♗xe7 ♖xe7 18.♘d2 b5 19.d5 ♕a4 20.♖b2 ♖c8∞) 17...♗f6 18.♘d2 b5 19.dxe5 ♘xe5 (19...♕a4 20.♘c4 ♘xe5 21.♘d6 ♖ed8 22.♖cd2±) 20.f4 ♕a4 21.♖cc1 (21.fxe5 ♕xc2 22.exf6 ♖xe4 23.♕f3 ♖d8⇄) 21...♘g6 22.♕f3 ♗e7 23.e5 ♗a3 24.♖b1 ♖ad8 25.♘b3 ♗f8 (25...♗e7!? 26.f5 ♖xd1+ 27.♖xd1 ♗d5 28.♖d4 ♕a6∞) 26.♘d4 b4 27.cxb4 c5 28.♕b3 ♕xb3 29.♘xb3 cxb4 30.♔f1 h5= Wang Hao-Dreev, Tromsø 2013] 17.h3 h6 [17...exd4 18.cxd4 ♕b5 19.♖d3 ♗d6∞] 18.♗g3 exd4 19.cxd4 ♗f8 20.d5 ♘c5? [20...cxd5!? 21.♖xc8 ♖xc8 22.exd5 g6∞] 21.d6 [21.♘e5 cxd5 22.♕h5 ♖xe5 (22...g6? 23.♕f3 ♗e7 24.exd5±) 23.♗xe5 dxe4⇄] 21...♖cd8 [21...♖xe4? 22.♖xc5 ♕a4 23.♕c2 ♗d6 24.♕xa4 ♖xa4 25.♖c2+-] 22.♖c4 [22.♘d4! ♖d7 23.♘b3 ♘xb3 24.axb3 ♕b4 25.♖xc6 ♖xe4 26.♕d3±] 22...f5 23.♘e5 ♕b5? [23...♖xd6!? 24.♖xd6 ♗xd6 25.♘xc6 ♕b5 26.♗xd6 ♕xc6 27.♖xc5 bxc5 28.e5 ♕d5 29.f4 g5⇄] 24.a4 ♘xa4 25.♕a2 ♔h7 26.♖xa4 ♖xe5 27.♗xe5 ♕xe5 28.d7 ♗d6 29.♖xa7 fxe4 30.♕c2 c5 31.♔f1 ♔h8 32.♖e1 c4 33.♖xe4 ♕b5 34.♕xc4 ♕h5 35.♕e2 1-0

Ding Liren
Ruslan Ponomariov
Tsaghkadzor Wch-tt 2015 (7)

1.d4 ♘f6 2.c4 e6 3.♘f3 d5 4.♘c3 c6 5.♗g5 ♘bd7 6.e3 ♕a5 7.cxd5 ♘xd5 8.♖c1 ♘xc3 9.bxc3 ♗a3 10.♖c2 b6 11.♗e2 ♗a6 12.0-0 ♗xe2 13.♕xe2 0-0 14.♖d1 ♖fe8 15.♗f4 ♖ac8 16.c4

16...c5N [16...♗e7 17.e4 ♕a4! 18.h3 ♘f8 19.♗e3 (19.c5 ♘g6 20.♗g3 (20.♗e3 bxc5 21.♖c4 ♕a5 22.dxc5 ♖ed8=) 20...♖ed8 21.♖c4 ♕a6⇄) 19...♘g6 20.g3 c5 21.d5 exd5 22.♖xd5 (22.exd5 ♗d6=) 22...♘f6 23.♕d3 ♘e7 24.♖d6 ♘c6= Tomashevsky-Dreev, Yugra-Kazan tt 2014; 16...♘f8 17.h3 ♕a4 18.♕d3 (18.c5 bxc5 19.♖c4 ♕a5∞) 18...h6 19.♕b3 (19.e4 ♖ed8∞) 19...♕a5 20.e4 ♖ed8 21.♗d2 (21.♗e2!?) 21...♕h5 22.♖e1 e5 23.d5 f5⇄ Brynell-Agrest, Sweden tt 2014] 17.♘e5 ♘xe5 18.dxe5 ♗b4 19.♕g4 ♔h8 [19...♖cd8 20.♖d6 ♕a4 21.♗h6 g6 22.♕e4±] 20.h4 [20.♖d7 ♘f8 21.♕e2 a6 22.♕d3 b5⇄] 20...♕a4 21.♖cc1 ♗a3! [21...♕xa2 22.h5 ♕b2 (22...h6? 23.♗xh6 gxh6 24.♕f4+-) 23.h6†] 22.♖b1 ♕xc4 [22...♕c2!?] 23.♖d7 ♖f8 [23...♗g8 24.h5 ♕c2 25.♖bd1 c4 26.♗h6⇄] 24.♖xa7 ♗b2 25.♕d1 ♖cd8 26.♕b3 ♕xb3 27.axb3 ♗c3 28.♖b7 ♗a5 29.♗g5 ♖d2 [29...♖d5 30.♗e7 ♖e8 31.♗d6 ♔g8 32.♗c7 ♖d7 33.♖a7±] 30.♗e7 ♖c8 31.♗d6 ♔g8 32.h5 h6 33.♖c1 f5 34.♖c4 [34.b4! ♗xb4 35.♖xb6±] 34...♖d3 35.♖a4 ♔h8 36.g4 fxg4 37.♖f4 ♖g8 38.♖ff7 ♗c3 39.♔g2 ♖d5 40.e4 ♖d3 41.♖xb6 ♖h3 42.f4 ♖a8 43.♖f8+ ♖xf8 44.♗xf8 ♖f3 45.♗xc5 ♖xf4 46.♖xe6 ♖xe4 47.♖e8+ ♔h7 48.e6 ♗f6 49.e7 ½-½

Artyom Timofeev
Alexandra Goryachkina
Khanty-Mansiysk 2014 (8)

1.d4 d5 2.c4 c6 3.♘f3 ♘f6 4.♘c3 e6 5.♗g5 ♘bd7 6.e3 ♕a5 7.cxd5 ♘xd5 8.♖c1 h6 9.♗h4 ♘xc3 10.bxc3 ♗a3 11.♖c2 b6 12.♗e2 ♗a6 13.0-0 ♗xe2 14.♕xe2 ♕a4 [14...0-0]

15.c4 [15.e4 0-0 16.e5 b5⇄] 15...0-0 16.e4 ♖fe8 17.♖d2 [17.♖d1 c5∞] 17...b5 18.c5 e5 19.♗g3 [19.♖fd1 ♗b4 20.♖c2 exd4 21.♖xd4 ♘f8∞] 19...♗b4 20.♖d3 exd4 21.♖xd4 ♘xc5 22.♘e5 ♘e6 [22...♖e6!? 23.♕h5 ♖f8 24.♗h4 ♕c2! 25.♖xb4 ♕c3 26.♘xc6 ♖xc6 27.♖xb5 ♕c4 28.♖a5 ♘xe4=] 23.♖d7 ♖e7 24.♖xe7 ♗xe7 25.♘xc6 ♗c5! [25...♗a3 26.♕d3 ♕c4 27.♕d5 (27.♕xa3 ♕xc6 28.f3 ♘d4 29.♕d3 ♖d8 30.♖d1 a5†) 27...♔f8 (27...♖e8 28.♖d1 a6∞) 28.♕d7 ♘c5 29.♕f5 (29.♕d6+!? ♔g8 30.♕c7 a5 31.♘e7+ ♔h7 32.♘d5±) 29...♘xe4 30.♗e5 ♘xg3 31.fxg3 ♕d4+ 32.♔h1 ♔g8 33.♕xf7+ ♔h7 34.♕f5+ ♔g8 35.♕e6+ ♔h7 36.♕g6+ (36.h3!? ♕e4 37.♔h2 a5 38.♖f7 ♗f8 39.♖f4 ♕b1 40.♘d7→) 36...♔g8 37.♘g4 ♔h8 38.♘xh6 gxh6 39.♕xh6+= Timofeev-B.Savchenko, Khanty-Mansiysk 2014] 26.♕d3 ♘d4 [26...b4 27.♕d5 ♖c8 28.♘e5 ♖d8 29.♘b7 ♕e8∓] 27.♗d6 [27.♘xd4 ♗xd4 28.♕d1 ♕c4∓] 27...♗xd6 [27...♘xc6 28.♗xc5 ♖d8 29.♕e2 ♘d4 30.♗xd4 ♖xd4∓] 28.♕xd4 ♕xd4 29.♘xd4 b4 30.♖c1 a5 31.♔f1 a4 32.♔e2 b3 33.axb3 a3 34.♔d3? [34.♘f3 f6 35.♖a1 a2 36.♔d3=] 34...♗e5! 35.♔e3 a2 36.♖a1 ♖d8

37.♖xa2 ♗xd4+ 38.♔e2 ♔f8 39.f4 ♔e7 40.e5 ♖b8 41.♔d3 ♗g1 42.g3 ♖xb3+ 43.♔e4 ♖b4+ 44.♔f3 ♔e6 45.♔g2 ♗d4 46.♔f3 ♗c5 47.♖a6+ ♔d5 48.♔g4 ♖b2 49.h4 ♖b3 50.h5 ♔e4 [50...♖a3–+ 51.♖xa3 ♗xa3 52.♔f5 ♗c5–+] **51.♖a4+ ♗d4 52.♖c4 ♗c3** [52...f5+ 53.♔h3 ♖b1–+; 52...f6 53.exf6 gxf6 54.♖c6 f5+ 55.♔h3 ♗f2–+] **53.♖b4 ♖c7 54.♖b8 ♖c3 55.♖b4 ♗a3** [55...f6–+] **56.♖c4 ♔d5 57.♖c7 ♔e6 58.♖c6+ ♔e7 59.♖c7+ ♔e8 60.♖c2 ♖d3 61.♖g2 ♖e3 62.♔f5 ♔e7 63.g4 ♖b3 64.♖c2 ♖b4 65.♖c7+ ♔e8 66.e6 fxe6+?** [66...♗e3! 67.exf7+ (67.♖c8+ ♔e7 68.♖c7+ ♔d8 69.♖d7+ ♔e8 70.♖d3 ♖xf4+ 71.♔e5 f6+–+) 67...♔f8 68.♔e6 ♖e4+–+] **67.♔xe6 ♖b6+ 68.♔f5 ♖b5+ 69.♔g6 ♖b6+ 70.♔h7 ♔d8 71.♖c4 ♗b2 72.g5 ♔d7 73.♖a4 ♔e6 74.♖a5 ♗c3 75.♖c5 ♗d4 76.♖a5 ♗c3 77.♖c5 ♗b2 78.♖a5 ♖b7 79.♔g6 ♗c1 80.f5+ ♔e7 81.f6+ gxf6 82.gxf6+ ♔e6 83.♖a8 ♗f4 84.♖e8+** ½-½

Aryan Tari
Dragisa Blagojevic
Reykjavik Ech-tt 2015 (1)

1.d4 d5 2.c4 e6 3.♘f3 ♘f6 4.♘c3 c6 5.♗g5 ♘bd7 6.e3 ♕a5 7.cxd5 ♘xd5 8.♖c1 h6 9.♗h4 ♘xc3 10.bxc3 ♗a3 11.♖c2 b6 12.♗e2 ♗a6 13.0-0 ♗xe2 14.♕xe2 ♕a4 15.c4 [15.e4 0-0 16.♖d1 ♖fe8 17.e5

17...b5 18.c4 bxc4 (18...♘b6!? 19.c5 ♘d5 20.♖b1 ♖ab8∞) **19.♖xc4 ♕xc4 20.♖xc4 ♖ec8∓**) 19...♗a6 20.♕c2 ♘b6 21.♖c6 ♖ac8 22.d5 (22.♖xc8 ♖xc8 23.♕b3 ♘d5⇄) 22...exd5 23.♖xc8 ♖xc8 24.♕f5 (24.♕b3 ♖c4↑) 24...♕e2 25.♖e1 ♕c2 26.♕h5 ♗b4 27.♖f1 ♕e4

28.h3 d4∓ Pecurica-Blagojevic, Podgorica ch-MON 2014] **15...0-0 16.♖d1 ♖fe8 17.c5** [17.♗g3 c5⇄] **17...e5 18.♖c4** [18.cxb6 axb6 19.♗g3 e4 20.♘e5 ♘xe5 21.♗xe5 c5∞] **18...♕a6 19.♕c2 b5 20.♖c3 e4! 21.♘d2 ♗b4 22.♖b3 ♗xd2 23.♖xd2 ♖ac8** [23...♕a4 24.f3 exf3 25.gxf3 ♘e5⇄] **24.f3 ♕a5 25.♖e2 f5 26.♖b1 ♕a3 27.♖b3 ♕a5 28.♗g3 ♕d8 29.♖b1 ♘f6 30.♗e5 ♘d5 31.♖f1 ♕g5 32.♔h1 ♘xe3** [32...♖f8 33.♕d2 ♖cd8=] **33. f4 ♘xc2 34.fxg5 ♗b4 35.gxh6 g6 36.g4 ♖f8 37.gxf5 ♖xf5 38.♖g1 ♔h7 39.♖xe4 ♖e8 40.♖e3 a5 41.♖eg3 ♖e6 42.a4 ♘d5 43.axb5 cxb5 44.♖c1 ♘e7 45.♖a3** ½-½

Tomashevsky's Novelty 13.♖xe2

Evgeny Tomashevsky
Alexander Ipatov
Reykjavik Ech-tt 2015 (1)

1.c4 c6 [To some extent this move already came as a surprise to me: Sasha's opening repertoire is rather broad and quite well prepared, and it was not easy to predict the Slav Defence, which in recent times he has rarely employed] **2.♘f3 d5 3.d4 ♘f6 4.♘c3 e6 5.♗g5 ♘bd7 6.e3 ♕a5** [And as for the Cambridge Springs Variation, he had never employed it at all! It is a sensible idea – to surprise the opponent with a recently prepared system, which also has a good reputation, but Alexander was a little unlucky: I had not only devoted much time to the resulting complicated strategic positions after a game with the 'guru' of the variation – Alexey Dreev (Loo 2014), but I had also made a cursory repetition of the main branches of this analysis before one of my games from the European Club Cup in October] **7.cxd5 ♘xd5 8.♖c1 ♘xc3 9.bxc3 ♗a3 10.♖c2 b6** [At the present moment this is probably the main branch of the entire variation, introduced in 2011 by Bart Michiels and 'circulated' by the future World Champion (Gelfand-Carlsen, London 2013)] **11.♗e2** [There are also plenty of subtleties after the bishop's development on d3, but at the present moment theory and practice 'vote'

for this more modest square] **11...♗a6 12.0-0 ♗xe2**

13.♖xe2!? [A principled novelty, associated with a new approach to the content of the position. Before this game everyone captured on e2 with the queen (what could be more natural?). After 'deserting' to the white side Magnus even won a brilliant game against Shakhriyar Mamedyarov (Shamkir 2014), but in May last year I was unable to find anything convincing for White. Speculative conclusions led to the following logical chain: Black has strategic advantages on the queenside and in the endgame, which suggests that he should seek counterplay involving attacks on the centre and exchanges; White dominates in the centre, which he would like to use for play against the opponent's king; capturing on e2 with the queen leaves the rook on the c-file, which will probably soon be opened, which favours exchanges and does not assist the attack. Of course, a concrete verification revealed that there were also 'pitfalls' after 13.♖xe2, but on the whole it convinced me of the practical suitability of the idea...] **13...0-0** [13...♕xc3?! is premature in view of 14.♖c2 ♕a5 15.♖xc6 0-0

16.♖c7 ♘f6 17.♗xf6 gxf6 18.♕c2±, Ikonnikov] **14.e4 ♖fe8!?** [At the first critical moment Sasha responded quickly and quite well, by choosing a flexible continuation, for the moment not disclosing all Black's cards. The most natural and principled is undoubtedly 14...♕xc3, after which White has an interesting choice mainly between 15.e5!? and 15.♖e3!? ♕a5 16.♕d3 with mind-boggling play in both cases, in which for a long time even the computer frequently 'gets confused' (15.♖c2?! ♕a5 16.♖xc6 ♖ac8 17.♕c2 ♕a6=, Ikonnikov). Another approach to the position is 14...e5, removing the opponent's most obvious attacking motifs. However, more often in this variation Black aims for ...c6-c5, and after the advance of the e-pawn and, say, 15.♕c2 ♖fe8 16.♖d1, White can claim some advantage] **15.♖e3** [This move took me quite a long time. The point is that I roughly remembered the variations from my home analysis, arising after 15.e5 ♕xc3 when the capture of the pawn is one of the best replies, and in this situation I preferred to make use of an additional possibility] **15...♗f8** [I spent a long time analysing the resulting type of position at home, I tested it at the board with full intensity and concentration, and all the same very many of my assessments during play and immediately after the game were, apparently, far from correct. Thus I considered the bishop manoeuvre to f8 to be dubious, and I assumed that the best and almost obligatory move was 15...e5!?, which is indeed sound and quite good, with the approximate continuation 16.♕c2 ♗e7 17.♗xe7 ♖xe7 18.♖d1 ♖ae8 19.g3 and slight pressure for White, thinking that the move in the game would allow me a fearsome attack. For some reason, 15...♗e7?! also seemed risky, on account of e4-e5 immediately or after the capture, which, to put it mildly, is questionable, for example: 16.♗xe7 ♖xe7 17.e5 ♕xa2 and if 18.♘g5 the reply 18...f6 19.exf6 ♘xf6 suggests itself, after which White has to concern himself with gaining sufficient compensation! (20.♕d3, Ikonnikov) Thus, if Sasha had retreated his bishop slightly less expansively, I would have had to relate differently to 15.♖e3...] **16.e5!** [During the game I felt extremely optimistic, considering for Black almost that variation which in fact occurred! Possibly

I was able to 'infect' my opponent with this confidence...] **16...♕xa2?!** [It is only after this loss of time, not justified by the slight material gain, that White's game genuinely becomes easy. It was essential to begin immediate counterplay in the centre with 16...c5! which in addition justifies the retreat of the bishop from a3] **17.♘d2** [Now Black cannot comfortably eliminate the wedge on e5, thanks to which his opponent obtains a great superiority in force on the kingside] **17...c5?** [Too late! For the defence of the king it was now time to adopt resolute measures: 17...f6 18.exf6 gxf6 (19.♗h4 ♗g7 20.♘e4↑ – Ikonnikov) or 17...f5 18.exf6 gxf6 with the continuation 19.♗h4 ♗g7 20.♘e4 ♖e7 21.♕g4 when White has a strong initiative for the pawn, but the defensive possibilities are not yet exhausted] **18.♘e4** [Four white pieces are attacking the king, whose residence the main defenders are unable to reach. The assessment of the position is undisputed. However, in the game numerous further events occurred...] **18...cxd4 19.cxd4 ♖ac8** [Little is changed by 19...♖ec8 20.♖h3 g6 21.♕g4 ♕d5 22.♕f4 with a decisive attack]

20.♕g4? [At this point I still had more than half an hour on the clock, but I rushed. 20.♖h3! wins quickly and without any questions: 20...♕c2 21.♕g4 and Black is absolutely helpless against the threat of 22.♕h4 h6 23.♗xh6! (e.g. 21...♔h8 22.♕h4 h6 23.♘d6+–, Ikonnikov)] **20...♖c4!** [Sasha exploits his opportunity! 'Thanks' to White's mistake the remaining part of the game became quite interesting] **21.♖f3?!** [As with Alexander on the 16th and 17th moves, 'mistakes do not occur singly'! In the variation 21.♗f6 ♖xd4 22.♗xg7 I missed the brilliant defence 22...♖xe4!!,

after which White has to force a draw by 23.♕g5 ♗xg7 24.♖g3 ♔f8 25.♕xg7+ ♔e7 26.♕g5+ ♔f8. And the variation 21.♖h3! ♖xd4 22.♕h5 h6 23.♗xh6! g6 24.♕h4 ♖xe4 25.♗f4! (25.♕xe4 ♗xh6 26.♖xh6 ♕d5 27.♕xd5 exd5 28.f4±, Ikonnikov) 25...♗g7 26.♕h7+ ♔f8 27.♗h6! ♗e7 (27...♗xh6? 28.♕xh6+ ♔e7 29.♕g5+ f6 30.exf6 ♘xf6 31.♖h7+ ♔d6 32.♕xf6+– – Ikonnikov) 28.♕xg7 ♖xe5 29.♖f3! ♔f8 30.♕h7!, when White's advantage is close to decisive, is not so easy to calculate correctly in the tense atmosphere of a team match] **21...♖xd4 22.♕f4!** [Of course, weak was 22.♘f6+? ♔xf6 23.♕xd4 ♘d5, when the advantage passes to Black. Now I was very pleased with myself: it appeared that the fine strategic plan of restricting the black pieces and creating a paradoxical weakness on f7 had been implemented very 'stylishly', and all the variations were 'knitting together' in my favour] **22...♖b8?** [The final mistake. Other rook moves or 22...♔h8 also do not save Black (23.♕xf7 ♖b8 24.♗f6+–, Ikonnikov), but 22...♘xe5! suggests itself, with a complicated justification in the form of 23.♕xe5 ♕c4!!. In my view it is such 'geometrical' moves that are especially difficult for humans to find, and they emphasize the difference between us and computers: 24.♖e1 (bad now is 24.♘f6+? gxf6 25.♕xf6 (25.♗xf6 ♖g4–+, Ikonnikov) 25...e5 when Black has the key resource ...♖g4!) 24...f5 25.♘d2 (25.♘g3!? ♗d6 26.♕e2 retains more fighting resources) 25...♕d5 26.♖xf5 ♕d7! and Black not so much gains saving chances, but is simply close to equality (27.♖f3 ♗b4=, Ikonnikov)! An amazing turn of events] **23.♕xf7+ ♔h8**

24.♗f6! [It was for calculating this natural winning move aesthetic and quite straightforward that the reserve of time, gained by quickly performing 20.♕g4?!, came in useful ☺] **24...♖xe4 25.♖g3 ♘xf6 26.exf6 g6 27.♖h3 h6 28.♕xg6 ♕d2** [28...♖g4 29.♕xg4 e5 30.♖d1+−, Ikonnikov] **29.♕xe4** [Initially after the game I seriously cursed myself for this 'blot on the canvas', but

later it transpired that other decisions deserved to be criticized ☺. And in slight time-trouble I remembered a piece of wisdom, ascribed either to Lasker or to Capablanca: 'If you have a choice between mate and the capture of a rook, take the rook – there may not be a mate'... However, after the obvious 29.♖g3 there

was a mate, and the capture on f2 with the queen could merely have deferred it by a few moves and for an instant embarrassed White] **29...♖c8 30.♖d3 ♕c2 31.♕xe6 ♕c6** [31...♕xd3 32.♕xc8+−, Ikonnikov] **32.♕g4 ♖c7 33.♕g6 ♕e6 34.♖d8** 1-0

Tomashevsky M/15-8-25

Exercise 1

position after 15.e4-e5

Can Black create counterplay here with ...c6-c5 ?
(solution on page 249)

Exercise 2

position after 16.♗g5-h4

Should Black worry about the reply 17.d5 after the logical 16...c5 ?
(solution on page 249)

Exercise 3

position after 15.♖e2-e3

What is the best defence for Black here?
(solution on page 250)

Slav Defence

What to Do against the 4.g3 Slav?

by Ivan Ivanisevic

1.	d4	d5
2.	c4	c6
3.	♘f3	♞f6
4.	g3	dxc4

A few years ago, at the 2013 European Team Championships in Warsaw, I was paired as Black with Alexander Grischuk. During my preparation for this game, I saw that on several occasions he had used an unfamiliar variation against the Slav – well, not entirely unfamiliar, but it had always been considered completely harmless for Black. After 3.♘f3 ♞f6 he had played 4.g3 in a few games, albeit mostly blitz and rapid games. Until then it had been thought that this early fianchetto allows Black to throw out his bishop, let's say to f5 or g4, getting a favourable version of the Réti Opening.

However, after 4...♗f5 White plays 5.♘c3, meeting 5...e6 with 6.♘h4 and chasing the bishop, as Carlos Matamoros observed in his Survey 'A

Catalan-Flavoured Slav' in Yearbook 113. In this position, I think that Black still hasn't obtained equality. The position is similar to the Slav with 4.e3 ♗f5 5.♘c3 e6 6.♘h4, with the difference that White's knight on h4 is defended, and so he can play e2-e4 at once.

I could not find a clear-cut solution, but I thought that it would be 'wise' to play 4...dxc4, followed by 5...g6, which would transpose to a variation from the Grünfeld Indian. I knew that it is not easy for White to win back the c4-pawn now; in fact he must be prepared to play a gambit.

In the end, this line never came on the board in my game against Grischuk, but my preparation caused me to think about what to play against this for a few more days. I finally came up with the idea that it was best to try to play this with white! The variation is quite rich, and it can transpose to various other openings. For example, if Black plays 4...e6, it leads to a kind of Catalan, if he plays 4...♗f5, we get a kind of Slav hybrid (see Matamoros's Survey in Yearbook 113, who restricted himself to this move and the other bishop move, 4...♗g4), if 4...g6, we have a Grünfeld Indian. If he plays 4...dxc4, followed by ...e7-e6 and ...b7-b5, we again have a Catalan, and

Alexander Grischuk

if 4...dxc4, followed by ...g7-g6, another Grünfeld.

In this Survey, I will only discuss variations in which Black plays 4...dxc4, followed by ...g7-g6, in different lines. More recently, I played a game against Balog in the Hungarian league. This game is important for the assessment of the position, and for the question of whether White will be able to achieve an advantage in this variation. I think that if White plays 6.a4, trying to win back the c4-pawn, Black will get a solid position, as witness the games Ivanisevic-Lampert and Tkachiev-Khairullin. The main test is the gambit that starts with the move 6.♘e5. Here, White must beware of the famous trick that occurred in the game Nikolic-Anand, where Nikolic played ♘e5 one move later, when Black had the strong response 7...♘g4!.

I think that in the variation starting with 5...♘bd7 6.0-0 g6, if White wants to get an advantage, he should play a gambit, as in the games Ivanisevic-Sedlak, Ivanisevic-Tokhirjonova, Avrukh-Motylev and Vinchev-Stefanov. If he wants to avoid risks, he can play as in Grischuk-Aronian, but here, after exchanging a single pair of knights, Black is still 'breathing more easily'.

Conclusion

I think 4...dxc4 is the best way for Black to fight against 4.g3. In order to seek an advantage, White has to play a gambit, so this line gives Black practical chances. On the other hand, if White plays it safe, the position is equal. A small problem is that those who play the Slav with black generally do not play the Grünfeld, so this line requires some flexibility. But otherwise, we are awaiting White's next move!

5...g6 6.♘e5

Ivan Ivanisevic
Imre Balog
Hungary tt 2015/16 (3)

1.d4 d5 2.c4 c6 3.♘f3 ♘f6 4.g3 [This is fashionable these days against the Slav] **4...dxc4 5.♗g2 g6** [Now we transpose into some Fianchetto Grünfeld!] **6.♘e5** [If White wants to react with ♘e5, he needs to do it fast. On the next move it is not possible because of a famous trick: 6.0-0 ♗g7 7.♘e5?! ♘g4! – see the blitz game Nikolic-Anand] **6...♗e6 7.♘a3 ♗d5 8.f3 b5 9.e4 ♗e6 10.0-0 ♗g7 11.f4 0-0 12.♘c2 ♕c8** [12...♘fd7!? 13.f5 (13.♗e3!? △ 13...♘xe5 14.dxe5) 13...♘xe5 (13...gxf5 14.♘xd7 ♗xd7 (14...♕xd7 15.d5 cxd5 16.exd5 ♖d8 17.♘e3 ♕e8 18.♗d2 ♗d7 19.♗c3±; 14...♘xd7 15.d5) 15.exf5 ♘a6 16.♕h5↑) 14.fxe6 ♘d3 15.♗e3∞]

13.♕e2 [A fine move, directed against ♗h3. 13.a4 ♗h3 – see the game Elianov-Malakhov] **13...a5** [13...♘bd7 14.a4 a6 15.♘b4! ♘xe5 16.dxe5↑; 13...♗h3 14.♗xh3 ♕xh3 15.g4 (15.f5 ♘fd7 16.♘g4↑) 15...♘fd7 16.♖f3 ♕h4 17.♕g2 ♕f6 18.g5 ♕d6 19.♘g4↑] **14.♗d2** [14.a4!?] **14...a4** [≥ 14...♘bd7

15.a4 c3 (15...b4 16.♘e3 (16.f5 gxf5 17.exf5 ♗d5∞) 16...♘xe5 17.dxe5 ♘d7 18.f5 (18.♖ac1 ♕a6 19.f5 c3 20.♕xa6 ♖xa6 21.bxc3 ♗b3 22.cxb4 ♘xe5∓) 18...♘xe5 19.fxe6 ♕xe6⊜)] **15.♗c3 ♗h3** [15...♗a6 16.♖ad1 and the white pieces are ready for action!] **16.♗xh3 ♕xh3 17.g4 ♘fd7 18.♘e3?!** [≥ 18.♖f3 ♕h4 19.♕g2 with serious threats, e.g. 19...c5 (19...♕f6 20.♘xd7 ♗xd7 21.e5 ♕e6 22.f5 ♕d5 23.♘b4 ♕e4 24.♖e1+−; the queen is trapped in the centre of the board!) 20.g5 cxd4 21.♗e1 ♕h5 22.♘xd7 ♗xd7 23.♖h3+−] **18...♕h4** [≥ 18...c5! 19.♖f3 ♕h4 20.♘xd7 (20.♘g2 ♕h6; 20.♕g2 cxd4 21.♖h3 ♕xh3 22.♕xh3 dxc3 23.bxc3 ♘xe5 24.fxe5 ♘c6∓) 20...♘xd7 21.e5 e6 22.g5 cxd4 23.♗xd4 (23.♗e1 ♕h5 24.♕g2 a3! 25.bxa3 (25.♖h3 axb2 26.♖b1 ♕xh3 27.♕xh3 ♖xa2−+) 25...♖xa3 26.♖h3 ♕xh3 27.♕xh3 ♖xe3 28.♕g2 ♘b6−+) 23...h6∓. Although this is a computer evaluation, it is not easy during the game to feel safe with your queen almost trapped, at the cost of one pawn...] **19.♘f3 ♕f6 20.e5** [20.f5!?] **20...♕xf4 21.♘d2 ♕h6 22.♘e4** [During the game I was really happy with this manoeuvre, and I evaluated this position as almost winning for me. However, the computer says that it is about equal!] **22...c5 23.♗d2 cxd4** [23...♘c6 was the subject of my calculation more than 23...cxd4. The computer says that a repetition of moves is the best solution.. did we reach the 30th move? 24.♕g2 ♕h4 25.♗e1 ♕h6 26.♗d2 ♕h4. Here White can try 27.♘d5 threatening ♗g5. White's initiative is obvious. 27...f6 and now 28.e6 ♘db8 29.dxc5 is interesting] **24.♘f5 gxf5** [24...♕h3 25.♘xe7+

(25.♘f2 d3! 26.♕d1 (26.♕e4 gxf5 27.♕xa8 ♕h4−+; 26.♘xe7+ ♔h8 27.♕e4 ♕h4 28.♕xa8 ♕xe7−+) 26...♕xf1+ 27.♕xf1 gxf5 28.gxf5 ♔h8 29.♕g2 ♖a6∓) 25...♔h8 26.♘g5 ♕d3 27.♕e1 ♘xe5 28.♗f4→ (28.♘xh7!?)] **25.♗xh6 ♗xh6 26.gxf5+− ♘xe5 27.f6!** [Closing in on the black king!] **27...e6 28.♕h5** [Black resigned as he cannot prevent new material losses] 1-0

Pavel Elianov
Vladimir Malakhov
Riga 2013 (1)

1.d4 d5 2.c4 c6 3.♘f3 ♘f6 4.g3 dxc4 5.♗g2 g6 6.♘e5 ♗e6 7.♘a3 ♗d5 8.f3 b5 9.e4 ♗e6 10.f4 ♗g7 11.0-0 0-0 12.♘c2 ♕c8 13.a4

13...♗h3 14.♗xh3 ♕xh3 15.♕e2 [15.g4!?; 15.f5!?] **15...♕c8 16.♗d2 ♘bd7 17.axb5** [17.♘b4!?] **17...cxb5 18.♗b4 ♖e8 19.♕f3 ♕b7 20.♘xd7 ♘xd7** [≥ 20...♕xd7] **21.f5** [≥ 21.e5] **21...♔h8 22.e5 ♕xf3 23.♖xf3 ♘b6 24.♘e3 ♔g8 25.♖a6 e6 26.fxe6 fxe6 27.♘g4 h5 28.♘f6+ ♗xf6 29.exf6 ♔f7 30.♗d6 ♘d5 31.♔f1 b4 32.♔e2 ♖ec8 33.♔d1 c3 34.b3 g5 35.♔c1 ♖d8 36.♗e5 ♖d7 37.♖f2 ♘e3 38.♖fa2 ♘f5 39.♖6a4 a5 40.♖xa5 ♖xa5 41.♖xa5**

♘xd4 42.♗xd4 ♖xd4 43.♖xg5 h4 44.gxh4 ♖xh4 45.♖g2 ♗xf6 46.♖f2+ ♔e7 47.♔c2 ♔d6 48.♔d3 ♔d5 49.♔e3 ♖h3+ 50.♔f4 ♔d4 51.♔g4 ♖h8 52.h4 ♖c8   0-1

5...g6 6.0-0 c6 7.♘e5

Predrag Nikolic
Viswanathan Anand
München blitz 1994
1.d4 ♘f6 2.c4 g6 3.♘f3 ♗g7 4.g3 d5 5.♗g2 dxc4 6.0-0 c6 7.♘e5?!
[Last call for 7.a4]

7...♘g4!∓ [This is the trick that White needs to remember and avoid!] 8.f4 [≥ 8.♘f3] 8...0-0 9.e3 ♘xe5 10.fxe5 c5 11.♘a3 ♘c6 12.♘xc4 cxd4 13.♗xc6 bxc6 14.exd4 ♗a6 15.b3 c5∓ 16.♗e3 ♕d5 17.dxc5 ♗xc4 18.bxc4 ♕xe5 19.♕f3 ♖ac8 20.♖ab1 ♕c3 21.♖fc1 ♕a3 22.♕e2 ♖c7 23.♗f2 ♖fc8 24.♖d1 e6 25.♖b3 ♕a5 26.♖b5 ♕a6 27.♖db1 ♗f8 28.♕d2 ♕c6 29.♖d1 ♕e8 30.♕a5 ♕c6 31.♕d2 a6 32.♖b6 ♕e4 33.♖xa6 ♗xc5 34.♗xc5 ♖xc5 35.♖d6 ♖xc4 36.♖d8+ ♖xd8 37.♕xd8+ ♔g7 38.a3 ♕e3+ 39.♔g2 ♖c2+ 40.♔h3 ♕e2   0-1

5...g6 6/7.a4

Ivan Ivanisevic
Jonas Lampert
Biel 2015 (8)
1.d4 d5 2.c4 c6 3.♘f3 ♘f6 4.g3 dxc4 5.♗g2 g6 6.a4

6...♘e4!? 7.♕c2 [7.0-0 ♗g7 8.♘a3!?] 7...♘d6 8.e4 ♘a6 9.0-0 ♗g7 10.e5 ♘f5 11.♕xc4 ♗e6 12.♕c3 ♗d5 13.♖d1 0-0 14.♘a3 ♘c7 15.♘c2 ♘e6⇄ 16.b4 [≥ 16.g4 ♘h6 17.h3 f5 18.exf6 exf6 (18...♖xf6 19.g5 ♖xf3 20.♗xf3 ♘f5 21.♗g4∞) 19.♘b4 f5 20.♘xd5 fxg4 21.hxg4 cxd5 (21...♕xd5 22.♘e5 ♕d6 23.♗e3∞) 22.♘e5∞] 16...♗e4 [16...♕d7 17.♗b2 ♖ad8] 17.♗b2 ♕d5?! 18.♖e1! ♗h6 19.♖xe4 ♕xe4 20.♖e1 ♕d5 21.g4 ♘f4 22.gxf5 ♘xg2 23.♔xg2 gxf5 24.b5 cxb5 25.♘b4 ♕d7 [25...♕c4 26.♕xc4 bxc4 27.♘d5 e6 28.♘f6+ ♔h8 29.d5±] 26.e6 fxe6 27.d5 ♖f6 28.dxe6 ♕d6 29.axb5 ♗g7 30.♔h1 ♖g6 31.♕b3 ♗xb2 32.♕xb2 ♖g4 33.♘c2 ♕d5 34.♕c3 ♖d8 35.h3 ♖g6 36.♘cd4 a6 37.bxa6 bxa6 38.♖a1 ♕e4 39.♖e1 ♕d5 40.♘c6 ♖e8 41.♘ce5 ♖g7 42.♘f7 h6 43.♘xh6+ ♔h7 44.♘f7 ♖eg8 45.♘e3 ♖g6 46.♕f4 a5 47.♘7e5 ♖f6 48.♔h2 ♕c5 49.♘h4 ♕d5 50.♘ef3 a4 51.♘g5+ ♔h8 52.♖g1 a3 53.♘f7+ ♔h7 54.♖xg8 ♔xg8 55.♕b8+   1-0

Vladislav Tkachiev
Ildar Khairullin
Khanty-Mansiysk blitz 2013 (5)
1.d4 d5 2.c4 c6 3.♘f3 ♘f6 4.g3 dxc4 5.♗g2 g6 6.0-0 ♗g7 7.a4 ♘e4

8.♘a3 ♘d6 [8...c3 9.♕c2 cxb2 10.♗xb2 ♘d6 11.e4 0-0 12.e5 ♘e8 (12...♗f5 13.g4 ♘h6 14.h3 ♘a6 15.♘c4⇆; 12...♗f5 13.♕e2 ♘e8 14.♘h4!?⇆ △ ♗e6 15.f4 or 14...♗c8 15.f4) 13.♘c4⇆. There are a few computer blitz games with this position] 9.♗f4 0-0 10.♖c1 ♘a6 11.♘xc4 ♘xc4 12.♖xc4 ♗e6 13.♖c1 ♘d5= 14.e3 ♕a5 15.♖e1 ♗e4 16.♘d2 ♗xg2 17.♔xg2 ♘b4 18.♕b3 ♕d5+ 19.♕xd5 ♘xd5 20.♘b3 ♖fd8 21.♘a5 ♖d7 22.♔f3 e6 23.g4 ♗f8 24.♘c4 f6 25.♗g3 ♘b6 26.b3 ♘xc4 27.bxc4 c5 28.♖ed1 ♖ad8 29.♖b1 b6 30.a5 cxd4 31.axb6 axb6 32.exd4 ♖xd4 33.♖xd4 ♖xd4 34.♖xb6 ♖xc4   ½-½

White Plays a Gambit 5...♘bd7

Ivan Ivanisevic
Nikola Sedlak
Montenegro tt 2014 (7)
1.d4 d5 2.c4 c6 3.♘f3 ♘f6 4.g3 dxc4 5.♗g2 ♘bd7 6.0-0 g6 7.♘c3 ♗g7 8.e4 ♘b6 9.a4 a5 10.h3 0-0 11.♕e2

11...e5 [11...♘e8!?] 12.dxe5 ♘fd7 13.♗g5 ♕e8 [13...♕c7 14.♗e7 ♖xe5 15.♗xf8 ♘xf3+ (15...♗xf8 16.♘xe5 ♕xe5 17.f4 ♗c5+ 18.♔h2 ♕e7 19.♖ae1↑) 16.♗xf3 ♗xf8 17.♗g4±] 14.♕e3 ♖a6 15.♖fd1 ♘xe5 16.♘xe5 [16.♖d8 ♕xd8 (16...♘xf3+ 17.♗xf3 ♕e5 18.♖ad1→) 17.♗xd8 ♖xd8 18.♘xe5 ♗xe5 19.♖d1±] 16...♕xe5 17.♗f4 ♕e6 18.♗c7 ♘d7 [18...♘a8 19.♗d6 ♖e8 20.f4±] 19.f4 ♖e8 20.♖d6 ♕f5?! [≥ 20...♕e7 21.♖ad1 ♖a8 (21...f5 22.♗f1! ♕f7 23.b3 cxb3 (23...♘e5 24.fxe5 ♕xc7 25.♗xc4+ ♔h8 26.♕g5!+−) 24.♖xa6 bxa6 25.e5±

22.♔h2±] **21.♖ad1 ♗f8 22.g4±
♕c5 23.♕xc5 ♘xc5 24.♖d8 ♖xd8
25.♖xd8 ♖a8 26.♖xf8+ ♔xf8
27.♗d6+ ♔g8 28.♗xc5+– f5
29.gxf5 gxf5 30.e5 ♗e6 31.♔f2 b6
32.♗d6 ♖c8 33.♔e3 ♔f7 34.♗f3
♔e8 35.♘e2 ♔d7 36.♘d4** 1-0

Boris Avrukh
Alexander Motylev
Eilat tt 2012 (3)

**1.d4 d5 2.c4 c6 3.♘f3 ♘f6 4.g3
dxc4 5.♗g2 ♘bd7 6.0-0 g6 7.♘c3
♗g7 8.e4 0-0 9.♕e2 ♘b6 10.a4 a5
11.h3 e5 12.dxe5 ♘fd7 13.♗g5
♕e8 14.♕e3 ♖a6 15.♖fd1 ♘xe5**

**16.♖d8 ♗xf3+ 17.♗xf3 ♕e5
18.♖ad1 ♗xh3 19.g4! f5 20.♖xf8+
♗xf8 21.♖d8 ♗xg4 22.♗h6?!** [≥
22.♗xg4 fxg4 23.♗h6 ♖a8 24.♕xb6
♖xd8 25.♕xd8 ♕d6 (25...♕e7
26.♕c8+–) 26.♕c8 g5 27.♗xf8 ♕xf8
28.♕xg4+–] **22...♖a8 23.♕xb6
♖xd8 24.♕xd8 ♕d6 25.♕xd6
♗xd6 26.♗xg4 fxg4 27.♗e3± ♔f7**
[27...♗c7] **28.♗b6 ♗b4 29.♘d1
♗d2 30.♔f1 h5 31.♔e2 ♗b4
32.♘e3 c3 33.b3** [33.bxc3 ♗xc3
34.♘c4 ♔e6 35.♘xa5 ♖xa5 36.♖xa5
b5 37.axb5 cxb5 38.♗d3+–] **33...♔f6
34.♔d3 ♗g5 35.♗c7** [35.e5±] **35...
h4 36.♘d1 ♗c5 37.♘xc3 ♗xf2
38.♔e2 ♗d4 39.♘d1 b6 40.♘f2
g3 41.♗d8+ ♔h5 42.e5 g2 43.♘h3
♔g4 44.♘f2+ ♔f5 45.♘h3 g1♕
46.♘xg1 ♗xg1 47.♗xh4 ♔xe5
48.♗d8 ♔e4 49.♔f1 ♗e3 50.♔e2
g5 51.♗c7 g4 52.♗g3 ♗f4** 0-1

Ivan Ivanisevic
Gulrukhbegim Tohirjonova
St Petersburg 2014 (1)

**1.d4 d5 2.c4 c6 3.♘f3 ♘f6 4.g3
dxc4 5.♗g2 ♘bd7 6.0-0 g6 7.♘c3**

♗g7 8.e4 ♘b6 9.a4 a5 10.h3 0-0
11.♕e2 h6 [In order to put the bishop
on e6, my opponent creates a potential
weakness on the kingside] **12.♗e3 ♗e6
13.♖ad1±**

13...♘fd7? [13...♖a6 14.♘e5 ♕d6
15.f4↑] **14.g4 ♘b8** [14...♘f6 15.♘e5±]
15.♘e5± g5 16.f4 [Opening up the
position of the black king] **16...f6?!** [16...
gxf4 17.♗xf4 ♘8d7 18.♘f3! ♘f6 19.♕d2
h5 (19...♔h7 20.g5 ♘g8 21.gxh6 ♗xh6
22.♘g5+ ♗xg5 23.♗xg5 f6 24.♗e3 ♗f7
25.♕f2+–) 20.e5+– hxg4 21.exf6 exf6
22.hxg4]

**17.d5   cxd5   18.exd5   ♗c8
19.♘g6+–   ♖e8   20.♗c5   ♔f7
21.♕e6+!** [Almost every move is
winning in this position, but I add an
exclamation mark for the nice picture!]
**21...♗xe6   22.dxe6+   ♔xe6
23.♖xd8   ♖xd8   24.♖e1+   ♔f7
25.♖xe7+   ♔g8   26.♗xb6   ♘c6
27.♗xc6   ♖d2   28.♗d5+   ♔h7
29.♗e4   ♔g8   30.♖xb7   ♖xb2
31.♘e7+   ♔h8 32.♘f5 ♗f8 33.♗d4
♖xb7 34.♗xf6+ ♔g8 35.♗xb7** 1-0

Simeon Vinchev
Plamen Stefanov
cr BUL 2012

**1.d4 ♘f6 2.c4 g6 3.♘c3 d5 4.♘f3
♗g7 5.g3 dxc4 6.♗g2 0-0 7.0-0**

♘bd7 **8.a4 a5 9.e4 c6 10.♕e2
♘b6 11.h3** [Via a different move order
we have reached our position] **11...♘e8**
[The idea is to prevent White's aggression
by playing ...f7-f5 at some point]

12.♖d1 [12.♗e3 f5!?] **12...♘d6** [12...
f5!?] **13.♗e3 f5 14.e5 ♘f7 15.♘d2
♗e6 16.f4± ♕c7 17.♖ac1 ♖fd8
18.d5! ♘xd5** [18...cxd5 19.♘b5 ♕c6
20.b3+–] **19.♘xd5 ♗xd5** [19...cxd5
20.♘f3 ♗c8 (20...♕c8 21.♘d4 ♔h8
22.b3±) 21.b3 e6 22.♘d4 ♕e7 23.bxc4
dxc4 24.♖xc4±] **20.♘xc4 ♗e6**
[20...♗xg2 21.♗b6 ♖xd1+ 22.♖xd1
♕c8 23.♔xg2±] **21.♖e1 ♖a6 22.♕f2
♗xc4 23.♖xc4 e6 24.♗f1± ♕e7**
[24...♗f8 25.♖cc1 ♖aa8 26.♗b6]
**25.♗c5 ♕e8 26.♗b6 ♖d5
27.♖cc1 ♖a8 28.♗c4 ♖d7 29.♕e3
♗f8 30.♕b3 ♘d8 31.♖ed1 ♗b4
32.♖xd7 ♕xd7 33.g4** [33.♖d1 ♕e7
34.♔g2] **33...fxg4 34.♖d1 ♕e7
35.hxg4 ♔f7** [35...♗c5+ 36.♗xc5
♕xc5+ 37.♔g2 ♕e7 38.♖d6±]
**36.♔g2 ♕e8 37.♖h1 ♕f7 38.♕g3
♗f8 39.f5 ♕d7 40.f6 h6 41.♕e3
♘f7 42.♕e2 ♖a6 43.♗f2 ♕c7
44.♗xe6 ♘g5 45.♗c4 c5 46.♖d1
♘e6 47.♕e4 ♔f7 48.♗e1 ♕c6
49.♕xc6 ♖xc6 50.♖d7+** 1-0
[I really like this game. Such a positional
treatment directed against the bishop on
g7...]

**White Avoids Risks
5...♘bd7**

Alexander Grischuk
Levon Aronian
London 2013 (13)

1.♘f3 d5 2.c4 c6 3.d4 ♘f6 4.g3
[Grischuk uses it, even in the Candidates'!]
4...dxc4 5.♗g2 ♘bd7

6.♕c2 ♘b6 7.♘bd2 g6 8.0-0 ♗g7 9.♘xc4 [9.e4!?. I first want to improve the position with ♖e1, h2-h3, and then pick up the c4-pawn] 9...♗f5 10.♕c3 ♘xc4 11.♕xc4 0-0 12.♖d1 a5 13.♕b3 ♕d6 14.♘e5 [Maybe 14.♗f4 ♕b4 15.♕xb4 axb4 16.♗d2 can pose some small problems to Black] 14...♘d7 [14...♘g4!?] 15.♘c4 ♕b4 16.♘e3 ♕xb3 17.axb3 ♗e6 18.d5 cxd5 19.♘xd5 ♘c5= 20.♖a3 ♗xd5 21.♖xd5 ♖ac8 22.♗g5 e6 23.♖d6 ♗xb2 24.♖xa5 ♗c1 25.♗f6 ♘xb3 26.♖b5 ♘d2 27.♖d3 b6 28.e3 ♘c4 29.♗f1 ♗a3 30.♖d1 ♖fe8 31.♖d7 ♗f8 32.♗xc4 ♖xc4 33.♖xb6 ♗g7 34.♗e7 ♖cc8 35.♔g2 ♖b8 36.♖c6 ♖bc8 37.♖b6 ♖b8 38.♖c6   ½-½

Exercise 1

position after 20...♔g8-f7

How does White win by force?
(solution on page 250)

Exercise 2

position after 17...♖f8-d8

How can White increase the pressure?
(solution on page 250)

Exercise 3

position after 7.♘f3-e5

Black to move.
(solution on page 250)

A Surprise against the Ragozin

by Vishnu Prasanna

1.	d4	♘f6
2.	c4	e6
3.	♘f3	d5
4.	♘c3	♗b4
5.	♕a4+	♘c6
6.	a3	

In Round 6 of the Hoogeveen Open 2015, I met the strong Dutch grandmaster and top seed of the event, Erwin l'Ami. I chose the main system of my repertoire against 1.d4, the Ragozin. I think my opponent had also expected this, because he quickly went 1.d4 ♘f6 2.c4 e6 3.♘f3 d5 4.♘c3 ♗b4 5.♕a4 ♘c6 6.a3!?. White's sixth move is quite rare, especially at the top level, although the younger Carlsen has played it and Kramnik also played it many years ago – unsuccessfully – in a blitz game. A few other GMs have played the variation on

occasion, but it has never been a serious option.

It does contain a bit of venom, though, and an unprepared black player would have to solve some tough problems. In my own game I quickly overcame my problems, until I unnecessarily weakened my position on move 11. After that I had to defend a long game to reach a draw.

Moving onto the theoretical part: after 6..a3 ♗xc3 (6...♗e7 does not look very logical to me) 7.bxc3 Black has three main options:

* 7....♗d7 is one of the main moves in the position. The critical game is Tran Quoc Dung-Ni Hua, 2014. There is an equalizing improvement for Black in that game, but I still believe it is not completely convincing for practical play.

* 7.....0-0 is a slightly more flexible way for Black. He reserves his option to play ...♗d7 for the future, but after 8.♗g5 h6 9.♗h4 the most likely way for Black is to transpose to 7...♗d7. However, in this position he has an interesting option after 9...g5 10.♗g3 ♘e4 11.♕c2 h5 12.♘e5 h4!?. It looks a bit suspicious, but I have been unable to refute it.

Paul Keres

* 7......♘e4 is probably the soundest way. It was my choice in the game, and I would probably repeat it if faced with this variation again. Black's position is sound and solid, and in all lines he is able to develop harmoniously.

Conclusion

The variation with 6.a3!? has its share of subtleties and nuances, but for a well-prepared black player it should not pose too much problems, although white players who are able to surprise their opponents have good chances of obtaining an edge from the opening.

Vladimir Makogonov
Paul Keres
Leningrad ch-URS 1947 (5)

1.d4 ♘f6 2.♘f3 d5 3.c4 e6 4.♘c3 ♗b4 5.♕a4+ ♘c6 6.a3 ♗xc3+ 7.bxc3 ♗d7 8.cxd5 exd5 9.♗g5 h6

10.♗xf6 ♕xf6 11.♕b3 ♕d6 12.e3 ♗f5! 13.♗e2 [13.♕xb7 ♖b8 14.♕a6 0-0 15.♗e2 ♖b2 16.0-0 ♖fb8−+] **13...0-0 14.0-0 b6 15.♘d2 ♘a5 16.♕a2 c5 17.♘b3?** [17.♗f3 ♖ad8=] **17...♘xb3 18.♕xb3 ♖ac8 19.♖ac1 ♖c7 20.♖fd1 ♖fc8 21.♗a6 ♖b8 22.♗f1 c4 23.♕b2 b5 24.♖e1 a5 25.f3 ♖e7 26.♖a1 g5! 27.e4 dxe4 28.a4 b4 29.fxe4 ♖xe4 30.♖xe4 ♗xe4 31.♗xc4 ♖c8 32.♕e2 ♗g6 33.♗d3 ♗xd3 34.♕xd3 ♖xc3 35.♕e4 b3 36.♖f1 ♕e6 37.♕xe6** [37.♕a8+ ♔g7 38.♕xa5 ♕e3+ 39.♔h1 ♖c1−+] **37...fxe6 38.♖b1 ♔f7 39.♔f2 ♖c2+ 40.♔f3 b2 41.h3 ♔e7 42.g4 ♔d6 43.♔e4 ♖h2−+ 44.d5 exd5+ 45.♔d4 ♖g2 46.♔c3 ♔c5 47.♖f1 d4+ 48.♔b3 ♖f2 49.♖e1 d3 50.♔a2 ♔c4 51.♖e8 d2** 0-1

Tran Quoc Dung
Ni Hua
Ho Chi Minh City 2014 (1)

1.d4 ♘f6 2.c4 e6 3.♘f3 d5 4.♘c3 ♗b4 5.♕a4+ ♘c6 6.a3 ♗xc3+ 7.bxc3 ♗d7!? [This was also the choice of Paul Keres way back in 1947] **8.cxd5** [8.♕c2 dxc4 9.e3 ♘a5 10.♘e5] **8...exd5 9.♗g5 h6 10.♗h4** [10.♗xf6 does not really test Black. 10...♕xf6 11.♕b3 ♕d6 12.e3 ♗f5 was okay for

Black in Makogonov-Keres, Leningrad ch-URS 1947] **10...0-0** [10...g5 11.♗g3 ♘e4 12.♕b3 ♗c8 13.e3 h5 14.♗d3 h4 15.♗e5 0-0 16.h3 ♘xe5 17.♘xe5 looks slightly better for White because the advanced black pawns on the kingside do not give him enough counterplay] **11.♕c2** [White seems to be well prepared. White prepares the exchange of knights and denies the f5-square to the black bishop]

11...g5 [11...♘a5!? is probably best, giving Black good counterplay: 12.e3 c5 13.♘e5 ♗e6 14.♗d3 (14.♗e2 ♖c8 15.♕b2 g5) 14...c4 15.♗e2 ♘b3 16.♖a2 ♕c8] **12.♗g3 ♘e4 13.e3 ♖e8 14.♘d2 ♗f5 15.♘xe4 ♗xe4 16.♕b2** [Black does not have enough compensation for his weak king and Black's two bishops] **16...♘a5 17.h4 f6 18.hxg5 hxg5 19.f3 ♗f5 20.♔f2 c6 21.♖e1 ♕b6 22.♕a2 ♔g7 23.e4 ♗g6 24.e5 ♕b3 25.exf6+** [25.♕d2±] **25...♗xf6 26.♗e5+ ♔f7 27.♕xb3** [27.♕d2 ♕c2 28.♕xc2 ♗xc2 29.♗h5±] **27...♘xb3 28.g3 ♘d2 29.♗e2 a5 30.♖h6 ♘c4 31.♗xc4 dxc4 32.f4 gxf4 33.gxf4 ♖e6 34.♖g1 ♖g8 35.♖g5 ♔e7 36.♖h1 ♖f8 37.♖hg1 ♗f5 38.♖g7+ ♖f7 39.♖xf7+ ♔xf7 40.♖g5 ♗e4 41.f5 ♖h6 42.♖g7+ ♔e8 43.f6 ♖h7 44.f7+ ♔f8 45.♗d6+** 1-0

Vladimir Kramnik
Alexander Grischuk
Moscow Wch blitz 2009 (16)

1.♘f3 ♘f6 2.c4 e6 3.♘c3 d5 4.d4 ♗b4 5.♕a4+ ♘c6 6.a3 ♗xc3+ 7.bxc3 0-0

8.e3 [I believe 8.♗g5 is more critical] **8...♗d7 9.♕c2 ♘a5! 10.cxd5 exd5 11.a4 ♖e8 12.♗d3 c5 13.dxc5 ♕c7 14.♗a3 ♘c4 15.0-0 ♘xa3 16.♖xa3 ♗xc5= 17.♕b2 b6 18.♖fa1 ♗e4 19.♘d4 ♖ac8 20.♗xe4 dxe4 21.a5 b5 22.a6 ♕g5 23.♖a5 ♖c5 24.♘e2 ♗e6 25.♖d1 ♗c4 26.♘f4 h6 27.♖aa1 ♕f6 28.♕b4 ♖c6 29.♘d5 ♕e5 30.♘f4 ♕f6 31.♖d7 ♖xa6 32.♖xa7 ♖xa7 33.♖xa7 ♖d8 34.♖a1 ♖d2 35.♕a5 ♔h7 36.♕a8 ♕xc3 37.♕xe4+ g6 38.♕b1 ♖b2 39.♕d1 ♖d2 40.♕b1 ♕c2 41.♕xc2 ♖xc2 42.♖b1 b4 43.h4 b3 44.e4 b2 45.♔h2 ♗a2** 0-1

Dmitry Svetushkin
Patrick van Hoolandt
Cutro 2009 (7)

1.d4 ♘f6 2.c4 e6 3.♘f3 d5 4.♘c3 ♗b4 5.♕a4+ ♘c6 6.a3 ♗xc3+ 7.bxc3 0-0 8.♗g5 h6 9.♗xf6 [9.♗h4] **9...♕xf6 10.e3**

10...♕g6! 11.♗e2 ♗d7 [11...♕xg2! is of course the main point of 10...♕g6: 12.♖g1 ♕h3] **12.cxd5 exd5 13.0-0 ♗h3** [13...♖ab8] **14.♘e1 ♖fd8 15.c4 a6 16.♖c1 dxc4 17.♗xc4 ♗e6 18.♕c3 ♖ab8 19.♘d3± ♗f5 20.♖fd1 ♖d6 21.♘f4 ♕f6 22.d5**

♕xc3 23.♖xc3 ♖bd8 24.♖e1 ♘e5
25.♖xc7 b5 26.e4 ♗xe4 27.♔f1
f5 28.f3 ♗xd5 29.♖xe5 ♗b3
30.♖ee7   1-0

Loek van Wely
Vadim Milov
Biel 2000 (10)

1.d4 ♘f6 2.c4 e6 3.♘c3 d5 4.♘f3
♗b4 5.♕a4+ ♘c6 6.a3 ♗xc3+
7.bxc3 0-0 8.♗g5 h6 9.♗h4

9...g5 [9...♗d7 transposes] 10.♗g3
♘e4 11.♕c2 h5 [11...f5 12.e3 h5
13.♘e5 f4 14.♘xc6 bxc6 15.f3 fxg3
16.fxe4 ♖f2 17.♕d1 g4 18.hxg3 ♕f6
19.e5 ♕f7 is highly unclear] 12.♘e5
h4 13.♘xc6 [13.f3!? ♘xe5 (13...♘xg3)
14.♗xe5 ♘d6 15.cxd5 exd5 (15...♘c4
16.dxe6 ♗xe6 17.e4 ♘xe5 18.dxe5 ♕e7
19.♕f2) 16.e4 f6 17.♗xd6 ♖xd6 18.exd5
♔g7 19.♗d3 ♖e8+ 20.♔f2 ♗d7 21.♗e4
♖e7 and Black has compensation for the
sacrificed pawn] 13...bxc6 14.f3 ♘d6
15.♗xd6 cxd6 16.e4 ♕f6 17.♗d3
dxe4 18.fxe4 c5 19.♕f2 ♕xf2+
20.♔xf2 ♗a6 21.dxc5 dxc5
22.e5 ♖fd8 23.♔e3 ♗d7 24.g3
♖ad8 25.♗e2 ♖d2 26.gxh4 gxh4
27.♖hd1 ♖xd1 28.♖xd1 ♖xd1
29.♗xd1 ♔g7 30.♔f4 f6 31.♗e2
♔g6 32.♔g4 fxe5 33.♗d3+
♔f6 34.♔xh4 ♗b7 35.♔g3 ♗c6
36.♔g4 ♗a4 37.♔f3   ½-½

Probably Soundest
7...♘e4

Magnus Carlsen
Humpy Koneru
Cap d'Agde 2008 (2)

1.d4 ♘f6 2.c4 e6 3.♘f3 d5 4.♘c3
♗b4 5.♕a4+ ♘c6 6.a3 ♗xc3+
7.bxc3 ♘e4

8.♗b2 0-0 [8...♘d6!] 9.e3 ♗d7
10.♕c2 ♘a5 11.♗d3 c5 12.0-0
cxd4 13.exd4 ♘f6 14.cxd5 exd5
15.♘e5 h6 16.♖ae1 ♕b6 17.♗c1
♗b5 18.♗xb5 ♕xb5 19.♕f5 ♕a6
20.♖e3 ♘b3 21.g4 ♘xc1 22.♖xc1
♖ae8 23.♖ce1 ♕e6 24.♕f4 ♕d6
25.h4 ♘d7 26.♘d3 ♕xf4 27.♘xf4
♖xe3 28.♖xe3 ♘b6 29.♖e7 ♖c8
30.♖xb7 ♖xc3 31.♖xa7 ♖c4
32.♘e2 ♖c2 33.♘g3 ♘c4 34.♘f5
♘d2 35.♘e7+ ♔h7 36.♘xd5 ♖c4
37.♖xf7 ♖xd4 38.♘e3 ♖a4 39.♔g2
♔g8 40.♖c7 ♘b3 41.h5 ♔f8
42.♖c4 ♖a7 43.a4 ♘a5 44.♖c3
♔f7 45.♘f5 ♔f6 46.♔g3 ♖b7
47.♖c5 ♖a7 48.♘d4 ♖d7 49.♖xa5
♖xd4 50.♖f5+ ♔e6 51.a5 ♖a4
52.f3 ♔e7 53.♔f2 ♖a3 54.♔e2 1-0

Nikolay Ogloblin
Dmitry Bocharov
Voronezh 2009 (3)

1.d4 d5 2.c4 e6 3.♘f3 ♘f6 4.♘c3
♗b4 5.♕a4+ ♘c6 6.a3 ♗xc3+
7.bxc3 ♘e4 8.♕c2 0-0 9.e3 b6

10.♗d3?! [Allowing Black to solve the
problem of the development of his bishop
easily; 10.cxd5!] 10...♗a6 11.0-0
♘a5 12.cxd5 ♗xd3 13.♕xd3
exd5 14.♘d2 ♕e7 15.♘xe4 dxe4
16.♕a6 ♕e6 17.a4 ♕c4 18.♕xc4

♘xc4 19.♖a2 ♖fe8 20.♗a3 a5
21.♖b1 f6 22.♔f1 ♔f7 23.♔e2 c6
24.♗c1 ♗e6 25.f3 d5 26.fxe4+
♔xe4 27.♗d2 f5 28.♖aa1 g6
29.♖b3 ♗e6 30.♖f1 ♖ae8 31.♖f3
h5 32.♖b1 ♔d5 33.♔d3 ♖e4
34.h3 ♖8e6 35.♖g3 h4 36.♖f3 f4
37.♖xf4 ♖xe3+ 38.♔xe3 ♖xe3+
39.♔c2 ♖e2+ 40.♔d1 ♖xg2 0-1

Laszlo Szabo
Mark Taimanov
Buenos Aires 1960 (8)

1.d4 ♘f6 2.c4 e6 3.♘f3 d5 4.♘c3
♗b4 5.♕a4+ ♘c6 6.a3 ♗xc3+
7.bxc3 ♘e4 8.♕c2 0-0 9.e3
b6 10.cxd5 exd5 11.♗d3 ♖e8
12.0-0

12...♗b7? [Here the bishop does not
contest White's light-squared bishop and
is quite passive. Black does not succeed
in equalizing in this game] 13.♘d2
♘a5 14.f3 [14.♘xe4 dxe4 15.♗e2
♕g5 16.c4±] 14...♘xd2 15.♗xd2
♘c4 16.♗xc4 dxc4 17.e4 ♕d6
18.♗e1 b5 19.♗g3 ♕b6 20.a4
[White patiently and successfully converts
his advantage] 20...c6 21.♗d6
a5 22.♕f2 ♕d8 23.♗c5 ♗c8
24.axb5 cxb5 25.d5 ♖a6 26.♕d4
♕f6 27.♕xf6 gxf6 28.g4 ♗d7
29.♔f2 ♖c8 30.♗e7 ♖e8 31.♗a3
♔g7 32.♖g1 ♖ea8 33.♗c5 ♖c8
34.♗d4 ♔f8 35.h4 ♔e7 36.♖a3
♖ca8 37.♖ga1 ♗c8 38.♗c5+
♔d7 39.♔e3 ♔c7 40.♔d4 ♗d7
41.♖3a2 ♔b7 42.g5 f5 43.exf5
♗xf5 44.♖e1 ♖d8 45.♖b2 ♗d7
46.♖e7 ♖c8 47.♖xf7 ♖e6 48.♗e7
♖e1 49.♗xd8 ♔xd8 50.♖xd7+
♔xd7 51.♖xb5 a4 52.♖a5 ♖h1
53.♔c5 ♖xh4 54.♖a7+ ♔e8 55.d6
♖f4 56.♔c6   1-0

Yury Shulman
Giorgi Kacheishvili

Wheeling 2009 (6)

1.d4 ♘f6 2.c4 e6 3.♘f3 d5 4.♘c3
♗b4 5.♕a4+ ♘c6 6.a3 ♗xc3+
7.bxc3 ♘e4 8.♕c2 0-0 9.e3 b6
10.cxd5 exd5 11.♗d3 ♖e8

12.c4?! [12.0-0 ♗f5 transposes]
12...♗a6 13.0-0 ♘a5 [13...♗xc4
14.♗xc4 dxc4 15.♕xc4 ♘a5 is
completely comfortable for Black] **14.♘d2
♗xc4 15.♗xe4 ♖xe4 16.♘xe4
dxe4 17.♕xe4 ♗xf1 18.♔xf1 c5
19.♗b2 cxd4 20.♖d1 ♘b3**   ½-½

Dmitry Svetushkin
Sergey Movsesian

Germany Bundesliga 2008/09 (1)

1.d4 ♘f6 2.c4 e6 3.♘f3 d5 4.♘c3
♗b4 5.♕a4+ ♘c6 6.a3 ♗xc3+
7.bxc3 ♘e4 8.♕c2 0-0 9.e3 b6
10.cxd5 exd5 11.♗d3 ♗f5

**12.c4 ♖e8 13.0-0 dxc4 14.♕xc4
♘d6** [I believe 14...♘a5! 15.♕a2 c5 is
the best way for Black to continue. Black's
strong control of the centre compensates for
White's bishop pair. 16.♗b2 ♗g4 is good
for Black] **15.♕c2 ♗xd3 16.♕xd3 b5
17.♗d2 ♘c4 18.♖fc1** [18.♕f5! ♗xd2
19.♘xd2 a6 20.♖fc1±] **18...a6 19.♗b4
♘6e5 20.♘xe5 ♘xe5 21.♕f5
♘c4 22.a4 c6 23.♖a2 g6 24.♕f3**

♕d5 25.♖ca1 ♘b6 26.axb5 ♕xf3
27.gxf3 axb5 28.♖a6 f5 29.♗c5
♘a4 30.♖xc6 ♖ac8 31.♖xc8
♖xc8 32.♗b4 ♖c2 33.♖b1 ♔f7
34.d5 ♘b6 35.e4 ♘c4 36.♗a5
♘d7 37.exf5 ♖c5 38.fxg6+ hxg6
39.♖d1 ♖c4 40.♗d8 b4 41.♖e1 b3
42.♖e7+ ♔g8 43.♖xd7 b2 44.♖b7
♖c1+ 45.♔g2 b1♕ 46.♖xb1 ♖xb1
47.♗c7 ♖d1 48.d6 ♔f7 49.♔g3
♔e6 50.♔f4 ♖d5 51.♔g4 ♖f5 52.f4
♖d5 53.♗b8   ½-½

Eva Moser
Tatiana Kosintseva

Rijeka 2010 (8)

1.d4 ♘f6 2.♘f3 e6 3.c4 d5 4.♘c3
♗b4 5.♕a4+ ♘c6 6.a3 ♗xc3+
7.bxc3 ♘e4 8.♕c2 0-0 9.e3 b6
10.cxd5 exd5 11.♗d3

11...♘a5 12.0-0 ♖e8 13.♘e5
[13.♘d2 ♗f5 14.f3 ♘xd2] **13...f6
14.♘f3 c5 15.dxc5 bxc5 16.c4**
[After 16.♖d1 ♕e7 17.♗b1 ♗g4 Black
has a very active and sound position]
**16...♘xc4 17.♗xc4 dxc4 18.♖d1
♕b6 19.♘d2 ♘xd2 20.♗xd2 ♗e6
21.♖ab1 ♕c6 22.f3 ♕a6∓** [Clearly
Black has won the opening battle] **23.
a4 ♖ad8 24.a5 ♖d3 25.e4 ♖ed8
26.♗c3 h5 27.♖e1 h4 28.h3
♕c6 29.♖bc1 ♕c7 30.♖b1 ♕c6
31.♖bc1 ♕c7 32.e5 f5 33.♕f2
♕e7 34.♖e3 ♕g5 35.f4 ♕h5
36.♖ce1 a6 37.♔h2 ♕h6 38.♔g1
♖c8 39.♔h1 ♗d5 40.e6 ♗e4
41.e7 ♔f7 42.♔g1 ♗xe7 43.♗e5
♔f7 44.♕a2 ♕e6 45.♕f2 ♕g6
46.♕a2 ♔f8 47.♖xe4 fxe4 48.f5
♕c6 49.♕xc4 ♕d5 50.♕xa6 ♖a8
51.♗xg7+ ♔xg7 52.♕g6+ ♔f8
53.f6 ♖g3 54.♕h6+ ♔g8 55.♕xh4
♖g6 56.♖xe4 ♕d1+ 57.♔h2
♕d6+ 58.♔h1 ♕xf6 59.♕e1 ♔f8**

♕d2 c4 61.a6 ♕xa6 62.♕d5+
♖f7 63.♖e8+ ♔g7 64.♕h5 ♕a1+
65.♔h2 ♖xg2+ 66.♔xg2 ♕f1+
67.♔h2 ♖f2+ 68.♔g3 ♖g2+   0-1

Deepan Chakkravarthy
P. Maheswaran

Sivakasi 2015 (6)

1.d4 ♘f6 2.c4 e6 3.♘c3 d5 4.♘f3
♗b4 5.♕a4+ ♘c6 6.a3 ♗xc3+
7.bxc3 ♘e4 8.♕c2 [This game explains
Erwin's choice of 8.♗f4 in our game]

8...♘a5! 9.e3 [Now the bishop is
restricted to c1, which limits White's
chances for an edge; 9.cxd5 exd5] **9...
b6 10.cxd5 exd5 11.♗b5+** [11.♗d3
♗f5 12.0-0 (12.♘e5 0-0 13.f3 (13.g4
♗e6; 13.c4 f6) 13...♘h4+−+) 12...0-0
13.♘e5 f6 14.♘f3 c5 is completely fine
for Black] **11...c6 12.♗d3 0-0 13.0-0
♖e8** [With a passive bishop on c1 White
does not have real chances of obtaining an
edge in this opening] **14.♘e5 f6 15.f3
♘g5 16.♘g4 ♗xg4 17.h4** [Black has
played quite well so far but now starts to
make some unusual mistakes] **17...♘e4**
[A very unusual decision; 17...♘xf3+
is simply much better for Black] **18.
fxe4 dxe4 19.♗xe4 f5 20.♗xf5
♗xf5 21.♖xf5 ♕xh4 22.♕a2+
♔h8 23.♗d2 ♖f8 24.♖af1 ♖xf5
25.♖xf5 ♕g4 26.♕f7 h6 27.♖f3
♕e4 28.c4 ♘b3 29.♗b4 ♕e8
30.♕f5 c5 31.♗c3 cxd4 32.exd4
♘c1 33.♔h1 ♘e2 34.♗b2 ♕a4
35.♕d3 ♖e8 36.d5 b5 37.♖h3
♔g8 38.♖xh6**   1-0

Erwin l'Ami
Vishnu Prasanna

Hoogeveen 2015 (5)

1.d4 ♘f6 2.c4 e6 3.♘f3 d5 4.♘c3
♗b4 5.♕a4+ ♘c6 6.a3 ♗xc3+
7.bxc3 ♘e4

8.♗f4!? [8.♕c2 ♘a5!] **8...0-0** [8...♘xc3 was possible, but I thought White had compensation after 9.♕c2 ♘e4 10.e3 0-0 11.♗d3 f5 12.h3±] **9.♕c2 b6** [9...e5 10.cxd5 (10.♘xe5 ♗f5 11.♕b2 ♘xe5 12.♗xe5) 10...f5] **10.cxd5 exd5 11.e3 g5?!** [Unnecessary, to say the least. My decision was based on a miscalculation on move 13 of the line

below: 11...♘a5 12.♗d3 ♗f5 13.0-0 (13.♘d2 ♖e8 14.f3 worried me during the game, and I stopped my calculations, but after 14...♘xd2 15.♗xf5 ♘dc4! the position remains slightly more than okay for Black) 13...♖e8 14.♖fd1 (14.♘d2 ♗g6) 14...♗e7 15.h3 ♖ac8 16.♗h2 c5] **12.♗g3 ♗f5 13.♗d3 ♖e8 14.0-0 ♘a5 15.♘d2 ♘c4 16.♘xc4 dxc4 17.♗xe4 ♗xe4 18.♕d1±** [I am not sure if I should judge this as slightly better for White or more, but I believe Black has not fully equalized yet] **18...c6** [18...c5! 19.♖e1 ♔g7 kept the balance for Black. Black should not allow White to expand with f2-f3/e2-e4] **19.f3 ♗d3 20.♖e1 ♕f6 21.e4 ♖ad8 22.♕d2 ♕g6 23.♖e3 ♖e6 24.♖ae1 h6** [Black has no options but to patiently wait and suffer] **25.h3 ♔h7 26.♕f2 f5? 27.d5!?**

cxd5 **28.exd5 ♖xe3 29.♕xe3 ♖xd5 30.♕e7+ ♕g7 31.♕e8 ♖d7 32.♗e5 ♕f7 33.♕h8+ ♔g6 34.♗d4** [34.h4! gxh4!] **34...f4** [Black is still under a lot of pressure but White no longer has an 'advantage'. Black has to be careful and patiently wait and not make mistakes] **35.♖e8 ♔h5 36.♔h2 ♗g6 37.♖e5 ♕h7 38.♕c8 ♗f5 39.♕f8 ♖f7 40.♕e8 ♗d7 41.♕d8 ♗f5 42.♖e8 ♖d7 43.♕f6 ♕f7 44.♕h8 ♗g6 45.♖e1 ♗f5 46.h4 ♕h7 47.♕e5 ♕f7 48.hxg5 hxg5 49.♔g1** [49.g4+ fxg3+ 50.♔xg3 ♔g6] **49...♔g6 50.♔f2 ♕f8 51.♖h1 ♕h7 52.♖e1 ♖d6 53.a4 ♖d6 54.♖h1 ♖e6 55.♕c7 ♕e7 56.♕xc4 ♕a3 57.♖e1 ♕b2+ 58.♔f1 ♖xe1+ 59.♔xe1 ♕c1+ 60.♔f2 ♕d2+ 61.♔g1 ♕e1+ 62.♔h2 ♕h4+ 63.♔g1** ½-½

Exercise 1

position after 14.♕c2xc4

What is Black's best move here?
(solution on page 250)

Exercise 2

position after 11...♕f6-d6

Find the best move for White.
(solution on page 250)

Exercise 3

position after 9...b7-b6

What should White play here?
(solution on page 250)

Queen's Indian Defence

The Bogo-Indian: Defence or Attack?

by Dejan Antic

1.	d4	♘f6
2.	c4	e6
3.	♘f3	♗b4+
4.	♘bd2	0-0
5.	a3	♗e7
6.	e4	d5
7.	e5	♘fd7
8.	♗d3	c5

The Bogo-Indian is certainly one of the openings which has gained great popularity in

Evgeny Tomashevsky

the last couple of years, with several games by the world's top grandmasters. The writer of these lines has written a few articles in the Yearbook about this opening, as well as a book, *The Modern Bogo* (with Branimir Maksimovic), published in 2014. Although the black position seems to be uncomfortable, Black usually undermines the white centre and conquers the strategically important square c5 for the black knight. One of the variations in which White tries to prevent this appeared for the first time at top level in the game Grischuk-Filippov, played last year. White won an impressive attacking game.

So, after the standard opening moves 1.d4 ♘f6 2.c4 e6 3.♘f3 ♗b4+ 4.♘bd2 0-0 5.a3 ♗e7 6.e4 d5 7.e5 ♘fd7 8.♗d3 c5, White continues with the offensive formation 9.♕c2 h6 10.0-0 ♘c6 and then the move 11.♘b3.

I have to admit that I myself have had some experience with this line, and I was not satisfied with the positions I achieved. During the World Cup in 2015, this position appeared in two rapid games between Maxime Vachier-Lagrave and Evgeny Tomashevsky. Although Black cannot boast about the result, the positions he achieved in these games were excellent, and now is the right moment to share some analysis of this line with the reader.

Play like Tomashevsky!

As I have already said, in the two games I played, I was not satisfied with the positions and the order of moves I chose. And yet I had a feeling that Black, even after the weakening of his pawn structure, had a dynamic game that compensated for all this. The right move order and the correct game plan were shown by GM Tomashevsky, although the results of his games against Vachier-Lagrave do not bear this out. I am absolutely positive that the result would have been much better in games with a standard time-control. I would like to point out that other options for White, such as 11.♖e1 (game Belous-Rozum), do not cause Black any trouble, and the alternatives and some other analysis are included in that game.

The Back-up Plan

To ambitious black players I suggest they pay attention to the plan followed in the game Rodshtein-Elianov, as well as in the game by GM Brkic. Instead of the standard 10...♘c6 and further piece development, Black plays 10...a5 – a prophylactic plan that is directed against 11.♘b3, so that he will be able to restrict that knight with 11...b6 and gain space later by advancing his a-pawn. This plan seems interesting, and further practice will show how this continuation should be evaluated. The classical chess school, though, prefers the development of pieces!

Conclusion

It is really nice to see that in the era of 'Grünfelds', a classical opening like the Bogo-Indian is seeing such a revival! Several years ago, while I was writing articles and preparing our book on this opening, I predicted that this variation would be tested by the world's best players. And it turned out I was right, despite the fact that, in practice, Black plays the Tarrasch Variation of the French Defence with a tempo less, at the same time giving White a full pawn centre. However, the facts are that White has spent a tempo on a2-a3, that the position of the knight on d2 is awkward and that this is an unfavourable version of the French Defence for White, since his c-pawn is on c4. All these factors convince us that we will witness more top-level games in this classical opening in the future, and you can rest assured that the writer of these lines will gladly share them with the readers of the Yearbook!

Play Like Tomashevsky! 11.♘b3

Alexander Grischuk
Anton Filippov

Tromsø ol 2014 (6)

1.d4 ♘f6 2.c4 e6 3.♘f3 ♗b4+ 4.♘bd2 0-0 5.a3 ♗e7 6.e4 d5 7.e5 ♘fd7 8.♗d3 c5 9.♕c2 h6 10.0-0 ♘c6 11.♘b3

11...cxd4 [11...a5 12.♖d1 a4 13.♘xc5 ♗xc5 14.dxc5 ♘dxe5 15.♘xe5 ♘xe5 16.cxd5 exd5 17.♗h7+ ♔h8 18.♗f5 (18.♗e4 ♗e6 19.♕c3 f6 20.♗e3±) 18...♗e6 19.♕c3 ♕f6 20.♗c2± Vasic-S. Maksimovic, Pancevo ch-SCG-w 2005] 12.♖e1 ♕b6 [12...♘b6 13.cxd5 (13.c5?! ♘d7 14.♗f4 a5 15.♕e2 ♗xc5 (15...a4 16.♘bxd4 ♘xc5∓) 16.♗b1 ♗b6 17.♕d3 f5 18.exf6 ♘xf6 19.♗xh6 gxh6 20.♕g6+ ♔h8 21.♕xh6+ ♔g8 22.♕g6+ ♔h8 23.♕h6+ ♔g8 ½-½ Balokas-Michelakos, Paleochora 2015)

13...♕xd5 14.♗f4 (14.♗h7+ ♔h8 15.♗e4 ♕c4 16.♕d1 ♖d8∞) 14...♗d7 15.♗h7+ ♔h8 16.♗e4 ♕c4 17.♕d1 ♖ad8? (≥ 17...♘d5 18.♖c1 ♕a4 19.♗g3 ♖ac8⩱) 18.♖c1± ♕b5 19.♗d3 ♕d5 20.♖e4 (20.♗g5!

20...♗xg5 (20...♗e8 21.♖xc6 hxg5 22.♖c7 ♖d7 23.♗e4±) 21.♖c5 ♘xe5 22.♘xe5 ♕d6 23.♘xd7 ♖xd7 24.♖xg5 ♘a4 25.♖g3 ♘xb2 26.♕g4±) 20...f5?! (20...♕g8 21.♗b1 f5 22.exf6 gxf6 23.♘bxd4 e5 24.♕e2 ♗f8 25.♘xc6 ♗xc6 26.♗g3±) 21.exf6 ♖xf6 22.♘bxd4± e5? (22...♘a4 23.♕xa4 e5 24.♘xc6 ♗xc6 25.♖xc6 ♖xf4 26.♖xf4 ♕xd3 27.♘e1 ♕d2 28.♖e4 bxc6±) 23.♗xe5 ♖xf3 24.♘xf3? (24.♖xc6!+− ♖xd3 (24...♗xc6 25.♕xf3; 24...bxc6 25.♘xf3 ♗f5 26.♖d4) 25.♖xh6+ ♔g8 26.♕xd3−+) 24...f5 25.♖d4 ♘xd4 26.♗xd4 ♖xd3 27.♕xd3 ♗f6 28.♖d1 ♕c4 29.♕c3 ♘e5 30.♘e1 ♘c6? (30...♖d7 31.♕c8+ ♖d8 (31...♔h7 32.♕c3=) 32.♕c3=) 31.♗xf6± ♖xd1 32.♗xd8 ♘xd8 33.g3 ♘c6 34.♔g2 1-0 (50) Parligras-Antic, Kragujevac tt 2015] 13.♗f4 a5 14.♖ad1 ♘c5 15.♘xc5 ♕xc5 16.♕e2 ♖d8 17.h4 ♔f8?! [17...♗d7 18.cxd5 exd5 (18...♕xd5 19.♗c4 ♕c5 20.♖c1 ♕b6 21.♗d3 ♗f8 22.♕e4 g6 23.h5 ♗e8→) 19.♕d2 ♗f8 20.♗b1 ♗g4 21.♖c1±] 18.♖c1 ♕b6 19.cxd5 exd5 [19...♖xd5 20.♕e4→] 20.♘g5!+− hxg5 [20...♗xg5 21.hxg5 hxg5 22.♗xg5+−; 20...♗e6 21.♘xe6+ fxe6 22.♕g4+−] 21.♕h5 ♗e8 22.e6 ♗xe6 23.♖xe6 gxf4 24.♗f5 g6 25.♖xg6 ♕c7 26.♖e1 fxg6 27.♕h8+ ♔f7 28.♗e6# 1-0

Maxime Vachier-Lagrave
Evgeny Tomashevsky

Baku (rapid) 2015 (3)

1.d4 ♘f6 2.c4 e6 3.♘f3 ♗b4+ 4.♘bd2 0-0 5.a3 ♗e7 6.e4 d5 7.e5 ♘fd7 8.♗d3 c5 9.♕c2 h6 10.0-0 ♘c6 11.♘b3 cxd4 12.♖e1 dxc4 13.♕xc4 ♘b6 14.♕c2 f5 15.exf6 ♖xf6 16.♗d2 [16.♕d1!? ♘d5?! (16...♗d7 17.♗c2 (17.♘bxd4 ♘xd4 18.♘xd4 ♗c5 19.♗c2 ♖c8∞) 17...e5! 18.♘xe5 ♘xe5 19.♖xe5 ♗d6 20.♖e2 (20.♖e1? ♖xf2!-+ 21.♖e4 (21.♗xf2 ♕h4+ 22.♔f1 ♗b5+ 23.♗d3 ♖f8+) 21...♘c6 22.♔xf2 ♗xe4 23.♗xe4 ♕h4+ 24.♔f1 ♕xe4-+) 20...♗g4 (20...♗b5) 21.f3 d3 22.♖xd3 ♗f5 23.♖d2 ♗xd3 24.♖xd3 ♘c4⩲ 17.♗c2 ♕b6 (½-½

S.Saric-Antic, Vrbas ch-SRB 2015) 18.♕d3±] **16...♗d7**

17.♘c5 ♗xc5 18.♕xc5 ♕f8 [18...♗e8 19.♖ac1 ♕d5 20.♕c2 (20.♕xd5 ♘xd5 21.♗b5 ♘de7⇄) 20...♕d6⇄] **19.♖ac1 ♕xc5 20.♖xc5 ♖af8** [20...♗e8!?] **21.♗e4 ♘d5 22.b4 a6 23.b5 axb5 24.♖xb5 b6 25.♗xd5 exd5 26.♖xd5 ♗g4?!** [26...♗e6 27.♖b5 (27.♖d6 ♗c4 28.♖xf6 ♖xf6 29.♘e5 ♗xe5 30.♖xe5=) 27...♘h3!∞] **27.♘xd4 ♘xd4 28.♖xd4± ♖xf2 29.♗xh6 ♗h3 30.♖d2 ♖xg2+ 31.♖xg2 ♗xg2 32.♗e3 ♗c6 33.♗xb6 ♖f3 34.♖c1 ♗e4 35.a4 ♗b3 36.♖c8+ ♔f7 37.a5 ♖b2 38.h4** [38.♖c7+ ♔g6 39.♖xg7+ ♔xg7 40.♗d4+ ♔f7 41.♗xb2 ♔e6 42.a6 ♔d7=] **38...g6 39.♖c3 ♖a2 40.♖e3 ♖a4 41.♔f2 ♔f6 42.♖c3 d5 43.♖c5 ♔e6 44.♗d8 ♔e5 45.♔g3 ♖a2 46.♗c7+ ♔e6 47.♔g4 ♖a4+ 48.♔f4 ♗e4 49.♔g5 ♗d3 50.♖e5+ ♔f7 51.♖d5 ♗e4 52.♖d7+ ♔e6 53.♖d6+ ♔e7 54.a6 ♖a5+ 55.♔h6 ♖h5+ 56.♔g7 ♖xh4 57.♗g3 ♖h3 58.♖d4 ♗h1 59.♗d6+ ♔e6 60.a7 g5 61.♗b4 ♖b3 62.♖d6+ ♔f5 63.♖f6+ ♔g4 64.♖b6 ♖b1 65.♖b8 ♖a1 66.♗c5 ♖a6 67.♗e3** ½-½

Maxime Vachier-Lagrave
Evgeny Tomashevsky
Baku (rapid) 2015 (3)

1.d4 ♘f6 2.c4 e6 3.♘f3 ♗b4+ 4.♘bd2 0-0 5.a3 ♗e7 6.e4 d5 7.e5 ♘fd7 8.♗d3 c5 9.♕c2 h6 10.0-0 ♘c6 11.♘b3 cxd4 12.♖e1 dxc4 13.♕xc4 ♘b6 14.♕c2 f5 15.exf6 ♖xf6 16.♗d2 ♗d7 17.♘bxd4 ♘xd4 18.♘xd4 ♖c8 19.♕d1 ♗c5 20.♘f3 ♗c6 [20...♘a4!?] **21.♗e4 ♘d5 22.b4 ♗b6 23.a4 a6 24.♕b3 ♕d7**

25.♔h1 [25.♖ed1 ♕e7 26.♖ac1 ♖d8 27.b5 axb5 28.axb5 ♗e8∞] **25...♕d6** [25...♖xf2 26.♖f1 ♗a7! (26...♗b6 27.♘e5 ♕d6 (27...♗xa4 28.♘xd7!) 28.♘xc6

28...♘cf8! 29.♖xf6 ♘xf6 30.♗f5 ♖e8 31.♗c3 bxc6 32.♗xf6 gxf6 33.♖e1⇄] 27.b5 (27.♘e5 ♗xa4 28.♕d3 ♕e8∓) 27...axb5 28.axb5 ♗xb5∓] **26.b5 axb5 27.axb5 ♗e8∞ 28.♖ac1 ♖xc1 29.♖xc1 ♗xf2 30.♖c8 ♖f8?!** [30...♕d7!] **31.♗xd5 exd5 32.♗b4↑ ♕e6 33.♖c2 ♗b6?** [33...♖xf3 34.♕xf3 ♗e3 35.♖e2 d4 36.♗d2 ♗xb5 37.♖e1 ♗c6+] **34.♗xf8 ♔xf8 35.♖d2± ♔f7 36.♕a3+ ♔g8 37.♕a8+ ♔h7?** [37...♕e8 38.♕xb7 ♕xb5 39.♖d1±] **38.♕xb7 ♕g6 39.♖d1 ♕c2 40.♖f1 ♕c4 41.♘d2** 1-0

S Dhopade Swapnil
Das Neelotpal
Nagpur ch-IND B 2015 (11)

1.d4 ♘f6 2.c4 e6 3.♘f3 ♗b4+ 4.♘bd2 0-0 5.a3 ♗e7 6.e4 d5 7.e5 ♘fd7 8.♗d3 c5 9.♕c2 h6 10.0-0 ♘c6 11.♘b3 ♘xd4 12.♘bxd4 cxd4 13.cxd5 exd5 14.b4 a5

15.♖b1 [15.♗d2±] **15...axb4 16.axb4 f6** [16...♖e8 17.♖e1 ♗f8 18.♗f4 ♕b6∞] **17.e6 ♘e5 18.♘xd4 ♕b6 19.♗e3 ♘xd3 20.♕xd3 ♗xe6 21.♗xh6 ♖f7 22.♗e3** [22.♘xe6 ♕xe6 23.♖fe1 ♕c6 24.♗e3±] **22...♗d7 23.♖fd1 ♕a6 24.b5 ♕a4 25.♘e2 ♗g4 26.♕xd5 ♖d8 27.♘d4?!** [27.f3±] **27...♗c6 28.♕xd8+ ♗xd8 29.bxc6 bxc6 30.♘xc6 ♗c7 31.♘d4 ♖d7 32.h3 ♕e4 33.♘f3∓** ½-½

Other Options for White 11.♖e1

Vladimir Belous
Ivan Rozum
St Petersburg ch-RUS rapid 2015 (8)

1.d4 ♘f6 2.♘f3 e6 3.c4 ♗b4+ 4.♘bd2 0-0 5.a3 ♗e7 6.e4 d5 7.e5 ♘fd7 8.♗d3 c5 9.♕c2 h6 10.0-0 ♘c6 11.♖e1 a5 12.cxd5 exd5

13.e6?! [13.♗f1 cxd4 14.♘g3 ♘c5 15.♗f5 ♗xf5 (15...♘xd3 16.♕xd3 (16.♘xe7+ ♕xe7 17.♕xd3 ♕c5∓) 16...♗xf5 17.♕xf5 ♕c8∓) 16.♗xf5 ♘e6 17.♗xh6 ♗g5? (17...gxh6 18.♖xe6 fxe6 19.♕g6+ ♔h8 20.♕xh6+ ♔g8 21.♕g6+ ♔h8=) 18.♗xe6 ♗xh6 19.♗h3 g6 20.♖ad1 ♕e7 21.g3 ♗g7 22.♔h1 ♖fe8 23.♘h4 ♖ad8 24.f4 ♕c7 25.♖xd4 1-0 (71) An.Bykhovsky-Kleiman, St Louis 2012; 13.♕d1 ♖e8 14.♗b1 ♘f8 15.dxc5 ♗xc5 16.♘b3 ♗b6 17.♗f4 ♘g4 18.♗g3 ♗c7 19.h3 ♗xf3 20.♕xf3 ♗xe5 21.♗xe5 ♘xe5 22.♕d1 ♕g5 23.♗a2 ♘fg6 24.♖e3 ♘f4 25.♖g3 ♕f6 26.♔h1 h5 27.♘d4 h4 28.♖e3 ♘ed3 29.♖xd3 ♕g6 30.♗xd5 ♘xd3 31.♕f3 ♖ad8 0-1 Kempinski-Naiditsch, Griesheim 2002; 13.♗f5 cxd4 14.♘b3 ♕b6 15.♗xd7 ♗xd7 16.♕d3 a4 17.♘bxd4 ♗xd4 18.♘xd4 ♖ac8 19.♖b1 ♖c4 20.♗e3 ♕a6 21.♖bd1 ♖fc8 22.h3 ♗f8 23.♔h1 ♕b6 24.♖e2 ♕c7∞ ½-½ (47) M.Socko-

Demina, Plovdiv Ech-W 2008; 13.dxc5
♘xc5 14.♘b3 ♖xd3 15.♕xd3 ♗g4
16.♘fd4 (≥ 16.♘bd4∞) 16...a4∓ 17.♕g3
♕c8 18.e6 ♗xe6 19.♗xh6 ♘f6 20.♘xe6
fxe6 21.♘c5 ♘d4 22.♖ac1 ♘f5 23.♕g6
♕e8 24.♕xe8 ♖fxe8 0-1 (37) Seel-Wahls,
Germany Bundesliga 2005/06] **13...
fxe6 14.♖xe6 cxd4∓ 15.♘b3 ♗f6
16.♗f4 a4 17.♘bd2 ♘b6 18.♖d6
♗d7 19.♗f5 ♗e7 20.♗xd7 ♗xd6
21.♗xd6 ♘xd7 22.♗xf8 ♕xf8
23.♕d3 ♘c5 24.♕b5 ♖a5 25.♕b6
d3 26.♖c1 ♕d8 27.♕xd8+ ♘xd8
28.♖c3 ♖b5 29.♔f1 ♘de6 30.♔e1
♖xb2 31.♘e5 d4 32.♖c1 ♖a2
33.♘ec4 b5 34.♘d6 ♘b3 35.♖xb3
axb3 36.♖b1 ♘c5 37.♘xb5 d2+
38.♔e2 ♘e4** 0-1

Andrey Esipenko
Evgeny Levin

Voronezh 2015 (2)

**1.d4 ♘f6 2.c4 e6 3.♘f3 ♗b4+
4.♘bd2 0-0 5.a3 ♗e7 6.e4 d5
7.e5 ♘fd7 8.♕c2 c5 9.♗d3 h6
10.0-0 ♘c6 11.♖e1 a5 12.♘b3 a4
13.♘xc5 ♘xd4 14.♘xd4 ♘xc5
15.♗f1 dxc4 16.♕xc4**

16...♕d5 [16...♗d7 17.♕c3 (17.♗e3±)
17...♖c8 18.♕g3 ♔h7 (18...♗h4)
19.♗d2 ♕b6 20.♗b4 ♖fd8 21.♖ad1
♗e8± Bar-Raznikov, Tortoreto 2015]
17.♘f5± ♗g5 18.♗xg5 [18.♕xd5
exd5 19.♘d6 ♗e7 20.♘xc8 ♖axc8

21.♗e3±] **18...♕xc4 19.♗xc4
hxg5 20.♘d6 ♗d7 21.♖ad1 ♗c6
22.h4 gxh4 23.♖d4 h3 24.gxh3 g6
25.♔h2 ♗g7 26.♔g3 ♖h8 27.♖e3
♖h6 28.h4 ♖f8 29.♗e2 f6 30.exf6+
♖xf6 31.♖e5 ♘b3 32.♖d1 ♖h8
33.♘e4 ♗xe4 34.♖xe4 ♘c5
35.♖b4 ♖c8 36.f4 ♖c7 37.♗f3 ♖ff7
38.♖b5 ♗f6 39.♖d4 ♔e7 40.♗d1
♖f5 41.♗xa4 ♘xa4 42.♖xf5 exf5
43.♖xa4 ♗d6 44.♖b4 ♔c5 45.♔f3
♖h7 46.♖b3 b5 47.♖c3+ ♔d4
48.♔g3 ♗e7 49.♔f3 ♖e1 50.♖b3
♔c4 51.♖c3+ ♔d4 52.♖b3 ♔c4
53.♖c3+ ♔d4 54.♖b3** ½-½

The Back-Up Plan
10...a5

Maxim Rodshtein
Pavel Eljanov

Khanty-Mansiysk ol 2010 (11)

**1.d4 ♘f6 2.c4 e6 3.♘f3 ♗b4+
4.♘bd2 0-0 5.a3 ♗e7 6.e4 d5 7.e5
♘fd7 8.♗d3 c5 9.♕c2 h6 10.0-0
a5 11.♘b3 b6**

12.cxd5 exd5 13.♗b5 [13.♗e3
c4 14.♗h7+ ♔h8 15.♘c1 b5 (15...g6?
16.♗xg6 fxg6 17.♕xg6 ♕e8 18.♕xh6+
♔g8 19.♘g5 ♕xg5 20.♕xg5+ ♔h7
21.♕h6+ ♔g8 22.♘e2+−) 16.♗f5
♘b6 17.♘e2 ♘c6 18.♘f4 ♖a7∞] **13...
a4 14.♘bd2 cxd4 15.b4?!** [15.♖e1

d3 16.♗xd3 ♘c5 17.♘d4∞] **15...
axb3 16.♘xb3 d3 17.♗xd3 ♘c5
18.♗h7+ ♔h8 19.♘bd4 ♗e6
20.♗f5 ♕d7 21.♖b1 ♖a6 22.♗e3
♘c6 23.♖fd1 ♘xd4 24.♘xd4
♖c8 25.♘xe6 fxe6 26.♗g4 ♕e8
27.♖dc1 ♖ca8 28.h3 ♕f7 29.♗e2
♖xa3 30.♖xb6 ♖a2** ½-½

Sarasadat Khademalsharieh
Ante Brkic

Dubai 2014 (2)

**1.d4 ♘f6 2.♘f3 e6 3.c4 ♗b4+
4.♘bd2 0-0 5.a3 ♗e7 6.e4 d5 7.e5
♘fd7 8.♕c2 c5 9.♗d3 h6 10.0-0
a5 11.♘b3 b6!? 12.♗e3 ♗b7** [≥
12...a4 13.♘c1 (13.♘bd2 cxd4 14.♗xd4
♘c6 15.♗c3 ♘c5) 13...cxd4 14.♗xd4
♘c6 15.♗c3 ♘c5 16.♗h7+ ♔h8 17.♖d1
♕e8!∞] **13.cxd5 exd5 14.♗f5** [14.
dxc5 a4 15.♘bd4 bxc5 16.♘f5 c4 (16...
d4?

17.♗xh6 ♗xf3 (17...gxh6 18.♕c1 ♗g5
19.♘xh6++−) 18.♗xg7 ♗g4 19.♗xf8
♗xf5 20.♗xf5 ♗xf8 21.♖ae1+−)
17.♗e2±] **14...♘c6** [14...a4] **15.e6
fxe6 16.♗xe6+ ♔h8 17.dxc5 ♖xf3
18.gxf3 ♘de5 19.♕d1?** [19.♘d2∆]
19...d4 20.f4 [20.♗d2 a4 21.f4 (21.♘c1
d3−+) 21...axb3 22.fxe5 ♘xe5−+] **20...
dxe3** [20...♕e8!] **21.♕xd8+?** [21.
fxe5] **21...♘xd8−+ 22.fxe5 ♘xe6
23.fxe3 ♗d5 24.♘d4 ♘xd4
25.exd4 bxc5** 0-1

Exercise 1

position after 19...e6xd5

How can White exploit his better development and the weakened position of Black's king?
(solution on page 250)

Exercise 2

position after 20.♖e5-e1

How can Black exploit his better development and White's exposed king?
(solution on page 250)

Exercise 3

position after 19.♕c2-d1

Try to exploit the weaknesses in White's ruined pawn structure on the kingside.
(solution on page 251)

Looking for material from previous Yearbooks?

Visit our website *www.newinchess.com* and click on 'Yearbook'.
In this menu you can find games, contributors and other information from all our Yearbooks.
Surveys are indexed by opening, by author and by Yearbook.

Grünfeld Indian Defence

A Lunge from the Armenian Laboratory

by David Vigorito

1.	d4	♘f6
2.	c4	g6
3.	♘f3	♗g7
4.	g3	d5
5.	cxd5	♘xd5
6.	♗g2	♘b6
7.	♘c3	♘c6
8.	e3	0-0
9.	0-0	♖e8
10.	♘h4	

In the Fianchetto Grünfeld Black has two main options. He can play the solid ...c7-c6 and ...d7-d5, which is popular amongst the world's elite, or he can play the more dynamic set-up with ...d7-d5, ...♘xd5. The former set-up will always retain some popularity due to its solidity, while the latter variation tends to fall in and out of favour. A few years ago this set-up was at its height of popularity and Black was scoring tremendously in the line 10.♖e1 a5 (see Yearbook 98).

White players started to look for alternatives with various waiting moves such as 10.h3!? and 10.a3!?. Please see

Viacheslav Zakhartsov's Survey in Yearbook 110.

In late 2013 the Armenian team came up with 10.♘h4!?, an exotic move which is the subject of this Survey. All these ideas are quite fresh and weren't yet considered in my 2013 book *Chess Developments: The Grünfeld*. In all cases White is trying to be prepared to meet Black's ...e7-e5 advance.

Black Advances 10...e5

After 10...e5 11.d5 ♘a5 White has a choice. 12.♕c2 was played in one of the original Armenian games, Sargissian-Kreisl, Warsaw Ech-tt 2013. Here Black should play the thematic 12...c6! 13.b4 ♘ac4 14.dxc6 e4! because after 15.cxb7? ♗xb7 Black's initiative is just too strong. The simple 12.e4 is also well met with 12...c6. See J.Cori-Gallego Alcaraz, Barcelona 2015.

White has been scoring well with the subtle 12.♖b1!. Against indifferent play White will play b2-b3 to isolate the a5-knight. If Black plays the immediate 12...♘ac4 then 13.b3 ♘d6 14.e4 with the idea a2-a4, ♗a3 should give White an edge. In our main game, Maletin-Sazonova, Izhevsk 2014, Black forces the pace with the logical 12...e4. After 13.♘xe4 ♘xd5 (a nice trap is 13...g5? 14.♘xg5! ♕xg5 15.b3 with the idea ♗d2, winning back material with

Gabriel Sargissian

a winning position) 14.♕a4! White has an annoying initiative and Black must be precise.

One critical line is 14...b6 (other moves are just bad) 15.b4 (15.♖d1!? N.Pert-Navarro Cia, Hinckley Island 2015) 15...♘c4 16.b5 (16.♕c6?! gave White a quick win in Kunte-Karthikeyan, Kottayam 2014, but after the precise 16...♗e6! Black gets a favourable version of the three minor pieces vs. queen) 16...♗e6 17.♕xc4 and now rather than 17...♘c3? (Maletin-Sazonova, Izhevsk 2014), Black should play 17...♘xe3!, which leads to an unclear position with White's three minor pieces against the black queen. Normally this would favour the pieces, but White's army is a little discombobulated, so matters are less clear.

As is typical in the Grünfeld, Black can also consider 11...♘b4 (Wang Hao-Li Chao, China tt 2013) or 11...♘e7 (Bai-Chirila, London 2014). More tests will be needed to see where Black should move his knight. White's play is pretty easy but the h4-knight can be a bit out of play, and it could also be a target itself.

Black Plays 10...a5

If Black does not want to break in the centre yet, a typical waiting move is 10...a5. Then another point of White's tenth move is revealed with 11.f4, stopping ...e7-e5 for the foreseeable future. Then 11...a4 already threatens 12...a3, when any move of White's b-pawn

would allow 13...♘xd4!. Normally White plays the multi-purpose 12.♖f2 (White can also try 12.♕e2 or 12.♘f3, see Nyzhnyk-Paragua, Rockville 2014). Both sides have some flexibility here, but White at least has more space. See the game Grachev-Sivuk, Loo tt 2014.

Other Moves

In the stem game, Aronian-Ragger, Warsaw Ech-tt 2013, the Austrian grandmaster played the modest 10...♗d7 and managed to hold off his famous opponent. This was quite a good result, especially considering the novelty that had been launched against him. The non-forcing nature of the play

means that both sides have a lot of options, but again, White has more space and feels a bit more comfortable.

Conclusion

The move 10.♘h4!? is a nice try for White and it has scored very well so far. Compared to other waiting moves such as 10.h3 and 10.a3, it changes the nature of the game. Black either has to allow White to play 11.f4 with a slow manoeuvring game, or else force the pace with 10...e5.

While I do not think that the Armenian idea should cause Black major problems, it is flexible and remains fresh, which is about all one can hope for against the Grünfeld these days.

Black Advances
10..e5

Gabriel Sargissian
Robert Kreisl
Warsaw Ech-tt 2013 (3)

1.d4 ♘f6 2.c4 g6 3.♘f3 ♗g7 4.g3 d5 5.cxd5 ♘xd5 6.♗g2 ♘b6 7.♘c3 ♘c6 8.e3 0-0 9.0-0 ♖e8 10.♘h4 e5 11.d5 ♘a5 12.♕c2

12...♘ac4 [12...c6! 13.b4 ♘ac4 14.dxc6 e4! △ 15.cxb7? ♗xb7–+] **13.e4 ♗d7 14.a4 a5 15.b3 ♘d6 16.♗e3± ♖c8 17.♕d2 c5 18.dxc6 ♖xc6 19.♖fd1 ♗e6 20.♘d5 ♘d7 21.♖ac1 ♗xd5**

22.♕xd5 ♘f6 23.♕d3 ♖xc1 24.♖xc1 ♗f8 25.f3 ♕b8 26.♗f1 ♖c8 27.♖c3 ♘de8 28.♗h3 ♖xc3 29.♕xc3 ♗b4 30.♕c2 ♕d6 31.♘g2 ♔g7 32.♔f1 ♘c7 33.♔e2 ♘e6 34.♕c4 ♘d7 35.♗xe6 fxe6 36.♕d3 ♕c6 37.♘e1 ♗c5 38.♕c3 ♕b6 39.♘c2 ♗xe3 40.♘xe3 ♔f7 41.♘g4 h5 42.♘xe5+ ♕xe5 43.♕xe5 ♕xb3 44.♕c7+ ♔f8 45.♕xa5 ♕c2+ 46.♔e3 ♕xh2 47.♕a8+ ♔g7 48.♕xb7+ ♔h6 49.♕b4 ♕g1+ 50.♔d3 ♕f1+ 51.♔d4 ♕xf3 52.a5 ♕xg3 53.♕f8+ ♔h7 54.a6 ♕g1+ 55.♔c4 ♕c1+ 56.♔b5 ♕b2+ 57.♕b4 ♕e5+ 58.♔c6 ♕a1 59.♔b6 ♕g1+ 60.♔b7 ♕d1 61.a7 ♕d7+ 62.♔a6 ♕c6+ 63.♕b6 ♕a4+ 64.♔b7 ♕xe4+ 65.♔b8 **1-0**

Jorge Cori
Andres Gallego Alcaraz
Barcelona 2015 (6)

1.♘f3 ♘f6 2.d4 g6 3.g3 ♗g7 4.♗g2 0-0 5.c4 d5 6.cxd5 ♘xd5

7.0-0 ♘b6 8.♘c3 ♘c6 9.e3 ♖e8 10.♘h4 e5 11.d5 ♘a5 12.e4

12...c6 [12...♘ac4 13.♕c2± △ b2-b3, a2-a4] **13.a4** [13.dxc6?! ♘xc6= 14.♘f3 ♗g4 15.h3 ♕xd1 16.♖xd1 ♗xf3 17.♗xf3 ♘d4 18.♗g2 ♖ac8 19.♗f1 a6 20.♖d3 ♘d7 21.♖b1 ♘c5 22.♖d1 b5↑ Stefansson-Ponizil, Teplice 2014] **13...cxd5** [13...♕e7!? looking to b4] **14. exd5 h6** [14...f5 15.d6□ e4 16.♘b5□ g5△ 17.♗d2! ♘c6 (17...♘ac4 18.♘c7 gxh4 19.a5! –+ !) 18.a5 ♘c4 19.♗xg5! ♕xg5 20.♘c7□] **15.♖e1** [15.b4 ♘ac4 (15...e4 16.♘xe4 ♘ac4 17.a5 ♗xa1 18.♗xh6 ♗h8 19.axb6∞) 16.a5 ♘d7

17.♗e3? (17.♕b3) 17...♘f6! 18.♕b3 (K. Grigoryan-J.Cori, Pune 2014) 18...♘xe3 19.fxe3 e4∓] **15...♗d7 16.♘e4 g5 17.♕h5!?** ♘b3 [17...gxh4 18.♗xh6 ♕e7 19.♗xg7 ♔xg7 20.d6 ♕e6 21.b4 ♘c6 22.a5] **18.♘xg5 hxg5 19.♗xg5 ♕b8?** [19...♕c7 20.♗e4 ♔f8 21.♖ad1!+−; 19...♗f6 20.♘g6! (20.♗e4 ♗xg5 21.♕h7+ ♔f8 22.♕h8+ ♔e7 23.♕xe5+ ♔f8 24.♕h8+ ♔e7=) 20...♗g4 21.♕h4! ♘d7□ 22.♗xf6 ♕xf6 23.♕xg4 fxg6 24.♕xd7 ♖xa1 25.♖xa1⩲] **20.♗e4+− ♕d6** [20...♔f8 21.♘g6+! fxg6 22.♕xg6+−] **21.♗h7+! ♔f8 22.♕f3! ♗h6 23.♗g6** 1-0

Dragos Nicolae Dumitrache
Milan Ollier
Avoine 2015 (5)

1.d4 ♘f6 2.c4 g6 3.♘f3 ♗g7 4.g3 0-0 5.♗g2 d5 6.cxd5 ♘xd5 7.0-0 ♘b6 8.♘c3 ♘c6 9.e3 ♖e8 10.♘h4 e5 11.d5 ♘a5

12.♖b1! ♗d7 [12...e4; 12...h6 13.♕c2 ♗g4 (13...♘ac4 14.b3 ♘d6 15.e4⩲) 14.b3 ♖c8? (Mareco-Navara, Gibraltar 2014) 15.♕e4!⩲ and ♕b4 is coming; 12...♘ac4 13.b3 (13.e4 c6 14.b3 ♘d6 15.dxc6 bxc6 16.♕e2⩲ Vasquez Schroder-Djukic, Tromsø 2014) 13...♘d6 14.e4 ♗d7 15.a4 a5 16.♖e1⩲ Gabuzyan-Chigaev, Al Ain 2013; 12...♕e7 13.e4 (13.b3!?) 13...♖d8 (13...♘ac4) 14.b3 ♘c6 15.♗b5! ♘d4?! 16.♗a3 ♕d7 17.♗xd4 exd4 18.♗c5 (18.♖c1⩲) 18...c6 19.♗xd4 cxd5 20.♗xg7 ♔xg7 21.♕d4+ ♔g8 22.exd5 (22.e5⩲) 22...♖xd5 23.♖fe1 ♘c7 24.♕f6 (24.♕a1⩲) 24...♕d6 25.♕xd6 ♖xd6 26.♖e7 ♗d7 27.♗xb7?! ♖b8 28.♗f3 ♘e6∓ e7, Jedlicka-Svoboda, Ostrava 2014] **13.b3 e4?** [13...c6 14.d6! ♗e6 (14...g5 15.♘f3 e4 16.♘d4 c5 17.♘de2±) 15.♗a3 ♗d7 16.♕d2 ♖c8

17.♗b4 b6 18.♖bc1 f5 19.♗xa5 bxa5 20.e4 f4 21.♖fd1 ♗f8 22.♘a4 c5 23.♖c3 c4 24.bxc4 ♖xc4 25.♖xc4 ♗xc4 26.♗h3 ♘f6 27.♕c2 ♗f7 28.d7 ♕a8 29.♕c8 ♕xe4 30.♘c3 1-0 Jojua-Chkhaidze, Tbilisi 2015] **14.♘xe4 g5** [Here we have a neat tactical point]

15.♘xg5! ♕xg5 16.e4!? [16.♕d2 is simpler, trapping the a5-knight: 16...♘ac4 17.bxc4 ♘xc4 18.♕d3 b5 19.e4±] **16...♕e7 17.♕d2 ♕c5 18.♗b2 ♗xb2 19.♖xb2 ♕a3 20.♕g5+ ♔h8 21.♖c2 c6 22.d6 ♘xb3?** [22...♖e6 23.e5±] **23.♕f6+ ♔g8 24.axb3 ♕xb3 25.♖c5** 1-0

Nicholas Pert
Miguel Navarro Cia
Hinckley Island 2015 (3)

1.d4 ♘f6 2.♘f3 g6 3.c4 ♗g7 4.g3 d5 5.cxd5 ♘xd5 6.♗g2 ♘b6 7.♘c3 ♘c6 8.e3 0-0 9.0-0 ♖e8 10.♘h4 e5 11.d5 ♘a5 12.♖b1 e4 13.♘xe4 ♘xd5 14.♕a4 b6

15.♖d1!? ♗d7 16.♕c2 ♘b4 17.♕e2 ♗b5?! [17...♖xa2 18.b4! ♘xc1 19.♖bxc1 ♘b3 20.♖b1 ♕e7 21.♖xb3 ♗a4 22.♖bb1 ♗xd1 23.♕xd1± ; 17...♕e7! 18.♗d2 (18.a3 ♗c6 △ 19.axb4 ♗xe4 20.♗xe4 ♕xe4 21.bxa5 ♕xb1) 18...♘xa2 19.♗xa5

bxa5 20.♘c5 ♕xc5 21.♗xa8 ♗a4⇄] **18.♖xd8 ♗xe2 19.♖xa8 ♖xa8 20.♗d2** [20.♘c3 ♖d8! 21.♘xe2 ♖xa2 22.♖a1 ♖d1+ 23.♗f1 ♖xc1 24.♖xc1 ♖xc1 25.♘xc1 ♗xb2 26.♘d3±] **20...♕d5 21.♖e1 ♕d3??** [21...♗g4] **22.♗xa5 bxa5 23.♘c5** 1-0

Denis Khismatullin
AR Saleh Salem
Sharjah 2014 (2)

1.d4 ♘f6 2.c4 g6 3.g3 ♗g7 4.♗g2 d5 5.cxd5 ♘xd5 6.♘f3 ♘b6 7.♘c3 ♘c6 8.e3 0-0 9.0-0 ♖e8 10.h4 e5 11.d5 ♘a5 12.♖b1 e4 13.♘xe4 ♘xd5 14.♕a4 b6 15.b4

15...♖xe4?! 16.♗xe4 ♘c3 17.♕c2 ♘xe4 18.bxa5 [18.♕xe4 ♗b7 19.♕c2 ♕d5 20.f3 ♘c4 21.♖d1 ♕c6 22.e4] **18...♗b7 19.f3 ♘c5 20.♗b2± ♗a6 21.♖bd1** [≥ 21.♖fd1 ♕g5 22.♕d2 ♗xb2 23.♖xb2 ♘d3 24.♖c2] **21...♕e7 22.♗xg7 ♔xf1 23.♕c3 ♗h3** [23...♗a6 24.♗f6 ♕e8] **24.♔f2 ♖e8 25.♗d4 ♘a4** [25...♘b7?! 26.axb6 axb6 27.♗f6 ♕e6 28.♗h8 f6 29.♗xf6 ♕xa2+ 30.♖d2 ♕f7] **26.♕c6 ♗d7?! 27.♕xc7 g5 28.♘g2 ♖c8 29.♕e5 ♕xe5 30.♗xe5 ♖c2+ 31.♔e1 ♘c5 32.axb6 axb6 33.♖d2 ♖xd2?!** [33...♖c1+ 34.♔f2 f5 △ ...g5-g4⇄] **34.♔xd2± ♗c6 35.♘e1 ♗b7 36.♗d4 f5 37.♔c3 ♔f7 38.♗b4 ♔e6 39.♗xb6 ♗d5 40.♗d8 h6 41.♔a3** [41.a4 ♘e5] **41...♘e5 42.f4 ♘c4+ 43.♔b4 g4 44.♘c2 ♔d7 45.♗f6 ♘d2 46.♘d4 ♗e4 47.a4 ♘f3 48.♘b3 ♗d5 49.♘c5+ ♔c8 50.♔c3 ♗c6 51.a5 ♘xh2 52.e4** [52.♗e6 ♘f1 53.♗h4 ♘xe3 54.♔d4±] **52...♘f1!= 53.e5 ♘xg3 54.♔d2 ♘e4+** ½-½

Abhijit Kunte
Pandian Karthikeyan

Kottayam 2014 (6)

1.d4 ♘f6 2.c4 g6 3.g3 ♗g7 4.♗g2 d5 5.cxd5 ♘xd5 6.♘f3 ♘b6 7.0-0 0-0 8.♘c3 ♘c6 9.e3 ♖e8 10.♘h4 e5 11.d5 ♘a5 12.♖b1 e4 13.♘xe4 ♘xd5 14.♕a4 b6 15.b4 ♘c4

16.♕c6?! ♗a6? [16...♗e6! 17.♖d1 (17.♕xc4 ♖xe3 18.♕xe6 ♖xe6 19.♗xe4 c6∓) 17...♖e5 18.♕c2 ♕e7∓] **17.♖d1± ♗e7?** [17...♘e5 18.♕xd5 ♕xd5 19.♖xd5 ♗d3 20.♖xd3 ♘xd3 21.♗d2±] **18.♕a4 ♗b5 19.♕c2 ♘d6 20.♗b2** 1-0

Pavel Maletin
Elena Sazonova

Izhevsk 2014 (1)

1.c4 ♘f6 2.♘f3 g6 3.♘c3 d5 4.cxd5 ♘xd5 5.g3 ♗g7 6.♗g2 0-0 7.0-0 ♘c6 8.d4 ♘b6 9.e3 ♖e8 10.♘h4!? e5 11.d5 ♘a5 [11...♘b4; 11...♘e7] **12.♖b1!** [△ b2-b3] **12...e4** [This is the most forcing, but White has some interesting ideas here] **13.♘xe4 ♘xd5** [One tactical point is that 13...g5? is met with 14.♘xg5! ♕xg5 15.b3 △ ♗d2+–. 15...♘d7 (15...♗f6 16.♗d2 ♕g7 17.♔h1!; even stronger than 17.♗xa5 ♗xh4 18.gxh4 ♗h3 19.♕f3 ♗xg2 20.♕xg2 ♘xd5 21.♖bc1±) 16.e4 ♕e7 17.♘f5 ♕f8 18.♕c2 (18.♗xg7! ♕xg7 19.♗b2 f6 20.♕d2 b6 21.♖fc1+–) 18...b6 19.b4 ♘b7 20.♕xc7+ Li Chao-Tomczak, Germany Bundesliga 2014/15] **14.♕a4! b6** [Other moves are just bad: 14...♘c6? 15.♖d1 ♗e6 (15...♘ce7 16.♘g5 h6 17.♗xf7 ♗xf7 18.e4) 16.♘c5± Kantor-Agdelen, Porto Carras 2015; 14...c6? 15.♗d2 b6 16.♗xa5 bxa5 17.♕xc6 ♖b8 18.♘d6 ♖e6 19.♘xf7!+– Radovanovic-Martic, Novi Sad 2015] **15.b4** [15.♖d1!? N.Pert-Navarro Cia, Hinckley Island 2015] **15...♘c4** [15...♖xe4?! Khismatullin-

Salem, Sharjah 2014] **16.b5** [16.♘f6+? ♗xf6 17.♗xd5 ♕xd5 18.♕xe8+ ♔g7→; 16.♕c6?! (Kunte-Karthikeyan, Kottayam 2014) 16...♗e6!]

16...♗e6 [16...♘a5 17.♗b2 (17.♖d1 ♗e6; 17...♗b7 18.♘c5!±) 17...♗xb2 18.♖xb2±] **17.♕xc4** [17.♖d1!? ♕c8] **17...♘c3?** [Overlooking White's reply. 17...♖xe3! 18.♕xe6!? (18.♕a4 (protecting the a2-pawn) 18...♗xf1 19.♗xf1 ♗d5 20.f3 (20.♗g2 a6! 21.bxa6 b5!∓) 20...c5 21.bxc6 ♖e6⇄. Most players will prefer two minor pieces to a rook and pawn in the middlegame, but White is not well coordinated) 18...♖xe6 19.♗xe3∞ ♖c8 20.♖fd1 ♕e7 21.♘d2 ♖xe3! 22.fxe3 ♕xe3+ 23.♔h1 ♖d8 24.♘hf3 ♕a3∞] **18.♕xc3!** [Perhaps Black had only considered 18.♕b4 ♘xb1 19.♕xb1 ♗c4 20.♘d2 (20.♖e1 ♗d3 21.♕b4 c5!⇄ 22.bxc6△) a5 23.♕a4 b5∓) 20...♗xf1 21.♔xf1±] **18...♕xc3 19.♘xc3+– g5 20.♘f3 ♕f6 21.♗b2 ♗c4 22.♘d5 ♕g6 23.♘f6+ ♔f8 24.♘e5 ♖xe5 25.♘d7+** 1-0

Wang Hao
Li Chao B

China tt 2013 (18)

1.d4 ♘f6 2.c4 g6 3.g3 ♗g7 4.♗g2 d5 5.cxd5 ♘xd5 6.♘f3 ♘b6 7.♘c3 ♘c6 8.e3 0-0 9.0-0 ♖e8 10.♘h4 e5 11.d5

11...♘b4 12.a3 [12.e4 c6 13.♕b3 ♘d3 14.♗e3 (Minko-Roiz, Minsk blitz 2015) 14...♘f4!=] **12...♘a6 13.♕c2** [13.e4 c6 14.dxc6 (14.a4 cxd5 15.exd5 f5 16.d6 e4 17.a5 ♘c4 18.♗f4 e6∓ Tadic-Vucinic, Kragujevac tt 2015 △ ...g6-g5) 14...bxc6 15.♕c2 ♘c5 16.♖d1 ♕e7 17.♗e3 ♘e6 18.♘a4 ♖xa4 19.♗xa4 c5? (19...♖b8!⇄) 20.♕f5!± Tan-Lei, Al Ain 2015] **13...♕e7** [13...f5 14.e4±] **14.e4 c6 15.dxc6 bxc6 16.♘f3 ♘c5 17.♗g5 ♘e6 18.♗e3 ♘b3 19.♖ad1 ♗a6 20.♖fe1 ♗c4 21.♘g5 ♕c8 22.♘a4 ♗a6 23.♘xb6 axb6 24.♖d7 c5 25.♘xf7!?** [25.♗f1 ♗xf1 26.♖xf1 ♗b5 27.♖xf7 h6 28.♖d1 hxg5 29.♖dd7 ♗h8 30.♗d1 exd4 32.♗g4 ♕d3□ 33.♖fe7 ♖xe7 34.♖xe7 ♕b3] **25...♗xf7 26.♖xf7 ♔xf7 27.♕xb3+ c4 28.♕c2 b5 29.♖d1 ♖ad8 30.♖d5 ♖xd5 31.exd5 e4 32.♗h3 ♕d6** [33.♗e6+ ♖xe6 34.dxe6+ ♕xe6=] ½-½

Jinshi Bai
Iion-Christian Chirila

London 2014 (7)

1.d4 ♘f6 2.c4 g6 3.♘f3 ♗g7 4.g3 0-0 5.♗g2 d5 6.cxd5 ♘xd5 7.0-0 ♘b6 8.♘c3 ♘c6 9.e3 ♖e8 10.h4 e5 11.d5 ♘e7 12.e4 ♗d7

13.♕b3 [13.b3 c6 14.♗g5 (14.d6 ♘ec8 15.♗a3 ♗f8 △ ...♖e6; 14.♗e3!? cxd5 15.exd5 e4 16.♘xe4 ♘exd5 17.♗d4) 14...h6 15.♗e3 cxd5 16.exd5 g5! 17.♘f3 (17.d6!?) 17...e4 18.♘xe4 ♘exd5 19.♘d4? (19.♗xb6 ♕xb6! 20.♘fxg5 (20.♕xd5 ♗c6∓) 20...♖e5 19...♕e7!∓ R.Burnett-Chirila, Saint Louis 2015] **13...c6 14.♗e3** [14.♗g5 cxd5 15.♘xd5 bxd5 16.exd5 ♕b6 17.♖fd1 ♕xb3 (17...♕c8) 18.axb3 f6 19.♗e3 g5?! (19...♗f8 20.♖xa7 ♖xa7 21.♗xa7 ♘c8 22.♗e3 ♘d6=) 20.♘f3 (20.d6

♘c6 21.♗d5+ ♔f8 22.♘f3±) 20...♔f8
21.♘d2! ♗c8 22.♘e4 ♔f7 23.d6±
♖d8 24.♘c5 ♗xd6 25.♗xb7 ♖ab8?
(25...♗g4□ 26.♗xa8 ♖xa8 27.♖d2±)
26.♖xa7 ♔g6 27.♖xd6 ♗xd6 28.♘xd7
1-0, Vocaturo-Baron, Warsaw Ech-tt 2013]
14...cxd5 15.exd5 ♖c8 [15...♘ec8!?]
16.♖ad1 [16.♖fd1] **16...♗g4 17.♖d3**
[17.♘b5!? ♗xd1 18.♖xd11] **17...♘c6
18.h3 ♘a5?** [18...♘d4□ 19.♗xd4 exd4
20.hxg4 dxc3 21.bxc3 ♘d7⇄] **19.♕b5
e4 20.♖d4!± ♗ac4 21.hxg4 ♘xe3
22.fxe3 ♗xd4 23.exd4 a6 24.♕b3
e3 25.♘e4 ♔h8 26.♕xe3 ♘xd5
27.♕h6 ♖c7 28.♘g5 f6 29.♘xg6+
♔g8 30.♘e6 ♕d6 31.♗xd5 ♕xd5
32.♘xc7 ♕xd4+ 33.♔h2** 1-0

**Black Plays
10...a5**

Illya Nyzhnyk
Mark Paragua

Rockville 2014 (6)

**1.d4 ♘f6 2.c4 g6 3.♘f3 ♗g7 4.g3
0-0 5.♗g2 d5 6.cxd5 ♘xd5 7.0-0
♘b6 8.♘c3 ♘c6 9.e3 ♖e8 10.h4
a5 11.f4 a4** [△ ...a4-a3, bxa3? ♘xd4!]

12.♕e2 [12.♕f2; 12.♘f3 a3 (12...♗f5
13.h3 ♘b4 14.e4 ♗c8 15.a3 ♘c6
16.♗e3 ♘a5 17.♕e2 f5 18.♘e5 e6?!
19.h4± Markus-Erdelyi, Hungary tt 2015)
13.bxa3 ♘a5 14.♖b1 ♘ac4 15.♘b3 ♘a5
16.♖b1 ♘ac4 17.♘e5! c5?! (17...♘xa3
18.♖xb6! cxb6 19.♕b3 ♗e6 20.d5+−;
17...c6) 18.dxc5 ♘xe5 19.cxb6 ♘d3
20.♘d5 ♖xc1 21.♖xc1+− Maletin-
Kovalev, Dubai 2014] **12...♗e6 13.♖d1
♗c4 14.♕f2 e6** [14...♘d5 15.e4
♘xc3 16.bxc3±] **15.♘f3 ♕e7 16.e4**
[16.♘e5 ♘xe5 17.dxe5 a6] **16...♖ad8
17.♗e3 ♕b4** [17...a3!? 18.b3 ♗a6
19.♖ac1 (19.♗f1 ♗xf1 20.♕xf1

f5!) 19...♘b4 20.♘e1 (20.♗f1 ♗xf1
21.♕xf1 f5) 20...♕d7∞] **18.♖ac1 ♗a6
19.d5! exd5 20.♘xd5** [20.exd5!? a3
(20...♘e7 21.♗c5 ♕a5 22.d6±) 21.bxa3
♕xa3 22.dxc6 ♘xc3 23.♘e5! ♖xd1+
24.♖xd1 ♗xe5 25.fxe5 bxc6 26.♗h6!♔]
**20...♘xd5 21.exd5 ♘e7 22.♘e5
♘f5 23.♗c5 ♕b5 24.♗a3 ♗xe5
25.fxe5 ♖xe5 26.♖xc7 ♖e2**

**27.♗f1 ♖xf2 28.♗xb5 ♘e3
29.♗xa6 ♘xd1 30.♗b7 ♖e2?!**
[30...♖f3 31.d6 (31.♗a6 ♖xd5 32.♗b7
♖fd3 (32...♘e3=) 33.♗xd5 ♖xd5)
31...♖xa3 32.bxa3 ♖xd6= 33.♗c6♗
♘c3 34.♗e8 ♔f8! 35.♗xf7 ♘b5=]
31.♗e7 ♖e1+ [31...♖b8 32.d6 ♘g7
33.g4!±; 31...♖xe7 32.♖xe7 ♘xb2
33.♗c6±] **32.♔g2 ♖xe7 33.♖xe7
♔f8** [33...♘xb2 34.♗c6±] **34.♖e4**
[34.♖c7 ♘e3+ 35.♔f3 ♘xd5 36.♖c4
♘b6 37.♖b4 ♖d6] **34...♖b8 35.♗c6
♖xb2+** [35...f5! 36.♖xa4 (36.♖e6 ♖xb2+
37.♔f1 ♖d2) 36...♖xb2+ 37.♔g1 ♖d2
38.♖a7 ♘e3 39.h3!? ♖g2+ 40.♔h1
♖f2 (40...♖xg3? 41.d6+−) 41.♗b5
♘xd5 42.a4±] **36.♗f1!+−** [36.♔g1
♖d2 37.♖xa4 f5!] **36...♖b1** [36...♖d2
37.♔e1! ♖d3 38.♔e2 ♘b2 39.♖xa4!+−]
37.♖e8+ ♔g7 38.d6 ♘e3+ 39.♔f2!
[39.♔e2? ♘f5 40.d7 ♘d4+ 41.♔e3
♖xc6 42.♖c8 ♖e1+ 43.♔f4 ♖d1
44.♖xc6 ♖xd7] **39...♘g4+ 40.♔f3 f5**
[40...♘f6 41.♗xa4 (41.d7+−) 41...♘xe8
42.d7!+−] **41.d7 ♖b2 42.♖e2 ♖b8
43.♗xa4** 1-0

Boris Grachev
Vitaly Sivuk

Loo tt 2014 (1)

**1.d4 ♘f6 2.c4 g6 3.♘f3 ♗g7 4.g3
0-0 5.♗g2 d5 6.cxd5 ♘xd5 7.0-0
♘b6 8.♘c3 ♘c6 9.e3 ♖e8 10.♘h4
a5 11.f4 a4 12.♖f2**

12...♗d7 [12...♘b4 13.♘e4 c6 14.♘c5
♘4d5 15.♘f3 ♘c7 16.♕c2 ♖a7 17.♗d2±
Predojevic-Obodchuk, Tromsø 2014; 12...
a3 13.bxa3 ♘a5 14.♖b1 ♘ac4 15.♕b3
♖a5 16.♘f3 (16.♘e4!?) 16...c5 17.d5
e6⇄ Chigaev-Martynov, St Petersburg
2014] **13.♘f3** [13.♘e4!? ♘a5 14.♘c5
♘c6 15.♘f3 ♘ac4 16.♕c2 e6 17.♗f1
♘d6 (17...♗xf3 18.♖xf3 ♘d6 19.a3±)
18.♘e5 ♘f5 19.♘xc6 bxc6 20.♗d2±
Ashwin-Nishant, Dubai 2014] **13...♕c8
14.♘e4 ♖d8 15.♘c5 ♗e8 16.♕f1**
[16.♗d2 e6 17.♖c1±] **16...e6 17.♗d2
♘d5 18.♕e1 b6 19.♘d3 ♗a6
20.♗f1 ♕a7 21.♖c1 ♘f6 22.♗c3
♘e4 23.♖fc2 ♖ac8 24.♗g2 ♘xc3
25.♖xc3 ♘e7 26.♘fe5 ♗b5 27.♘c6
♘xc6 28.♗xc6 ♕a5 29.♕d1
♗xd3 30.♕xd3± ♗f8 31.♗b7
♖b8 32.♖xc7 ♘d6 33.♖c8 ♖bxc8
34.♗xc8 ♕d5 35.b3 axb3 36.axb3
b5 37.♗a6 b4 38.♗b5 ♕a8 39.♕c2
♗e7 40.♗c6 ♕a5 41.♗e4 ♗d6
42.h4 ♔g7 43.♕b2 ♕a3 44.♕b1
♖d7 45.♔f2 ♖c7 46.♗c6 ♕a5
47.♖c4 ♕a6 48.♕c2 ♕a1 49.♗e4
♖a7 50.♕b1 ♕a5 51.g4 f5 52.♗f3
♖c7 53.♕c2 ♖xc4 54.♕xc4 ♕d8
55.g5 ♕d7 56.♕c6 ♕xc6 57.♗xc6
♔f7 58.♔e2 ♗f8 59.♔d3 h6
60.♔c4 hxg5 61.hxg5 ♗d6 62.♗d7
♔e7 63.♗c8 ♔f7 64.♔b5 ♔e7
65.♔c6 ♗b8 66.♗d7 ♔f7 67.♔b7
♗d6 68.♗b5 ♗f8 69.♔c6 ♔e6
70.♗e2 ♔d8 71.♗a6 ♔e8 72.♔b5
♔d8 73.♗b7 ♔e8 74.♗g2 ♔d8
75.♗f1 ♔c7 76.♗c4 ♔d7 77.♔b6
♔d6 78.♗b5 ♔e7 79.♔c7 ♗g7
80.♗c4 ♗f8 81.♔c6 ♗g7 82.♔c5
♗f8 83.♔xb4 ♔d7+ 84.♔a4 ♗g7
85.♗b5+ ♔d8 86.b4 ♔e7 87.♔c6
♔d8 88.♗a5 ♗f8 89.♔b5 ♔d6
90.♔c4 ♔e7 91.♗b7 ♔d7 92.♗a6
♔d8 93.♗b3 ♔d7 94.♗c4 ♔e7
95.♔a4 ♔d7 96.♔a5 ♗f8 97.b5 ♗a3**

98.b6 ♗c1 99.♗xe6+ ♔d8 100.♔a6 ♗xe3 101.b7 ♗xf4 102.♔a7 ♔e7 103.♗d5 ♗c7 104.b8♕ ♗xb8+ 105.♔xb8 ♔d6 106.♗f3 1-0

Other Moves

Levon Aronian
Markus Ragger
Warsaw Ech-tt 2013 (3)

1.d4 ♘f6 2.c4 g6 3.♘f3 ♗g7 4.g3 d5 5.cxd5 ♘xd5 6.♗g2 ♘b6 7.♘c3 ♘c6 8.e3 0-0 9.0-0 ♖e8 10.♘h4!? ♗d7 [10...♘b4 11.a3 ♘4d5 12.♕e2!? e5 13.dxe5 ♗xe5 14.e4 ♘e7 15.♕c2 ♘c6 16.♘f3 ♗f6 17.h3 ♕e7 18.♘c3 ♗e6 19.♗f4 ♗c4 20.♖fe1 ♕e6?! 21.♘d5 ♗xd5 22.exd5 ♕xd5 23.♘e5 ♕a5

24.b4 ♕a6 25.♘xc6 ♗xa1 26.♖xa1 bxc6 27.♗xc6 ♕e2 28.♕xe2 ♖xe2 29.♗xa8 ♘xa8 30.♖d1± Gordievsky-Paravyan, Loo ch-RUS jr 2014]

11.f4! a5 [11...e6 12.♘f3 a5 13.♖b1 a4 14.♕e2 ♕e7 15.♘e4 (15.♗d2±) 15...♘b4 (15...♘a7!? 16.♘c3 ♗c6) 16.a3 ♘a6 17.♗d2 ♗c6 18.♘c3 (18.♘f2!?) 18...♗d5 19.♖fe1 ♗c4 20.♕f2 c5⇄ Holm-

Elishev, Gibraltar 2015; 11...♕c8!? △ ...♗h3] **12.♘e4 ♘d5 13.♘f2** [13.♘f3!?; 13.♗d2!?] **13...e6** [13...♘b6!?] **14.e4 ♘b6 15.♘f3 a4 16.e5 ♘e7 17.♘e4 ♗c6= 18.♖e1 ♘ed5 19.♕e2 ♘d7 20.a3 f5 21.exf6 ♘5xf6 22.♘c3 ♘d5 23.♗h3 ♘xc3 24.bxc3 ♗d5 25.♘g5 ♘f8 26.♗e3 b5 27.♗f2 ♖b8 28.♖ab1 ♗c4 29.♕b2 ♗d5 30.♖e3 h6 31.♘f3 ♘d7 32.♕c2 ♕f6 33.♗f1 c6 34.♖be1 g5 35.f5 ♕f7 36.c4 bxc4 37.fxe6 ♖xe6 38.♘xg5 ♕g6! 39.♕xg6 ♖xg6 40.♘e6 ♗h8 41.♘f4 ♖d6 42.♖e8+ ♖xe8 43.♖xe8+ ♘f8 44.♖c8 ♗g7 45.♗e3 ♗f7 46.♗f2 ♗xd4 47.♗xd4 ♖xd4 48.♖xc6 ♖d2+ 49.♔e3 ♖a2 50.♗xc4 ♖xa3+ 51.♔e4 ♗xc4 52.♖xc4 ♖a1 53.♔f5 a3 54.♖a4 a2 55.♖a7 ♘e6 56.h4 ♘xf4 57.gxf4 h5** ½-½

Exercise 1

position after 13...g6-g5

Black has sacrificed a pawn but apparently is winning a piece. What is the best way for White to deal with this attack on his knight?
(solution on page 251)

Exercise 2

position after 16.♕a4-c6

White is attacking the a8-rook and the c4-knight. How should Black deal with this double attack?
(solution on page 251)

Exercise 3

position after 19...e5-e4

Both sides have pieces hanging. White can get two minor pieces for a rook. What is the best way to do this?
(solution on page 251)

Grünfeld Indian Defence

Svidler's 'Stonewall' against the Grünfeld

by Tibor Fogarasi

1.	d4	♘f6
2.	c4	g6
3.	♘c3	d5
4.	cxd5	♘xd5
5.	♗d2	♘b6
6.	e3	♗g7
7.	f4	

Peter Svidler is a world-famous specialist of the Grünfeld Defence. Lately, the Russian grandmaster has enriched the theory of his favourite opening with interesting ideas for White as well. The move 7.f4!? was played by him for the very first time in 2013(!!) against Boris Gelfand. It is quite shocking that you can come up with a novelty at such an early stage of the game... In the computer age, such unpleasant surprises pose difficulties even to top theorists. With this 'Reversed Stonewall' of d4-e3-f4, White aims to prevent the central break ...e7-e5. Black's only remaining idea of active counterplay is under-mining the centre by ...c7-c5. The big question of the whole line is whether the second player should play it immediately, or after some preparation? The problem is that Black is often unable to pull it off if he postpones it.

The move 7.f4!? has enjoyed great popularity in the two years since the first try. It has been given a go by super grandmasters like Wang Hao, Li Chao, Kasimdzhanov, Moiseenko and Korobov, to name but a few.

Variation A

After 7...0-0 8.♘f3 we have a crossroads:

A1) 8...♗e6 is a more recent move. Black eyes the weak c4-square, and tries to prepare the break ...c7-c5. After 9.♗e2 (9.♘e4 ♘c4! 10.♘c5 ♘xd2 11.♕xd2 ♗c8 12.♗d3 b6 13.♗e4 c6 14.♘a4 ♗e6 15.♘c3 and White was better in Ulibin-Jarmula, Teplice 2015) 9...♘8d7 10.e4 ♗g4 11.♗c1 e6 12.0-0 c5! 13.dxc5 ♘xc5 14.♗e3 ♖c8 15.e5 ♕e7, White could have obtained the upper hand by 16.♕e1! in Blübaum-Ragger, Mitropa Cup 2015.

A2) 8...♗g4 is Peter Svidler's reaction to his own weapon. It is interesting that a surprised Gelfand played the same move in the very first game of this line: 9.h3 ♗xf3 10.♕xf3, and now 10...♘8d7 was Svidler's improvement, but White's position is preferable after 11.0-0-0 e6 12.♔b1 c5 13.e4!

♕e7 14.♗e2, especially as he has the bishop pair.

A3) 8...♘8d7 is Morozevich's favourite: 9.♘e4 (White prevents the immediate ...c7-c5) 9...♘f6 10.♘xf6+ exf6!?, and a position with chances for both sides arose in Li-Zakhartsov, Guben 2014. 9.b4 also looks good for White. After 9...♘f6 10.♗d3 ♘bd5 11.♘xd5 ♕xd5 12.♖c1 c6 13.♖c5, it is not advisable to take the a2-pawn. 13...♕d6 14.0-0 ♗e6 15.a4 ♘d7 16.♖c1 leads to a position with chances for both sides.

Variation B

7...c5 8.dxc5 ♘6d7 9.♘e4 (White follows a central strategy. Black equalizes both after 9.♘a4 e5! 10.♘f3 exf4 11.exf4 0-0 12.♗c4 ♘xc5 13.♘xc5 ♕e7+ 14.♕e2 ♕xc5 15.♖c1 ♕b6 and 12.♗e2 ♕e7 13.0-0 ♘xc5 14.♘xc5 ♕xc5+ 15.♔h1 ♘c6 16.♖c1 ♕b6, as in Savina-So, Montpellier 2015) 9...0-0 10.♘f3 ♗xb2 11.♖b1 ♗g7 12.♗c4.

This is the position White plays for in the line with 7.f4. The first player's pawn structure is far from ideal, but his actively placed pieces provide ample compensation for the weaknesses. Black has to play very precisely: 12...♘a6!? (12...♘f6 13.♘eg5 (13.♘xf6+ ♗xf6 14.e4 is also quite unpleasant for Black) 13...e6 14.♘e5, and White has a dangerous initiative) 13.♗xa6 bxa6 14.♕a4 ♘b8! 15.c6 ♕e8 16.♖c1 ♘xc6 17.♕xc6 ♕xc6 18.♖xc6 ♗b7 19.♖c4 ♗d5 20.♖a4 ♗c6 and the game was drawn by repetition (Korobov-Sedlak, Croatia tt 2014).

Conclusion

After 7...c5, Black has to tread a narrow path, but he seems to be able to equalize by Nikola Sedlak's 12...♘a6. The moves 8...♗e6 and 8...♘8d7 are also playable for Black. The computer often gives the annotation '=' quite easily, but I feel that White is a bit better if Black cannot play ...c7-c5...

Peter Svidler

Evgeny Tomashevsky
Alexander Morozevich
Tromsø 2013 (4)

1.d4 ♘f6 2.c4 g6 3.♘c3 d5 4.cxd5 ♘xd5 5.♗d2 ♘b6 6.e3 ♗g7 7.f4 ♘8d7 8.♘f3 c5 9.d5

9...f5 10.♕b3 0-0 11.♖d1 ♔h8 12.a4 c4?! [12...♘f6!?] 13.♗xc4 ♘c5 14.♕b4 ♘xc4 15.♕xc4 b6 16.0-0 [16.b4 ♗a6 17.b5 ♗b7 18.0-0 ♖c8≅] 16...♗a6 17.♘b5 ♘e4 18.♗b4! ♖c8 19.♕b3 ♕d7 20.♘fd4 ♖fe8 21.♘c6 e6 22.♘cxa7 ♗xb5 23.♘xb5 h5 24.d6 e5 25.♖c1 [25.♘c7±] 25...exf4 26.♖xc8? [26.♖c7! ♖xc7 27.dxc7 fxe3 28.♕xe3+−] 26...♖xc8 27.♖xf4 ♔h7 28.♖f1 ♗e5 29.♕d5?! [29.♖d1! h4 30.♗c3 ♘xc3 31.♘xc3±] 29...♗xb2 30.♘d4 ♘f6 31.♕b3 ♗xd4 32.exd4 ♘e4! 33.♕d5 ♖d8

34.♖c1 ♕xa4 35.♕f7+? [35.♕b7+ ♔h6 36.♕xb6 ♖c8 37.♖b1! (37.♖e1? ♕a2!−+) 37...♕a2 (37...♕c2 38.♗e1 ♖a8→) 38.♗c5 ♕f2+ 39.♔h1 ♖a8≅] 35...♔h6 36.♕e7?? [36.♖b1 ♕c2 37.♕b3 ♕f2+ 38.♔h1 ♕xd4−+] 36...♕xb4−+ 0-1

Aryan Tari
Victor Mikhalevski
Berlin Wch blitz 2015

1.d4 ♘f6 2.c4 g6 3.♘c3 d5 4.cxd5 ♘xd5 5.♗d2 ♘b6 6.e3 ♗g7 7.f4 ♘8d7 8.♘e4

8...♘d5 9.♗c4 e6 10.♘f3 0-0 11.0-0 b6 12.♖c1 ♗b7 13.♕c2 c5 14.♘d6 ♗c6 15.e4 [15.♘e5! ♘b8 16.dxc5 bxc5 17.♘e4 ♘b4 18.♗xc6 ♘8xc6 19.♕b1±] 15...♘7f6 [15...♕e7 16.♘b5 a6 17.exd5 ♗xb5 18.♖fe1→] 16.e5 [16.dxc5 bxc5 17.exd5 exd5 18.♗xf7 ♖xf7 19.♘e5 dxc4 20.♘xc6 ♕d5 21.♘e5 ♘e4⇄] 16...♘e8 17.dxc5 bxc5 18.♘e4 ♘b4 19.♕b1 ♕b6 20.♗e3 ♗xe4 21.♕xe4± ♖c8 22.♔h1 ♘c7 23.♗g1 ♘bd5 24.b3 ♖fd8 25.♖fd1 ♗f8 26.♖e1 ♘e7 27.♘g5 ♘f5 28.♗f2 ♘b5 29.♘f3 ♘a3 30.♗f1 a5 31.g4 ♘e7 32.♗h4 ♕b4 33.♕e2? [33.♗a6 ♖c7 34.f5±] 33...♕xf4 34.♘g5? [34.♕e4!] 34...♖d2 35.♘h3 ♖xe2 36.♘xf4 ♖xa2−+ 37.♖ed1 ♘c6 38.♗f6 ♘d4?? 39.♖a1?? [39.♖xd4+−] 39...♖xa1 40.♖xa1 ♘ac2 41.♖xa5 ♘xb3 42.♖a4 ♘d2 43.♗d3 ♘e3 44.♖a2 ♘f3 45.g5 c4 46.♗e4 c3 47.♘d3 ♘d2 48.♗b7 ♖c7 49.♗g2 ♘b3 50.♘e1 c2 51.♘xc2 ♖xc2 52.♖xc2 ♘xc2 53.♗e4 ♘e3 54.h4 ♘c5 55.♗f3 ♘d3 56.h5 ♘c4 57.h6 ♘cxe5 58.♗e4 ♗d6 59.♔g2 ♘c5 60.♗c2 ♘ed7 61.♗c3 ♗f4 62.♔f3 ♗xg5 63.♗g7 ♗f6 64.♗b1 ♗xg7 65.hxg7 ♔xg7 66.♔g4 h5+ 67.♔g5 f6+ 68.♔h4 ♔h6 0-1

Matthias Blübaum
Markus Ragger
Zillertal 2015 (5)

1.d4 ♘f6 2.c4 g6 3.♘c3 d5 4.cxd5 ♘xd5 5.♗d2 ♘b6 6.e3 ♗g7 7.f4 0-0 8.♘f3 ♗e6 9.♗e2 ♘8d7 10.e4 ♗g4 11.♗c1 [11.♗e3!? ♗xf3 (11...e6!?) 12.♗xf3 (12.gxf3 e6 13.h4∞) 12...♘c4 (12...c5!?) 13.♕e2±] 11...

e6 12.0-0 c5!⇄ 13.dxc5 ♘xc5
14.♗e3 ♖c8 15.e5 ♕e7

16.♘d4?! [16.♕e1! ♖fd8 (16...f6?!
17.♕h4!) 17.♕g3 ♗xf3 18.♕xf3±]
16...♘c4! 17.♗c1 ♗xe2 18.♕xe2
♘d7 19.♘e4 f6 20.♘d6? [20.exf6
♘xf6 21.♗g5 e5 22.♘de6 exf4 23.♖xf4
(23.♗xf4 h6!) 23...b5⇄] 20...♘xd6
21.exd6 ♕xd6 22.♕xe6+ ♕xe6
23.♘xe6 ♖fe8 24.f5 [24.♘xg7 ♔xg7
25.♖d1 b6∓] 24...gxf5 25.♘d4 ♗f8
26.♔h1 ♘e5 27.♗d2?! [27.♘xf5 ♘d3
28.♗e3 ♘c5 29.♖ad1! ♖xb2 30.♘h6+
♔h8 31.♗xc5 ♖xd1 32.♗d4 ♔g7
33.♘f5+ ♔g6 34.♘d6 ♖ed8 35.♖xf6+
♔h5 36.♖f5+ ♔g6 37.♖f6+=] 27...♘c4!
28.♗c3 ♘e3 29.♘f3 ♘d5 30.♘xf5
♘xc3 31.bxc3 ♖e2∓ 32.♘g3 ♖e5
[32...♘c2 33.♘e4 ♗e7 34.♘xf6+ ♗xf6
35.♖xf6 ♖8xc3 36.♖af1 ♖c7 37.a4∓]
33.♖d1 ♗f7 34.h3 ♖ce8 35.♖d7+
♖8e7 36.♖d6 ♖5e6 37.♖dd3 ♗a6
38.♖f2 ♖e1+ 39.♔h2 ♗c5 40.♖b2
[40.♖f1 ♖xf1 41.♘xf1 ♖xa2 42.♖d7+
♔g6 43.♖xb7 ♖c2-+] 40...♗g1+
41.♔h1 ♗d4+ 42.♔h2 ♗e5?!
[42...♗b6! 43.♖e2 (43.♖xb6 ♗g1+!
44.♔h1 ♗xb6+ 45.♔h2 ♗g1+ 46.♔h1
♗d4+ 47.♔h2 ♗e5-+) 43...♖xe2
44.♘xe2 ♗e5+ 45.♔g1 ♖b2 46.♔f2
♔e8-+] 43.♖xb7+ ♔e6 44.♖xh7
♖xa2 45.♖dd7 f5 46.♖de7+? [≥
46.h4! f4 47.♖he7+ ♔f6 48.♖h5+ ♔f5
49.♖xa7 ♖xa7 50.♖xa7 ♔g4 51.g3! fxg3+
52.♘xg3 ♗xg3+ 53.♔g2] 46...♗d6
47.♖xa7 ♖e3!! [47...♖xa7 48.♖xa7
♖e3 49.♖g7!] ♖xc3 50.♖g5 ♔e6 51.h4=]
48.♖ag7 ♖ee2!-+ 49.♖g6+ ♗c5
50.♖f7 ♖xg2+ 51.♔h1 ♖h2+
52.♔g1 ♖ag2+ 53.♔f1 ♖f2+
54.♔g1 [54.♔e1 ♗xc3+ 55.♔d1 ♖d2+
56.♔c1 ♗b2+ 57.♔b1 ♖d1+ 58.♔a2
♖a1+ 59.♔b3 ♖a3#] 54...♖hg2+
55.♔h1 ♖xg3 56.♖xg3 ♗xg3   0-1

David Anton Guijarro
Wei Yi
Leon 2015 (1)

1.d4 ♘f6 2.c4 g6 3.♘c3 d5 4.cxd5
♘xd5 5.♗d2 ♘b6 6.e3 ♗g7
7.f4 0-0 8.♘f3 ♗e6 [8...♗f5 9.♖c1
(9.♗e2!?) 9...♘8d7 10.e4 ♗g4 11.♗e3
e6 12.♗e2 ♘xf3 13.♗xf3 c5 (13...♘c4
14.♕e2 ♘db6 15.e5±) 14.dxc5 ♘c4
15.♕e2 ♘xe3 16.♕xe3 ♖c8 17.c6 (17.
b4 b6!) 17...♖xc6 18.e5 ♕b6 19.♕xb6
♖xb6 20.b3 ♖b4 21.♘e4 g5 22.♖c7
♘b6 23.fxg5 ♘d5 24.♖d7 ♗xe5 25.0-0±
Alexandrov-Jumabayev, Khanty-Mansiysk
2013] 9.♘e4 [9.b3!?]

9...♘c4! 10.♕c2?! [10.♘c5! ♘xd2
11.♕xd2 ♗c8 12.♗d3 (12.♗c4!?) 12...
b6 (12...♘d7!?) 13.♗e4! c6 14.♘a4 ♗e6
15.♘c3 ♘d5?! (15...♘d6 16.0-0 ♘d7
17.♖ad1±) 16.♘xd5 cxd5 17.♗d3 ♘d7
18.0-0 ♘f6 19.♖fc1 ♖c8 20.♖xc8 ♕xc8
21.♖c1 ♕e6 22.♖c7 ♗g4 23.♖xa7 h6
24.♘e5 ♗xe5 25.dxe5 f6 26.exf6 ♗xf6
27.g3± Ulibin-Jarmula, Teplice 2015]
10...♘xd2 11.♘fxd2 ♘d7 12.♘g5
c5 [12...♗f5 13.e4 ♗g4 14.h3 h6 15.♘xf7
♖xf7 16.♗c4 e6 17.hxg4 ♘xf4 18.♗xe6+
♔h8 19.♘f3 ♘f8 20.♗b3 c5 21.0-0-0
cxd4 22.♔b1±] 13.dxc5?! [13.♘xe6
fxe6 14.dxc5 ♖c8 15.♗c4 ♘xc5 16.0-0±]
13...♘d5 14.e4 ♘c6 15.♗c4 ♕a5
16.♖c1 e6! 17.0-0 ♕xc5+ 18.♔h1
♕e7! 19.♘gf3 ♖ac8 20.♕b1
[20.♕b3!?] 20...♕b4 21.♗b3 ♘c5!
22.♖c4 ♕b6 23.♖cc1 ♖fd8∓
24.f5? [24.e5 ♗xf3 25.♘xf3 ♘xb3
26.axb3 ♕xb3∓] 24...exf5 25.exf5
♗xf3 26.♘xf3 ♘xb3 27.axb3
♕xb3 28.fxg6 hxg6 29.♖xc8 ♖xc8
30.♘g5 ♕xb2 31.♕e1 ♗f6-+
32.♘e4 ♗e7 33.h3 ♕e5 34.♕b1
♖c4! 35.♘d2 ♖c7 36.♕a2 ♗d6
37.♘f3 ♕e3 38.♘d2 ♗f4 39.♖d1
♕e2   0-1

Mikhail Ulibin
Michal Wisniewski
Police 2015 (1)

1.d4 ♘f6 2.c4 g6 3.♘c3 d5 4.cxd5
♘xd5 5.♗d2 ♘b6 6.e3 ♗g7 7.f4
0-0 8.♘f3 ♗e6 9.♘e4 ♘8d7
10.♕c2 f6? [10...h6!?]

11.♘c5! ♘xc5 12.dxc5 ♘d7
13.♘d4 [13.♗c4 ♘xc4 14.♕xc4+ ♔h8
15.♘d4±] 13...♗f7 14.c6! e5 [14...
bxc6 15.♘xc6 ♕e8 16.♗a6±] 15.cxb7
exd4 16.bxa8♕ ♕xa8 17.♗c4
♕xg2 18.0-0-0 f5 19.h4 ♘b6
20.♗xf7+ ♖xf7 21.exd4 ♗xd4
22.h5 c5 23.hxg6 hxg6 24.♗c3+-
♕g3 25.♕h2! ♕e3+ 26.♔b1
♕e4+ 27.♔a1 ♖g7 28.♕h8+
♔f7 29.♖he1 ♖g8 30.♕h7+ ♔g7
31.♕h4 ♕b7 32.♖xd4! cxd4
33.♗xd4   1-0

Alexander Moiseenko
Rustam Khusnutdinov
Tromsø ol 2014 (7)

1.d4 ♘f6 2.c4 g6 3.♘c3 d5 4.cxd5
♘xd5 5.♗d2 ♘b6 6.e3 ♗g7 7.f4
0-0 8.♘f3 ♗e6 9.♖c1 ♘8d7 [9...c5
10.dxc5 ♘c4 11.b3 ♘xd2 12.♕xd2 ♘c6
13.♗b5 ♕a5 14.♗xc6 bxc6 15.♘d4
♖ad8 16.♘ce2 ♕xd2+ 17.♔xd2 ♘d5
18.♖hg1 ♖fe8≌ 19.♘c3 ½-½ Rusev-
Grover, Golden Sands 2013]

189

10.♘e4 a5 11.a3 ♘f6 12.♘c5 ♗d5
13.♗d3 ♘bd7 14.♘xd7 ♕xd7
15.♘e5 ♕d6 16.0-0 ♘e4! 17.♕c2
[17.♗e1 ♖fc8 18.♕c2 f5⇄] 17...♗b3
18.♕xb3 ♘xd2 19.♕xb7 ♖fb8
[19...♘xf1 20.♗xf1∞] 20.♕xc7 ♘xf1
21.♗xf1 ♖xb2 22.♕c3 ♖bb8
23.♘c6 ♖c8 24.a4 ♕e6 25.♗b5
♗f6 26.♕d3 ♕d6 27.♖c4! ♔g7
[27...♖c7 28.♕c3!] 28.♘xa5 ♖xc4
29.♘xc4 ♕b4 30.♔f2 e6 31.♔e2
♖c8 32.g3 [32.g4? ♗h4!] 32...♖c7
33.♔f2 ♖c8= 34.♔e2 [34.e4?! ♖d8
35.e5 ♗e7+] 34...♖c7 35.♔f1 ♖c8
36.♔f2 ♖c7 37.h4 ♖c8 38.♔f1
♖c7 39.♔e2 ♖c8 40.♔f2 ♖c7
41.♔f1 ♖c8 42.♔e2 ♔g8 43.♔f1
♔g7 44.♔e2   ½-½

Variation A2
7...0-0 8.♘f3 ♗g4

Peter Svidler
Boris Gelfand
London 2013 (5)
1.d4 ♘f6 2.c4 g6 3.♘c3 d5 4.cxd5
♘xd5 5.♗d2 ♘b6 6.e3 ♗g7 7.f4
0-0 8.♘f3 ♗g4 9.h3 ♗xf3 10.♕xf3
c6

11.h4! ♘8d7 12.h5 e6 [12...c5
13.hxg6 hxg6 14.♕h3 ♖e8 15.d5±] 13.
hxg6 hxg6 14.e4 f5 [14...♘xd4?
15.♕h3 ♗g7 16.♕h6+ ♔f6 17.f5!→;
14...♕e7!?] 15.g4 [≥ 15.e5±]
15...♘f6 16.gxf5 exf5 17.e5 ♘g4
18.d5! cxd5 [18...♘xd5? 19.♗c4+–]
19.0-0-0 d4 20.♘b5?! [20.♗e1?!
♖c8 21.♔b1↑] 20...♕d5 21.♕h3
♖fc8+ 22.♔b1 ♖c6 23.e6?!
[23.♘d6 ♖xd6 24.exd6 ♘f2 (24...♕xd6
25.♗g2±) 25.♕h7+ ♔f8 (25...♔f7
26.♖c1+–) 26.♕xg6! ♕f7 (26...♘xh1
27.♖e1! ♕f7 28.♕g1!!±) 27.♕xf7+

♔xf7 28.♗g2±] 23...♕xe6 24.♗g2
♕f2 25.♕h7+ ♔f7 26.♖de1 ♕f6
[26...♘e4? 27.♗xe4 fxe4 28.f5!+–]
27.♗xc6 bxc6 28.♘c7 ♖h8
[28...♘xh1 29.♖e6 ♕h8 30.♖xf6+
♔xf6 31.♘e8+ ♖xe8 32.♕xh1 ♖e6∞]
29.♕xh8 ♖xh8 30.♘e8 ♖xh1?!
[30...♕d8 31.♖xh8 ♕d5 32.♖h7+ ♔g8
33.♖g7+ ♔f8 34.♖b7 ♕h4 35.♘d6
♘e4 36.♘xe4 fxe4 37.♖xe4 ♕f2⇄]
31.♘xf6 ♘g3 [32.♘h7 ♘e4 33.♘g5+
♘xg5 34.fxg5∞]   ½-½

Rustam Kasimdzhanov
Peter Svidler
Tbilisi 2015 (5)
1.d4 ♘f6 2.c4 g6 3.♘c3 d5 4.cxd5
♘xd5 5.♗d2 ♘b6 6.e3 ♗g7 7.f4
0-0 8.♘f3 ♗g4 9.h3 ♗xf3 10.♕xf3

10...♘8d7 11.0-0-0 e6 12.♔b1
c5 13.dxc5 ♘xc5 14.e4! ♕e7
15.♗e2 ♖ad8 [15...♘ca4!? 16.e5
(16.♘xa4 ♘xa4 17.e5 f6⇄) 16...f6⇄]
16.♖he1 [16.h4!?] 16...♖d4 17.e5 f6
18.♘b5 ♖d5 [18...♖d7!⇄ (△ ...♘d5)]
19.♗b4 fxe5 20.♕a3 ♘bd7 [20...
a5! 21.♕xa5 ♖xd1+ 22.♗xd1 (22.♖xd1
♘d5⇄) 22...♘c4⇄] 21.♗g4 ♖xf4
[21...♖xd1+ 22.♖xd1 h5 23.♗f3 exf4
24.♘c3 b6 25.♕xa7⇆] 22.♖xd5 exd5
23.♘c3 ♖f7? [23...♖c4 24.♗xd7
(24.♘xd5 ♕d6 25.♘e3 ♖e4 26.♗xd7
♕d3+! 27.♕xd3 ♘xd3 28.♗e6+ ♔h8
29.♗d2 ♘xe1 30.♗d4 ♖d4 31.♗xe1
♗h6 32.♗c3 ♘xe3 33.♗xd4 exd4
34.♗xb7=) 24...♕h4! 25.♗xc5 ♕xe1+
26.♔c2∞] 24.♘xd5 ♕d6 25.♖d1 b6
26.♕xa7+– e4 [26...♘f6 27.♕xb6
♕xb6 28.♘xb6 ♗f8 29.♖d8+–]
27.♗xd7 e3 [27...♖xd7 28.♗xc5 bxc5
29.♘e7+ ♖xe7 (29...♕xe7 30.♖xd7
♕f8 31.♖xg7+! ♕xg7 32.♕xg7+ ♔xg7
33.a4+–) 30.♕a8++–] 28.♘xe3
♕e5 29.♕a8+   1-0

Variation A3
7...0-0 8.♘f3 ♘8d7

Li Chao B
Viacheslav Zakhartsov
Guben 2014 (5)
1.d4 ♘f6 2.c4 g6 3.♘c3 d5 4.cxd5
♘xd5 5.♗d2 ♘b6 6.e3 ♗g7 7.f4 0-0
8.♘f3 ♘8d7 9.♘e4 ♘f6 10.♘xf6+
[10.♗d3 ♘xe4 11.♗xe4 ♘c4 12.♖c1
♗e6 13.♘g5 ♗d5 14.♕b3?! (14.b3
♘xd2 15.♗xd5 ♕xd5 16.♕xd2 ♖ac8
17.♖c5 ♕d7 18.♕c2 c6 19.0-0±) 14...
b5! 15.♕xb5 c6 16.♕c5 ♘xb2 17.♕c3
♘c4 18.♗d3 ♕d6 19.0-0 f5 20.♕a3
a5 21.♖c5 ♘b7 22.♖xd5 cxd5 23.♘e6
♕d6 24.♕xd6 ♘xd6 25.♘xf8 ♗xf8
26.♖b1±   Tomashevsky-Morozevich,
Tromsø 2013]

10...exf6!? 11.♕c2 [11.♗d3!?]
11...♖e8 [11...♗f5 12.♗d3 ♗xd3
13.♕xd3 f5 14.0-0 ♖e8⇄] 12.♗d3 f5
13.0-0 ♗e6 14.b4 ♗d5 15.♘e5
c6 16.a4 ♖c8 [16...f6 17.♘c4
♘xc4 18.♗xc4 ♕d7=] 17.♖ae1
♘d7 18.♖e2 ♘xe5 19.dxe5
f6 20.e4! fxe4 21.♗xe4 ♗xe4
[21...fxe5 22.f5!≌] 22.♖xe4 fxe5
23.♖fe1 ♕d5 [23...♕d7 24.fxe5 ♖e6
25.♗c3±] 24.♗c3 ♖cd8 25.fxe5
♕d3 26.♕a2+ ♔h8 27.♖4e3
♕d5 28.♕f2! ♕c4 29.♕g3±
♕e6 30.♕h4 ♔g8 31.♖h3 h5?!
[≥ 31...h6] 32.♖f3 ♖d5 33.h3 ♖ed8
34.♕e4 ♔h7 35.♕c2 ♖8d7
36.♔h1 a6 37.a5 c5 38.bxc5
♖xc5 39.♕e4 ♖dc7 40.♖ee3
♖c4 41.♕b1 ♕c8 42.♕e1
♖4c6 43.♖d3 ♖e6 44.♕d2
♖ec6 45.♕e3 ♖e6 46.♕g5 ♕e8
47.♖d8 ♕e7 48.♕xe7 ♖exe7
49.♖d5 ♖e6 50.g4 ♖ce7 51.g5
♗xe5 [51...b6 52.♗b4 ♖e8 53.axb6
♖xb6 54.♗d6±] 52.♗b4 ♖e8

[52...♖c7? 53.♖e3!+−] **53.♖f7+**
♔g8 54.♖xb7 ♗a1 55.♖b6! ♗e5
56.♖d8!+− ♔f7 [56...♖xd8 57.♖xe6
♖d4 58.♗e1+−] **57.♖d7+ ♔g8**
58.♔g2 ♗f4 59.♖bb7 ♗e5 60.h4
1-0

Evgeny Gleizerov
Cyril Ponizil
Teplice 2014 (7)
1.d4 ♘f6 2.c4 g6 3.♘c3 d5 4.cxd5
♘xd5 5.♗d2 ♘b6 6.e3 ♗g7 7.f4
0-0 8.♘f3 ♘8d7 9.b4 [9.a4 a5
10.♘e4 ♘d5 11.♕b3 ♘7f6 12.♗d3
♘xe4 13.♗xe4 ♘f6 14.♗d3 b6 15.0-0
♗b7 16.♖fd1 ♘d5 17.♕c2 ♗xf3 18.gxf3
c5 19.dxc5 bxc5 20.♘c3 ♕b6 21.♗c4
e6 22.♖d2 ♕c6 23.♔f2 ♘d5 24.♗xg7
♔xg7 25.♖ad1 ♘b6 26.♗b5 ♕c7
27.♕c3+ ♔g8 28.♖d6± Stachowiak-
Sieciechowicz, Legnica 2014] **9...♘f6**
10.♗d3 ♘bd5 11.♘xd5 ♕xd5
12.♖c1 c6 13.♖c5

13...♕xa2?! [13...♕d6 14.0-0 ♗e6
15.a4 ♘d7 16.♖c1 f5∞] **14.♗c4 ♕b2**
15.♖a5! ♗e6 [15...♗f5 16.0-0 ♗c2
(16...♕c2 17.♕e2+−) 17.♕e2 ♗b1
(17...♗b3 18.♗d3 ♗a2 19.♖c1+−)
18.♕e1 b5 19.♗xf7+ ♔xf7 20.♕xb1
♕xb1 21.♖xb1 ♘e4 22.♖c1 ♖fc8
23.♖a6 ♗e6 24.♖cxc6+ ♔d5 25.♖xc8
♖xc8 26.♖xa7 ♖c2 27.♗e1± Gleizerov-
Tosic, Obrenovac 2013] **16.♗xe6 fxe6**
17.♘g5 [17.♘e5! (△ ♘c4, ♘d3)
17...♘d5 18.♘d3 ♗xe3 19.♕xb2 ♗xd1
20.♔xd1±] **17...e5 18.dxe5 ♘d5**
19.♕a1 [19.♗e6 ♖f7 20.0-0 ♘xb4
21.♗c1 ♕c3 22.♕d7±] **19...♕xa1+**
[19...♕c2!?] **20.♖xa1 ♘c7 21.♔e2**
♖fd8 22.g4 e6?! [≥ 22...♖d5] **23.h4**
h6 24.♘e4 ♔f7 25.h5 gxh5 [25...g5
26.fxg5 ♗xe5 27.♖af1+ ♔g7 28.gxh6+
♔xh6 29.♖f7+−] **26.♖xh5 ♘b5**
27.♖f1 ♔e7 28.f5!+− exf5 29.gxf5

♗xe5 30.f6+ ♗xf6 [30...♔e6
31.♘c5++−] **31.♖xf6** 1-0

Robert Aghasaryan
Vladislav Artemiev
Yerevan 2014 (4)
1.d4 ♘f6 2.c4 g6 3.♘c3 d5 4.cxd5
♘xd5 5.♗d2 ♘b6 6.e3 ♗g7 7.f4
0-0 8.♘f3 ♘8d7 9.e4

9...♘b8 10.♗e3 ♗g4 11.♗e2
♘c6 12.♘e5!? [12.f5 ♗xf3 13.♗xf3
♘c4 14.♕e2 ♘xe3 15.♕xe3 ½-½
Radovanovic-Grigoriants, Skopje 2014]
12...♗xe2 13.♘xe2 ♘xe5 14.dxe5
♘c4 15.♕b3 [15.♗d4 c5! 16.♗xc5
♘xb2 17.♕xd8 ♖fxd8 18.♗xe7 ♖d7
19.♗f6 ♖c8!∓] **15...♘xe3 16.♕xe3**
e6 [16...c6!?] **17.♘c3?** [≥ 17.0-0] **17...**
g5! 18.g3 f6! 19.♖d1 gxf4 20.gxf4
♕e7 21.exf6 ♕xf6 22.0-0 ♗h6
23.♘e2 ♕xb2 [23...♖f7!?] **24.♖b1**
[24.♖d7 ♕b6!? 25.♕xb6 axb6 26.♖xc7
♖xa2 27.♖f2∓] **24...♕xa2 25.♔h1**
♔h8 26.♖xb7 ♖f7 27.♘g3 [27.♖c1
♕a5∓] **27...♕a6! 28.♖bb1** [28.♖fb1
♗xf4 29.♖b8+ ♖xb8 30.♖xb8+ ♔g7
31.♕f3 ♕a1+ 32.♔g2 ♕e5∓] **28...♕d6**
29.♘h5 c5 30.♕e2 [30.♖bd1 ♕e5!!]
30...♖af8 31.♖bd1 ♕c6∓ 32.♖g1
c4 33.♖d4 ♖c7 34.♖c1 c3 35.♕d3
♕c5! 36.e5 c2−+ 37.♘f6 ♕c6+
38.♖e4 ♗xf4 0-1

**Variation A
7...0-0 8.♘f3: Alternatives**

Wang Hao
Alexander Grischuk
Beijing 2013 (3)
1.d4 ♘f6 2.c4 g6 3.♘c3 d5 4.cxd5
♘xd5 5.♗d2 ♘b6 6.e3 ♗g7 7.f4
0-0 8.♘f3 a5 9.♖c1 [9.♗e2 ♘a6
10.♘e4 ♕d5 11.♘f2 a4 12.0-0 c5 13.e4

♕d8 14.dxc5 ♘d7 (14...♘xc5 15.♗e3
♘bd7 16.♖c1 b6 17.e5 ♗b7 18.♗c4±)
15.c6! ♘dc5 16.e5 bxc6 17.♗e3 ♗e6
18.♖c1 ♕a5 19.♕e1 ♕xe1 20.♖fxe1
♘d7 21.♘d4 ♗xa2 22.♘xc6±
Bernadskiy-Gupta, Albena 2013]

9...♘a6 10.♘a4 ♘xa4 11.♕xa4
b6 12.♕c6 ♖a7 13.♗xa6!? ♗xa6
14.♔f2 ♕d6 [14...♗c8!?] **15.♘e5**
♖c8 16.♖hd1 ♗xe5 17.dxe5 ♕xc6
18.♖xc6 ♗b7 19.♖cc1 [19.♖c3 c5
20.♗e1 ♗e4=] **19...♗d5! 20.♖a1**
♗e4 21.g4 c5 22.♗e1 ♗f8 23.a3
♔e8∓ 24.♖ac1 ♖d7 25.♖d4 ♗c6
26.♖xd7 ♔xd7 27.b4! cxb4
28.axb4 a4 29.b5! ♗xb5 30.♖xc8
♔xc8 31.♗b4 ♗d3 32.♔f3 ♔d7
33.e4 ♗c2 34.♔e3 h5 35.gxh5
gxh5 36.h4= e6 37.♔d4 ♗c6
38.♗a3 ♗b5 39.♔c3 ♗xe4 40.♗f8
♗g6 41.♗a3 ♗c6 42.♔d4 ♗h7
43.♗f8 ♗g8 44.♗a3 ♗d7 45.♗b4
♔c6 46.♗a3 ♔d7 47.♗b4 ♔c6 ½-½

Momchil Nikolov
Muhammad Khusenkhojaev
Golden Sands 2014 (3)
1.d4 ♘f6 2.c4 g6 3.♘c3 d5 4.cxd5
♘xd5 5.♗d2 ♘b6 6.e3 ♗g7 7.f4
0-0 8.♘f3 ♘a6

9.♗xa6 [9.♘e4!? ♗f5 10.♘g3 ♗e6
11.♗xa6 bxa6 12.0-0 c5 13.♗c3 ♘d5

14.♕d2 ♘xc3 15.bxc3 ♕a5 16.♘e4
cxd4 (16...♖ac8!?⇄) 17.cxd4 ♕xd2
18.♗fxd2 ♖ab8 19.♘c5 d5 20.♘db3
♖fc8 21.♖xa6 ♖b6 22.♘ac5 h6 23.♖fc1
g5 24.f5 (24.fxg5 hxg5 25.e4±) 24...e5
25.♘d7 ♖xc1+ 26.♖xc1 ♖a6 27.♖c8+
♔h7 28.♘bc5 ♖xa2 29.e4 ♖a1+
30.♔f2 ♖a2+ 31.♔e1 ♗c4 32.f6 exd4
33.fxg7 ♔xg7 34.♘e5 ♗b5 35.♖c7+−
Fedoseev-Grischuk, Moscow 2014] 9...
bxa6 10.0-0 ♗b7 11.♕c2 c5!⇄
12.dxc5 ♘c4 13.♖ad1 ♕a5
14.♘a4 ♘xd2 15.♖xd2 ♗c6 16.b3
♖ac8 17.♖c1 ♖c7 18.♕d3 ♗xa4
19.bxa4 ♖xc5 20.♖xc5 ♕xc5
21.♔f2=   ½-½

Variation B
9.♘a4

Anastasia Savina
Wesley So
France tt 2015 (5)

1.d4 ♘f6 2.c4 g6 3.♘c3 d5 4.cxd5
♘xd5 5.♗d2 ♘b6 6.e3 ♗g7 7.f4
c5 8.dxc5 ♘6d7 9.♘a4 e5! 10.♘f3
exf4 11.exf4 0-0 12.♗e2

12...♕e7 [12...b6 13.0-0 ♘xc5
14.♘xc5 bxc5 15.♗c3 ♘xc3 16.bxc3
♘d7 17.♖b1 ♘b6 18.♘e5 ♗f5 19.♗b5
♕c7 20.♘g4 ♖ad8 21.♕f3 f6 22.♗xf5
gxf5 23.♘c4 ♔h8 24.♘xb6 axb6
25.♖fb1 ♖d6 26.a4 ♕d8 27.h3 ♖g8
28.♖1b2 ♖d3 29.♕h5 ♖xc3 30.♕xf5
♕d4+ 31.♔h2 ♖c1 32.♖f2 ♕a1 0-1
Wang-Giri, Beijing 2013] 13.0-0 ♘xc5
14.♘xc5 ♕xc5+ 15.♔h1 ♘c6
16.♖c1 ♕b6 17.♗c4? [17.b4 ♗e6
18.b5 ♘e7=] 17...♗xb2 18.♘g5
♗f5! 19.♖c3 ♗xc3 20.♗xc3 h6
21.♕a1 [21.♘f3 ♕c5 22.♕b3 ♖ac8∓]
21...♖ad8! 22.♘f3 ♔h7 23.♕e1
♕c5 24.♗b3 f6−+ 25.♗b2 ♗g4

26.♘h4   ♗f5   27.♘xf5   ♕xf5
28.♕f2 ♕a5 29.♕g3 ♕d4 30.♗a3
♕b5! 31.♖g1 ♘e2 32.♕e1 ♖fe8
33.♗f7 ♘xg1 34.♗xe8 ♕xe8   0-1

Wang Hao
Fabiano Caruana
Bucharest 2013 (4)

1.d4 ♘f6 2.c4 g6 3.♘c3 d5 4.cxd5
♘xd5 5.♗d2 ♘b6 6.e3 ♗g7 7.f4
c5 8.dxc5 ♘6d7 9.♘a4 e5! 10.♘f3
exf4 11.exf4 0-0 12.♗c4

12...b6 [12...♘xc5 13.♘xc5 ♕e7+
14.♕e2 ♕xc5 15.♖c1 ♕b6 16.♘e5
♗e6=] 13.0-0 ♗a6 14.♗xa6
[14.♕b3!? bxc5 15.♘c3±] 14...♘xa6
15.c6 ♘dc5 16.♘xc5 ♘xc5
17.♘c3 [17.♕c2!? ♖c8 18.♗c3!±]
17...♗xc3 18.bxc3 ♖c8 19.♘d4
♘e6 20.♘xe6 fxe6 21.♕a4 ♕c7
22.♖ad1 a5 23.g3 [23.♖d7 ♕xc6
24.♕d4 ♕xc3 25.♕xb6 ♕c5+ 26.♕xc5
♖xc5=] 23...♕xc6 24.♕xc6 ♖xc6
25.♖fe1 ♖f7 26.♖d2 ♖fc7 27.♔f2
♔f7 28.♖b1= ♖b7 29.♖d3 ♔e7
30.g4 ♖c4 31.♔g3 b5 32.♖b2
♖c5 33.a4 ♖d7 34.♖xd7+ ♔xd7
35.axb5 ♖xc3+ 36.♔h4 ♖c5 37.b6
♔c8 38.♖e2 a4 [38...♖c6 39.♖e5
a4 40.♖a5 ♖c4 41.♖a7 h6 42.♔g3=]
39.♖xe6 ♖a5 40.♖e5 ♖xe5 [40...♖a6
41.f5!] 41.fxe5 a3 42.e6 a2 43.e7
♔d7 44.b7 a1♕ 45.e8♕+ ♔xe8
46.b8♕+ ♔f7 47.♕c7+ ♔g8   ½-½

Variation B
Main Line

Anton Korobov
Nikola Sedlak
Croatia tt 2014 (2)

1.d4 ♘f6 2.c4 g6 3.♘c3 d5 4.cxd5
♘xd5 5.♗d2 ♘b6 6.e3 ♗g7 7.f4

c5 8.dxc5 ♘6d7 9.♘e4 0-0 10.♗c4
♗xb2 11.♖b1 ♗g7 12.♘f3

12...♘a6!? 13.♗xa6 [13.c6 bxc6
14.0-0 ♘b6 15.♗b3 ♗f5∓] 13...bxa6
14.♕a4 [14.0-0 ♕c7 15.♘d4 ♖b8
16.♖xb8 ♕xb8=] 14...♖b8! 15.c6
[15.0-0 ♗d7 16.♕a3 ♗b5 17.♖fd1
♕d3 18.♘c3 ♗c6⇄] 15...♕e8
16.♖c1 ♘xc6! 17.♕xc6 [17.♖xc6?
♗d7−+] 17...♕xc6 18.♖xc6
♗b7 19.♖c4 ♗d5= 20.♖a4 ♗c6
21.♖c4 ♗d5 22.♖a4 ♗c6 23.♖c4
♗d5   ½-½

Evgeny Tomashevsky
Teimour Radjabov
Baku 2014 (8)

1.d4 ♘f6 2.c4 g6 3.♘c3 d5 4.cxd5
♘xd5 5.♗d2 ♘b6 6.e3 ♗g7 7.f4
c5 8.dxc5 ♘6d7 9.♘e4 ♗xb2
10.♖b1 ♗g7 11.♗c4 0-0 12.♘f3
♘f6

13.♘eg5 e6 14.0-0 [14.♘e5 ♘d5
(14...♕c7!?) 15.♘gf3?! (15.e4!?
♗xe5 16.fxe5 ♘c3 17.♗xc3 ♕xg5
18.♕f3 ♘d7 19.h4 ♕e7∞) 15...♘d7
16.♘xd7 (½-½ Prusikin-Fogarasi,
Germany tt 2015) 16...♗xd7! 17.0-0
(17.♖xb7 ♕c8↑) 17...♗c6∓] 14...
h6 15.♘xf7!? ♖xf7 16.♘e5 ♖f8
[16...♘e4!?] 17.♘xg6 ♖e8 18.f5

[18.♕c2!? ♘bd7 19.♖fd1 ♕c7
20.♗b4⩱] **18...♘a6 19.c6! bxc6
20.fxe6 ♗xe6** [20...♖xe6 21.♘f4 ♘c7
22.♕c2⩱] **21.♗xa6 ♘e4! 22.♗b4**
[22.♗e1 ♗xa2 23.♕xd8 ♖axd8 24.♖c1
♗d5 25.♘f4=] **22...♗xa2** [22...♕g5
23.♘f4 ♗xa2 24.♖c1 ♖ab8 25.♕c2
♗f7∞] **23.♘e7+ ♔h8 24.♕xd8
♖axd8 25.♘xc6 ♗xb1 26.♘xd8
♖xd8 27.♖xb1 ♖b8! 28.♗d3
♘c3 29.♗xc3** [29.♖b3?? ♗d5–+]
**29...♖xb1+ 30.♗xb1 ♗xc3=
31.♔f2** ½-½

Evgeny Gleizerov
Benjamin Bok

Sarajevo 2014 (3)

**1.d4 ♘f6 2.c4 g6 3.♘c3 d5
4.cxd5 ♘xd5 5.♗d2 ♘b6 6.e3
♗g7 7.f4 c5 8.dxc5 ♘6d7 9.♘e4
♗xb2 10.♖b1 ♗g7 11.♘f3 0-0
12.♗c4** [12.♕c2 ♘f6 13.♗d3 ♘c6
14.0-0 ♕c7 15.♘xf6+ ♗xf6 16.♗e4
♗d7 17.♗c3 ♖ac8 18.♖fd1 ♗xc3
19.♕xc3 ♖fd8 20.♘e5 ♗e8 21.♗xc6
♗xc6 22.♘xc6 (22.♘g4 f6!) 22...♕xc6
23.♕e5 ♖xd1+ 24.♖xd1 ♕c7 25.♕c3
f6 26.♖d5 ♔g7 27.♕d4 ♕c6 28.h3=
Parligras-Radjabov, Tromsø 2014;
12.♖c1 ♘f6 13.♘xf6+ ♗xf6 14.♗e2
♕c7 15.e4 ♗e6 16.♕a3 ♘c6 17.♗e3
a5 18.0-0 ♘b4 19.e5 ♗g7 20.♖b2

♖fd8 21.♘d4 ♗d5 22.♘b5 ♕c6
23.♘c3 e6 24.♘xd5 ♖xd5 25.♗f3 ♗f8
26.♖fb1 ♖d7 (Tunik-Gupta, Al Ain 2013)
27.♖b5±] **12...♘f6 13.♘xf6+ ♗xf6
14.e4**

14...e5? [14...♕c7 15.♗e3 (15.e5
♗g7 16.♗e3±) 15...♘c3+ 16.♘d2
♗g7 17.0-0 ♘c6 18.♘f3 ♗d7
19.♗d5±] **15.fxe5 ♗g7 16.0-0
♘c6 17.♗c3 ♕xd1 18.♖fxd1
♘d8 19.♗a5 ♘e6 20.♖d5!±
♗h6 21.♔f2 ♗d7 22.♗xb7
♗a4 23.♗xa8 ♖xa8** [23...♗xd1
24.♖xd1 ♖xa8 25.c6 ♖c8 26.♘d4!
♘xd4 27.♖xd4 ♖xc6 28.♖d8+ ♔g7
29.♗b4 g5 30.♗e7+–] **24.♖d5 ♗c2
25.♖b4+– ♘f4 26.c6! ♗xe4**
[26...♘d3+ 27.♖xd3 ♗xd3 28.c7 ♖c8
29.♖d4 ♗a6 30.♖d8+ ♗f8 31.e6!+–]
**27.c7 ♗xd5 28.♖b8+ ♔g7
29.♖xa8 ♘d3+ 30.♔f1** 1-0

Alexander Moiseenko
Aryan Tari

Tromsø ol 2014 (2)

**1.d4 ♘f6 2.c4 g6 3.♘c3 d5 4.cxd5
♘xd5 5.♗d2 ♘b6 6.e3 ♗g7 7.f4
c5 8.dxc5 ♘6d7 9.♘e4 0-0 10.♘f3
♗xb2 11.♖b1 ♗g7 12.♗c4 ♘c6
13.0-0 ♘f6 14.♘eg5 h6**

**15.♘xf7! ♖xf7 16.♘e5 e6 17.♘xf7
♔xf7 18.♕c2 ♕c7?!** [≥ 18...♘e7
19.♗c3 ♘f5 20.♖f3→] **19.f5! gxf5
20.♖xf5 ♗e7?** [20...♔g8 21.♖bf1 ♘g4
22.♖5f4 ♘ge5 23.♗c3!→] **21.♖f4 ♘e5**
[21...♕e5 22.♖bf1 ♕xc5 23.♗c3!+–]
**22.♗c3 ♗d7 23.♖xf6! ♗xf6
24.♕h7+ ♔d8 25.♕g8+ ♔e7**
[25...♗e8 26.♖d1++–] **26.♕xa8+–
♗c8** [26...♘xc4 27.♗xf6+ ♗xf6
28.♕f8+ ♔g6 29.♕g8+ ♔h5 30.♕f7+
♔g5 31.♕g7++–] **27.♗e2 ♗f7
28.♕xa7** 1-0

Exercise 1

position after 47.♖e7xa7

Against the seemingly very
strong 47...♖xa7 48.♖xa7 ♗e3,
White prepared the spectacular
counterblow 49.♗g7!!. Does Black
have another opportunity?
(solution on page 251)

Exercise 2

position after 55...♗a1-e5

How can White strengthen his
initiative?
(solution on page 251)

Exercise 3

position after 25...♘e6-f4

What is the simplest win for White?
(solution on page 251)

King's Indian Defence

A Powerful Weapon

by Krisztian Szabo

1.	d4	♘f6
2.	c4	g6
3.	♘f3	♗g7
4.	g3	0-0
5.	♗g2	d6
6.	0-0	♘bd7
7.	♘c3	e5
8.	e4	exd4
9.	♘xd4	♖e8
10.	h3	a6
11.	♖e1	

In this position, White has some space advantage and his pieces are well placed. Basically he would like to play on the kingside with f2-f4 and sometimes even g3-g4 as well. Black's position looks a little passive, but he is always threatening to break out with ...♖b8, ...c7-c5 and ...b7-b5, so his main battlefield is the queenside. White can try to prevent this with a2-a4 or put pressure on the d6-pawn.

In this Survey we will concentrate on the move 11.♖e1. Usually with the rook on e1, the c1-bishop develops to b2, but to play b2-b3 White usually needs to prepare with ♖b1, otherwise he could be in trouble on the long diagonal.

The Tempting 11...♘e5

In the game Airapetian-Solak, St Petersburg 2012, Black played 11...♘e5. This is a tempting move, because it looks active, and Black immediately attacks the pawn on c4. On the other hand, the g7-bishop's diagonal is closed even more, so now White can continue with 12.b3 without having to prepare this with ♖b1. 12...c5 This looks a dangerous move, because Black weakens not only the d5-square but also his d6-pawn. However, White can't attack it so easily and the black knight is ready to go to c6 after f2-f4. 13.♘c2 ♗e6 14.♗b2 ♘c6 Now the knight controls the d4-square, so it isn't logical for White to aim for ♘e3-d5. 15.♘d5 ♘d7 16.♗xg7 ♔xg7, with a balanced position.

The Straightforward 11...♖b8

11...♖b8 Black continues his straightforward plan and still doesn't decide where he will put his d7-knight.
12.♘c2 occurred in Khismatullin-Mamedyarov, Khanty-Mansiysk rapid 2013, and now 12...♘e5. This is a provocative move. White will protect the c4-pawn, and if he attacks the knight with f2-f4, Black simply

Dragan Solak

goes back to d7. 13.♘e3?! A logical move, because White doesn't want to weaken the long diagonal with b2-b3. On the other hand, the knight is positioned strangely on e3, and Black gets easy play on the kingside. Therefore 13.b3 was the natural reply, for example: 13...b5 14.cxb5 axb5 15.f4 ♘ed7 16.♗b2 ♗b7 17.♖b1 ♘h5, and now we can understand the point of the provocative 12...♘e5, as Black can exert some pressure on the kingside now. 13...b5 13...♗e6 was also possible. 14.cxb5 axb5 with a complicated middlegame. 12.♗e3 was seen in Werle-A. Vovk, Trieste 2015. 12...c5 12...♘e5 was also possible, e.g. 13.b3 c5 14.♘de2 b5, and now 15.f4 ♘ed7 16.♕xd6 leads to a highly forced line: 16...b4 17.e5!

Bxc3 18.Nxc3, with some initiative for the piece. **13.Nc2** The engine suggests the strange 13.Nf3!?. **13...b5 14.cxb5 axb5 15.Qxd6 b4 16.Na4 Bf8 17.Qd1**, and here Black should have played **17...Bb7!?**, with good compensation for the pawn.

In the game Marin-Wojtaszek, Spain tt 2009, White played the most common move, **12.Rb1**. Basically, this is a prophylactic move, which prepares b2-b3 after stepping out of the pin by the g7-bishop. **12...Nc5 13.b4** White immediately attacks the knight. In case of 13.Qc2 Bd7 14.Be3 b5, Black looks OK. **13...Ne6 14.Nde2** 14.Be3 and 14.Nb3 have also been tried. **14...b5 15.cxb5 axb5 16.Be3 Nd7** The typical regrouping. Now Black prepares ...Ne5. **17.f4 Nb6**, and here White can probably take the pawn with **18.Nxb5!?**, which is a typical risky engine move. Marin continued with the more human **18.Qd3 c6**, with an unclear middlegame.

12...Ne5 is the best reply to 12.Rb1. Now 13.Bf1?! is a logical move, controlling the b5-square and preventing ...b7-b5. It is also an inaccuracy, because Black can still play ...b7-b5: 13...c5 14.Nc2 b5! occurred in the game Vachier-Lagrave-Mamedyarov, Tromsø Olympiad 2014. This is a very strong breakout. Black can achieve his main aim and White can't take the pawn because of

the tactical blow 15.cxb5 axb5 16.b4 (16.Bxb5? does not work in view of 16...Rxb5 17.Nxb5 Qd7!, followed by 18...Qh3, with a decisive attack, and 16.Nxb5 would be met by 16...d5! 17.f4 Nc6 18.e5 Ne4, with a great initiative for Black. 16...c4 17.Nd4 d5, and Black looks nicely placed.

In Marin-L.Vajda, Bucharest 1999, White played **13.b3**, which is the most natural reply. **13...c5 14.Nc2 Nc6!?** White's usual plan is Ne3-d5, but now he needs to control the d4-square, too. 14...Be6 was also possible. **15.f4 Nd4?!** This is too early. The strange **15...Nb4!?** would have been more accurate. And now White should have played 16.Nxd4 cxd4 17.Nd5 Nxd5 18.cxd5 Qb6 19.Bb2, and White is slightly better.

In our illustrative game So-McShane, Las Vegas rapid 2015, White continued with **12.a4**, which is the most radical solution to prevent ...b7-b5. On the other hand, this move involves some dark-square weaknesses on the queenside. **12...Ne5** 12...a5!? was also possible, to fix the pawns and gain the b4- and c5-squares. **13.b3 Nfd7** 13...c5!? is also possible: 14.Nc2 Be6 (the typical 14...Nc6 was the alternative) 15.Bb2 h5, with a double-edged middlegame. **14.Be3 Nc5** White's position looks very healthy; he is better developed. On the other hand, Black is active and his pieces

are powerful. **15.Bf1?!**. A logical move, because it protects the d3-square. But the e4-pawn is loose now. **15.Be2!** was more accurate. **15...Nc6!**. Suddenly White is in trouble because the e4-pawn is hanging and the b3-pawn is also under pressure. 16.Rb1 Ne4 17.Nce4 Re4 18.Nc6 bc6 19.Bg2 Re5, and later White managed to equalize with some nice play.

Conclusion

This is a really complex opening. At first sight, White's position looks more comfortable, because he gains some space in the early middlegame and his pieces are well placed. White's natural plan is to play on the kingside with f2-f4, while keeping Black under pressure in the centre, too. Black's position is passive, but he is always ready to break out with ...Rb8, ...c7-c5, ...b7-b5 – his main battlefield is the queenside. So this variation is more ambitious for Black than other lines, because he takes risks in order to create active counterplay.

Actually, this line is not so popular as the plans with 8...c6, followed by ...Qb6, but it is also a very powerful weapon. Theoretical knowledge is important here, because after any inaccuracy, both Black and White can get into in trouble very quickly. Moreover, the middlegames are full of specific motifs.

Wesley So
Luke McShane
Las Vegas 2015 (4)

1.♘f3 ♞f6 2.c4 g6 3.♘c3 ♝g7 4.g3
0-0 5.♗g2 d6 6.0-0 e5 7.d4 ♘bd7
8.h3 ♖e8 9.e4 exd4 10.♘xd4 a6
11.♖e1 ♖b8

12.a4 ♘e5 [12...c6 13.a5 (13.♗e3!?;
13.♘c2 ♘e5 14.♘e3 ♗e6 15.b3 ♘fd7
16.♗d2 (16.♗b2?! ♘c5∓) 16...♘c5
17.♖f1 b5! (17...♘ed3 18.♖b1 a5 19.f4
f5 20.exf5 gxf5 (20...♗xf5!? 21.♘xf5
gxf5 22.♔h2 ♕f6∞) 21.♔h2 ♗d7∞
Kasparov-Topalov, Linares 1999) 18.axb5
axb5 19.b4 (19.f4 bxc4 20.fxe5 cxb3‼)
19...♘xc4 20.bxc5 b4 21.♘a4 ♗xa1
22.♘xc4 ♘xc4 23.♕xa1 ♖xf1 24.♗h6
f6 25.♕xf1⇄) 13...♘e5 14.♗f1 (14.b3 c5
15.♘c2 ♘c6∓) 14...c5 15.♘c2 (15.♘b3
♗e6 16.f4 ♘c6∞) 15...♗e6 16.♘d5
♘fd7 17.♗d2 ♘c6 18.♕c1 ♘d4 19.♖a3
♗xd5 20.cxd5 ♘b5 21.♖b3 ♘e5 22.f4
c4 23.♖be3 ♘d3 24.♗xd3 cxd3 25.♖xd3
♖c8 26.♕b1 ♖c4‼ Tadic-Damljanovic,
Neum 2014; 12...♘c5 13.a5 (13.b4
♘e6 14.♗e3 c5 15.bxc5 dxc5 (Arnett-
Brenninkmeijer, New York 1993) 16.♘xe6!
♗xe6 17.♘d5±) 13...♘fd7 (13...h6
14.♖a3 ♘e6 15.♘c2 ♘g5 16.♔h2 ♗e6
17.f4 ♘gh7 18.♘d5± Inarkiev-Svidler,
Sochi blitz 2014) 14.♗e3 ♘e5 15.b3
(15.♗f1 ♘c6! 16.♘xc6 bxc6 17.♕c2 ♘b3
18.♖ad1 c5 19.♘d5 ♘xa5∓ Rustemov-
Golubev, Minsk 1993) 15...♘c6∞; 12...a5
13.♗e3 (13.♘db5 ♘c5 14.♗f4 (14.♗e3
b6!? (14...♗d7 15.♕c2 b6 16.♖ad1 ♕c8
17.g4 ♕d8 (Bareev-Khalifman, Pardubice
1994) 18.f4±) 15.♕c2 ♗b7 16.♗d4
(Vukic-Itkis, Cetinje 1993) 16...c6⇄)
14...♘fd7 (14...♘e6 15.♗e3 (15.♘xc7!?
♘xc7 16.♕xd6 ♕xd6 17.♗xd6 ♘a6

18.♗xb8 ♘xb8 19.e5 ♘fd7 20.f4±)
15...♘f8 16.♘d5 ♘d7 17.♘f4 ♘dc5
18.♕c2 c6 19.♘c3 ♕b6∞ Baburin-Van
Wely, Skei 1993) 15.♘d5 ♘e6∞; 13.b3
♘c5 14.♗b2 c6 15.♕c2 ♕b6 16.♖ad1
♗d7 17.♗c1 ♖bd8 18.♗e3 ♗c8 19.f4
♘fd7 20.♗f2 ♘b8 21.g4 ♘ba6 22.♔h1
♘b4 23.♕e2 ♘ba6∞ Matlakov-Maze,
Berlin blitz 2015) 13...♘c5 14.♕c2 ♗d7
15.♖ad1 b6!? (15...♕e7 (Ardiansyah-
Gagunashvili, Jakarta 2011) 16.♘db5±)]
13.b3 ♘fd7 [13...c5!? 14.♘c2 (14.♘de2
♗xh3!? 15.♗xh3 ♘f3+ 16.♔g2 ♘xe1+
17.♕xe1 ♘xe4 18.♗e3 b5! (18...♘d4?
19.♘xd4 cxd4 20.♗xd4 ♘xg3 21.♕d2+−
Cosma-Nisipeanu, Romania ch 1992)
19.axb5 axb5⇄) 14...♗e6 (14...♘c6
15.♖b1 b6 (15...♕a5!?; 15...♗e6!?)
16.♗b2 ♘a5 17.♘a1 ♗b7 18.♕d2 ♖c8
19.♘d5 ♘xd5 20.♗xg7 ♘f4 21.♕xf4
♔xg7 22.♖bd1 ♖e6 23.♖d3 ♕e7=
Kunte-Jones, Parramatta 2010) 15.♗b2
(15.♖b1 h5 16.f4 ♘c6 17.♘d5 ♘h7
18.h4 b5 19.axb5 axb5 20.cxb5 ♖xb5
21.♕d3 (Kirov-C.Bauer, Besancon 1998)
21...♖b8 (21...c4!?) 22.♗b2 ♗xb2
23.♖xb2 ♘f6‼) 15...h5 (15...♕d7 16.f4
(16.♔h2 h5 17.♘d5 ♗xd5 18.exd5 ♕f5
19.♗xe5 ♖xe5 20.♖xe5 ♕xe5 21.♕d3
h4‼ Danilov-Nisipeanu, Romania tt 1992)
16...♘c6 17.g4±) 16.♖b1 ♘h8 17.♘e3
♘c6 18.♘cd5 ♘xd5 19.cxd5 ♘d4
20.♘c2 ♘xc2 21.♕xc2 ♗d7 22.f4 ♗xb2
23.♕xb2 b5∞ Agrest-Radjabov, Khanty-
Mansiysk 2010] 14.♗e3 [14.f4 ♘c6
15.♗e3 ♘c5 16.♖b1 ♘b4 17.♕d2 c6
18.♘c2 a5 19.♔h2 f5⇄ Thejkumar-Solak,
Albena 2012] 14...♘c5 15.♗f1?!
[15.♖e2! ♗d7 16.♗d2 ♕c8 17.♔h2 ♘c6
18.♘de2 ♗e6 19.♖b1 ♘b4∞ Kunte-
Pradeep, New Delhi 2015]

15...♘c6! 16.♖b1 ♘xe4 17.♘xe4
♖xe4 18.♘xc6 bxc6 19.♗g2 ♖e5
20.♗xc6 ♗xh3 [20...♕f5!?] 21.♗a7

♖a8 [21...♖c8!?] 22.♖xe5 ♗xe5
23.♗d4

23...♗xd4 [23...♖b8! 24.♗a7
♗f5!∓] 24.♕xd4 ♖b8 25.b4 ♗d7
26.♗xd7 ♕xd7 27.♕a7 ♕c8
28.b5 ♖a8 29.♕d4= ♕e8 30.c5
dxc5 31.♕xc5 ♕e4 32.♖c1
♕xa4 33.bxa6 ♕xa6 34.♕xc7
♕f6 35.♕c6 ♕d8 36.♔g2 h5
37.♕f3 ♖b8 38.♖a1 ♔g7 39.♖a7
♕e8 40.♕c3+ ♔g8 41.♕f6
♕e4+ 42.♕f3 ♕e8 43.♕f6
♖b5 44.♕f3 ♔g7 45.♖a8 ♕e1
46.♖c8 ♕e5 47.♖c7 ♖f5 48.♕c3+
♕xc3 49.♖xc3 ♔h6 50.♖c4 ♔g5
51.♖d4 ♖a5 52.♖f4 f6 53.♖b4
♖d5 54.♔h3 ♖f5 55.♖f4+ ♔e5
56.♖a4 ♖d2 57.♔g2 ♖d4 58.♖a5+
♔e6 59.♖a6+ ♔e5 60.♖a5+ ♖d5
61.♖a4 ♔f5 62.♖f4+ ♔g5 63.♖a4
♔h6 64.♖f4 ♖d6 65.♖a4 g5
66.♖a5 ♔g6 67.♖a8 ♖d4 68.♖g8+
♔h7 69.♖a8 h4 70.gxh4 ♖xh4
71.♔g3 ♔g6 72.♖g8+ ♔f5 73.♖a8
♖g4+ 74.♔f3 ♖g1 75.♖a5+
♔g6 76.♖a8 ♖b1 77.♔g2 ♔h5
78.♖a6 f5 79.♖a5 ♔g4 80.f3+
♔f4 81.♖a4+ ♔e3 82.♖a3+
♔d4 83.♖a4+ ♔e5 84.♖a5+ ♔f6
85.♖a6+ ♔f7 86.♔g3 ♖b4 87.♖c6
♖h4 88.♖c5 ♔g6 89.♖c6+ ♔h5
90.♖f6 ♖f4 91.♔g2 g4 92.fxg4+
♖xg4+ 93.♔f3 ♔g5 94.♖f8 ♖f4+
95.♔g3 ♖g4+ 96.♔f3   ½-½

Gor Airapetian
Dragan Solak
St Petersburg 2012 (4)

1.d4 ♞f6 2.c4 g6 3.g3 ♝g7 4.♗g2
0-0 5.♘c3 d6 6.♘f3 ♘bd7 7.0-0

e5 8.h3 ♖e8 9.e4 exd4 10.♘xd4 a6 11.♖e1 ♘e5 [11...c5?! 12.♘f3 ♘b6 13.♕d3 ♗e6 14.b3 ♕c7 15.♗f4 ♖ad8 16.♖ad1± Kustar-L.Vajda, Budapest 2004; 11...♘c5 12.♖b1 ♖b8 13.b3 ♗d7 14.♗b2 ♕c8 15.♔h2 (15.b4 ♘e6∞) 15...b5 16.cxb5 axb5 17.b4 ♘a4 18.♗xa4 bxa4∞ Akopian-Piket, Groningen 1991; for 11...♖b8 see 11...♖b8 games] **12. b3** [12.♗f1 c5 13.♘f3 ♘xf3+ 14.♕xf3 ♗d7 15.♕g2 ♘e5 16.f4 ♘c6 17.♗e3 ♘d4 (17...f5 18.♗f2! ♘d4 19.exf5 ♗xf5 20.♖xe8+ ♕xe8 21.♖e1 ♕f7 22.♘e4 ♕c7 23.♘g5± Richardson-Turner, England 4NCL 2014) 18.♘d5 ♗e6⇄]

12...c5 13.♘c2 ♗e6 [13...♘c6 14.♖b1 (14.♗b2 ♗e6 transposes to the text move) 14...♗e6 15.♘d5 b5 16.♗g5 ♗xd5 17.cxd5 ♘e5 18.♕d2 ♖c8 19.a4 c4 20.♘b4 c3 21.♕c2 ♕a5 22.♘c6 ♘xc6 23.dxc6 bxa4 24.♗f4 (24.e5?! ♖xe5 25.♖xe5 ♕xe5 26.♗f4 ♕c5⇄ Leitao-Bachmann, Villa Martelli 2010) 24...a3⇄] **14.♗b2** [14.♗e3 h5 15.f4 ♘c6 ½-½ Payen-Brodsky, St Petersburg 2005] **14...♘c6** [14...♖b8 15.♘d5 ♗xd5 16.cxd5 ♗d7 17.♖b1 f5⇄ Toma-Jianu, Arad 2012] **15.♘d5 ♗d7 16.♗xg7 ♔xg7 17.♕d2 ♗xd5 18.cxd5 ♕a5 19.b4 ♘xb4 20.♖ed1** [20.♘e3⧻] **20...♕d8 21.♘xb4** [21.♘e3!?] **21...cxb4 22.♕xb4 ♘c5 23.f4 f6 24.♖ac1 ♖c8 25.♖e1 ♗d7 26.♕b6 ♕d8 27.♕b4 ♕d7 28.♕b6 ♕d8 29.♕b4 ♕d7** ½-½

The Straightforward 11...♖b8

Denis Khismatullin
Shakhriyar Mamedyarov
Khanty-Mansiysk 2013 (3)
1.d4 ♘f6 2.c4 g6 3.g3 ♗g7 4.♗g2 0-0 5.♘c3 d6 6.♘f3 ♘bd7 7.0-0

e5 8.h3 ♖e8 9.e4 exd4 10.♘xd4 a6 11.♖e1 ♖b8 12.♘c2 [12.b3 c5 13.♘c2 b5 14.♕xd6 ♗b7 15.cxb5 axb5 16.♗f4 ♘h5 17.e5 ♖e6 18.♕d2 ♗xg2 19.♔xg2 ♘xe5 20.♕xd8+ ♖xd8= Onischuk-Flores, Khanty-Mansiysk 2009; for 12.♖b1 see 12.♖b1 games] **12...♘e5**

13.♘e3?! [13.♘a3?! ♗e6 14.f4 ♘xc4!? (14...♘c6 15.♗e3 ♕c8 16.♔h2 h5 17.♖c1 ♗d7 18.♕d2 ♘c5 19.♘d5 f5 20.♗xc5 dxc5 21.e5↑ Staniszewski-B.Socko, Polanica Zdroj 1999) 15.f5 ♘xa3 16.fxe6 ♘c4 17.exf7+ ♔xf7 18.♕b3 b5∓; 13.b3 b5 14.cxb5 axb5 15.f4 ♘ed7 16.♗b2 (16.♘b4?! ♗b7 17.e5 c5! 18.♘c6 ♗xc6 19.♗xc6 dxe5 20.♗xb5 ♕a5 21.♗b2 exf4 22.♖xe8+ ♘xe8 23.♕xd7 ♗d4+! (23...♗xc3? 24.♗c4! ♘d6 25.♕xd6 ♖f8 26.♖b1! ♕xa2 27.♗xc3 ♕xb1+ 28.♗f1+- Timman-Danielsen, Helsingor 2013) 24.♔h1 ♘f6 25.♕d6 ♖xb5 26.♘xb5 ♗xb2-+; 16.e5!?) 16...♗b7 17.♖b1 ♘h5∞] **13...b5** [13...♗e6 14.b3 (14.♗f1!?) 14...♘fd7 15.♗b2 ♘c5 16.♗f1 b5 (16...a5!?) 17.cxb5 axb5 18.♗xb5 (18.♖b1? b4∓ Matnadze-Arakhamia Grant, Tbilisi 2005) 18...♘ed7⇄ h3, e4] **14.cxb5 axb5 15.a3?!** [15.a4!?] **15...♘fd7 16.f4 ♘c4 17.♕c2 ♘c5 18.♖b1 ♗b7∓ 19.b4 ♗xc3 20.♕xc3 ♘xe4 21.♗xe4 ♖xe4 22.♗b2 ♘xb2 23.♘g4! ♘a4 24.♕a1 ♔f8 25.♘f6?** [25.♕h8+ ♔e7 26.♕f6+ ♔d7 27.♕xf7+ ♔c8 28.♖xe4 ♗xe4 29.♕e6+ ♔d7 30.♕xd7+ ♔xd7 31.♘f6+ ♔c6 32.♘xe4 ♘b6∓] **25...♖e6!-+ 26.♖xe6** [26.♘xh7+ ♔g8-+] **26...fxe6 27.♘d7+ ♕xd7 28.♕h8+ ♔e7 29.♕g7+ ♔d8 30.♕f6+ ♕e7** 0-1

Jan Werle
Andrey Vovk
Trieste 2015 (6)
1.♘f3 ♘f6 2.c4 g6 3.d4 ♗g7 4.g3 0-0 5.♗g2 d6 6.0-0 ♘bd7 7.♘c3 e5 8.e4 exd4 9.♘xd4 ♖e8 10.♖e1 a6 11.h3 ♖b8 12.♗e3 c5 [12...h6 13.♕c2 (13.b3!?) 13...c5 14.♘de2 b5 15.♖ad1 b4 16.♘d5 ♗b7 17.♘ef4 ♘h7 18.♖e2 ♘e5 19.h4 a5 20.♘ed2 a4 21.b3 axb3 22.axb3 ♖a8 23.♘d3 ♘g4⇄ Tica-L.Vajda, Malinska 2015; 12...e5 13.b3 c5 (13...♘fd7!? 14.f4 ♘c6 15.♕d2±) 14.♘de2 b5 15.f4 (15.cxb5 axb5 16.a4 bxa4 17.♖xa4 ♗e6 18.♘c1 ♕b6∓ Pascua-Mozharov, Olongapo City 2015) 15...♘ed7 (15...♘c6? 16.e5!±) 16.♕xd6 b4 17.e5 bxc3 18.♖xc3 (18.exf6? ♖xe6 19.fxg7 ♖b6 20.♕d1 (20.♗c6? ♖e6 0-1 Ayyad-Vakhidov, Abu Dhabi 2015) 20...♖be6∓) 18...♘h5 19.g4 ♖f8 20.♕d2 ♘g7 21.♖ad1 (Espinosa Aranda-Illescas Cordoba, Madrid rapid 2015) 21...♗e6 22.♘e4 ♘d4 23.♗xd4 cxd4 24.♕xd4 ♕a5∞]

13.♘c2 [13.♘f3!?] **13...b5 14.cxb5 axb5 15.♕xd6 b4 16.♘a4 ♗f8 17.♕d1 ♕a5?!** [17...♗b7!?] **18. b3 ♘e5 19.♗f4 ♗b7 20.♘e3 ♖bd8 21.♘d5 ♘fd7 22.♗g5 ♖c8 23.f4± h6 24.♘f6+** [24.♗h4!±] **24...♗xf6 25.♗xf6 ♘c6 26.♘b2** [26.e5] **26...♖a6 27.f5?!** [27.e5!↑] **27...♗g7 28.♗xg7 ♔xg7 29.♕d2 ♕c7∞ 30.♕f2 ♘d4 31.♖ac1 gxf5 32.♔h2?** [32.♘a4] **32...fxe4 33.♖xe4 ♖xe4 34.♗xe4 ♖e8 35.♕xd4+ cxd4 36.♖xc7 ♖xe4 37.♖c2 d3 38.♔f2 ♖e2 39.♔g2 ♖c2 40.♔f3 d2 41.♘d1 ♖xa2 42.♔e3 ♖a3 43.♖xd2 ♖xb3+ 44.♔f4 ♖d3 45.♖xd3 ♗xd3 46.♔e3 ♗f5 47.♔d4 ♗e6 48.♘f2 b3 49.♔c3 ♔f6 50.♘d3 ♔f5**

51.♔d4 h5 52.♔e3 ♗c4 53.♘b2 ♗f1 54.h4 ♔g4 55.♔f2 ♗b5 56.♘d1 f5 57.♘e3+ ♔h3 58.♘d1 ♗c6 59.♘b2 f4   0-1

Mihail Marin
Radoslaw Wojtaszek
Barbera del Valles 2009 (3)

1.♘f3 ♘f6 2.g3 g6 3.♗g2 ♗g7 4.0-0 0-0 5.c4 d6 6.d4 ♘bd7 7.♘c3 e5 8.e4 a6 9.h3 exd4 10.♘xd4 ♖e8 11.♖e1 ♖b8 12.♖b1 ♘c5!? [12...c5 13.♘f3!±; for 12...♘e5 see 12...♘e5 games]

13.b4 [13.♕c2 ♗d7 (13...♘fxe4? 14.♘xe4 ♘xd4 15.♗g5 ♕d7 16.♕d2!±) 14.♗e3 b5 (14...h6 15.♔h2 b5 16.cxb5 (16.b4 ♘e6 17.♘xe6 ♖xe6 18.c5 ♘d7 19.♖bd1 dxc5 20.bxc5± Izeta Txabarri-Gonzalez Garcia, Santa Clara 1994) 16...axb5 17.b4 ♘e6 18.♖bd1±) 15.cxb5 axb5 16.b4 ♘e6 17.♘b3 c5 18.bxc5 b4 19.♘d5 ♘xd5 20.exd5 ♘xc5 21.♘xc5 ♖c8 22.♘b7 ♖xc2 23.♘xd8 ♖xd8 24.♖xb4 ♖xa2=] 13...♘e6 14.♘de2 [14.♗e3 ♘xd4 (14...h6?! 15.f4 c6 16.♖b2 ♘xd4 17.♗xd4 ♗e6 18.c5± Tukmakov-Gallagher, Zurich 1994) 15.♗xd4 ♗e6 16.♘d5 (16.♗f1 ♘d7 17.♗xg7 ♔xg7 18.♘d5 c6 19.♘e3 ♘f6 20.♕d4 b5 21.♖bd1 bxc4 22.♘xc4 d5⇄) 16...c6 17.♘e3 (17.♗xf6+ ♗xf6 18.♗xf6 ♕xf6 19.♘xd6 ♖bd8 20.♘c5 ♗d2⊠) 17...b5⇄; 14.♘b3 ♗d7 15.♘d5 ♘e5 16.♘e3 ♘c6 (16...b5!?) 17.b5 axb5 18.cxb5 ♘cd4 19.♘xd4 ♘xd4∞ Portisch-Golubev, Biel 1995] 14...b5 [14...♘d7 15.f4 b5 (15...♘b6 16.♕d3 a5 17.a3 axb4 18.axb4 ♖a8 19.♗e3 ♘a4 20.♘b5 ♗d7 21.♕c2±) 16.cxb5 axb5 17.♕d3 ♘b6 18.♖d1 (18.♘xb5? ♗a6-+) 18...♕d7∞] 15.cxb5 [15.♕d3 bxc4 (15...♘d7 16.cxb5 ♘e5 17.♕c2 axb5 18.f4 ♘c4 19.♘xb5) 16.♕xc4 ♘d7 17.f4

a5 18.a3 ♘b6 19.♕d3 axb4 20.axb4 ♖a8⇄] 15...axb5 16.♗e3 ♘d7 17.f4 ♘b6 18.♕d3 [18.♘xb5!? ♘c4 19.♗f2 ♖xb5 (19...♘b2!?) 20.♕d3!±] 18...c6 [18...♘c4 19.♗f2 ♘a3 20.♖bd1 ♗b7∞] 19.♗f2 ♘a6?! [19...♖a8! 20.♖ed1 ♗f8 21.f5 (21.h4 ♘g7 22.♘d4 ♗d7 23.♗f3 ♕c7 24.♖dc1 ♕b7∞; 21.g4 ♘c4! (21...♖a3 22.f5!) 22.a4 ♗a6 23.axb5 ♖xb5 24.♘xb5 cxb5∞) 21...♘g7 22.♘d4 ♗d7 (22...♗b7? 23.♘dxb5! cxb5 24.♕xb5±) 23.g4 (23.e5 d5 24.e6 fxe6 25.fxg6 e5 26.gxh7+ ♔h8 27.♘de2 ♗f5∓) 23...♘c4⇄] 20.a4! ♘c7 21.axb5 ♘xb5 22.♖a1?! [22.♘d4! ♘xc3 23.♕xc3 ♗b5 24.e5 dxe5 25.♘xc6 exf4 26.♕xg7+ ♔xg7 27.♘xd8 ♖exd8 28.gxf4± Marin] 22...♕c8 [22...♖a8? 23.♖xa6! ♖xa6 24.♘xb5 cxb5 25.♕xb5+-] 23.♖a2 [23.♕c2 ♘xc3 24.♘xc3 ♘c4⇄] 23...d5! 24.e5 [24.exd5 ♘xc3 25.♖xa6 ♘cxd5∓] 24...♘xc3 25.♕xc3 [25.♖xa6 ♘c4! 26.♖a7 ♘xe2+ 27.♖xe2 ♖b7∞] 25...♗xe2 26.♖exe2 ♘c4 27.♗c5 ♗f8 28.♗xf8 ♖xf8= 29.♖a7 ♕d8 30.♕d4 [30.♖a6=] 30...♕b6 31.♕xb6 ♖xb6 32.♖c7 ♖xb4 33.♖xc6 d4 34.♗e4 ♖d8 35.♖c2 ♘e3 36.♖c8 ♖b8   ½-½

Maxime Vachier-Lagrave
Shakhriyar Mamedyarov
Tromsø ol 2014 (4)

1.♘f3 ♘f6 2.g3 g6 3.♗g2 ♗g7 4.c4 0-0 5.d4 d6 6.♘c3 ♘bd7 7.0-0 e5 8.e4 exd4 9.♘xd4 ♖e8 10.h3 a6 11.♖e1 ♖b8 12.♖b1 ♘e5

13.♗f1?! [For 13.b3 see Marin-L.Vajda, Bucharest 1999] 13...c5 14.♘c2 b5! 15.cxb5 axb5 16.b4?! [16.♗xb5? ♖xb5 17.♘xb5 ♕d7! 18.♘xd6 ♕xh3-+; 16.f4 ♘c6∞; 16.♘xb5 d5! 17.f4 ♘c6 18.e5 ♘e4⇄] 16...c4 17.♘d4 [17.♗f4

♘h5!] 17...d5! [17...♗d7 18.♗e3 ♕c8∞ Frare-Disconzi da Silva, Sao Jose de Rio Preto 2005] 18.♗g5 [18.f4?! ♘xe4! 19.♖xe4 (19.♘xe4 ♘d3!-+) 19...dxe4 20.fxe5 ♗xe5-+; 18.exd5 ♘xd5 19.♘cxb5 (19.♘xd5? ♕xd5-+) 19...♗b7! (19...♕d7!?) 20.♗g2 ♕b6-+] 18...dxe4 19.♘xe4 ♗b7 20.♗g2 ♗xe4 [20...♕b6! 21.♗xf6 ♗xf6 22.♘xf6+ ♕xf6 23.♗xb7 ♖xb7 24.f4 ♕d7! 25.fxe5 ♖xe5-+] 21.♖xe4 ♕b6 22.♗xf6 ♗xf6 23.♕e2 ♖e7 24.♘c2 ♖d8 25.♖e1 ♖dd7 26.♘e3 ♔g7∓ 27.♖d1 ♕d3?! [27...♖d3; 27...♕d8] 28.a4 ♖xe4 29.♗xe4 ♖d4 30.a5 ♕d6 31.♕g4 ♔h6 32.♘c2 ♘xf2! 33.♖xd4 ♗xd4 34.♕h4+ ♔g7 35.♗xg6! ♘g4+ 36.♔f1 hxg6 37.♘xd4 ♖xd4 38.♕xg4 ♕d3+ 39.♕e2 [39.♔f2 c3-+] 39...♕xg3 40.a6 ♕h3+ 41.♔g1 ♕g3+ 42.♔f1 ♕c3 43.♕a2 ♕h3+ 44.♔g1 c3 45.♕a1 [45.a7 ♕e3+ 46.♕f2 (46.♔f1 ♕c1+ 47.♔e2 c2-+; 46.♔g2 ♕d2+ 47.♔xd2 cxd2 48.a8♕ d1♕-+) 46...♕xf2+ 47.♔xf2 c2 48.a8♕ c1♕-+] 45...♕g4+ 46.♔f1 ♕f3+ 47.♔g1 ♕e3+ 48.♔f1 ♔h7 [48...♔h7 49.♕a2 ♕c1+ 50.♔e2 ♕b2+-+]   0-1

Mihail Marin
Levente Vajda
Bucharest 1999 (6)

1.♘f3 ♘f6 2.c4 g6 3.g3 ♗g7 4.♗g2 0-0 5.0-0 d6 6.d4 ♘bd7 7.♘c3 e5 8.e4 exd4 9.♘xd4 ♖e8 10.h3 a6 11.♖e1 ♖b8 12.♖b1 ♘e5 13.b3 c5 14.♘c2 [14.♘f3 ♘xf3+ 15.♕xf3 b5 16.♗f4 ♘h5 17.♗d2 f6 18.♗f4 ♘h5 19.♗d2 f6 ½-½ Khuzman-Van Wely, Leeuwarden 1993]

14...♘c6!? [14...b5?! 15.f4 (15.cxb5 axb5 16.f4 ♘ed7 17.♕xd6 ♘h5 (≤ 17...

b4 18.♘a4 ♖e6 19.♕d2 ♕e7 (19...♗b7 20.e5 ♗xg2 21.♔xg2±) 20.e5±; ≤ 17...♕a5 18.b4 ♕a7 (Labedz-Kadric, Dallas 2014) 19.e5!±) 18.♕d3 (18.♖e3 b4 19.♘e2 (19.♘d5 ♗b7⇄) 19...♕a5⇄) 18...b4 (18...c4?! 19.♘e3 (19.bxc4? bxc4 20.♕xc4 ♗xc3 21.♖xb8 ♗xe1−+; 19.♕f3 cxb3 20.♖xb3 ♗b7 21.♖xb5 ♖c8!♕) 19...cxb3 (19...b4 20.♘d5 ♕a5 21.bxc4 ♕xa2 22.♕b3± Timoshenko-Golubev, Alushta 1994) 20.♖xb3 ♘b6 21.♖d1 ♕c7 (Arkell-Gupta, Douglas 2014) 22.♘b4±) 19.♘d5 (♘b6∞) 15...♘ed7 (15...♘c6? 16.e5±) 16.♕xd6 (Hjartarson-Hillarp Persson, Reykjavik 1997) 16...♘h5 17.♘e2 (17.♖e3 bxc4 18.e5! (18.bxc4? ♗xc3 19.♖xb8 ♘xb8 20.♕xd8 ♖xd8 21.♖xc3 ♖d1+−+) 18...cxb3 19.♖xb3 ♗f8∞; 17.♕d3 bxc4 18.♕e3!; 18.bxc4? ♗xc3 19.♖xb8 ♗xe1∓) 17...♕a5 (17... bxc4 18.g4 ♘hf6 19.e5 ♖e6 20.♕d2

♘e8 21.♗d5±; 17...♗b7 18.g4 (18.e5!?) 18...♖xe4 19.♗xe4 ♖xe4 20.gxh5 ♖b6 21.♕d2+−) 18.e5↑; 14...♘h5 15.♘e3!? (15.g4 ♘f6 (Luch-Guimaraes, Porto 2013) 16.♗b2±) 15...b5 (15...♗xc4 16.♗xc4 ♗xc3 17.♗d2♕) 16.cxb5 axb5 17.♗b2 b4 18.♘cd5 ♗a6 (Marin-Golubev, Bucharest 1996) 19.♘f5!↑; 14...♗e6 15.f4 ♘c6 16.♗b2 h5 (16...♘h5!?) 17.♘d5 ♘h7 18.♗xg7 ♔xg7 19.♕d2 b5 (19...♗xd5 20.cxd5 ♘a7 21.b4 b6 22.♖b3↑ Marin-Dragomirescu, Predeal 2006; 19...h4 20.♕c3+ ♔g8 21.g4±) 20.♘de3!? (20.b4?! ♗xb4 21.♘cxb4 cxb4 22.♕xb4 bxc4 23.♕c3+ (23.♕xc4?) ♘f6∓ Delchev-Gallagher, Heraklio 2007) 23...♔g8 24.♕xc4∞) 20...bxc4 21.bxc4 ♖xb1 22.♖xb1± **15. f4** [15.♘d5 ♘xd5 16.cxd5 ♘d4 17.♗b2 ♘xc2 18.♕xc2 b5 (18...b6 19.♗xg7 ♔xg7 20.f4± Naumann-Thiede, Germany

Bundesliga 2009/10) 19.♗xg7 ♔xg7 20.f4 ♗d7∞; 15.♖e2 b5 16.♖d2 ♖e6 17.cxb5 axb5 18.b4 ♕f8 19.a3 ♗a6 20.f4 ♘h5 21.♖d3 ♘d4 22.g4 ♘xc2 23.♖xc2 (Pantsulaia-Jones, Dresden ol 2008) 23...♗d4+ 24.♖xd4 (24.♔h2 ♘f6∞) 24...cxd4 25.♘d5 ♘f6 26.♘xf6+ ♖xf6 27.♗b2♕] **15...♗d4?!** [15...♘b4!?] **16.♗e3** [16.♘xd4 cxd4 17.♘d5 ♘xd5 18.cxd5 ♕b6 19.♗b2 ♗b4 (19...♗d7 20.♕d2±) 20.♖c1 ♗d7 21.♔h2±] **16...♕a5?** [16...♘xc2 17.♕xc2 b5 18.cxb5 axb5 19.b4 ♗d7 20.bxc5 b4 21.♘d1 dxc5 22.♘f2 ♗f8⇄] **17.b4!± cxb4 18.♘xb4 ♘e6 19.♕xd6 ♗f8 20.♕b6 ♕a3 21.♘bd5 ♘xd5 22.♘xd5 ♗g7 23.♕b3 ♕xb3 24.axb3 b5 25.f5 gxf5?!** [25...♘d8 26.f6 ♗f8 27.♗f4 ♖b7 28.♘c7+−; 25... bxc4 26.fxe6 fxe6 27.♘b6+−] **26.exf5 ♘d8 27.♗f4** 1-0

Exercise 1

position after 14.♘d4-c2

How can Black continue in this seemingly passive position?
(solution on page 251)

Exercise 2

position after 16...♕d8-a5

How can White exploit his advantage in development?
(solution on page 252)

Exercise 3

position after 16.♗f1xb5

What is Black's strongest continuation?
(solution on page 252)

Benoni Defence

Benko Gambit   BI 25.3 (A58)

Two New White Weapons against the Modern Volga

by Milos Perunovic

1.	d4	♘f6
2.	c4	c5
3.	d5	b5
4.	cxb5	a6
5.	bxa6	g6
6.	♘c3	♗g7

This is a new variation which appeared two years ago. Sergey Kasparov wrote a Survey on it in Yearbook 114, called 'The Benko Is Still Alive! (only without ...d7-d6)'. At first sight, the variation makes no sense: Black allows White to play e2-e4 and castle. However, in the main line after 6...♗xa6 7.e4 ♗xf1 8.♔xf1 d6 9.♘f3 ♗g7 10.g3 0-0 11.♔g2 ♘bd7 12.a4!, Black still hadn't found the right way to create counterplay.

In our variation with 6...♗g7, Black wants to take the initiative in a non-standard way, compared to the 'classical Volga'. One of the main differences is that Black attacks White's central squares with ...e7-e6 instead of the classical move ...d7-d6. Of course, according to opening

principles, White should play e2-e4. If White tries to play according to one of the other standard schemes against the Volga, with ♘f3, g2-g3, ♗g2 and 0-0, Black doesn't capture the pawn on square a6; he can first play the knight (...♘bd7-♘b6), when the position of the black bishop on square c8 prevents one of White's main ideas in this variation: ♖b1, b2-b3, ♗b2 (with ...♗f5).

After 7.e4 0-0 we will look at two possibilities (the drawbacks of the push 8.e5 were explained by Kasparov in his Survey):
The main line is 8.♘f3 ♕a5, attacking pawn e4, when White has two main possibilities: 9.♗d2 or 9.♘d2. The move 9.♗d3? isn't good, as witness 9...♘xd5! (Gelfand-Carlsen, Zürich 2014, and Onischuk-Perunovic, Berlin Wch rapid 2015). After both continuations I think Black has good counterplay, as was shown by Sergey Kasparov in Yearbook 114.

The Tricky 8.a7

8.a7 is one of the new proposals for White. One of the main ideas is to force Black to put his rook on square a7 and to prevent the move ...♕a5, since after ♗d2 the threat will be ♘b5. For example: 8...♖xa7 9.♘f3 e6 (the classical move for this variation; if 9...♕a5? 10.♗d2) 10.♗e2 (the other possibility is 10.dxe6,

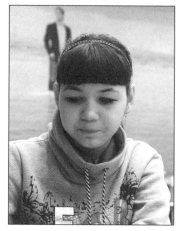

Alexandra Goryachkina

when Black has two options: 10...fxe6, as in the game Peralta-Felgaer, and the non-standard move 10...dxe6!?; both moves lead to unclear positions) 10...exd5 11.exd5 d6 12.0-0 ♘a6 13.♗b5 (the idea of this move is multiple: it prevents the black rook to move to e8, and also White wants to put this bishop on c6 from where it could defend the weak pawn on d5. White's next idea is ♘d2-♘c4. If the knight immediately heads for c4 with 13.♘d2, then after 13...♘c7 (13...♖e8 was Demuth-Giri from the French team championships, 2015) 14.♘c4 ♗a6, with the idea of ...♕a8, Black has good counterplay) 13...♘c7!. In the game L'Ami-Perunovic, Reykjavik Ech-tt 2015, Black played 13...♕b6, but after 14.a4, with ♘d2-♘c4 next, White is probably better. After 13...♘c7 I think Black has counterplay, but he has to play very carefully.

The Interesting 8.♗e2

8.♗e2!? is an interesting move. White is planning to play e4-e5 – not straight away but after he has finished his development, and he wants to develop the bishop before playing ♘f3 in order to prevent Black's move

...♘g4 after e4-e5. For example: 8...♕a5 9.♗d2 ♗xa6 10.e5 ♘e8 11.♘f3 d6 12.e6 ♗xe2 (12...fxe6?! 13.♘g5 was seen in Cheparinov-Melkumyan, Berlin Wch blitz 2015) 13.♕xe2 ♕a6 – a standard manoeuvre in this type of position. The position is very unclear. In the analysis of that game we show some possibilities, but definitely this position requires deeper analysis.

Conclusion

I think 8.a7 is a good way to fight for the advantage, and Black must play very precisely to find compensation. After 8.♗e2 the position is very interesting for further analysis, and both sides have chances here. This is still a new variation, in which both sides have a lot of possibilities. These are only two of the various proposals for White to fight for an advantage.

The Tricky 8.a7

Fernando Peralta
Ruben Felgaer
Buenos Aires ch-ARG 2015 (10)

1.d4 ♘f6 2.c4 c5 3.d5 b5 4.cxb5 a6 5.bxa6 g6 6.♘c3 ♗g7 7.a7 ♖xa7 8.e4 0-0 9.♘f3 e6

10.dxe6 fxe6 [10...dxe6!? is a strange move for this type of position, but it definitely requires deeper analysis. Let me show you some of the possibilities in this position: 11.♕xd8 (11.♗e3 ♕b6⇄) 11...♖xd8 12.♗e3 ♘a6 13.♗c4 (13.♗xa6?! ♗xa6 14.♗xc5 ♖b7 15.♗a3 ♖c8 and Black is two pawns down, but he has a tremendous initiative; 13.♘d2 ♘g4→; 13.♘b5?! ♘b4!; 13.♖d1 ♖xd1+ 14.♔xd1 ♘g4) 13...♗b7 14.♘d2 ♘g4 15.♗g5 ♖b8 16.0-0 ♘e5 17.♗f4 ♘b4 18.a3 ♘bc6 19.♘b5 ♖aa8 20.♗e2 ♗a6⇄ and I think Black has compensation] **11.♗d3 d5 12.0-0 ♘c6** [12...dxe4 13.♗xe4!] **13.♗g5 h6 14.♗xf6 ♗xf6 15.♖c1** [15.exd5 exd5 16.♗xg6 ♖g7 17.♗h5 (17.♗d3 ♗h3 18.g3 (18.♘e1? ♗xc3 19.bxc3 ♗xg2-+) 18...♗xc3 19.bxc3 ♕f6 20.♗e2 ♗xf1

21.♕xd5+ ♕f7 22.♕xf7+ ♖gxf7 23.♔xf1 ♖xf3 24.♗xf3 ♖xf3∓; 17.♗c2? ♗h3 18.g3 ♗xc3 19.bxc3 ♗g4-+) 17...♗a6 (17...♗h3!?) 18.♕xd5+ (18.♘xd5 ♗xb2∞; 18.♖e1 ♘b4⇄) 18...♖xd5 19.♘xd5 ♗xb2 20.♖ab1 ♗xf1 21.♔xf1 ♖b8∞] **15...♗g7?** [15...♖af7 16.exd5 exd5 17.♗xg6 ♖g7 18.♗h5 ♗a6 (if 18...♗h3 19.♖e1 ♗e6 Black has some compensation, but not enough) 19.♕xd5+ ♖xd5 20.♘xd5 ♗xb2 21.♖xc5 ♗xf1 22.♔xf1±; 15...♗e5 (Black must play very aggressively) 16.♘xe5 ♗xe5 17.exd5 exd5 18.♘xd5 (18.♗xg6 ♗a6∞; 18.♘b5 ♖xa2 19.♖xc5 ♖xb2 20.♗xg6 ♗xh2+! 21.♔xh2 ♖fxf2 22.♗f7+ (22.♗c2 ♕h4+ 23.♔g1 ♖xg2+ 24.♔xg2 ♗h3+ 25.♔f3 ♗g4+ 26.♔e3 ♕g5+ 27.♔d3 ♗xd1 28.♖c8+ ♔g7 29.♖c7+ ♔g6 30.♖c6+ ♔g7=) 22...♖xf7 23.♖xc8 ♕xc8 24.♘d6 ♕c7 (24...♖xg2+ 25.♔xg2 ♖g7+ 26.♔h2 ♕g4 27.♕xd5+ ♗h7=) 25.♕xd5 ♕xd6+ 26.♕xd6 ♖xf1=) 18...♔g7, and the position is very dangerous, but I think Black has compensation: 19.♗c4 (19.♖xc5 ♗xh2+!) 19...♗xb2 20.♖c2 ♗d4∞]

16.exd5 exd5 17.♘b5 ♖xa2 18.♖xc5 ♘b4 19.♖c7+ ♖f7 [19...♗d7] **20.♖xf7+ ♔xf7 21.♗b1**

♖a5 22.♘bd4 ♕b6 23.♕c1 ♗a6 24.♖e1 ♘d3 25.♖xd3 ♗xd3 26.♕xh6 ♗e4 27.♕h7+ ♔f8 28.♕d7 ♖a8 29.♘g5 **1-0**

Alexandra Goryachkina
Ekaterina Kovalevskaya
Kazan ch-RUS W 2014 (9)

1.d4 ♘f6 2.c4 c5 3.d5 b5 4.cxb5 a6 5.bxa6 g6 6.♘c3 ♗g7 7.e4 0-0 8.a7 ♖xa7 9.♘f3 e6 10.♗e2 exd5 11.exd5 d6 12.0-0 ♘a6 13.♘d2 ♘c7 14.♘c4 ♖e8

15.♗f4 ♘cxd5 16.♘xd5 ♘xd5 17.♕xd5 ♖xe2 18.♘xd6 ♗d4 19.♕c6 ♗a6 20.♗e3 ♖xe3 21.fxe3 ♗xe3+ 22.♔h1 ♗xf1 23.♖xf1 ♖e7 24.♘c4 ♗d3 25.♘xe3 ♖xe3 26.♕f6 ♕d5 27.a4 ♖e2 28.♖g1 ♖xg2 29.♖xg2 ♕d1+ 30.♖g1 ♕d5+ 31.♖g2 ♕d1+ 32.♖g1 ♕d5+ 33.♖g2 ♕d1+ ½-½

Adrien Demuth
Anish Giri
Montpellier 2015 (5)

1.d4 ♘f6 2.c4 c5 3.d5 b5 4.cxb5 a6 5.bxa6 g6 6.♘c3 ♗g7 7.e4

0-0 8.a7 ♖xa7 9.♘f3 e6 10.♗e2 exd5 11.exd5 d6 12.0-0 ♘a6 13.♘d2

13...♖e8 [13...♘c7 14.♘c4 ♗a6 15.♗g5 (15.♗f4 ♘h5 (15...♖e8 16.♗xd6 ♘fxd5 17.♘xd5 ♘xd5 18.♕xd5 ♖xe2 19.♕xc5 ♖d7⇄) 16.♗e3 (16.♗xh5 ♖xc4 17.♗e2 ♗xe2 18.♕xe2 ♗xc3 19.bxc3 ♘xd5∞) 16...f5∞) 15...♕a8 (15...h6 16.♗h4 ♘b5 17.♘xb5 ♗xb5 18.a4 ♗a6⇄) 16.♗xf6 ♗xf6 17.♘xd6 (17.♘b6 ♕b7 (17...♕d8!?) 18.♘d7 ♗xc3 19.bxc3 ♗xe2 20.♕xe2 ♖fa8⇄) 17...♗xe2 18.♕xe2 ♘xd5 19.♕f3 ♗xc3 20.bxc3 ♖a3 21.♖ac1 ♕c6 (21...♖xa2 22.♖fd1 ♘c7 23.♕e3 ♕c6 – White has some pressure but the position is about equal) 22.♘c4 ♖xa2=] **14.♗b5 ♗g4** [14...♗d7 15.♗xd7 ♕xd7 16.♘c4 ♘e4 17.♗d2 ♘c7] **15.f3** [15.♕b3 ♗d7 16.♘c4] **15...♗d7 16.♘c4?** [16.♗xd7 ♕xd7] **16...♘h5?!** [16...♘xd5! 17.♘xd6 (17.♕xd5 ♗xc3 18.♗xd7 ♗d4+ 19.♔h1 ♘b4 20.♕xd6 ♖xd7 21.♘g3 ♗f6∓) 17...♘xc3 18.bxc3 ♗xb5 19.♘xb5 ♖d7 20.♕a4 ♘b4∓] **17.g4?** [17.♗xd7 ♗d4+ 18.♔h1 ♖xd7 19.g3±] **17...♗xc3 18.♗xd7 ♗d4+ 19.♕xd4** [19.♔h1 ♕xd7 20.gxh5 ♘c7∓] **19...cxd4 20.♗xe8 ♕xe8 21.gxh5 ♘b4–+ 22.♗f4 ♘xd5 23.♘xd6 ♕d7 24.♗g3 ♖a6 25.♘e4 ♖c6 26.♗e5 f5 27.♘f2 ♘e3 28.♖fc1 ♕d5 29.♖xc6 ♕xf3**

0-1

Frode Urkedal
Rune Djurhuus
Oslo 2015 (2)

1.d4 ♘f6 2.c4 c5 3.d5 b5 4.cxb5 a6 5.bxa6 g6 6.♘c3 ♗g7 7.♘f3 0-0 8.a7 ♖xa7 9.e4 e6 10.♗e2 exd5 11.exd5 d6 12.0-0 ♘a6 13.♗c4

13.♗f4 ♘c7 14.♖e1 ♗b7 15.♕d2 [15.b3 ♘fxd5! 16.♘xd5 ♘xd5 17.♕xd5 (17.♗g5 ♘f6) 17...♗xa1 18.♕xd6 (18.♖xa1 ♕f6∓) 18...♗c3 19.♖c1 ♗b4∓] **15...♘fxd5!** [An excellent tactical motif] **16.♘xd5 ♖xb2 17.♕d1 ♘xd5 18.♕xd5 ♖xe2 19.♖xe2 ♗xa1 20.♕xd6** [20.♕xd6?! ♗g4] **20...♗b7** [Also possible was 20...♗e6! 21.♕xc5 ♖e8⇌] **21.♕xc5 ♖e8** [White is a pawn up, but Black has excellent compensation] **22.♖xe8+** [22.♕c7 ♗c6 23.♖xd8 ♖xd8 24.♗b4 h5⇌] **22...♕xe8 23.♕c7 ♗d5?** [23...♗c6!⇌] **24. h3?** [24.a4! h6 25.a5±] **24...h6 25.a3 ♗b2 26.♘e5 ♗d4 27.♗e7 ♗e6 28.♘g4 ♗xg4 29.hxg4 ♕a4 30.♕b8+ ♔h7 31.♕f4 ♕d1+ 32.♔h2 ♔g7 33.♕b8 ♔h7 34.♕f4 ♔g7 35.♗b4 g5 36.♕e4 ♕a1 37.♗d6 ♕b2 38.f3 ♕a1 39.a4 ♕g1+ 40.♔h3 ♕h1+ 41.♔h2 ♗g1 42.♕e5+ f6 43.♕c7+ ♔g6 44.♕b8 ♔g7 45.♕b7+ ♔h8 46.♕c8+ ♔g7 47.♕c7+ ♔g6 48.♕g3 ♗xh2 49.♕xh2 ♕a1 50.f4 ♕xa4 51.f5+ ♔g7 52.♕c7+ ♔g8 53.♕d8+ ♔f7 54.♕h8 ♕a1 55.♕h7+ ♔e8 56.♕g8+ ♔e7 57.♕e6+ ♔f8 58.♕c8+ ♔g7 59.♕e8 ♕c3+ 60.g3 ♕a1 61.♕g6+ ♔f8 62.♕xh6+ ♔e8 63.♕h8+ ♔d7 64.♔h2** ½-½

Yuri Vovk
Ray Robson
Baku 2015 (1)

1.d4 ♘f6 2.c4 c5 3.d5 b5 4.cxb5 a6 5.bxa6 g6 6.♘c3 ♗g7 7.♘f3 0-0 8.a7 ♖xa7 9.e4 e6 10.♗e2 exd5 11.exd5 d6 12.0-0 ♘a6 13.♗c4

13...♗f5?! [The idea of this move is ...♘e4, but here it was better for the bishop to stay on c8 because then it can still go to b7 or a6: 13...♘c7! 14.♗g5 (14.♗f4 a6; 14.♖e1 ♗a6 15.♗b3 ♕a8) 14...a6 15.♖xa6 (15.b3 h6 16.♗xf6 ♕xf6 17.♖c1 ♗xc4 18.bxc4 ♗a3 19.♘e4 ♕f4 20.♖e1 ♖fa8=; 15.♘d2 ♕a8) 15...♖xa6 16.♕d2 ♕a8 17.♖ad1 ♖b8 (17...♖e8 18.♖fe1 ♖xe1+ 19.♘xe1 ♕b7⇌) 18.♖fe1 ♘b5⇌] **14.♗d2** [14.♖e1! (aimed against ...♘e4) 14...♘b4 15.♖e2 ♖e7 16.♖xe7 ♕xe7 17.♗f4] **14...♘c7** [14...♘e4 15.♘xe4 ♗xe4 16.♗c3 ♗b4 17.♗xg7 ♔xg7 18.a3 ♗xf3 19.♕xf3 ♘c2 20.♕c3+ ♘d4±] **15.♖e1 ♘d7 16.a4?!** [16.♗f4 ♘b6 17.♗f1] **16...♘b6 17.b3 ♕a8 18.♖c1 ♘bxd5 19.♘xd5 ♘xd5 20.♗xd5** [20.♗g5 ♘b6 21.♗f1 ♘d5] **20...♕xd5 21.♗f4 ♗b7 22.♕xd6 ♕xb3 23.♕xc5 ♕xa4 24.♗e5 ♖a5 25.♕c3 ♖c8 26.♕d2 ♖xc1 27.♕d8+ ♗f8 28.♖xc1 ♖a6 29.h3 ♕d7 30.♕b8 ♕a7 31.♕d8 ♕d7 32.♕b8 ♕d5 33.♖a1? [33.♗b2=] 33...♗xh3 34.♖e1 ♗d7 35.♘e5 ♗e6 36.♕b2 ♕b3 [36...f6 37.♘f3 ♗f7∓] 37.♕xb3 ♗xb3 38.♘d7 ♗e7 39.♗d4 ♗d6 40.♗c5 ♖xd7 41.♗xe7 ♔g7 42.♗b4 g5 43.f3 h5 44.♔f2 ♗e6 45.♖e5 ♗g6 46.♗c3 h4 47.♗b4 ♖c7 48.♖c5 ♖b7 49.♗c3 ♖a7 50.♗a5 ♖b7 51.♗d8 ♖b2+ 52.♔g1 f6 53.♖c2 ♖d2 54.♖xe6 ♖xd8 55.♖a6 ♖d1 56.♔f2 ♖d1 57.♖b6 ♔f7 58.♖b8 ♔e6 59.♖a8 ♔e5 60.♔e3 f5 61.♖e8+ ♔f6 62.♖f8+ ♔g6 63.♖g8+ ♔h6 64.f4 g4 65.♖h8+ ♔g6 66.♖xh4 ♖a1 67.♔f2 ♖a2+ 68.♔g3 ♖a3+ 69.♔f2 ♖a8 70.♖h1 ♖a2+ 71.♔g3 ♖a3+ 72.♔f2 ♖b3 73.♖h8** ½-½

Erwin l'Ami
Milos Perunovic
Reykjavik Ech-tt 2015 (3)

1.d4 ♘f6 2.c4 c5 3.d5 b5 4.cxb5 a6 5.bxa6 g6 6.♘c3 ♗g7 7.e4 0-0 8.a7 ♖xa7 9.♘f3 e6 10.♗e2 exd5 11.exd5 d6 12.0-0 ♘a6 13.♗b5

13...♕b6 [13...♘c7 14.♗c6 (14.♗c4 ♗a6♔) 14...♗b7 (14...♖a6 15.♗f4 ♖b6 16.♘a4 (16.♕d2 ♗g4) 16...♖b4 (16...♖a6) 17.♗d2 ♘fxd5 18.♗xd5 ♘xd5 19.♗xb4 ♘xb4♔) 15.♗f4 (15.♗xb7 ♖xb7♔) 15...♘h5 16.♗g5 ♕a8 17.♗e7 (17.♗xb7 ♕xb7 18.♕d2 (18.♗e7 ♕xb2) 18...♖b8♔; 17.♖e1 ♖b8; 17.a4 ♗xc6 18.dxc6 ♕xc6 19.♗e7 (19.♘b5 ♖a6) 19...♖fa8 (19...♖e8 20.♕d6 ♕a8♔) 20.♕xd6 ♕b7♔) 17...♖c8 18.♗xb7 (18.♗xd6 ♗xc6 19.♗xc7 (19.dxc6?! ♖d8∓) 19...♗xc3 20.dxc6 ♗xb2 21.♖b1 ♖axc7 22.♖xb2 ♘xc6; 18.♗d7 ♖b8 19.♗xd6 ♖d8 20.♗xc7 ♖xd7 21.♗b6 ♖a6 22.♗xc5 ♘f4♔; 18.♖e1 ♗xc3 19.bxc3 ♘xd5 20.♗xb7 ♕xb7 21.♗xd6 ♘xc3∞) 18...♖xb7 19.♗xd6 ♖xb2 20.♖c1 (20.♗e5 ♘f4 21.♗xf4 ♗xc3 22.♖c3 (22.d6 ♘d5 23.♗g3 c4) 22...♗xc3 23.♖c1 ♗f6♔) 20...♗xc3 21.♗xc7 ♖xc7 22.♖xc3 ♘f4 23.d6 ♖d7 24.♖xc5 ♕a6 25.a4 (25.g3 ♖xd6 26.♖c8+ ♔g7 27.♕a1 ♘e2+ 28.♔g2 ♕xa2=) 25...♖xd6 26.♕a1 ♖db6♔; 13...♗b7 14.♗f4 ♘b4 15.♗c4 ♗a6 16.♗xa6 ♘xa6 17.♘b5 ♖d7; 13...♖b4 14.♗f4 ♕b6 15.a4; 13...♗f5 14.♗f4 ♕b8 15.a4 ♘b4 16.♖c1] **14.a4 ♗b7** [14...♘c7 15.♘d2 ♕b8 16.♘c4 ♘fxd5 17.♘xd5 ♘xb5 18.♗f4 ♕b7 19.axb5 ♖xa1 20.♕xa1 ♕xd5 21.♘xd6; 14...♘b4 15.♘d2 ♕b8 16.♘c4+] **15.♘d2 ♘xd5 16.♘c4 ♘xc3 17.bxc3 ♕d8 18.♘xd6** [18.♕xd6 ♘c7 19.♗e3 ♗xc3 20.♖ad1 ♕xd6 21.♖xd6 ♘e6

22.♗c4 ♗a6 23.♘b5 ♗xb5 24.axb5 ♖b8] **18...♗a8** [18...♘c7] **19.♗e3 ♗xc3?** [19...♗e5 20.♘c4 ♗xc3 21.♗h6 ♗xa1 (21...♘d4 22.♘e3 ♗xa1 23.♕xa1 ♘d4 24.♕c1! ♖c8 (24...♖d8 25.♖d1 ♕h4 26.♖xd8+ ♕xd8 27.♗xa6 ♖xa6 28.♕b2 f6 29.♕a2+ ♔h8 30.♕f7 ♕g8 31.♕e7+−) 25.h3!+−; 21...♕xd1 22.♖axd1 ♖b8) 22.♕xa1 ♕d4 23.♗xf8 ♕xa1 24.♖xa1 ♔xf8 25.♘b6] **20.♖a3** [20.♘xf7 ♖axf7 21.♕xd8 ♖xd8 22.♖ac1 ♗d4 23.♗xd4 (23.♗xa6 ♗xe3 24.fxe3 ♖d2=) 23...♖xd4 24.♗xa6 ♗d5±] **20...♗e5 21.♘c4?** [21.♘xf7! ♖axf7 (21...♕xd1 22.♘h6+ ♔g7 23.♖xd1 ♗f4 24.♗g4 h5 25.g3 ♗xe3 26.♘xe3±) 22.♕xd8 ♖xd8 23.♗xa6±; 21.♖d3] **21...♗d4 22.♖d3** [22.♗h6 ♘c7 23.♗xf8 ♘xb5 24.♖g3 ♘c3 25.♖xc3 ♔xf8♔] **22...♕d5= 23.f3 ♘c7 24.♗xd4 cxd4 25.♖xd4 ♕c5 26.♔h1 ♘xb5 27.axb5 ♕xb5 28.♘d6 ♕b2 29.♖d2 ♕b4 30.♖e1 ♗c6 31.♖d4 ♕b2 32.♘c4 ♕c3 33.♘e5 ♖a2 34.♘xc6 ♕xc6 35.♖d2 ♖xd2 36.♕xd2 ♖e8 37.♖xe8+ ♕xe8 38.h3 h5 39.♕d4 ♕e1+ 40.♔h2 ♕e6** ½-½

The Interesting 8.♗e2

Ivan Cheparinov
Hrant Melkumian
Berlin Wch blitz 2015 (14)

1.d4 ♘f6 2.c4 c5 3.d5 b5 4.cxb5 a6 5.bxa6 g6 6.♘c3 ♗g7 7.e4 0-0 8.♗e2 ♕a5 9.♗d2 ♗xa6 10.e5 ♘e8 11.♘f3 d6 [11...♗xe2!? 12.♕xe2 ♕a6 13.♕xa6 (13.♗f4 d6) 13...♘a6 14.0-0-0 (14.a3 f6♔) 14...d6] **12.e6**

12...fxe6?! [12...♗xe2 13.♕xe2 (13.♘xe2 ♕b5 14.♘g5 f5 15.♘c3

♕c4∞) 13...♕a6 14.exf7+ (14.♔g5 ♕xe2+ 15.♔xe2 f5 16.♘f7 (16.h4 ♘f6∞; 16.a3 ♘a6 17.♖hd1 ♘f6) 16...♘a6 17.♔h6+ ♔h8 18.♘f7+ ♔g8=; 14.♕e4 f5 15.♕h4 ♘f6 16.♖d1 ♕b7 17.0-0 ♘a6♔) 14...♖xf7 15.♘g5 (15.♘b5 ♕b7 16.0-0 (16.♘g5 ♖f5 17.0-0 (17.♕e6+ ♔h8 18.0-0 ♕xb5 19.♘f7+ ♖xf7 20.♕xf7 ♘f6 21.♕xe7 ♕d7) 17...♕xd5 18.♕xe7 (18.a4 ♘c6) 18...♖e5 (18...♘c6) 19.♘c3 ♕xg2+ 20.♔xg2 ♖xe7∞) 16...♕xd5 17.♘c3 ♗xc3 18.♗xc3 ♘c6 19.♖fd1 ♕f5 20.a4) 15...♕xe2+ 16.♔xe2 (16.♘xe2?! ♖f5) 16...♖f5 17.g4 (17.♘e6 ♗xc3 18.♗xc3 ♖xd5∞) 17...♗xc3 18.gxf5 ♗xb2 19.♖ab1 ♖xa2 20.fxg6 hxg6♔] **13.♘g5 ♗xe2** [13...♗d4 14.0-0 ♘g7 15.♘b5 ♕b6 16.♘xd4 cxd4 17.b4±]

14.♘xe2 [14.♕xe2! e5 15.♕g4±, White has a strong initiative] **14...♕a4?!** [14...♕a6! 15.♘xe6 ♗f5 16.♘xg7 ♗xg7 17.♗c3 ♗c4 18.0-0 ♖xd5 19.♕e1 ♘c6∞] **15.♕xa4 ♖xa4 16.♘xe6± ♖f7 17.♘xg7 ♗xg7 18.0-0 ♘f5 19.♘c3 ♗d4 20.♖fd1 ♘a6 21.♗e3 ♖b4 22.♖d2 ♖f8 23.♖e1 ♘c7 24.h3 h5 25.♗g5 ♔f7 26.a3 ♖d4 27.♖de2 ♘xd5 28.♘xd5 ♖xd5 29.♗xe7 ♖e8 30.♗g5 ♖xe2 31.♖xe2 ♘d4 32.♖e7+ ♔f8 33.♖d7 ♖xg5 34.♖xd6 ♔e7 35.♖b6 ♘e2+ 36.♔f1 ♘f4 37.g3 ♘xh3 38.a4 c4 39.♖c6 ♖f5 40.f4 g5 41.♔g2 g4 42.♖xc4 ♖d5 43.b4 ♖d2+ 44.♔f1 ♖f2+ 45.♔e1 ♖a2 46.b5 h4 47.♖c3 ♖a1+ 48.♔d2 ♖a2+ 49.♔c1 ♘g1 50.♖e3+ ♔d6 51.gxh4 ♘f3 52.♔b1 ♖xa4 53.h5 ♖xf4 54.h6 ♖f7 55.♖c3 g3 56.♖c6+ ♔e5 57.♖g6 ♔f4 58.♖g7 ♖f5 59.h7 ♖xb5+ 60.♔c2 ♖h5 61.♖f7+ ♔g4 62.♖g7+ ♘g5** 0-1

Alexander Riazantsev
Dinara Dordzhieva

Khanty-Mansiysk 2015 (3)

1.d4 ♘f6 2.c4 c5 3.d5 b5 4.cxb5 a6 5.bxa6 g6 6.♘c3 ♗g7 7.e4 0-0 8.♗e2 ♕a5 9.♗d2 ♗xa6 10.e5 ♘e8 11.♘f3 d6 12.e6 f5 13.h4 h5 14.♘g5 ♗xe2? [14...♘f6 15.0-0±]

15.♕xe2? [15.♘xe2! – this knight will go to f4: 15...♕a4 16.♘f4+−] 15...♕a6 16.♘h3 [16.♕f3 ♕c4 17.♘h3 ♘f6 18.♘f4 ♔h7 19.♕g3 ♘g4 20.f3 ♘e5 21.b3 ♕d4 22.♔e2±] 16...♘f6 17.♗g5 ♕xe2+ 18.♔xe2 ♘a6 19.♘f4 ♔h7 20.♖hd1 ♖fb8 21.♖d2 ♖a7 [21...c4!⯐] 22.♖c1 ♘b4 [22...c4] 23.a4 [23.a3 ♘a6 24.f3] 23...♘g4 24.b3 ♘e5 25.♘b5 ♖ab7 26.♔d1 ♖a8 27.♔e2 ♖ab8

28.♘h3 ♖a8 29.♗f4 ♖a6 30.♘g5+ ♔g8 31.♗xe5 ♗xe5 32.♖c4 ♗f6 33.♘f7 ♔g7 34.f3 ♔h7 35.g4 ♖b8 36.♘g5+ ♗xg5 37.hxg5 hxg4 38.fxg4 ♔g7 39.♖f4 ♖h8 40.gxf5 ♖h2+ 41.♖f2 ♖xf2+ 42.♔xf2 gxf5 43.♘c3 ♖a8 44.♔g3 ♖h8 45.a5 ♔g6 46.♘a2 ♖a6 47.♘c3 ♔b4 48.♔h2 ♖xh2 49.♔xh2 ♔xg5 50.♘b5 ♖xd5 51.a6 ♖b6 52.a7 ♔f4 53.♘xd6 ♔g5 54.♘b5 ♘a8 55.♔g3 ♖f6 56.♔f4 ♔xe6 57.♘c3 ♗f6 58.♘d5+ ♔e6 59.♘e3 ♔d6 60.♔xf5 ♔c6 61.♔e6 ♔b7 62.♔xe7 ♔xa7 63.♔d6 ♔b6 64.♘c4+ ♔b5 65.♘d2 ♘b6 66.♘e4 c4 67.bxc4+ ♘xc4+   ½-½

Alexander Riazantsev
Zaven Andriasyan

Minsk 2015 (20)

1.d4 ♘f6 2.c4 c5 3.d5 b5 4.cxb5 a6 5.bxa6 g6 6.♘c3 ♗g7 7.e4 0-0 8.♗e2 ♕a5 9.♗d2 ♗xa6 10.e5 ♘e8 11.♘f3 d6 12.e6 f5? 13.h4 ♗xe2 [13...♘f6 14.h5! ♘xh5 15.♘g5 ♗xe2 16.♕xe2 ♕a6 17.♕f3 ♘f6 (17...♘f6 18.♘xh7! ♘xh7 19.♕g3 g5 (19...♖f6 20.♕h3 ♘f8 21.♘h6+−) 20.♗xg5 ♘xg5 21.♕xg5+−) 18.♖xh5!

gxh5 19.♕xh5 h6 20.♘f7±] 14.♕xe2 ♕a6

15.h5+− ♕xe2+ 16.♔xe2 ♗f6 17.hxg6 hxg6 18.♖h6 ♘a6 19.♖xg6+ ♗g7 20.♖h1 ♘ac7 21.♗g5 ♘f6 22.♗h6 ♘fe8 23.♖h3 ♖f6 24.♖xf6 ♗xf6 25.♗d2 ♘g7 26.♖g3 ♖b8 27.b3 ♖a8 28.♔d3 ♔h7 29.♘g5+ ♔g8 30.♘f7 ♘a6 31.a3 ♘c7 32.a4 ♖b8 33.♔c2 ♘a6 34.♖h3 ♘e8 35.♘b5 ♗g7 36.♖g3+ ♔h7 37.♘g5+ ♗xg5 38.♖xg5 f4 39.♖h5+ ♔g6 40.♖h8 ♔g7 41.♗c3+ ♔g6 42.♖d2 ♔f5 43.f3 ♔g6 44.♖f8 c4 45.b4 ♔h7 46.♔e2 ♔g6 47.♔f2 ♔h7 48.♔g1 ♔g6 49.♔h2 ♘f6 50.♖xb8 ♘xb8 51.♘c7 ♘h5 52.a5 ♘g3 53.b5 ♘e2 54.a6 ♘xa6 55.bxa6 ♘xc3 56.a7   1-0

Exercise 1

position after 20...♗c3-e5

White to move.
(solution on page 252)

Exercise 2

position after 16.♘d2-c4

Black to move.
(solution on page 252)

Exercise 3

position after 17...♘h5-f6

White to move.
(solution on page 252)

Another Carlsen Surprise Weapon

by Mark van der Werf

1.	d4	d5
2.	♗f4	♘f6
3.	e3	c5
4.	c3	♘c6
5.	♘d2	e6
6.	♘gf3	

The London System is an ideal weapon for players who don't want to learn lots of theory, but do like a sound position after the opening. White plays d2-d4, ♘f3, ♗f4, e2-e3, c2-c3 and ♘bd2 one way or another and then just sits and waits to see what strategy Black will adopt. The London System is more than a hundred years old, but never got popular among top players – until recently. Gata Kamsky, who likes to avoid theory, has been a London fan for quite some time, but now Alexander Grischuk, Vladimir Kramnik and even Magnus Carlsen use it to their benefit as well. Magnus Carlsen beat Yangyi Yu in brilliant style in a blitz game during the

tiebreak match that decided the Qatar Open. With the World Champion's stamp of approval, it is time to take a closer look.

From the above diagram position, Black has two main options:
A) 6...♗d6 and
B) 6...♗e7.

The Popular Choice
Most top players move the king's bishop to d6. After **6...♗d6** White usually plays **7.♗g3** in order to keep controlling square e5. The only serious alternative is 7.♘e5, but if Black challenges the knight immediately with 7...♕c7 8.♘df3 ♘d7, White should go for an equal position with 9.♘xd7 ♗xd7 10.♗xd6 ♕xd6 11.dxc5 ♕xc5 12.♗e2 0-0 13.0-0. In the game Giri-Hou Yifan Black simply played 8...0-0 and was soon better after an inaccuracy from White.
7...0-0
Castling is probably better than 7...♗xg3 8.hxg3 ♕d6 9.♗b5 ♗d7 10.♗xc6 ♗xc6 11.♘e5, which gave White some advantage in the game J. van Foreest-Welling (see Game Section).
8.♗d3
A recent try is 8.♗b5 a6 9.♗d3 b6 10.e4, as seen in the game Grischuk-Karjakin.

Jorden van Foreest

8...b6
The strange move 8...a6 leads to the game Carlsen-Yu, which actually had a more logical move order. Black can also prepare ...e6-e5 with 8...♕e7, but White has the advantage after 9.♘e5. The game Kamsky-Shankland is a very instructive and spectacular example.
9.e4
A common alternative is 9.♘e5 ♗b7 10.0-0 ♖c8, followed

by the committal 11.f4. In the game Kosic-Korobov Black answered accurately with 11...♘e7 as the start of a very instructive plan.

9...♗e7
This is much better than 9...dxe4 10.♘xe4 ♘xe4 11.♗xe4 ♗b7 12.♕a4 ♕c7 13.dxc5 bxc5 14.0-0-0, and White has the initiative.

10.e5 ♘h5 11.a3
This position is about equal, and indeed the game Grischuk-Nakamura ended in a draw after wild complications.

The Solid Choice
The alternative **6...♗e7** is more modest and extremely solid. Black threatens to swap the bishop on f4, starting with 7...♘h5. Note that the immediate 6...♘h5 allows 7.♗g5, when White has some advantage, which the game Dgebuadze-Savchenko illustrates. After the text-move White can play 7.♘e5 in order

to preserve his bishop. Then, after 7...♘xe5 8.♗xe5 0-0, the chances are equal. A better idea is to ignore the threat by playing 7.♗d3 ♘h5 8.♗g3. Black will have to trade on g3 at some point, opening the h-file for the white rook. See the game Heberla-Mi.Bartel. White can also decide to make some room for his bishop with **7.h3 0-0 8.♗d3**

See the games Gelashvili-Gulamali, Matlakov-Alekseenko, V.Georgiev-Quesada Perez, and last but not least Carlsen-Tomashevsky.

Move Order
Although White can play the moves given in the intro without much thought, it can be beneficial to postpone ♘f3. In a Survey in the SOS series (Vol. 5, chapter 12) I used substantial space to write about the specific nuances, but top players don't seem to bother. Nevertheless, the game Kamsky-Wang Yue is a nice example of where the London System specialist uses this move order to score a clean positional victory.

Conclusion
White should not expect to have a clear edge after the opening if Black knows his stuff. He can, however, expect to get a decent playing position without having to know complicated move sequences. Therefore, this system is not only a useful weapon for club players, but also for the best players in the world, who increasingly like to avoid opening theory.

**Anish Giri
Hou Yifan**
Wijk aan Zee 2016 (13)
1.d4 ♘f6 2.♘f3 e6 3.♗f4 d5 4.e3 c5 5.c3 ♘c6 6.♘bd2 ♗d6 7.♘e5 ♕c7 8.♘df3 0-0 [Black can get a good position with 8...♘d7 and then 9.♘xd7 is probably best because after 9.♘xc6 ♗xf4 10.♘xa7 ♖xa7 11.exf4 ♕xf4 12.♗b5 0-0 or; 9.♗b5 cxd4 10.exd4 f6 11.♘xd7 ♗xf4 12.♘c5 0-0 13.0-0 ♗d6 Black's position is fine. After 9.♘xd7 Black has no problems either: 9...♗xd7 10.♗xd6 ♕xd6 11.dxc5 ♕xc5 12.♗e2 with equal chances] 9.♗d3 b6 10.♘xc6 ♕xc6 11.♘e5 ♕c7 12.♕f3?! [Much better is 12.0-0 a5 13.♕e2 ♗b7 with an equal position]

12...♘e4! [Now White cannot take on e4 and 13...f6 is a major threat. Black has a clear edge already] **13.♘c4** [13.♗xe4 dxe4 14.♕xe4 ♗b7 15.♕d3 cxd4 16.cxd4 ♗xg2 17.♖g1 ♕b7 is very good for Black and 13.0-0 f6 14.♘c4 (or 14.♘g4? e5!) 14...♗xf4 15.♕xf4 ♕xf4 16.exf4 ♗a6 17.♖fe1 cxd4 18.cxd4 ♗xc4 19.♗xc4 dxc4 20.♖xe4 ♔f7 gives Black the better endgame. Probably 13.♘g4

♗xf4 14.♕xf4 ♕xf4 15.exf4 is the best way for White to control the damage] **13...♗xf4 14.♕xf4 ♕xf4 15.exf4 ♗a6 16.♗xe4** [16.♘e5 ♗xd3 17.♘xd3 cxd4 18.cxd4 ♖ac8 is also very good for Black] **16...dxe4 17.♘d2 cxd4 18.♘xe4 f5 19.♘g5 dxc3 20.0-0-0** [White has to do something special because 20.bxc3 h6 21.♘f3 ♖ac8 22.♖c1 ♗b7 is very bad for him] **20...♗c4?!** [Nothing is wrong with the logical 20...cxb2+ 21.♔xb2 ♗c4 22.♖d7 h6 23.♘f3 ♖fd8] **21.b3 ♗d5 22.♖he1 ♖fe8 23.♖e3 ♖ac8 24.♖dd3 ♗xg2 25.♖d7** [Now White has some counterplay. He is two pawns down, but a7, c6 and e6 are weak] **25...♖ed8 26.♖xd8+ ♖xd8 27.♘xe6 ♖d6 28.♘g5 ♗c6 29.♖xc3?!** [29.♖e6 ♖xe6 30.♘xe6 ♗e4 31.♘g5 gives White serious drawing chances. Now Hou

Yifan improves her position gradually]
**29...h6 30.♘h3 ♗b5 31.♖e3 ♗f1
32.♔g1 ♖d4 33.♖e1 ♗g2 34.♘e2
♖e4 35.♔d2 ♗f3 36.♘g3 ♖xf4
37.♖e8+ ♔f7 38.♔e3 g5 39.♖h8
♔g7 40.♖c8 ♗g4 41.♖c7+ ♔f6
42.h3 ♖f3+ 43.♔d4 ♗xh3 44.♖c6+
♔e7 45.♖xh6 ♗g4 46.♖g6 ♖xf2
47.♖xg5** [Black is a clean pawn up,
but there is still a technical task ahead]
**47...♔f7 48.b4 ♖f3 49.♘e2 ♖h3
50.♘c3 ♖h8 51.♘d5 ♖e8 52.a3
♖e4+ 53.♔d3 ♗e2+ 54.♔d2
♖d4+?!** [The rook ending is not so clear.
Black should have kept the bishop and
knight on the board with 54...♗a6. Then
55.♖xf5+ is prohibited because Black plays
55...♔e6 followed by 56...♖d4+, winning
the knight] **55.♔xe2 ♖xd5 56.♖h5
♔g6 57.♖h8 ♖d7 58.a4 ♔f6 59.a5
♔e5 60.♖c8 bxa5 61.bxa5 ♖d5
62.a6 ♖a5 63.♖c6 ♔d5 64.♖f6
♔e4 65.♖e6+ ♔f4 66.♔d3 ♖a4
67.♖g6 ♔f3 68.♖c3 f4 69.♔b3
♖a1 70.♔b4 ♔e3?** [70...♔e4
71.♔b5 f3 72.♖f6 ♖a2 73.♖f7 f2 is
completely winning for Black] **71.♔b5
f3 72.♖e6+ ♔d4 73.♖f6 ♖b1+
74.♔a4 ♖f1 75.♔b3 ♔e3 76.♖e6+
♔d2 77.♖d6+ ♔e3 78.♖e6+ ♔d4
79.♖f6 ♔e4 80.♖f7 ♖a1** [After 80...
f2 81.♔b2 Black cannot make progress
either] **81.♖e7+ ♔d4 82.♖f7 ♔e3
83.♖e7+ ♔d2 84.♖d7+ ♔e1
85.♖e7+ ♔f1 86.♖xa7 f2 87.♔c4
♔e2 88.♖e7+ ♔d2 89.♖f7 f1♕+
90.♖xf1 ♖xf1 91.♔b5 ♔c3 92.a7
♖f8 93.♔c6 ♔b4 94.♔b7 ♖f7+
95.♔b6 ♖xa7** ½-½

Jorden van Foreest
Gerard Welling
Schwäbisch Gmünd 2016 (4)

**1.d4 d5 2.♘f3 ♘f6 3.♗f4 e6 4.e3
c5 5.♘bd2 ♘c6 6.c3 ♗d6 7.♗g3
♗xg3** [7...0-0 is the usual move, but
Black's idea is simple: playing ...e6-e5 as
soon as possible] **8.hxg3 ♕d6 9.♗b5**
[And the youngest Dutch grandmaster
finds a way to prevent this] **9...♗d7
10.♗xc6 ♗xc6 11.♘e5** [A few years
ago I had to defend this position with
black, and didn't succeed. White has given
up his bishop but is in total control of e5,
which is the key square in this position]

11...♗b5 12.♕f3 ♕e7 [Now the
black king is permanently in trouble. 12...
h6 13.g4 ♘f8 14.♕f4 0-0-0 is a more
logical continuation] **13.g4 h6 14.♕g3
a5 15.0-0-0 cxd4** [Black tries to force
matters, but this backfires. However, he
is in trouble anyway because White's
attack is faster and more dangerous after,
for example: 15...a4 16.a3 ♖ac8 17.f4
♘d7 18.g5] **16.exd4 ♗e2 17.♖de1
♗xg4** [This clever sequence only helps
White] **18.f3 ♗f5 19.♕xg7 ♖h7
20.♕g3 b5 21.♘f1 ♖g8 22.♕f4
b4 23.♘e3 ♗g6 24.c4** [Now Black's
counterattack is gone and his position
collapses immediately. Note that ♘e5
is still the hero of the position] **24...
dxc4 25.♘xg6+ fxg6 26.♕xd6+
♔xd6 27.♘xc4+ ♔d7 28.♘xa5
♖a8 29.♘b7 ♖xa2 30.♔b1 ♖a8
31.♘c5+ ♔c8 32.♖xe6** [A model
game by Van Foreest] 1-0

Alexander Grischuk
Sergey Karjakin
Berlin Wch blitz 2015 (18)

**1.d4 ♘f6 2.♗f4 d5 3.e3 e6 4.♘f3
c5 5.♘bd2 ♘c6 6.c3 ♗d6 7.♗g3
0-0 8.♗b5** [We see this move in other
variations as well. If the ♘c6 moves, or
is removed, White gains control over e5]
8...a6

9.♗d3 [But Grischuk has other plans. He
thinks ...a7-a6 is a queenside weakening.
Compare this to the game Carlsen-Yu where
Black voluntarily plays ...a7-a6!] **9...b6
10.e4** [This is the best answer to 9...b6. It
is wise to play e3-e4 before Black controls
this square] **10...♗e7** [After 10...dxe4
11.♘xe4 ♘xe4 12.♗xe4 ♗b7 13.dxc5
♗xc5 14.♕e2 White has a slight edge]
11.dxc5 [11.e5 is the main alternative,
which leads to positions similar to those
in the game Grischuk-Nakamura] **11...
bxc5 12.0-0 ♘h5** [12...♗b7 13.exd5
exd5 14.♗h4 is about equal] **13.♘e5
♘xe5 14.♗xe5 g6 15.♖e1** [I would
prefer 15.h3 because now Black could
have played 15...f6 followed by 16...♘xg3]
**15...♗f6 16.exd5 exd5 17.♕f3 ♗b7
18.h3 ♖e8 19.♗xf6 ♕xf6 20.♕xf6
♘xf6** [White has a minuscule advantage]
**21.♗c2 ♘f8 22.♘b3 ♖ac8 23.♖ad1
♘h5 24.f3 ♘f4 25.♔f2 ♘e6 26.h4
♖b8 27.♘c1 ♗c6 28.b3 c4?!** [This
is a positional concession. Better is 28...a5
29.♘d3 f6 with equal chances, for example
30.g4 ♔f7 31.f4 c4 32.f5 gxf5 33.gxf5 ♘c7
34.♖xe8 ♖xe8 35.♘f4 ♘b5 36.♘xd5
♗xd5 37.♖xd5 ♘xc3 38.♖d2 ♘e4+
39.♗xe4 ♖xe4 40.bxc4 ♖xc4] **29.♘e2
♖ec8 30.b4 ♖d8 31.♘d4 ♗d7
32.a4 ♖e8 33.a5 ♘xd4 34.♖xd4
♖xe1 35.♔xe1 ♗c6** [Black's pawns
are all on the wrong color, and d5 is a
permanent weakness. White has a clear
advantage] **36.♔f2 ♖e8 37.♖d2 ♖e6
38.g4** [White cannot make progress on the
queenside and therefore creates a second
front] **38...h6 39.f4 g5?!** [This makes
White's task easier, but remaining passive
is always difficult, and especially in a blitz
game] **40.hxg5 hxg5 41.fxg5 ♔g7
42.♗f5 ♖e8 43.♖e2 ♖d8 44.♖e7 d4
45.♖c7 ♗b5 46.cxd4 ♖xd4 47.g6**
[White is winning] **47...c3 48.♖xf7+
♔h6 49.♖h7+ ♔g5 50.♖c7 ♔f6
51.♖xc3 ♖xb4 52.♖e3 ♗c4 53.♖e4
♖b2+ 54.♔e3 ♗d5 55.♖e8 ♖b5
56.♗d3 ♖xa5 57.♖f8+ ♔g7 58.♖f5
♔h6 59.♖h5+ ♔g7 60.♔d4 ♖a4+
61.♔xd5** 1-0

Gata Kamsky
Sam Shankland
Sturbridge 2014 (4)

1.d4 ♘f6 2.♗f4 d5 3.e3 e6 4.♘d2
[Kamsky seems to use a different move

order in every game] **4...c5 5.c3 ♘c6 6.♘gf3 ♗d6 7.♗g3 0-0 8.♗d3 ♕e7?!** [This move seems inaccurate because White can prevent Black from playing ...e6-e5]

9.♘e5 ♘d7 [9...♕c7 is an interesting alternative, but it is difficult to play from a psychological point of view because Black just moved the queen to e7. However, it is important to put pressure on the ♘e5. After 10.f4 ♘e7 11.0-0 ♘f5 12.♗f2 ♗e7 chances are equal] **10.♘xd7 ♗xd7?** [If Shankland had foreseen the coming events, he would have played 10...♕xd7. The reason becomes clear in a few moves] **11.♗xd6 ♕xd6 12.dxc5 ♕xc5?** [12...♕c7 or 12...♕e7 is absolutely necessary. Still, Black has not enough compensation for the pawn] **13.♗xh7+!** [A classical sacrifice but in an original version. White gets a powerful attack against the black king] **13...♔xh7 14.♕h5+ ♔g8 15.♘e4 ♕c4** [15... g6 would have been the solution if Black had played 10...♕xd7. Now 16.♘xc5 gxh5 17.♘xd7 wins a very healthy pawn] **16.♘g5 ♖fd8** [16...♕d3 is the natural defence, but White can block the b1-h7 diagonal effectively with 17.e4!. After 17...♖fd8 18.♕xf7+ ♔h8 19.♖d1 ♕c4 20.f4 White has several winning ideas, with ♖h1-f1-f3-h3 being the simplest] **17.♕xf7+ ♔h8 18.♕h5+ ♔g8 19.♖d1** [White has no direct win, so he brings the rook into play] **19... e5 20.♕f7+ ♔h8 21.e4** [A multi-purpose move. It threatens ♖xd5 and it prevents the black queen from helping on the kingside. Black can only prevent ♕h5+-h7+-h8+-g7+ by returning a piece] **21...♘e7 22.♕xe7 ♗b5 23.♖d2 ♕xa2** [23...d4 is more tenacious, but after 24.f3 White's king is safe and his position is completely winning] **24.♕f7**

♕a1+ 25.♖d1 ♕xb2 26.♕h5+ [White finally has a forced sequence that wins him the game] **26...♔g8 27.♕h7+ ♔f8 28.♕h8+ ♔e7 29.♕xg7+ ♔d6 30.♖xd5+ ♔c6 31.♕f6+** 1-0

Magnus Carlsen
Yangyi Yu
Doha blitz playoff 2015 (1)
1.d4 ♘f6 2.♗f4 [Magnus plays the London System in this very important blitz game, and he gets what he wants: a non-theoretical position] **2...d5** [White has played ♗f4 very early. Black has numerous options, but we focus on the classical set-up] **3.e3 e6 4.♘f3 a6?!** [I think Black should avoid this move if it is not really necessary] **5.♗d3 c5 6.c3 ♗d6 7.♗g3 ♘c6 8.♘bd2 0-0 9.♘e5**

9...♗e7 [Black tries to swap White's bishop against a knight, but he will not succeed. Better is 9...♕c7 and only after 10.f4 he should play 10...♗e7, like in the game Kosic-Korobov] **10.0-0 b6 11.♗h4! ♘f5 12.♗g5 h6 13.♗f4** [A lot of bishop moves by the World Champion, but it is a good investment] **13...♗b7** [After this move both players were down to approximately one and a half minute] **14.h3 ♗e7 15.a4 ♘d6 16.f3** [What a difference with the game Kosic-Korobov! White controls the important centre squares] **16...♘d7 17.♕e2 ♘f6** [Clearly Black doesn't know what to do and waits for Carlsen to attack] **18.♗h2 ♕c8 19.♖ac1 a5 20.g4!** [And he doesn't have to wait for long] **20...♕d8 21.♕g2 ♘d7 22.f4** [Now that square e4 is sufficiently covered, White plays f2-f4, to support the kingside attack] **22...♖c8** [Note that

Black cannot occupy e4 with 22...♘f6 23.g5 hxg5 24.fxg5 ♘fe4 because after 25.g6 White has a devastating attack] **23.♖ce1 cxd4 24.exd4 ♗a8 25.g5** [White's advantage is obvious now. His attack is progressing smoothly and Black has no counterplay at all] **25... hxg5 26.fxg5 ♘xe5 27.♗xe5 ♘c4 28.♘f3** [Better is the logical 28.g6 but both players had less than 30 seconds on the clock] **28...♘xe5 29.♘xe5 ♗d6 30.♖e2 g6 31.♕g4 ♔g7 32.h4 ♖h8** [Now Magnus plays an excellent sacrifice, taking into account the limited time] **33.♖xe6! fxe6 34.♕xe6** [Black can only defend g6 by giving back a bishop, but he is completely lost anyway] **34...♕e8 35.♕xd6 ♖c6** [35...♕e3+ 36.♔g2 ♕xd3 37.♕d7+ ♔g8 38.♕xc8 is mate in eight] **36.♕e5+ ♕xe5 37.♘xe5** [Very nice! Material is about equal, but the position is completely winning for White] **37...♖xh4 38.♖f7+ ♔g8 39.♖a7 ♖c8 40.♗xg6 ♗c6** [Blunders a rook, but it isn't important for the result] **41.♗f7+ ♔f8 42.♘g6+** [Many people would be proud of this game if it had been played with a classical time control. As a blitz game it is brilliant] 1-0

Dragan Kosic
Anton Korobov
Reykjavik Ech-tt 2015 (2)
1.d4 ♘f6 2.♘f3 c5 3.c3 e6 4.♗f4 ♘c6 5.e3 d5 6.♘bd2 ♗d6 7.♗g3 0-0 8.♗d3 b6 [Developing the bishop to b7 is definitely Black's best option. It is important to control at least one central square] **9.♘e5** [All part of the plan, but top players also like 9.e4] **9...♗b7 10.0-0** [In the game Karjakin-Adams, Wijk aan Zee 2016, White played 10.f4 immediately. Black replied in a similar way as Korobov: 10...♘e7 11.♕f3 ♘f5 12.♗f2 ♗e7 13.g4 ♘d6 14.g5 ♘fe4 After 15.0-0-0 Black launched an attack with 15...c4 16.♗c2 b5 and won convincingly] **10...♖c8** [10...♕c7, challenging the knight, is a good alternative, but top players tend to favour the text move] **11.♕e2** [In an earlier game Korobov faced 11.f4 ♘e7 12.♕b1 and managed to win convincingly against Kamsky. See Exercise 1 for more details] **11...♕c7 12.f4** [Black was waiting for this move. Safer was bailing

out with 12.♘xc6 ♕xc6 13.♗xd6 ♕xd6 14.♘f3 with equal chances. Now Black carries out an instructive plan]

12...♘e7! [The knight goes to f5, the bishop drops back to e7 and then the knight comes to d6. There is nothing White can do to prevent this plan] **13.♘f3 ♘f5 14.♗f2 ♗e7 15.♖ad1 ♘d6 16.♗h4 ♘fe4** [Black has carried out his plan and has a clear edge now] **17.♗xe7 ♕xe7 18.♕h3 f6 19.♘ef3 ♗c6 20.♗c2 ♗d7** [Black is manoeuvring comfortably and is gradually making progress] **21.♘xe4 dxe4 22.dxc5 bxc5 23.♘d2 f5 24.b3 ♖cd8 25.♘b1 ♗c8 26.♕g3 ♕f6 27.♕e1 ♘f7 28.♖xd8 ♖xd8 29.♕e2 e5 30.fxe5 ♕xe5 31.♖d1 ♖xd1+ 32.♕xd1 g5 33.♕e1 ♗b7 34.♕g3 f4?** [Black has played very well, but now he throws away his advantage, which he could have retained with 34...♕xg3 35.hxg3 ♘e5] **35. exf4 ♕xf4 36.♕xf4 gxf4 37.b4?** [White returns the favour. With 37.c4 ♘d6 38.♘c3 ♔g7 39.♘e2 he could have won a pawn although Black has sufficient compensation. Now the position is still drawish, but Black has some practical chances] **37...e3 38.bxc5 ♘e5 39.♘a3 a6 40.♗b3+ ♔g7 41.♘c2 ♘d3 42.♘d4 ♘xc5 43.g3** [43.♘e2 is perhaps the easier option. Now Black gets an annoying passed pawn on the h-file] **43...fxg3 44.♘f5+ ♔f6 45.♘xe3 gxh2+ 46.♔xh2 ♔e5 47.♘g4+ ♔f4 48.♘f6 ♘xb3 49.axb3 ♔e3 50.♘d7?** [White's last chance to secure a draw was the obvious 50.♘xh7 ♔d3 51.c4 ♔c3 52.♘f6 ♔xb3 53.♘d7, and this position is a draw according to the endgame database] **50...♔d2 51.♘c5 ♗c8 52.♘e4+ ♔d3 53.♘d6 ♗d7 54.c4 ♔c3 55.♘e4+ ♔b4 56.♔g3 ♗c6 57.♔f4 a5 58.♘d2 ♔c3 59.♔e3 h5**

60.♘f3 ♗b7 61.♘d2 h4 62.♘e4+ ♔b4 63.♔d3 h3 64.♘f2 h2 65.♔c2 ♔c5 66.♔c3 ♗c6 67.♘d3+ ♔d6 68.♘f2 ♗e6 69.♔d4 ♔f5 70.♔e3 ♗b7 71.♔e2 ♔f4 72.♔e1 ♔g3 73.♔e2 ♔g2 74.♔e3 ♗f3 [Zugzwang! The h-pawn will decide the game] **0-1**

Alexander Grischuk
Hikaru Nakamura
Skopje tt 2015 (7)
1.d4 d5 2.♘f3 ♘f6 3.♗f4 e6 4.e3 ♗d6 5.♗g3 c5 6.♘bd2 ♘c6 7.c3 0-0 8.♗d3 b6

9.e4 ♗e7 [9...dxe4 10.♘xe4 ♘xe4 11.♗xe4 ♗b7 12.dxc5 ♗xc5 13.♕a4 ♖c8 14.♖d1 gives White a clear edge. Exercise 2 features a frightening example] **10.e5 ♘h5** [Of course Black targets the bishop. Not good is 10...♘d7, after which White has excellent attacking chances on the kingside] **11.a3 a5 12.♕e2 ♖a7** [This is an improvement over the rapid game Kramnik-S.Zhigalko, Berlin 2015, where Black played 12...c4 immediately. After 13.♗c2 b5 14.♘g5 ♗xg5 (14... g6 15.♘xh7 is no option) 15.♕xh5 g6 16.♕e2 f5 17.exf6 ♕xf6 18.h4 ♗f4 19.♗xf4 ♕xf4 20.g3 White had a clear advantage, because his bishop is superior to Black's] **13.0-0 c4 14.♗c2 b5 15.h4** [It is not easy to start a kingside attack in another way. However it is very tricky. Note that after White has castled kingside, 15.♘g5 g6 is not dangerous anymore] **15...g6** [The logical move 15...♘xg3 16.fxg3 b4 17.♕e3 b3 18.♗d1 f6 seems to give Black a substantial advantage without risk] **16.♗h2** [A strong pawn sacrifice. The h-file gives White enough compensation] **16...♗xh4 17.g4 ♘g7 18.♘xh4 ♕xh4 19.♔g2 f5 20.exf6 ♕xf6 21.♗d6 ♖ff7 22.f4** [It looks like

White has prevented ...e6-e5 for good, but 22.♕e3 was a better way to do this] **22...e5** [Anyway!] **23.dxe5 ♕h4** [White cannot defend g4 properly and decides to gamble:] **24.f5 gxf5** [Better is 24...♘xf5! 25.♗xf5 (25.gxf5 gxf5 followed by ...f5-f4 gives Black a crushing attack) 25...gxf5 26.♘f3 ♕xg4+ 27.♔f2 ♔g7 28.♖g1 ♕f4 29.♕e3 and White is two pawns down, but positional compensation and the bishops of opposite colours give him some drawing chances] **25.♖h1 ♕d8** [25...♕g5 26.♘f3 ♕f4 27.♖h4 ♘e6 28.gxf5 ♕xh4 29.♘xh4 ♕f4+ 30.♔f2 ♖xe2 31.♔xe2 is another crazy variation. Here White has abundant compensation for the exchange] **26.♕e3 d4 27.cxd4 ♘e8 28.♖h6?!** [The position is so complex that the momentum is swinging from one side to the other. Here White can keep the initiative with 28.d5 ♘xd6 29.dxc6 ♘e8 30.♘f3] **28...♖g7 29.♖g1 ♖ad7?** [29...♖xg4+ 30.♔f1 ♖g1+ 31.♕xg1+ ♔g7 32.♕e3 ♘e7 is just equal] **30.d5?** [30.♔f1 ♘xd6 31.exd6 looks much better for White] **30...♘e7 31.♗xe7 ♖dxe7 32.♕d4 ♗b7** [32...♖xg4+ 33.♔f1 ♖eg7 34.♖xg4 ♖xg4 is still better for Black. Now the game peters out to a draw] **33.♔f2 ♕xd5 34.♕xd5+ ♗xd5 35.♗xf5 ♖xe5 36.♖e1 ♖xe1 37.♔xe1 b4 38.axb4 axb4 39.♗e6+ ♗xe6 40.♖xe6 ♘c7** [Draw agreed. That looked like an unlikely result about 15 moves ago] **½-½**

The Solid Choice
6...♗e7

Alexandre Dgebuadze
Stanislav Savchenko
Ubeda 1998 (5)
1.d4 d5 2.♘f3 ♘f6 3.♗f4 c5 4.e3 e6 5.c3 ♘c6 6.♘bd2

6...♘h5 [This move is premature, because White can keep his bishop] **7.♗g5 ♕b6** [7...♗e7 8.♗xe7 ♕xe7 leaves the knight misplaced. After 9.♗d3 0-0 10.0-0 ♘f6 11.dxc5 ♕xc5 12.e4 White has a slight edge] **8.dxc5 ♗xc5 9.b4 ♗e7** [9...♗f8 is an interesting alternative, although White is better after 10.e4] **10.b5 ♘b8 11.♗xe7 ♔xe7 12.c4** [White tries to open the position because Black's king is stuck in the centre] **12...♘f6 13.cxd5 exd5 14.♗e2 ♗e6 15.a4 ♕d6 16.0-0 ♘bd7 17.♕b1 ♖hc8 18.♕b2 ♘b6?!** [Black has succeeded in completing his development, but now he is helping White. Better was 18...♔f8 19.♘d4 ♘c5] **19.♘d4 ♔f8 20.a5 ♘bd7 21.♖fc1 ♘e5 22.h3 ♗d7 23.♘2f3 ♘xf3+ 24.♗xf3 ♖xc1+ 25.♖xc1 ♖c8 26.♖xc8+ ♗xc8 27.♕c2 ♗d7** [Swapping the rooks hasn't done much for Black. White still has a nagging advantage based on his powerful knight and control of the c-file] **28.♗g4 ♘xg4 29.hxg4 g6 30.g5 ♔e7 31.♕c3 b6** [Black should remain passive. Now White can access Black's fortress] **32.axb6 axb6 33.♕a1 ♕b4** [33...♕c7 34.♕a3+ ♕c5 35.♕a7 is more tenacious, but Black will not be able to defend all his weaknesses] **34.♘c6+ ♗xc6 35.♕f6+** 1-0

Bartlomiej Heberla
Michal Bartel

Katowice 2015 (4)

1.d4 ♘f6 2.♗f4 e6 3.e3 c5 4.♘d2 d5 5.c3 ♘c6 6.♘gf3 ♗e7 7.♗d3 [7.h3 is preferable in my opinion; 7.♘e5 is met by 7...♘xe5 and now neither 8.♗xe5 0-0 nor 8.dxe5 ♘d7 gives White any advantage] **7...♘h5 8.♗g3**

8...♗d7 [There is no need to hurry with 8...♘xg3 although after 9.hxg3

h6 10.g4 0-0 White has no immediate threats] **9.♕e2 ♕b6 10.♖b1 ♖c8 11.a3 h6 12.dxc5 ♕xc5 13.e4 ♘xg3?!** [Black has been very patient, but still there was no need to capture the bishop. Better was 13...0-0 14.0-0 ♘xg3 15.hxg3 ♖fd8 with an equal position] **14.hxg3 dxe4 15.♘xe4 ♕b6 16.g4!** [Of course. Now White has a clear plan] **16...e5 17.g5 ♗g4 18.gxh6 f5 19.♘ed2 ♖xh6** [19... e4 would be a consistent follow-up, but 20.♘xe4 fxe4 21.♕xe4 ♗xf3 22.♕xf3 gives White excellent compensation for the knight] **20.♖xh6 gxh6 21.♘c4 ♕c5 22.b4 ♕d5 23.♘e3 ♕e6 24.b5 ♘d8 25.♘xg4 fxg4** [Better was 25...e4. After 26.♘d4 exd3 27.♘xe6 dxe2 28.♘g7+ ♔f8 29.♘xf5 ♖xc3 30.♔e2 ♖xa3 31.♘xe7 ♔xe7 32.♘xh6 White is a pawn up but there is still some work to be done] **26.♘xe5 ♖xc3 27.♔f1 ♗xa3?** [27...♗d6 28.♘xg4 ♕xe2+ 29.♗xe2 is required. The text move is too greedy] **28.♗c4 ♖xc4** [28...♕e7 29.♕e4 and White is winning] **29.♘xc4 ♕xe2+ 30.♔xe2** [Now Black defends stubbornly, but the result is inevitable] **30...♗c5 31.♖h1 ♗e6 32.♔f1 ♘d4 33.b6 axb6 34.♖xh6 b5 35.♘e5 b4 36.♘d3 b6 37.♔e1 b3 38.♔d2 ♔f7 39.♔c3 g3 40.fxg3 ♘e2+ 41.♔xb3 ♗e3 42.♖h3 ♗f6 43.g4 ♗g1 44.♖h5 ♔g6 45.♖e5 ♘d4+ 46.♔c4 ♘c2 47.♘f4+ ♔f6 48.♖f5+ ♔g7 49.♔d3 ♘e3 50.♖e5 ♘d1 51.g5 ♘f2+ 52.♔e2 ♘g4 53.♖e7+ ♔f8 54.♘g6+ ♔g8 55.♔f3 ♘h2+ 56.♔f4 ♗c5 57.♖b7 ♘f1 58.♘e5 ♘e3 59.♘d7 ♘xg2+ 60.♔g3 ♘e3 61.♘f6+ ♔f8 62.g6 ♘f5+ 63.♔g4 ♘e7 64.♔h5 ♔g7 65.♘d5 ♔f8 66.♘xe7 ♗xe7 67.♔h6 ♗d6 68.g7+ ♔g8 69.♔g6 b5 70.♖d7** 1-0

Maxim Matlakov
Kirill Alexeenko

St Petersburg 2014 (7)

1.d4 d5 2.♘f3 ♘f6 3.♗f4 e6 4.e3 c5 5.c3 ♘c6 6.♘bd2 ♗e7 7.h3 0-0 8.♗d3 ♘h5 [For me 8...b6 9.0-0 ♗b7 10.♕e2 is the most logical continuation – it leads to the game V.Georgiev-Quesada Perez] **9.♗h2 f5** [This changes the structure of the game. For White it is now essential to keep control over square e5]

10.dxc5 ♗xc5 11.0-0 ♘f6 12.c4 [If White hesitates for too long, Black will play ...♘b6 and ...e6-e5] **12...♗d6 13.♗xd6 ♕xd6 14.♖c1 f4** [14... e5 is not an option because of 15.cxd5 ♘xd5 16.♗c4 ♘h8 17.♘g5 h6 18.♘df3 ♘ce7 19.♗xd5 ♘xd5 20.e4 with a clear edge for White] **15.♖e1 fxe3 16.♖xe3 ♗d7 17.a3 ♖ae8 18.b4** [It is difficult for Black to improve his position, but the text move hands over square e4 to White] **18...d4?! 19.♖e1 e5 20.c5 ♕c7 21.♘e4 ♘xe4 22.♗xe4 f5** [22...a6 is probably better, but pawn e5 is doomed in the long run] **23.b5 ♗xe4 24.♖xe4 ♘d8 25.♕e2** [White confiscates pawn e5 and has a winning advantage] **25...♘f7 26.♘xd4 ♘g5 27.♖e3 ♕a5 28.♕c4+ ♔h8 29.♘b3 ♕d8 30.c6 bxc6 31.bxc6 ♕f6 32.♕e2 ♖c8 33.♖xe5 ♕g6 34.♕g4 ♕f7 35.♕xg5 ♕xb3 36.♕e3 ♕b2 37.c7 h6 38.f3 ♕b7 39.♖e7 ♕b2 40.♖c6 ♔h7 41.♕xh6+ ♔g8 42.♕e6+ ♔h8 43.♖c4** 1-0

Tamaz Gelashvili
Kazim Gulamali

Orlando 2011 (8)

1.d4 ♘f6 2.♘f3 d5 3.♗f4 e6 4.e3 c5 5.c3 ♘c6 6.♘bd2 ♗e7 7.♗d3 0-0 8.h3

8...♗d6 [An interesting idea, because 9.♗g3 is impossible and we know that 9.♘e5 is not dangerous for Black] **9.♗xd6** [9.♗g5 h6 10.♗h4 e5 promises White no advantage] **9...♕xd6 10.0-0 e5 11.dxc5** [The standard procedure in this kind of position. After 11.dxe5 ♘xe5 12.♘xe5 ♕xe5 Black is already better] **11...♕xc5 12.e4 ♗e6 13.♖e1 ♖ae8** [13...♖ad8 14.exd5 ♗xd5 15.♕c2, with an equal position, is a more natural continuation] **14.♕c2 h6 15.b4 ♕d6 16.a3 a6 17.exd5 ♘xd5** [17...♗xd5 is also possible] **18.♘c4 ♕c7 19.♘cxe5 ♘xe5 20.♖xe5 ♕xc3 21.♕xc3 ♘xc3** [After an interesting exchange sequence White is still slightly better] **22.♖c1 ♖c8 23.♖c5 ♖xc5 24.bxc5 ♘a2** [This is risky. I would prefer to put the knight in the centre of the board] **25.♖c2 ♗b3 26.♖b2 ♗d5 27.♘d4 ♘c3?!** [This gives White a chance to increase his advantage] **28.♘f5?!** [28.♖c2 ♘a4 29.c6 bxc6 30.♘xc6 ♗b3 31.♘e7+ ♔h8 32.♖c7 gives Black a hard time keeping the position together] **28...♖e8 29.♘d6 ♖e1+ 30.♔h2 ♘a4 31.♖c2 ♖e5 32.f4 ♖e3 33.♗c4 ♗c6** [Safer is 33...♗xc4 34.♖xc4 b5 35.♖c2 ♖d3 36.♘b7 ♗d7 37.c6 ♖c7] **34.♘xf7 ♔f8 35.♘e5 ♘xc5?** [35...♗e4 36.c6 bxc6 37.♖d2 is necessary. Now Black remains a pawn down and is in serious trouble] **36.♘xc6 bxc6 37.♗f1 ♘d7 38.♖xc6 ♖xa3 39.♗xa6** [It is far from easy to win this position, but it is also very difficult to defend it] **39...♘f6 40.♗e2 ♖e3 41.♗d1 ♖d3 42.♗c2 ♖d4 43.♖c8+ ♔e7 44.♖c7+ ♖d7 45.♖c4 ♖d2 46.♔g3 ♘d5 47.♔f3 ♘b6 48.♖c6 ♖d6 49.♖c3 ♔f6 50.h4 g5 51.fxg5+ hxg5 52.h5 ♘d7 53.♔g3 ♘e5 54.♖b3 ♘f7 55.♖b7 ♖c6 56.♗e4 ♖c3+ 57.♔f2 ♘h6 58.♖b6+ ♔e5 59.♗f3 ♗f5 60.h6 ♖c7 61.♗e2 ♖f7 62.♔g1 ♖f6 63.h7 ♖f8 64.♗g6 ♖h8 65.♗d3 ♘e7 66.♖xg5+ ♔f6 67.♖g3** [Black resigned. White will put his king on h6, then play ♖f3 and ♔g7, and there is nothing Black can do about it] **1-0**

Vladimir Georgiev
Yuniesky Quesada Perez
Merida 2006 (1)

1.d4 ♘f6 2.♘f3 e6 3.♗f4 b6 4.e3 ♗b7 5.♘bd2 ♗e7 6.h3 c5 7.c3

0-0 **8.♗d3 ♘c6 9.0-0 d5 10.♕e2** [A very different move order leads to a well-known type of position] **10...♗d6 11.♗g5** [11.♗xd6 ♕xd6 12.dxc5 bxc5 13.e4 is an equally good possibility] **11...h6 12.♗h4 ♗e7** [12...e5 13.dxc5 bxc5 14.e4 d4 leads to an equal position] **13.♗g3 ♘d7 14.♖ad1 ♖e8 15.a3 a5 16.e4 ♕c8 17.♖fe1 c4 18.♗b1 b5** [This resembles the position in the game Grischuk-Nakamura, but there is a huge difference: White hasn't played e4-e5 yet]

19.exd5 exd5 20.♘f1 ♘f6 21.♗e5 [21.♘e3, keeping an eye on d5 and f5, is more logical and probably better] **21...♘e4 22.♘e3 ♘xe5 23.dxe5 ♗c5 24.♔h2 ♖a6** [24...♗c6 25.♖f1 ♕b7 26.♖de1 ♖ad8 is a good alternative because 27.♘xd5 is impossible due to 27...♗xf2] **25.♖f1 ♕a8 26.♖de1** [Now 27.♘xd5 is a threat because of the possibility of 28.♘c7, forking Black's major pieces] **26...♕a7?!** [26...♕b8 prevents 27.♘xd5. After 27...♕g5! 28.♘xg5 hxg5 the knight on d5 has no natural retreat] **27.♘xd5 ♘xf2?** [A knight on f2 looks nice, but it is actually in trouble. Black should have played 27...♗xd5 28.♗xe4 ♗xe4 29.♕xe4 ♗xf2 30.♖e2 ♗c5 with only a slight edge for White] **28.♘f4 ♖f6 29.♕d2 ♖a6** [Not an impressive manoeuvre] **30.♘d4 ♘d3 31.♘xd3 cxd3 32.♗xd3?!** [32.e6! followed by 33.♕xd3 was immediately winning] **32...♕b8 33.♕f4 ♖f6 34.♕g3 ♖b6 35.b4 axb4 36.axb4 ♗xd4 37.cxd4 ♗d5 38.♖c1 ♖c8 39.♗f5 ♖c4 40.♕f4 ♖bc6** [Black should play 40...♕d8 followed by ♕g5, but it is still not pleasant] **41.♗d3 ♖xc1 42.♖xc1 ♕b7 43.♗f1 ♖xc1 44.♕xc1 ♕d7 45.♕c5 ♕f5** [45...♗c6 is better. Black cannot save the queen ending] **46.♕xd5**

♕xf1 **47.♕a8+ ♔h7 48.♕e4+ ♔g8 49.♕a8+ ♔h7 50.♕e4+ ♔g8 51.d5 ♕c4** [The pawn ending seems to be drawn...] **52.♕xc4 bxc4 53.d6** [... but it isn't. After the forced 53...♔f8 Black gets mated after 54.b5] **1-0**

Magnus Carlsen
Evgeny Tomashevsky
Wijk aan Zee 2016 (6)

1.d4 ♘f6 2.♘f3 e6 3.♗f4 b6 4.e3 ♗b7 5.h3 ♗e7 6.♗d3 0-0 7.0-0 c5 8.c3 ♘c6 9.♘bd2 d5 10.♕e2 [The World Champion plays the standard moves, including h2-h3. Although it looks innocent, Black has not achieved full equality yet] **10...♗d6** [An interesting idea. Black spends an extra tempo to exchange bishops. Perhaps 10...♘h5 11.♗h2 ♗d6 12.♗xd6 ♕xd6 is a better way to do this] **11.♖fe1 ♘e7** [11...♗xf4 12.exf4 cxd4 13.♘xd4 ♘xd4 14.cxd4 ♕d6 15.g3 is better for White. Note that 11...♘h5?! is not a good idea. White can play 12.♗xh7+ ♔xh7 13.♘g5+ ♔g6 14.♕d3+ f5 15.dxc5 bxc5 16.♘xe6 ♕d7 17.♘xf8+ ♖xf8 18.♗xd6 ♕xd6 19.g4 and the attack continues] **12.♖ad1 ♘g6?!** [Now White has an instructive method to claim a clear edge]

13.♗xg6! hxg6 14.♗xd6 ♕xd6 15.♘e5 [This type of position occurs a lot in this opening, but this is a good version for White. Because of the double pawn on g6 and g7 Black is unable to chase away White's powerful knight] **15...g5** [Black sees an attack coming and tries to prevent 16.f4, but White plays it anyway – and it is really strong] **16. f4! gxf4 17.♖f1!** [The logical follow-up because 17.exf4 cxd4 18.cxd4 ♖ac8 gives Black to much counterplay along the open c-file] **17...♘d7** [17...fxe3 is very dangerous. White gets excellent attacking chances after 18.♖xf6 exd2 (after 18...gxf6 19.♕g4+ ♔h7 20.♖f1! White can checkmate his opponent even quicker) 19.♖xd2!, but it may be the best way to proceed. Black should play the cool 19...♕e7 (19...gxf6 20.♕g4+ ♔h7 21.♖f2 is mate in six!) 20.♖f4 ♕g5 21.♖g4 ♕h6 and White has an edge, but it is not decisive yet] **18.♕h5 ♘f6** [18...♘xe5 19.dxe5 ♕e7 20.♖xf4 followed by ♖h4 and 18...g6 19.♕h6 ♘xe5 20.♖xf4 g5 21.dxe5 ♕xe5 22.♖g4 are both winning for White] **19.♕h4 ♕d8** [19...fxe3 is not a viable alternative anymore. White's queen is much better placed on h4 than on e2: 20.♖xf6! gxf6 (or 20...exd2 21.♖xd2) 21.♕g4+ ♔h7 22.♖f1 exd2 23.♖f4 and mate is inevitable] **20.♖xf4 ♘e4?** [Black is obliged to move the knight, but he should exchange on d4 first] **21.♘xe4 ♕xh4 22.♖xh4 dxe4 23.dxc5** [Now White's rook enters the black position, winning at least a pawn] **23...bxc5 24.♖d7 ♖ab8 25.b3 a5 26.♖c7 a4 27.bxa4** [Black has to do something, but the a-pawn turns out to be an important asset] **27...♗a8 28.a5 ♖b7 29.♖xc5 ♖a7 30.♘c4** [Here Black resigned a bit prematurely, but he had apparently had enough. Again

a very successful London game by the World Champion!] 1-0

Move Order

Gata Kamsky
Wang Yue
Beijing blitz 2013 (12)

1.d4 ♘f6 2.♗f4 e6 3.e3 c5 4.c3 ♘c6 5.♘d2 d5 6.♗d3 [Kamsky likes to vary the move orders. Postponing ♘f3 gives White additional opportunities] **6...♗d6 7.♗xd6 ♕xd6**

8.f4 [Very nice. If Black doesn't act quickly, White gets an easy advantage after 9.♘gf3 and 10.0-0] **8...cxd4 9.cxd4**

♗d7 [9...♘b4 10.♗e2 ♕b6 11.♕b3 ♗d7 12.a3 ♘c6 13.♖xb6 axb6 gave an approximately equal position in the game V.Kovacevic-Beliavsky, Plovdiv 1983] **10. a3 0-0 11.♘gf3 ♘e7 12.0-0 ♗c6 13.♘e5** [White has a comfortable edge] **13...♘d7 14.♕h5 f5 15.♘xd7** [Of course he takes the knight] **15...♕xd7 16.♘f3 ♕e8 17.♕xe8 ♖fxe8 18.♖fc1 ♖ec8 19.h3 ♗e8 20.♘e5 ♘c6 21.♔f2 ♘xe5 22.dxe5** [Again White has a good bishop against a bad one for Black] **22...♔f8 23.g4 g6 24.♔g3 a5 25.h4 h5?** [This looks suspicious. Now White gets the g-file to work with. In addition, pawn h5 is weak] **26.gxh5 gxh5 27.♔f2 a4** [All pawns on the light squares?] **28.♔e2 ♖c6 29.♔d2 ♖ac8 30.♖c3 ♖xc3 31.bxc3 b5 32.♖g1 ♖c7 33.♗e2 ♖g7?** [If Black stays passive, it is not easy for White to make progress, for instance: 33...♖e7 34.♖g5 ♖h7 35.♔d3 ♔e7 36.♔d4 ♔f8 37.♔c5 ♖c7+ 38.♔b4 ♖c6 and White cannot take on b5, while taking on h5 gives Black enough counterplay: 39.♗xh5 ♖c4+ 40.♔a5 ♗xh5 41.♖xh5 ♖xc3 42.♔xb5 ♖xa3] **34.♖xg7 ♔xg7 35.♔d3** [And White marches into Black's position with devastating force] 1-0

Exercise 1

position after 12.♕d1-b1

How does Black gain control of e4?
(solution on page 252)

Exercise 2

position after 14.♖a1-d1

What should Black play: 14...♕e8, 14...♕e7 or 14...♕f6 ?
(solution on page 252)

Exercise 3

position after 12...♕d6xc5

What is the logical result after ♗xh7+: 1-0, draw or 0-1?
(solution on page 253)

English Opening

The Old and the Young

by Mihail Marin and Valentin Stoica (special contribution by Wesley So)

1.	c4	e5
2.	♘c3	♘f6
3.	g3	♝b4
4.	♝g2	0-0
5.	e4	

Henrique Mecking

During their frequent chats about the perennial issue of the relationship between classical and modern chess, the authors of this Survey usually adopt diametrically opposed positions. Somewhat surprisingly, the more experienced (and supposedly more traditionalist) one thinks that chess has progressed a lot due to computers, while the younger one, staying far from a revolutionary approach, continues searching for inspiration in what he considers to be the golden era of chess, somewhere between the 1950s and '80s.

One of the central questions of our debates is whether the engines can cause abrupt changes in the evaluation of classical lines, overshadowing the knowledge accumulated over decades and opening a completely new, really 'correct' direction for analytical investigation and practical rehearsal. The variation examined in this Survey is quite illustrative.

The tabiya depicted in the above diagram was submitted to intensive practical testing in the early '70s, with such great names as Kortchnoi with white, Portisch on both sides and Mecking with black. Due to Black's good results, the variation based on 5.e4 soon disappeared from top-level tournaments.

The younger author has recently tried to breathe some new life into White's traditional plans, but the latest discovery seems to prove that even though it was wearing the seal of some of his favourite players, his area of research was not necessarily the best. The purpose of this article is to review the classical perception of this set-up, with frequent insertions from recent practice between the old games, in order to allow us to understand the merits of the truly star game.

What strikes the eye in the above position is the weakness of the d4-square. The natural plan for Black is to occupy it with ...♘c6, ...♝c5 and ...♘d4, but this allows White to attack on the kingside with f2-f4-f5.

Paradoxically, one of the most illustrative games for the dangers awaiting Black in such cases is Jobava-Mchedlishvili, featuring a completely different line, in which White plays e2-e4 at a much later stage. For a brief review of the 5.e4 ♘c6 set-up we have chosen the game Byrne-Portisch.

Even though things are not entirely clear in the above line, Black is best advised to try and achieve an early pawn break in the centre in order to exploit White's slight delay in development. True, 5...c6 6.♘ge2 d5 does not offer Black enough compensation, as can be seen in the game Kortchnoi-Taimanov, so Black usually starts with 5...♝xc3, giving White an important choice between 6.dxc3 and 6.bxc3. Since our main game features the latter move, we will start with examining the former.

Clearing the d-File

Since 6.dxc3 clears the d-file for the white queen, Black cannot think of a successful break with ...c7-c6 and ...d7-d5, so play continues 6...d6 7.♕e2, defending e4 and preparing ♘g1-f3, possibly followed by ♘f3-h4-f5.

How should Black continue? The stereotypical 7...♘c6 lacks flexibility, transposing to a reversed Rossolimo Sicilian with two important differences. Being a tempo down, Black will be slow carrying out the plan ...♗e6, ...♕d7 and ...♗h3. In addition, he has already castled kingside, making the attack based on ...h7-h5 ineffective. At the same time, White's pressure along the d-file could become telling. See Markowski-Strzemiecki. The attempt to stabilize on the dark squares with ...a7-a5, followed by ...♘d7-c5, has similar drawbacks, as we see in Marin-Louis.

Black's main plan is to undermine White's control in the centre with ...a7-a6 and ...b7-b5. True, the consequences of rushing this

idea (7...a6 8.♘f3 b5) are not necessarily annoying for White. In Kortchnoi-Kuzmin, White chose to radically change the structure with 9.c5!?, while in Miezis-Krasenkow he ignored the tension with 9.0-0. In both games the evaluation hovers between a slight advantage for White and equality.

The most consistent idea is to prepare the pawn break with ...♘b8-d7-c5, as in Kortchnoi-Mecking. White did not find anything better than keeping control of d5 with b2-b3 (... bxc4, bxc4), leading to a complex position with some space advantage for White to compensate for the relative weaknesses.

More Ambitious

Optically, 6.bxc3 looks like the more ambitious recapture.

White strengthens his control in the centre, and if he is allowed to complete his development with d2-d3, ♘f3 and 0-0, he has every reason to claim a long-term advantage. True, Black can still go for ...a7-a6 and ...b7-b5, but with accurate play White should keep his initiative, as in Marin-Vuilleumier.

However, Black does not need to be so 'cooperative'– he can start

active play in the centre with 6...c6. Practice has shown that after 7.♘e2 d5 White is by no means better. In fact, he should play energetically in order to avoid getting the worst of it. See Li-Wang. The same applies to the attempt of delaying Black's counterplay with 7.♕b3, which is a premature queen development, as in Portisch-Mecking.

After all the decades that have passed since the 5.e4 set-up started being tested at top level, the evidence speaks strongly against 6.bxc3. This is a bit confusing, since strategically this should be the way to go. The missing dot on the 'i' was added in the featured game Giri-Anand, in which the Dutch super GM played 7.♘f3. This is surely the most logical move, as it develops the knight to the best square, putting pressure on the black centre. In the past, players were probably put off by the fact that the e4-pawn is hanging, but any reasonably strong computer puts the move in its top-3 list. Remarkably, even such a well-prepared player as Anand was caught by surprise and went down rather quickly.

Conclusion

It is too early to give a definitive evaluation of the stunning new move 7.♘f3, but it surely makes the best of White's positional potential after 6.bxc3. Oh, and the younger author sees no reason to deny that on this occasion his colleague's perception about the progress of our favourite game was more accurate...

Weakness of the d4-Square

Baadur Jobava
Mikheil Mchedlishvili
Tbilisi 2007 (9)

1.c4 e5 2.♘c3 ♘f6 3.♘f3 ♘c6 4.g3 ♘d4 5.♗g2 ♘xf3+ 6.♗xf3 ♗b4 7.0-0 0-0 8.♗g2 h6 9.d3 ♖e8 10.e4 d6 11.f4 c6 12.♔h1 ♗c5 13.♖b1 a6

14.f5 b5 15.g4 b4 16.♘a4 ♗d4 17.g5 hxg5 18.♗xg5 c5 [18...♗f8 19.♖f3 ♔e7 20.♖h3 △ ♖h7] 19.♕e1 ♗d7 [19...♔f8 20.♘c3!?] 20.♕h4+− ♗xa4 21.♖f3 ♗d7 [21...♗f8 22.♕h8+ ♔e7 23.♕xg7+−] 22.♖h3 ♔f8 23.♕h8+ ♘g8 24.♗xd8 ♖exd8 25.♖h7   1-0

Donald Byrne
Lajos Portisch
San Antonio 1972 (3)

1.g3 e5 2.c4 ♘f6 3.♘c3 ♗b4 4.♗g2 0-0 5.e4 ♘c6 6.♘ge2

6...♗c5 7.0-0 d6 8.d3 [8.h3 a6 (8...♘d4 9.d3 c6 10.♔h1 ♘e8 11.♘xd4 ♗xd4 12.♘e2 ♗b6 13.d4 ♕e7 14.♗e3 ♘f6 15.♕d3 ♖e8 16.♘c3± Portisch-Ree, Wijk aan Zee 1969) 9.♔h2 ♖b8 10.a3 b5 11.b4 ♗a7 12.d3 ♘d4 13.f4 exf4 14.♗xf4 ♘d7 15.cxb5 (15.c5 dxc5

16.♘xd4 cxd4 17.♘d5 c6 18.♗xb8 ♗xb8 19.♘f4 ♘e5♔) 15...axb5 16.a4 ♘xe2 17.♘xe2 bxa4 18.♖xa4 ♗b6 19.d4 ♗b7 20.♘c3 ♕f6 21.b5 ♕g6 22.♗f3 ♗f6 23.♖e1 (23.e5 dxe5 24.♗xe5=) 23...♖fe8 24.d5 ♘d7 25.♖f1 ♕f6 26.♕d2 ♘e5♔ Hartoch-Portisch, Amsterdam 1971] 8...a6 [8...♗g4 9.h3 ♗xe2 10.♘xe2 ♘d4 11.♔h2 c6 12.f4 ♘d7 13.f5 f6 14.h4 b5 15.g4 ♘xe2 16.♕xe2 a5 17.♗f3 ♕e7 (½-½ Voloshin-Laznicka, Brno 2006) 18.cxb5 cxb5 19.♖g3] 9.h3 ♖b8 10.a3 b5 11.b4 ♗a7 12.♘d5 ♘xd5 [12...h6 13.♗e3 ♗xe3 (13...♘d4 14.f4) 14.♘xe3 ♗d7 (Murray-Ree, Vancouver 1971) 15.d4!?] 13.cxd5 ♘e7 14.d4± f5 15.dxe5 dxe5 16.♕b3 ♔h8 17.♗e3 ♗xe3 18.fxe3 fxe4 19.♘c3 ♗b7 20.♖xf8+ ♕xf8 21.♗xe4 ♘g8 22.♗g2 ♘f6 23.e4 ♕d6 24.♔h2 h6 25.♕b2 ♖f8 26.♕e2 ♕b6 27.♖f1 ♗c8 28.♖f3 ♗d7 29.♘d1 ♖e8 30.♘f2 a5 31.♕b2 axb4 32.axb4 ♕d6   ½-½

Early Pawn Break in the Centre

Viktor Kortchnoi
Mark Taimanov
Leningrad 1973 (3)

1.c4 e5 2.♘c3 ♘f6 3.g3 ♗b4 4.♗g2 0-0 5.e4 c6 6.♘ge2

6...d5 7.cxd5 cxd5 8.exd5 [8.♘xd5 ♘xd5 9.exd5 ♗f5 10.0-0 ♘d7 11.d3 (11.d4!?) 11...♖e8 12.♗e3 ♘f6 13.♕b3 a5 Ivkov-Ree, Amsterdam 1968 =/∞ Kortchnoi] 8...♗f5 9.d4! [9.a3 ♗c5 10.b4 ♗d4 11.d3 ♘g4 12.♗d2 a5♔ Arutinian-Galstian, Moscow 2004; 9.0-0 ♗d3♔ Kortchnoi] 9...e4 10.♗g5 [10.0-0 ♘bd7 11.h3 h6 12.♕b3 ♕a5 13.a3 ♗xc3 14.♘xc3 ♘b6 15.♗d2 ♕a6

16.♖fc1 ♕c4 17.♕d1 ♗fxd5 18.♘xe4 ♕xd4 (Speelman-Pritchett, Brighton 1972) 19.♗b4 ♕xd1+ 20.♖xd1 ♘xb4 21.axb4 ♖ad8 22.♘c5±] 10...♘bd7 [10...♕xd5 11.♗xf6 gxf6 12.0-0± Kortchnoi] 11.♕b3 ♕b6 12.0-0 h6 13.♗f4! [13.♗xf6 ♘xf6 14.a3 ♗a5 15.♕a2 ♕d6 Kortchnoi] 13...♖fe8 14.♘a4 ♕a5 15.a3 ♗f8 16.♘ec3 g5 17.♗e3 ♖ac8 18.♖fc1± ♘g4 19.♕xb7 ♖b8 20.♕c6 ♖ec8 21.b4 ♖xc6 22.bxa5 ♖a6 23.♗xe4 ♗xe4 24.♘xe4 ♖xa5 25.♘ac5 ♘xc5 26.dxc5 f5 27.♗d2 ♖a4 28.♘d6 ♖d4 29.♗b4 ♖xd5 30.♖d1 ♘f6 31.c6 ♗xd6 32.♗xd6 ♖c8 33.c7 ♔f7 34.♖xd5 ♘xd5 35.♖e1 ♔f6 36.f4 gxf4 37.♖e5 ♘b6 38.♖c5 fxg3 39.♗xg3 h5 40.♔f2 ♔e6 41.♖e5+ ♔f6 42.♖a5 ♔e6 43.♖xa7 ♔d7 44.♖a5 ♖f8 45.♗f4 ♔c6 46.♖e5 ♔b7 47.♖b5 ♔c6 48.a4 ♖a8 49.♔f3 ♖f8 50.♖b4 ♖e8 51.a5 ♘c8 52.♖d4 ♗b7 53.a6+   1-0

Clearing the d-File 6.dxc3

Tomasz Markowski
Zbignieuw Strzemiecki
Warsaw 2012 (4)

1.c4 ♘f6 2.♘c3 e5 3.g3 ♗b4 4.♗g2 ♗xc3 5.dxc3 d6 6.e4 0-0 7.♕e2 ♘c6 8.♘f3 h6 9.0-0 ♘h7?! [9...♗e6 10.♖e1 ♕d7 11.♘c2 ♗h3 12.f3 ♗xg2 13.♔xg2 ♘d8 14.♗e3 ♘e6 15.b3 a5 16.♗a3 b6 17.♖ad1 △ ♗c1, ♘f5/d5]

10.♘h4 ♗e6 11.♗e3 ♕d7 [11...b6 12.♘f5 ♕d7?! 13.♘g4 ♗xf5 14.exf5 ♘f6 15.♕h4 e4 (15...♘h7 16.♗xh6 gxh6 17.f6±) 16.g4 (16.♗xh6 ♕xf5) 16...♘e6 17.h3± ♘c4? 18.♗xh6!] 12.c5± g5?!

13.♘f5 [13.f4!? exf4 (13...gxh4 14.f5→; 13...♗g4 14.♘f3±) 14.gxf4 gxh4 15.f5 ♔h8 16.♔h1 ♗g8 17.cxd6 ♕xd6 18.♖ad1 ♕e5 19.fxe6 ♖xe6 20.♕h5↑] 13...♗xf5 14.exf5 ♕xf5 15.cxd6 [15...♔b5 ♖ab8 16.cxd6 cxd6 17.♖ad1 ♘g6 18.♖d2 ♖fd8 19.♖fd1↑] 15...cxd6 16.♖fd1?! [16.♖ad1 ♖ad8 17.f4 (17.♖d2!? e4?! 18.f3↑) 17...gxf4 (17...exf4 18.gxf4 g4 19.♘d5↑) 18.♔b5 (18.gxf4 e4) 18...♕h5 (18...♕g6 19.gxf4 e4 20.f5±) 19.gxf4 ♘f6 20.♖d2↑] 16...♖ad8 17.♖d2 ♘f6 [17... e4 18.♖ad1 d5] 18.♖ad1 d5 [18...♕e6 19.h4↑] 19.♗xd5 ♘xd5 20.♖xd5 ♖xd5 21.♖xd5 ♖d8 22.♖xd8+ ♘xd8 23.♗xa7 ♘c6 24.♗e3 e4 [24...♕b1+ 25.♔g2 ♕xa2 26.♕b5±] 25.♔g2± ♘e5 26.h3 ♘d3 27.♔b5 b5 28.♕g4 ♕d5 29.c4 bxc4 30.♕c8+ ♔h7 31.♕xc4 ♕f5 32.♔g1 ♕f3 33.g4? [33.♗d4± ♘e1 34.♕f1 ♕d1? 35.♗c3 ♘f3+ 36.♔g2 ♘h4+ (36...♔d7 37.♕c4 ♕f5 38.a4+−)] 33...♘e1 34.♕f1 ♕d1= 35.f4 [35.a4 ♘f3+ 36.♔g2 ♘h4+ 37.♔g1=] 35...♘f3+ 36.♔f2 ♕c2+ 37.♕e2 ♕c3 38.fxg5 hxg5 39.♔f1 ♕a1+ 40.♔g2 ♘h4+ 41.♔f2 ♘f3 [△ ...♕g1] 42.♔g2 ♘h4+ 43.♔f2 ♘f3 44.♔g2 ♘h4+ ½-½

Mihail Marin
Thibault Louis
Helsingor 2015 (3)

1.c4 ♘f6 2.♘c3 e5 3.g3 ♗b4 4.♗g2 0-0 5.e4 ♗xc3 6.dxc3 d6 7.♕e2 a5 8.♘f3 ♘bd7 9.0-0 ♘c5 10.♘h4 ♖e8 11.b3 c6 12.♗a3 ♕e7 [12...g5 13.♖ad1!? (13.♘f5 ♗xf5 14.exf5 e4∞) 13...♘cxe4 (13...♕e7 14.♘f5 ♗xf5 15.exf5 e4 16.f3!?) 14.♗xe4 ♘xe4 15.♕xe4 gxh4 16.♖xd6 g5 17.♗c1 ♕g4 18.♕e3±] 13.♖ad1 g6 [13...♗g4 14.f3 ♗e6 15.♘f5 ♗xf5 16.exf5 ♖ad8 17.♖d2±]

14.♖d2 [△ ♖fd1, f2-f3, ♗f1, ♘g2-e3] 14...b5?! 15.cxb5 cxb5 16.♖fd1 ♗b7 [16...♗a6 17.♕e3 ♖ed8 (17...♗g4 18.♕f3 ♘f6 19.♖xd6 ♘fxe4 20.♕e3+− with pressure on ♘c5, ♘e4) 18.f3 (18.♗g5 ♕h8 19.♗xc5 dxc5 20.♖xd8+ ♖xd8 21.♖xd8+ ♕xd8 22.♕xe5 ♕d1+ 23.♗f1 ♔g7 24.♔g2±) 18...♖ac8 19.♗f1 ♗g7 20.♘c4 ♕e8 18...♖xc5 21.♖d6! ♖xc3 22.♘f5+!!) 21.♕g5 ♔f8 22.♖xd8+ ♖xd8 23.♖xd8+ ♕xd8 24.♕xe5±] 17.f3 ♗a6 18.♕e3± [With pressure on ♘d6] 18...♖ed8 19.♗f1 ♖ac8 20.♘g2 [20.♗xc5 ♖xc5 (20...dxc5 21.♖xd8+ ♖xd8 22.♖xd8+ ♕xd8 23.♕xc5±) 21.♖xd6± ♖xc3? 22.♖xd8+ with an attack] 20...♔g7 21.♖xd6!+− b4 22.♖xd8 ♖xd8 23.♖xd8 ♕xd8 24.cxb4 ♗xf1 25.♔xf1 ♕d1+ 26.♘e1 ♕e6 27.bxa5 g5 28.♗b2 ♕d6 29.♕b6+− 1-0

Viktor Kortchnoi
Gennady Kuzmin
Moscow 1973 (17)

1.c4 e5 2.♘c3 ♘f6 3.g3 ♗b4 4.♗g2 0-0 5.e4 ♗xc3 6.dxc3 d6 7.♕e2 a6 8.♘f3 b5

9.c5 ♗b7?! [9...dxc5 10.♘xe5 ♕e7 (10...♖e8 11.f4 ♗b7 12.0-0 ♘bd7 13.♖d1±) 11.f4 ♗b7 12.0-0 ♘bd7 13.♘xd7 ♘xd7 14.♖e1±; 9...♗e6 10.cxd6 cxd6 11.b3 (11.♕c2 h6 12.0-0 ♕c7 13.♘h4 ♘c6; 11.♗g5 ♗g4 12.f3 ♗d7; 11.0-0? ♗c4−+) 11...♘bd7 (11...♕c7 12.0-0 ♕xc3?! 13.♗a3⩱ ♖d8 14.♖fd1 ♕c7 15.♕d2 △ ♖xd6 15...♘xe4?! 16.♖ac1 ♕b6 17.♕e2 d5 18.♘xe5 ♘d7 19.♘c6 ♖e8 20.♗xe4 dxe4 21.♕xe4↑) 12.0-0 ♘c5 13.♘h4∞] 10.cxd6 cxd6 11.♘h4 d5 [11...♘bd7 12.♘f5 ♕c7 13.0-0 ♘c5 14.f3 ♗c8 15.♗g5 ♗xf5 16.exf5 ♘cd7 17.a4↑] 12.♗g5! h6 [12...dxe4 13.♖d1 ♕b6

14.♘f5↑] 13.♗xf6 ♕xf6 14.exd5 ♘d7 15.0-0 ♖fe8 [15...♘b6 16.a4!? ♘xa4 17.c4 ♘b6 18.b3±] 16.a4± bxa4 17.♖xa4 [17.♖fd1 ♘b6 18.♗e4 g6 19.♘g2±] 17...♘b6 18.♖a5 e4 [△ ...g7-g5] 19.d6!? [19.f3 ♘xd5 20.fxe4 ♘f4! (△ ...♘b6+ 20...♘b6+ 21.♕f2 ♔xa5? 22.♕xf7+ ♔h7 23.exd5+−) 21.♕f2 ♕xg2 22.♕xf6 gxf6 23.♔xg2 ♖xe4∞] 19...♖ad8?! [19...g6!, restricting the ♘h4] 20.♘f5!↑ ♘c8 21.♕e3 [21.♖d1 ♘xd6 22.♘e3±] 21...♘xd6 22.♕b6 ♘xf5 23.♗xb7 ♖b8 24.♕d5 g6 25.♗xe4 ♖bd8 26.♕c6 ♖e6 27.♕a4 ♘d4 28.♗g2 ♘e2+ [28...♘f3+ 29.♗xf3 ♕xf3 30.♖xa6 ♖e2 31.♖b6 ♖dd2±] 29.♔h1 ♖d2 30.♕a1 ♖b6 31.♖a2 h5 32.c4 ♖bxb2 33.♖xb2 ♖xb2 34.c5 ♔g7 35.c6 ♖c2 36.♗e4 ♖c5 37.♕xa6 ♘d4 38.♕a3 ♕e5 ½-½

Normunds Miezis
Michal Krasenkow
Bad Wiessee 2001 (4)

1.c4 e5 2.♘c3 ♘f6 3.g3 ♗b4 4.♗g2 0-0 5.e4 ♗xc3 6.dxc3 d6 7.♕e2 a6 8.♘f3 b5 9.0-0 [9.♗g5 ♘bd7 10.♘d2 h6 11.♗xf6 ♕xf6 12.0-0 (Damljanovic-Riff, Pamplona 2011) 12...♘b6; 9.♘d2 ♕e8 10.0-0 ♘c6 11.♖e1 ♗e6 12.♗f1 bxc4 13.♘xc4 ♘bd7] 9...bxc4

10.♖d1 ♘bd7 11.♕xc4 a5 12.♕e2 [12.♗e3 ♗a6 13.♕a4 ♕b8 14.♖d2 ♗b5 15.♕c2 ♗g4 16.♗g5 h6 17.h3 hxg5 18.hxg4 f6∓ V.Georgiev-Pelletier, Batumi 1999] 12...♗a6 13.c4 a4 14.♕c2 ♗b7 15.♘h4 ♖a6 [15...g6 16.f3 ♘c5 17.♗e3 ♕e7 18.b4 axb3 19.axb3±; 15...♘c5 16.♗e3 ♘e6 (16...♘cxe4 17.f3+−; 16...♘fxe4 17.f3+−; 16...♗xe4 17.♗xe4 ♘cxe4 18.f3+−) 17.c5↑] 16.♘f5 ♘c5

17.♗e3 ♘e6 18.c5 ♘g4 19.cxd6 ♘xe3 20.♘xe3 [20.fxe3! cxd6 21.♕d2, pressurizing the ♘d6] 20... cxd6 21.♗f1 ♖b6 22.♘c4 [22.♕xa4 ♘c5 23.♕a3 ♘xe4] 22...♖c6 23.♕xa4 ♘d4 24.♘a5 [24.♘e3!? △ ♖xd4‡] 24...♕a8 25.♕b4 ♖c2 [25...♖c7 26.♖xd4 exd4 27.♘xb7 ♕xb7 28.♕xd4⩲] 26.♖xd4 exd4 27.♘xb7 ♖b8 28.♕xd4 ♖xb7 29.b4♕ ♕a7 30.♖d1 [30.♕xa7 ♖xa7 31.a4 ♖b2 32.b5 ♖a5 33.♖c1 ♔f8 34.♖c4 ♔e7 35.h4!?±/=] 30...♕xd4 31.♖xd4 ♖xa2 32.e5 d5 33.♖xd5 g6 34.b5 ♖b2= 35.h4 ♖a7 36.♖d6 ♖a1 37.♔g2 ♖e1 38.♖d5 ♖c1 39.♖d6 ♖e1 40.♖d5 ♖c1 41.♖d6 ♔g7 [41...♖cc2 42.♖f6 ♖c5 43.e6=; 41...♖c5 42.e6 ♖f5 43.e7 ♖bxf2+ 44.♔h3 ♖e5 45.♖d8+ ♔g7 46.e8♕ ♖xe8 47.♖xe8 ♖xf1=] 42.h5? [42.♖d4 ♖cc2 43.♖f4 ♖c5 44.♗c4] 42...♖c5! 43.hxg6 hxg6 44.e6 ♖f5 45.♔g1 [45.e7 ♖bxf2+ 46.♔h3 ♖h5+ (46...♖e5‡) 47.♔g4 f5#] 45...fxe6 46.♖xe6 ♖fxf2‡ 47.♖e3 ♖fc2 48.♖f3 ♔h6 49.♖e3 ♖g5 50.♖e4 ♖c3 51.♗e2 ♖xg3+ 52.♔f2 ♖c3 53.♖e8 ♖cb3 54.♖e5+ ♔f4 55.♖e6 ♖f3+ 56.♔e1 ♖e3 57.♖f6+ ♔e4 58.♖e6+ ♔d4 59.♖d6+ ♔c3 60.♖c6+ ♔b3 **0-1**

Viktor Kortchnoi
Henrique Mecking
Augusta 1974 (1)

1.c4 e5 2.♘c3 ♘f6 3.g3 ♗b4 4.♗g2 0-0 5.e4 ♗xc3 6.dxc3 d6 7.♕e2 ♘bd7 8.♘f3 ♘c5 9.♘h4 a6 10.b3

10...b5 11.♗a3 ♘fd7 12.0-0 ♗b7 13.f3 [13.♘f5 g6 14.♘h6+ ♔g7 15.♗c1 bxc4 16.♕xc4 a5 17.♕e2 f5⇄] 13...♗c6 [13...g6!?, to restrict the ♘h4] 14.♘f5 [14.♖fd1 g6!? 15.♗h3

(15.♗f1 f5 16.exf5 g5) 15...♘e6=] 14... bxc4 [14...g6 15.♘e3] 15.bxc4 [15.♕xc4? ♗b5] 15...♘a4 16.♕d2 ♘dc5 17.♘e3 ♖e8 18.♖ad1 ♖b8 19.♘d5 ♗d7 20.♗b4 ♗e6 21.♖fe1 c6 22.♘e3 ♕b6 23.♕c2 [23.♖xd6? ♖bd8 24.♕xe5 ♘d3‡] 23...♖bd8 24.♗f1 [24.f4!?] 24...a5 25.♗a3 ♕c7 26.♖d2 ♖d7 27.h4 f6 28.♔h2 g6 29.♖ed1 ♖ed8 30.♖f2 ♖e8 31.♕d2 ♘b6 32.♔h1 ♘b7 33.♕c2 ♖ed8 34.h5 ♖g7 35.♖h2 [35.hxg6 hxg6 36.♖h2 △ ♗h3 36...♖h7 37.♖dd2 ♖dd7=] 35...gxh5 [35...♘c5 36.♗h3 ♗xh3 37.♖xh3 ♘ba4 38.♔g2± △ hxg6, ♖1h1] 36.♕f2 [36.♗h3! ♗f7 (36...♗xh3 37.♖xh3 ♖g5 38.♗c1; 36...♗xc4? 37.♘xc4 ♖xc4 38.♗e6++-) 37.♘f5 ♖g5 (37...♖xc4 38.♘xg7 ♔xg7 39.♗c1 d5 40.exd5 cxd5 41.g4↑) 38.c5 dxc5 39.♖xd8+ ♕xd8 40.♗xc5+) 40.♖d2 ♘c7 41.♗b1 ♗c4 42.♕g1±] 36...♘a4 37.♖c1 ♕f7 38.♗e2 [38.♗h3!? ♗xc4 39.♘f5 ♖g6 40.♕a7⩲] 38...♘ac5 39.♖h4 ♔h8 40.♖g1 ♖dg8 41.♗c1 f5↑ 42.exf5 ♗xf5 43.♘xf5 ♕xf5 44.♕h2 ♕c2 45.♖xh5 ♕xc3 46.♗h6 ♖f7 47.♖g5 ♖xg5 48.♗xg5 ♘e6 49.♗h6 ♕c2 50.♗d1 ♕xh2+ 51.♔xh2 ♘d4 52.♗g2 ♘c5 53.♗d2 ♘d3 54.♗c3 ♖b7? 55.f4! ♘b2 56.fxe5 dxe5 57.♗b3 a4 58.♗xb2 axb3 59.♖a1! bxa2 [59...♘c2 60.♖c1] 60.♖xa2 ♖b4 61.c5 ♖c4 62.♗xd4 exd4 63.♖a8+ ♔g7 64.♖d8 ♖xc5 65.♖xd4 ♖f5 66.g4 ♖f6 67.♖d7+ ♖f7 68.♖d6 ♖f6 69.♖d7+ ♔g6 70.♔g3 h6 71.♖a7 ♔g5 72.♖g7+ ♖g6 73.♖f7 ♖d6 74.♖f5+ ♔g6 75.♔h4 ♖f6 76.♖c5 ♖e6 77.♖f5 ♖e8 78.♖c5 ♖c8 79.♔g3 ♔f6 80.♖h5 ♖h8 ½-½

More Ambitious 6.bxc3

Mihail Marin
Alexandre Vuilleumier
Helsingor 2015 (5)

1.c4 e5 2.♘c3 ♗b4 3.g3 ♗xc3 [The relevant move order for our Survey is 3...♘f6 4.♗g2 0-0 5.e4 ♗xc3 6.bxc3

♘c6 7.d3 d6 8.♘f3, transposing back to the game] 4.bxc3 ♘f6 [4...♘e7] 5.♗g2 0-0 6.d3 ♘c6 [6...c6 7.♘f3±; 6...♖e8 7.e4 (7.♘f3 e4) 7...♘c6 8.♘f3 d5 9.cxd5 cxd5 10.exd5 ♘xd5⇄] 7.e4 d6 8.♘f3

8...a6 9.a4 ♘d7 10.♘h4 ♘c5 11.0-0 b6 12.f4 [12.d4 ♗b7 13.♘f5 ♘ca5 14.♖b1± ♗e6 (14...♘xc4? 15.♗h6! ♗xf5 16.exf5) 15.♕g4 g6 16.♗h6 ♖e8 17.c5 bxc5 18.dxe5 dxe5 19.f4↑] 12...♘a5 [12...exf4 13.♗xf4 g5 14.♘f5 ♗xf5 15.exf5 gxf4 16.♗xc6 fxg3 17.f6 ♔h8 18.d4 ♘e6 19.♕h5+-] 13.♖a2 f6 14.♘f5 ♗e6 [14...♗d7 15.fxe5 fxe5 16.d4 ♘cb3 17.♗a3±] 15.♘e3 [15.d4 ♗xc4 16.♕g4 g6∓; 15.♕g4 ♗xf5 16.exf5 ♘xd3∓] 15...b5 16.fxe5! [16.axb5 axb5 17.fxe5 dxe5 18.♗a3 ♘ab3!] 16...dxe5 [16...♘xa4 17.♖xa4 bxa4 18.♕xa4 (18.exd6 cxd6 19.♕xa4 ♕b6 20.d4) 18...♘b7 (18... c5 19.exd6 ♖b8 20.♘d5±) 19.exd6 cxd6 20.e5 ♘c5 21.♕d1±; 16...fxe5 17.♖xf8+ ♕xf8 18.axb5 axb5 19.♖f2 ♕e8 20.♘d5±] 17.♗a3 ♘xa4 [17...♘xd3 18.♗xf8 ♔xf8 19.axb5 axb5 20.♕e2 bxc4 21.♖fa1 c6 22.h4 ♘c5 23.h5 h6 24.♔h2±; 17...♗ab3 18.d4+-] 18.♗xf8 ♕xf8 19.♖c2?! [19.♕c2! ♕c5 20.♖e1±] 19...bxc4?! [19...♖d8!] 20.d4!± exd4 [20...♘b3!?] 21.cxd4 c3 22.e5 ♖d8 23.exf6 ♗b3 [23... gxf6 24.♖cf2 (24.♘g4 f5 (24...♗b3 25.♘xf6+ ♔h8 26.♕h5 ♗xc2 27.♕e5) 25.♖cf2+-) 24...♖b3 25.♕h5 (25.♗d5+) 25...♕e8 26.♕g4+ ♕g6 27.♕h4 ♕g5 28.♕e4+-] 24.fxg7 ♕xg7 25.♘f5 ♕g5 26.h4 ♗xc2 [26...♕f6 27.♕h5 ♔h8 28.♘h6 ♕xd4+ 29.♔h2 ♗xc2 30.♘f7+ ♔g8 31.♘xd8 ♕xd8 32.♗d5+ ♔h8 33.♕e5+] 27.♕xc2 ♕d2 28.♕xa4 c2 29.♕a2+ ♔h8 30.♕f7 **1-0**

Li Chao B
Wang Hao

Zaozhuang 2015 (6)

1.c4 e5 2.♘c3 ♘f6 3.g3 ♗b4 4.♗g2 0-0 5.e4 ♗xc3 6.bxc3 c6 7.♘e2

7...d5 8.cxd5 cxd5 9.exd5 ♘xd5 10.0-0 [10.d4 exd4 11.♕xd4 (11. cxd4 ♗g4 12.f3 ♗e6∓ 13.0-0 ♘c6 14.f4 ♗g4 15.♕b3 ♗xe2 16.♖f2 ♘b6 17.♗xc6 ♗c4, Steindorsson-Stefansson, Reykjavik 2005) 11...♗e6 12.0-0 (12. c4 ♘c6∓) 12...♕a5 (12...♘c6 13.♕c5 ♖e8 (13...♖c8 14.♖d1) 14.♗f4 (14.♖d1 ♕f6) 14...♘xf4 15.♗xf4 ♖c8 16.♕b5 ♕e7±) 13.c4 ♘c6 14.♕b2 ♘b6 15.c5 ♕xc5 16.♘f4♔, with pressure on b7 and the h1-a8 diagonal] **10...♘c6 11.♖b1** [11.d3 ♗g4 12.♗b2 ♕d7 13.♖e1 (Turov-Edouard, Wijk aan Zee 2013) 13...♖ad8∓; 11.d4 exd4 (11...♗g4 12.f3 ♗f5 13.g4 (13.c4 ♘db4∓; 13.dxe5 ♘xe5 14.f4 ♘d3) 13...♗g6 14.dxe5 (14.f4 exf4 15.♗xd5 ♕xd5 16.♘xf4 ♕d7) 14...♘xe5 15.f4 ♕b6+ 16.♔h1 ♘xg4 (16...♘d3 17.f5±; or 17.♗xd5±) 17.♕xd5 ♘f2+ 18.♖xf2 ♕xf2 19.♕f3 ♕e1+ 20.♕f1 ♕xf1+ 21.♗xf1 ♗d3∞/=) 12.♕d2!?N ♘xc3 (12...♖e8 13.♘xd4± 13.♗xc3 dxc3 14.♕xc3 ♗e6 (14...♘d4? 15.♖e1±; 14...♕d4 15.♕xd4 ♘xd4 16.♗a3 ♖e8 17.♗c5 ♘c6) 15.♖e1 (15.♗b2 f6 16.♖fe1 ♗f7 17.♖ad1 ♕c7 with the idea ...♖ad8) 15...♕d4 16.♕xd4 ♘xd4 17.♗xb7 ♖ab8 18.♗e4 f5 19.♗e3 ♖fd8 20.♗xd4 ♖xd4=] **11...♘b6** [11...♖b8 12.c4 (12.♗a3 ♖e8 13.♖b5 ♗e6 14.♕b1 ♕d7∓ Budnikov-Naumkin, London 1993; 12.d4 ♗g4) 12...♘b6 13.d3 ♗f5 14.♖b3 ♕d7 15.♗e3 ♖fd8 16.♗xb6 axb6 17.♗d5 ♘e7 18.♘c3 ♘xd5 19.♘xd5 ♗e6 20.♘xb6 ♕c6♔ Teske-Meins, Germany Bundesliga 2003/04]

12.d4 ♗e6 [12...♗f5?! 13.♖b5 (13.♖b3?! ♗e6 14.d5 ♗xd5 15.♗xd5 ♘xd5 16.♗a3 ♖e8 17.♖xb7 ♕c8∓, Nakamura-Carlsen, Oslo blitz 2009) 13... a6 (13...♕d7 14.dxe5 ♗d3 15.♖c5 ♖fe8 (15...♗a6 16.♕c2) 16.♗xc6 bxc6 17.♖e1 ♗e4 18.♘d4±) 14.♖b2 ♖b8 15.♕b3 ♘d7 16.dxe5 ♘cxe5 (16...♘c5 17.♕b6) 17.♖d2±; 12...exd4 13.♘xd4 ♘xd4 14.cxd4 ♗f5 15.♖b5 ♕d7 16.♖c5±] **13.a4** [13.♕d2 d5 14.dxe5 ♘xe5 15.♗xd5 ♘xd5 16.♘h1 ♕a5 17.c4 ♕xd2 18.♗xd2 ♘xc4 19.♖xb7 ♖fe8 20.♗e3 Ivkov-Olafsson, Wijk aan Zee 1971; 13.dxe5 ♘xa2 (13...♘xe5 14.♗xb7 ♖b8 15.♗g2 ♗xa2 (Zwardon-Zakhartsov, Pardubice 2012) 16.♖b5 f6 17.♗e3) 14.♗a3 ♖e8 15.♖b2 ♘c5 16.♗xd5 (16.♖d2? ♗xg2 17.♖xd8 ♖axd8∓) 16...♕xd5 17.♕xd5 ♘xd5 18.♖xb7 ♘xe5=] **13...♗d5** [13...♗c4 14.♖e1 ♕d7 15.♗a3 ♖fd8= Pribyl-Hecht, Bamberg 1972] **14.♖b5 ♗xg2 15.♔xg2 a6 16.♖c5** [16.♖b1 ♘c4 17.♗xb7 ♕d5+ 18.f3 ♖fd8♖] **16...♘d7 17.♖d5 ♗e7 18.♖d6 ♘c8 19.♖d5 ♘cb6 20.♖d6 ♘c4 21.♖d5 ♕c7∓ 22.dxe5 ♕c6 23.f3 ♘dxe5 24.♘f4 ♖fe8 25.♖e1 h6 26.h4 ♘g6 27.♖xe8+ ♖xe8 28.♘xg6 ♕xg6 29.♖d8 ♖xd8 30.♕xd8+ ♔h7 31.♕d5** ½-½

Lajos Portisch
Henrique Mecking

Petropolis 1973 (5)

1.c4 e5 2.♘c3 ♘f6 3.g3 ♗b4 4.♗g2 0-0 5.e4 ♗xc3 6.bxc3 c6 7.♗a3 ♖e8

8.♕b3 b6 [8...♗a6 9.♘e2 b6 10.0-0 ♗b7 11.c5 ♕c7 (11...♘xc5 12.♗xc5 ♗a6 13.♗d6 ♖e6 14.♖fe1 ♗xe2 15.♗xe5 ♖xe5 16.♖xe2 d5 17.d4 ♖xe4 18.♗xe4 dxe4 19.♖f1 ♕d6 20.f3±

Istratescu-Pelletier, Switzerland tt 2008) 12.cxb6 (12.♖fb1 ♘xc5 13.♗xc5 ♗a6 14.♕a3 ♗xe2 15.♗d6 ♕b7∞) 12... axb6 13.♖fb1 b5 14.c4 b4 15.♗xb4 c5 16.♗c3 ♗xe4=] **9.♖d1** [9.d3 ♗b7 10.♘f3 d5 11.♕d2 (Hübner-Christiansen, München 1992) 11...dxe4 12.♘xe4 ♘xe4 13.♗xe4 ♘d7 14.0-0 ♘f6 15.♖ad1 ♘xe4 16.dxe4 ♕g5 17.c5 ♗c8⇄; 9.♘e2 ♗b7 10.♗d6 ♖e6 11.♗xb8 (11.♕a3 c5 12.♗xb8 ♗xe4! 13.♗xe4 ♗xe4∓ (White will lose the ♗b8) Grigoriants-Sadvakasov, Subotica 2000) 11...♖xb8 12.0-0 d5∓ Bruzon Batista-Sadvakasov, Istanbul ol 2000; 9.♘h3 ♗b7 10.c5 h6 11.0-0 ♗a6 12.♖fe1 bxc5 13.♗xc5 d5= M.Sulyok-Chernin, Austria Bundesliga B 2007/08] **9...♗b7 10.♘e2 dxe4 12.dxe4 ♕c8 13.c5** [13.0-0 c5 14.f3 ♘c6∓ △ ...♘a5, with pressure on ♘c4] **13...♗a6 14.f3 ♘bd7 15.♗h3 ♕b7 16.♘c1 ♖ab8** [16...♕c7 17.cxb6 axb6 18.♗d6 ♕a7∓ with play on the a-file] **17.cxb6 ♘xb6 18.♗d6 ♖bd8 19.♔f2 ♗b5 20.♕c2 ♖xd6!?** [20...♗a4 21.♘b3 ♘c4 22.♗c5 ♘xa7 23.♖a8 24.♗e3 ♖eb8 25.♖he1 c5 △ ...♘a3, ...c5-c4 26.♗c1 ♘a5∓] **21.♖xd6 ♘c4 22.♖d3 ♕b6+ 23.♗g2 ♘e3+ 24.♖xe3 ♕xe3 25.♖d1= ♕b6 26.♕f2 ♕xf2+** [26...g6!?= △ ...♔g7] **27.♔xf2 ♔f8 28.♗f1 ♖xf1 29.♔xf1 ♗e7 30.♘d3 ♘d7 31.♖b1±/= 31...♖a8 32.♔e2 f6 33.♖b7 ♗d8 34.f4 ♗c8 35.♖b4 ♔c7 36.♖b1 ♖e8 37.♗f3 f5 38.♘f2 fxe4+ 39.♘xe4 exf4 40.gxf4 ♘b6 41.♖g1 ♗e7 42.h4 ♘d5 43.c4 ♘b6 44.c5 ♘d5 45.f5 ♔b7 46.♖b1+ ♔a6 47.♖b8 ♖e5 48.♘d6 ♘f6 49.♖b7 ♖xc5 50.♖xg7 ♖d5 51.♘c8 ♖xf5+ 52.♔g2 ♖f4 53.♖xa7+ ♔b5 54.♖f7 h5 55.♘a7+ ♔c5 56.a4 ♖g4+ 57.♔f3 ♘d5 58.♖f5 ♖xh4 59.a5 ♖h3+ 60.♔g2 ♖a3 61.♖xh5 ♖xa5 62.♘xc6 ♔xc6** ½-½

Anish Giri
Viswanathan Anand

Bilbao 2015 (4)

1.c4 e5 2.♘c3 [Against 2.g3, Vishy plays 2...c6, so I suppose White was trying to avoid exactly that] **2...♘f6 3.g3 ♗b4** [The typical reaction to 3.g3] **4.♗g2 0-0 5.e4** [I actually had this position recently, and I was Black. It went 5.♘f3 e4 6.♘d4 ♘c6 7.♘c2 ♗xc3 8.dxc3 h6 9.0-0 ♖e8 10.♘e3 d6 11.f3 ♘e5 12.b3 ♗d7 13.♕c2 exf3 14.exf3 ♕c8 with a very stable position. I won in 40 moves (Maghsoodloo-So, Baku 2015)] **5...♗xc3** [This is considered to be the standard reaction. White is not allowed to connect his forces with ♘ge2 and has to double his pawns. Looking at this line briefly, I wonder what is wrong with 5...d6 6.♘ge2 ♘c6 7.0-0 ♗c5 8.d3 a6 9.h3 (9.a4, to prevent ...b7-b5, deserves attention) 9...b5 10.cxb5 (10.b3 ♘d4) 10...axb5 11.♘xb5 ♗a6 12.♘ec3 ♖b8 13.a4 ♘b4 with an equal position. Probably both 5...♗xc3 and 5...d6 should be okay for Black] **6. bxc3 c6** [Less than a year earlier, in the Qatar Open, Shakhriyar Mamedyarov played this line (5.e4) against Anish: 6...♖e8 7.d3 c6 8.♘e2 (I'm sure White was planning an improvement somewhere. Perhaps here 8.g4!? d5 9.g5 ♘fd7 10.cxd5 ♘c5 11.♗e3 ♘ba6 with a very unclear game; or simply 8.♘f3) 8...d5 9.cxd5 cxd5 10.exd5 ♕xd5 11.♖b1 ♘c6 12.0-0 ♗g4 13.f3 ♗f5! 14.♖xb7 ♘b6 15.f4 e4 16.♕b3? (a blunder, but it was hard to defend already) 16...♗e6 17.♕b5 exd3 18.♖xb6 dxe2 19.♖e1 ♗c4! 20.♕xc6 ♕d1! 21.♔f2 ♖ad8 0-1, Mamedyarov-Giri, Doha 2014]

7.♘f3! [A new idea. It's a very nice move, and it's strong too. Now Vishy has to solve new problems over the board] **7...♘xe4** [7...d6 8.d3 is better for White. He can choose to open up the centre after finishing his development, and eventually make use of his bishop pair; 7... d5 8.exd5 e4 9.♘d4 cxd5 10.cxd5 ♕xd5

11.0-0 ♗g4 12.♕b3 ♕d7 and Black looks slightly worse here too] **8.0-0 d6** [8...♖e8 9.♖e1 and no matter what Black does, White will regain the pawn and retain his bishop pair] **9.♘xe5 dxe5!** [A good choice. Black might have some tempting options here but White is better after all of them and you can be sure that Anish has analysed them too. 9...♘xf2 fails due to 10.♖xf2 dxe5 11.♗a3 ♖e8 12.♖xf7! ♘d7 (12...♔xf7 13.♕h5+ ♔g8 14.♗e4 g6 15.♗xg6 hxg6 16.♕xg6+ ♔h8 17.♖f1 ♗e6 18.♖f6 and there is no more hope left for Black here) 13.♕h5 ♘f6 14.♖xf6 gxf6 15.♗e4 f5 16.♖f1 and White is clearly better; 9...♘xg3 10.fxg3 dxe5 11.♗a3 ♖e8 12.♖xf7 is the same as 9...♘xf2; and also 9...♘g5 10.♘g4 f5 11.f4; or 9...♘xc3 10.♗xf7; or 9...♘xd2 10.♘xf7 ♖xf7 11.♕xd2 favour White] **10.♗xe4 ♗e6?** [A blunder, and very uncommon for Vishy's usual precise and solid play. I assume that his first intention was 10...♘d7 11.d4 ♘f6, which is quite okay. Perhaps Vishy didn't like to defend a slightly worse position: 12.♗g2 exd4 13.cxd4 ♗g4 14.♕d2 ♖e8 15.d5. White still has some initiative, and it can be unpleasant to defend this over the board] **11.♗a3** [Suddenly Black is losing a pawn by force. I was watching this game, which was being played on the board beside me, and I remembered White had barely used 10 minutes on his clock. All preparation, I thought, but the fight would have been better if Vishy hadn't gone 10...♗e6?] **11...♖e8** [11...f5 12.♗xf8 fxe4 13.♗a3 does not give enough for the exchange; 11...♗xc4 12.♗xf8 ♗xf1 13.♗xg7! is also winning] **12.♕b1** [Maybe the move that Black missed] **12...♕xd2** [Desperation, but it doesn't work against Anish. 12...♘d7 was the lesser of evils. White can now take on b7 or go for 13.♗xh7+ ♔h8 14.♗f5 when White is a pawn up and the complications are in his favour after 14...♗xc4 15.♕xb7 ♗xf1 16.♖xf1 ♘f6 17.♕xf7 ♕xd2 18.♗e7 (also strong is 18.♗c1 ♕d5 19.♕g6) 18...♘d5 19.♗c5] **13.♕xb7 ♘d7 14.♗xc6 ♖eb8** [It's not easy to pick a good move in a bad position. Even after Black's

best option 14...♕xc3 White should be close to winning: 15.♗d6 ♖ad8 16.♖ac1 ♕d3 17.♖fd1 ♕f5 18.c5 and Black can hardly move. Alternatively, 14...♖ab8 15.♕xa7 ♕xc3 16.♗d6 doesn't help Black at all] **15.♕a6 ♖b6 16.♕a4 ♖c8 17.♖ad1 ♕xd1** [Black attempts to set up a fortress, which shouldn't work. Vishy is hoping for some kind of miracle] **18.♖xd1 ♗bxc6 19.♕xa7 ♖6c7 20.♕e3 ♖xc4 21.♗b4** [Consolidating the queenside. Now the a-pawn is ready to start running. From now on Anish starts to carefully nurse his advantage to a win] **21...h6 22.a4 ♘f6 23.♕xe5** [Even simpler was to push the passed pawn: 23.a5 e4 24.a6 ♘d5 25.♕d2, winning] **23...♖e4 24.♕a5 ♔h7** [24...♗b3 25.♖d8+ forces exchanges, and makes the conversion easier: 25...♖xd8 26.♕xd8+ ♖e8 27.♕c7 ♗xa4 28.c4 and White wins] **25.f3 ♖e2 26.♕b5 ♖a2 27.g4** [Slowly gaining space on the kingside and preventing ...♗h3 ideas. 27.a5 ♗h3 might look a little scary] **27...♖e8** [Or 27...h5 28.g5 ♘e8 29.a5 ♗h3 30.♕b7 and wins] **28.♗c5** [There is no need to rush, White carefully centralizes his bishop to d4. Any move should be good here as Black is simply too far behind in material] **28...♔g8 29.♖e1** [29.♗f2 ♖a8 30.♖d4 is also good enough] **29...♖a8 30.♗d4 ♖2xa4 31.h4** [31.♔f2 might be easier, to remove any back-rank problems] **31...♖a2 32.♕b1 ♗d5?** [A further mistake, but Black was very low on time. 32...♘d7 is most stubborn, though in the long run White should find a way to break through after 33.♕e4 ♘f8 34.h5] **33.♕f5 ♗e6 34.♕f4** [34.♖xe6 fxe6 35.♕xe6+ also wins. White has too many pawns. For example: 35...♔h8 36.♗xf6 gxf6 37.♕xf6+ ♔h7 38.h5 ♖2a6 39.♕f7+ ♔h8 40.♔f2 ♖c6 41.c4 ♖ac8 42.f4 ♖xc4 43.♕f6+ ♔h7 44.♕g6+] **34...♘d7 35.♖f1 ♘f8 36.♖f2** [Defending the second rank. Keep in mind that exchanges help the player who is up in material] **36...♖2a5 37.♕g3 ♗c4** [Here Black lost on time, but I don't think he can set up a fortress anyway after 38.♖b2] **1-0**

Exercise 1

position after 10...c7xd6

The e4-pawn is attacked and the positional threat ...d6-d5 is looming. How would you neutralize Black's apparent initiative?
(solution on page 253)

Exercise 2

position after 35...g6xh5

In this complex position with mutual weaknesses, White missed the strongest continuation. Can you do better?
(solution on page 253)

Exercise 3

position after 15...b6-b5

Black seems to have overtaken his opponent in the fight for the initiative, but White can stay on top. How?
(solution on page 253)

Looking for material from previous Yearbooks?

Visit our website *www.newinchess.com* and click on 'Yearbook'.
In this menu you can find games, contributors and other information from all our Yearbooks.
Surveys are indexed by opening, by author and by Yearbook.

Takacs' Underestimated Line

by Jan Timman (special contribution by Levon Aronian)

1.	c4	c5
2.	♘f3	♘f6
3.	♘c3	d5
4.	cxd5	♘xd5
5.	e4	♘b4
6.	♗c4	♘d3+
7.	♔e2	

Levon Aronian

In the Symmetrical English, if Black occupies the centre immediately with 3...d5, White has a choice after exchanging on d5: 5.g3, 5.d4, 5.e3, or the sharpest move 5.e4. This move was introduced by Alekhine in a game against Landau, Scarborough 1926. Landau withdrew his knight to c7, so we don't know what Alekhine had in mind against the crucial move 5...♘b4.

White has two options: Kholmov's 6.♗b5+, which was rather popular in the 1970s and 1980's, and 6.♗c4, which was introduced by Takacs almost half a century earlier. The Hungarian player Sandor Takacs (1893-1932) had only a short career. He started playing international chess when he was more than twenty, and died young. Takacs played the line with 6.♗c4 in 1928 against Spielmann, and a year later against Rubinstein. Since he won both games, it would be justified to call it 'The Takacs Variation'.

In his notes to his game against Topalov from the London Classic, 2015, Aronian observes that 6.♗c4 leads to more tactical play than the alternative 6.♗b5+. This is true, but if Black plays 6...♗e6, the game takes on quite a strategic nature. Black allows a serious disruption of his pawn structure in order to guarantee a firm outpost for his knight on d3. The line is complicated, with chances for both sides.

In this Survey I will concentrate on the line after 6...♘d3+ 7.♔e2. There are, in fact, few other openings in which the white king moves up at such an early stage. Black has two choices here:

A) The Old 7...♘xc1+

7...♘xc1+ is the old move that was played by both Spielmann and Rubinstein. Black goes for the bishop pair, hoping to finish his development. This is not so easy to accomplish, however. Nowadays this position is rare in tournament practice. Still, it is not easy to prove an advantage for White. After 8.♖xc1 Black has different choices:

1. Black Prevents the Push of the d-Pawn by 8...♘c6

Takacs reacted with 9.♕b3 in his game against Spielmann, but this is certainly not White's best option. Black will have to play ...e7-e6 anyway. The crucial move is 9.♗b5, as Botvinnik played against Rabinovich in Leningrad 1933 (7...♘xc1 8.♖xc1 ♘c6 9.♗b5; see the game Pelletier-Sutovsky in the Game Section).

2. Black Continues Kingside Development with 8...e6

This led to disaster in an old game Botvinnik-Kasparian, Leningrad 1938, and has hardly ever been played afterwards. Still, in a lot of cases it transposes to positions arising from Black's 3rd option.

3. Black Takes Square b5 from White with 8...a6

This is Rubinstein's choice, and most likely Black's best (9.d4 – see the game Takacs-Rubinstein).

B) The Modern 7...♘f4+

7...♘f4+ is the modern move, and by far the most popular one. After 8.♔f1 Black has to make a 5th consecutive knight move. Normally he withdraws it to e6, keeping firm control of square d4. An interesting alternative is to return with the knight to d3. It is the computer's first or second move, so it is surprising that it was not played before 2013. The idea of 8...♘d3 is that White has to move his queen to dislodge the knight, after which the push of White's d-pawn is not imminent (9.♕e2 – see the game Sutovsky-Nepomniachtchi).

So the most common move is 8...♘e6. In his comments for ChessBase, Ribli observes that both sides stand badly after this move: White because he has lost the right to castle, and Black because his knight on e6 is in the way. These are small problems that can be resolved, however. If White goes for the quiet 9.d3, Black should not have any opening problems. In Jakovenko-Svidler, Rhodos 2013, there followed 9...♘c6 10.h4 h5 11.♘g5 g6 12.♘xe6 ♗xe6 13.♗xe6 fxe6 14.♘e2 ♕d6, with equality.

White has two main moves here:

1. White Hinders Black's Development with 9.♘e5

This was first played by Averbakh against Bondarevsky, Moscow 1946. Black has various moves now. Giri tried 9...♘c6 against Nakamura in 2014, and after 10.♘xc6 bxc6 11.♘a4 he sacrificed a pawn with 11...♘d4. Aronian, in his comments, observes that Giri, despite being a pawn down, achieved his favourite result. A rather venomous remark which, actually, is not quite justified here; if you play like this with black, you are taking risks. Anyway, I can't really recommend the knight move. Reliable is 9...g6 (see Larsen-Timman, Bugojno 1984).

2. The 'Drunken Evans Gambit': 9.b4

The name was invented by Nigel Short. In fact this gambit is much more dangerous than the Evans Gambit. If Black turns down the offer, he has to sacrifice a pawn himself. It is not sure whether this gives him enough compensation (9...♗g7 – see Khairullin-Naiditsch). If Black takes the pawn, White has two good squares for the knight. If he withdraws it to e2, Black probably has to play his king's knight for the 7th time: the best square is c5 (9...cxb4 10.♘e2 ♘c5 – see the game Miles-Hort). Aronian threw his knight forward with 10.♘d5. After 10...g6 White again has two options. The first one is 11.♗b2, intending to exchange bishops and win back the pawn on b4. This was Seirawan's favourite (10.♘d5 g6 11.♗b2 ♗g7 12.♗xg7 ♘xg7 13.♘b4 – see the game Seirawan-Sax). Aronian chose the sharper 11.d4, establishing a strong centre. It is amazing that this position appeared only for the fourth time in tournament practice. Aronian's 13.♖c1 was new. In my view it is the most natural move (for 11...g6 12.♗e3 ♗g7 13.♕d2 see the game Piket-Van

Wely). Topalov was obviously surprised by White's opening choice. We will have to wait for further practical tests. First of all: what does White have in mind after 13...0-0, which is the natural way to develop? After 14.h4 Black has the reply 14...h5. The position is sharp, and full of strategic and tactical ideas. It should be noted that the knight on e6 is no longer a bad piece, as long as White's knight stands on d5. The centralized white knight is quite strong, although it is hindering further action, in a way.

Conclusion

The line introduced by Takacs leads to sharp play, both in a positional and in a tactical sense. Black can solve his opening problems if he knows what he's doing. The line with 7...♘xc1+ is certainly not as bad as its reputation. Nepomniachtchi's bold play against Jakovenko in particular needs further tests. The line in which the knight retreats to d3 has also hardly been played, but it seems that Black will be able to get a playable position. The fact that Caruana tried it with black is a clear sign that it is, in fact, a reliable method. If Black wants a real fight, he can opt for the line with 8...♘e6. Probably White's most promising line is the one in which he puts his knight on d5. As Aronian points out, Black can hold his own in that case. White normally opts for this line to get unusual positions, not primarily to get an opening advantage.

It is surprising that this variation is not played more often. We will have to await further practical tests before we will be able to draw more conclusions.

The Old 7...♘xc1+ 8...♘c6

Yannick Pelletier
Emil Sutovsky
Heraklio 2007 (1)

1.♘f3 ♘f6 2.c4 c5 3.♘c3 d5 4.cxd5 ♘xd5 5.e4 ♘b4 6.♗c4 ♘d3+ 7.♔e2 ♘xc1+ 8.♖xc1 ♘c6 9.♗b5! [It is important to pin the knight in the fight for the control of square d4]

9...♗g4 10.♕a4 ♕d7 11.♖hd1 [In Botvinnik-Rabinovich, White played the immediate 11.d4, which led to sharp complications after 11...cxd4 12.♘d5 ♖c8 13.♘b4 a6 14.♕xa6 (a better try for an advantage is 14.♗xc6 bxc6 15.♖xc6 ♖xc6 16.♕xc6 e5 17.♕a8+ ♔c8 18.♕xc8+ ♗xc8 19.♖c1 with some initiative) 14...e5 15.♘b8 and now Black should have played the cold-blooded 15...♖xb8! 16.♖xc6 bxc6 17.♗xc6 ♖xb2+ 18.♔d3 f6 19.♗xd7+ ♗xd7 20.♕a8+ ♔f7 when White has to find the ingenious 21.♖c1! ♗b5+ 22.♖c4 in order to equalize] **11...e5 12.♘d5 ♗xf3+** [Black could have waited with this exchange. More accurate was the immediate 12...♖b8] **13.♔xf3** [Pelletier wants to keep his kingside structure intact. Taking with the g-pawn was strong, because White has an interesting attacking plan: 13.gxf3 ♖b8 14.♖c3 ♗d6 15.♖d3 0-0 16.♖g1 f5 17.♘e3! and White is better] **13...♖b8 14.b3 ♗d6 15.♗xc6** [White could have kept the tension with 15.g3 with the idea ♔g2. He has a slight positional plus] **15...bxc6 16.♘e3 0-0 17.♖c4 ♗e7 18.♔e2 ♗g5!** [The best solution. Black is going to exchange the strong knight] **19.h3** [White has to control the g4-square. After 19.♖xc5 ♗xe3 20.fxe3 ♕g4+ Black is fine] **19...♖b5 20.♕a3 a5** [More accurate was 20. ...♖fd8] **21.♕c1 ♖d8 22.♕c3 ♗xe3 23.♕xe3 ♕e7 24.♖dc1 ♖d4**

25.a4 [White is content with a draw. By playing 25.f3! he could have kept a long-lasting edge] **25...♖b4 26.♖xb4 cxb4 27.d3**   ½-½

The Old 7...♘xc1+ 8...a6

Sandor Takacs
Akiba Rubinstein
Rogaska Slatina 1929 (6)

1.c4 ♘f6 2.♘f3 c5 3.♘c3 d5 4.cxd5 ♘xd5 5.e4 ♘b4 6.♗c4 ♘d3+ 7.♔e2 ♘xc1+ 8.♖xc1 a6 9.d4

9...cxd4 [In a rapid game Jakovenko-Nepomniachtchi, Moscow 2012, Black played the daring 9...b5 and after 10.♗d5 ♖a7 11.dxc5 e6 12.♗b3 (interesting is the piece sacrifice 12.♕d4, but after 12...exd5 13.exd5 ♗e7 Black seems to be OK) 12...♖d7 13.♕c2 ♗b7 14.♖hd1 ♖xd1 15.♘xd1 ♗e7 Black had sufficient compensation for the pawn. It is not easy to improve on White's play] **10.♕xd4 ♕xd4 11.♘xd4 e6 12.♘a4 ♘d7 13.♖hd1**

13...b5 [In Botvinnik-Kasparian, Leningrad 1938, Black played 13...♗e7? and after the obvious sacrifice 14.♘xe6 the great endgame composer resigned. This miniature

is quite well known and has not done the reputation of the 7...♘xc1+ line any good] **14.♘xe6!** [Also here this is White's best option] **14...fxe6?** [It is certainly not easy to refrain from taking anything if three of your opponent's minor pieces are en prise. Still, Black should have played the incredible 14...♖b8!, after which it is difficult to prove an advantage for White, e.g. 15.♘c7+ ♔d8 16.♗xf7 bxa4 17.e5 ♖xb2+ 18.♔f1 ♗a3 19.e6 ♖xf2+! and the game will finally peter out into a draw] **15.♗xe6 bxa4 16.♖xc8+ ♖xc8 17.♗xd7+ ♔d8 18.♗g4+** [The winning move] **18...♗d6 19.♗xc8** [I think that Rubinstein must have missed this move in his calculations. After 19.♖xd6+ ♔c7 a draw would have been the likely result] **19...♔e7 20.♗xa6 ♖b8 21.♖b1!** [The most accurate] **21...g5 22.b3 h5 23.♗d3 a3 24.♗c4 h4 25.h3 ♖f8 26.♖d1 ♖f4 27.f3 ♖f8 28.♖d5 ♗f4 29.♔d3 ♗c1 30.b4 ♖b8 31.♔c3 ♔f6 32.b5**   1-0

The Modern 7...♘f4+ 8...♘d3

Emil Sutovsky
Ian Nepomniachtchi
Poikovsky 2013 (4)

1.♘f3 ♘f6 2.c4 c5 3.♘c3 d5 4.cxd5 ♘xd5 5.e4 ♘b4 6.♗c4 ♘d3+ 7.♔e2 ♘f4+ 8.♔f1 ♘d3 9.♔e2 ♘f4+ 10.♔f1 ♘d3 11.♕e2 [After repeating the moves, Sutovsky decides to play for a win. Black is now forced to exchange on c1] **11...♘xc1 12.♖xc1 e6 13.h4** [Preparing to bring the rook to h3; a typical recipe in this type of position] **13...a6** [Also here Black prepares for the development of his knight by first controlling square b5]

14.e5 [An absolutely mandatory push. White needs the e4-square for his pieces] **14...♘c6 15.h5 h6 16.♖h3 b5 17.♗d3 ♗b7 18.♗e4 ♕b6** [It is not easy to say whether Black should develop his queen to d7 or b6. In many cases there will be a bishop swap on b7 later on, in which case it doesn't matter] **19.a4** [A thematic move. White is aiming to get square c4 for his knight] **19...b4 20.♘b1 0-0-0** [A very risky decision. The king is not very safe on the queenside. A better move was 20...a5 in order to relieve the pressure. Black can keep his king in the centre, aiming for the exchange of queens. At a later stage his king may be safe on the kingside] **21.d3 ♕a5 22.b3 ♕c7 23.♘bd2 ♔b8 24.♖g3** [More accurate was 24.♘c4. Now Black gets a chance to complicate matters] **24...♖g8** [Black decides to remain passive. It was difficult to calculate, but it was possible to take the e-pawn. After 24...♘xe5 25.♗xb7 ♘xd3 26.♗e4 ♘xc1 27.♕xa6 ♕a7 28.♕c4 f5 29.♘e5 ♖xd2 30.♕xc1 ♖d6 White is slightly better, although Black's position is defensible] **25.♗h7 ♖h8 26.♗e4 ♖g8 27.d4** [For unclear reasons Sutovsky decides to force matters. The pawn sacrifice doesn't yield the right result and gives away the advantage] **27...♘xd4 28.♘xd4 ♖xd4 29.♗xb7 ♕xb7 30.♖f3 g6** [Creating enough counterplay] **31.♘c4 gxh5 32.♘a5 ♕d5 33.g3** [Safer was 33.♔g1] **33...♗e7** [Now White has to undertake some quick action, otherwise Black will take over] **34.♖xa6!** [The start of a combination that will eventually lead to a draw] **34...♕xf3 35.♕b6+ ♔c8 36.♖xc5+ ♗xc5 37.♕xc5+ ♔d7 38.♕xd4+ ♔e8 39.♕xb4 ♕d1+ 40.♔g2 ♕d5+ 41.♔h2 ♕xe5 42.♘c4 ♖g4 43.♘d6+ ♔d7 44.♕b7+ ♔xd6 45.♕b8+ ♔d5 46.♕b5+ ♔e4 47.f3+** [The point of the combination. White wins back the rook] **47...♔f5 48.♕d3+ ♔f6 49.fxg4 hxg4 50.♕d2 h5 51.a5 ♔g6 52.a6 h4 53.a7 hxg3+ 54.♔g2 ♕h8 55.♔xg3 ♕h3+ 56.♔f2 ♕h2+ 57.♔e3 ♕g3+ 58.♔d4 ♕d6+ 59.♔e3 ♕g3+ 60.♔d4 ♕d6+ 61.♔e3 ♕e5+ 62.♔f2 ♕h2+ 63.♔e3 ♕g3+** ½-½

Bent Larsen
Jan Timman

Bugojno 1984 (3)

1.♘f3 ♘f6 2.c4 c5 3.♘c3 d5 4.cxd5 ♘xd5 5.e4 ♘b4 6.♗c4 ♘d3+ 7.♔e2 ♘f4+ 8.♔f1 ♘e6 9.♘e5 g6 [An alternative is 9...♕d6 10.f4 ♘c6 11.♕a4 and now Black lost quickly in Suba-Sax, Hastings 1983, after 11...♘ed8 12.d4. Better is 11...g6 and the computer believes that the position after 12.d4 cxd4 13.♘b5 ♕d8 14.f5 ♗g7 is playable for Black. I don't think that many people would volunteer to play this with black. 9...♘c6 is an anti-positional approach that has been played by both Ljubojevic and Giri. After 10.♘xc6 bxc6 White's simplest continuation is 11.d3 (White can also immediately go for the c5-pawn with 11.♘a4.

In Nakamura-Giri, Wijk aan Zee 2014, Black sacrificed a pawn by 11...♘d4. He did not have full compensation after 12.♘xc5 g6 13.♘b3 ♗e6 14.♗xe6 ♘xe6 15.♕c2. In a rapid game Piket-Ljubojevic, Monaco 2002, Black played 11...♕d6 12.d3 ♘d4 13.♗e3 e5. This may actually be acceptable for Black, since he can swing his queen to g6) 11...g6 12.♗e3 ♗g7 13.h4 h5 14.♖c1 with a positional plus for White (Anastasian-Yegiazarian, Yerevan 2007). 9...♕d4 was played in Averbakh-Bondarevsky, Moscow 1946. After 10.♕a4+ ♗d7 11.♘xd7 ♕xd7 White has a full extra tempo compared with the game Larsen-Timman. Best now was 12.♕xd7+ ♔xd7 13.b3 with an edge. Instead he went 12.♗xe6 fxe6 13.♕xd7+ ♔xd7 14.d3 ♘c6 ♘c6 with equality] **10.♕a4+ ♗d7 11.♘xd7 ♕xd7 12.♗xe6 fxe6 13.♕xd7+ ♔xd7**

14.d3 [In Vallejo-Fernandez, Dos Hermanas 2002, White chose an ambitious, but risky plan: 14.e5?! ♗g7 15.♘e4 b6 16.f4 ♖f8 17.d4 ♘c6 18.g3 and White got full compensation for the pawn. Stronger is 15...♗a6!, after which White has no time to execute his plan: 16.f4 ♖hf8 17.d4 cxd4 18.♔e2 ♖ac8 and the black rook will invade on c2] **14...♘c6 15.♗e3 b6 16.h4** [The best way. White is looking for active play on the kingside] **16...♗g7 17.h5 ♖af8 18.hxg6 hxg6 19.♔e2 ♗d4 20.♖af1 e5** [Strengthening the position in the centre] **21.♔d2 g5** [A strong move, after which it is clear that Black is fighting for the initiative. White cannot really take the g-pawn since after 22.♖xh8 ♖xh8 23.♗xg5 ♖g8, the black rook invades] **22.b3 ♗xc3+** [At the right moment. Otherwise White would move his knight to b5 or e2] **23.♔xc3 g4 24.♖xh8 ♖xh8 25.g3 ♘d4 26.a3 a5 27.♖a1 ♘e2+ 28.♔d2 ♘d4 29.♔c3 ♔d6 30.♔b2 b5 31.b4** [A good defensive measure. Larsen is already planning a positional exchange sacrifice] **31...cxb4 32.axb4 a4 33.♖c1 ♘b3 34.♖c3 ♔d7 35.♖xb3** [Guaranteeing the draw. White has a fortress] **35...axb3 36.♔xb3 ♖c8 37.♔b2 ♖c6** ½-½

Ildar Khairullin
Arkadij Naiditsch

Moscow 2009 (6)

1.♘f3 c5 2.c4 ♘f6 3.♘c3 d5 4.cxd5 ♘xd5 5.e4 ♘b4 6.♗c4 ♘d3+ 7.♔e2 ♘f4+ 8.♔f1 ♘e6 9.b4 g6 10.bxc5 ♗g7

11.♗xe6 [The principal continuation. White gives up the bishop pair to keep his pawn and build up a strong centre] **11...♗xe6 12.d4 0-0** [The position has become a kind of Grünfeld with an extra white pawn on c5, in which White has to endure more pressure than in a normal Grünfeld. Black has to take sharp measures to get compensation for the pawn. The main alternative is 12...♘c6. After 13.♗e3 Black has two possibilities:

A) 13...♗g4 14.♕e2 f5 15.h3 with a clear advantage for White in Seirawan-Miles, London 1982. In Navara-Naiditsch, Wijk aan Zee 2006, Black altered the move order: 12...♗g4. Navara played the unusual 13.♖b1 now, which was insufficient for an advantage. It is not entirely clear what Naiditsch intended to do after 13.♗e3. If 13...0-0 then 14.h3 is strong again, to take back with the pawn on f3;

B) 13...♗c4+ 14.♔g1 ♕a5. This was first played in a simultaneous game Kasparov-Shirov, USSR sim 1986. The game continued 15.♕d2 0-0-0 16.♖c1 f5 and Black was fine. Better is 15.♖c1 0-0-0 16.♘b1! as in Vallejo Pons-Leko, Linares 2003. Leko played 16...♕a6 but was clearly worse after 17.d5. Crucial was 16...♕xa2. Ribli now recommends 17.♘bd2 in ChessBase, but after 17...♗d3 18.d5 ♘b4 19.♘d4 f5! the game is unclear. Probably the direct 17.d5 is White's best, for example: 17...♘b4 18.♘d4 ♘d3 19.♖c2 ♘b2 20.♕e1 ♕a1 21.h4 ♗e5 22.c6! and White is better, although the position remains very sharp after 22...b5.

13.♗e3 f5 [A new approach. Black opens up the kingside to exert pressure on White's centre] **14.exf5 ♖xf5 15.h4** [The thematic move that is White's best option here] **15...♘c6 16.h5 ♕d7** [An interesting alternative was 16...gxh5 17.♔g1 ♕f8 to bring the other rook to

d8. It is not so easy for White to prove an advantage] **17.hxg6 hxg6 18.♕d2** [Inaccurate. The queen often has better squares at its disposal. White could keep an edge by the natural 18.♔g1] **18...♖af8 19.♖h4 ♕h5** [It is surprising that Naiditsch refrained from the obvious exchange sacrifice 19...♖xf3. After 20.gxf3 ♖xf3 21.d5 ♗h3+ 22.♔g1 ♘e5 Black has full compensation] **20.♖xh5 gxh5 21.♕d3** [Now White is better again] **21...♗f5 22.♕c4+ ♔h8 23.♖d1 e6 24.♖d2 ♘a5 25.♕b4 ♘c6 26.♕c4** ♕f7 [Black avoids a repetition of moves, but this doesn't mean that he is playing for a win. After 26...♘a5 Khairullin had probably planned 27.♕b4 ♘c6 28.♕a4 and White is better] **27.♘b5 ♗g4 28.♘d6 ♕g6 29.♕d3 ♕xd3+ 30.♖xd3 ♗xf3 31.gxf3 b6 32.cxb6** [White could have preserved better winning chances by keeping his passed pawn. The alternative 32.f4 gave good winning chances] **32...axb6 33.d5 ♘b4 34.dxe6 ♘xd3 35.e7 ♘b4 36.a4 ♘d5?** [The losing move. After 36...♖g8 37.e8♕ ♖xe8 38.♘xe8 ♘d5 could have easily held the endgame] **37.exf8♕+ ♗xf8 38.♘c4** [The winning move. Black must enter a hopeless knight ending] **38...♗c5 39.♔g2 ♔g7 40.♔g3 ♔f6 41.♔h4 ♔g6 42.♗xc5 bxc5 43.a5 ♘b4 44.♘e3 ♘a6 45.f4 ♘b4 46.f5+ ♔f6 47.♔xh5 c4 48.♘xc4 ♔xf5 49.♔h6 ♘e4 50.♘d2+ ♔d5 51.f4 ♘c6 52.♘b3 ♔c4 53.f5** 1-0

Anthony Miles
Vlastimil Hort
London 1983 (4)

1.c4 c5 2.♘f3 ♘f6 3.♘c3 d5 4.cxd5 ♘xd5 5.e4 ♘b4 6.♗c4 ♘d3+ 7.♔e2 ♘f4+ 8.♔f1 ♘e6 9.b4 cxb4 10.♘e2

10...♘c5 [The main alternative is 10...♘c7, which has appeared quite often in practice. After 11.d4 e6 12.h4 Black has the following options:

A) 12...♗d6 13.h5 (13.♗g5 looks stronger; after 13...f6 14.e5! ♗e7 15.exf6 gxf6 16.♗h6 White has very good compensation for the pawn) 13...h6 14.♖h4 ♘d7 15.♗b2 ♗e7 16.♖h3 ♘f6 with sharp play and chances for both sides (Hübner-Tukmakov, Wijk aan Zee 1984);

B) 12...b5 13.♗d3 ♗b7 14.h5 h6 15.♖h4 ♘d7 16.♗f4 a6 and Black was fine in Loginov-Van Wely, Moscow 2002. Again, 14.♗g5 was the right way to play, with excellent compensation;

C) 12...♘d7 13.♗g5! ♗e7 14.♖c1 ♘b6 15.♗d3 f6 16.♗f4 ♘a6 17.h5 0-0 18.♕b3 ♗d7 19.♘g3 and White had built up a promising attacking position in the simultaneous game Kasparov-Grunberg, Germany 1985]

11.♕c2 [In Giri-Kasimdzhanov, Zug 2013, White played the weaker 11.♘g3 and after 11...♗e6 12.♗xe6 ♕d3+! 13.♔g1 ♘xe6 14.♗b2 ♘c6 Black was better. It is important for White to control square d3] **11...e6 12.d4 ♘cd7 13.♗b2** [Also under these circumstances the alternative 13.♗g5 was probably preferable. After 13...♗e7 14.♗xe7 ♕xe7 15.♗xe6 0-0 16.♗b3 ♘b6 White has won back the pawn and kept his centre. Black has easy play, however. Chances are about even. The disadvantage of the text is that Black will have a quick queenside development] **13...♘b6 14.♗d3 ♗d7 15.♖c1 ♘a6 16.♕d2 ♖c8 17.h4 ♖xc1+ 18.♗xc1 ♕c7** [Much better was 18...♘c7! with the strategic idea 19...♗b5. Black gets an excellent game after the bishops are swapped] **19.h5 h6 20.♖h4 ♗a4 21.♖f4 ♗d6 22.♖g4 ♘c4 23.♕e1** [The game is very interesting. Chances are probably equal, but White's position is easier to play] **23...♘a3?** [Black collapses under the pressure. He had to retreat with his bishop by 23...♗f8] **24.e5 ♗e7 25.♗xa3 bxa3 26.d5!** [Suddenly Black's queen's bishop is hanging] **26...♘c5 27.♕c3 ♕b6 28.♖b4 ♕a5 29.d6** [This looks crushing, but Black has a hidden defence. Stronger was 29.dxe6 ♘xe6 30.♖xb7 and after the exchange of queens the position is technically winning] **29...♘xd3** [The only move was 29...♗d7!, because 30.dxe7 ♘xd3 doesn't give White anything. White keeps an edge by 30.♗c2, but Black can still fight with 30...♗d8] **30.♖xb7** [Winning immediately] **30...♗d8 31.♖e7+ ♔f8 32.♕xa5 ♗xa5 33.♖xa7 g5 34.hxg6 ♗c6 35.♖xa5** 1-0

Yasser Seirawan
Gyula Sax

Linares 1983

1.c4 ♘f6 2.♘c3 c5 3.♘f3 d5 4.cxd5 ♘xd5 5.e4 ♘b4 6.♗c4 ♘d3+ 7.♔e2 ♘f4+ 8.♔f1 ♘e6 9.b4 cxb4 10.♘d5 g6 [An interesting alternative was 10...♘c5. In Yermolinsky-Tseshkovsky, Telavi 1982, Black got a good game after 11.♘g5 f6 12.d4 fxg5 13.dxc5 e6. Much better is the natural 11.♕e2. White is on top after 11...e6 12.d4 ♘a4 13.♗g5 f6 14.♗f4]

11.♗b2 ♗g7 12.♗xg7 ♘xg7 13.♘xb4 [White must take a time-out to take back the pawn. In Seirawan-Peters, South Bend 1981, Black was better after 13.♕c1 ♘c6 14.d4 ♗e6 15.h4 ♖c8] **13...0-0 14.h3** [A necessary precaution. In Hübner-Portisch, Abano Terme m 1980, and Polugaevsky-Kortchnoi, Buenos Aires m 1980 – both games were played around the same time –, Black was better after 14.d4 ♗g4] **14...e5** [A straightforward move. Black wants to get enough ground in the centre. A good alternative was 14...♕d6. In Seirawan-Böhm, Lugano 1983, White was better after 15.♖b1 ♘c6 16.♘xc6 bxc6 17.♕c2 ♗e6 18.♕e2 c5 19.♖b7. The right method is first 15...♗e6, with a good game for Black] **15.g3 ♗e6 16.♖c1 ♘d7 17.♘d5 ♘f6** [An alternative was 17...f5, e.g. 18.d3 ♘b6

19.♘xb6 axb6 20.♗xe6+ ♘xe6 21.♕b3 ♕f6 22.♘g5 ♖fe8 with equal chances] **18.♘xf6+ ♕xf6 19.♔g2 ♖fd8** [More accurate was 19...♖ad8 20.♕b3 b6, to answer 21.♕b2 with 21...♖fe8, and the e-pawn is protected] **20.♕b3 ♖d7 21.♕b2** [Now White has some pressure] **21...♖ad8 22.♗e2 ♖e7 23.♖c5 ♖d7 24.♖d5 ♖de8 25.♗b5 ♗xb5 26.♖xb5 ♕c6 27.d3 f6 28.♖c1 ♕d7 29.♖d5 ♕e6 30.♕a3 b6 31.♖d6 ♕f7 32.♖cc6 ♘e6** [Sax has defended well and it is hard for White to increase the pressure] **33.h4 ♖d7 34.d4 ♖xd6 35.♕xd6 exd4 36.e5** [Seirawan tries to win at all costs. This winning attempt is still justified since White doesn't risk anything] **36...fxe5 37.♘xe5 ♕f5 38.♘f3** [White is starting to drift. The best move was 38.♕d7 with equal chances] **38...d3** [Suddenly Black is better] **39.♕d7??** [A horrible blunder in time pressure] **39...♘f4+** 0-1

Jeroen Piket
Loek van Wely

Escaldes 1998 (4)

1.♘f3 ♘f6 2.c4 c5 3.♘c3 d5 4.cxd5 ♘xd5 5.e4 ♘b4 6.♗c4 ♘d3+ 7.♔e2 ♘f4+ 8.♔f1 ♘e6 9.b4 cxb4 10.♘d5 ♘c6 [Note the unusual move order in this game. White can go for 11.♗b2 now, hindering the development of Black's kingside] **11.d4** [Probably Piket had planned to play this in any case] **11...g6 12.♗e3 ♗g7 13.♕d2** [White's idea is to give the d-pawn optimal protection and then move the bishop to h6] **13...0-0** [In Kraai-Esserman, Edmonton 2009, Black played the dubious 13...h6. After 14.♖d1 ♕a5 15.h4 ♗d7 16.g3 he opted for 16...0-0-0, which was more than Black's position could take. The sharp 17.a3! could have given White a decisive advantage, e.g. 17...♕xa3 18.♔g2 ♘a5 (otherwise the queen is lost) 19.♘xe7+ ♔b8 20.♗d5 ♕c3 21.♕e2 and Black's position looks utterly hopeless. Instead of castling queenside, 16...♖c8 was better, but then White slowly strengthens his position by 17.♔g2. Van Wely's approach is much more sensible. He doesn't fear a direct attack, since he has enough influence in the centre] **14.♖d1**

14...a5 [Black protects his b-pawn, but this was not really necessary. The best move was 14...b6! to fianchetto the bishop. Black actually has a good game. I think that Aronian mainly refrained from Piket's set-up because of this possibility; with the rook on c1 the fianchetto is hardly possible for Black] **15.h4 h5 16.♗h6** [All according to plan] **16...♔h7** [A strange move. A natural developing move like 16...♗d7 looked better. Black also had the option to sacrifice an exchange by 16...♘cxd4, e.g. 17.♘xd4 ♗xd4 18.g4! b5 (fighting for the initiative) 19.♗xf8 ♕xf8 20.♗xb5 hxg4 21.h5 g5 22.♗e2 and in this sharp position White's chances are preferable] **17.♗xg7 ♘xg7 18.♘g5+ ♔g8 19.♕f4** ½-½

Levon Aronian
Veselin Topalov

London 2015 (7)

1.c4 [At the age of 11, under the influence of a book by Dvoretsky that I had read about the strategy of choosing an opening repertoire, I [LA] began actively playing the English Opening, since it sometimes transposed into my favourite Sicilian with an extra tempo. The main idea of the opening, as I sincerely believed at that time, was to play c2-c4, g2-g3, ♗g2, ♘c3, and push the b-pawn if possible, without especially being diverted by Black's plans] **1...c5** [The first surprise. Veselin usually plays either 1...e5 or 1...c6] **2.♘f3 ♘f6 3.♘c3 d5** [I also did not expect this. Most elite players have switched to the more tedious 3...♘c6] **4.cxd5 ♘xd5 5.e4** [In two games before this I employed 5.d4 and 5.e3. The move in the game leads to more tactical play] **5...♘b4 6.♗c4** [Some strong players, including Alexander Grischuk, one of the drivers of modern opening fashion, have played 6.♗b5+. In view of my love for

Chess960, normally I am not against having my king in the centre] **6...♘d3+** [A curious fact: the well-known game in which Nimzowitsch played his famous ♘g3-♘h1 with the manoeuvre of his knight via f2-h3 to g5 and won against Rubinstein, Dresden 1926, was played with this very variation. Rubinstein chose the solid move 6...e6, and this move is better than its reputation. Another move which can be recommended is 6...♗e6] **7.♔e2 ♘f4+ 8.♔f1 ♘e6** [Here the paradoxical 8...♘d3 is also possible. To me the move in the game seems sounder] **9.b4** [The most critical continuation. In a game between two stars of modern chess played in 2014, Nakamura chose 9.♘e5 and after 9...♘c6 10.♘xc6 bxc6 11.♘a4 ♘d4 12.♘xc5 he acquired an extra pawn, which, however, did not prevent Giri from achieving his favourite result] **9...cxb4** [9...g6 is a serious alternative. As in games of the old masters, Black replies to a gambit with a counter-gambit] **10.♘d5** [10.♘e2 gives Black more choice and therefore demands more home preparation. Since other variations after 1.c4 are more often employed, I did not spend much time on this variation, and I aimed for the unusual position which arose in the game] **10...g6 11.d4** [Far more common is 11.♗b2, which also leads to interesting play. The positions arising after the move in the game are rather curious. The two knights on d5 and e6 restrain each other, and often semi-zugzwang positions can arise, where both sides apparently have everything developed and stand well, but what to aim for subsequently is not clear. Ideally White needs to deploy everything towards the centre and try to exchange the dark-squared bishops, move his knight from d5 and trample the black pieces with the central pawns. For his part, Black wants to play ...♘c7 as soon as possible, with the exchange of his awkward e6-knight, or by ...♗d7/...a7-a5, and then either ...♘a7-♘b5 or ...a5-a4, with the ideas of ...b4-b3/...♘a5, to provoke exchanges, which will enable him to find posts for his minor pieces] **11...♗g7 12.♗e3 ♘c6 13.♖c1** [This move had not occurred before in practice, although it does not change much. In the game Piket-Van Wely, Escaldes 1998, Jeroen played

13.♕d2 and placed his rook on d1, which is also quite logical]

13...♗d7 [My opponent handles the position in the spirit of modern chess. Without hurrying to castle, Black aims to quickly develop his queenside. 13...0-0 is more natural, but it is possible that, on seeing the furious speed with which I was making my moves, Veselin decided to choose a move which I might not have studied] **14.♕d2** [Not a bad move, but after the game I realized that the developing 14.h4 h5 15.g3 was stronger. I thought that h4 would never run away from me, but I did not notice an important resource] **14...♕a5** [We both thought that the b4-pawn was hanging, and for this reason Veselin chose an inaccurate plan. Black should have either supported his pawn by 14...a5 or continued his plan with 14...♖c8 since after 15.♘xb4 ♘xb4 16.♕xb4 he has the good move 16...b5, which I had overlooked, after which Black achieves important exchanges. For example, after 17.♕xb5 ♖xc1+ 18.♗xc1 0-0 Black has excellent play] **15.h4** [An invitation to an endgame, which Black should have accepted. The more forceful move 15.♗b3 seemed to me to be not so convincing on account of 15...♕b5+ 16.♔g1 0-0 with the idea of ...♖fe8 and ...♘a5, although now, after analysis, I realize that Black does not have time for all this, since after h4-h5 White's attack develops of its own accord] **15...♖c8** [But now Black cannot escape into a slightly inferior endgame. From the practical point of view, this is the decisive mistake. As Veselin rightly commented after the game, Black was obliged to play 15...b3 and after 16.♕xa5 ♖xa5 17.axb3, although White has a pleasant position, for the moment nothing terrible has occurred] **16.♗b3 ♕b5+** [Topalov

is well known for his resourcefulness, and with this move he tries an original method of defence, which does not work on account of White's great range of attacking ideas. In the event of the simple 16...h5 17.g3, because of the ridiculous position of the queen on a5, Black has no convenient moves, since 17...0-0 loses to 18.♖xc6 ♗xc6 19.♘xe7+ ♔h8 20.d5 ♖cd8 21.♕c1 ♗b5+ 22.♔g2 when the white pieces are dominant] **17.♔g1 h6** [Black tries to find time to play ...♘a5 in order to simplify the position, but I find an easy solution] **18.♔h2 g5** [After 18...♘a5 19.♖xc8+ ♗xc8 20.♖c1 White has too many threats. 18...g5 is a part of Black's defensive plan begun with 16...♕b5] **19.♖hd1 ♔f8** [Here 19...g4 was consistent, after which White had the very strong 20.♘e5 ♘xe5 21.♖xc8+ ♗xc8 22.dxe5 ♘xe5+ 23.g3 with a winning attack, which, however, would have demanded energetic play by him. After the passive move in the game White is no longer obliged to play accurately] **20.♔g1 ♖d8** [Now if 20...g4 the reply 21.♘e5 gains in strength, since the king is worse placed on f8 than on e8] **21. hxg5 hxg5 22.♗xg5 ♘xg5** [This is equivalent to resignation. 22...♖h5 23.♗e3 ♗e8 was more resilient, with a lost position, but not yet automatically won by White] **23.♕xg5**

[And now there is no acceptable defence against the threats of ♖c5 and ♖xc6] **23...♗h6 24.♕h4 ♗g7 25.♕f4 ♗h6** [After 25...♗e8 26.♘g5 ♖d6 27.♘c7 Black suffers great loss of material] **26.♘g5 ♗xg5 27.♕xg5** [On seeing that after 27...♗e6, apart from a forced win by 28.♖xc6, White has at least five easy ways of winning, my opponent resigned] 1-0

M/16-1-77 Aronian

Exercise 1

position after 17.♗e3xd4

White exchanged on d4. How should Black take back?
(solution on page 253)

Exercise 2

position after 17.♖h1-e1

Black played 17...♕a5. Was this sharp move justified?
(solution on page 253)

Exercise 3

position after 22.♖d1xd3

White intends to push his d-pawn. What should Black do about it?
(solution on page 253)

English Opening

More than Just an Experiment?

by Mihail Marin and Valentin Stoica

1.	c4	c5
2.	♘f3	♞c6
3.	d4	cxd4
4.	♘xd4	♞f6
5.	g3	e5
6.	♘b5	

The early stages of the so-called Symmetrical English are often characterized by a fight for the opening of the centre with d2-d4 or ...d7-d5 respectively.

Alberic O'Kelly de Galway

One of White's problems is that after 1.c4 c5 2.♘f3 ♞c6 3.d4 cxd4 4.♘xd4 ♞f6 5.♘c3 e6 Black has good opportunities for counterplay after either 6.g3 ♛b6 or 6.♘db5 d5 (or even 6...♝b4). This is how 5.g3 became popular, with the obvious aim of avoiding an early pin on the queen's knight. But nothing is perfect in chess, and this move has the drawback of failing to put immediate pressure on the centre, justifying the wave of popularity at top level of the somewhat exotic 5...e5. White's only hope of an advantage is 6.♘b5 (otherwise Black would gain space in the centre with 6...d5), reaching the starting point of this Survey.

We should start by mentioning that this line is a frequent guest in top-level rapid and blitz games, which shows that it is still regarded as an experiment.

If we compare the above position to similar ones arising from the Sicilian, lines like the fashionable Sveshnikov and the almost forgotten Labourdonnais and O'Kelly immediately come to mind. For the sake of free piece development, Black has weakened the d6- and d5-squares. White will obviously try to consolidate his control of those squares, while Black should try to undermine the white centre with either ...d7(6)-d5 or ...a7-a6 and ...b7-b5.

Not Entirely Satisfactory

The Labourdonnais approach with 6...a6 does not seem to offer Black an easy life, as can be seen from the comments to Panteleev-Kreuzer.

The Sveshnikov pattern based on 6...d6 is a lot sounder but, in our view, not entirely satisfactory either.

Even though fighting for the d5-square with ♝c1-g5 is thematic, 7.♝g5 is premature here due to 7...♝e6, posing White early problems in the centre based on his poor development. See Romanov-Naiditsch.

The plan with 7.♝g2 (planning to meet 7...♝e6 with 8.♘1a3, preventing ...d6-d5) is better. The other developing move 7.♘1c3 is equally good, but these lines tend to transpose to each other with the possible move orders 7.♝g2 ♝e6 8.♘1a3 ♝e7 9.0-0 a6 10.♘c3 0-0 or 7.♘1c3 a6 8.♘a3 ♝e7 9.♝g2 0-0 10.0-0 ♝e6.

The most natural plan is 11.♗g5, which was the choice of one of the authors when facing this line. Even though this ensures White the control of d5, giving away the bishop pair is to some extent double-edged. See Iturrizaga-Moiseenko.

The less obvious 11.b3, followed by ♗b2, offers White chances of a perfectly harmonious development, as in Artemiev-Gabrielian. Both plans offer White some slight advantage, and choosing between them is purely a matter of taste.

The O'Kelly Approach:

Black's best chance of equality is offered by the O'Kelly approach: 6...♗b4+. Since

7.♘5c3 now allows 7...d5, White has a choice between 7.♘1c3 and 7.♗d2.

The idea behind 7.♘1c3 is to provoke the exchange on c3 with a2-a3.

The neutral 7...0-0 allows White to carry out this plan unhindered, as in Svidler-Nepomniachtchi.

The critical move is 7...d6, speeding up the attack against the c4-pawn with ...♗e6. Analysis proves that after 8.a3 ♗xc3+ 9.♘xc3 ♗e6 White should not waste time on defending the pawn. Ivanchuk-Leko went 10.♗g2, with reasonable compensation for the pawn but not more. In Kramnik-Grischuk, White preferred 8.♗g2, but this

forced him to make structural concessions, offering Black excellent play.

Since 7.♘1c3 does not seem to offer an advantage, 7.♗d2 looks like White's best try. With his dark squares in danger, Black should react energetically with 7...a6. 8.♘5c3 d5 leads to a typical Catalan position, in which White's pressure along the long diagonal is fully compensated for by Black's excellent development, as in Iturrizaga-Rodshtein.

In our opinion, the crucial line for this whole set-up starts with 8.♗xb4. Here, too, White sacrifices a pawn, but in the featured game Vallejo-Leko the always well-prepared Hungarian grandmaster was clearly in the ropes in the middlegame. More practical games are needed in this latter line, of course.

Conclusion

Our conclusion is that this line has every right to exist, but we expect new ideas for White to pop up in the near future.

Petar Panteleev
Gerhard Kreuzer
Germany 2004 (3)

1.♘f3 c5 2.g3 ♘c6 3.c4 ♘f6 4.d4 cxd4 5.♘xd4 e5 6.♘b5 a6 7.♘d6+ [7.♘5c3 is too passive, allowing Black to start his counterplay at once: 7... b5!? 8.cxb5 axb5 9.♘xb5?! ♕b6 10.a4 (½-½ J. Horvath-Claverie, Val Thorens 2002) 10...♗b7 11.e3 (11.♗g2 ♘d4-+) 11...♘b4 12.♖g1 ♗e7∓] **7...♗xd6 8.♕xd6 ♕e7** [8...♘e4 9.♕d3 ♕a5+ (9...♘c5 10.♕d1±) 10.♘c3 ♘xc3 11.♗d2 d5 12.♗xc3 dxc4 13.♕d6!? ♕d8 14.♗xe5 ♕xd6 15.♗xd6 ♗e6 16.♗g2 0-0-0 17.0-0-0±] **9.♕xe7+ ♘xe7 10.♘c3** [10.♗g2 d5 11.cxd5

♘fxd5 12.0-0 ♗e6 13.♗d2 0-0 (Heinig-Lick, Dresden 2012) 14.♘c3±]

10...d5 [Due to White's bishop pair, the counterplay based on 10...b5 is not entirely satisfactory: 11.cxb5 (11.♗g2 ♖b8 12.cxb5 axb5 13.a3 b4 14.axb4 ♖xb4 15.0-0 0-0 16.f4!?±) 11...♗b7 12.♖g1 axb5 13.♘xb5 0-0 14.♗d2±]

11.cxd5 ♘exd5 [11...♘fxd5 12.♗g2 ♗e6 (12...♘xc3 13.bxc3 0-0 14.♗a3 ♖e8 15.0-0 ♘c6 16.♖fb1) 13.♗d2 0-0 14.0-0 f6 15.♘a4†] **12.♘xd5** [12.♗d2!? ♘b4 13.♖c1 0-0 14.♗g2 ♗e6 15.a3 ♘c6 16.0-0 h6 17.♗e3±] **12...♘xd5 13.♗d2 ♗e6 14.♖c1** [14.♗g2 0-0 15.0-0 f5 16.e4±] **14...0-0 15.♗g2 ♖ac8** [15...f5 16.e4 (16.0-0 e4) 16... fxe4 17.♗xe4 ♘f6 18.♗g2 (18.♗b1 ♗h3) 18...♖f7 19.b3 ♗d5 20.0-0 ♗xg2 21.♔xg2 ♖d7 22.♗c3 ♖e8=/±] **16.0-0 b5?!** [Instead of weakening the dark squares, Black should have consolidated them with 16...f6!?] **17.f4?!** [The same type of mistake: White weakens the light squares. 17.e4! ♘e7 18.♗b4±] **17...exf4 18.gxf4 f5 19.b3 ♘f6 20.♗b4 ♖xc1** [20...♖fe8=] **21.♖xc1 ♖c8 22.♖xc8+ ♗xc8 23.♔f2 ♔f7**

24.♔e3 [24.h3 ♔e6 25.♔e3 ♘d5+=]
24...♔e6 [24...♘g4+ 25.♔d4 ♘xh2]
25.♔d4 h6? [After 25...♘e4!?= it is hard to see how White could get more than a drawn opposite-coloured bishops ending with an extra pawn] 26. e3 g5? 27.♗f8± gxf4 28.exf4 h5 29.♗g7 ♘e4 30.h4 ♗d7 31.♗f3 ♗e8 32.b4 ♗g6 33.♗d1 ♔d6 34.♗b3 ♗e8 35.♗f8+ ♔c7 36.♔e5 ♗d7 37.♗c2 ♘g3 38.♔f6 ♘e4+ 39.♔g6 ♔d8 40.♔xh5 ♗e6 41.♔g6 ♗f7+ 42.♔xf7 ♘g3 43.♗g7 1-0

Evgeny Romanov
Arkadij Naiditsch
Warsaw 2011 (8)

1.c4 ♘f6 2.♘f3 c5 3.g3 ♘c6 4.d4 cxd4 5.♘xd4 e5 6.♘b5 d6 7.♗g5

7...♗e6 8.e3!? [8.b3 d5 9.♗g2 (9.cxd5 ♗b4+) 9...dxc4 (9...♗b4+ 10.♘d2 dxc4) 10.0-0 a6∓ Parfenov-Lanin, Smolensk 2005; 8.♘d2 d5 9.cxd5 (9.♗xf6 gxf6 10.cxd5 ♗xd5 11.e4 ♗e6 12.♗c4 ♗b4) 9...♗xd5 10.e4 ♗e6 11.♗c4 ♗b4 12.♗xe6 fxe6 13.0-0 0-0 14.a3 ♗xd2 15.♗xd2 ♘xe4∓ Filippov-Moiseenko, Bydgoszcz 1999; 8.♘1a3? d5 9.cxd5 (9.♗xf6 ♕a5+!−+) 9...♘xd5!? 10.♗xd8 ♗b4+ 11.♘c3 ♘xc3∓ 12.♕c2? ♘xa2+ 13.♔d1 ♖xd8+−+] 8...♖c8 [8...d5 9.♗xf6 gxf6 10.cxd5 ♗xd5? 11.♕xd5!+−] 9.♗xf6 ♕xf6?! [9... gxf6 10.♘5c3 f5 11.♗e2 g7 12.♘d5 (12.0-0 e4 13.♘a3 a6) 12...b5!? 13.♘bc3 (13.cxb5? ♗xd5 14.♕xd5 ♗b4 15.♕d1 ♘c2+) 13...bxc4 14.♗xc4 0-0 15.0-0 e4∞] 10.♘5c3 [10.♘1c3 ♕d8 11.♘d5 ♕a5+ 12.♕d2 ♕xd2+ 13.♔xd2 ♗d7 14.♗g2 f5 15.♖ac1±] 10...♕d8 11.♘d5 h5 [11...♕a5+ 12.♘bc3 (12.♕d2 ♕xd2+ 13.♔xd2 g6 14.♘bc3

♗g7 15.♗e2 f5∞) 12...♘b4 13.♕b3 ♘xd5 14.cxd5 ♗d7= 15.♕xb7? ♖xc3! 16.bxc3 ♕xc3+ 17.♔e2 e4 (and ...♗g4+ is coming. 17...♕xa1? 18.♕xd7+! ♔xd7 19.♗h3+ ♔c7 20.♖xa1±) 18.♕a8+ ♔e7 19.♕xa7 (19.♕b7 ♗f6!∓ and ...♗g4+ is coming) 19...♔d8 (19...♗f6? 20.♕d4+!+−) 20.♕b8+=] 12.h4 g6 13.♘bc3 f5 14.♗h3 e4? [14...♗g7 15.0-0 0-0 16.b3 ♗f7 17.♖c1 e4] 15.♘xe4± ♗g7 16.0-0 ♗xd5 17.cxd5 ♘e5 18.♘g5 ♕b6 19.e4 ♗f6 20.exf5 ♗xg5 21.hxg5 h4 22.fxg6 ♖c7 23.♕a4+ ♔e7 24.g7 ♖g8 25.♕f4 ♖xg7 26.g6 hxg3 27.♕h4+ ♔f8 28.♕d8# 1-0

Eduardo Iturrizaga Bonelli
Alexander Moiseenko
Berlin 2015 (9)

1.♘f3 c5 2.c4 ♘c6 3.d4 cxd4 4.♘xd4 ♘f6 5.g3 e5 6.♘b5 d6 7.♗g2 ♗e6

8.♘1a3 ♗e7 9.0-0 a6 [9...0-0 10.♗g5 ♘e8 11.♗e3 ♘f6 12.♘c3 ♕d7 13.♘d5 ♖fc8 (13...♗xd5 14.cxd5±) 14.♕d2 ♘g4 (Marin-Lupu, Andorra 1996) 15.♖ad1 ♗f8 16.♘b5±; 9...h6 prevents ♗g5 at the cost of an important tempo: 10.♘c3 0-0 11.♘d5 ♖c8 12.♗e3 (12.b3!? as we will see, this plan is viable even if Black does not play ...h7-h6) 12...♕d7 13.♗b2 ♖fd8 14.♘b5±; 12.♘b5!?) 12...♘g4 (12...a6 13.♖c1 ♘g4 14.♗b6) 13.♗d2 f5 (13...a6 14.e4!?) 14.♗c3 h5 (14...a6 15.♘c2 h5 16.b3!? h4?! 17.e4 f4? 18.♗h3+−; 14...♕d7 15.e3 ♘f6) 15.♘b5 a6 16.♘xe7+ ♕xe7 17.♘xd6 ♖cd8 18.c5± Z.Rahman-Jumabayev, New Delhi 2006] 10.♘c3 0-0 11.♗g5 ♖c8 [11...♕d7 12.♕d2 ♖fd8 (12...♘g4 13.♗xe7 ♘xe7 14.♖ad1 ♖ad8 15.♘e4 d5 16.♘c5 ♕c7 17.♘xe6 fxe6 18.♖c1

d4 19.c5±) 13.♗xf6 ♗xf6 14.♘d5 ♗xd5 (14...♖ab8 15.♘xf6+ gxf6 16.♕h6±) 15.♕xd5 (15.cxd5 ♗e7 16.♘c4 ♖ab8 17.a4 g6 18.e4 ♗g7 19.a5 f5 20.♗h3±) 15...♖ab8 16.♖fd1 ♗e7 17.♕a5 e4? (17...g6 18.♘c2 ♕e6 19.♘e3 e4) 18.♗xe4 ♗xb2 19.♖ab1 ♗xa3 20.♕xa3± Keitlinghaus-Schmittdiel, Prague 1990] 12.♕d2 h6 [12...♘a5 13.♗xf6 ♗xf6 14.b3 e4 15.♖ad1 ♗xc3 16.♕xc3 b5 17.♘xe4 bxc4 18.b4 (18. bxc4 ½-½ Garcia Ilundain-Speelman, Escaldes 1998) 18...♘c6 19.b5 axb5 (19...♘e7 20.♗b7 ♖c5 21.bxa6±) 20.♘xb5 d5 21.♗xd5 ♗xd5 22.e4 ♕b6 (22...♘e7 23.exd5 ♖c5 24.d6 ♖xb5 25.dxe7 ♕xe7 26.♕xc4±) 23.♖xd5 ♘e7 24.♘d6 (24.♖d7 ♕xb5 25.♖xe7±) 24...♘xd5 (24...♖c6 25.♖b5 ♕a6 26.♖a5 ♕b6 27.e5±) 25.♘xc8 ♕xf2+ (25...♘xc3 26.♘xb6 ♘xe4 27.♘xc4±) 26.♖xf2 ♘xc3 27.♘e7+ ♔h8 28.♖c2 ♘xe4 29.♖xc4±] 13.♗xf6 ♗xf6 14.♖fd1 [It makes more sense to keep this rook on f1, keeping the threat f2-f4-f5 in reserve and avoiding a pin along the long dark diagonal: 14.♖ad1 ♗g5 (14...♕b6 15.b3 ♕a5 16.♘c2 b5 17.cxb5 axb5 18.♘e4 ♗e7 19.♕xa5 ♘xa5 20.♘e3 ♖fd8 21.♘d5±) 15.e3 ♗g4 16.f3 ♗h5 (16...♗e6 17.f4) 17.g4 ♗g6 18.f4 exf4 19.exf4 ♗f6 20.f5 ♗h7 21.♘e4± – the h7-bishop is completely out of play] 14...♕b6 [14...♗g5!? 15.e3 ♗g4] 15.b3 ♖fd8?! [15...♕a5! 16.♘d5 (16.♘c2?! e4!; 16.♖ab1 b5!?⇄) 16...♕xa3 17.♘xf6+ gxf6 18.♕xh6= White will give perpetual soon] 16.♘c2 [16.♘d5 ♗xd5 17.cxd5 ♘e7 18.♘c4 ♕a7 19.e3±] 16...♗g5 17.e3 ♕a7 18.♕d3 [18.h4 ♗e7 19.♘d5±] 18...♗e7 19.♗d5± ♖f8 20.♖d2 ♔h8 21.♗xe6 fxe6 22.♕g6 ♖f6 23.♕g4 ♖cf8 24.♘e4 ♖f5 25.♕g6 ♘d8 26.♘xd6 ♗xd6 27.♖xd6 ♘f7 28.♖xe6 ♘g5 29.♖e8 ♖xf2 30.♖xf8+ ♖xf8 31.♖f1 ♕b8 32.♕d3 e4 33.♕d1 ♘f3+ 34.♔g2 ♖d8 35.♘d4 ♕a7 36.♖f2 b5 37.cxb5 axb5 38.♘xb5 ♖xd1 39.♘xa7 g5 40.♔h3 h5 41.g4 ♖g1 42.♖g2 ♖e1 43.gxh5 ♖xe3 44.♔g4 ♖e1 45.♘b5 ♘e5+ 46.♔f5 ♘d3 47.♔g6 ♘f4+ 48.♔xg5 ♘xg2 49.♘d6 e3 50.♔g6 ♘f4+ 51.♔g5 e2 0-1

Vladislav Artemiev
Artur Gabrielian

Izhevsk 2014 (6)

1.♘f3 c5 2.c4 ♘c6 3.d4 cxd4 4.♘xd4 ♘f6 5.g3 e5 6.♘b5 d6 7.♘1c3 a6 8.♘a3 ♗e7 9.♗g2 0-0 10.0-0 ♗e6 11.b3 ♖c8 [11...♘d7 12.♘c2 ♘h8 13.♘d5 (13.♗a3 ♘c5 14.♘e3±) 13...f5 14.♗a3 ♘c5 15.♘xe7 ♕xe7 16.♕d2 ♖fd8 17.♖ad1 ♖ac8 18.♘e3± Tkachiev-Milov, Cannes 2006; 11...♕d7 12.♘d5 ♖ab8 13.♕d3!?± b5 14.♘xe7+ ♘xe7 15.♖d1 ♖fd8 16.♗b2±] **12.♗b2** [12.♘d5 ♗g4 13.f3 ♗e6 14.e4 b5 15.♗e3 (15.♗b2!? bxc4 16.♘xc4 ♗xd5 17.exd5 ♘b4 18.f4 e4 19.g4↑) 15...bxc4 16.♘xc4 ♗xd5 17.exd5 ♘b4∞ (pressure on the ♗e3) Gomez-Pulanu, playchess.com 2007] **12...h5** [12...♕a5 13.♘c2 (13.♘d5 ♖fe8 14.♘c2 b5 15.♘ce3±) 13...♖fd8 (13...b5!?) 14.♘e3 b5 (Cramling-Bellon Lopez, Oviedo 1993) 15.♘cd5± bxc4?! 16.♘xc4 ♕c5 17.♗a3 ♕a7 18.♘xe7+ ♘xe7 19.♘xd6± ; 12...b5!? 13.♘d5 (13.cxb5 axb5 14.♘axb5 d5 15.e3 ♕a5 16.a4 ♖fd8∞) 13...bxc4 14.♘xc4 ♗xd5 15.♗xd5 ♘h3 16.♗g2± with the idea ♘e3-d5] **13.♘d5 h4**

14.♘c2 [14.♕d3±] **14...b5 15.cxb5 axb5** [15...♘xd5 16.bxc6!] **16.♘ce3** [16.e4!? hxg3 (16...♗xd5 17.exd5 ♘a5 18.♘b4±; 16...♘b8 17.♘cb4±) 17.hxg3 ♖e8 18.♘ce3±] **16...♘xd5 17.♘xd5 hxg3 18.hxg3 ♗g5 19.e3 ♘e7 20.♗a3 ♘xd5 21.♗xd5 ♗e7 22.♗b4± ♕b6 23.♗f3 ♖fe8 24.♕d2 d5 25.♗xe7 ♖xe7 26.a4 bxa4 27.bxa4 ♖d7 28.a5 ♕a7 29.♖fb1 d4 30.exd4 exd4 31.♖b6 d3 32.♔g2 ♖c2 33.♕f4 ♖d8 34.♕h4 f6 35.♖h1 ♔f8 36.♕h8+ ♗g8 37.♖xf6+ gxf6 38.♕xf6+ ♔e8 39.♖e1+ ♖e2 40.♗xe2** 1-0

Peter Svidler
Ian Nepomniachtchi

Sochi 2015 (5)

1.♘f3 c5 2.c4 ♘f6 3.d4 cxd4 4.♘xd4 ♘c6 5.g3 e5 6.♘b5 ♗b4+ 7.♘1c3 0-0

8.a3 ♗xc3+ [8...♗e7 9.♗g5 ♘e8 (9...d6 10.♗xf6 gxf6 11.♘d5 a6 12.♘bc3 f5 13.e3 ♗f6 14.♕h5 e4 15.0-0-0±; 9...a6 10.♗xf6+) 10.♗xe7 ♘xe7 11.♗g2 ♕b6 (Vokoun-Londyn, Prague 2014) 12.♕d2 a6 13.♘a4 ♕e6 14.♘bc3 ♖b8 15.c5±; 8...♗c5 9.♗g2 d6 10.b4 a6 11.bxc5 axb5 12.cxb5±] **9.♘xc3 d6 10.♗g2 ♗e6 11.b3 h6 12.0-0 ♖c8 13.h3** [13.a4 a6 (13...a5 14.♗a3 ♘b4 15.♗xb7±) 14.♗a3 ♕b6 15.♖a2 ♖fd8 16.e3 (16.♕d2 ♘d4) 16...♘b4 17.♖d2 ♖d7 18.e4 (18.h3 ♖cd8 19.e4) 18...♗g4 19.♕b1 ♖cd8 20.h3 ♗e6 21.♕d1±] **13...♕d7 14.♔h2 ♘e7 15.e4± a6 16.a4** [16.f4!± exf4 17.gxf4 ♕c7 18.f5 ♗d7 19.♗f4 ♘e8 20.f6!+−] **16...♘c6 17.♗e3 ♘e7 18.♖a2 ♘d7 19.♖d2 ♘c5 20.f4** [20.♖xd6 ♘d4 21.♖xd4 exd4 22.♗xd4± ♘xb3 23.♕xb3 ♗xc4 24.♕b2 ♗xf1 25.♘d5 ♕e6 (25...♕e8 26.♗xg7+−) 26.♗xf1+− ♕xe4?! 27.♗g2 ♕e6 28.♗xg7] **20...f6** [Closing the a1-h8 diagonal, and opening the 7th rank] **21.♖xd6 ♘d4 22.♖xd4 exd4 23.♗xd4 ♘xb3?!** [23...♖fd8 24.♘d5±] **24.♕xb3 ♗xc4 25.♕b2?** [25.♘d5! ♕f7 26.♕b2 ♗xf1 27.♗xf1±] **25...♗xf1 26.♗xf1** [26.♘d5? ♕e8 27.♗xf1 ♕xe4] **26...♖fd8∞ 27.♗f2** [27.♘d5? ♕xe4] **27...a5 28.♘d5?** [28.♗b6∞] **28...♕xe4∓ 29.♗g2 ♕c2! 30.♕b6 ♔h8 31.♗f3** [31.♘xf6 ♖d2 32.♘e4 ♖e2∓] **31...♕c6** [31...♕d2!−+ 32.♘xf6 (32.♘e7 ♖c2

33.♔g1 ♖b2 34.♕c5 b6 35.♕e3 ♕xe3 36.♗xe3 ♖d3) 32...♖d6 33.♘e4 ♖xb6 34.♘xd2 ♖b2 35.♘e4 b5 36.axb5 a4] **32.♕xa5 ♖a8 33.♕b5 ♖xa4 34.♕b3 ♕c4 35.♕xb7?! ♖a2 36.♔g1 ♕c1+ 37.♔g2 ♕c5** 0-1

Vassily Ivanchuk
Peter Leko

Beijing 2014 (2)

1.♘f3 ♘f6 2.c4 c5 3.d4 cxd4 4.♘xd4 ♘c6 5.g3 e5 6.♘b5 ♗b4+ 7.♘1c3 d6 8.a3 ♗xc3+ 9.♘xc3 ♗e6

10.♗g2 [10.e3 0-0 11.f3 (11.♗e2 ♘a5 12.b3 d5∓) 11...♖c8 (11...♘a5 12.b3 d5∓) 12.e4 ♕b6∓ Bachmann-Quintiliano Pinto, Florianopolis 2015; 10.e4 0-0 11.h3 ♖c8 (11...♘a5 12.b3 b5! 13.♘xb5 ♘xe4∓) 12.♗e3 b6 13.♖c1 ♕e7 14.b3 ♘d7 15.♗g2 ♘c5 16.b4 ♘b7 17.♘d5 ♗xd5 18.cxd5 ♘b8 19.0-0-0 Ivanchuk-M.Muzychuk, Cap d'Agde blitz 2013] **10...♗xc4 11.♗g5** [11.♗xc6+ bxc6 12.♕a4 ♗b5 13.♕xb5 cxb5 14.♕xb5+ ♕d7 15.♕d3 h6= Piorun-Bobras, Germany Bundesliga 2014/15] **11...0-0 12.♖c1** [12.♘e4 d5 13.♗xf6+ gxf6 14.♗h6 ♘d4 15.e3 ♗e2 16.♕d2 (16.♕b1 ♖e8 17.exd4 exd4 18.♔d2 ♕b6→) 16...♘f3+ 17.♗xf3 ♗xf3∓ Lagno-Karjakin, Berlin 2015] **12...♘d4** [12...h6 13.♗xf6 ♕xf6 14.♘e4 ♕e6 15.♕xd6 ♘d4 16.♕xe6 ♗xe6 17.♘c5 ♖ac8 18.♗xb7 ♖c7 19.♗a6 ♖b8 20.b4 ♖b6 21.♗d3 a5 22.♖b1 (22.0-0!? axb4 (22...♘h3 23.♘a4! ♖bb7 24.♖xc7 ♖xc7 25.♖d1±) 23.♘xe6 ♖xc1 (23...♘xe6 24.♖xc7 ♘xc7 25.♖c1 ♘e8 26.♖c8 ♔f8 27.a4 ♔e7 28.a5±) 24.♖xc1 fxe6 25.♘b3 26.♖c8+ ♔f7 27.axb4 ♖xb4+) 22...♘a2 23.♖a1 ♘d5 (Lagno-Muzychuk, Geneva 2013) 24.0-0±; 12...♖c8!?] **13.e3 ♘b3** [13...♘b3 14.♕d2 ♗e6 15.♗xf6

♕xf6 16.♘e4 ♕g6 17.♘xd6 ♖ad8 18.0-0 b6 19.♕b4±; 13...♖e8!? 14.♗xf6 gxf6 15.♗d5 ♗xd5 16.♘xd5 ♕a5+ 17.♘b4 (17.♘c3 ♗a6!) 17...♘c6 18.0-0 ♗xb4 19.♕g4+ ♔h8 20.axb4 ♕d8 21.♖fd1♕] **14.♗xf6** [14.♖c2 ♗c5 15.♗xf6 ♕xf6 16.♘d5 ♗xd5 17.♕xd5♕] **14...♕xf6** [14...gxf6 15.♖c2♕/±] **15.♘e4 ♕e6 16.♘g5 ♘xc1!** [16...♘c8 17.♖c3+— △ ♕c2] **17.♘xe6 ♘d3+ 18.♔d2 fxe6♕ 19.f4 ♖ac8** [19...♘f2 20.♕c2 d5 21.♖a1 ♖ac8 22.♕a4 ♗d3 23.♖c1 ♖xc1 24.♔xc1 ♖c8+ 25.♔d2 ♖c2+ 26.♔e1 ♖e2+ 27.♔f1 ♖xb2+ 28.♔g1 b5 29.♕xa7 ♗g4 (△ ...♖b1+) 30.♗xd5□ ♖b1+□ (30...exd5? 31.♕a8+ ♔f7 32.♕xd5+) 31.♔g2 ♖b2+=] **20.♕b1** [20.♕a4!? ♘xb2 21.♕xa7 b5∞] **20... d5 21.b3 ♗a6 22.b4 ♗c4 23.♗f1 e4?** [23...♘f2! 24.♗xc4 (24.♖g1 ♘e4+ 25.♔e1 ♗xf1 26.♖xf1 ♖c3—+) 24...dxc4 25.♖f1 ♖fd8+ 26.♔e2 ♘d3=] **24.♕a1!** [a1-h8] **24... e5** [24...♘f2 25.♗xc4 dxc4 26.♖c1 ♖fd8+ 27.♔e2±] **25.♗xd3 ♗xd3 26.♖c1 exf4 27.exf4** [27.♖xc8! fxe3+ 28.♔xe3 ♖xc8 29.♕e5 ♖d8 30.♕e7 d4+ 31.♔f4 ♖f8+ 32.♔e5±; 27.gxf4!?±] **27...♗c4= 28.♕d4 a6 29.h4 ♖c6 30.h5 ♖f7 31.♕e5 h6 32.a4 ♔h7 33.a5 ♖fc7 34.♕f5+ ♔g8 35.♕e5 ♔h7 36.♕e8 ♖c8 37.♕d7 ♖8c7 38.♕f5+ ♔g8 39.♕e5 ♔h7 40.f5 ♖f7 41.♖g1 ♗d3 42.♖c1 ♗c4 43.♖g1 ♗d3 44.♖c1 ♗c4 45.♖g1** ½-½

Vladimir Kramnik
Alexander Grischuk
Kazan 2011 (2)

1.♘f3 c5 2.c4 ♘c6 3.d4 cxd4 4.♘xd4 ♘f6 5.g3 e5!? 6.♘b5 ♗b4+!? 7.♘1c3 d6 8.♗g2N a6 9.♘a3 [9.♕a4 ♗d7∓; 9.a3? axb5−+]

9...♗xc3+! [9...♗xa3?! 10.bxa3 0-0 11.0-0 ♗e6 12.♗d5±] **10.bxc3 0-0 11.0-0** [11.♗g5 ♕a5!? 12.♕c1 ♘d7 13.0-0 ♘c5⇄] **11...h6!?** [11...♗e6 12.♗g5 h6 13.♗xf6 ♕xf6 14.♕xd6 ♖fd8 15.♕c7 ♖d7 16.♕b6 ♕d8♕] **12.♘c2** [12.♖b1!?] **12...♕c7 13.♘e3 ♗e6 14.♗a3 ♖fd8 15.♗b4?** [15.♘d5 ♗xd5 16.cxd5 ♘a5∓; 15.♖b1 ♘a5 (15... b5!?) 16.♕d3 ♖ac8!? (16...♖ab8 17.♖fd1 ♘xc4 18.♘xc4 ♗xc4 19.♗xd6 ♗xd3 20.♗xc7 ♗xb1 21.♖xb1±; 16...♗xc4 17.♘xc4 ♘xc4 18.♖xb7 ♕c8 19.♖b3 ♖a7=) 17.♖b4 b6!? 18.♘d5 ♗xd5 19.cxd5 b5⇄] **15...♖ac8** [15...♘xc4!? 16.♘xc4 ♘xb4 17.cxb4 ♕xc4 18.♗xb7 ♖ab8 19.♖c1 ♕xa2∓] **16.♖b1**

16...e4!∓ 17.♕a4?! a5 [17...b5! 18.cxb5 axb5∓ 19.♕xb5?! ♖a8! 20.♘f5 ♔h8! 21.♖d6 ♕d7] **18.♗a3 ♘e5 19.c5!? dxc5 20.c4 ♘eg4** [20...♘d4 21.♗b2; 20...♗d2!? 21.♖b2 ♖d4 22.♖c2 ♘fg4∓] **21.♗xg4 ♗xg4 22.♕c2 ♕d7 23.♗b2** [23.♖fd1 ♕e6 (23...♗e7 24.h3 ♗f5 25.♖xd8+ ♖xd8 26.♖b5) 24.♖xd8+ ♖xd8 25.♗xc5 e3!∓ 26.♗xe3? ♗f5−+] **23...♕d2! 24.♕xd2 ♖xd2 25.♗xf6 gxf6 26.♗xe4 ♗xe2 27.♖fc1 ♖cd8 28.♗xb7 ♖xa2 29.♗d5 ♖d7 30.♖b5 ♖c7 31.♖cb1 a4 32.♖a5 ♔g7 33.♔g2 ♗d3 34.♖b8 f5 35.♖ba8 ♗c2 36.♔f3 ♗e4+?!= 37.♗xe4 fxe4+ 38.♔e3 ♖c2 39.♖xa4 ♖e7 40.♖d8** ½-½

Eduardo Iturrizaga Bonelli
Maxim Rodshtein
Baku 2015 (1)

1.♘f3 ♘f6 2.c4 c5 3.g3 ♘c6 4.d4 cxd4 5.♘xd4 e5 6.♘b5 ♗b4+ 7.♗d2 a6 [7...♗c5 8.♗e3 ♗b4+ (8...♗xe3 9.♘d6+ ♔f8 10.fxe3±) 9.♘1c3 0-0 10.a3 ♗xc3+ 11.♘xc3 b6 12.♗g5

---

h6 13.♗xf6 ♕xf6 14.♗g2± Tratar-Rodriguez Gonzalez, San Sebastian 2015; 7...♗e7 8.♗g2 0-0 9.0-0 d6 10.♘1c3 a6 11.♘a3 ♗e6 12.♘d5 (12.♗g5) 12...♖c8 13.♖c1±; 7...♗xd2+ 8.♕xd2±] **8.♘5c3**

8...d5 9.cxd5 ♘xd5 10.♗g2 ♗e6 11.0-0 ♘b6 [11...0-0 12.♘xd5 ♗xd5 13.♗xb4 ♗xg2 (13...♗xb4 14.♘c3) 14.♔xg2 ♗xb4 15.♘c3 ♕xd1 16.♖fxd1 ♖fd8 17.♖ac1± Schlosser-Areshchenko, Yerevan 2014] **12.♘a4** [12.♗e3 ♘c4 13.♕c1 0-0 14.♖d1 ♕c7 15.a3 (15.♘d5 ♗xd5 16.♖xd5 ♘xe3 17.♕xe3 ♘d4!) 15...♘xe3 16.♕xe3 ♗a5 17.♘d2? (17.♘d5∞) 17...♗b6 18.♕f3 ♖ad8! Aronian-Nakamura, London 2012; 12.♘e4 ♗e7 13.♗e3 ♘c4 14.♘c1 ♕xd1 15.♖xd1 ♘d4 16.♘bc3 0-0-0 17.♖f1 h6 18.b3 ♘a3 19.e3 ♘dc2 20.♗xa3 ♘xa3 21.♘a4 ♔b8 22.♘ec5 ♗d5 23.e4 ♗c6 24.♖ac1 ♗b5 25.♖fe1 ♗g5 26.f4 exf4 27.h4 ♗e7 28.e5 ♖d2 29.♘e4 ♖d4 30.gxf4 ♗xh4 31.♖ed1 ♖c2 32.♗f3 ♖hd8 33.♗d6 ♖xf4 34.♗xb7 ♗f2+ 35.♔h2 ♗e3 36.♘xb5 ♖h4# Shchekachev-Edouard, Caen 2011] **12...♗e7** [12...♗xd2 13.♗xc6+ bxc6 14.♗xb6 ♕xb6 15.♕xd2 0-0 16.♘c3 ♖fd8 17.♕c2 c5 18.♖fd1 ♖d4 19.e3 ♖b4⇄ Shimanov-Barbosa, Katowice 2014] **13.♘bc3** [13.♘xb6 ♕xb6 14.♘c3 ♖d8 15.♕c1 0-0 16.♗e3 ♘d4∓ Lalith-Istratescu, Hastings 2011] **13...0-0 14.♘xb6** [14.b3 ♘xa4 15.♘xa4 ♖c8 16.♗e3 ♗a5 17.♕b1 f5 18.♘b6 ♖c7 19.♘c4 ♗xc4 (19...♕b5!?=) 20.bxc4 ♗c5 21.♗d5+ ♔h8 22.♗xc5 ♕xc5 23.♕b2 ♕e8 24.♖ab1± Iljin-Elianov, Loo tt 2013] **14...♕xb6 15.♘d5 ♗xd5** [15...♕xb2!?] **16.♗xd5 ♘d4** [16...♖ad8!?= 17.e4 (17.♗c3 ♗c5) 17...♗c5] **17.♗c3 ♖ad8 18.e4 ♔h8 19.♗xd4 exd4 20.♖c1 f5 21.♕d3 ♗f6 22.♖c2± g6 23.♖fc1 ♗g7 24.♖e2 f4 25.♖ec2 ♗e5 26.♖c5**

♕f6 27.♖1c2 h5 28.♗xb7 h4 29.♖c6 ♕g5 30.♗xa6 fxg3 31.hxg3 ♖f7 32.♖c8 ♖xc8 33.♖xc8+ ♔g7 34.♗c4 ♕g4 35.♗xf7 ♕xc8 36.♗c4 hxg3 37.fxg3 ♕h3 38.a4 ♔h7 39.a5 ♗xg3 40.♕d2 ♕g4 41.♕e2 ♕g5 42.a6 ♗b8+ 43.♔f1 ♕c1+ 44.♔g2   ½-½

Francisco Vallejo Pons
Peter Leko
Reykjavik Ech-tt 2015 (7)

1.♘f3 ♘f6 2.c4 c5 3.d4 cxd4 4.♘xd4 ♘c6 5.g3 e5 6.♘b5 ♗b4+ 7.♗d2 a6

8.♗xb4 axb5 9.♗d6 ♕a5+ [9...♘e4 10.♗g2 ♕a5+? (10...♘xd6 11.♕xd6 bxc4) 11.b4! ♘xb4 12.♗xe4 ♘c2+ 13.♔f1 ♘xa1 14.♗xe5 (14.♘a3+−) 14...♕xa2 15.♗xg7+− Bacrot-Vachier-Lagrave, Bastia rapid 2012] 10.♘d2 [10.♘c3 b4 11.♘b5 b3+ 12.♘c3 (12.♕d2 ♕xd2+ 13.♔xd2 ♘e4+ 14.♔e3 ♖xa2 15.♗g2 ♘xd6 16.♘xd6+ ♔e7 17.c5 ♘b4⇄) 12...♘e4 13.♕d3 (S. Ernst-Bruzon Batista, Wijk aan Zee 2012) 13...♘xd6 14.♕xd6 ♘b4↑; 10.♕d2 ♘e4 11.♕xa5 ♘xa5 12.♗xe5 (12.♗a3 (J.Milosevic-Lingur, Khanty-Mansiysk 2015) 12...♘xc4∓) 12...♘b3 13.♗g2 f6! (13...♘xa1 14.♗xe4 f6 15.♗c3) 14.♗f4 ♘xa1 15.♗xe4 ♖xa2 16.♘c3 ♖xb2 17.♗c1 ♖b4 18.♘xb5 d5 19.♗xd5 ♗d7∓] 10...♘e4 [10...bxc4 11.♗g2 b5 12.0-0 ♗b7 13.a4±] 11.c5 ♘xd6 12.cxd6 ♕b4 [12...h5 13.♗g2 ♖h6 14.♕c2 ♖xd6 15.♖d1 ♖h6 16.0-0 h4⇄] 13.♗g2 ♕xd6 [13...♕xb2 14.♖b1 ♕d4 15.e3 ♕xd6 16.♖xb5 ♖xa2 17.♗d5♔] 14.0-0 0-0 15.♘e4 ♕e6 [15...♕xd1 16.♖fxd1 b6 17.♘d6 b4 18.e3±] 16.♘c3 b4 17.♘d5♔ ♖a5 18.♕d2 [△ e2-e3, ♘xb4] 18...e4 [18...d6 19.♘xb4 ♘xb4 20.♕xb4 ♖xa2 21.♗h3 f5 22.♖xa2 ♕xa2 23.♖d1±] 19.♖fd1 b3 [19...d6 20.e3 (20.♕xb4 e3!) 20...♖c5 21.♘xb4±] 20.axb3 ♖xa1 21.♖xa1 d6 22.♖d1 f5 23.b4± ♕f7 24.♘b6 [24.b5 ♘e5 25.♖c1 ♘d3 26.exd3 ♕xd5 27.♕b4+ ♕xd3? 28.♗f1 ♕d5 29.♗c4+−; 24.f3 exf3 25.exf3 ♕e7 26.f4±] 24...♕b3+ 25.♘xc8 [25.♕d5+ ♕xd5 26.♖xd5 ♗e6 (26...♘xb4 27.♖xd6 ♔f7 28.f3 e3 29.f4±) 27.♖xd6 ♔f7 28.g4!? g6 29.gxf5 gxf5 30.f3 exf3 31.♗xf3 ♗e7 32.♖d2 ♘xb4 33.♔f2±; 25.g4!?] 25...♖xc8 26.g4 ♖d8 27.gxf5 d5 28.♖c1 [28.h4 ♔f7 29.h5 h6 30.♔h2 ♕c4 (30...♔f6 31.♖c1 ♕xb4? 32.♖xc6+!) 31.f6!? gxf6 32.♗h3↑ ♕xb4? 33.♕xh6] 28...♕xb4!= 29.♕xb4 ♘xb4 30.♖c7 b6 31.h4 ♖d6 32.♔h2 ♖c6 33.♖b7 ♖c2 34.♖xb6 ♖xb2 [34...♘c6=] 35.♔g3 ♔f7 36.f3 ♘d3 37.♖xb2 ♘xb2 38.fxe4 dxe4 39.♗xe4 ♘f6 40.♔f4 ♘c4 41.♗d5 ♘e5 42.♗g8 h6 43.♗d5 ♘d7 44.♗c6 ♘e5 45.♗b5 ♘f7 46.♗c4 ♘e5 47.♗b5 ♘f7 48.♗c4   ½-½

Exercise 1

position after 7...♗c8-e6

How would you defend the c4-pawn?
(solution on page 253)

Exercise 2

position after 13...♗e7xf6

Which rook would you develop to d1?
(solution on page 254)

Exercise 3

position after 23.♗e3-d4

With two pawns for the exchange and his domination in the centre, White has an overwhelming advantage. Black tried 23...♘xb3 24.♕xb3 ♗xc4. Your answer?
(solution on page 254)

VIEWS

FEATURING

Reviews
& Solutions to Exercises

Reviews

Having Fun!?

by **Glenn Flear**

Englishman Glenn Flear has travelled plenty and currently lives in the south of France. For every Yearbook he reviews a selection of new chess opening books with a man of the world's eye. Being a grandmaster and a prolific chess author himself, Flear's judgment is severe but sincere, and always constructive.

For more book information we refer to our website: www.newinchess.com

There is a natural tendency these days to blindly follow an engine's assessment. Well, of course, they are rather strong, aren't they? Everyone acknowledges that they can be useful tools, but treating them as the ultimate oracle is not a good idea. Do I need to remind you that you should strive to think for yourself, use your own judgement, and then, from time-to-time, call upon the services of your silicon friend? It should remain your assistant, not your master.

Liberated authors will stress the 'practical chances' in a variation in order to emphasize their own sentiments about the type of position on the board. It's like they are aiming to put across the message, 'I know the engine gives such-and-such an assessment, but in an over-the-board game it's far more difficult to handle for...', which brings me to the Dave Smerdons of this world. They have a tendency to play tricky lines that lead to exciting chess. Apart from bringing enjoyment, this approach pays off more often than not. Imagine, for a moment, 'sacrificing' a pawn with black for easy play but objectively only partial compensation. The analysis engine may shake its virtual head and insist that it's +0.5 for White. However, a human opponent, whilst all alone (hopefully!), would have to find a string of precise moves to maintain any advantage. Meantime, it can be great fun watching an opponent sweat!

In contrast, a lot of positional main lines are around the +0.2 mark for White. Unfortunately, despite the achievement of near-equality, you may end up with boring games with virtually no winning chances. Is that what you call fun?

David Smerdon
Smerdon's Scandinavian
Everyman Chess

The Scandinavian with 2...♕xd5 has been featured in a number of previous books, but the affable Australian GM is building his repertoire around 1.e4 d5 2.exd5 ♘f6. This is quite an ambitious project in that it doesn't have a great reputation, although I have seen it played a fair bit at a lower level.

You might start having your doubts as soon as you begin reading the Introduction: 'This opening is unsound'. A great sales pitch (or

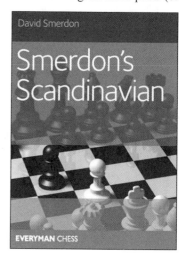

not?) from the author! The rest of the book however does show that Black can play in a daring way and obtain decent 'practical chances' against whatever White comes up with.

This thick book is jam-packed full of original analyses and curious, if not weird, ideas. On certain pages the author puts the analysis to one side and instead waxes lyrical about all sorts of themes, approaches, and general psychology. I could describe him as modest and self-effacing, even to the point of calling himself a deranged lunatic at one point! Smerdon is many things: funny, lively, passionate, thorough, and courageous, but certainly not a wuss (see page 162)!

An enjoyable read for those who like 'something a little different', that is both on their bedside table and at the chessboard.

At times Smerdon is almost persuading the reader to persist along with him in his attempts to make it all palatable. I suppose the barrier for many players is psychological: 'It just can't be good', they will exclaim. However, time and time again, Smerdon, the player, has been able to win from these optically dicey positions, so we certainly should respect Smerdon, the author, in his efforts.

Often, one just has to get past the stage of worrying about only getting half-a-pawn's worth of compensation. If you were, for example, to enter the first few moves of the Benko Gambit and ask your analysis engine to give a judgement, what does it come up with? On mine it's about +0.5. Well, experience has taught me that many resulting middlegames are more difficult to play with white. In practice, Black scores as well in such positions as he does in the main lines of various mainstream defences.

So can Black do something similar against 1.e4 ? If so, it could be

in Smerdon's Scandinavian! In many lines Black shakes matters up with a pawn gambit here or there and the 'compensation' can be of the long-term variety which is sometimes under-estimated by the engines. Take for example in the Icelandic Gambit.

1.e4 d5 2.exd5 ♘f6 3.c4 e6!? 4.dxe6 ♗xe6 5.♘f3 ♕e7 6.♕e2 ♘c6 7.d4 ♗f5! 8.♕xe7+ ♗xe7 9.a3 ♘a5 10.♘bd2 c5

A typical position where White's computer-edge is compensated for in the real world by Black's activity and various 'human' emotions.

The author is quite open about pointing out some promising options for White. In the past, he hasn't been unduly worried what his opponents have come up with, as he knows that his experience in such positions will generally be a plus that counteracts any preparation. Maybe things will change, now that the book has been published! Here are a couple of annoying lines, which might help you if you are playing Dave soon!

1.e4 d5 2.exd5 ♘f6 3.♘f3 ♗g4
Naturally it's possible for Black to change tack and opt for 3...♕xd5 4.♘c3 ♕a5 or 4...♕d6.

4.♗b5+ ♘bd7 5.h3
As recommended by a number of authors.

5...♗h5 6.♘c3 a6 7.♗e2 ♘b6 8.d4 ♘fxd5 9.♘xd5 ♕xd5
Material equality has been re-established with White having the plan of playing for

c2-c4 in order to obtain a slight preponderance in the centre.

10.0-0 e6

'... I must concede that White's position is optically more pleasant... [after] many hours studying this position, my conclusion is that it is objectively equal.'

11.b3 ♗e7 12.c4 ♕d8 13.♗e3 0-0 14.♘e5 ♗xe2 15.♕xe2
Now Smerdon (coincidentally, sitting next to me) played his novelty...

15...♘d7
... in a team rapid game.

16.♖ad1 ♘xe5 17.dxe5 ♕c8
Hodgson-Smerdon, Daventry team rapid 2014, and although your analysis engines will prefer White, Smerdon assures the reader that '... Black can hold the white forces at bay with minimum discomfort'. So although this line isn't particularly thrilling, from Black's point of view, it is pretty solid.

If you prefer something more active then you could try the following, which DS calls the 'correspondence refutation'.

1.e4 d5 2.exd5 ♘f6 3.d4 ♗g4 4.f3 ♗f5 5.g4 ♗g6 6.c4

6...e6

'The only way to combat White's attempt at an outright refutation is to stand up to the challenge and fight fire with fire.' (DS) That's all very noble until you get yourself burnt! (GF).

Otherwise there is 6...c6 (which is also on the hot side!), e.g. 7.♘c3 cxd5 8.g5 ♘fd7 9.cxd5 (Smerdon's novelty) 9...♞a6. Now the author states: 'White can keep an advantage from this position with precise play, but Black retains good practical chances.' In order to further increase his understanding the author has invited chess club colleagues to test this position at blitz. He has also run some engine versus engine matches. I don't think that many authors go to that much trouble! He obviously felt a bit nervous about this line, but apparently Black did pretty well in these informal encounters.

He feels that Black's sacrifice may not be 'objectively sound', but adds that one shouldn't 'be too dismissive of Black's chances'.

7.♘c3 exd5

Here 7...c5!? is a creative idea that hasn't been played yet: 8.♗e3 (Bücker) 8...exd5 (DS) 9.dxc5 (Houdini), and I can't see anything that smacks of compensation for Black.

8.g5 ♘h5

Or 8...♘fd7 9.♘xd5 ♘c6 10.h4 ♘b6 11.♕e2+ ♗e7 12.♘xe7 ♘xd4 (12...♘xe7 13.h5 ♗f5 with another case of 'White being better, but in practice it isn't easy to handle) 13.♘c6+ ♘xe2 14.♘xd8 ♘xg1 15.♖xg1 ♖xd8 with a two-bishops pull for White.

9.f4 ♘c6 10.♗e2 dxc4 11.♗xh5 ♗xh5 12.♕xh5 ♘xd4 13.♔f2

Iv.Popov-Laylo, Quezon City 2014, and White can maintain his advantage.

Tightrope walking aside, is this why Smerdon states that his version of the Scandinavian isn't really sound?

In the book, White and Black are given the pronoun 'she' rather than the conventional 'he'. I'm not sure if this is a pun or intended as a gesture towards gender equality, but it came across as odd. In most books 'she' is only used when a player is known to be female. In France, where I live, White and Black are plural entities and thus 'ils' (which translates to a masculine-leaning 'they') is standard. Perhaps a non-binary reference is the most politically correct?

The title is appropriate as the author has been at the helm in the development of the theory over the last 15 years or so. The work has much to offer, especially at club player level where one can 'get away' more readily with such bravado. I personally find this approach to be too risky (maybe I respect my analysis engine too much, or I'm just a boring old codger?), but there are no doubt other GMs around who are willing to take calculated risks in the opening. So summing up, the book is for adventurous spirits.

Gawain Jones
Grandmaster Repertoire:
The Dragon (Volumes 1 & 2)
Quality Chess

It has always taken a certain breed to want to live in the land of Dragons. I remember in my youth in England many young aggressive players being attracted to this fiery variation. In fact, it is no exaggeration to state that the Sicilian Dragon was the Black opening par excellence that fuelled the British Chess phenomenon of the seventies.

The amazing combinations and tactical ideas are still exciting even in the computer age. So what is different in 2015?

Nowadays, an engine will tell you after the game if a sacrifice is sound, but the emotions at the

board are the same. In the famous Yugoslav Attack, there is still the thrill of launching a dangerous queenside initiative mixed with the alarm at what White is doing down the h-file. Perhaps the biggest difference now is that with the highest-level analysis available at one's fingertips, your preparation can tip the balance of power in your direction.

The author is a high-level regular Dragon practitioner and has also previously published analyses and counter-analyses elsewhere. So there are not many around who are as authoritative as Gawain and, not surprising, he gives the opening the full Quality treatment (i.e. he analyses the key variations until the pips squeak).

Why are there two volumes? Each one is over 300 pages, and Quality has clearly decided to avoid 600+ page books. However, this means that to get the full story according to Jones you will have to fork out the princely sum of €48.98. Another negative is that you have to learn an awful lot theory if you want to play this variation.

On the plus side, the author's deep and measured analysis concludes that Black is holding his own. Here is an example of one of the English GM's improvements.

1.e4 c5 2.♘f3 d6 3.d4 cxd4 4.♘xd4 ♘f6 5.♘c3 g6 6.♗e3 ♗g7 7.f3 0-0 8.♕d2 ♘c6 9.♗c4 ♗d7 10.0-0-0 ♖c8 11.♗b3 ♘e5 12.♔b1 ♘c4 13.♗xc4 ♖xc4 14.g4 b5 15.h4 h5 16.gxh5 ♘xh5 17.♘ce2 ♕c7 18.♗h6 ♖c8 19.♗xg7 ♔xg7 20.♖c1

Now, instead of 20...a5 21.♖hg1 e6 22.f4, Pogonina-Sudakova, Elista 2002, with some advantage to White, Jones takes the opportunity to control some squares on the kingside with...

20...♖h8 21.♘c3

Here 21.♖cg1!? looks more natural to me.

21...♕c5=.

The Yugoslav Attack is actually the subject of the author's attention for over 400 pages, i.e. all of Volume Two plus more than a third of Volume One.

Here is another key line where Black seems to be perfectly okay.

1.e4 c5 2.♘f3 d6 3.d4 cxd4 4.♘xd4 ♘f6 5.♘c3 g6 6.♗e3 ♗g7 7.f3 0-0 8.♕d2 ♘c6 9.♗c4 ♗d7 10.0-0-0 ♖c8

For those who like to note such things, there is a typo on the summary page missing a pair of moves out, which (being a Dragon layman) confused me for a while.

11.♗b3 ♘xd4 12.♗xd4 b5 13.♘d5 ♘xd5 14.♗xg7 ♔xg7 15.exd5 a5 16.a3 ♔g8 17.h4 b4 18.axb4 axb4 19.h5 ♗f5 20.hxg6 ♗xg6

As it isn't draughts, White isn't obliged to capture on b4! So Negi examines 21.♕e3!?, whereas Pavlovic and now Jones give 21.♕d4!?.

Instead...

21.♕xb4

... was played in D.Ledger-R.Pert, Hastings 2011, whereupon Jones gives the following:

21...♖b8 22.♕c3 ♕b6=.

Nor could other Quality authors Pavlovic (2010) and now Negi (2015) find any advantage for White in this, the so-called Topalov Variation. So it looks like the Dragon is still as hard to slay as ever.

It's good to see the author give plenty of space to White's rapid queenside castling, as this has been often chosen by certain authorities as their anti-Dragon weapon.

1.e4 c5 2.♘f3 d6 3.d4 cxd4 4.♘xd4 ♘f6 5.♘c3 g6 6.♗e3 ♗g7 7.f3 0-0 8.♕d2 ♘c6 9.0-0-0 d5

Books for 'average' players sometimes suggest less-trustworthy alternatives such as 9...♗d7, but as usual, the Quality author doesn't shirk from the main line.

10.♕e1

The author has already faced this cunning retreat himself a couple of times recently.

10...e5 11.♘xc6 bxc6 12.exd5 ♘xd5 13.♗c4 ♗e6 14.♔b1

This recent development was recommended in *Modernized: The Open Sicilian* by Amanov & Kavutskiy and was also given a closer look in Van der Tak's Survey in Yearbook 116.

14...♖b8 15.♘e4 f5

'...an interesting attempt to sharpen the struggle' – Amanov & Kavutskiy.

16.♘g5 ♗c8 17.h4 h6 18.♘e4

At this point A & K stop, preferring White slightly. Jones looks at this position for 8-9 pages(!), and

suggests more than one promising way for Black to continue...

18...fxe4

GJ admits that White keeps some advantage after 18...♗e6, as played in Edouard-Jones, London 2014.

Otherwise there is 18...♕c7!?, a novelty prepared by Jones and Palliser, who continue with 19.♘c5 ♔h7 20.h5 g5 21.c3 and now either 21...e4!? or 21...♕b6.

19.fxe4 ♖f4!?

Lampert-Jones, Wunsiedel 2015, with good play.

Volume 2 deals with all the other white attempts such as the Classical, Levenfish and Fianchetto. Here too the author has some great suggestions. The following isn't his move, but it's one that caught my eye! Coincidentally it puts a spanner in the works of one of Tim Taylor's lines in *Slay the Sicilian* (Everyman 2012).

12...♘xe4! 13.♘xe4 ♗xf5

... with excellent compensation.

If we compare the Dragon and Smerdon's Scandinavian we note that in both cases Black obtains complicated play (and thus arguably potential winning chances). The Dragon is based around a tried-and-tested structure and is probably sounder, but there is more to learn. The type of Scandinavian in question goes off the beaten track right from the beginning, but can be highly risky even if you know your stuff.

Even in the old days, the Dragon needed good preparation, so these analysis-rich volumes won't put off the die-hards and may well inspire the stronger echelon of the book-buying public. However I can't see weaker players being able to benefit much from the latest wrinkles. The doubt arises for those who can be considered as 'somewhere in-between'. If you are in this category and are tempted to dabble (but don't know the Dragon very well), then make sure that you have plenty of time on your hands!

It's the moment to sum up. These latest volumes in the Grandmaster Repertoire series are well-researched, nicely written, and diligently put together. Hopefully the high standards continue in this excellent, highly recommended series.

Alexander Delchev &
Semko Semkov
Understanding The Queen's
Gambit Accepted
Chess Stars

Semko Semkov was involved in an earlier QGA project along with Konstantin Sakaev in 2003. This time his partner is fellow Bulgarian Alexander Delchev.
Both of these Chess Stars works feature fairly loose repertoires with a number of options depending on taste. In some cases, the authors suggest a

radical solution for Black, but still supply the necessary information to enable the reader to fall back on mainstream theory. The short Introduction already lays out the salient points of where the repertoire is taking you.

Delchev, who is still an active player, seems to have tried out a number of the suggestions himself in recent tournaments. Here is one quite rare idea that the book brings to our attention.

1.d4 d5 2.c4 dxc4 3.♘f3 ♘f6 4.e3 ♗g4 5.♗xc4 e6 6.♘c3 ♘c6!?

D & S vaunt the merits of this move whilst pointing out the drawbacks of the alternatives.

7.♗b5

Similar is 7.h3 ♗h5 8.♗b5.

7...♗d6 8.e4

Instead 8.♕a4 ♗xf3 9.gxf3 0-0 10.♗xc6 bxc6 11.♕xc6 ♖b8 (Edouard-Delchev, Linares 2013) gives Black excellent practical compensation.

8...♘d7 9.♗e3 0-0 10.h3 ♗h5

11.e5!?

At first, 11.♗e2 ♘b6 12.0-0 f5! 13.♘g5 is given by the engines as a shade better for White. D & S persist and after the following almost forced sequence: 13...♗xe2 14.♘xe2 ♕d7 15.♕b3 ♖ae8 16.e5 h6 17.♘xe6 ♕xe6 18.♕xe6+ ♖xe6 19.♘f4 ♖ee8 20.exd6 g5 21.d5 gxf4 22.♗xb6 cxb6 23.dxc6 bxc6, play leads to a 'drawn' endgame according to the authors.

11...♗e7 12.♗e2 ♘b6 13.g4?!
Maybe 13.a3!?=.

13...♗g6 14.h4 ♗b4!?
The calm 14...h6!? comes into consideration: Can White achieve something on the kingside or will he just over-press?

15.h5 ♗e4 16.h6 g6 17.♔f1
Better is 17.0-0.

17...♗xc3 18.bxc3 f6!³
Maki Uuro-Brynell, Izmir 2004.

I am quite impressed as this looks like a convenient development set-up for Black. However, if this doesn't appeal then the privileged reader can choose between the fashionable 3...a6 (not much theory, but it can easily lead to drawish simplification) or the main-line Classical with 3...♘f6 4.e3 ♘f6 and so on.

As in a number of Chess Stars publications, each section is divided up in a way which facilitates the reader's task of getting to understand the material: a winning formula that some other publishers could learn from. The 'Main ideas', 'step-by-step' and 'annotated games' are self-explanatory by name and ideally presented by nature.

I must note that the quality of the English language used in the text is quite high, and contrasts quite markedly from the 2003 work mentioned above.

I particularly liked the authors' readiness to show why certain variations don't work very well

for Black. Here is one which has received great attention of late:

1.d4 d5 2.c4 dxc4 3.e4 b5?!

S & D don't believe this to be fully correct. So they don't include it as part of the repertoire, however in Chapter 3 they are able to '... show Black's problems in that topical line'. Here are some ideas that go beyond what Bogdan Lalic mentioned in Yearbook 116.

4.a4 c6 5.axb5 cxb5 6.♘c3 a6 7.♘xb5 axb5 8.♖xa8 ♗b7

9.♖a1

D & S also examine 9.♖a2!?, e.g. 9...e6 10.f3!? (10.♘e2 ♗b4+ 11.♗d2 ♘c6 12.b3 (it's convenient that the rook on a2 defends the bishop on d2) 12...♘ge7 (12...♘f6! is critical) 13.bxc4 bxc4 14.♕b1 (14.♕a4!) 14...c3 15.♗xc3 ♗xc3+ 16.♘xc3 ♕xd4 17.♘b5 ♕e5, Vidit-Tari, Berlin World Blitz 2015) 10...♘c6 11.♘e2 ♗b4+ 12.♗d2 ♘ge7 13.b3 0-0 14.bxc4 bxc4, Hambleton-Ganguly, Edmonton 2015, and now D & S suggest 15.♕c1! ♕b6 16.♕xc4 ♖c8 17.♘f4 (instead of this, my engines propose 17.♘g3, equally with some white advantage) with a pull.

9...e6 10.♘e2

Rare, but even the better known 10.f3 could be favourable, e.g. 10...f5 11.♘h3 fxe4 12.fxe4 ♘f6 13.♘g5 ♕b6, Kovalenko-Heberla, Katowice 2015, and now the authors give the improvement 14.♗e2! ♘xe4 15.0-0±.

10...♘f6 11.f3 ♘c6 12.♗e3 ♗b4+ 13.♘c3 0-0

14.♔e2!

An amazing looking move and apparently Morozevich's idea according to D & S. Certainly the engines prefer White, as does the analysis in the book.

In the following example, the authors reveal a way in which the reader can counter a repertoire promoted by both Avrukh and Kornev.

1.d4 d5 2.c4 dxc4 3.e3 e5 4.♗xc4 exd4 5.exd4 ♗d6! 6.♘f3 ♘f6 7.0-0 0-0 8.h3 ♘c6 9.♘c3 h6 10.♕c2 ♘b4 11.♕b1 ♗e6 12.♗xe6 fxe6 13.♖e1

Delchev's comment is: 'I have always wondered why... Avrukh prefers White's position.'

Kornev is also keen on White here.

13...♕d7

Similar is 13...♕e8!? 14.♗d2 ♘bd5 15.♖e2 ♕f7 (this could also arise from 13...♕d7) 16.♘e5 ♕h5 17.♕d3 ♕f5 18.g4 ♕xd3 19.♘xd3 (Avrukh), and now the UTQGA improvement goes 19...♖fe8 20.♖ae1 ♔f7 21.♘b5 a6 22.♘xd6+ cxd6 23.♗f4 ♖ad8=.

14.♗d2

D & S point out the following route to equality that improves on Avrukh's 2008 repertoire...

14...♖ae8!

... as in Avrukh-Golod, Jerusalem 2013.

15.♖e2 ♘c6 16.♕d3 e5=

The book also examines other options (for both colours) from the diagram, leading to the conclusion that Black doesn't have any real problems here.

The authors also mention a couple of previous books where the recommendation for White is to employ the Exchange Variation (where 7.dxc5 occurs in the Classical, leading to an early trade of queens). I like D & S's comment that those other works 'prefer to discuss irrelevant variations while "timidly" evading the most topical lines'. So on pages 66 to 70, D & S aim to point out what really matters in these types of position with poignant examples and some words of advice such as 'I repeat once again: the main factor is piece activity'.

One of the problems with playing the Queen's Gambit Accepted is when White delays or omits c2-c4, but even here a chapter (albeit a short one) is supplied offering some useful ideas for Black.

The book is a manageable size and will suit those who will want to carry it around!

What more can you ask for? For me, this is an absolute gem of a book. Get it!

Alexey Bezgodov
The Double Queen's Gambit
New in Chess

It was such a good idea of the author to write about this subject. If Black can get away with 2...c5, and even equalize with it, then it requires proper investigation.

The early ...c7-c5 thrust arises quite often in queen's pawn openings, and yet I don't believe anyone else has given it as much attention as Alexey Bezgodov. The curious aspect of this work is that the bibliography contains more than a hundred references, despite the fact that 2...c5 rarely gets a look in! Perhaps this is a reflection of the author's style with thoughts and input coming from all directions. Further evidence of this universal approach can be seen by looking at the titles of Chapters Three to Five, which involve transpositions into the Sicilian Alapin, the Slav Exchange, and the Panov Attack!

Furthermore, although the cover lays out the defining position after 1.d4 d5 2.c4 c5, the author's idea is to react with ...c5 against most white second moves, and in particular 2.♘f3, 2.♗f4, and 2.♗g5.

A novel idea is the 'retro-training' section, which actually involves a series of exercises from games of the past. So you can combine some illustrative games, history, and the pleasure of solving problems.

Another pleasant point is the large number of diagrams. The author has also opted for light notes with plenty of text, so the lay-out is clear, informative and entertaining.

However, there are aspects of this book that baffled me. The

chapter headings are a little difficult to understand so I found myself turning quite a few pages in order to work out what they meant. Unfortunately, the most frustrating aspect of this work is more serious. Although the author gets close, he has a nasty habit of avoiding crunch questions. Here is an example:

Firstly, after 1.d4 d5 2.♗f4 c5 the big issue is whether 3.e4 is any good.

The author mentions it in passing, but that's all. Then 3...dxe4 4.d5 is a reversed Albin Counter-Gambit with White having the extra, useful move ♗f4. It's dangerous, double-edged, and even dastardly, but the author has nothing to add. Some sources suggest that 3...♘c6 is better, but this too leads to sharp complications (for example 4.exd5 ♕xd5 5.♘c3 ♕xd4 6.♘d5). Sadly, you'll have to investigate elsewhere if you want any guidance.

Even more frustratingly, a key game is missing from this book. On page 216 the author states 'there are more details on this in the next game'. Unfortunately the chapter ends abruptly a few lines later and the next section is quite different in character!

However, in Chapter 20 on page 233, the author addresses White's fianchetto more seriously, but still misses White's most challenging try. Incidentally, Avrukh recommended something similar, but it seems that Laurent Fressinet has found the best way.

Flear-Degraeve

St.Affrique 2010

1.d4 d5 2.c4 c5 3.cxd5 ♕xd5 4.♘f3 cxd4 5.♘c3 ♕a5 6.♘xd4 ♘f6 7.g3 e5 8.♘b3 ♕c7

9.♗g2

Here 9.♗g5 is Avrukh's suggestion from his Grandmaster Repertoire 1.d4 volume 1 from 2008, which is absent from the Bibliography. He continues with 9...♗b4 (this is better than 9...♕c6 10.♗xf6 gxf6 11.♘d5± ♗b4+? 12.♘xb4 ♕xh1 13.♕d6 ♗e6 14.♘c5+−, Migot-Moussard, Nancy 2013) 10.♖c1 ♘e4 (if 10...♘bd7 then simply 11.♗g2 0-0 12.0-0; plausible however is 10...♕c6 11.♗xf6 gxf6 12.f3 ♗e6 13.a3 ♗xc3+ 14.♖xc3 ♕b6 15.e3 ♘d7 16.♕c2 0-0 17.♘d2 ♖fd8 with a reasonable game) 11.♗d2 (Bezgodov seems unaware that he was following Avrukh) 11...♘xd2 (11...♗xc3 12.♗xc3 ♕b6 13.♗d4 ♕b4+ and now AB analyzes both 14.♘d2 and 14.♕d2 to equality) 12.♘xd2 ♘c6 13.♗g2 and claims some advantage, but the engines don't think it is much.

9...♗b4 10.♗d2

The strongest way for White could well be Fressinet's 10.♕d3! (which is not mentioned at this point by AB at all) 10...0-0 11.♗g5 when I can't see a way for Black to equalize: 11...♖d8 (11...a5!? 12.0-0 a4 13.♗xf6 gxf6 White) 12.♕f3 ♗xc3+ (nor do other tries impress: 12...♘bd7 13.0-0 h6 14.♘d5 ♕d6 15.♘xf6+ ♘xf6 16.♗xf6 ♕xf6 17.♖fd1;

12...♗g4?! 13.♕xb7±; 12...a5 13.♖c1 a4 14.♗xf6 gxf6 15.a3! ♗xc3+ 16.♖xc3 ♘c6 17.♘c5 with an edge) 13.♕xc3 (being able to capture with the queen gives White a promising game whether Black captures or not) 13...♘c6 (or 13...♕xc3+ 14.bxc3 ♘c6 15.♘c5 h6 16.♗xf6 gxf6 17.♖d1 ♖b8 18.♖xd8+ ♘xd8 19.♔d2) 14.0-0 ♗e6 15.♖ac1 ♖ac8 16.♗xc6 with a pull to White, Fressinet-Degraeve, Belfort 2010.

10...0-0 11.0-0

On pages 215-6, we find Nemet-Blum, which continued 11.♖c1 ♘c6 12.0-0 ♖d8 and now instead of 13.a3 (0-1 in 15!) Bezgodov states that 13.♕c2! ♗e6 14.♗g5 'is better. This is where further analysis is promised in the 'next game'. For the record, it would then be about equal according to the engines.

11...♖d8 12.♕c1 ♗e6 13.♗g5 ♗xc3?!

Here 13...♘bd7! 14.♘e4 ♖ac8= would have been correct.

14.♕xc3 ♕xc3 15.bxc3 ♘bd7 16.♗xb7

16.♘a5!? is also promising.

16...♖ab8 17.♘a5

with an edge for White.

So despite the author's charming style and great intentions this book is not rigorous enough for my liking. There are plenty of model games which are agreeably annotated, but this work won't suit players who want to delve into the critical theory.

Solutions to Exercises

Exercise 1 (page 48) **SI 1.3**
Colovic-Christiansen (analysis)
Reykjavik 2014 (2)

After **10...exd5 11.e5!** White regains the piece while retaining an advantage. Black should play 10...♞g4!, with a good position.

~

Exercise 2 (page 48) **SI 1.3**
Palac-Kadric
Bol na Bracu 2014 (2)

After **20...♝e6?**, played in the game, White seized the initiative: **21.♝xe6 fxe6 22.♕b1 ♖c8 23.♖b7**. Black should have played 20...♕c8 with a small edge for White.

~

Exercise 3 (page 48) **SI 1.3**
Safarli-Grandelius
Dubai 2015 (8)

Black played **47...♕f5??** and after the forcing **48.♕h6++− ♔f7 49.♖f4 exf4 50.♖e1** he had to resign, whereas 47...♕f3 48.♕h6+ ♔f7 49.♕h7 ♔e6 50.♕xg6+ ♔f6 would have led to a small advantage for Black.

~

Exercise 1 (page 58) **SI 14.7**
Kenes-Li
Al Ain 2013 (10)

15...♝e6! The f7-pawn should not always be left en prise. The highly attractive 15...♝g4!? was played in the game, but it worked only because White took with the queen in the wrong way. **16.♝xe6 fxe6** with a strong initiative for Black due to his powerful bishop. A sample line is **17.♖xh6 ♖f8 18.♕h5+ ♔d7 19.♕h3 ♖ab8!**. The rooks are perfectly placed as well and Black is ready to break through. **20.♔f1 ♖xb2 21.♘d1 ♕b5+ 22.♔g1 ♖xc2**, winning material as **23.♖xe6 ♔d8 24.♕h7 ♖h8! 25.♕xe7+ ♔c8 26.♖xe5 ♕f1+!!** leads to a pretty mate!

~

Exercise 2 (page 58) **SI 14.7**
Rajlich-Dub
Budapest 2000 (2)

Black played **16...a4! 17.♘xa4 ♖xa4! 18.♝xa4**, but missed the magnificient

intermediate move **18...♖h8!!**. After the game continuation 18...♕xb2? 19.♝xc6+ ♝d7 20.♝xd7+ ♔xd7 21.♕e2 ♖c8 White could claim an advantage by means of 22.♖hb1! ♕xc2 23.♖b7+ △ 23...♔e6?! 24.♖c1!+−. **19.♖xh8+** 19.♖f1? ♕xb2−+ △ 20.♝xc6+ ♔f8. **19...♝xh8 20.♝xc6+ ♔f8! 21.♝b5! ♕xb5** After 21...♕xb2 22.♖b1 ♕g1+ 23.♝f1 ♝a6! 24.c4 ♝xc4 25.♕xb2 ♕xf1+ 26.♔d2 ♕d3+ Black has a draw at least. **22.c3** The diagonal, weakened by 16.f3, can once again be used in case of 22.c4?! ♕c5!. **22...♘e5 23.0-0-0 ♘c4** and Black has the initiative thanks to his active minor pieces.

~

Exercise 3 (page 58) **SI 14.7**
Azarov-Dydyshko
Minsk 2002 (9)

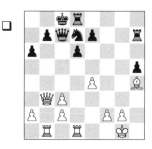

The powerful blow **23.♖xd6!** won a second pawn: **23...exd6 24.♝xd8 ♔xd8 25.♕g8+ ♘f8 26.♕xf8+ ♔d7 27.♕f5+ ♔e8 28.♖d1 ♖h6 29.e5! dxe5 30.♖d5** and Black had had enough.

~

Exercise 1 (page 64) **SI 14.12**
Howell-Neverov
Hastings 2010 (4)

10.e5! ♝xg2 11.exf6 ♝xf1 12.fxe7 ♕xe7 13.♕xf1±

Exercise 2 (page 64) **SI 14.12**
Fedorchuk-Almagro Mazariegos
Navalmoral 2012 (3)

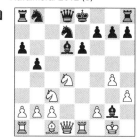

13.♘xe6!+− **fxe6** **14.♕xd6 ♗b7 15.♕xe6+ ♔f8 16.♗g5 1-0**
16...♕xg5 17.♕e8#; 16...♘f6 17.♗xf6 gxf6 18.♖ad1+−.
~

Exercise 3 (page 64) **SI 14.12**
Van Koningsveldt-Jonsson
Email 2012

16.g5!± ♗f8 16...♘e4 17.♕h5+ ♔g8 18.♗xe4 dxe4 19.g6+−; 16...♗b4 17.♗d2 (17.c3; 17.♗e3!?) 17...♗xd2 18.♕xd2 ♘e4 19.♕f4 ♔g8 20.f3; 16...♗c5 17.♗e3! ♗xe3 18.gxf6 ♗xf2+ 19.♔xf2 ♕b6+ (19...♕xf6?? 20.♕h5++−) 20.♕d4±. **17. gxf6 ♖xe1+ 18.♕xe1 ♕xf6 19.♘e3 ♕e5 20.♕d1±**
~

Exercise 1 (page 74) **SI 23.6**
I.Almasi-Szabo
Budapest 2015 (5)

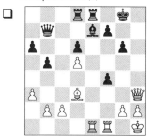

25.♗xg6!! fxg6 26.♕h6!+−

Exercise 2 (page 74) **SI 23.6**
Meszaros-Antal
Hungary tt 2005

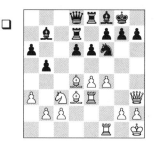

19.♘d5!!N ♘g4 19...♘xe4 20.♗f6!+−; 19...exd5 20.♗xf6+−; 19...♘xd5 20.exd5 g6 21.dxe6+−. **20.♕xg4 exd5 21.e5 g6 22.f5** 22.e6+−. **22...dxe5 23.♗xe5 ♗g7 24.fxg6! fxg6 25.♗xg6 hxg6 26.♕xg6 d4□ 27.♗xg7** 27.♖h3? ♗e4!!. **27...♕xg2+ 28.♕xg2 ♖xg7 29.♖g3 ♖ee7 30.♖g1+−**
~

Exercise 3 (page 74) **SI 23.6**
Leko-Wang Yue (analysis)
Beijing 2014 (6)

28.f6!! ♗xf6 29.♖xf6 ♘xf6 30.♗xh6+−
~

Exercise 1 (page 79) **SI 29.1**
Bahmatsiy-Nikolovsky
Prague jr 2012 (4)

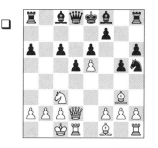

13.♘e4! 13.♗e2 was played in the game. **13...♗e7** 13...♘xg3?! 14.♘f6+ ♔xf6 (14...♔e7

15.♕b4+) 15.exf6 ♘xh1 16.♗d3 ♘xf2 17.♕xf2+−; 13...♖b8 14.♕c3. **14.♕c3±**
~

Exercise 2 (page 79) **SI 29.1**
Debashis-Gupta
Abu Dhabi 2015 (9)

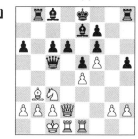

16.♔b1?! 16.a3!± was a good prophylactic move with the idea ♔b1-♖e3-♖d3-♘a4 and c2-c4-c5: 16...d5 17.exd5 cxd5 18.♕xd5 ♖xd5 19.♘xd5. **16...♖b4!**
~

Exercise 3 (page 79) **SI 29.1**
Debashis-Gupta
Abu Dhabi 2015 (9)

20...♗f8?! 20...♕d2! 21.♕f1 (21.♕xd2 ♖xd2 22.♖c2; 21.♕f3 ♕d3+ 22.♕xd3 ♖xd3 23.c5 dxc5 (23...d5 24.♘b6) 24.♘b6 (24.♘xc5 ♕d2) 24...♗b7 25.♘c4 ♗d8 26.♖ed1 ♖xd1 (26...♖d4? 27.♖xd4+−) 27.♖xd1 ♗c7) 21...♕d3+ 22.♕xd3 ♖xd3 23.c5 dxc5 24.♗d1!! ♖d2 25.♗f3!±.
~

Exercise 1 (page 86) **SI 33.7**
Petrosyan-Garcia Guerrero
Katowice 2014 (5)

A space advantage: **18...♕xd2 19.♖xd2 ♗xd5 20.♖xd5 ♖a2 21.♗f1 ♘c5 22.b4** etc.

~

Exercise 2 (page 86) SI 33.7
Odeev-Sevdimaliev
Konya 2015 (6)

To exchange on f6 and establish a knight on d5: **13...♗e6 14.f4 ♖fc8 15.b3 axb3 16.axb3 ♕b4 17.f5 ♗d7 18.♗xf6 ♗xf6 19.♘d5** etc.

Exercise 3 (page 86) SI 33.7
Zakhartsov-Bressac
Cappelle-la-Grande 2011 (5)

To exchange pieces without allowing changes to the pawn structure.

~

Exercise 1 (page 96) SI 34.8
Analysis

20.h4 ♖f7! 20...fxe4 21.h5 g5 22.fxg5 ♖f7 23.g6 ♖g7 24.0-0∓ is much less clear.

21.h5 g5! Suddenly the white queen is in danger. **22.♘f6+** 22.fxg5 ♗f8–+; 22.0-0 ♗f8 (22...fxe4–+) 23.♕xg5+ ♖g7 24.♕f6 fxe4–+; 22.♘xg5 ♗f8 23.♘xf7 ♗xh6 24.♘xh6+ ♔g7–+. **22...♗xf6** 22...♔h8!? **23.exf6 g4 24.♕g5+ ♔h8 25.0-0 ♗b7** and Black's position is strategically winning.

~

Exercise 2 (page 96) SI 34.8
Malakhov-Ganichev
St Petersburg 2014 (6)

17.c4! Although 17.♗e3 and 17.♖d1 are good, this move is stronger. After **17...♕d4+** (17...♕b7 18.a4 0-0 19.♗d3+– is winning for White) **18.♗e3 ♕xa1 19.♖g1!** Black's queen is lost. Material will be balanced, but White's better coordination decides.

~

Exercise 3 (page 96) SI 34.8
Kurmann-Moiseenko
Tromsø 2014 (6)

17...exf4! 17...♗d4 18.♕xc7 ♖xc7 19.♖b1 exf4 20.♔d1 is less clear. **18.♗b2** 18.bxc5 ♕e5+ 19.♔f3 (19.♔f2 ♕d4+ 20.♔e1 ♕xa1–+) 19...♕xa1 20.♗b2 ♕e1 21.♕c3 ♕xc3+ 22.♗xc3 ♖b8 23.♔f2 ♖b3∓; 18.♕c3!? ♕d6! 19.♗b2 (19.bxc5 ♖xc5 20.♕d4 ♖c4 21.♕d2 ♕c5–+) 19...d4 20.♕b3 ♗b6∓. **18...♗e3 19.♕xc7 ♖xc7 20.♔d3 d6∓** Three pawns for the piece and an initiative with his active pieces are more than enough compensation for Black.

Exercise 1 (page 105) SI 45.1
Tabakov-Adorjan
Varna 1969

19...♗xc3!–+ 20.bxc3 20.♘xc3 ♗xd1 21.♕xd1 dxc5–+. **20...♕b5+ 21.♔a1 ♕xe2 22.♕xe2 ♗xe2 23.♖d2 ♗h5** and Black won easily, on move 41.

~

Exercise 2 (page 105) SI 45.1
Kaaber-Molvig
Copenhagen 2002 (6)

17...♗xg2 18.♔xg2 ♖xc5! 19.♗xc5 ♕d5+ 20.♕f3 ♕xc5 21.d4 ♕b6 22.dxe5 ♘e3+ 23.♔h1 ♘xf1 24.♖xf1 ♕xb2 25.♖f2 ♕b6 and Black won on the 60th move.

~

Exercise 3 (page 105) SI 45.1
Spassky-Larsen
Malmö 1968 (3)

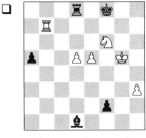

50.e6! ♖xd5+ 51.♔h6! 51.♔g6 ♗h5+ 52.♘xh5 ♖g5+ (52...f1♕ 53.e7++–) 53.♔xg5 f1♕. **51...♖h5+** 51...♗h5 52.e7+ ♔f7 53.e8♕++–. **52.♔g6**

Exercise 1 (page 108) PU 3.6
Dobrin-Hassan
Email 2001

11.♕e2! ♛b6+ 12.♔h1 ♗e7 12...♖c8
13.♖d1 ♗e7 14.♘c3 ♘xc3 15.bxc3 ♘c5
16.♗e3 0-0 17.♕xc4±. **13.♕xc4 0-0
14.♕e2 ♖ac8 15.c4 ♕a6 16.b3
♗f6 17.♗b2 ♘xb2 18.♕xb2 ♘c5
19.♘c3 ♘e3 20.♖g1 ♖fd8 21.♕e2
♕a5 22.♘e4 ♘xe4 23.♕xe3 ♘c5
24.♖gd1+−**

~

Exercise 2 (page 108) PU 3.6
Andreeva-Fominykh
Heraklio 2004 (5)

15...♘fd7!? Heading for e5. Both sides
need to arrange their development. **16.♖e1**
♘e5 **17.♕c2 ♕f6 18.♖e4 h5 19.h3
g5 20.♘e2 ♗h6** 20...g4!?. **21.♗c3!**
♕g6 **22.♗xe5 dxe5 23.g4 ♗g7
24.♘g3 hxg4 25.fxg4 ♕f6+ 26.♘f5±**

Exercise 3 (page 108) PU 3.6
Tinture-Guilloux
cr 1995

Exercise 1 (page 116) RG 3.1
Solak-Volkmann
Istanbul 2003 (8)

18...b5 18...♖e8? was played in the game.
19.♗f1 19...♗d3 c4 20...♗f1 ♘d5. **19...c4∓**

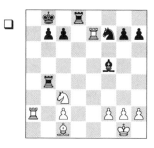

21.h3 21.♖xf7?? loses because of
21...♖b1!!−+ and after 22.g4 (both 22.♘e2
and 22.♘xb1 run into mate on d1) 22...♖xc1+
23.♔g2 Black wins with 23...♗e6!.

~

Exercise 2 (page 116) RG 3.1
Siwirkski-Wolochowicz
Warsaw 1985

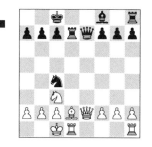

No! The move **13...♕b4??** loses
immediately. Correct was 13...♕xe2
14.♘xe2 ♗c5∓. In the game White gave
a forced mate with **14.♕e8+! ♖d8
15.♕xd8+!! ♔xd8 16.♗g5++**.

Exercise 3 (page 116) RG 3.1
Horstmann-Bogenberger
cr 2003

None! Both ways of castling lose
immediately!! The right move is **12...
f6!±** as played in the game. If 12...0-0??
13.♖d5!+−; 12...0-0-0?? 13.♖d5!+−. The
funny thing is that among 11 games that
came to the diagram position, Black played
12...f6 only two times; seven games saw
12...0-0-0?? (but only 3 times White played
13.♖d5!+− and four times White played
13.♘b5??); 2 games saw 12...0-0?? but in
both White played 13.♘b5??. Unbelievable!

~

Exercise 1 (page 126) RL 17.4
Rodriguez-Vajda
Canberra 2012 (4)

The answer is no; without rooks White has
less practical chances in the endgame.
23.a3 is better. **23.♖xe8+?! ♖xe8
24.♖e1?** 24.a3. **24...♖xe1+ 25.♕xe1
b4! 26.cxb4 ♕a7 27.♕c3 axb4
28.♕xb4 ♕xa2**

~

Exercise 2 (page 126) RL 17.4
Vocaturo-Ubilava
Benasque 2015 (7)

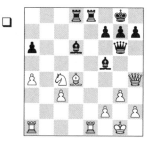

27.♖e3 27.♗xg7! ♔xg7 28.♖xe8 ♗xg3
(28...♖xe8? 29.♕d4+ ♔g8 30.♘xd6+−)
29.hxg3 ♖xe8 30.♕d4+±. **27...♖b8?**
And now again 27...♗c7. **28.♗xg7!
♖xe3 29.♘xe3 ♔xg7 30.♕d4+
♔g8 31.♘xf5** would have led to a big
advantage for White.

Exercise 3 (page 126) RL 17.4
So-Onischuk
Saint Louis 2015 (7)

23...♗e6!= would have solved all the problems according to Ivan Sokolov! **23... cxb5 24.a3 ♘c6** 24...♖ed8 25.♗c3 ♘d3 26.♖e3±. **25.♘g5 ♗h5 26.♗c3** would have led to a small but durable advantage for White because of his active bishops.

~

Exercise 1 (page 132) RL 27.11
Svidler-Motylev
Moscow 2004 (9)

27...♖c1+ 28.♖e1 28.♖xc1 ♕xc1+ 29.♖e1 ♕xf4. **28...♕c2! 29.♕xc2 ♖xc2 30.e6** 30.♖xa6 d3 31.♖d1 ♖xb2 32.♔h2 ♖xb3−+. **30...fxe6 31.♖xe6 ♗c5−+**

~

Exercise 2 (page 132) RL 27.11
Bulmaga-Olsarova
Braila 2014 (3)

24...♗f6!! 24...♖xa2? was played in the game: 25.♖xa2 ♗xf7 26.♖a6±; 24... bxc3 25.bxc3 ♘f6 26.♖e6∞; 24...♗xg5 25.♘xg5∞. **25.♗xf6** 25.♔g2 ♗xg5 26.♕xg5 (26.♘xg5?? ♖xa2!−+) 26...♕xg5

27.♘xg5 d2∓. **25...♕xf6 26.♔g2** 26.♗d5 ♖xa1 27.♖xa1 ♘e7∓. **26...♘d8∓**

~

Exercise 3 (page 132) RL 27.11
Caruana-Giri
Stavanger 2015 (9)

29...♗e4! 29...♕xe5?= was played in the game. **30.♖e1** 30.♘f5 g6 31.♘g3 ♗d5∓. **30...♗a8!! 31.♘f5** 31.♕xd3? ♕c6 32.f3 ♘c5 33.♕c2 ♘xb3 34.♕xb3 g5−+. **31...♖d8 32.♖e3 ♘f4∓**

~

Exercise 1 (page 139) KP 4.4
Van Delft-Ree
Netherlands tt 2010 (4)

11.♘d5 ♗xd5 12.exd5 ♘ce5 13.♘d4 13.♖b1 was played in the game. **13...♖e8 14.b3 ♘c5 15.♗b2 ♕d7 16.♖e1±**

~

Exercise 2 (page 139) KP 4.4
Howell-Berkovich
La Massana 2008 (4)

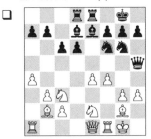

16.f5! d5 17.fxg6 ♗c5+ 18.♔h1 hxg6 19.♖xf6 gxf6 20.♕f1±

Exercise 3 (page 139) KP 4.4
Meier-D.Popovic
playchess.com 2005

15.a4!± limits Black's play (15.a3 b5!= was played in the game).

~

Exercise 1 (page 147) KP 12.1
Haas-Schroeder
cr 2014

23...♘e4!! 24.♕f4 ♕xf4 25.♗xf4 ♘xc3 26.♖xe7 ♘xh7□ 27.♗e5 ♘e2+□ 28.♔f1 ♗a6=

Exercise 2 (page 147) KP 12.1
Schroeder-Elison (analysis)
cr 2014

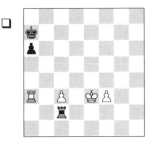

53.f4 ♔b6 54.f5 ♖h2 55.♔f4 Or 55.♖b3++−. **55...a5 56.♔g3 ♖h8 57.♔g4 ♔b5 58.f6 a4 59.♖a1 ♖c8 60.♖b1+ ♔a5 61.♖c1 a3 62.♔f5 ♖c7 63.♔g6 ♖c6 64.♔g7 ♖c4 65.f7 ♖g4+ 66.♔h6 ♖f4 67.♔g6 ♖f2 68.♖a1 ♔a4 69.♖b1 ♖g2+ 70.♔h5**

♖h2+ 71.♔g4 ♖h8 72.♖b7 a2 73.♖a7+ ♔b3 74.♔g5 ♖c8 75.♔g6 ♔b2 76.♔g7 a1♕ 77.♖xa1 ♔xa1 78.f8♕+−

~

Exercise 3 (page 147) KP 12.1
Schroeder-Elison
cr 2014

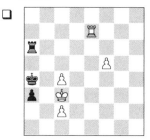

65.♖b7 65...a2 66.♔b2 ♖f6 67.♖a7+ (67.♖b5?? ♖c6 68.c3 ♖f6 69.♔xa2 ♖xf5=) 67...♔b4 68.c3+ ♔c5 69.♖a5+ ♔xc4 70.♖a4+ ♔d3 71.♖d4+ ♔e3 72.♔xa2□ ♖xf5 73.♖d8+−.

~

Exercise 1 (page 153) VO 17.2
Dunlop-Maitre
cr 2012

9.♕c2 △ ♕e4+. **9...d5 10.e3 ♕a5 11.♘ge2±** 11.♖xc4 dxc4 12.♔f1± Kolanek-Vasquez Nigro, Lechenicher SchachServer 2012.

~

Exercise 2 (page 153) VO 17.2
Analysis

9.h5± Black cannot prevent both h5-h6 and ♗h4 (analysis of Jobava's tricky move order 5...♘c6!?).

~

Exercise 3 (page 153) VO 17.2
Riazantsev-Tjurin
Voronezh 2004 (3)

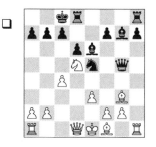

13.♖h5! Black resigned because on **13...♕g4 14.♗e2 ♕e4 15.f3 ♕g6 16.♘e7+** wins the queen.

~

Exercise 1 (page 158) VO 19.6
Lampert-Szabo
Budapest 2015 (4)

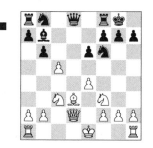

11...♘bd7! 11...bxc5 was played in the game.

~

Exercise 2 (page 158) VO 19.6
Analysis

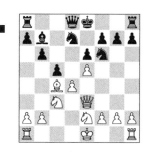

11...♘g4! 12.♕g3 cxd4!

Exercise 3 (page 158) VO 19.6
Analysis

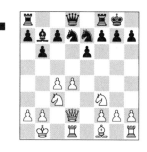

11...a6! with the idea 12...b5.

~

Exercise 1 (page 165) QO 15.7
Carlsen-Mamedyarov
Shamkir 2014 (1)

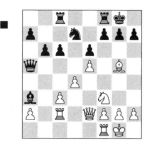

No, after **15...c5 16.d5! exd5 17.e6** White is clearly better.

~

Exercise 2 (page 165) QO 15.7
Gelfand-Carlsen
London 2013 (3)

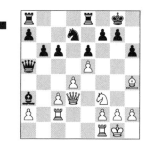

No, **16...c5!** and if **17.d5 c4!**.

Exercise 3 (page 165) QO 15.7
Tomashevsky-Ipatov
Reykjavik 2015 (1)

15...e5! to stop White's e4-e5.

~

Exercise 1 (page 170) SL 1.4
Ivanisevic-Tokhirjonova
St Petersburg 2014 (1)

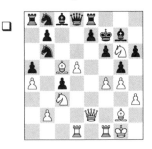

21.♕e6+! ♗xe6 22.dxe6+ ♔xe6
22...♔xg6 23.♗e4+ f5 24.♗xf5+ ♔f6
25.♘e4#; 22...♔g8 23.♖xd8 ♖xd8
24.♗xb6+–. **23.♖xd8 ♖xd8 24.♖e1+**
♔f7 25.♖xe7+ ♔g8 25...♔xg6
26.♗e4+ f5 27.♗xf5+ ♔f6 28.♘e4#.
26.♗xb6+–

~

Exercise 2 (page 170) SL 1.4
Vinchev-Stefanov
cr 2012

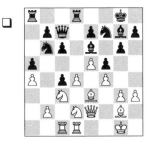

18.d5!

Exercise 3 (page 170) SL 1.4
Nikolic-Anand
München blitz 1994

7...♘g4!∓

~

Exercise 1 (page 175) NI 27.4
Svetushkin-Movsesian
Germany Bundesliga 2008/09 (1)

14...♘a5 (14...♘d6 was played in the
game) **15.♕c2 c5** frees Black's position.

~

Exercise 2 (page 175) NI 27.4
Makogonov-Keres
Leningrad ch-URS 1947 (5)

12...♗f5! preventing White from
developing the bishop to d3.

Exercise 3 (page 175) NI 27.4
Ogloblin-Bochorov
Voronezh 2009 (3)

10.cxd5! The game move 10.♗d3 is bad
because it allows Black to develop his bishop
easily: 10...♗a6. **10...exd5 11.♗d3**

~

Exercise 1 (page 180) QI 1.11
Grischuk-Filippov
Tromsø ol 2014 (6)

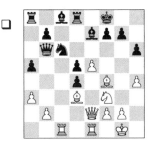

20.♘g5! hxg5 20...♗xg5 21.hxg5
hxg5 22.♗xg5–+; 20...♗e6 21.♘xe6+
fxe6 22.♕g4–+. **21.♕h5 ♔e8 22.e6**
♗xe6 23.♖xe6 gxf4 24.♗f5–+

~

Exercise 2 (page 180) QI 1.11
Saric-Antic
Vrbas 2015 (7)

20...♖xf2! 21.♖e4 21.♔xf2 ♕h4+
22.♔f1 (22.♔e2 ♖e8+–+) 22...♗b5+
23.♗d3 ♖f8+–+. **21...♗c6! 22.♔xf2**
♗xe4 23.♗xe4 ♕h4+ 24.♔f1
♕xe4–+

Exercise 3 (page 180) **QI 1.11**
Khademalsharieh-Brkic
Dubai 2014 (2)

19...d4! 20.f4 20.♘d2 a4 21.f4 (21.♘c1
d3–+) 21...axb3 22.fxe5 ♘xe5–+.
20...♕e8! 21.♗f5 21.fxe5 ♘xe5–+.
21...dxe3 22.fxe5 ♘xe5 23.fxe3
♕c6 24.e4 ♖d8 25.♕c2 a4–+

~

Exercise 1 (page 186) **GI 1.10**
Li Chao-Tomczak
Germany Bundesliga 2014/15 (3)

14.♘xg5! ♕xg5 15.b3! Now the a5-
knight is in trouble. Black can save it, but
the price is too high. **15...♘d7** 15...♗f6
16.♗d2 ♕g7 17.♔h1! (17.♗xa5 ♗xh4
18.gxh4 ♗h3 19.♔f3 ♗xg2 20.♕xg2
♘xd5 21.♖bc1±). **16.e4 ♕e7 17.♘f5**
♕f8 18.♕c2 Even stronger is 18.♘xg7!
♕xg7 19.♗b2 f6 20.♕d2 b6 21.♖fc1+–.
18...b6 19.b4 ♘b7 20.♕xc7±

~

Exercise 2 (page 186) **GI 1.10**
Kunte-Karthikeyan
Kottayam 2014 (6)

16...♗a6? 16...♗e6! 17.♖d1 (after
17.♕xc4 ♘xe3 18.♕xe6 ♖xe6 19.♗xe3
c6∓ △ ...♕e7 Black has a queen for
three minor pieces, but his coordination is
much better) 17...♘e5 18.♕c2 ♕e7∓.
17.♖d1±

~

Exercise 3 (page 186) **GI 1.10**
Bai-Chirila
London 2014 (7)

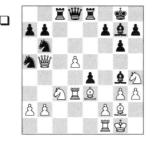

20.♖d4!± After 20.♖d2 ♗xc3 21.bxc3
♘ac4 22.hxg4 ♘xd2 23.♗xd2 ♕xd5
24.♕xd5 ♘xd5 25.♖c1 ♖c4 the position
is unclear. White has two bishops for a rook
and pawn, but Black has some initiative and
the h4-knight will take time to come back
into the game. **20...♘ac4 21.hxg4**
♘xe3 22.fxe3 ♗xd4 23.exd4 a6
24.♕b3 e3 25.♘e4 ♔h8? 25...e2.
26.♕xe3+–

~

Exercise 1 (page 193) **GI 3.3**
Blübaum-Ragger
Zillertal 2015 (5)

47...♖e3!! 47...♖xa7 48.♖xa7 ♖e3
49.♔g7!! ♖xc3 50.♖g5 ♔e6 51.h4=.
48.♖ag7 ♖ee2! 49.♖g6+ ♔c5
50.♖f7 ♖xg2+ 51.♔h1 ♖h2+
52.♔g1 ♖ag2+ 53.♔f1 ♖f2+
54.♔g1 54.♔e1 ♗xc3+ 55.♔d1 ♖d2+
56.♔c1 ♗b2+ 57.♔b1 ♖d1+ 58.♔a2
♖a1+ 59.♔b3 ♖a3#. **54...♖hg2+**
55.♔h1 ♖xg3 56.♖xg3 ♗xg3–+

Exercise 2 (page 193) **GI 3.3**
Li Chao-Zakhartsov
Guben 2014 (5)

56.♖d8! ♔f7 56...♖xd8 57.♖xe6 ♖d4
58.♗e1+–. **57.♖d7+ ♔g8 58.♔g2**
♗f4 59.♖bb7 ♗e5 60.h4+–

~

Exercise 3 (page 193) **GI 3.3**
Gleizerov-Bok
Sarajevo 2014 (3)

26.c6! ♗xe4 26...♘d3+ 27.♖xd3 ♗xd3
28.c7 ♖c8 29.♖d4 a6 30.♖d8+ ♗f8
31.e6!+–. **27.c7 ♗xd5 28.♖b8+ ♔g7**
29.♖xa8 ♘d3+ 30.♔f1

~

Exercise 1 (page 199) **KI 64.4**
Vachier-Lagrave-Mamedyarov
Tromsø ol 2014 (4)

14...b5! 15.cxb5 axb5 16.b4?!
16.♗xb5? ♖xb5 17.♘xb5 ♕d7! 18.♘xd6
♕xh3–+; 16.f4 ♘c6∞; 16.♘xb5
d5! 17.f4 ♘c6 18.e5 ♘e4⇄. **16...**
c4 17.♘d4 17.♗f4 ♘h5!. **17...d5!**

17...♗d7 18.♗e3 ♛c8∞. **18.♗g5** 18.
f4?! ♘xe4! 19.♖xe4 (19.♘xe4 ♘d3!–+)
19...dxe4 20.fxe5 ♛xe5–+; 18.exd5 ♘xd5
19.♘cxb5 (19.♘xd5? ♛xd5–+) 19...♗b7!
(19...♘d7!?) 20.♗g2 ♛b6–+. **18...
dxe4 19.♘xe4 ♗b7 20.♗g2** and now
20...♛b6! 21.♘xf6 ♗xf6 22.♘xf6+ ♛xf6
23.♗xb7 ♖xb7 24.f4 ♖d7! 25.fxe5 ♖xe5–+.

~

Exercise 2 (page 199)   KI 64.4
Marin-Vajda
Bucharest 1999 (6)

**17.b4! cxb4 18.♘xb4 ♘e6 19.♛xd6
♗f8 20.♛b6 ♛a3 21.♘bd5+–**

~

Exercise 3 (page 199)   KI 64.4
**Vachier-Lagrave-
Mamedyarov (analysis)**
Tromsø ol 2014 (4)

**16...♖xb5! 17.♘xb5 ♛d7! 18.♘xd6
♛xh3–+**

~

Exercise 1 (page 204)   BI 25.3
l'Ami-Perunovic
Reykjavik 2015 (3)

21.♘xf7! 21.♘c4 was played in the
game. **21...♖axf7** 21...♚xf7 22.♖d3
♛f6 (22...♛h4 23.f4 ♗f6 24.♖d7+ ♖xd7
25.♛xd7+ ♚g8 26.♗xa6+–; 22...♛e7
23.♗h6 (23.♗xa6+–) 23...♖b8 24.♗c4+
♚e8 25.♖e1+–) 23.f4 ♗b2 (23...♖b8
24.♗c4+ ♚g7 25.♗d2+–) 24.♖d6
♛c3 25.♗d2 ♛a3 26.f5+–; 21...♛xd1
22.♘h6+ ♚g7 23.♖xd1±. **22.♛xd8
♖xd8 23.♗xa6±**

~

Exercise 2 (page 204)   BI 25.3
Demuth-Giri
Montpellier 2015 (5)

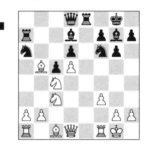

16...♖xd5! 16...♘h5 was played in the
game. **17.♘xd6** 17.♛xd5 ♗xc3 18.♗xd7
(18.bxc3 ♗xb5∓) 18...♗d4+ 19.♚h1
♘b4 20.♛xd6 ♖xd7 21.♛g3 ♗f6∓.
**17...♗xc3 18.bxc3 ♗xb5 19.♘xb5
♖d7 20.♛a4 ♘b4∓**

~

Exercise 3 (page 204)   BI 25.3
Analysis

18.♘xh7! ♘xh7 19.♛g3 g5 19...♖f6
20.♛h3 ♘f8 21.♗h6 ♖xe6+ 22.dxe6 d5
23.♗xg7 ♛xe6+ 24.♚f1 ♛xg7 25.♖e1+–;
19...♘f6 20.♛xg6 ♛c4 21.♗g5!+– –
the threat is ♖h4 and ♗h6. **20.♗xg5
♘xg5 21.♛xg5 ♛b7** 21...♘d7 22.exd7
♛b7 23.♖h3 f4 24.♚f1+–. **22.♖h3 f4
23.♛h5 ♖f6 24.♖b1!+–** with the idea
♛h7, ♖h5-♖g5. 24.0-0-0+–.

Exercise 1 (page 212)   QP 9.4
Kamsky-Korobov
Antalya 2013 (1)

12...♖c7! A very strong move. Black
intends to move his queen to a8 and gain
control over square e4. **13.♗h4 ♘g6
14.♗g5 ♛a8!** Black is not afraid of
15.♗xf6 gxf6 because White cannot take
advantage of the weakened kingside. In fact,
the open g-file is a potential asset. In the
game White played 15.f5, but he was just a
pawn down after 15...♘xe5 16.dxe5 ♗xe5
and eventually lost the game.

~

Exercise 2 (page 212)   QP 9.4
Sedlak-Prusikin
Germany tt 2014

14...♛e7 is the best move. After 15.0-0
♖fd8 16.♖fe1 White is slightly better.
Immediately losing is 14...♛e8?? 15.♗xh7+
♚xh7 16.♛h4+ ♚g8 17.♘g5 and Black
resigned in the blitz game Grachev-
Gorodetzky, Minsk 2015; and 14...♛f6
is suboptimal because the queen gets
into trouble. After 15.0-0 ♛a8 (15...♖fe8
16.♖d7 (16.b4 ♗f8 17.b5 ♘a5 18.♗xb7
♖c4!± was played in the game) 16...♗a8
17.♖c7+–) 16.b4 ♛e7 17.b5 ♘a5 18.♗h4
♖c4 19.♗xf6 ♖xa4 20.♗xe7 ♗xe4
21.♗xf8 ♚xf8 22.♖d4 ♖xd4 23.♘xd4
White is an exchange up.

Exercise 3 (page 212) QP 9.4
Delchev-Rusev
Sunny Beach 2015 (6)

13.♗xh7+ ♔xh7 14.♕h5+ ♔g8 15.♘e4 This is the game Kamsky-Shankland, but with Black's bishop on c8 instead of d7, and that is the difference between losing and drawing. **15...g6** In the mentioned game this defence was not possible! **16.♕g5 ♕e7 17.♘f6+ ♔g7 18.♘h5+ ♔g8** and draw by repetition.

~

Exercise 1 (page 220) EO 11.5
Kortchnoi-Kuzmin
Moscow 1973 (17)

11.♘h4! In conjunction with the next move this is the best way of fighting for the light squares in the centre. **11...d5** Otherwise White would install his knight on f5 with all the comfort. **12.♗g5!**

~

Exercise 2 (page 220) EO 11.5
Kortchnoi-Mecking
Augusta 1974 (1)

36.♗h3!± Indeed, this is the best moment to take control of the f5-square since the c4-pawn is not really hanging.

~

Exercise 3 (page 220) EO 11.5
Marin-Vuilleumier
Helsingor 2015 (5)

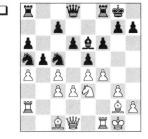

16.fxe5!± The only move, forcing Black to weaken either the f-file or the a3-f8 diagonal before he can capitalize on his queenside pressure.

~

Exercise 1 (page 228) EO 42.9
Piket-Ljubojevic
Monaco 2002 (2)

17...cxd4 Worse is 17...exd4 18.♘xc5 ♗xc5 19.♗b3. Black doesn't get enough compensation for the pawn. **18.♘b6 ♕h6 19.♖c2 axb6 20.♕xa8 0-0** Now Black has excellent compensation for the exchange. It is very hard for White to connect his rooks.

~

Exercise 2 (page 228) EO 42.9
Suba-Fernandez Troncoso
Coria del Rio 2002 (2)

No, it was not. He should have played 17...d3 or 17...♘xa4 with equality in both cases. Now after **18.♗c2 d3 19.b4 dxc2 20.♘f6+!** White had a winning advantage.

~

Exercise 3 (page 228) EO 42.9
Psakhis-Vaganian
Lvov 1984 (11)

22...0-0 Vaganian played 22...♕e7, but after 23.d5 exd5 24.♗xf6 ♘e6 he would have been in serious trouble if White had found 25.♕d2! (instead of 25.♕e3). It is also possible to play 22...♖c8 since 23.d5 (23.♘e1!) 23...exd5 24.exd5 ♘cxd5 25.♕e5+ ♔f8 is OK for Black. After 23.♘e1 the defense is not so easy, however. **23.d5 ♘ce8 24.d6 ♕a5!** and Black holds his own.

~

Exercise 1 (page 234) EO 46.11
Romanov-Naiditsch
Warsaw rapid 2011 (8)

8.e3!? 8.b3 d5 9.♗g2 (9.cxd5 ♗b4+) 9...dxc4 (9...♗b4+ 10.♘d2 dxc4) 10.0-0 a6∓ Parfenov-Lanin, Smolensk 2005; 8.♘d2 d5 9.cxd5 (9.♗xf6 gxf6 10.cxd5 ♗xd5 11.e4 ♗e6 12.♗c4 b4) 9...♗xd5 10.e4 ♗e6 11.♗c4 ♗b4 12.♗xe6 fxe6 13.0-0 0-0 14.a3 ♗xd2 15.♗xd2 ♕xe4∓ Filippov-Moiseenko, Bydgoszcz 1999; 8.♘1a3? d5 9.cxd5 (9.♗xf6 ♕a5+!−+) 9...♘xd5!? 10.♗xd8 ♗b4+ 11.♘c3 ♘xc3+ 12.♕c2? ♘xa2+ 13.♔d1 ♖xd8+−+. **8...♖c8 8...**d5 9.♗xf6 gxf6 10.cxd5 ♗xd5? ♕xd5!+−. **9.♗xf6**

Exercise 2 (page 234) EO 46.11
Iturrizaga Bonelli-Moiseenko
Berlin Wch blitz 2015 (9)

Exercise 3 (page 234) EO 46.11
Svidler-Nepomniachtchi
Sochi tt-RUS 2015 (5)

14.♖fd1 It makes more sense to keep this rook on f1, keeping the threat f2-f4-f5 in reserve and avoiding a pin along the long dark-squared diagonal: 14.♖ad1 ♗g5 (14...♕b6 15.b3 ♕a5 16.♘c2 b5 17.cxb5 axb5 18.♘e4 ♗e7 19.♕xa5 ♘xa5 20.♘e3 ♖fd8 21.♘d5±) 15.e3 ♗g4 16.f3 ♗h5 (16...♗e6 17.f4) 17.g4 ♗g6 18.f4 exf4 19.exf4 ♗f6 20.f5 ♗h7 21.♘e4±; the h7-bishop is completely out of play. **14...♕b6** 14...♗g5!? 15.e3 ♗g4. **15.b3 ♖fd8?!** 15...♕a5! 16.♘d5 (16.♘c2?! e4!; 16.♘ab1 b5!?⇄) 16...♕xa3 17.♘xf6+ gxf6 18.♕xh6=, White will give perpetual soon.

25.♕b2? 25.♘d5! ♕f7 26.♕b2 ♗xf1 27.♗xf1±. **25...♗xf1 26.♗xf1** 26.♘d5? ♕e8 27.♗xf1 ♕xe4. **26...♖fd8∞**

Not yet a subscriber?

**If you buy single copies of the Yearbook,
please realize that subscribing has many advantages:**

> **It's cheaper:** you can save up to 25% on the bookshop price
> **It's prompt:** you will always receive new issues within one week of publication (so nobody will be able to surprise you!)
> **It's convenient:** you will receive every issue at home, on your doormat
> **It's refreshing:** every three months your opening repertoire will be refreshed – guaranteed!
> **It's complete:** you will never miss an issue, and always have, at home, full access to all Surveys
> **It saves time:** armchair shopping means you will have more time to actually study
> **It's magical:** you pay absolutely NO delivery costs!

Find out why thousands of Yearbook readers from all over the world have taken out a subscription. Go to www.newinchess.com, click on **'Subscribe now'**, fill out the form, and it's done.

– 1000 pages a year of opening news, on your doormat –

We've rolled back prices of Yearbook volumes!

Year	Issues	4 paperbacks	4 hardcovers
2013	106-109	€ 59.95 £ 49.95 $ 67.50	€ 69.90 £ 59.40 $ 79.90
2012	102-105	€ 59.95 £ 49.95 $ 67.50	€ 69.90 £ 59.40 $ 79.90
2011	98-101	€ 54.95 £ 49.95 $ 59.95	€ 64.95 £ 54.95 $ 74.95
2010	94-97	€ 49.95 £ 39.95 $ 59.95	€ 64.95 £ 54.95 $ 74.95
2007	82-85	€ 39.95 £ 32.75 $ 44.95	€ 54.95 £ 38.95 $ 64.95
2006	78-81	€ 39.95 £ 32.75 $ 44.95	
2005	74-77	€ 39.95 £ 32.75 $ 44.95	€ 54.95 £ 38.95 $ 64.95
2000	54-57	€ 24.95 £ 19.95 $ 27.95	

THE CHESS PLAYER'S GUIDE TO OPENING NEWS